Blind Eye to Murder

BLIND EYE
TO MURDER

BRITAIN, AMERICA AND THE PURGING OF
NAZI GERMANY – A PLEDGE BETRAYED

Tom Bower

ANDRE DEUTSCH

First published 1981 by
André Deutsch Limited
105 Great Russell Street London WC1
Copyright © 1981 by Tom Bower
All rights reserved
Printed in Singapore by Toppan

ISBN 0 233 97292 7

'Retribution for these crimes must henceforth take its place among the major purposes of the war.'

Winston Churchill 25 October 1942

'Revenge is, of all satisfactions, the most costly and long drawn out; retributive persecution is of all policies, the most pernicious. Our policy, subject to the exceptional cases I have mentioned, should henceforth be to draw the sponge across the crimes and horrors of the past – hard as that may be – and look for the sake of all our salvation, towards the future. There can be no revival of Europe, without the active and loyal aid of all the German tribes . . .'

Winston Churchill 28 October 1948

To Juliet

CONTENTS

List of Illustrations 8
Preface and Acknowledgements 9
1 'It was very civilized' 13
2 'This rather wild story' 27
3 'Still somewhat sceptical' 45
4 'We seem to be short of ideas' 62
5 'A broad programme' 85
6 'A substantial lack of national policy' 111
7 'What kind of Germany we want' 137
8 'Systematic and meticulous imbecility' 161
9 'Until the crack of doom' 197
10 'We just plain turned them loose' 241
11 'We've tried the corporals, now the generals must be tried too' 268
12 'The men of 39' 293
13 'It would be jolly good for them' 308
14 'They were not Nazis, they were businessmen' 334
15 'Masterly inactivity' 351
16 'All German industrialists were really on trial' 366
17 'Shaking these people out as fast as we can' 379
18 'If you're concerned about morality, go to church' 404
19 *Schlusstrich* 422

Bibliography 418
Notes 422
Index 469

LIST OF ILLUSTRATIONS

1. *The fight for the UN Commission*
Sir Cecil Hurst (BBC Hulton Picture Library); Herbert Pell (Associated Press); Lord Simon (BBC Hulton Picture Library)

2. *Lack of enthusiasm at the War Office*
John Lawson (BBC Hulton Picture Library); Sir Frederick Bovenschen (Imperial War Museum); Viscount Bridgeman (Imperial War Museum)

3. *Two who tried*
Sir Hartley Shawcross (BBC Hulton Picture Library); Patrick Dean (BBC Hulton Picture Library)

4. *Belsen*
Scenes in the camp shortly after liberation (Camera Press and Imperial War Museum)

5. *Nazi-hunters*
Colonel Clio Straight; Group Captain Tony Somerhough; The British War Crimes Group

6. *The Malmedy Massacre*
The scene of the massacre (United Press International); The defendants at the trial (US Army photographs)

7. *The fates of two wanted men*
Gustav Wagner, living in exile; The execution of Oswald Pohl (US Army photograph)

8. *British Successes*
Colonel Gerald Draper with Rudolph Höss; Josef Kramer and Irma Grese (Imperial War Museum)

9. *Antagonists*
Generals Clay and Sokolovsky (Associated Press); Bishop Wurm (Deutsche Presse-Agentur)

10. *The Governments of Occupation*
General Clay with Sir Sholto Douglas (Associated Press); General Robertson and John McCloy (Associated Press)

11. *The deportation of the French Jews*
Ernst Heinrichsöhn (Deutsche Presse-Agentur); Kurt Lischka and Herbert Hagen (Deutsche Presse-Agentur); Ernst Achenbach (Deutsche Presse-Agentur)

12. *The New Germany – and the old*
Konrad Adenauer and Hans Globke (United Press International); The Managing Board of I.G. Farben; Hermann Abs and Franz Ulrich (Deutsche Presse-Agentur)

Those photographs which are not credited have been obtained from private sources.

PREFACE AND
ACKNOWLEDGEMENTS

Like many others born in the postwar years in Britain and the United States, I grew up to believe that the Second World War was a just and moral crusade, ending in the victory of righteousness over tyranny. By the time I entered my teens I had read every book in my local library which told of the heroism of those who fought in the struggle against Nazism. The image of the sacrifice of those who died in that struggle has always haunted me; for many it was the outcome of reasoned consideration and a determination to fight for the principles that they believed in. Among those principles, especially for those who fought a longer and grimmer war in the occupied countries, was the belief that with victory would come justice: those who had done evil would be punished, and those who had died would be avenged.

During the war, the leaders of the Western Alliance went to some lengths to assure the world that this would be so; and after the war those who had lived through it, and those of my own generation who followed, were assured that this had indeed happened, at Nuremberg and elsewhere. The tiny minority of criminals who had escaped to South America could safely be ignored. It was only in the Sixties, as it became increasingly commonplace to say that if Germany had lost the war she had certainly won the peace, that I began to visit West Germany frequently. I quickly came to realize that the architects of the country were very often the same men who had held high positions in the regime which my boyhood heroes had fought to overthrow.

It was not until 1977 that I was finally prompted to begin an investigation of this inexplicable paradox. A short newspaper clipping then caught my eye; it reported that a former SS officer, Hubert Kappler, who had been convicted of the murder of 335 Italians, had escaped from Italy to Germany. Apparently, as a German citizen, he was safe from deportation back to Italy. Some war criminals, it seemed, did not have to search so far afield as South America to find safe refuge.

It quickly became clear to me that there was an issue more important even than the fact that mass murderers remained at large and undisturbed. What really merited investigation was that those who gave the orders for murders, deportation, plunder and slavery had not just survived, they had, in many instances, returned to their desks and were again in a position to give orders.

No ready explanation lay to hand. Nothing had been published which drew upon the official documents or, in an organized fashion, upon the recollections of those who were responsible for what happened in post-war Germany. Much of what had been written was evidently concerned with glossing over rather than elucidating the truth.

The only aspect of the subject which had been explored in detail – and is for that reason largely ignored in this work – was the proceeding of the International Tribunal at Nuremberg. Many excellent accounts are available, but all subscribe to a greater or lesser extent to the comforting myth that Nuremberg somehow took care of the whole problem. As I have tried to show, this was far from the case. And when it comes to the subsequent trials, the prosecution of those actually responsible for atrocities and concentration camps and the removal of nazis from power and influence, the published record is exceedingly sparse. The facts that had appeared had simply been reported as such, with no attempt at explanation. To my surprise, I quickly found that the reasons which began to emerge were very different to those I had expected. The thousands of files which I read in Washington, London and in Germany suggest that those who fought for justice were betrayed by their own side; worse still, the rhetoric of their leaders concealed a reluctance, often a refusal, to see their pledges put into effect when the time came.

The scale of the documentation was intimidating, and its content often breathtaking. In contrast to the heroism of those who fought in the front line, the cynicism and weakness of those who directed them seemed shocking. I have tried to record their dilemmas and problems fairly and without bias – that record must speak for itself. But the completion of this book gives me satisfaction, not only because it fulfils a long-held ambition, but also because so many people tried to convince me, some for their own reasons, that what I suspected was either not so or could not be established.

I am grateful to many people whose patience, knowledge, experience and encouragement has helped me in my task. Firstly, I must thank my colleagues. Christopher Capron, a past editor of BBC Television's *Panorama* programme, unhesitatingly allowed me to pursue my initially vague notion, and with characteristic generosity gave me opportunities to develop my knowledge and understanding of Germany; John Gau and others at Lime Grove studios gave me leave of absence to write this book.

During the research I interviewed over two hundred people in Britain, France, Germany, Eastern Europe, and North and South

America. Many, for their own good reasons, must remain anonymous. Of the remainder, those who were most helpful were:

Hermann Abs, Foster Adams, Lord Annan, Jacob Beam, Wolfgang Benz, General Sir Alec Bishop, the late Joe Borkin, Martin Broszrt, Professor Arthur Bülow, Lady Chambers, Henry Cleaver, Sir Patrick Dean, Roger Elliot, Dwight Fanton, Walter Freud, John Fried, John Gimbel, Charles Gunston, Colonel Richard Halse, Isser Harel, Edward Helmuth, John Kellam, Joe Leniewski, John Liddle-Simpson, John McCloy, Neil McDermott, Professor Keith Mant, the late Airey Neave, Lutz Niethammer, Alan Nightingale, Lord Paget, William Perl, John Rathbone, Jacques Reinstein, James Riddleberger, Sir Frank Roberts, Jan Rocha, Kurt Schwedersky, Harry Schweiger, Lord Shawcross, the Right Honourable Emanuel Shinwell, Drexel Sprecher, General Clio Straight, Telford Taylor, Simon Wiesenthal, Lord Wilberforce and Lawrence Wilkinson.

I owe special thanks to James Weingartner for his help on Chapter 12, to Professor Gerald Draper for answering endless questions, and to Ray Brislin for hospitality in Washington. To the staff at the Suitland Records Centre outside Washington I owe more than can be recorded. George Chalou, Will Mahoney and John Mendelson efficiently and uncomplainingly produced the enormous number of documents I wanted to see, and on their own initiative guided me into areas of which I would have otherwise remained ignorant. I owe them, and Brewster Chamberlain, an enormous debt.

In Germany I owe a special debt to Sebastian Cobler and especially to Bernt Engelmann, whose help and knowledge was so valuable. Equally, in France, Serge and Beate Klarsfeld, tireless champions of their cause, were very helpful at the outset.

Few books about this subject and period have been written without acknowledgement to Martin Gilbert, but I owe an even greater debt to his wife Susie, whose meticulous research at the beginning produced the documentary proof that my suspicions were in fact true. I am grateful to Claire Selarie and Elaine Davenport for additional research. The work of Nick Makris and Anne Watson in New York and Liz Rives-Brown in London saved much time. Thanks also to Shelley Cassidy, Margaret Hoffmann, and Jackie Valledy for typing the manuscript.

I received enthusiastic support from the outset from my agent, Robert Ducas. His total belief in the project was reassuring and infectious. Thanks to him, the book was edited by Piers Burnett, whose contribution has been inestimable. Not only did he turn a manuscript into a book, but his constructive involvement added perspicacity and fluency.

Finally, an acknowledgement for which words are inadequate. To my parents, who have always been reassuring and helpful; and to Juliet, without whom none of what follows would ever have been written.

1

'IT WAS VERY CIVILIZED'

The end came as no surprise. The distant thunder of artillery had become quieter. The voice on the radio had warned listeners to stand by for a special announcement. In a suite in Hamburg's luxury Vierjahreszeiten Hotel, forty-three-year-old Hermann Josef Abs knew it was time to pack and leave before the British soldiers arrived. It was the afternoon of 3 May 1945. The commander of the Wehrmacht unit defending the city had just surrendered to officers of the British 7th Armoured Division. By nightfall, those same officers had requisitioned the Vierjahrerzeiten as a club and were enjoying the fruits of victory. The booty that night was the hotel's well-stocked cellar.

By then Hermann Abs was, as he believed, safely hidden in the nearby home of a friend. He stayed inside and off the streets for the next six weeks, uncertain whether his brilliant career was now finished. Thirty-five years later, he was to claim with innocent charm that he fell asleep that first night relieved about the Allied victory. 'My conscience was clear, my memory was good.'[1]

Five days later Germany signed the instrument of unconditional surrender and formally acknowledged that the fate of the nation and its citizens rested entirely in the hands of the three powers whose armies occupied the country. It would not be unreasonable to say that the fate the victors decreed for Abs would be a fair test of their intentions towards his country. Certainly, Abs' name was not unknown to them. While he remained concealed, at least two organizations within the Allied armies were searching for him. One group wished to find him because they wanted to restore him to a position of power in which he could help them rebuild Germany. The other group sought him because they felt that one of the reasons they had fought the war was to ensure that men like Hermann Abs could never again achieve power of any kind in Germany: moreover they hoped to hold Abs accountable for the way in which he had used his power prior to 3 May 1945.

Hermann Abs was, and is, a banker. German banks have traditionally had much closer links with industry than their counterparts in America or Britain. In the absence of a stock market on the scale of Wall Street or the London Stock Exchange, it was to the banks that industrialists looked for finance, and to the banks that they confided their plans and reported their results; as a consequence, the big German banks almost always had a voice in the decisions, and a seat in the boardroom, of their major industrial clients. As Germany expanded to become one of the world's great industrial powers in the first part of the twentieth century, so German banking became one of the power centres of the world economy.

Abs served his apprenticeship in the small elite world of international banking in the fifteen years prior to 1938; in that year he emerged as one of its leaders, a member of the *Vorstand*, or managing board, of the mighty Deutsche Bank, the largest in Germany. He had studied his profession not only in his own country, but in Paris, London, New York, Amsterdam, the Far East and South America. He was already a partner in the important private bank, Delbruck, Schickler, and obviously a man being groomed for great things. His training had not only introduced him to the firmament in which he was to shine, but also to some of its established constellations and their member stars. It was a world in which personal relationships and mutual respect counted for a great deal. By 1939 there were few people of any importance in the whole world of banking whom Abs did not know well, and scarcely any who did not know of and respect him.

One fellow banker who had come to admire and respect Abs was an affable, polyglot Englishman called Charles Gunston, who had first come to Germany in 1925, sent by the Bank of England as a trainee to the Reichsbank in Berlin. Selected by Sir Montagu Norman to manage the bank of England's German desk at a time when the power and influence of the City of London was still immense, Gunston was a man to be feted and respected in Germany. After 1933, the man most anxious to win Gunston's confidence was the new president of the Reichsbank, Hjalmar Schacht.

Schacht's political allegiances were on record. He had successfull; lobbied German industrialists and bankers to contribute to Hitler's 1933 election fund. In office, he was to use a mixture of cunning and charm to defraud the Western world's governments and bankers of hundreds of millions of pounds to finance Germany's crash programme of rearmament and industrial expansion. The money was borrowed without any intention of repaying it. Appointed in 1935 as 'General for the War Economy', Schacht admitted after the war that it had always been his intention to raise the money for rearmament ('armaments second to none'), knowing that Hitler intended to declare war on Russia.

Winning other people's confidence was the essence of getting their money. In the case of Montagu Norman and Gunston, it was not very difficult. Both were great admirers of Germany – even Nazi Germany. Gunston went so far as to spend his 1934 summer holidays in the *Reichs-arbeitdienst*, a Nazi party work camp. About the rigorous daily routine of work and military drill, Gunston now says: 'I enjoyed it. It was quite fun. The Germans thought I was a lunatic.'[2] To those Germans who wanted to listen to him, Gunston would explain how sympathetic he was to Germany's resentment over the Versailles Treaty. Amongst those who heard his views were two young bankers whom Schacht suggested he should meet because he had marked them as rising stars. They were Karl Blessing and Hermann Abs.

Blessing was personal assistant to Schacht. He joined the Nazi party in 1937 and became a member of the Himmler Circle, a select group of bedrock Nazi industrialists and bankers who paid generous contributions into a secret account for the SS leader's benefit and who played a vital role in Germany's rearmament. Twice, Blessing went with twenty-one other members of the circle to visit concentration camps. It was a sort of excursion trip, with Himmler as their personal guide. The list of Blessing's fellow tourists to Dachau and Orianneberg reads like a roll call of the accused at the postwar Nuremberg war crimes trials.[3] Yet Gunston, who went skiing in Silesia with Blessing, says of the Reichsbank official: 'Raising his arm and shouting "*Sieg Heil*" was all for show. It was clear to me that the Germans in the Reichsbank were, to a man, anti-Nazi.' Interrogated after the war, Blessing said of the Himmler Circle: 'I thought it was just for beer evenings. Nothing else.'[4] Blessing also denied that he had visited concentration camps or even knew they existed.

Abs was not then, or at any other time, a member of the Nazi party, but Schacht recognized his commercial and diplomatic skills and trusted him with the most sensitive missions. One of these was to attend the meetings of the Bank for International Settlements in Basle, where Abs' task was to resist the attempts by Germany's creditors to obtain repayment of the vast loans made after the First World War. Briefed by Schacht, Abs' role was to lie convincingly about the state of Germany's reserves, to explain, for example, that in 1937 they amounted to only seventy million reichsmarks in gold, whereas the true figure was nearer five hundred million. Gunston met Abs regularly at those meetings. He remembers him, with admiration as being: 'Very urbane. Always a velvet glove around an iron fist.'

In the months before war broke out, Abs travelled extensively to London, Paris and New York. Old friendships were renewed, new contacts made. In London, the partners of Kleinworts, the merchant bank, which handled a lot of Delbruck, Schickler and Deutsche Bank business, always gave him a warm welcome. In New York, the partners of J. Henry Schroeder and Dillon Reed were anxious to welcome their guest. There was some self-interest in the attention he received. All of these banks had lent Germany a lot of their money and Abs held one of the keys to its eventual repayment.

Yet, strangely, none of the Anglo-American bankers really probed Abs about the circumstances of the Deutsche Bank's sudden and phenomenal growth. It had absorbed the Jewish-owned Mendelsohn's bank, Germany's biggest private bank, and had purchased Adler and Oppenheimer, another big Jewish company. These and many other companies had been the victims of aryanization, the forced purchase of Jewish companies at knockdown rates. Nor did they ask him about the full circumstances of his bank's takeover of Austria's giant Creditanstalt Wiener Bankverein: with its vast assets in eastern and south-eastern Europe, its sudden absorption was equivalent to the disappearance of Barclays or the Bank of America. There were similar aryanizations and strange 'acquisitions' after the German takeover of Czechoslovakia, when Czech banks and industry became German overnight. But before September 1939 many Anglo-American bankers still made a delicate distinction between those who terrorized with the jackboot and those who followed to reap the profits.

Even before he became a director of the Deutsche Bank, Abs was not far removed from the centres of Nazi power. Among the clients of Delbruck, Schickler were Adolf Hitler and the Nazi philosopher Alfred Rosenberg; Schacht used the bank to channel secret funds from his own account, 1-c, to that of the foreign minister, Ribbentrop. But after 1938 Abs was at one of the nerve centres of Germany's ambition. As the director in charge of the Deutsche Bank's Foreign Department, he bankrolled much of the industrial expansion which followed in the wake of the Wehrmacht's conquests. He watched as his clients integrated the factories, mines and transport systems of a dozen conquered nations into a series of industrial empires unmatched in European history.

For Germany industry, the first four years of the war were a period of immense opportunity and profitability. The industrial resources of three quarters of Europe were theirs for the taking, and the German war machine would eagerly buy and consume all that they had to offer. And a shrewd banker was not slow to identify his interests with those of his clients. The Deutsche Bank was shrewd.

By 1945, its directors sat on 197 different company boards. The bank's wealth had quadrupled during the twelve years of Nazi rule.[5] But its phenomenal success was not due entirely to sheer financial savvy. It outstripped its competitors because it had good relations with the government. Some of the bank's directors had been deliberately appointed to please the party. Others were convinced Nazis. Phillip Reemstsma, the tobacco magnate, Albert Pietsch, adviser to Rudolf Hess, and Wilhelm Zangen, the leader of the Reichsgruppe Industrie, representing all German industrialists, were all early party supporters. Alongside them sat high-ranking SS and SA officers. Regularly and discreetly, the bank paid large contributions into private funds for Hitler and Himmler. Wherever the Wehrmacht went, so did the directors of the bank, only pausing on the way to squabble over the spoils with their rivals, the Dresdener Bank.

Hermann Abs was responsible for the bank's foreign investments, yet he did not become a party member, pleading his devout Catholicism. But his religion did not prevent him joining two Nazi party affiliated organizations, the DAF and NSV. He now claims that the more fanatical party members in the bank demanded that he either join the party or resign, but that his other colleagues protected him by insisting that he was indispensable. He did however get a new assistant, Franz Heinrich Ulrich, a member of the SS since 1933. But Abs' loyalty was never in doubt. He spoke and wrote regularly about the new postwar Europe, under German control. He, unlike most other Germans, admits that he never even contacted the resistance.

Abs was valued in the citadels of Nazism. Interrogated after the war, Emil Puhl, the vice-president of the Reichsbank, said that 'Abs impressed everybody'. Baron von Schroeder, the Nazi party's key pre-1933 banker, told his interrogators: 'Abs proved very valuable to the party and the Government.' According to Schacht, Abs was 'the only German who can clarify Germany's past financial operations'.[6]

To be a successful banker in wartime Germany did, of course, demand certain departures from peacetime practice. One of the features that must have taken a little adjustment was that the clients of the Deutsche Bank, along with other German industrialists, had reintroduced the slave trade into Europe. At least six million Europeans of all nationalities and all religions were captured and herded into Germany's factories and mines. Men, women and children were literally worked to their deaths. Many of those companies that used slave labour were financed by the Deutsche Bank.

Siemens, the electrical company, made an agreement with Himmler's SS to get cheap labour in Auschwitz, Buchenwald and Ravensbrück concentration camps. Discipline was maintained by the SS.'[7] Mannesmann used slave labour in its own German factories. British prisoners of war who survived swore depositions about the slow starvation towards death inside Mannesmann factories. BMW drew its slave labour from the nearby Dachau concentration camp.[8] IG Farben actually built its own concentration camp adjacent to Auschwitz. IG Auschwitz, as it was called by the directors, was designed to produce artificial rubber. At least fifty thousand inmates died of starvation, exhaustion, exposure and torture building the factory in the alternately freezing or swampy wasteland of Eastern Poland. Some of those who died were buried as they fell in the cement foundations. Others were the victims of the daily 'selection'. Judged unfit for further work at the 4 am rollcall, they were taken to the neighbouring gas chambers at Birkenau and cremated later that day. IG Farben inmates rarely survived more than three months, the time it took for the body to burn up its own fat – as part of company policy, IG supplied little food. Evidence produced at the Nuremberg trial of the IG Farben managing directors showed that even the SS complained about the company's 'waste of labour'. There was not, the directors were told, an infinite supply.[9]

IG Auschwitz cost two hundred and fifty million dollars (at 1941 prices), the giant company's biggest investment. The Deutsche Bank was the company's main banker. Hermann Abs was the Bank's representative on the company's supervisory board (*Aufsichtsrat*). He claims he never knew about the investment, because the decision, he insists, was taken by the managing board (the *Vorstand*). 'If I had, I would have resigned,' he now says.

By the Spring of 1944, the same shrewd self-interest which had led the Deutsche Bank and its clients to devote their loyalties to the Nazis suggested that the time might be coming when they would have to change horses. From early 1944, Abs was a member of a small group of Germany's leading bankers, industrialists and economists who discussed and laid plans for the postwar period, after Germany's defeat. None of them were members of the resistance. They were just pragmatic businessman, anxious to protect their interests when the horse they had backed for the past twelve and more years finally lost the race. Cloaked in considerable secrecy, two groups had been formed in early 1943 after the German defeat at Stalingrad, to discuss and plan economic and industrial policies for the aftermath of Germany's defeat. The members of one group, the *Arbeitskreis für Aussenwirtschaftsfragen* (the AAF – Committee for Foreign Economic Affairs), were financiers and industrialists. The members of the second group, the *Kleine Arbeitskreis* (the KA – Small Working Group), were purely industrialists.[10]

Abs belonged to the AAF. One of the few surviving documents of their activities is an invitation from Karl Blessing to sixteen leading bankers and industrialists to a meeting on 30 May 1944 at the Hotel

Esplanade in Berlin. The purpose of the meeting was to collect the names of those industrialists and bankers in Britain and America who might be sympathetic towards Germany after the war. The hope was that they could find allies for the inevitable postwar negotiations between Germany and its creditors to settle the still outstanding debts. The group continued to meet until February 1945. Among the inner circle was Karl Blessing, at the time supremo for Germany's oil industry, Ludger Westerick, head of Germany's aluminium industry, Hermann Abs and Ludwig Erhard, at the time a finance and economics expert.

Erhard was the link between AAF and the *Kleine Arbeitskreis* of industrialists which had been set up by Wilhelm Zangen, the president of the Reichsgruppe Industrie, the organization representing German industrialists. His work in the committee was closely coordinated by Otto Ohlendorf, at the time a senior SS officer and departmental chief in the Ministry of Economics, but previously the head of *Einsatzgruppe D*, an SS murder battalion which had operated in Russia. The battalion had, on his own admission, executed ninety thousand civilians who had been buried in mass graves. Ohlendorf had been ordered back to Berlin after an argument with Himmler.

Members of the KA were Friedrich Flick, the coal and steel baron, Phillip Reemstsma, Germany's leading cigarette manufacturer, Heinrich Dinkelbach, one of Germany's largest steel manufacturers, and Hermann Schmitz, chairman of IG Farben. Like Zangen, all of these industrialists had been enthusiastic and early supporters of the Nazis. All of them had pledged heavy contributions to Nazi party funds. Like Zangen too, they had become concerned about the future of their industries. Masterminding their work was Zangen's deputy, Rudolf Stahl, who like Zangen, was a director of the Deutsche Bank. Stahl was in regular correspondence with both Erhard and Ohlendorf.

The evidence of the activities of these two groups, although scattered, is persuasive on one issue. German industrialists and bankers who had invested heavily in Hitler were determined, despite the dangers, to protect their future. The measure of their foresight is that most of those named, and the others who took part, became leaders of postwar Germany's industry, banking and government.

Abs certainly played his part as a director of the Deutsche Bank right up to the end. He left Berlin on 16 April 1945. His departure had been delayed until the last moment. The ten other members of the bank's *Vorstand* could not agree whether the young Abs should become the new chairman at the provisional headquarters in Hamburg. The sound of the nearby battle for Berlin had prevented their argument lasting very long, but Abs could quote in his favour that Franz Urbich, one of the bank's most distinguished directors, had, on his eightieth birthday in July 1944, entrusted Abs with the task of rebuilding the bank after the war.

In practical terms, the previous month Abs had organized a convoy of lorries to take the records of his department to Hamburg. When the question of the Bank's assets of eleven billion reichsmarks, about five and a half billion dollars, arose, other members of the *Vorstand* had insisted that they be moved to Erfurt. Then, just days before the final board meeting, they heard that a map seized from a captured Allied pilot showed that Erfurt was in the proposed Soviet zone. The bank's fortune was immediately moved to Hildesheim. Abs' prophecy of the Allied zonal arrangements had been proven correct.

Six weeks after the German surrender, most of Abs' friends and former associates had been arrested and were interned either as security suspects or suspected war criminals. He thought the same fate was awaiting him when a British jeep stopped outside the house of Prince Wittgenstein where he was staying, and there was a loud banging on the door. Captain Sutton of the British Military Government's Finance Division asked him to get into the jeep. But, instead of going to the nearest internment camp, Abs was driven to the Finance Division's headquarters in the Esplanade Hotel, one of the few undamaged buildings in Hamburg. Instead of being roughly manhandled into an interrogation room, the German banker was courteously invited to meet the head of the Division's Banking Section – Charles Gunston.

According to Gunston: 'I don't know who was more pleased to see the other. He complained that he had lost his shaving gear, but he looked shaven and exactly as before. Not a hair out of place. I immediately asked him whether he would help us rebuild the German banking system. Happily he agreed.'

For Gunston it was 'like old times'. 'I didn't ask him about the war. It didn't matter. They had been financing their war effort, like we had been financing ours. Politics just didn't come into it.' Gunston admits that he was not interested in the German extermination camps like Auschwitz and Majdanek, nor in the concentration camps like Buchenwald and Dachau. He was not interested in the atrocity stories or what had happened during the war. Charles Gunston says he is not interested in politics. For Gunston and the British Treasury, Abs was the recognized genius of the German banking system, a friend who had to be protected.

He had to be protected because not everyone in the Allied camp shared Gunston's feelings. Like nearly all prominent Germans, Abs featured on the lists of people who were to be automatically arrested by the Allied armies. Arrested because their influence and authority in Germany made them a threat to the occupation forces, and because an essential part of the Allied plan for Germany was the removal of all who held power and influence under the Nazi regime. It was a realistic working proposition that, party member or not, anyone of importance in the political, social and economic life of Germany had at least compromised with, if not actually supported, the Nazis.

Moreover, in the case of the leaders of German business and industry there was another consideration. It might be, in order to ensure that German ambition and German power were destroyed for good, that the whole machinery which had provided the sinews for Hitler's wars would have to be demolished. It was not, however, an idea on which the wartime Allies found much common ground. As Abs himself wryly put it: 'The dissensions between the *western* Allies were one of the phenomena of the postwar years.'

Essentially, British and American policies were so at odds that the intended victims of denazification became its beneficiaries. While both Allies were agreed on the destruction of Germany's military power, they disagreed on the destruction of the German economy. The Americans wanted a harsh, penal peace settlement. The British did not want to crush Germany and make it dependent on other countries for support.

A leading member of the anti-American lobby in Whitehall was Edward Playfair of the Treasury. In conversations with US Treasury officials in early 1944, Playfair explained that he could see no reason for the Allies to deprive the German bankers and industrialists of their wartime plunder and profits. In his view they had just produced what the government had ordered, like their British and American counterparts.[11] To his considerable surprise, the American officials vehemently attacked him for apparently not believing that Nazi industrialists had done anything wrong. In particular they insisted that what they saw as the enormous concentration of power in one hundred people and two giant banks had to be broken.

Colonel Bernard Bernstein was one of those American postwar planners who drew up a blueprint for nothing less than a frontal assault on German capitalism. The German economy was to be decentralized and decartelized. Once it had been crushed to splinters, it would be allowed to resume limited activities. At interdepartmental meetings in Whitehall during March and April 1945, Playfair did not hide his outrage at Bernstein's plans.

The Americans wanted everyone appointed to an official position after 30 January 1933 to be vetted with a bias in favour of removal. 'That means everyone would be sacked,' Playfair said on 25 April, 'Where are we going to find replacements? Only those who are really bad should be removed. The rest should be kept on.' It was only the restraining hand of Ivonne Kirkpatrick, a Foreign Office diplomat, which prevented Playfair openly declaring war on American policies before the war in Europe had ended.[12] 'It would have the effect of exploding the political dynamite,' Kirkpatrick counselled. 'Gentle persuasion is the only answer.' Negotiations with the Americans did not resolve the differences. Opinion at SHAEF* remained permanently divided, the British insisting that to follow Bernstein's plan would mean the 'confusion will become more confounded'. British policy remained to get the Germany economy working.

The head of the British Military Government's Finance Division, directly responsible for the Banking Section, was Paul Chambers. He was on secondment from the Inland Revenue, where he had invented the British Pay As You Earn tax scheme. Later he was to become chairman of the British chemical giant, ICI. Before leaving for Germany, he had been given elaborate and complicated briefs and statistical surveys of German industry and finance. But, to his confessed surprise, he arrived to find the policy manuals obsolete. 'The first and most important job for the Finance Division staff was to separate the sewage from the water.' The manuals were thrown away. Chambers wrote twenty years later: 'My most valuable contribution to Germany after that was to get German industry going . . . despite French, American and Russian opposition and criticism.'[13] The key to that achievement was the reopening of the German banks. Hermann Abs was the architect of that operation.

Even if Chambers discovered that the manuals which Whitehall provided were obsolete, he was still, in theory, bound by directives from the Supreme Allied Headquarters in Europe, in particular by the 'Financial and Property Control Technical Manual' on the denazification of the banks. It was quite explicit:

Many of the persons who must be removed may not have conspicuous Nazi party ties. The absence of such ties however, does not mean that they are not active Nazis or ardent sympathizers. From the point of view of Military Government, they represent as dangerous and unreliable elements as do notorious Nazi Party members.

Because control in the financial field is highly centralized, it is probable that no person holds a key financial post unless he is acceptable to the Nazis, has been found by them to be dependable and has acted in support of Nazi

*Supreme Headquarters Allied Forces Europe, Eisenhower's headquarters organization for the invasion of Western Europe.

aims. The holders of some key financial positions have been responsible to a large extent for the mobilization and organization of the German economy in war. They have been instrumental in carrying out the policies of German domination and exploitation in the annexed, occupied or Axis countries. In many cases they have acted as intelligence agents and in the seizure and liquidation of property belonging to persecuted minority groups . . . The Finance Officer must ensure that such [persons] are removed at once. Convenience of administration must not be allowed to delay the denazification programme. Even if the removal programme entails in practice the closing of financial institutions, that must not interfere with carrying out the policy.[14]

Chambers says of this instruction: 'So far as I was concerned, this problem of preventing Nazis getting any hold on finance, banking or heavy industry, was quite fundamental to the whole purpose.'

However, Chambers left the crucial matter of the selection of the staff who were to denazify German finance and banking to an acquaintance, a 'city man', as he describes him, whom he met by chance in Berlin. 'Lord Robert Rockley offered to become my deputy in order to smooth the process of the transfer of men from the 21st Army Group (the British army in Germany) who were willing to serve in the Finance Division and who could be "vetted" by him (on my behalf) and taken onto the staff of the Finance Division without my having to do any work personally in this choosing. Some time later, when this work was over and the process completed, Rockley withdrew and returned to his City work in London.'[15]

Rockley, in fact, returned to his own bank, Kleinworts, which had close links to Delbruck, Schickler, the Deutsche Bank and Abs.

The men Rockley left in charge of commercial banking were Albert Haynes and Edward Hellmuth. Haynes had worked for Kleinworts since 1923 and consequently knew Abs very well. Hellmuth worked for the Midland Bank, the Deutsche Bank's correspondent bank in London. Rockley's interest in Abs was not purely philanthropic. Kleinworts had a large stake in the Settlement and Schacht loans. Abs represented a key to an eventual settlement of these and would hopefully remember Kleinworts with favour.

It was Gunston however who found Abs and flew to Berlin to get Chambers' agreement to his employment. Neither Chambers nor the Banking section seem to have found anything dubious in the prospect of employing Abs, or considered that they were contravening the strict denazification regulations. They were technocrats, interested in obeying Playfair's instructions to get the economy working. All of them were dispassionate about Germany's wartime activities. They were entrusted with a job and the prosecution of war criminals was not their concern.

That however, was not the attitude taken by Bernstein and the Finance Division in the American zone. Every suspected banker and industrialist they had found was arrested on the spot and held as a suspected war criminal. When Bernstein heard not only that Gunston was using Abs to re-establish the banking system in the British zone, but that Abs was using his base in Hamburg to re-establish the Deutsche Bank throughout Germany, he exploded. He demanded that Abs be arrested and extradited to the American zone for interrogation. Gunston refused.

American pressure on Gunston increased when Bernstein discovered that the Deutsche Bank in Hamburg had not only instituted a secret courier service between branches, to avoid Allied censorship, but had also forbidden bank employees in other zones to cooperate with the Allies.[16] Under Bernstein's pressure, Gunston at last agreed that Abs could be interrogated, but in Hamburg, not in the American zone. John Kellam, a British accountant in the Banking Section, was present throughout the three-day interrogation in order to, as he puts it, 'see that there was fair play'.[17]

The interrogator was Major Andrew Kamark, who according to Kellam was 'a Jewish official from the US Treasury'. Kamark suffered from the same problem as the vast majority of Allied interrogators in those first postwar months: he did not know the correct answers to his own questions. Abs quickly realized that Kamark was asking out of ignorance and was not in a position to confront him with the documentary evidence to prove that he was either lying or hiding anything. Abs was more sophisticated and more intelligent. It was to lead to a fatal, but inevitable, conclusion.

According to Kellam, when the American asked Abs about Hitler's account at Delbruck, Schickler: 'Abs' memory, which we all knew to be excellent, suddenly became blurred.' Kamark excitedly shouted: 'I put it to you Herr Abs, you have a convenient lapse of memory.' Abs replied: 'Major Kamark, you are unfair, unkind and unjust. But you are in a position to say it.' 'That reply,' remembers Kellam, 'set Kamark aback. We all felt that Abs had stood up very well. The Americans wanted to get their eye-for-an-eye revenge. I knew that the Germans had blotted their copyback, but we had to live with them for the next three hundred years.' According to Hellmuth: 'The Americans wanted to be rough with him. They didn't appreciate his banking experience. They believed him to be a Nazi. But he wasn't a member of the party, so we gave him protection.'

The Banking Section even hid the truth about their work from their superiors at the British Control Commission in Lübeck. At the eighth meeting of the Standing Committee on Denazification on 4 December

1945 the Finance Division reported on the results of denazification in banking: 'Denazification of banking institutions has been prosecuted vigorously since the beginning of the occupation in accordance with the detailed directive issued by SHAEF . . . . The rigid application of this policy to banks was virtually completed by 31 October 1945 in so far as arrest, mandatory removal or suspension was concerned.'[18]

The statistics given for Hamburg were that out of 4,689 employees, nine had been arrested, 595 removed and forty-two suspended – just under fourteen per cent of the total employees in all. None of those removed were vital to Abs' operation. By comparison, in Hanover, which was not an important commercial centre, 303 employees had been arrested and 2,284 removed. The Banking Section were not unique in pretending that they were denazifying. The oil, agriculture, shipping, coal, economics and industrial sections all did the same. The chairman of the committee noted meekly at the end of the 30 November meeting: 'Apart from the *ad hoc* examination of certain prominent individuals, little or nothing has been done by way of denazification of industry or commerce.'

It was a situation which pleased Playfair, who confessed to the Foreign Office, after visiting Gunston, that he was otherwise 'very gloomy' about American pressure. The Americans were making, he reported, 'a good deal of fuss about denazification'.[19]

Temporarily, at the end of 1945, Bernstein won. Gunston remembers that only one member of the Banking Section, a Colonel Rose, was unsympathetic about the use of Abs. 'He threatened me that unless I fired Abs, he would expose me in the *Daily Mirror*.' At that, Gunston's resistance broke. He told Abs: 'There is political pressure to get you and I can't stop it.'

Hellmuth was chosen to strip Abs of his forty-five directorships in accordance with Military Law 52. The occasion was, according to Hellmuth, deliberately surrounded with some solemnity. 'I did it with dignity, in my best German. He appreciated my approach. At the end I told him that I hoped that the Midland and Deutsche Banks could work together in the future. It was very civilized.'

Hellmuth is proud of that occasion. He believes it is one of the reasons why, twenty years later, when he was the International Director of the Midland Bank, Abs rang him from Frankfurt to invite the Midland and not another British bank to join EBIG, an international consortium of banks. The tactful handling of Abs' dismissal, Hellmuth feels, paid off handsomely.

But the dismissal was not enough for the Americans. Gunston returned to England at the beginning of January. On 16 January, Abs was arrested as a suspected war criminal. Within days, Kellam arrived at

Hamburg's Altona jail to ask Abs for more advice. Abs refused. His cooperation, he said, was dependent on his getting out of jail. It took Kellam 'three months of very hard work' to get the banker out of cell ninety-three. 'I finally got permission from British intelligence and drove him to his apple farm at Remagen in the French zone. I winkled him out of American hands. Gunston and I deserve the credit for that.'

Today, Abs is the chairman of the Deutsche Bank, Europe's second largest bank, with a controlling interest in nearly one third of West Germany's industry. Other past members of the AAF have also had impressive careers in postwar Germany. Westerick became secretary of state in the prime minister's office; Blessing became president of the Federal Bank; and Erhard became Chancellor of the Republic.

During the war none of them would have considered themselves as war criminals. They were neither soldiers nor politicians, and have forever denied that they had any responsibility for the fate of the millions who perished. After all, they did not pull the triggers or release the Zyklon B gas into the packed chamber below.

Whether, without white collar support, the Third Reich could have sustained itself in war, is as disputed now as it was in 1945. To some Americans, the executive supplying poison gas, employing slave labour, or plundering other countries, was as much a war criminal as those who shot an unarmed prisoner of war. To others, there was a sharp distinction between the actual murderer and the middle-class technocrat sitting behind his desk.

But until Germany's final defeat, neither group had more than the vaguest of ideas of the extent of the criminality, and the daunting obstacles which stood in the way of any programme of doing justice to it. Only a dwindling handful would have the stamina, courage and conviction to pursue the justice for which the war had ostensibly been fought. At the end it would seem as if the Allies had turned a callous and blind eye to the murder of twelve million Europeans.

2

'THIS RATHER
WILD STORY'

A natural consequence of the Chamberlain government's appeasement
policy was that it deliberately played down reports of Nazi brutality and
persecution. To comment on them officially would not only have
undermined government policy, but would also have breached the well-
established convention of not interfering in another country's affairs.
Hilter was, according to the official view, a dangerous and difficult
child, prone to tantrums, who was not to be needlessly provoked by
criticism.

So it was not until shortly after the declaration of war that the ample
evidence of Nazi crimes contained in British government files was officially put on the record, in a White Paper entitled *The Treatment of
German Nationals in Germany*.[1] The document explained that the
information, including the existence of Dachau and Buchenwald concentration camps, had been withheld up to that point because 'it would
have been wrong to embitter relations between the two countries.' It
added: 'Even after the outbreak of war HMG felt reluctant to take action
which would have the effect of inspiring hatred.'

Given the resources which the Foreign Office had at its disposal for
gathering information, the White Paper was not a particularly impressive document. The eyewitness accounts of 'barbarous treatment, the
flogging and torture which are the order of the day' in Germany, were
out of date and scarcely revelatory. Certainly there was no impression
that the events described would call for any action on the part of the
British or Allied governments in the event of a German defeat. The
crimes had been committed by Germans against Germans and would
remain a German affair. At most they indicated the detestable nature of
the enemy.

Although Britain had given refuge to some tens of thousands of
refugees from Germany and Austria, mainly Jews, trade unionists and
socialists, there was no precedent for one side in a war concerning itself
with the way an enemy treated its own nationals. Nevertheless, among
the various Whitehall departments the Foreign Office had the greatest
sympathy and understanding for the circumstances which had driven
these people into exile. It was, in contrast to the Home Office and the

27

War Office, well aware that their hatred of Nazism for outweighed any residual loyalty they might have to their countries, and it was far more alive to the possibilities of harnessing their motives to the war effort. But any idea of imposing a judicial remedy for their wrongs in a postwar world was quite alien to current realities or historical precedent.

British officialdom was not unaware of the nature of Hitler's regime – diplomatic reports and the press had made that quite obvious over the past eight years – but in 1939 the business of the government machine was to mobilize and organize the nation and the Empire for war. A war which would presumably end, like earlier wars, with an armistice and a peace treaty, and with the replacement of National Socialism by an alternative German government whose business it would be to remedy the wrongs which the Nazis had done to their fellow Germans.

War crimes, breaches of the rules of war by the military, and crimes committed by one belligerent against the citizens of another, were a different matter. They were a legitimate field of interest and concern. But the precedents of the First World War were not encouraging. The Foreign Office felt it had every reason for approaching the subject with caution.

In Paris, on 3 February 1920, Baron von Lersnera, the German ambassador, was formally presented with a list of 896 Germans wanted by six countries* for trial. Under Article 228 of the Versailles Treaty, the German Government had recognized the right of the Allies to try Germans for the 'violation of the laws and customs of war'. Those listed were to be handed over, along with any documentary evidence and eye-witnesses the Allied courts needed.

Heading the list was the Kaiser, accused of offences against 'international morality and the sanctity of treaties'. Others included on the list were Field-Marshals Hindenburg and Ludendorff and Admiral Tirpitz; the former Chancellor Bethmann – Hollweg and the Duke of Würtemberg. Further down the list were the names of those responsible for the mass shooting of Belgian civilians and French prisoners of war, and for the torpedoing of British hospital ships.

Emerging onto the street, Lersnera emotionally told a crowd of newsmen that he would resign rather than allow the listed men to be handed over to the Allies. Back in Germany, where the myth that the German army had been betrayed by the socialists and not defeated by the Allies had already taken root, the protests were less diplomatically restrained than the Baron's. Bluntly the Allies were told that the men would not be

---

*The Americans did not list anyone.

handed over. There was little they could do. No Allied soldiers were based in Germany and neither the German army nor the police were answerable to the Allies. A compromise was reached: the Germans were to hold the trials, and the original total of 896 would be reduced to forty-five. There was a face-saving provision that the Allies could re-try the accused if they were dissatisfied by the outcome.

For the Allies, it was the beginning of a traumatic and humiliating nightmare. Many of the wanted men had by then disappeared. Witnesses were also untraceable and even many of those found refused to go to Germany. When the trials finally opened in Leipzig on 23 May 1921, the courtroom atmosphere was more like a political rally. The first British cases to be heard were against the two U-boat commanders who had torpedoed the hospital ships *Dover Castle* and *Llandovery Castle*. Lieutenant-Commander Karl Neumann, whose submarine U86, which torpedoed the *Llandovery Castle*, although obeying his commander's orders, knew that the commander was acting against his orders. Compounding the crime, after the submarine surfaced it had successfully shelled all but one of the crowded lifeboats. In court, according to *The Times*, the two commanders were 'unashamed and proud to be barbarians'.[2] Defiantly, both refused to make statements and were sentenced to four years imprisonment as accomplices. A German newspaper headline the following day read: 'Four Years Imprisonment for U-boat Heroes'. Within six months, with the help of prison officials, both had escaped.

Another case featured General Stenger, who was charged with issuing orders for surrendering Allied soldiers to be shot. A Major Cruscius was charged with carrying out that order. Hundreds of French POWs were shot, many by Cruscius himself in a first aid post. Cruscius pleaded guilty, but claimed that he had obeyed Stenger's orders. As the German judges acquitted Stenger and convicted Cruscius, the packed courtroom burst out in applause mixed with hoots of derision aimed at the French observers. No one heard Cruscius' sentence of two years for manslaughter. Stenger was carried out shoulder high, garlanded in flowers, the crowd cheering him for giving the orders that no quarter should be given. On 11 July a paid advertisement from Stenger appeared in the German press thanking everyone for their congratulations and saying that he had received too many letters for individual replies. The Allies had been mocked.

The six cases which followed underlined their humiliation. A few months' imprisonment for systematic brutality in POW camps, and acquittals for murder. In January 1922 the Allies withdrew their observers in protest. But their proposal that the remaining accused be surrendered for trial, as agreed at Versailles, was defiantly rejected by the

Reichswehr, the rump of the German army. To break the stalemate, the Leipzig judges unilaterally decided in June 1922 to continue the trials, without the Allies, of all of those on the original list and others named afterwards. It was a mere gesture. In closed court, the politicians were tried and acquitted, while the soldiers were tried and 'their innocence proved'. Of the 901 Germans finally prosecuted, only thirteen were convicted. Taken to prison, all of them 'escaped' within a few months. The prison warders who helped them were publicly feted and congratulated.

The lesson of Leipzig was clear. The attempt to force Germany to hand over alleged criminals to the justice of the victors had been an humiliating failure. It had only contributed to the sense of injustice felt by Germans, which had aided the rise of Hitler and led to the new war. Since any idea of a victory that would lead to the military occupation of Germany was very far from official minds in the days of the 'phoney war', it seemed obvious that any repetition of the fiasco at Leipzig was to be avoided at all costs. Officials were also, perhaps, uncomfortably aware that public hatred of the Germans in the aftermath of the last war had been fuelled by atrocity stories which were, frequently, the deliberate inventions of Allied propaganda. The accounts of hordes of Uhlans violating Belgian nuns and similar fanciful tales had been valuable in persuading the British people that they were fighting and working in defence of civilization against barbarism. But they were usually quite untrue.

Moreover, the events of the inter-war period did not suggest that propagandists had become any more scrupulous in their use of atrocities to inflame public opinion. Both the Italian invasion of Abyssinia and the Spanish Civil War had produced tales of atrocities that were graphic and horrifying, and had been used freely by all sides. The atrocities of the other side, real or alleged, were clearly becoming an almost routine weapon of war – useful, no doubt, in simplifying the issues for the public, but government officials were aware that they would be wise to treat them with scepticism. This scepticism had to be, in the British view, particularly rigorous when those involved were foreigners – likely to be hysterical and to exaggerate such things for their own ends. The German Jews were, of course, foreign, and while there was no doubt that they had been treated abominably it must be born in mind, as an assistant under-secretary, Reginald Leeper, put it, that: 'As a general rule the Jews are inclined to magnify their persecutions.'[3]

The Foreign Office reaction to the first suggestion that Britain should involve itself with war crimes was, therefore, entirely predictable. The suggestion came from the Polish government-in-exile. The German invasion of Poland had brought a spate of reports of rape, murder, mass arrests and deportations, attested to by both refugees and observers within the country. By early 1940 the Polish authorities were pressing the British and French governments, not for public condemnation alone, but also for some commitment to seek out and punish those responsible. The Poles were spurred on not only by anger, but also by the fear that a compromise peace was not impossible in the near future. As well as sympathy and private assurances, they wanted a public statement which would commit their allies. They offered the draft of a tripartite declaration which concluded with a commitment to 'hold those responsible for these crimes, which cannot go unpunished'.

Whitehall's reaction to the suggestion that the British government should openly commit itself to bringing Germans to justice for crimes committed in another country, a country as far away as Czechoslovakia had been in 1938, was adamant – the idea was unthinkable. Yet obviously the Poles could not simply be ignored. A form of words had to be found that expressed condemnation and sympathy but avoided anything that could be construed as a commitment to future action. Various drafts were produced. The Foreign Secretary, Lord Halifax, thought that something about 'righting wrongs' sounded best, though it carried an unfortunate undertone of obligation. There was a consensus, according to one official, Roger Makins, that it would be inadvisable to 'single out the barbarities inflicted on the Jews' for special mention, and it was agreed that it was essential to avoid committing Britain to the 'same trouble as after the last war about drawing up lists of criminals who were to be personally punished.'[4]

Only one dissenting voice was raised within the Foreign Office hierarchy: that of Sir Robert Vansittart. On 26 February 1940 he wrote to Halifax:

> There is no analogy in the world between isolated atrocities such as took place in Belgium in the last war, still less atrocities on a relatively small scale at sea, on the one hand, and on the other the deliberate attempt to exterminate a whole nation. These are totally different things. The latter, to the best of my knowledge, has not been attempted for at least eight hundred years. It would seem to me unthinkable that we should, in any event whatever, pass a sponge over these wholesale horrors. Were we to do so, it would put a premium on international crime in the twentieth century, and, above all there would be no further incentive to better behaviour on the part of that section of Germany which, with all its brutality, cannot stomach what has been done in Poland.[5]

But Vansittart's long, almost singlehanded, campaign within the

Foreign Office against the policy of appeasement was hardly likely to have endeared him to Halifax, one of the most convinced advocates of the policy; and he took little trouble to disguise his relentless suspicion and contempt for the German nation. His advice was not likely to carry much weight; something he himself probably recognized when he concluded his minute: 'A protest to the conscience of the world doesn't mean much *in practice* [emphasis in origin] when the world is busily demonstrating, under the influence of fear, that it hasn't got one.' The inference was unlikely to be lost on, or to appeal to, a statesman who had supported British submission at Munich.

In the end the most acceptable draft seemed to be the one produced by William Strang. Its conclusion suggested that the three governments: 'make a formal and public protest to the conscience of the world against the crimes committed by the German government and their agents against the Polish population. They must hold the German government responsible for these crimes, and they reaffirm their determination to right the wrongs inflicted on the Polish people.'

On 27 February the acting first secretary at the Foreign Office, Frank Roberts, flew to Paris to present the proposed British draft to the other two governments. The Poles were bitterly disappointed and angry. They threatened that they would refuse to sign the declaration unless it contained some promise of retribution. Roberts returned the next day and, in recording the discussions for the file, commented: 'If the Poles remain obdurate, it is their funeral . . . it would be unfortunate to commit ourselves to punishing Germans for atrocities.'[6]

Ultimately the Poles had no alternative but to give way, and the three governments signed the declaration in the form in which Strang had drafted it. Its substance failed to give the Poles what they wanted, as did its manner of propagation. It was published in *The Times* on 18 April 1940 – on page six. It cannot have brought comfort to many of the citizens of occupied Poland, nor is it likely that any of the Germans then busy suppressing their conquered territory were influenced in their conduct.

By the middle of 1941, with German armies occupying Western Europe from North Cape to the Pyrenees and sweeping across Russia towards Moscow in an apparently invincible blitzkrieg, it was quite evident in London that any comparison between the atrocities of the earlier war and the activities of Nazi Germany was meaningless. Mass deportations in Western Europe had been reported in both the Axis and the neutral press; the *New York Times* had carried frequent reports from Berlin, Vienna and Paris on the treatment of Jews, trade unionists, socialists and clergy. The various resistance movements and the governments-in-exile provided a mass of accurate, detailed and first-hand reports of wholesale executions of innocent hostages in reprisal for the death of German soldiers. No one in an official position concerned with policy towards Europe could have been in the least doubt that the behaviour of the German conquerors went far beyond the rules of warfare, and even beyond the limits of civilization.

At the time, the British response was limited to frustrated gestures. Unable to help occupied Europe militarily, Churchill felt that Britain could at least support morale and foster the resistance movements, promising to eventually 'set Europe ablaze'. In his early broadcasts, which were more products of his temperament than of calculated policy, he promised the Europeans not only ultimate victory but also revenge. In broadcast speeches in October 1940 and May 1941, he even hinted that Britain was committed to exacting justice for Nazi crimes. In a broadcast on 22 June 1941 he seemed to go even further towards a commitment:

> Any man or State who fights against Nazism will have our aid. Any man or State who marches with Hitler is our foe. This applies not only to organized states, but to all representatives of that vile race of Quislings who make themselves the tools and agents of the Nazi regime against their fellow countrymen and against the lands of their birth. These Quislings, *like the Nazi leaders* [emphasis added], if not disposed of by their fellow countrymen – which would save us trouble – will be delivered by us on the morrow of the victory to the justice of the Allied tribunals.

On 8 July Captain Strickland put a question in the House of Commons. He asked the government 'whether a record is being kept of the names of Nazis, fascists and their allies responsible for deeds of cruelty and oppression committed against defenceless men, women and children . . . with a view to future proceedings as and when possible?'

As Foreign Secretary, it fell to Anthony Eden to reply. In preparing his brief, Foreign Office officials minutely scanned the Prime Minister's statements, searching for anything that could be construed as a commitment, fearful lest Churchillian rhetoric had preempted Britain's freedom from obligation.[7] The broadcast of 22 June obviously raised problems. It seemed to contain a clear suggestion that Allied tribunals would be created to mete out justice to war criminals, which would include the Nazi leaders. To prevent any notion of commitment taking root, Sir William Malkin, a Foreign Office legal adviser, decided that the speech had really been addressed to Quislings, not war criminals. 'I doubt,' he minuted, 'whether the PM's reference to "Nazi leaders" was intended to [cover offences against the laws of war committed by enemy nationals in occupied territory].' It was obviously a sensitive area where the government had to tread with great caution. Efforts were made to get the question withdrawn. When they failed, Éden simply replied that the question was premature, and sat down without further comment. It would not be possible, however, for the Foreign Office to continue using these stonewalling tactics for long.

To the stream of atrocity reports from Western Europe were now added those from Russia. The Foreign Office continued to treat these with scepticism, but there was concern elsewhere in Whitehall. On 25 September, Dr Hugh Dalton, minister for economic warfare and a Labour member of the coalition government, wrote to Eden about the reports that there had been mass executions of French hostages by the Germans in retaliation for attacks on German soldiers. He suggested that Eden might issue a declaration that: 'we do not intend to allow these criminals to go unpunished. We should tell the people of Europe that the names of all those connected with the shooting of hostages, from the commander of the occupying forces downwards, are being duly noted. We should say that after the war these men will be hunted down, tried for the murders now being committed, and if they are convicted, summarily executed.[8]

It fell to Roger Makins to comment, and he could not resist a burst of sarcasm at Dalton's expense: 'Although the vision of Dr Dalton as a witch doctor smelling out the German criminal from one end of Europe to the other is a terrifying one, the question whether it should be revealed to Europe is by no means easy to decide.' He then went on to outline the standard Foreign Office response. Significantly he did not underestimate the extent or enormity of Nazi crimes, but nevertheless reaffirmed that any commitment to 'hunt down and try thousands of Germans after the war' would be 'virtually impossible to carry out'. The government, he suggested, should 'studiously refrain from saying what we propose to do with them in the unlikely event of our catching any after the war'.

Makins' views were supported by four senior colleagues, Sir Alexander Cadogan, the permanent under-secretary, Sir Orme Sergeant, the deputy under-secretary of state, Strang and Malkin, when the five of them met on 29 September 1941 to draft a reply to Dalton. Sergeant stressed that there must be no mention whatever of any records or lists being kept. Such an admission would be 'halfway towards being committed to trying war criminals,' and the government could 'safely leave the Germans to the vengeance of their neighbours without undertaking ourselves to wield the flaming sword.' The most they were prepared to offer Dalton was a joint declaration similar to the one that had been issued with the Poles in 1940. It would, of course, 'again leave vague the threat of retribution'. The declaration would be drafted by the Foreign Office and presented to the Cabinet by Eden.

Drafting the declaration was Malkin's responsibility. Again ignoring Churchill's speeches, which Frank Roberts pointed out to him 'certainly commit HM Government to the principle of retribution', Malkin sought to produce a piece which might suggest an intention to punish, but would certainly not imply a commitment. He found the beginning easy to write. It was peppered with phrases like 'lust for conquest', 'the German yoke', and the 'spirit of the enslaved peoples'. Such rhetoric was harmless, but the conclusion presented problems. The signatories to the proposed declaration, he suggested, should declare that 'the brutalities which are being committed in the occupied countries' were 'contrary to the dictates of humanity; are a reversion to barbarism and will meet with. . .' At this point the five officials could not agree whether the brutalities should meet with 'retribution sure sudden and complete' or simply with 'exemplary retribution'. The choice was put to Eden, who selected the first form of words.

But while prepared to debate what kind of retribution was to be expected, no one at the top of the Foreign Office would even consider suggesting to Eden that he specify who was going to mete it out. Introducing the draft to Cabinet on 5 October,[9] Eden explained that he did not want to encourage futile resistance or issue any specific threats, as he was convinced that any commitment to 'try the war criminals' should be avoided. The declaration should be seen as a boost to the morale of the resistance movements, no more. The Cabinet did not agree. Other ministers wanted the declaration to end with a positive conclusion that those responsible for atrocities would be punished, and argued that it should suggest that lists of names should be compiled and, if possible, sent to London. Eden was asked to submit a revised draft.

Back at the Foreign Office Makins set about defusing this firework which threatened to demolish the policy so carefully maintained over the past two years. While meeting the Cabinet's wishes, his revised draft studiously avoided stating who was to carry out the retribution or to compile the lists of those who might expect it. The conclusion ran: '. . .world opinion will not allow the criminals to escape just punishment for their crimes. The facts are being put on record so that in due time the world may pronounce its judgement. With victory will come retribution.'[10] It is clear that Makins' wording was deliberately vague. On the same day that he produced the draft he sent a minute to Sergeant pointing out that the previous evening, while fire-watching, he had heard a BBC broadcast to Europe which said that lists were being prepared of 'persons guilty of infamous conduct'.[11] Within forty-eight hours the BBC had been instructed that it was not to mention such lists again.

Not everyone in London was ready to treat the matter with the same caution as the Foreign Office. Reports from Moscow intensified the pressure from the Allied governments for action. Daily broadcasts from Russia detailed horrific mass killings and atrocities, and in early October Moscow Radio described the discovery of a massacre outside Kiev. Thanks to Heydrich's precise report, history now knows that on 29 September, 33,771 Jews had been taken to the ravine known as Babi Yar and individually executed with a bullet in the back or neck, while standing on a plank projecting over the ravine. Within a week foreign journalists on a tour round Kiev were asking their German guides for confirmation of the reports. Cavendish – Bentinck at the Foreign Office was less inquisitive. He dismissed the reports as 'products of the Slavic imagination'. Besides, the Russians were widely mistrusted. 'We ourselves put out rumours of atrocities and horrors for various purposes and I have no doubt this game is widely played.'[12]

Reports from Western Europe were not so easy to dismiss. At the end of September 1941, Hitler had issued the *Nacht und Nebel* (Night and Fog) decree. Instead of shooting hostages and trying partisans, which created martyrs and stiffened resistance, suspects were to be brought in 'night and fog' across the frontier into Germany and kept isolated. The resulting spate of sudden disappearances was immediately reported to London, where the governments-in-exile were getting impatient with the British.

After reading the Foreign Office's proposed Allied declaration, Dejean, the French representative, told British officials that he wanted something less cold and 'more arresting'.[13] When the British demurred, he defiantly told them that the French would draft their own declaration. On 13 October the Poles and the Czechs, to the intense irritation of the Foreign Office, submitted an alternative draft. The Foreign Office reaction was that if the declaration was not in the form they proposed, then the British government should not be party to it at all. Eden needed little persuasion to agree. When Hankey, the former Secretary to the Cabinet, added his advice against joining in the declaration, the foreign secretary described it as 'a glimpse of the obvious'.

According to Roberts, quite apart from his natural caution about becoming embroiled in troublesome commitments, Eden was openly uninterested in the 'war crimes business'.[14] This could well have been the product of what Oliver Harvey, Eden's private secretary, describes as Eden being 'hopelessly prejudiced' against the Jews. Writing in his Diaries in the context of the Palestine problem, Harvey noted: 'This is largely due to the blind pro-Arabism of the FO which A.E. has never resisted. Indeed he is a blind pro-Arab himself'.[15] Distrustful of rhetoric and disdainful of populism, Eden took a mandarin view of foreign affairs. But at the head of the government was a rhetorician and populist supreme.

Churchill's utterances had already involved the Foreign Office in some delicate hair-splitting in the field of war crimes. Now worse was threatened. In early October he suggested to Eden that he should broadcast on the subject of German atrocities. Though on 8 October Eden had told the Prime Minister that he thought it a good idea, he quickly realized that it was also a dangerous one and revised his opinion: 'I am not sure subject is large enough for the PM.'[16]

In the event, the issue was forced. On 25 October President Roosevelt publicly protested about the execution of 'scores of innocent hostages'. His statement ended with the words: 'It only sows seeds of hatred which will one day bring a fearful retribution.' Churchill had only been warned that the President was going to issue the statement a few hours before it appeared, and since it would obviously be embarrassing for him to remain silent while the leader of a nation still officially neutral spoke out, a statement was quickly drafted for simultaneous release. After condemning 'Nazi butcheries in France . . . and above all behind the German front in Russia', it ended with the declaration that: 'Retribution for these crimes must henceforth take its place among the major purposes of the war.'[17]

This surely marked defeat for the Foreign Office, final and complete. Yet they seem to have been undeterred. There was even some advantage to be found in Churchill's precipitate action. On Orme Sergeant's advice, Eden put it to the Cabinet on 27 October that after the Prime Minister's statement further British participation in any joint declaration with the Allies could only fall flat. The Cabinet agreed that Britain should not join in the declaration and the Allies were abandoned to, in Cadogan's words, 'say what they like'.

Having disposed of the problems of the Allied declaration, the next difficulty seemed to be the matter of compiling lists of war criminals. Not only did Churchill's statement seem to carry a very obvious implication that some record of Nazi crimes and their perpetrators would be kept, but Eden himself felt that he had given such an undertaking. On 10 October he had scribbled an instruction that this should be done because, 'I have so assured Parliament'.[18] Surprised, Roberts set about minutely scrutinizing every ministerial utterance in order to establish that no undertaking had been given. The Foreign Secretary could not be allowed to assume such a responsibility if it could be avoided. Eden was thinking of either a statement he had made in the House on 8 October, when he said that 'note is being taken of these German atrocities and they will not be forgotten' or the revised draft of the joint Allied declaration, which, following the Cabinet's decision, had to promise the compilation of lists. Roberts, however, was quick to see that the Parliamentary statement was far from a promise that the British themselves would keep any lists. He minuted: 'We know that note is in fact being taken by the Allied governments. . . . The Secretary of State did not, however, state that note was being taken by *H.M. Government*' (emphasis in original).

British reservations applied not only to the principle of retribution for war crimes, but also to the practical aspects. At that stage of the war it looked as if the British would have to be responsible for carrying out the threats and promises which Britain's Allies were so anxious to make publicly; and if this was to be done then it would be mainly on the basis of information supplied by those Allies. The Foreign Office was fairly clear that much of this information was likely, in their view, to be unreliable. As one official put it, it seemed that the representatives of the various occupied countries were 'in unhealthy competition', spreading 'tales embroidered for propaganda purposes'.[19] The Foreign Office's instinct to keep their heads down and avoid commitment, even if it involved somewhat undignified logic-chopping, remained as strong as ever.

The Allies, having been in effect cold-shouldered by the British, proceeded to act on Cadogan's advice and 'say what they liked'. The representatives of eight nations – Belgium, Czechoslovakia, Greece, Luxemburg, the Netherlands, Norway, Poland and Yugoslavia – together with the French National Committee drew up their own draft for the declaration and presented it to the Foreign Office. Everyone was happy with the condemnations of Nazi rule and brutality, but the British were horrified by one sentence which stated that the oppressors could expect 'punishment, through the channel of organized justice, of those guilty of or responsible for these crimes, whether they have ordered them, perpetrated them or participated in them.'[20]

'This is getting pretty near the "Hang the Kaiser" thing,' Orme Sergeant told Eden. In a more ponderous minute Makins commented that the draft: 'Throws the net very wide and takes us into paths we are very reluctant to tread.'[21] In chorus, the officials begged their minister to stop the Allies before it was too late. Politically, however, the whole issue had become too hot for the British to control. Even the Soviets were now anxious to join the nine signatories; they insisted, however, on the reference to Germans being changed to Nazis.[22] As the Western Allies were belatedly to realize in 1945, it was not a minor distinction, and Russian involvement was finally to founder on this point. When the signing ceremony finally took place at St James's Palace on 13 January

1942, they, like the British and the Americans, attended as observers.

If the Allies could not be prevented from issuing the declaration, Britain could at least be distanced from its more unfortunate provisions. In his welcoming speech to the Allied representatives, Eden was careful to point out that the pledges of trials and punishment were an Allied and not a British policy. The Australian delegation went even further, they attended 'under protest', explaining to the Foreign Office that this was because they would have liked the declaration to 'remain vague'.[23]

Officially and intentionally, until spring 1942 the Foreign Office maintained a detached, if sympathetic, attitude towards the tribulations of occupied Europe, coupled with scepticism towards much of the information they received from their Allies. But the entry of Japan into the war and the collapse of British resistance in the Far East changed official attitudes and brought them under far greater pressure from public opinion. Now the reports coming into London were of British prisoners being tied up and bayoneted; of European women being raped and herded into communal brothels by the Japanese; of Britons being left to die of disease and starvation in flagrant breach of the international conventions. When Eden confirmed the stories in the House of Commons on 10 March 1942 he was clearly shocked.

The news from Europe was equally horrifying. On 29 May Heydrich was assassinated in Prague by a group of resistance fighters organized and armed by the British. In retaliation the entire population of the village of Lidice, 1,288 people, including children and the elderly, had been either shot or transported to the concentration camps. Throughout Britain independent groups began to be set up to press for strong action and for a pledge of reprisals against the guilty men at the end of the war.

After the reports of Japanese atrocities against British captives appeared, the Law Officers had suggested that they look into the matter, and Cadogan had agreed to this. Their recommendations were sent to the Foreign Office by early April,[24] but it was not until 11 June that Cadogan called an interdepartmental meeting to consider them.[25] In issuing invitations to the meeting, Malkin explained that there was a need to re-examine the 'detached attitude' that had so far been official policy.[26] The Cabinet would have to take decisions on policy in order that the Foreign Office could again give a lead and forestall any embarrassment from the Allies or public opinion. In fact, when Eden put the question before the Cabinet after the meeting, on 6 July, he stressed that the last thing he wanted to do was to make a statement of policy; what he hoped was that some 'guiding principles' could be established which would enable conversations to take place with the Allied governments, thus reducing the risk of any unfortunate decisions being reached which 'might afterwards prove embarrassing'.[27] Eden based his suggestions on the survey of war crimes produced by the Law Officers, Sir Donald Somervell, the Attorney-General, and Sir Maxwell Fyfe, the Solicitor-General. Both were clearly still heavily influenced by Leipzig and confused about what to do in the new situation. Their assessment managed to raise questions, but proposed few answers other than to conclude that massive retaliations on the part of the conquered peoples towards the end of the war would save the need for trials.

Eden's proposals, called 'The Treatment of War Criminals', represented the Foreign Office's fallback position. If it was now politically impossible to avoid a commitment to action in the future, then it was still feasible to limit the commitment and make it as vague as possible. It dismissed out of hand the possibility of arraigning Hitler and the Nazi leadership before a court. Their guilt was 'so black' that no conceivable judicial procedure was appropriate: their fate must be a political decision. This section was, no doubt, based on the Law Officers' memorandum, which had suggested that while Hitler had committed 'crimes against civilization' they 'were not recognized as crimes under international law to be dealt with and punished by a court. . . It may be doubted whether any tribunal that could be assembled would be regarded by those in enemy countries as impartial'.

In the case of less politically exalted criminals, Eden's recommendation was that they should be tried by military courts as soon as possible after an armistice and judged by existing laws. The aim was to prevent reprisals and to forestall the possibility of trials 'dragging on for years and so delaying the return to a peaceful atmosphere in Europe'. He suggested that negotiations should soon be started to prevent wanted men finding refuge in neutral countries. While the necessity for lists to be drawn up was now admitted, neither Eden nor the Law Officers had anything to suggest when it came to ways and means of actually finding the wanted men. The latter felt that 'there was nothing useful that can be said . . . at this stage of the war'. Nor was this to be in any way a British responsibility: finding and arresting war criminals was a problem to be left to the country that wanted them.

If, as Churchill had proposed, retribution for Nazi crimes was now 'among the major purposes of the war', it was not one to which the Foreign Office was prepared to give a great deal of forethought. Certainly the paper which the Foreign Secretary laid before the Cabinet made no concessions to those who felt that some principles of justice might be at stake. The attitude was clearly that if some commitment was inescapable, then it was essential to minimize it and the damage it might be expected to bring about. In any case there was still a chance that if all concerned kept their heads the business might quietly disappear from the agenda.

The War Office took an equally pragmatic view. Briefing their minister for the Cabinet discussion, his officials supported the argument of the Law Officers that the need for trials was likely to be obviated by the massive reprisals that could be expected to be inflicted on the Germans at the end of the war.[28] (It was, of course, assumed that any foreseeable armistice would find the Germans still *in situ* in the occupied territories.) 'This paper,' the War Office commented, 'does not leave a very clear-cut impression of definite proposals, and AG [The Adjutant-General] regards the whole problem as set out in it as "completely theoretical" because when the break-up occurs the injured nations will take the law into their own hands.'

Guy Lambert, the deputy under-secretary, made the War Office's views clear when he wrote to Roberts at the Foreign Office asking him to remove the proposal that there would be trials for 'breaches of the rules of war committed in actual operations'. Individual officers, he insisted, could not be held responsible for obeying superior orders, and any who had committed illegal acts would be dealt with by those who carried out the reprisals that were seen as inevitable.[29]

Combining the Foreign Office's opinion that the Nazi leadership could not be prosecuted with the War Office's opinion that superior orders would be an acceptable plea would obviously have meant, in effect, that there could be no trials at all. One member of the government felt that this was all a little too easy. Shortly before the Cabinet meeting on 6 July, when Eden's paper was due to be discussed, Lord Simon, the Lord Chancellor, wrote to Churchill saying that the proposals in the Paper would fail 'to satisfy public opinion or achieve a substantial measure of justice'.[30] In particular, he objected to the suggestion that Hitler and Himmler should be dealt with on political criteria, while their subordinates would be tried and hanged as war criminals. He pointed out that if the plea of superior orders was accepted, the inevitable conclusion would be that the atrocities would go unpunished.

Simon had not so far been consulted. As a prominent appeaser he was disliked by both Churchill and Eden, and his intervention at this point might have been unproductive. However, it is clear that Churchill sensed the Foreign Office's coolness and detachment and felt that Simon at least shared his own anger and understanding of public feeling. It was better to have Simon as an ally than no one at all, especially as the Prime Minister had just returned from Washington, where he had proposed, and the President had agreed to, the establishment of a United Nations Commission on Atrocities. Churchill had suggested that such a body, investigating and collecting evidence, would provide good propaganda.[31]

By publicly naming those responsible for atrocities it would 'let them know that they are being watched by the civilized world, which will mete out swift and just punishment on the reckoning day'. Roosevelt's aide, Harry Hopkins, had worked out a detailed proposal for the two leaders. Eden's reaction to the plan had been cool. 'There may be little harm in the idea,' he wrote. 'What do we do next?'[32] His officials were no more enthusiastic. At best they felt that it would provide a useful means to 'head off the Allies'; providing, of course, that it was prevented from achieving any real substance or momentum. Simon, however, was eager.

Churchill's proposal was put to the Cabinet, along with Eden's paper on the 'Treatment of War Criminals', at the meeting on 6 July 1942.[33] The Foreign Office paper was passed over without comment and the Cabinet agreed to back Churchill's proposal for the commission. Simon was given the job of chairing a ministerial committee to work out a war crimes policy. While the Foreign Office scarcely welcomed the appointment, it also supposed that the lack of comment on the paper which Eden had presented meant that it now represented official British policy.

This was certainly Eden's understanding when he attended the first meeting of Simon's committee on 27 July.[34] At the meeting Simon set out his own views: British policy should not involve international tribunals or new retrospective laws. On the other hand, in contradiction to the Foreign Office view, Simon was against making any distinction between the Nazi leaders and their subordinates. Either because of mutual dislike, or Eden's lack of interest, the disagreement was not discussed. Instead, the meeting agreed on the importance of winning American support for the United Nations Commission, and its only decision was to begin talks about the establishment of the commission.

Certainly the Foreign Office did not see Simon's appointment as in any way limiting their pre-eminence in matters of policy. Without consulting him, they resolved to stand firm against Allied pressure to publicly endorse the St James's Palace Declaration.[35] Although it seemed that, six months after the Declaration had been signed, British policy, as decided in Cabinet, had now caught up with the Allies, the Foreign Office continued to refuse any public acknowledgement of this, despite pressure from the Allied governments for the British to endorse the Declaration. The concern and embarrassment of the Foreign Office was increased when, on 21 August, Roosevelt issued a statement warning those responsible for 'barbarous crimes . . . [which] may even lead to the extermination of certain populations . . . that the time will come when they shall have to stand in the courts of law in the very countries which they are now oppressing and answer for their acts'.[36]

It seemed that even the Americans were conspiring to force Britain into making a commitment which would be deeply troublesome in the future. The White House's initiative was all the more exasperating when the Foreign Office discovered that the State Department in Washington had been deliberately holding back messages to Roosevelt, especially on the subject of war crimes. Their irritation is understandable, even if it seems in retrospect that loss of diplomatic face was of more consequence than the news from Europe.

On 10 August 1942 at 6.25 pm an unclassified telegram had arrived at the Foreign Office from the British consul-general in Geneva. It was a message from Gerhart Riegner, secretary of the World Jewish Congress, to be passed to the Labour Member of Parliament, Sidney Silverman. It read:

> Receiving alarming reports stating that, in the Führer's Headquarters, a plan has been discussed, and is under consideration, according to which all Jews in countries occupied or controlled by Germany numbering three and a half to four millions should, after deportation and concentration in the East, be at one blow exterminated, in order to resolve once and for all the Jewish question in Europe. Action is reported to be planned for the autumn. Ways of execution are still being discussed including the use of prussic acid. We transmit this information with all the necessary reservation, as exactitude cannot be confirmed by us. Our informant is reported to have close connections with the highest German authorities, and his reports are generally reliable. Please inform and consult New York.[37]

Dennis Allen, a Foreign Office lawyer, who read the message that evening, commented that while there had been many reports of Jews perishing in large numbers because of bad conditions or lack of food, 'they do not of course amount to "extermination at one blow".' The German policy, he wrote, 'seems to be rather to eliminate "useless mouths" but to use able bodied Jews as slave labour. . . I do not think we should be wise to make use of this story in propaganda to Germany without further confirmation. . . We should not help matters by taking any further action on the basis of this rather wild story.'

The telegram was given to Silverman the following day, but he was not permitted to telephone Rabbi Stephen Wise, head of the American Jewish Congress, in New York. However, the next day he did ask Eden for a debate on German atrocities. Eden's comment on this request showed that the scepticism of which Allen's remarks were typical reached right to the top. 'I don't see why the House of Commons should have a debate,' the Foreign Secretary minuted.[38]

Riegner's message did finally reach Rabbi Wise in America, but only on 28 August. The State Department had withheld it 'in view of the unsubstantiated nature of the information',[39] and Sumner Welles, the undersecretary of State, persuaded Wise not to publicize the contents until they were confirmed. It was not until November that the message was released. By then Berlin radio was enthusiastically reporting the deportation of Western European Jews to Poland. The 'extermination of certain populations' which Roosevelt had hinted at was in full swing. It was over a year since the *Einsatzgruppen* had set about their atrocious work behind the lines of the German armies in Eastern Europe and since Richard Heydrich had been asked by Goering to think about future plans for the Jews.

Those in London who were best placed to know about such things were unable and unwilling to acknowledge them as true or even really plausible. They had not yet accepted that this was a war in which the truth about the enemy far exceeded the wildest fantasies of imaginative propagandists. They had not begun to address themselves to the question of what, if anything, could be done about such evil.

3

'STILL SOMEWHAT SCEPTICAL'

On 31 August 1942 SS Unterscharführer Ernst Heinrichsohn sent a telegram marked 'urgent top secret' from 72 Avenue Foch in Paris to Department IV B 4 in Berlin.[1] Marked for the attention of SS Obersturmbahnführer Adolf Eichmann, it was confirmation that train number 901/41 had left Drancy at 08.55 with one thousand Jews on board. Its stated destination was Auschwitz concentration camp in Poland. Enough food for fourteen days had also been loaded onto separate trucks. The food, provided by the French government, ostensibly for the Jews, was in fact untouched throughout the journey and was taken by the German guards at the camp.

Such telegrams to Berlin had become quite routine for Heinrichsohn. He had spent the past weeks making the Foreign Office's 'rather wild story' a reality. He had supervised the loading and departure of twenty other trains from the Drancy internment camp on the outskirts of Paris since 19 July. Twenty-five thousand Jews had already been sent to Auschwitz, but Eichmann was still dissatisfied with the deportation programme from France. He constantly complained that too little had been achieved in the two years of occupation. There were still nearly three hundred thousand Jews at large.

Heinrichsohn had been posted to France soon after its capitulation. Then aged twenty, he had been assigned as an assistant to Kurt Lischka, the deputy chief of the Paris Gestapo. Lischka, a veteran SS man, had laid the foundations of the Gestapo's bureau for Jewish affairs in Berlin before the war; he had supervised the deportation of twenty thousand Polish Jews in 1938 and had been one of the organizers of the *Kristallnacht*, the attack on Jews in Berlin on 9 November 1938. During the first year of the occupation, the efforts by the Gestapo to round up Jews had been frustrated by a major disagreement between Heydrich and Keitel in Berlin. The French had succumbed to occupation surprisingly fast, and the army did not want the delicate balance disturbed. But the SS were more irritated by the Vichy government's attitude on the Jewish question. Aryanization decrees had been published, but not fully enforced, and by the end of 1941 none of the Jews so far arrested had been deported owing to French government opposition. Negotiations with Laval, the Vichy prime minister, were handled by two professional diplomats, Otto Abetz and Ernst Achenbach, both assigned to the German embassy in Paris. The stumbling block was the resistance to deportations of the aged Marshal Pétain. In May 1942 the SS finally lost their patience and assigned a French-speaking SS major, Herbert Hagen, to Paris to speed the negotiations for mass arrests and deportations.

Intelligent and sophisticated, Hagen had joined the SS in 1933 and was recruited by Dr Alfred Six, one of the Nazi party's chief ideologues on Jewish affairs, to write antisemitic articles and books. Amongst his prolific output was *World Jewry: Its Organizations, Its Power, Its Politics*, and *Britain, Hinterland of World Jewry*. He was a frequent lecturer to party officials on the problems of Jewry and a critical connoisseur of all anti-semitic propaganda. Once he commented to Eichmann that he found that the latest issue of *Der Stürmer* lacked its 'usual objectivity'.

By the time Hagen arrived in Paris, Eichmann had successfully over-come army opposition to deportations. Agreement to deportations had also been given by Karl Rademacher, a senior Foreign Office official responsible for Jewish affairs, on condition that at first only stateless and non-French Jews were deported. Hauptsturmführer Theodor Dannecker, Eichmann's personal representative in Paris, had, after con-siderable work, arranged for enough railway trucks and locomotives to be available for a train to leave Paris every other day. Now all that remained was to arrest the Jews. For that French cooperation was vital.

On 5 May Heydrich himself arrived in Paris to impress the French with the need for cooperation and speed. Little progress was made during his short visit, but he left behind, as the new SS chief, Karl Oberg, whose size, shaven head and reputation for ruthlessness com-bined to make him a living caricature of an SS man.

On 4 July, on Oberg's orders, Hagen and Lischka met French govern-ment officials. According to the ten-page report minuting their dis-cussions, the two Germans told the French that Hitler had personally ordered the solution to the Jewish problem in France. Arrests and deportations had to begin forthwith. The French finally agreed that stateless, but not French, Jews could be arrested. Four days later Dannecker and Heinrichsohn met eight French police chiefs to discuss the proposed arrests. Dannecker explained that he wanted at least twenty-two thousand arrested and wanted them temporarily housed in four transit camps. He had already chosen the sports stadium, the Vélodrome d'Hiver, as one centre.

Three days later, at another joint meeting, a senior representative of the SNCF, the French railways, also came to iron out any transport prob-lems. Speaking loudly, Dannecker said that he now wanted between twenty-four and twenty-five thousand arrested. Over two thousand

French police were to be assigned to the mass arrests. Dannecker was already nervous. Eichmann had phoned from Berlin several times leaving no doubt that he was irritated by the lack of progress. Dannecker had now, however, got final agreement for the arrests to start on 16 July. Masterminding the operation was Kurt Lischka.

Just before 4 am on 16 July, squads of French police burst into the cheap hotels and boarding houses all over the capital where the Jews lived. Discovering their whereabouts was not difficult. In accordance with the law, most had registered with the local police. Amid terrible scenes of fear, panic, tears and screams, the arrests continued for two days. In full view of the Parisians, busloads of Jewish families arrived at the Vélodrome d'Hiver and Drancy. But, at the end of the operation, Heinrichsohn reported to Lischka that only 12,884 had been arrested. Amongst them were 4,051 children.

Oberg and Lischka were displeased, and two days later, on 20 July, Eichmann rang Dannecker from Berlin. The previous exceptions, women over fifty-five, men over sixty and mothers with children under two, were to be lifted. Clearly in a controlled rage, Eichmann ordered the rapid arrest of as many Jews as possible, before the operation was discredited in Berlin. Eichmann was apparently still dissatisfied when he arrived in Paris on 28 August to speak to all the SS officers involved. Hagen now says that Eichmann only came to give a pep talk, but according to the record, Eichmann insisted that a further two hundred thousand Jews had to be deported by the end of the year. Each of the deportees, he added, at the request of the Auschwitz commandant, was to bring warm clothing because of winter conditions in Poland. Four days later, Hagen went to see Laval demanding greater French cooperation and amendments to the laws to allow the many thousands of naturalized Jews to be deported. Eichmann's target was never met, despite the intensive efforts of his faithful servants.

For those who had been arrested on 16 July and crowded into the Vélodrome d'Hiver, conditions were appalling. A total of 4,051 children and 2,800 adults waited for five days without food or water; babies were born, others died, some became insane, everyone was filthy. There were only ten lavatories for 6,900 people. At the end, mothers were separated from their children, the former sent direct to Auschwitz, the children to Drancy.

Madame Odette Béaticle is one of the very few to have survived internment at Drancy. After several months of internment, her husband arranged a temporary pass for her, and having left she never returned, which saved her from Auschwitz. But what she saw in those months has haunted her ever since. In particular, the two days when Heinrichsohn supervised the shipment of the four thousand unaccompanied children to

Auschwitz. Béaticle remembers Heinrichsohn, looking very handsome, his blonde hair sharply contrasting with his black uniform and shining boots, standing outside the barracks where the children had lived, barking orders for the French police and internees to speed up the loading. 'I was shocked to see this very handsome young man being so hard, without any sympathy for the children. Most of them were crying: "Maman, maman", but Heinrichsohn was impenetrable, like marble.'

Today, Heinrichsohn finds it easy to justify his role: 'I was told that the children were being reunited with their families. And I must confess I was so young and naive that I did not realize that I might possibly be doing wrong. I was just obeying Lischka's orders.'

Lischka now says that he was just 'doing his duty', while Hagen insists that he believed that the deportations were part of the grand plan to build the Jewish State. Auschwitz, according to Hagen, was just an assembly point, a halfway stage on the journey to Palestine.

Only 196 of the hundreds of Germans directly involved in the deportations of French Jewry were named after the war. Of those, about thirty were convicted by the French in their absence, but only two, Oberg and Knochen, served prison sentences. It was left to the Israelis, fifteen years later, to find, capture and execute Eichmann. It was only in 1980, thirty-eight years after the events, that Hagen, Lischka and Heinrichsohn were finally convicted, but only as 'accomplices' to murder, by a German court in Cologne.[2]

Yet the existing German documentation leaves little doubt that all the SS officers in France knew the object of the deportations; their memoranda contain references to the *Endlösung* (final solution) and the fact that the Jews were to be *ausgerottet* (exterminated). These words were even used in the course of their discussions with French officials. As Eichmann toured Europe, visiting his subordinates, he briefed them on plans and progress. In Paris, he told his friend Hagen exactly what would happen to the Jews when they reached their destination in Poland.

The deportees themselves had no illusions about the fate that awaited them. According to Odette Béaticle, those at Drancy had no doubt that the trains would take them to their deaths; only the manner of their execution remained uncertain until the moment when they stood naked in the gas chambers at the final end of the journey which Lischka, Hagen, Heinrichsohn and their colleagues had organized so carefully.

But in London and Washington the mounting evidence that the 'Final Solution' was an appalling reality continued to be treated with scepticism and caution. One looks in vain through the official papers for an expression of more than conventional sympathy or shock, or any indication that the news from occupied Europe might merit the setting aside of political calculations and the niceties of diplomacy. While Berlin Radio reported the deportations from Drancy, Jewish lobbyists in Britain and the United States were failing to make much impact upon the bland facade of doubt, and even indifference, which was still the official reaction to war crimes.

In theory the wheels that would propel the engines of retribution and justice were already turning, but it was an agonizingly slow process.

On 5 August, John Winant, the American ambassador in London, forwarded Simon's detailed proposals for the United Nations Commission to the State Department.[3] But he had received no reply by the time the Simon Committee next met on 2 September.[4] Eden had sent an urgent reminder asking for a reply. Included was a request for an American view on the suggestion that, instead of leaving the disposal of the war criminals for an eventual peace treaty, any armistice should contain a clause demanding their immediate surrender.[5]

On 28 September Eden received a vague and unsatisfactory reply which seemed to suggest American agreement to the idea.[6] Clarification was necessary but there was little time. Pressure was intensifying in England for an official statement; Jewish lobbyists had won sympathy among politicians, especially from Lord Maugham, and were all pushing for a commitment to prosecute war criminals.[7] The Foreign Office urged Winant to obtain more definite replies from Washington. In some embarrassment he had to admit that, after sending three telegrams, he had just been told that his original letter of 5 August had been mislaid.[8]

Under pressure from the exiled governments, Eden had set 7 October as the date for the announcement of the creation of the Commission. He sent a copy of his proposed statement direct to Roosevelt, with a plea for a decision before his deadline. The agreement arrived at the last moment, on 6 October.[9] The Americans proposed a title, the United Nations Commission for the Investigation of War Crimes (it was finally called the United Nations War Crimes Commission, UNWCC), and the State Department had made one small, but very significant, change in the text. As a result, the Presidential statement issued in Washington said that: 'Punishment small be meted out to the ringleaders responsible for the organized murder of thousands.'[10] The corresponding passage in Lord Simon's statement to the House of Lords read: 'The aim is the punishment of individuals . . . who are proved to be themselves responsible whether as ringleaders or actual perpetrators.'[11] The difference between the two forms of words was the difference between a few score men and a multitude running into tens of thousands.

In the Lords, Simon outlined his own view of the Commission's work. It would 'investigate war crimes committed against nationals of United Nations, recording the testimony available, and the Commission will report from time to time to the governments of those nations cases in which such crimes appear to have been committed, naming and identifying wherever possible the persons responsible. The Commission should direct its attention in particular to organized atrocities.' To his credit, Simon realized that this would not in itself be enough to ensure justice. It was vital to collect the evidence and to create investigative machinery which could find the wanted men. 'We can all discuss these fine points about the right Court until the crack of doom, but, unless the criminal tribunal has got those two conditions satisfied, it cannot exercise its powers.' The practical implications were not understood, however, until it was far too late. And even if they had been understood, the tasks involved were ones which called for the skills of policemen and detectives, not panels of lawyers and politicians.

After that announcement, the Foreign Office felt that they had gone quite far enough towards agreement for lists to be drawn up. Officials thought that, at best, the surrender of those listed could be demanded as one of the terms of an armistice, but considered it foolish and even dangerous to look beyond that. Significantly, Eden protected himself from the danger that he might have to comment or answer questions about the establishment of the Commission, or about the general British policy towards war crimes, by managing to restrict the government statement to the House of Lords. Nothing was said in the Commons.[12] In the meantime, the practicalities of actually establishing an international commission posed problems that threatened a stillbirth with damaging repercussions.

The British had deliberately not consulted the Soviets about the establishment of the Commission.[13] It had, after all, arisen out of discussions between Churchill and Roosevelt; and the Foreign Office, at least, was deeply distrustful of any alliance with the Soviets – an attitude which was reciprocated. Memories, of the Nazi-Soviet pact on the other hand, and of the Allied intervention after the Bolshevik revolution on the other, had created a strong feeling of permanent and mutual antagonism. The distrust extended to British and Allied scepticism over Moscow's accounts of Nazi atrocities in Russia. Previous attempts by the Russian to discuss the problem with British officials, including Eden himself, had been effectively curtailed by British coolness.[14] It was therefore natural for the Foreign Office to aim first for an agreed Anglo-American position before even consulting the Russians.

However, having set a deadline for the announcement of the Commission, it was necessary for Britain's other allies to be rapidly informed, and on 3 October invitations were delivered by hand to Allied embassies asking them to join in discussions aimed at setting up the Commission. Unfortunately, it subsequently emerged, 3 October being a Saturday, the doorman at the Russian embassy, after signing for its receipt, had forgotten about the letter.[15] To Moscow it seemed as if they had only received it on the 6th, just twenty-four hours before Simon's statement in the House of Lords. Britain and America were immediately accused of acting 'without prior consultation with the Soviet government'. In a public denunciation in *Pravda* the Soviet government went on to accuse the British of secretly negotiating a peace treaty with Germany. British talk of prosecuting war criminals could only be bluff when the country was, in *Pravda*'s words, 'a refuge for gangsters'. The gangster in question was Rudolf Hess, the Deputy Führer, who had flown to Britain on a bizarre unofficial mission on 10 May 1941.

The Russians claimed that the British could prove the sincerity of their intention to prosecute war criminals by putting on trial one of Hitler's closest confidants and a prime architect of Nazi policy.[16] In fact, the British had quickly, and to their own disappointment, discovered that Hess was mentally unstable. Even Hitler's frantic concern that Hess might be persuaded to broadcast propaganda to Germany had proved groundless. The notion of trying him had been discounted by all shades of British opinion – even eventually by the communist *Daily Worker* newspaper. A trial would at best create a martyr, and at worst would provoke retaliation against British prisoners of war. His fate, it was decided, was a matter for Allied agreement after the war.[17]

The task of saving the Commission from premature extinction fell to the British ambassador in Moscow, Sir A. Clark Kerr. Using the opportunity to chastise the Russians, according to his own report[18], he took an aggressive and self-righteous line when he saw Stalin on 5 November. Inevitably, the ambassador was ignorant of Stalin's real feelings on war crimes policy. When at the outset Kerr related the saga of the delayed invitation, Stalin contented himself with the comment: 'And you are the people who try to give us lessons in collaboration.' But when the subject of Hess was raised, it became clear that, rather than exploiting the situation as a convenient stick with which to beat an errant ally, the Russians genuinely saw it as a serious test of British good faith. Stalin, Kerr reported, 'showed signs of restiveness and impatience' and was 'clearly disturbed', as he asked: 'It is the custom after the war to repatriate prisoners of war. Will Hess be repatriated? Secondly, if Goebbels were to land in Britain tomorrow will he too become a POW and then be sent back to Germany?' What Stalin wanted, Kerr reported,

BLIND EYE TO MURDER

was 'immediate action to satisfy the people who had suffered at the hands of the criminals.'

Curtly, Clark Kerr replied that all this would be a subject for discussion, and that of course Hess would not be sent back to Germany. He then turned to what was clearly, to his mind, the main subject of the meeting. 'I renewed my efforts to pin him down . . . to wring any admission of guilt from him' (over the *Pravda* article). He was evidently successful in winning some retraction from Stalin, who ingenuously explained that there were differences of opinion in Russia and he had not personally written the piece. Ten days later the Foreign Office cabled appreciatively to Kerr: 'I approve your language and congratulate you.'[19] Kerr apparently also thought that he had won Russian participation in the Commission. On the same day as his meeting with Stalin he reported that the 'Extraordinary State Commission' which had been set up on 14 October to investigate the 'misdeeds of the Hitlerites' would submit material to the UN Commission.

Stalin however insisted that Russian participation was subject to an agreement that war criminals would be tried by an international tribunal as soon as they were found, and that their fate would not be left to a political decision. 'Otherwise it would be said that Churchill, Roosevelt and Stalin were wreaking vengeance upon their political enemies.'[20] This was not acceptable to the British. The Foreign Office loftily cabled Kerr on 15 November: 'The Soviet Government will hardly expect us at this stage to go into further details regarding the formalities which would accompany a political decision in respect of outstanding war criminals.'[21] The Russians remained dissatisfied, and resurrected the issue of Hess. On 24 November Molotov told Kerr that if he were not immediately tried, 'the whole question of war criminals would lose most of its immediacy'.[22]

The Foreign Office, however, was determined to persist with its policy of what the Russians saw as 'talking and doing nothing practical' – a charge which Frank Roberts admitted was accurate,[23] and to which Dennis Allen lamely commented: 'We hitherto received no indication from the Soviet Government of any desire to discuss the punishment of war criminals.'[24] The Foreign Office believed, moreover, that there were serious and real reasons for caution in announcing plans for war crimes trials. Public announcements, they feared, would lead to reprisals against British POWs. It was not a consideration that can have carried much weight with the Russians. Their POWs were being murdered, starved or worked to death by the Nazis, and those who survived were to be treated in much the same fashion when they returned to Russia.

Nevertheless, on 24 January, Britain and Russia seemed to have settled their differences over the UNWCC, although nothing had been done in the meantime to actually set it up.[25] The Americans remained ignorant about the Anglo-Russian differences and were not interested enough to ask about progress. Only Simon seemed concerned. On 12 January he wrote to Eden: 'I am concerned lest there may not be a challenge to our government as to why we have not got further with this business.'[26] There was no immediate reply. But the Foreign Office was facing mounting pressure for action from others in London.

Officials had managed to fend off a Commons debate in early November. Malkin told Richard Law, Eden's minister of state, that 'a debate would be undesirable and might even do a certain amount of harm. We don't particularly want public attention focused on this subject at the present stage.'[27] Roberts agreed: a debate would 'concentrate attention upon a subject that is best left in a dim light for the time being'. The officials were still unwilling or unable to believe the evidence from Europe. In early November a telegram had arrived from Berne 'confirming' the reality of the 'Final Solution'. 'I am still somewhat sceptical about this story,'[28] commented Geoffrey Harrison, a first secretary, and the other officials concurred.

Despite pressure from every government in exile, from Maisky at the Soviet embassy, from the Chief Rabbi, MPs and the press, the Foreign Office succeeded in holding the line until the end of November.

On 25 November Sidney Silverman handed Law a twenty-page dossier containing the evidence of extermination: there were accounts of Auschwitz, Chelmno, Belsen and Treblinka, of mass shootings, mobile gas trucks and the fate of three hundred and eighty thousand inhabitants of the Warsaw ghetto. Silverman wanted the government to organize a four-power declaration, which Law was unable to promise; he knew that Eden wanted Britain to remain uncommitted. But, writing an account of his conversation with Silverman, he said: 'I think we would be in an appalling position if these stories should prove to have been true and we have done nothing whatsoever about them.'[29]

Roberts' attitude was more cautious and measured: 'A statement would have to be vague, since we have no actual proof of these actrocities, although I think that their probability is sufficiently great to justify action . . . if this is considered essential with a view to satisfying Parliamentary opinion here . . . it would I think be dangerous to embark on a propaganda campaign lacking a foundation of quotable and proved facts.'[30] Roberts had what he considered to be good arguments to back him up. Both he and Dennis Allen could point to Jews who, like Rabbi Perlzweig, had repeatedly warned that any declaration would make the situation worse. Roberts also feared it might 'irritate' Hitler, who was 'in a very difficult mood about POWs.'

Moreover, a public admission that Britain accepted the evidence for the extermination of the Jews could have wide-ranging repercussions. It would make it very much harder to resist the pressure to allow those Jews who could still escape – from Hungary, Bulgaria and the Balkans – to settle in Palestine. Such emigration could only weaken Britain's already strained grip upon the Middle East.

But calculated detachment could not last forever. The Foreign Office might still tell the BBC on 2 December, in relation to the Final Solution, that they were 'soft-pedalling the whole thing as much as possible for the moment,'[31] while denying that they were 'deliberately trying to kill the story', but Law's argument that the price of silence could be too great was gaining ground. When, on the same day, Maisky, briefed by Silverman, called on Eden and urged a declaration that 'might give the unhappy Jews some comfort,' Eden realized he had no choice but to agree.

The British drafted a document and sent it to Washington for approval.[32] It had already arrived when Rabbi Wise handed the President a dossier similar to Silverman's, entitled 'Blueprint for Extermination'. Even more than the Foreign Office, the State Department had found it possible to maintain a detached attitude and to deplore the idea of a declaration which, they felt, would 'divert the war effort.' After reading the British draft, Robert Reams, a Foreign Service officer, commented: 'While the statement does not mention the soap, glue, oil and fertilizer factories, it will be taken as additional confirmation of those stories and will support Rabbi Wise's contention of official confirmation from State Department sources.'[33]

Had Reams' arguments been as successful as those of British officials, there would have been no declaration. Politically, however, there was no alternative but to publish it. The British declaration stated that the information from Europe:

> . . . leaves no room for doubt that the German authorities, not content with denying to persons of Jewish race, in all the territories over which their barbarous rule has been extended, the most elementary human rights, are now carrying into effect Hitler's oft repeated intention to exterminate the Jewish people in Europe. From all the occupied countries Jews are being transported, in conditions of appalling horror and brutality, to Eastern Europe. In Poland, which has long been the principal Nazi slaughterhouse, the ghettos established by the German invaders are being systematically emptied of all Jews except a few highly skilled workers required for war industries. None of those taken away are ever heard of again. The able-bodied are slowly worked to death in labour camps. The infirm are left to die of exposure and starvation or are deliberately massacred in mass executions.

The number of victims of these bloody cruelties is reckoned in many thousands of entirely innocent men, women and children . . . . [The governments] condemn in the strongest possible terms this bestial policy of cold-blooded extermination[34]

The American version was slightly different, instead of the definitive 'leaves no room for doubt,' Cordell Hull modified the wording so that the story was attributed to 'numerous reports'.[35]

The declaration was published in Moscow, read out in Washington by Roosevelt and delivered in the House of Commons by Eden, who noted in his diary that: 'It had a far greater dramatic effect than I had expected.'[36] Officials on both sides of the Atlantic hoped that the effects of the declaration could remain purely dramatic. They strenuously resisted any suggestion that there should be a relaxation of rules to allow Jewish immigration from occupied Europe to Britain, Palestine or the United States. Nor were they ready to devote time and energy to making good the declaration's concluding pledge that 'those responsible for these crimes shall not escape retribution, and [the Allies will] press on with the necessary practical measures to this end.' Ironically, the pledge was taken more seriously by those committing the crimes.

Recalling the day's events in Warsaw on 25 January 1943, Hans Frank, the German governor of Poland, responsible for organizing the ghettoization and deportation of at least two and a half million people in Poland, wrote: 'After a lot of talk about anti-Jewish measures . . . I point out that all of us assembled here want to remember that we are on Roosevelt's war crimes list. I have the honour of being at the top of the list. We are all accomplices in a world historical sense.'[37] No one suggested that the pace of work should be relaxed, but no one doubted that, individually, they were marked men should Germany lose the war.

One hundred miles south-east of Warsaw, deep in a forest, Gustav Wagner, the Austrian deputy Commandment of the Sobibor extermination camp, spent that night like all the others, drinking and playing cards with his fellow SS men.[38] Trained before the war at Schloss Hartheim, a so-called 'euthanasia institution', in the practicalities of cold-blooded murder, Wagner had arrived in Poland in March 1942. In a clearing next to a railway branch line he had organized the construction of a purpose-built killing centre with a production line as sophisticated as a complex modern factory. In just fifteen months, at least two hundred and fifty thousand men, women and children stepped off the train in the morning, were gassed by lunchtime and their corpses burnt before dawn the next day. By then their luggage had been sorted and packed for shipment to Germany.

The victims were gassed by the carbon monoxide fumes of a captured Russian tank. Wagner watched as thousands of people jumped and fell out of cattle trucks and were shipped towards the gas chambers. Eyewitnesses remember that Wagner killed people with his own hands, daily. Thomas Blatt, one of the few survivors, remembers:

> He didn't kill the same way as the other Germans. He didn't shoot, he tortured. He used an axe, a shovel, a whip, even his bare hands. I saw him pick up a shovel and simply split a man's head in two. He didn't need a reason for doing it. Perhaps the man was moving too slow. But when he killed he smiled. Murdering was his pleasure – you could see it in his face. He didn't consider it a duty, it was more a private matter.[39]

Sam Lerer, another survivor, saw Wagner use an axe handle to beat to death a father and son standing next to each other: 'It just took a few minutes. He and another SS man just kept on hitting them. The sound of the cries of those two men sounded like wild animals.' In Sohibor Wagner was known as 'The Angel of Death'.

Until 1979, Wagner lived an untroubled and, according to him, 'very pleasant' life in Brazil. He arrived there, using his own name, in 1952. 'We had a feeling,' he told me, 'that if we lost the war we would be saddled with the consequences.' Despite his fears, Wagner was never prosecuted for his crimes. Yet in Sobibor he realized that if recognized and caught by the Allies after the war, his fate would be the same as his victims', albeit in less gruesome circumstances. That Wagner, and the majority of those involved in the murders, successfully escaped prosecution after Germany's defeat, was the direct result of the indifference to war crimes shown by Allied officials during the war.

Having finally, it seemed, reached an agreement with the Russians over the establishment of the UNWCC, the Foreign Office, urged on by Simon, sent out further and more detailed proposals on 4 March 1943.[40] Three weeks later Maisky told Eden that there was a new problem.[41] The British had suggested that the Commission should include representatives from all the Allies and from the British Dominions. The Russians objected to the inclusion of the latter. They had not previously been mentioned and they were not countries that had directly 'suffered' at the hands of the Nazis. Eden pointed out that soldiers from Australia, Canada, New Zealand, South Africa, Burma and India were all fighting in the Allied cause; however he agreed to investigate the possibility of a special arrangement.

A further three weeks passed before Maisky returned to say that, if the Dominions were to be included, the Russians would demand the addition of the Baltic states, Lithuania, Latvia and Estonia. This, the Foreign Office realized, was politically explosive. The three states had been seized by Russia under the terms of the Molotov-Ribbentrop pact, and the Russian proposal looked very like a brazen attempt to obtain recognition of an illegal annexation. Eden patiently explained that the Dominions were, in contrast to the three Baltic countries, independent sovereign nations, and even delivered a short historical dissertation to back up this argument. Stubbornly, Maisky remained unwilling to be convinced. It was a deadlock that was to prove unbreakable.

However preparations went ahead, albeit slowly. By June, all the participants had named their representatives. The Foreign Office had clearly offered some fairly broad hints as to the sort of people they felt were needed. Forwarding the British proposals of 4 March to Washington, Freeman Matthews from the American embassy commented: 'The Foreign Office believes that while the question of war crimes is hardly one directly connected with the prosecution of the war, those whose time and thought would be devoted to its study are probably precisely those who are not fully occupied with the war effort.'[42]

It was a delicate and diplomatic way of saying that Whitehall did not feel that the Americans need disturb their war effort by seeking out the brightest or the best to fill the post on UNWCC. The State Department officials found it very hard, even so, to find a suitable man. Several professors of law rejected the offer and it was not until 12 June that the job was filled. It was Roosevelt himself who proposed fifty-nine-year-old Herbert Pell, a former New York congressman and Democratic party faithful, who had frequently advertised himself as available for work.[43]

Told to contact the State Department urgently, as 'it is desired that you shall proceed to London as soon as possible,' Pell arrived in Washington with no very clear idea of the job he had undertaken, but with a very clear idea of the sort of status that was his due. Horrified officials heard that he would have to stay at either the Ritz or Claridge's in London and that he would require staff and expenses on a lavish scale. He then returned to the Knickerbocker Club in New York to prepare for his imminent departure. He waited five months.

The State Department was fighting its own delaying action, much aided by the confusion and apparent lethargy that marked the Foreign Office's attempts to establish the Commission. Efforts were still being made in London to get the Russians back into the UNWCC fold. As a compromise, it was suggested that the Dominions might just participate in cases involving their own nationals, but this was rejected out of hand. Clearly the matter was not considered important, since it was not on the agenda when the Prime Minister met Stalin in Moscow in October.

On 14 July the Foreign Office told the State Department that 'it would be unwise to assume that the Commission would be set up in the near future.'[44] A fortnight later they announced to the Americans that the first meeting would be at the end of September. But the second message also revealed that the Commission's tasks now included deciding the form and procedure of the courts which would be used in war crimes trials. An anxious State Department official wrote: 'these plans are quite different from those which the Department understood at the time that Mr Pell was designated.'[45]

Pell himself was also getting impatient. At the end of August, having been told several times that 'the time is not ripe,' and having made and cancelled two sets of transatlantic reservations for himself and his wife, he had approached the President himself, who in turn asked Cordell Hull, the Secretary of State, for an explanation. Hull replied evasively that they were still waiting to hear from the British.[46] On 29 October the President again sent a note to the State Department: 'What is the status of the war criminals' trials? What is Pell and his group doing?'

The answer was that: 'Pell's group met without Pell.'[47] The first meeting of the Commission had taken place in London a week previously, on 19 October, without the Russians; and without Pell, who, the State Department maliciously explained to the White House, 'would not travel without his wife.' On 9 November, Pell descended upon Foggy Bottom in person. He complained to Graham Hill, a State Department official, about not being in London and about inadequate briefing.

To Hill's discomfort, Pell then saw the cursory reports of the first meeting which had reached Washington, and he accurately discerned that little progress had been made. There was no decision about the kinds of courts that would be required or the sort of law they would apply; without knowing that, Pell pointed out, it was going to be impossible for the Commission to know what kind of evidence it should set about gathering. Seizing the opportunity he went on to tell Hill that: 'in the absence of instructions, he would, should the occasion arise, act on his own initiative, would use a "strong hand".'[48] The meeting confirmed the State Department's belief that Pell's appointment was a painful mistake. Pell, however, was ready and eager to set about remedying the Commission's deficiencies when he arrived in London in early December.

Pell had every reason for feeling that it was time for the Commission to seriously set about its task. Not only were the Germans beginning to retreat on the Eastern front, but with the invasion of Italy in September and the build-up of forces for the opening of a second front in Europe, the time was clearly approaching when the pledges of the past two years were going to have to be acted upon. Moreover, yet another declaration had been made by the three major Allies, this time in a form which hardly seemed to admit of equivocation.

Early in October 1943 reports had come into London of a massacre of a hundred Italian officers carried out by German forces on the Greek island of Kos. At a Cabinet meeting on 8 October Churchill referred to this report and to other instances of German 'frightfullness'; he proposed a new declaration, to be signed by the foreign ministers of Britain, the US and Russia, who were due to meet in Moscow later in the month.[49] Eden, who was leaving for Moscow the following day, was not at the meeting, he was automatically critical of Churchill's initiative. He wrote to wrote to his officials: 'I am far from happy about all this war crimes business. When I come back I want to have a departmental discussion about it all. Broadly I am most anxious not to get into the position of breathing fire and slaughter against war criminals and promising condign punishment and a year or two hence have to find pretexts for doing nothing. I realize difficulty caused by our pledges.'[50] His feelings were shared by his senior advisers.

So it was once again Churchill who had to produce a draft of the declaration and a covering message to Roosevelt, in which he explained that he was sure that atrocities in Poland had been reduced by previous declarations, and suggested that a threat to send those guilty back to the scene of their crimes might further inhibit the murderers, and would, he felt, especially appeal to Stalin.[51]

The draft and the message to the President were sent to Cadogan at the Foreign Office for comment and for him to send on to Washington. In his minister's absence, but well aware of Eden's views, Cadogan fought a delaying action. For three days he did nothing and, when Churchill asked why his telegram had not been dispatched, Cadogan replied that a reference to the Allies pursuing war criminals to the 'uttermost ends of the earth' must be removed.[52] 'It suggests,' wrote Cadogan, 'that we should disregard attempts by neutrals to grant asylum.' Churchill brusquely overrode the objection and ordered the draft sent in its original form.[53]

The plan was accepted by Roosevelt and Stalin, and the Declaration was initialled in Moscow by the three foreign ministers, Eden, Cordell Hull and Molotov, and published on 1 November. Over the following days it was widely broadcast, and became the theoretical cornerstone of postwar war crimes policy. It committed the Allies to the principle that, after the armistice, those responsible for atrocities, massacres and executions:

will be sent back to the countries in which their abominable deeds were done in order that they may be judged and punished according to the laws of those liberated countries. . .Those Germans who take part in wholesale shootings of Italian officers or in the execution of French, Dutch, Belgian or Norwegian hostages or of Cretan peasants or who have shared in the slaughters inflicted on the people of Poland, or in the territories of the Soviet Union which are now being swept clear of the enemy, will know that they will be brought back to the scene of their crimes and judged on the spot by the people they have outraged. . .most assuredly the three Allied powers will pursue them to the uttermost ends of the earth and will deliver them to the accusers in order that justice may be done. The above declaration is without prejudice to the case of the major criminals whose offences have no particular geographical location and who will be punished by a joint decision of the governments of the Allies.[54]

Owing, apparently, to confusion, the version broadcast by London and Washington substituted for the 'Italian officers', who had been the pretext for Churchill's original proposal, the words 'Polish officers', while Moscow stuck to the original. Goebbels' propaganda ministry was quick to seize on this discrepancy as evidence that the Allies were not agreed on responsibility for the Katyn massacre of the Polish officer corps.[55] This minor victory was the only discernible evidence that the Declaration had been noticed by the Germans. It has even less effect on British and American policy. On the contrary, when the first opportunity to consider its application arose, it was conspicuously ignored.

Only a few days before the signing of the Declaration, the British and American governments were faced with their first opportunity to put all their fine words about war crimes into effect. Military telegram NAF 476,[56] dated 18 October 1943, from General Eisenhower at Allied headquarters in Algiers, North Africa, to the American Chiefs of Staff in Washington was a request for permission to put on trial a group of captured Italian officials who were known to have killed Yugoslav civilians by torture and starvation. It was received as a bolt out of the blue. No one in Washington had devoted much thought to war crimes, least of all the military. The Foreign Office was asked for advice. They were less surprised, but endorsed the opinion of Harold Macmillan, the resident British minister in Algiers, that 'this whole question is leading us towards very deep water.'[57]

Both Dennis Allen and Sergeant were in no doubt that the reply to Eisenhower must be to do as little as possible. The UNWCC had only just held its first meeting. Nothing had been decided. Even the suggestion that war crimes trials were contemplated, the Foreign Office feared, might provoke retaliation against Allied POWs. Nor were just practicalities at issue. There were also delicate political questions, such as whether an American court could try Italians for crimes against Yugoslavs. Despite the threats and the pledges, there was still a vacuum where there should have been a policy.

Based on London's advice, the Chiefs of Staff signalled Eisenhower on 21 October: 'It has not been determined where responsibility for trial of persons so designated will lie. Facts regarding suspected war criminals should be transmitted to London for consideration by Commission.'[58] During the next two days the fear of reprisals grew. On 28 October the Chiefs sent another signal ordering Eisenhower not to hold any trials while the Allies decided their policy, and not to segregate the suspects for fear that Allied intentions of holding war crime trials would become known. Secrecy over postwar intentions, the officials decided, was vital.[59]

The Russians had interpreted the text of the Declaration very differently. Not being members of UNWCC, and apparently oblivious, or insensitive, to the possibility of reprisals, they interpreted the pledge with a fierce simplicity that came from direct experience of the atrocities it referred to. On 23 December, in an announcement which made direct reference to the Declaration, Moscow Radio reported the conviction of three members of a German *Einsatzgruppe* and a Russian collaborator. All of them were hanged in public, slowly and painfully. The well-publicized three-day trial in Kharkov appalled both the State Department and Foreign Office. Fearing reprisals, the Foreign Office briefed journalists to explain that the Declaration only applied to the handover of criminals after the armistice.[60] The State Department, in even greater panic, sent messages to the German government through Switzerland, promising that, in accordance with the Geneva Convention, German soldiers would not be tried.[61] Hull publicly announced that the United States did not regard 'direct handling of war criminals' as falling within the terms of the Moscow Declaration.[62] The headlong rush for dissociation confirmed Moscow's worst suspicions of its allies' intentions.

4

'WE SEEM
TO BE SHORT
OF IDEAS'

Sir Cecil Hurst, aged seventy-three, was appointed British delegate to
the United Nations War Crimes Commission in November 1942. His
distinguished legal career included a period as a judge on the International Court at the Hague and service as a legal adviser to the Foreign
Office. By the time Herbert Pell arrived in London thirteen months
later, Hurst, who was also the Commission's chairman, was already
exasperated by the problems and frustrations that were to bedevil it.

Hurst's first move had been to ask for the evidence of war crimes that
his own government had so far accumulated. The response was not
encouraging. Three individuals within the Whitehall machine were, in
theory, responsible for collecting and assessing information. Peter Kent
had been recruited from retirement and appointed in 1942 as an assistant
in the Treasury Solicitor's office, with the task of collecting evidence. By
September 1944 Kent's list included only twelve names. Unaware of
Kent's existence, the War Office had appointed one of their own staff,
Cyril Gepp, to compile a list of crimes committed against British
soldiers. At the Foreign Office, a South Wales solicitor, Roger Allen,
had been given the task of recording 'German breaches of the rules of
warfare'.

The first response of the Foreign Office to Hurst's request for their
own list of war crimes was hesitant, on the grounds that some of it was
confidential and could not be released.[1] In fact, Allen had very little to
offer to the Commission; sticking rigidly to the legal definition, his list
included crimes such as invasions, attacks on merchant shipping and the
bombing of hospitals. Sometimes he went to dockyards to interview
returning seamen, but on his own admission: 'I do not attempt to keep a
full record.'[2] His major source of information were German newspaper
clippings and transcripts of monitored broadcasts supplied by the
Ministry of Information. Nevertheless his work was praised by
Cavendish – Bentinck because it had the merit of being 'sceptical of
unsubstantiated stories'.[3]

But even when stories were well substantiated there were reasons for denying them to the Commission. Intelligence agencies had amassed an enormous file on nearly one hundred thousand Germans at all levels of responsibility. In late 1942, MI9 had sent the Foreign Office astonishingly detailed reports on Sachsenhausen, Buchenwald and Natzweiler concentration camps. Obtained from escapees who had arrived in England, the reports not only described the minutest details of corruption, sexual activities, armaments, shortages and sketch plans of mobile crematoria in the camps, but also gave a long list of SS men at camps 'who were particularly brutal.' No less than seventeen were named at Buchenwald, with particular descriptions of their sadistic interests.[4] The Foreign Office did not give the Commission the list. Anything that could be even slightly connected with intelligence was barred.

Later, in September 1944, the Foreign Office invented further reasons for denying evidence to the Commission. Robert Eisenstadt wrote from Bubendorf in Switzerland to the British embassy giving details about his escape from the Lublin Majdanek extermination camp, where he had been sent from Germany.[5] Enclosed in the letter were twenty names and even addresses of SS and Gestapo men involved in the Final Solution in Frankfurt, Buchenwald and Majdanek. Dennis Allen dismissed the letter as of little legal value and not to be passed on, because Majdanek would be under the Russians, who did not recognize the London-based Poles. The Foreign Office had ordered the Commission to steer clear of involvement in any cases or areas where Russian-sponsored communists were operating. Nor, said Allen in response to a query from his colleague, Con O'Neil, was there anyone else who could use the information. For the same reason Malkin had ruled out handing the Commission detailed evidence, with names, which had arrived about German atrocities in the Baltic states, firstly because Russia was not a member of the Commission, and secondly because Britain did not recognize Russia's claim to the territories.[6]

Gepp at the War Office had also imposed rigid limitations on his brief. By March 1943 his list included forty-three cases of British soldiers who had been shot dead after capture as well as instances of bombing of hospitals and the ill-treatment of POWs, but no evidence as to who had been responsible.[7]

Gepp's criterion for including a case in his list required that the informants' reliability must be judged 'good' by the interrogators. It was on these grounds that the War Office list included the evidence of James Graham only in its 'doubtful category' and thus excluded it from the British contribution to the UNWCC lists. Graham alleged that twenty British POWs had been shot by Germans in 1940, near the village of 'Casshel (Belgium or France)' (in fact Cassel is in France), and that another eighty had been driven into a barn by German soldiers who had then thrown hand grenades inside, killing all but four.

Graham had got back to Britain in March 1941 after a harrowing escape which left him seriously handicapped. When he was first interrogated by MI9 he had not told them the story of the massacre. It was only in October 1942 that he had written to tell the army that he had heard the massacre story while in captivity. The army did not believe him because he had failed to report it in March 1941. In April 1943, Private Albert Pooley,[8] his legs severely wounded, arrived in England from Germany, the beneficiary of a Red Cross exchange of wounded POWs. Pooley told his interrogators that on 24 May 1940 he was a surviving member of a severely battered battalion of the Royal Norfolk Regiment desperately fighting off a vastly superior force from the SS *Totenkopf* Division. One hundred survivors, cut off from Dunkirk, retreated to Le Paradis, a small French village near Béthune and Cassel. Exhausted and outnumbered, their commander ordered them to raise a white flag and surrender. They were then taken to a field where the Germans ordered the one hundred British soldiers to kneel down. Suddenly two machineguns opened fire. Pooley was wounded but lay hidden under a pile of dead bodies. The SS soldiers having left the field, Pooley crawled to a farmhouse. He and one other were the only survivors. Some weeks later he was found by German soldiers in a local hospital.

Pooley's interrogators, MI9 officers whose identities have never been discovered, were clearly sceptical about the story from the outset. One yawned, while the other pared his nails. Pooley became immediately resentful. By the end they had in effect told him that he was suffering from delusions, 'barbed wire-itis'. The interrogators were convinced that German soldiers would never commit such an outrage. Pooley's story was never compared to Graham's 'doubtful' account of the massacre of 'twenty men' at 'Casshel'.[9]

Graham's account of the second massacre of 'eighty soldiers' in a barn also did not appear on British war crimes lists. It in fact occurred at Wormhoudt, also in northern France, just two days after the massacre at Le Paradis. The SS general, Sepp Dietrich, commander of the *Leibstandarste SS Adolf Hitler*, was trapped under British fire in a ditch outside Wormhoudt. In the bitter fighting to rescue their commander, his troops captured about one hundred and fifty members of the Royal Warwickshire Regiment. Fifty were separated from the others, pushed into a barn, and then subjected to grenade and rifle fire. After the shooting, Sepp Dietrich ordered every officer to swear an oath of silence. At least one British soldier escaped to reveal after the war that the SS officer who gave the command for the shooting was a Captain Moenke.[10]

With such reluctance to accept evidence when it was offered, or to try and corroborate it, it is not surprising that the War Office vetoed a suggestion from Hurst that they should appeal to British troops for witnesses.[11] Realistically, they replied that such an appeal would only attract a flood of volunteers, eager for a free trip back to London.

When the three departments finally met at the Foreign Office on 14 May 1944 to pool their evidence, the list they produced contained just thirty-three names of wanted men.[12] If one arm of the British government had conceived of the UN Commission, it looked very much as if another had gone a long way towards ensuring its failure.

Indeed, having reluctantly acquiesced in the birth of the Commission, the Foreign Office had no enthusiasm for breathing life into this unwanted child. In July Hurst met with Dennis Allen and explained that if the Commission was to be totally reliant on governments for the supply of information, its own role could be little more than a supervisory one.[13] Allen soon after commented that this amounted to no work at all and added that Hurst seemed to have 'some rather odd ideas'.

Allen soon found the ideas of Herbert Pell odder still. A fierce antagonism rapidly developed between the American delegate and the Foreign Office. When they first met on 7 December, both Hurst and Pell had to confess that their respective governments had failed to provide them even with the meagre evidence they had so far collected. Nor was the position any happier when it came to the governments-in-exile. The information from occupied Europe was either non-existent or imprecise. The Foreign Office had disallowed a suggestion that the BBC should broadcast an appeal for evidence to be collected, since 'no doubt everything possible was already being done on these lines by the people in the occupied countries themselves'.[14]

Moreover there was a fear that such an appeal would provoke reprisals – even reprisals in kind since, as Cadogan told Sir Edward Bridges in the Cabinet Office, he believed that the British were also breaching the rules of war.[15] Happily, perhaps, no one in London was keeping any record of those breaches either.

Even when the governments-in-exile were able to produce evidence and names, there was no guarantee that they would find their way into the Commission's list. Still believing that the precedent of 1918 would be followed and that the final result of the Commission's work would be a list of names that would be handed to the German authorities, Malkin at the Foreign Office ordered Hurst to ensure that evidence and allegations presented by the exiled governments should be judicially tested before each individual name could be listed. It was inevitable that information reaching London from the inferno of occupied Europe would fail such a test. Although the requirement kept some doubtful cases off the list, it also meant that by August 1944 the Poles had failed to get a single one of the Germans responsible for the murder of three million Polish Jews onto the official list; while the French had only managed to get Robert Wagner, the notorious Gauleiter of Alsace Lorraine, who was undoubtedly responsible for scores of murders, included on mere petty offences. In disgust, Pell compared the process to the failure to convict Al Capone of anything more serious than tax offences.[16]

Pell's difficulties were not due solely to the British and the handicaps which they imposed upon the Commission. His own government was as much to blame. The State Department had equipped him with an assistant, Lawrence Preuss, a Department official who was soon at loggerheads with his chief. But they had done little else to arrange for the American contribution to the Commission's work. Indeed, the Department had not even decided who in Washington was to be responsible for collecting evidence and passing it to the Commission. When Preuss wrote on 22 January 1944 to Green Hackworth, the legal adviser at the State Department, suggesting that whatever evidence the Department had should be forwarded to London, and that an official should be appointed to collect future evidence, Hackworth was puzzled. 'If the cases are to be prepared by the governments', he wrote, 'I should suppose the Commission would have very little to do.'[17] The view of State Department officials was that the Commission was a British invention, and, having produced a delegate in the form of Pell, nothing further was required of them. They sought to pass responsibility to the Department of War.

At the end of February the acting Secretary of State, Edward Stettinius, wrote to Stimson at the War Department suggesting that his Department would be in a better position to do the job.[18] The War Department, however, was plainly uninterested in the Commission because it was a State Department creation. Writing on 13 March Stimson confirmed that the War Department accepted responsibility for War Crimes policy but mentioned, almost in passing, that, 'in view of the shortage of personnel,' it would be impossible for his Department to pass information about cases involving Americans to the Commission.[19] Grateful that they had successfully shed a responsibility, State Department officials apparently felt no need to query this excuse. Nor did they protest when, four months later, for 'security reasons', the War Department refused to supply the Commission with the names of any Germans in positions of authority in Europe.[20] In June, the US Joint Chiefs of Staff informed the State Department that they formally rejected the possibility of referring any cases to the Commission since it would limit the jurisdiction of American military courts and cause delays.[21] Thus, as far as the US government was concerned, the Commission remained a State Department problem, and one best ignored.

Within two months of his arrival in London, Pell's anger and frustration were acute. He put the blame for the Commission's obvious failure to come to grips with its task squarely on the Foreign Office. It was, he concluded, the result of Eden's lack of interest and the restrictions with which his officials had beset the Commission. The result, he wrote to the assistant secretary of state, Breckenridge Long, on 28 January, would be 'that the punishment of war guilt would degenerate into another farce as it did after the last war'.[22] Long asked Hackworth to draft some instructions for Pell in the hope that this would dispel 'the lack of organization and real lack of purpose amongst members of the Commission'. In the event, all that Pell received was a letter from Stettinius in mid-February containing some 'rough suggestions submitted for your guidance' which amounted to no more than an affirmation of American support for an international court.[23]

Pell's distrust of the Foreign Office hierarchy was wholly reciprocated. His assistant, Preuss, got a sympathetic hearing from Frank Roberts in April when he confided – 'speaking frankly' – that Pell was making 'dangerous mistakes'.[24] Preuss went on to describe the Czech member of the Commission, Dr Ecer, as 'wild, unbalanced and indiscreet', and the Polish and Belgian representatives, Dr Glaser and General de Baer, as 'difficult and rather apt to get out of hand'. Just over a month later, Preuss, who had by now openly quarrelled with Pell, and was returning to America, lunched with Malkin and had little difficulty in convincing him that the Commission was positively dangerous.[25]

All Pell's suspicions would have been confirmed by the Foreign Office reaction to a report on the Commission's first four months' work which Hurst submitted to Lord Simon on 1 April. Hurst's conclusion, contained in the first paragraph, was that: 'it will not be possible for the Commission to accomplish with satisfaction either to itself or to the governments which appointed it, the task which it was set up to perform'.[26] The very few cases which were listed were trivial, he claimed, and many nations were not even submitting cases. 'Drastic changes seem to be necessary,' wrote Hurst, if the politicians' pledges, which he quoted at length, were to be fulfilled. Some of the impediments to progress were: the insistence on sticking to formal definitions of a war crime, such as breaches of the rules of war, because these did not cover many of the mass atrocities; the refusal to allow the Commission to consider cases where the victims were not Allied nationals (but Germans, Hungarians and Austrians); and insistence on detailed evidence when the underground sources of information often did not give the victims' nationality. One solution he recommended was to put collective responsibility on all members of the Gestapo, arrest them all and then investigate each one while they were under arrest.

Simon was not convinced by Hurst's pessimism, but realized there was a problem.[27] Malkin however was scathing. Hurst's paper was unimpressive, he commented, and the proposals for widening the Commission's work were just an attempt to cover up his failure.[28] 'A provisional comment,' wrote Roberts, 'is "How lucky the Russians are not to be members".'[29]

The Foreign Office officials were by now convinced that anything proposed by the Commission was unacceptable. Arresting all the Gestapo was derided by Allen as 'impractical and unnecessary',[30] while Cadogan rejected it, firstly because many of the Gestapo officers wore civilian clothes and would therefore, be unidentifiable and, secondly because the frontier police, while technically Gestapo, were relatively innocent – a view which would have puzzled those who had been pulled off trains by the frontier police and shot while 'trying to escape'. But Simon's legal argument seemed to be conclusive. The British, he claimed, never prosecuted groups.[31]

The same fate struck a proposal from the Commission that it should have representatives in Europe, attached to SHAEF, investigating war crimes.[32] It was, said Malkin, just one of 'a number of proposals of varying degrees of unwisdom'[33] and he promptly wrote to John Foster at the War Office that he should not even discuss the idea with the Commission, whose members were 'rather leaky tubs . . . rather inclined to lay their hands on things which are really not their business.'[34]

Similarly Malkin contemptuously dismissed de Baer's proposal for an international court to judge war crimes, saying: 'I would not send these documents to anybody. The Commission is a stamping ground for every crank in the country and I should not be disposed to pay too much attention to its products.'[35]

The opposition was all quite unnecessarily destructive, and in some cases not even well-founded. While the Foreign Office officials derided the suggestion that the Gestapo might be arrested en bloc, the three-power European Advisory Committee, set up in London to coordinate Allied policy in the liberated territories, which was a Foreign Office responsibility, was giving serious consideration to an exactly similar proposal,[36] and Simon's claim that it was impossible in law to prosecute groups did not apply to the German or other Continental legal systems.

By summer 1944, the State Department was also becoming concerned at the evident failure of the Commission to make any headway. On 7 July Hackworth told British embassy officials that his Department was now seriously worried and that they blamed the British for the Commission's failure.[37] Hackworth 'was somewhat troubled', the embassy reported to Malkin, 'by the apparent absence of action in a straight line . . . if the war ended suddenly we should be totally unequipped to deal with the war criminal situation'. The report went on to raise the point that had become absolutely central to the Commission and its future: 'As far as he could understand it, the Commission was being diverted into irrelevant channels, such as consideration whether Germans who had persecuted Jews before 1939 could be tried as war criminals.'

The question of crimes committed before September 1939, or against people who were either stateless or citizens of Germany and her allies, was to polarize attitudes and policies towards war crimes in a way that no previous issue had done. Ultimately it was to break the deadlock that the creation of the UNWCC had only succeeded in institutionalizing.

Until spring 1944 British and American officials were agreed that there was no way, legal or otherwise, in which these crimes, which were not war crimes in the legal sense as defined at the time, could be dealt with by the UNWCC. Simon's speech in the House of Lords, in which he announced the setting up of the UN Commission, had specifically limited its scope to crimes committed against nationals of the United Nations.

Two days after Simon's speech, Leon Rosengarten, the secretary of the Jewish Aid Committee for Emigration in Zurich, had written posing the question in the clearest possible manner: 'Is it to be understood that cruelties and massacres of stateless persons who formerly were German, Austrian and Rumanian Jews are included?'[38] (Nazi legislation had deprived Jews of their nationality). The Foreign Office was in no doubt that they were not included. It was simply against international law. Roger Allen minuted: 'The question is surely too big for the Commission: it is nothing less than a question of indicting Nazi internal policy during the whole period of the regime. This is a political, not a legal issue, and should be dealt with as such.'[39] Jews and stateless people, wrote Allen, could not be represented on the Commission and it was 'difficult to envisage an appropriate tribunal' for trials. Even Dennis Allen's suggestion that a distinction be made between stateless Jews killed in Germany and those murdered 'on the territory of the United Nations' was dismissed because it would be impossible to decide which frontiers at which date should be adopted.

There the matter rested as far as the Foreign Office was concerned. If international law failed to provide for the circumstances, then obviously nothing could be done. It might be regrettable, but it was also highly convenient.

There was however a momentary breach in that resolute position when the Commission formally suggested that it also collect evidence of crimes against 'persons of no nationality or against local inhabitants'.[40] At first Allen suggested that he saw no reason to oppose the extension of the Commission's investigations as long as 'phrases are not used which might create the impression that the Jews are being regarded as the equivalent of a separate nationality of their own.' Malkin went even further and wrote that although he would personally prefer the Commission not to deal with offences against German Jews, 'if they do, I do not think that we can object.' Within a few days however, they had been brought firmly back into line and were insistent that the Commission could only deal with atrocities which were strictly war crimes, as legally defined.

Pell had arrived in London with different ideas. From the first he had been determined that the Commission should collect evidence of all atrocities, even those committed by Germans against Germans at any time since 30 January 1933 – he even went so far as to press for the investigation of crimes against those who had, with Allied encouragement, committed acts of sabotage for which they had been punished by the Germans.[41]

Preuss was the first to experience the strength of Pell's feelings on the whole subject – it was indeed the principal reason for their falling out. Legalisms, Pell shouted, would have to be brushed aside. 'New laws will have to be created if necessary. The failure to prosecute would be a mockery of justice.'[42] Preuss was appalled by Pell and terrified by his encouragement to visiting Jewish representatives, who were urged to 'build a fire'[43] under the governments by organizing a passionate press campaign. But he was too weak to oppose him. Neither of them had arrived with any instructions, and Pell silenced all protests by claiming to have been personally appointed by the President.

Impetuously, seeing that the State Department were not prepared to send instructions, Pell wrote to Roosevelt on 16 February 1944, about what he called the 'very thorny question of the Jews in Germany.' He wanted the President's 'direct and affirmative support.' 'If this question is not taken up by the War Crimes Commission, there seems to be no organization in the world that can touch those who have persecuted these unfortunate people on account of their religion and their race.'[44]

The White House passed the letter to Stettinius, who asked Hackworth to draft a reply after consulting John Pehle, the acting director of the War Refugees Board.[45] Pehle was distinctly unpopular in the State Department as a vehement advocate of the Jewish cause. He had expressed his disgust at the State Department for conspiring with the British to deny refuge in Palestine to those Jews who could still escape, and he had lobbied Roosevelt for the past four months on behalf of

Jewish organizations which were concerned at the omission from the Moscow Declaration of any reference to the extermination of the Jews – an endeavour which bore fruit in March when the President issued a separate declaration on the subject, drafted by Pehle. Pehle's interest in the subject of war crimes, together with his direct access to the White House, made him a real danger to the detached and level-headed approach which the State Department hoped could still be maintained.

Hackworth saw the threat and decided to ignore the instruction to consult Pehle, explaining disingenuously that: 'since these are separate matters it might be well to keep them separate.'[46] The reply that went out to Pell followed that which Allen had given to Rosengarten in October 1942: crimes committed in peacetime could not be tried by the Allies as war crimes – though, added Hackworth, 'they will have to be dealt with by the United Nations.' It was to be expected, added Hackworth, that those Germans responsible for murdering Jews would also be found to have been responsible for the murder of Allied nationals, and would therefore be tried in any case.

Pell's interpretation of the reply was deliberately obtuse and distorted. He reported to the Secretary of State on 24 March that, eight days previously, he had told the other Commission members that the American government supported the prosecution of cases involving German Jews as 'crimes against humanity'. 'I believe I have interpreted the President's instructions correctly,' Pell wrote, 'although there may be some criticism on technical grounds.' Justifying his decision, he said: 'if the War Crimes Commission does not consider these offences, they will, almost certainly, go unpunished . . . it seems to me an unduly narrow point of view to say that we are only interested in our own nationals, and hypocritical if, at the same time, we say we are fighting for humanity and justice.'[47] Fortunately for Pehle his letter went to the assistant secretary, Adolph Berle, who instead of reprimanding him for this blatant misrepresentation of American policy, tried to see if the policy could not be changed. Berle arranged for the State Department to re-examine its position on the subject.

In the meantime the Department continued to support the British line. An instruction to Pell which had originally read, when drafted in May, that the Commission could 'well consider ways and means of dealing with the perpetrators'[48] of crimes against German citizens, was amended before its dispatch in July to a more considered version which merely suggested that the Commission 'might be authorized by the participating Governments to examine the question'.[49] On 15 July Stettinius wrote to Rabbi Wise that the State Department: 'knows of no reason for in any wise undertaking to limit the punishment of war crimes to those committed in invaded territories. In fact it considers that

war crimes, wherever committed, should be adequately punished.'[50]
But the letter rejected Wise's suggestion that the Commission investigate prewar crimes and the idea of separate representation on the Commission for the Jews. Ignoring the diplomatic tiptoeing in Washington,
Pell exploited his alleged connection with Roosevelt and persuaded the
miserable and frustrated Hurst to write on 16 May, asking the British
government to reconsider its own position.[51]

Hurst's initiative was well timed. The previous day Adolf Eichmann had
given the orders for the deportation of Hungarian Jewry to Auschwitz.
Mass arrests and internment had already begun on 15 April on Hitler's
orders after he had split irrevocably with his erstwhile ally Horthy.
Within a month, German soldiers had rounded up over five hundred
thousand Jews. Packed, sometimes ninety at a time, into cattle trucks,
they left for Auschwitz at the rate of twelve to fourteen thousand per
day. Each truck had two buckets, one with water, one for excreta. The
screams of those inside, often suffocating to death, could be plainly heard
as the trains slowly passed through villages en route for Poland. It lasted
forty-six days. About three hundred thousand were killed. Many were
gassed, others were shot because the gas chambers and crematoria could
not cope with the vast numbers. Thousands just stood waiting for their
turn.

In the case of the Hungarian Jews, neither the British nor the
American governments could deny knowledge of what was happening.
Indeed, they had been warned that just such a catastrophe was imminent
for months past. The Jewish Agency had begged the Foreign Office to
allow the Hungarian Jews into Palestine while they were still free to
leave. Their pleas had been refused. Roosevelt's declaration of 24 March
on the murder of the Jews had been deliberately timed as a final effort to
deter the Germans from destroying the last surviving group of European
Jews under German control. The BBC was even allowed to broadcast
warnings to the Germans that they would be prosecuted for the
deportations.[52]

The Hungarian Jews, as citizens of an Axis ally, were in exactly the
same position as the German Jews. Hurst and Pell realized that the wave
of public horror aroused by reports of the deportations gave them an
ideal opportunity to press their own case. On 31 May Hurst wrote to
Eden with a new tone of confidence and aggression. He explained that
the Commission was under strong pressure to include those responsible
for Axis killings on racial, political or religious grounds in their lists, but
their terms of reference, much to everyone's disappointment, prevented
it. Perhaps, asked Hurst rhetorically, the governments had other plans

for prosecuting those cases. If so, they should be publicized, since 'the Commission feels that a public announcement to this effect would be helpful, in order that the public at large may understand that effective steps will be taken to ensure that the authors of these atrocities are brought to justice.'[53]

Hurst knew that the Cabinet was about to discuss the whole question of war crimes.[54] Simon had already prepared a paper for the meeting.[55] It recommended that the Cabinet should reject Hurst's suggestion (of 16 May) that the government reconsider its policy on the treatment of crimes against the stateless and crimes committed prior to the outbreak of war. Simon argued that to include such crimes in the Commission's lists would be 'confusing'. Privately, he told Hurst that in his view even the murder of Poles, Frenchmen and Americans in concentration camps was probably legal under German law, and that he doubted whether international law would be effective in such cases.[56]

Cadogan had given swift Foreign Office support to Simon's argument. To list cases involving the German Jews would be impractical, he wrote, because 'it would in practice be impossible to initiate proceedings on the scale necessary'.[57] Somewhat perfunctorily, he added: 'the Jews in Hungary, however, seem deserving of attention.' The attention, though, was to be restricted to those Jews who were Allied nationals and had sought refuge in Hungary. This rigid interpretation of the law seems strange when compared, as we shall see, with Cadogan's support for Churchill's plan to execute one hundred Nazi leaders within two hours of identification and without trial. There was no justice or international law to support that idea.

Over two hundred thousand Hungarian Jews had already arrived in Auschwitz when Simon's paper finally came before the Cabinet on 28 June.[58] Moreover, American pressure on the British to allow those who remained to enter Palestine had intensified; and news had leaked out about the extraordinary mission of Joel Brand. Brand, a Hungarian Jew, had arrived in Istanbul on 25 May with an astonishing offer to the British and Americans from Adolf Eichmann in Budapest. The organizer of the Final Solution offered to barter the lives of Hungary's Jews. In return for Allied supplies of tons of coffee, tea, cocoa, soap and ten thousand trucks, they would be allowed to leave for Palestine. Unable to make any progress in Turkey, Brand had sailed to Cairo.

British intelligence, after long interrogation and consultation with the Foreign Office, arrested Brand as a suspected Gestapo agent trying to split Britain from its Russian ally. It was a convenient way out. The British were unwilling to damage their relations with the Arabs. Yet only Simon seemed to understand the probable effect if the public suddenly realized the wide gap between the government's words and its deeds.

In his paper, which included the recommendation that Hurst's request of 31 May be refused, Simon reviewed the Commission's work. 'Very little progress' had been made, he reported, in collecting evidence. The seventy cases so far reported were trivial and incomplete. 'If one contrasts this minute result with the pronouncements that have been made of the intentions of the Allies . . . one appreciates the anxiety of the Chairman of the Commission as to the position.'[59] Simon argued that this created a political problem. The public were convinced that the Commission was busily preparing to prosecute huge members of war criminals, whereas the truth was that the results were 'exceedingly meagre'.

The limited concession proposed to the Cabinet by Simon was that the Commission should be allowed, where there was not the possibility of judicially listing someone as a suspected war criminal, to at least collect the evidence for eventual use by prosecutors.[60] It was a very limited expansion of the Commission's role, expecially as it was again refused permission to collect evidence of the murders of Hungarian and German Jews, and other stateless people. The Cabinet agreed to the modest proposal.[61]

For Hurst and Pell, who had not only seen the Hungarian Jews as a lever to activate the moribund Commission, but who had also become deeply committed to the idea that justice should be done to those responsible for the horrors they were witnessing, the Cabinet's decision was a bitter blow. The Commission was again left working in a vacuum. Neither Allied government had agreed on an effective war crimes policy.

It was to be a further four months before Eden answered Hurst's letter of 31 May, but it was quite clear to the Commission that their initiative had been rejected; their attempt to tackle an appalling crime happening at that very time had failed. Officials at the Foreign Office and the State Department now began minutely to examine and define the pitifully small margin by which they *had* gained ground.

On 4 July ten Foreign Office officials met under the chairmanship of Sir William Strang, the British representative on the European Advisory Committee, to re-examine the Commission's task in the light of the Cabinet's decision.[62]

At the end, Dennis Allen was delegated to re-examine policy towards the German Jews. Guided by what Allen himself called 'influence on the side of restraint,'[63] he thoroughly searched through all the public statements and concluded that: 'none of these declarations appears to involve HMG in an inescapable commitment to bring to trial the perpetrators of crimes against Jews and others in enemy countries.'[64] Satisfied with that conclusion, he then embarked on a series of legal somersaults which left even Eden perplexed. If a Hungarian Jew, Allen suggested, was

WE SEEM TO BE SHORT OF IDEAS

murdered in Poland, which was Allied territory, then those who loaded
him onto the train in Hungary could be classed as war criminals. In the
next paragraph he contradicted himself, saying that atrocities committed for racial, political or religious reasons in enemy countries could
not be war crimes, and therefore the Commission could not list those
responsible. It was what Cadogan called 'the inevitable conclusion'.[65]
The Commission and the Allies could only prosecute crimes committed
against Allied nationals or in Allied countries.

Eden was unsure. On 11 July, four days after the deportations from
Hungary ended, Churchill had written to him rejecting any negotiations based on the Brand message, concluding that all that remained was
to make public declarations 'so that everyone connected with it will be
hunted down and put to death.'[66]

Allen's report went against everything that Churchill wanted and
believed. '*Maybe*,' Eden wrote at the end of Allen's report, 'but am I not
pledged in some of my numerous statements about Jewish persecutions
to punish those responsible and is it possible to square this with the conclusions in this paper?' Allen replied smugly: 'Such assurances as have
been given have always been worded in general terms and we have been
careful to apply them to German occupied Europe generally.' He went
on to suggest that the only way in which the guilty could be brought to
justice was by pressure on a new German government. While gratefully,
accepting that he was politically covered, Eden knew that that very idea
had been repeatedly discarded as futile by all Foreign Office officials,
including Allen himself. Now, with no acceptable alternative policy, it
was resurrected as a convenient reply to any critics.

The Foreign Office was clearly uncertain, and had to convince itself,
that it was at all necessary for Germans to be punished for murdering
their fellow citizens. Commenting on Allen's suggestion, O'Neil
wrote: 'Clearly these crimes were vile and should be punished. . . The
men who committed them would be from all points of view, not least
from our own as occupying authorities, better put away than left
running round free in Germany.'[67] Yet the feeling of the German people
about Allied pressure was considered important. 'The German people as
a whole,' wrote O'Neil, 'would probably resent less the punishment of
persons guilty of torturing Jews than the task of elaborating steps to
restore the Jews, in a starving country, to their pre-Nazi financial
status.' Summarizing what even O'Neil saw as a theoretical question,
Harrison wrote: 'I imagine conditions will anyhow be such that it will
not be practical to pursue this question.'[68]

Significantly, throughout the discussion, no one had suggested the
amendment of international law to cover those responsible for millions
of deaths. Nor can it be seen as anything other than a deliberate

omission. The draft terms of surrender gave the Allies 'supreme authority with respect to Germany.' Legally, there was nothing to prevent the Allies prosecuting Germans for crimes against Germans.

Jack Troutbeck, the Foreign Office official responsible for negotiating the terms with the Americans and Russians, spelled it out to SHAEF headquarters. The Allies were not to use their legal powers but would rather 'bring pressure to bear on a future German government to carry out the necessary punishments themselves'.[69] Non-prosecution was a clear policy and not a legal decision. Yet, significantly, Simon himself had initiated a change in the law so that British courts could try the *Peleus* case; an instance of a merchant ship being torpedoed and its crew machinegunned to death by the German submarine, because 'the accused were Germans, the victims Greeks and the crime was committed on the high seas.'[70]

In the same letter in which he told Eden of the need for this change in the law, Simon confirmed the real reasons why the Commission should not be allowed, even temporarily, to collect evidence on Axis cases. 'We should, I fear, be only raising false hopes if we encouraged the idea that investigation by the UNWCC would lead to the punishment of the black-guards. It is a sorry conclusion and you will be able to judge whether it is likely that Mr Roosevelt will be able to accept it in view of the big Jewish electorate in the USA.'

A statement of British policy was sent to the State Department on 15 August.[71] It reaffirmed that the Commission should not be allowed to list German cases involving Axis nationals, and that it should be left to the Allies to put pressure on the German government. Any alternative, said the Foreign Office 'would give rise to serious difficulties of practice and principle'.[72]

Emotions had run very high in America over the plight of the Hungarian Jews. Cordell Hull had himself started negotiations with the Germans on buying the lives of some of those still in Hungary. Money in a Swiss bank was later used for that purpose. American pressure had forced the British to issue five thousand 'bogus' Palestinian immigration certificates to Hungarian Jews which were accepted by the Germans.[73] Washington had also sympathetically supported the Swede Raoul Wallenberg's successful ploy of housing five thousand Hungarian Jews in specially designated 'Swedish diplomatic houses'.

For three years Washington had been content to leave war crimes policy to the British. Such interest as there had been existed mainly in the State Department, which had been happy to support the line adopted by the Foreign Office. Pehle had been able to influence Presidential statements, but he had not been successful in persuading those responsible for policy that any more active interest need be taken. The War Department had simply gone its own way, disapproving of the Department of State's apparent collusion with the British, but unwilling to become involved in the international aspects of the subject. Things were about to change very radically.

Even within the State Department there were people who were beginning to doubt that present policy could be either right or honourable. On 1 August Pell sent a cable asking to whom the information so far collected by the Commission should be addressed.[74] There were, he warned, 'a great many cases and a great amount of data.' The query ended up on the desk of Fletcher Warren of the Foreign Activity Correlation Department. Warren went round the Department but no one seemed in the least interested. After three weeks he became angry and confronted Hackworth. The legal adviser was plainly uninterested. He disliked Pell, thought the Commission was a British responsibility, and told Warren that as far as the US was concerned war crimes were now a War Department matter. Warren then phoned the War Department and asked if they would like the list. To his surprise the Department had still not appointed anyone to be responsible for collecting evidence. Now furious, he confronted both Hackworth and Katherine Fite, Hackworth's assistant, insisting that something had to be done. Nothing was. In a 'Memorandum for the Files' dated 26 August he set down his angry opinion, 'not officially but simply as an American,' that the Department's failure to accept responsibility or even take an interest would cause an uproar when it became public.[75]

The State Department took two months to consider the Foreign Office statement of 15 August, and in the meantime Pell's fury threatened to overflow in public. He proposed to hold a press conference at which he would expose Allied policy for the fiasco it was.[76] At first the Foreign Office, under the impression that Pell's idea had official American support, acquiesced in the plan for a press conference.[77] Indeed, Pell had supporters in Washington – Pehle, for one, urged Stettinius to support the plan. But he also had adversaries, and their influence proved the stronger.

When Preuss resigned as Pell's assistant the War Department had secured the appointment of one of their own officials, Lieutenant-Colonel Joseph V. Hodgson, in his place. At first they merely wanted to ensure that they were kept informed, being happy to go along with a British policy that seemed directed at ensuring that the Commission remained impotent; they certainly did not support Pell's activist ambitions. After all, as the Secretary of War told Henry Morgenthau, when the latter tried to enlist, his support against the British and the State

Department at the beginning of August, if the US were empowered to punish Germans for killing Germans before the war, then 'Germans would have the right to intervene in our country to punish people who are lynching negroes.'[78]

Hodgson was quick to warn his superiors of Pell's intentions, and within hours of his cable arriving in the Pentagon a stinging rebuke was on its way to London from the State Department. Pell was reprimanded for calling a press conference on 'such a delicate subject' without the President's authorization.[79]

But the secret of the Commission's failure was not to be concealed for long.

On 30 August 1944 Sir Cecil Hurst chaired the War Crimes Commission's first press conference, a hurriedly arranged affair.[80] Four days earlier de Gaulle had proudly marched down the Champs Elysées. The liberation of Paris and first-hand reports from British and American correspondents of German brutality during the occupation immediately renewed interest in war crimes. The pressure for reassurance about the Allied governments' intentions was irresistible, and it came from a wider public than the interested pressure groups alone. For nearly two years the Commission's existence had been the American and British governments' stock answer to all questions about plans for postwar prosecutions. But previous attempts to get details of the Commission's work had been blocked by the State Department and Foreign Office 'in the interests of security.' The fear of reprisals was the excuse for secrecy, but officials, politicians and Commission members left no one in doubt that a mass of information had been gathered.

Minutes after the conference started, Hurst was asked, as a routine opener, whether Hitler was on the Commission's list. Hurst stumbled and then tried to evade answering. No detailed case against Hitler had been prepared, he admitted, but if the Commission were suddenly asked for one 'it would do its best.' Pressed, he admitted that Hitler was not on the list. He did not explain, as he might have, that the State Department had ordered Pell, soon after he arrived, to prevent any mention of putting Hitler on trial because it might be 'provocative'.[81]

The next question was: 'How many people are on the list?' 'The list of war criminals is not a very long one,' said Hurst. 'It is meagre.' There was uproar, but Hurst resolutely refused to give the number. The Commission's failure was headline news on both sides of the Atlantic the following day. There were, in fact, just 184 names on the list, fourteen of them for being jointly responsible for pulling a statue from its pedestal and cutting its head off.[82] Lord Simon's worst fears were realized.

The State Department continued to remain calm in the face of a public row and Hackworth wrestled with the task of preparing a reply to the British suggestions for enlarging the Commission's brief. Elsewhere in Washington consciences were not so easy. Having accepted responsibility for war crimes the War Department had been content to do as little as possible, blandly ignoring the UN Commission on the grounds that, as a child of the State Department, it must be their responsibility to deal with their troublesome offspring. But the Department contained powerful figures, including several lawyers whose anger had been aroused by the reports of atrocities in Europe and by the fate of the Hungarian Jews in particular. Nor were they averse to exposing what they considered to be a shameful and humiliating failure on the part of their colleagues in the Department of State.

Exactly what the sequence of events was, is not clear, but it is evident that the War Department resolved to take a more active interest in the whole war crimes field, and the first fruit of that interest was evident in the reply which Hackworth finally sent to London on 4 October.[83] The British proposals sent in August were, he suggested, 'too broad in scope'; the Commission should be permitted to consider the cases of non-German nationals taken to Germany and subsequently murdered. Most significantly, the British pledge to bring pressure on a successor government in Germany to deal with the cases of German nationals had to be 'carefully considered' in favour of 'more direct methods'.[84] The last phrase puzzled the British, until, twenty-four hours later, Hackworth spelled it out over the phone to the embassy. The words meant what they said: military, not diplomatic, pressure had to be used on Germany to bring the criminals to trial.

Malkin was seriously disturbed. He knew that Hackworth had always shared his own desire for a 'detached attitude'. Both agreed that, legally, these murders could not be considered war crimes.[85] But some agreed text had to be arrived at which could be handed to the Commission as a statement of the policy that they were supposed to be carrying out. After phoning Hackworth in Washington, Malkin noted that it was agreed that the Commission could not be given freedom to deal with German cases, but the State Department 'was anxious for election and other reasons not to give the impression that we are not proposing to do anything about such cases. This is very much our view.'[86] Sticking to his line that, ultimately, the Commission was a British responsibility, Hackworth left it to Malkin to construct a form of words that would be meaningless and yet avert the furore which would be provoked by an outright admission that there were no plans for the Allies to ensure the punishment of those responsible for crimes against German citizens. Malkin told Allen to 'insert something' that would avoid a 'minor storm' in the press if leaked by Hurst or Pell.[87] Allen was in favour of simply telling the Commission to keep out of such cases and leaving them to be resolved by 'pressure', but a colleague, James Wardrop, warned him that the danger was to great – 'if by mischance *PM* [an American magazine] or similar publications were to get hold of so concrete an undertaking the consequences would be disastrous.'[88]

Thinking that they had finally secured agreement with Washington, Foreign Office officials on 9 November produced an agreed draft of Eden's answer to Hurst's letter of 31 May. 'It would be a mistake,' the letter said, 'for the Commission to undertake this additional and heavy burden, although HM Government sincerely hope that those who have been responsible for these atrocities may one day have the punishment which their actions deserve.'[89]

It was in effect the *coup de grâce* for the Commission as an effective instrument for investigating war crimes. Just over a month later Herbert Pell arrived back in America. Spitefully, the State Department had for weeks rejected his requests to return briefly to see his ninety-year-old mother and attend his only son's marriage, claiming his presence in London was too important. Suddenly they reversed their opposition and agreed.

Soon after his arrival he read newspaper reports that, by extraordinary misfortune, a Congressional committee had refused to appropriate the necessary funds for him to continue as US representative on the Commission. Without more ado, the State Department announced Pell's resignation. Pell instantly offered to do the work without pay. That was refused, and he began a public campaign against State Department officials who 'do not want to punish Nazi criminals as thoroughly as they advocate.'[90] For the Jewish lobbyists, the War Refugee Board and other interested organizations, Pell became a martyr, the victim of the insensitive, obstructive and antisemitic bureaucrats.

Pell's martyrdom turned into a full crisis at the beginning of the new year following the announcement from London of the 'resignation due to ill health' of Sir Cecil Hurst. Both Eden and Simon were content to let it be known that Hurst had suffered a nervous breakdown and was not expected to recover.[91] He lived until 1963. In fact, he resigned in anger at the Foreign Office's refusal to treat the Commission and war crimes prosecution seriously. Letters and proposals from the Commission to the Foreign Office remained unanswered, and SHAEF refused to cooperate with the Commission. Hurst's resignation was followed by that of the Norwegian representative and by the threatened resignation of the Australian, Czech and Polish representatives. Fed on rumours that

Churchill wanted to use the German army against the Russians, Bruce, the Australian representative, accused Hurst of resisting every proposal to improve the Commission and Foreign Office of deliberate sabotage because they feared that Poland and Czechoslovakia would become communist after the war.[92] Stung by the attack, British officials openly cursed the day they had championed Dominion membership and not backed the Russians.

For a few days the Foreign Office toyed with the idea of closing the Commission down. Roberts hoped it would just 'fade away' while another official commented that it was 'a great bore and probably a great mistake.'[93] The idea was smartly dropped when Hackworth suggested the same to the British embassy.[94] It would, Roberts told the embassy, confirm that the British were to blame if the initiative to close it down had been an American one.

Belatedly, the Foreign Office blamed the failure on the Americans, on the other participating nations, on everyone except themselves.[95] On 12 December Strang presented a paper on war crimes to the European Advisory Committee. It was rejected peremptorily by the Soviets as being too legalistic and ineffectual. Bruised, Strang complained to his officials that the brief they had given him consisted only of background material. 'We seem to be short of ideas. Let us start drafting directives and then we will find a policy.'[96]

If the demise of the UN Commission in all but name represented the end of one strand of British policy, another had already expired. It had never been intended that the resounding phrases of the Moscow Declaration should cover, nor that the Commission should deal with, the Nazi leaders – those whose guilt was 'so black', and whose crimes so generalized, that their fate had to be a 'political decision'.

In late October 1943, excited by his triumph in securing agreement to the Moscow Declaration and, perhaps, encouraged by the fact that Eden had not yet returned to London, Churchill turned his mind to what that 'political decision' should be. On 3 November he asked Cadogan to read the proofs of a paper he had prepared for the Cabinet. Entitled 'The Punishment of War Criminals',[97] it dealt with the fate of those 'major criminals whose notorious offences have no geographical location.' The Prime Minister's solution for 'Hitler and the Mussolini gangs, the Japanese War Lords and Quislings' was naively simplistic. Between fifty and one hundred should be listed, by agreement, and declared world outlaws. When any of those listed was arrested by an Allied soldier, he could be 'shot to death' within six hours of identification by a major-general or above without need for reference to higher authority.

Churchill believed that dealing with the Nazi leadership was an international responsibility, while the other war criminals were the direct responsibility of those countries who had suffered. 'The British nation at any rate would be incapable of carrying out mass executions for any length of time, especially as we have not suffered like the subjugated countries'. Shooting the leadership out of hand would avoid all the inevitable delays of trials, 'the tangles of legal procedure'. Regardless of its obvious imperfection, it avoided a repetition of Leipzig and was therefore desirable.

Piqued by Churchill's unexpected initiative, Dennis Allen delighted in itemizing the paper's mistakes, faulty assumptions, and misconceptions. The neutrals would be offended, the term 'world outlaws' no longer existed, prosecuting Quislings was not an international responsibility, other ministers and departmental interests had been ignored, while Russia's demand for an international tribunal was not taken into account. He was nevertheless attracted to the idea of summary executions.[98]

The Cabinet was split when it considered the slightly amended paper on 10 November.[99] Shooting the German leaders on sight, however attractive in the short term, worried those concerned with the Allied claim that they were fighting for justice. Approval might also have provoked Moscow to demand the immediate execution of Hess. The issue was shelved for Simon and Somervell, the Attorney-General, to reconsider. Once again there was no progress. Four declarations had been issued threatening punishment but there was a vacuum where there should have been policy. Only Roosevelt liked Churchill's idea when they met one month later in Cairo, but that meant next to nothing.[100]

In London there was not only deadlock, but also a bankruptcy of ideas. Simon lacked the legal imagination to cope with the unprecedented criminality. At the Cabinet meeting on 13 March, ministers could not agree what the charges were against the Nazi leadership.[101] Simon wanted 'conducting a barbarous war,' Morrison wanted a charge relating to genocide, others wanted a charge for starting the war, while Churchill insisted that shooting the top hundred was the best solution of all. It would, he believed, create a gulf between the leaders and the people.

Unable to agree on charges or on summary execution, the Cabinet asked the Foreign Office to draw up the list – 'A list of those whose crimes would be so notorious to the conscience of mankind that their fate decided by political decision would not only be accepted but expected.'[102] But officials found that the criterion for inclusion, 'responsibility for bringing about the war and directing its conduct against the United Nations, explicitly excluding those guilty of war crimes in the strict sense,' created more problems than it solved. Hitler's ministers of transport and education were as guilty as all other politicians, but in their view less so than the individual SS officer: could they be shot on sight? Everyone knew where to begin – 'Hitler, A.' – but no one knew where to stop.

For two months nothing happened. There was no list and Eden did not, as directed by Churchill, start discussions with the State Department.[103] Prompted by Churchill, the Foreign Office finally produced a list and a proposed policy in a paper called 'Treatment of Major War Criminals'.[104] It was condemned by Simon for failing 'to come up to its title',[105] and even Eden was obviously unenthusiastic. He wrote: 'I have so little taste for this subject that I am prepared to agree to all that is proposed here.'[106] Instead of one hundred names, it was a list of thirty-two Germans and five Italians. Amongst those selected for immediate execution, besides the most obvious leaders, were Max Amann, the director of the Nazi party publishing house, Arthur Axmann, the Reich Youth leader, and Bernhard Rust, the minister of education – men who were totally unknown to the British, and probably even to the German, public. Even Eden felt that at least seven should not have been listed.

Attlee did not hide his anger. He criticized the absence of any military leader other than Keitel, and the complete absence of industrialists. 'Officers who behaved like gangsters should be treated as such,'[107] he wrote, and also demanded that industrialists' property should be confiscated. Eden justified the exclusion of all the military leadership on the grounds that beyond Keitel, 'it becomes practically impossible to distinguish between general political responsibility and the responsibility of professionals who are merely carrying out the regime's orders'. Industrialists were excluded, he explained, 'because it was impossible to draw any satisfactory dividing line'.[108]

The Cabinet discussed the problem, along with Hurst's demand for a wider brief for the UN Commission, on 28 June.[109] The outcome was yet another deadlock. Everyone agreed on rapid justice, but not on its implementation or on the list. The problem was again handed over to Simon and Somervell.

Ten weeks later Simon had reduced the list to five (Hitler, Himmler, Goering, Goebbels and Ribbentrop) and reaffirmed the by now meaningless point that it was a 'political and not a judicial question.'[110]

At the end of September, Churchill and Roosevelt met in Quebec. As a last recourse, Churchill sought Roosevelt's active support for the 'immediate execution' policies. The President was still quite prepared to leave war crimes policy to the British: he agreed without question.[111] Moreover, the idea assorted well with Henry Morgenthau's draconian plans for the complete destruction of postwar Germany, then favoured in the White House. It was left to Churchill to get Stalin's agreement. Six weeks later Churchill telegraphed Roosevelt: 'U[ncle] J[oe] took an unexpectedly ultra respectable line. There must be no executions without trial otherwise the world would say we were afraid to try them. I pointed out the difficulties in international law but he replied there must be no death sentences.'[112] Stalin had, in fact, said exactly the same thing two years previously to the British ambassador, Clark Kerr.

By November 1944 it was clear to everyone except the Foreign Office that the half-hearted British attempt to organize a war crimes policy on behalf of the two Western Allies and occupied Europe was a hopeless failure. Allied armies stood on the threshold of the Reich itself. Already enormous numbers of potential witnesses and vast amounts of evidence were in Anglo-American hands. Not only had no effective policy been decided upon by which the pledges of justice and retribution were to be redeemed, but, much worse, the long-drawn-out fiasco had actually prevented any preparations being made to carry out the practical tasks of gathering evidence, tracking down wanted men, interrogating witnesses and suspects, establishing courts – in short doing all those tasks without which, as Simon had clearly foreseen two years previously, no policy could be effective.

The new policies which were about to be born in the Department of War in Washington might belatedly fill the vacuum which the Foreign Office and the State Department had contrived; but the failure to lay plans and to organize institutions and procedures was irretrievable. While the diplomats argued by what laws and in what courts the murderers of ten million innocents should be tried, they quite overlooked the obvious fact that a precondition of any trials at all was the appointment of a police force to ensure the presence of the accused and to equip the prosecution with some evidence.

5

'A BROAD
PROGRAMME'

If the initial failure to produce a war crimes policy was the fault of the Foreign Office and State Department, then the failure to create the necessary machinery after the two departments had decided on the need for a programme was certainly the fault of the military. While the War Department in Washington realized that the responsibility for war crimes, which they had taken on so casually in early 1944, might prove to be more than a formality, the military in London had been deliberately excluded from the subject from the very outset. Explaining that the presence of the Secretary of State for War would not be required on Simon's ministerial committee when it was set up in July 1942, the secretary to the Cabinet, Sir Edward Bridges, wrote to Sir Frederick Bovenschen, the permanent secretary at the War Office: 'You will be informed of any matters that may concern you from the military point of view.'[1] Apart from Cyril Gepp, who continued to be responsible for compiling his rather inadequate list of crimes against British soldiers, that was the last anyone in the higher echelons of the War Office heard on the subject for almost two years

So far as the army's legal section, the Judge Advocate-General's Department, was concerned, their interest in war crimes only extended to those which might be committed in the course of actual combat. No consideration was given to providing the army with a list of wanted men; indeed they would not have known where to send them if they discovered any. In January 1944 the Foreign Office had proposed to the Americans that the military should hand suspects over to the UN Commission, but the suggestion was passed to the Joint Chiefs of Staff and remained in limbo until they rejected it six months later, in July.[2]

At SHAEF, (the headquarters of the Supreme Commander, Allied Forces Europe, or SCAEF) detachment reigned in the months before D-Day. Nobody there accepted any responsibility for war crimes work – nobody had asked them to. Nevertheless, in early April, John Foster, of SHAEF's legal department, circulated a memo[3] explaining that the accepted definition of a war criminal was a person who featured on the Commission's list – at the time the list contained sixty-eight names. Foster went on to explain that included among SCAEF's orders would be one to arrest anyone suspected of being a war criminal. The following month, having talked to Hurst, he produced a paper[4] outlining SHAEF's responsibilities for arresting wanted men; the document in fact listed the unanswered questions that existed rather than laying down any directives, but it did propose that the task should be carried out by G2, the Intelligence Division. Clinging rigidly to old theories, G2 was to arrest anyone whose name was on the Commission's list and, after an armistice, present the list of remaining names to the German authorities.

On 6 May, Brigadier-General T.J. Betts, deputy to the assistant chief of staff at SHAEF, rejected Foster's apparently modest proposal. SHAEF, wrote Betts, was not responsible for trials of war criminals, and G2 refused to accept any responsibility for collecting evidence because that was a job for the Allied governments. As for arresting war criminals, 'this is a function of the police power rather than of counter-intelligence which is concerned primarily with the maintenance of military security. It is suggested that consideration be given to allocating the searching for such individuals to law enforcement agencies.'[5]

Hurst and Pell were well aware of the need for the kind of 'police' work which Betts pinpointed so succinctly and so unhelpfully. By mid-June the armies under SHAEF's command were actually ashore in Europe and, in desperation, Hurst wrote on the 15th suggesting that representatives of the Commission should be attached to SHAEF with a staff of lawyers and detectives to form an agency which would identify war criminals, conduct investigations and prepare cases for trial.[6]

At the same time, Hurst and Pell persuaded Foster that he should put pressure on the G2 division to reconsider its refusal to become involved.[7] Colonel H.G. Sheen of G2 told Foster[8] that if the Division did accept the responsibility, someone would have to authorize a massive increase in staff, all of whom would have to be given a ninety-day specialized investigative training at a special police college in Chicago, and that at least eighty-five per cent of them would have to be qualified French and German linguists – a qualification which very few intelligence personnel possessed. Underlining Sheen's objections, Major-General K.W.D. Strong, G2's second assistant chief of staff, added that investigation would only be possible with more staff and based on a centralized authority.[9]

At the end of August, SHAEF went even further and refused outright to investigate any war crimes committed before D-Day, or against civilians whenever they occurred, or against POWs not involved in the D-Day operation.[10] Similarly, Belgian and Dutch government representatives who asked SHAEF for help in investigating atrocities committed during their countries' liberation were bluntly turned away.[11]

A meeting of Foreign Office officials on 4 July considered Hurst's proposal for the new agency. They agreed among themselves that the plan should be rejected but that the Commission should only be told that its ideas were being referred to Washington for the American government's reaction.[12]

Simultaneously a new draft directive to the Allied armies for trials of war criminals was produced by the combined Chiefs of Staff and was sent to the American Joint Chiefs on 7 July for their comments.

Opposing any direct relations between the Commission and SHAEF, Roberts had argued that since the Russians were not members, they would object to the agency being set up in enemy territory; and, that, since SHAEF did not have a formal war crimes mandate yet, it could not work with the Commission even in Britain. Contacts, even for transmitting the lists between the two, could only be through the British or American governments.[13] The firm conclusions of the officials, displaying the evident lack of urgency which they attached to the subject, makes somewhat depressing reading.

Less than two weeks earlier, the Foreign Secretary had made a solemn pledge to the House of Commons which very clearly implied the need for some such agency as Hurst was proposing. It was given as a result of the Foreign Office receiving information of what was to be the single most notorious war crime committed by the Germans against British nationals.

On 24 March 1944, seventy-nine air force officers from nine nations had daringly escaped from Stalag Luft III, a German POW camp at Sagan in Silesia[14] – a story immortalized in *The Great Escape*. They had successfully dug a tunnel under the perimeter fence and, in disguise, attempted to make their way to Britain. Only three succeeded. Of the seventy-six recaptured, fifty were executed by the Gestapo on Hitler's personal orders. Twenty-five of those murdered were British. At first the deaths were reported to the Foreign Office by the Swiss representative acting as the Protecting Power. The Germans insisted that they had been killed 'while trying to escape'. The Swiss representative commented in his report that he doubted the German account.

On 23 June Eden made a statement about the deaths in the House of Commons. An official note received from the German government accused the Allied General Staff of provoking the escape as a military and political objective and justified the severe measures as necessary to prevent German public security being endangered. In a sombre tone, Eden denounced these 'cold-blooded acts of butchery', and pledged that the British government would 'never cease in their efforts to collect the evidence to identify those responsible. They are firmly resolved that these foul criminals shall be tracked down to the last man, wherever they may take refuge. When the war is over they will be brought to exemplary justice.' It was a rousing threat which went down well, but it provided no noticeable encouragement for the Foreign Office hierarchy to find some way to begin the efforts which Eden so solemnly and worthily promised.

The first hint that the War Office received that war crimes might, after all, involve them came when Hurst sent a copy of his letter of 15 June to Guy Lambert, the assistant under-secretary.[15] But Lambert did not feel any action was called for, and when his minister, Sir John Grigg, attended the 28 June Cabinet, which reviewed the whole subject, his departmental brief advised him that; 'the War Office is not directly concerned with the machinery for bringing to trial the perpetrators of war crimes, that is the business of the United Nations War Crimes Commission. . . . The War Office is indirectly concerned as being one of the sources of information and evidence of such crimes. As such a source the War Office is not likely to be able to produce very much evidence.' Nor, said the brief, could the War Office offer soldiers to provide any oral evidence.[16]

But doubts had begun to creep in. On 4 August the director of Military Intelligence, G.R. Way, sent a memo to Lambert pointing out that his section had 'a very sensitive finger on the pulse of PW feelings, and there is no doubt whatever that any undue delay in bringing criminals to justice and still more any default of justice through failure to obtain strict evidence, would give rise to serious disillusionment among repatriated prisoners of war, and would also I think, have perjorative repercussions on civilian morale. It cannot be sufficiently emphasized that returned prisoners will have themselves seen and heard of the most flagrant war crimes and criminals, and will have every justification for expecting to see speedy and exemplary justice administered.' Way then suggested that there would be an outcry if trials could not be held because of restrictive rules of evidence.[17]

Lambert shared Way's concern, though his instinct favoured evasion rather than action. Realizing that nothing had been organized by the government which would actually produce the results, he immediately contacted Sir Henry MacGeagh, the Judge Advocate-General, suggesting that he should protect himself, lest 'you might find yourself saddled at the last moment with considerable responsibility in this field. . . It might be necessary for S. of S. to exercise some pressure at Cabinet level to prevent you from being landed with an impossible task at the last minute.'[18]

MacGeagh nevertheless supplied a draft directive on the prosecution of war crimes a month later, but by then Lambert's doubts had turned to grim suspicion. He was still determined to do his best to fend off the inevitable. Within hours of Hurst's disastrous press conference on 30 August, he waspishly wrote to Patrick Dean, asking with bland innocence whether the Foreign Office had done anything about Hurst's suggestion that the Commission be attached to SHAEF. In particular, Lambert wanted to know how the Foreign Office intended to investigate the Stalag Luft III murders. A MI9 summary naming suspected personalities had been given to Kent at the Treasury Solicitor's office, 'but neither he nor the War Crimes Commission have means of pursuing that information when our troops got into Germany . . . so far as I can see the necessary machinery does not exist.'[19]

Lambert was, of course, totally correct. Not only did no machinery exist, but there seemed no means by which it could be brought into existence. The Commission had at least tried; but its proposal had found no favour in the Foreign Office, and was now languishing in the State Department, which also disapproved of it. The War Department in Washington, nominally the American agency responsible, had not yet turned its mind to the subject; the War Office and SHAEF both hoped that involvement on their part could be avoided. Apart from Fletcher Warren, filing his lonely protest in the State Department, and the members of the Commission itself, no one seemed to even feel any indignation over the situation.

Hurst was near despair. His press conference had been a public humiliation; Pell's outrage with the Foreign Office had reached the point at which he was openly threatening Hurst with public exposure of Whitehall's unconcern which would, he said, destroy the American public's goodwill towards Great Britain.[20] Hurst could not defend the Foreign Office: he was only too aware of the lack of interest, and of answers, which his many approaches had met with.

Moreover, a new possibility now lent urgency to his worries: it seemed all too possible that, before any action was agreed upon, let alone taken, the wanted men might have escaped from Europe. Exiled governments in London had for some time been getting reports that the Gestapo and SS had set up an elaborate escape organization, providing everything from false papers to civilian clothes, for all their members. Other reports to the Foreign Office from embassies in the neutral countries described attempts by leading Nazis to get immediate asylum for their families. From Stockholm, there was a report of Nazis parachuting to asylum, and from Spain accounts of Nazis leaving, disguised as Spanish seamen. Allegedly every neutral ship leaving Spain was stopped by the Royal Navy in their search for escapers, but by September 1944 there were confirmed reports of German submarines taking both people and booty from Spain to South America.[21]

Several of the Allied declarations promising the Nazis retribution for their crimes had also warned the neutrals not to give asylum. The threat had been opposed by both Foreign Office officials and some ministers. The Chancellor of the Duchy of Lancaster had gone so far, in July 1943, as to suggest that if they did get asylum, 'it would probably prove the best from the point of view of posterity' because it would avoid the trials.[22]

The neutrals felt they had nothing to fear. Some Foreign Office officials seemed, in fact, to treat the whole subject with frivolity. Told by the Czechs that the escapees were even sending official telegrams to their next of kin announcing their own deaths, Elvyn Williams asked: 'I wonder how the Germans decide what is and what is not a war criminal?'[23] Pressure by both the United States and British embassies in Eire, Spain, Sweden, Switzerland, Argentina and the Vatican to persuade the governments concerned to publicly declare that would-be escapees would be refused asylum, had produced no results. On the contrary, the governments' unanswered queries about the definition of a war criminal, and their previous sympathies towards the Nazis, made such declarations very unlikely.[24]

Hurst had reported the rumours to the Foreign Office on 24 July.[25] The letter was among those that still awaited an answer. Frustrated and angry, he determined upon a final effort. He asked Lord Wright, a senior and respected British judge who was sitting on the Commission as the nominal Australian representative, to warn Churchill of the impending disaster. Melodramatically, Wright insisted that his short memorandum be sent immediately to Churchill, who was then in Quebec. In it he wrote:

> I am increasingly concerned at the risk that many war criminals may, unless some change in the present procedure for dealing with them may be devised, escape their just retribution. I wish therefore to urge the immediate inauguration and staffing of a system of Military Courts, established under the various Supreme Allied Commanders, for the trial of war criminals. This would be coupled with the task of collecting evidence as nearly as possible to the time and place of the crime. This is a practical matter but there should be in the armies a sufficient number of men capable either to investigate the cases or to try them. It could be easily effected if the fiat of the supreme authorities were issued. What is essential is that time is not lost – otherwise evidence disappears, and the criminals escape. Germans are extraordinarily clever in ruses and devices to cover up their tracks.[26]

There was nothing new in the suggestion of military courts. Simon had proposed the same system in 1942. But Wright's letter had the desired effect of sounding the alarm. Churchill immediately sent copies of the memorandum to Simon and Eden with the comment:

> It is clear that he feels strongly that, unless the procedure of the War Criminals Commission is changed and greater progress made, the whole business may be brought into disrepute, and his criticisms in some respect run so closely with the criticisms made in the Lord Chancellor's memorandum of 2 June 1944 as to cause me uneasiness. [27]

Four days later, on 20 September, Simon wrote to Wright thanking him on his own and Hurst's behalf for sending the 'excellently written' memorandum. [28] Meanwhile, at the Foreign Office, Patrick Dean had been considering matters with due deliberation. At the end of September he delivered an answer to Lambert's pointed inquiry. SHAEF would take the initial responsibility for investigating war crimes while the war continued, he said. Afterwards, it would pass to the Control Commission, a body that had recently been created as the embryo government authority for what would be the British zone of Germany. [29]

In September 1944, the Control Commission was in fact little more than a letterheading and a handful of staff who were not considered important for the war effort. Nevertheless, Dean's colleague Oliver Harvey wrote just days earlier to its director, Major-General Stanley W. Kirby, breaking the news of this new responsibility which was being offered to his wretchedly understaffed organization. 'We think,' he wrote with studied innocence, 'it would be extremely useful if you could work out plans with SHAEF . . . taking into account the War Crimes Commission's recommendations.' [30] Pushing the responsibility onto a non-existent organization and asking it to negotiate with SHAEF, which had already rejected any broad responsibility, was pressing political fortune too far.

In any case, events were now moving beyond the Foreign Office's control. On 18 September, Simon had hastily arranged a meeting with General E.C. Betts from SHAEF's Legal Division. Betts was pursuaded that the armies should be at least allowed to arrest concentration camp guards, though he refused to go further and permit them to pursue those guards who might escape. [31] Betts also agreed to support the Commission's proposal that a War Crimes Agency should be attached to Eisenhower's headquarters. But that was dependent, Betts emphasized, on SHAEF getting a directive from the Combined Chiefs.

Four days later Simon chaired a meeting in his office to discuss with others, including Dean, Hurst's complaint that proposals made by the Commission were being ignored by the Foreign Office, Wright's memorandum to the Prime Minister, and how war crimes investigations could be started as soon as possible.

Dean was on the defensive when the Lord Chancellor brusquely asked why a French government representative had been prevented from interrogating a German officer named Hackel, then a POW in Britain. According to the resistance, Hackel had, with his own hands, killed two Frenchmen in front of their homes in La Valonne for having shown sympathy towards Poles working in the German army. (It was in fact not the first British refusal to allow interrogations; Lambert had earlier told Hurst that interrogations could only be allowed after the war.[32]) Dean defended the decisions, saying that examination in the French sense 'was a serious matter', and just as there were to be no trials until after the war because of the risk of reprisals, there should be no interrogations either. He rejected the distinction between getting evidence and trials, an excuse Simon brushed aside.[33]

The unpleasant coolness between Simon and Dean during that meeting was one consequence of a letter which had just arrived at the Foreign Office. Determined to upset what they saw as that department's calculated obstructiveness, Simon and Hurst had taken the offensive. On 21 September Eden received a personal letter from Simon criticizing his department's record of failing to reply to the Commission's recommendations, especially the one of 15 June suggesting direct contacts between the Commission and SHAEF: Simon wrote: 'It is so urgent that something effective should be done without further delay that I trust you will forgive me writing to you on this matter. My great fear is that we may reach a point where public opinion will demand to know what had been done about war criminals, and will by no means be satisfied about the answer'.[34]

Simon also wrote to Churchill to acknowledge the copy of Wright's memorandum and to explain matters as he saw them. He told the Prime Minister that he was 'far from satisfied with the present position', although blame could not be put on the Commission because Hurst had 'a very difficult team to drive – the American member I gather is most troublesome, and the smaller European nations raise all sorts of technical complications.' Nevertheless, to rely on the existing machinery would be a recipe for failure. 'It must be remembered,' Simon wrote, 'that very strong and confident assurances as to our intentions that the guilty would be punished have made on many occasions.' Therefore an organization had to be established to investigate and arrest the war criminals. Those guilty of crimes against British nationals should be tried by British military courts, the remainder being dealt with according to the

Moscow Declaration.[35]

Simon's letter to Eden and a copy of his report to the Prime Minister arrived at the Foreign Office in quick succession. Eden scribbled on the head of the first before passing it to Richard Law: 'I have much sympathy with the Lord Chancellor in this. Who is dealing with this at the FO? We have many legal advisers and it is unsatisfactory if it is true that we have been so dilatory. Does anyone at the FO ever see Sir Cecil Hurst?'[36] The casual tone of the last question was a revealing indictment of the Foreign Secretary's disdain for the subject.

It fell to Dean to construct the Foreign Office's defences. Tall, giving an impression of absent-mindedness, he was not then a career diplomat; today he does not deny that the Foreign Office did little about war crimes:

I wouldn't like to say there was no thought, but I would say there was very little thought given to it. We had a lot of other problems on our hands. We just didn't think or know very much about the difficulties involved for catching them and putting them on trial, or realized how many were involved. However a lot of officials did find it rather tedious. After all the main work in the Foreign Office, and what people are interested in, is the formulation of foreign policy, and there were a lot of political questions about what was to be done about Germany, relations with America and Russia. So I expect a lot of people were bored with it. It took a lot of time, detailed troublesome work, when there were a lot of other big issues which they were really trying to work on.[37]

Dean was eventually to become one of the very few officials convinced of the need for a war crimes programme, but as he confronted the two documents from the Lord Chancellor, his chief feeling, shared by his colleagues, was anger that Simon, the 'appeaser', should seek to lay blame at the doors of the Foreign Office and indignation that Eden should apparently consider the criticism justified. Oliver Harvey voiced the rancour for all: 'I think Lord Simon is as usual thinking to some extent about his own alibi.'[38]

It no longer was a question of the validity of criticism, but a settling of old scores. Roberts caustically commented: 'The Lord Chancellor has overlooked several developments of which I think he has been informed,' adding in handwriting: 'generally although we have not troubled him with the details of a lengthy correspondence.' Among the matters to which Roberts referred was none other than the 'Foreign Office being active in recent months in tying up arrangements between the Commission and SHAEF'. The activity amounted to one telegram and one letter. Dean, equally unconvinced of Simon's case, commented that; 'in spite of Lord Wright's and Lord Simon's criticisms, it is safe to say that although the UNWCC is in many ways not very satisfactorily, the general plans to detect and apprehend German war criminals who may be captured is not so gloomy as their letters and minutes make it appear.' – a conclusion which, to say the least, put a gloss on reality. Dean even added that Simon wanted to close the Commission down – a suggestion which his letters did not confirm.

After the spleen had been vented, Roberts minuted Eden that the record of the Foreign Office's Central Department on war crimes was unsatisfactory because it was grossly understaffed, heavily overworked, and war crimes needed a full-time official. The alternative, warned Harvey, was a 'breakdown'. Eden sympathized with the labour shortage and an extra official, James Wardrop, was appointed. Wardrop's contribution was to be something less than nothing; at one stage he actually queried whether evidence about Auschwitz could be handed to the Commission.[39] A more fruitful decision was to make Dean the official responsible for war crimes matters within the Foreign Office.

On 3 October Eden replied to Churchill.[40] Naturally, there was no mention of the Foreign Office's internal problems. Any failure was due to the inadequacies of the Commission, to Washington's tardiness in replying, to Russia's refusal to join the Commission. Arrangements were under way, Eden told the Prime Minister, for SHAEF and the Control Commission to build a war crimes organization. Separately, the Foreign Secretary wrote to Simon, hoping that: 'you will do your best to correct any impression that may exist to the effect that the Foreign Office held matters up, since I am satisfied such an impression is not in accordance with the facts.'[41]

Eden's assurances to Churchill were wholly unjustified. Dean had in fact spoken to both the British and the American military authorities, and had been told that neither could spare a single man for war crimes work.[42] The embryo Control Commission was equally unhelpful; only three days after Eden wrote his letter, the Foreign Office received a formal reply to its suggestion that the Control Commission should take on the job. Its director, Kirby, wrote that there was little he could do without knowing 'the method and place of trial and nature and extent of evidence required. I should be most grateful if you would let me know whether these directions are to be supplied by the Foreign Office?' Nobody at the Foreign Office knew the answer. Dennis Allen commented: 'I am afraid I am not clear what the position now is about all this'; while Dean advised that any answer should be 'very short'.[43]

The Cabinet discussed war crimes on 4 October, but the only outcome was a decision that the cases should be tried by military courts.[44] Simon had pressed for legislation in the form of a War Crimes Bill that would provide for the trials to take place in Britain. Although it at first had Churchill's support, the proposal was rejected on the grounds that it might provoke the Germans to retaliation. However, encouraged no doubt by Eden's reassurances, Churchill continued his interest in war crimes, and on 5 October he sent a note to Eden suggesting that he take an account of British preparations to Moscow to show Stalin on his forthcoming visit. It would, Churchill felt, emphasize the strength of the British commitment to punishing war criminals.[45] Rejecting the idea with commendable, if inescapable, honesty, Dennis Allen commented: 'It would merely tend to confirm their views as to the inadequacy and half-heartedness of our own arrangements for dealing with war criminals as compared to their own.'[46]

The comparison, however disturbing, did not provoke the Foreign Office into precipitate action. As far as they were concerned, matters still stood as they had on 7 July when they sent Washington the Commission's 15 June proposal for SHAEF to create a war crimes agency. It was in the form of a draft directive drawn up by the British Chiefs of Staff. They were still waiting for the American reaction. The presumption then was that, whatever the eventual form the war crimes agency took, it would be a SHAEF responsibility. But before it could come into being or start work, there would have to be Anglo-American discussions to settle the details; draft directives for the agency's establishment and responsibilities would wind their way through Whitehall to the War Cabinet and on to the Chiefs of Staff and the military authorities; a parallel course in Washington would lead to the Joint Chiefs of Staff and the Department of War.[47] Until then SHAEF's directives strictly limited its interest in war crimes to those committed against Allied forces after D-Day.

In the meantime, at the War Office, presentiments of disaster were deepening. Hundreds of thousands of Germans had already been captured; the US 1st Army was across the frontiers of the Reich and pressing towards Aachen, the Red army was poised for an assault on Eastern Prussia. The Foreign Office had been pressing for some weeks to draw the War Office into what looked, after the criticisms of Wright and Simon, more and more like a political minefield.

Sir Frederick Bovenschen was determined to resist the pressure. A stubborn man, he was intent on preventing the hard-pressed War Office assuming any more responsibilities, especially if they would not aid the war effort. Neither then, nor in the future, was he interested even in investigating crimes committed against British soldiers. Yet, remembering the dire warnings contained in Way's memorandum,

Bovenschen decided that it would be prudent to at least try to clarify the position. He wrote to the Cabinet secretary, Sir Edward Bridges, on 2 October, asking four direct questions: which department had overall control for war crimes; who was preparing the necessary lists of wanted men and how were the military to be told; which courts would try the cases; and who would provide the jailers and executioners? The letter ended: 'You may suggest that I am butting into business which is no concern of mine. All I am concerned with is to be sure that at a later stage the War Office and the army are not expected to have planned or to do things which they have not in fact planned and have not prepared themselves to do.'[48]

Bridges' reply,[49] which he admitted was 'vague . . . and slightly pontifical on issues of policy which have not been determined', was in truth simply confusing. The only decision to date, said Bridges, had been the Cabinet decision on 4 October that military courts would be used. Otherwise nothing had been determined, except that the subject remained a Foreign Office responsibility. Everything hinged on agreeing a Combined Chiefs of Staff directive to SHAEF, after which the War Office would get responsibility. It was not the reply Bovenschen wanted, although he clearly expected it. Now at least he knew what he had to fight.

The other result of Bovenschen's inquiry was an invitation from Malkin to a joint meeting at the Foreign Office to discuss SHAEF's directive, and the setting up of an investigatory agency.[50] The meeting took place on 20 October. Minor amendments were suggested for the draft directive, which had come back from Washington a week earlier. It was reaffirmed that SHAEF would ultimately be made responsible for war crimes. Nothing useful was accomplished.[51]

None left the meeting more disappointed than Patrick Dean. He had arrived at the meeting irritated by Lambert's lack of interest and influenced by reports of the disastrous failure to create the necessary machinery to investigate German war crimes in Italy which he had heard from Hurst. Having failed in a plea for an organization to be planned, Dean contrived to get Sir Thomas Barnes, the Treasury Solicitor, who had also been at the meeting, to send a detailed letter to Lambert.

Marked 'Urgent and secret' and sent five days after the meeting, Barnes' letter argued that a special investigatory organization was vital to prevent the trail going cold and evidence disappearing. He wanted on-the-spot trained investigators working directly for him, nothing less than a special branch working with the army as soon as possible would suffice. He also wanted the War Office to send him the evidence directly, rather than through the Foreign Office, from whom he got next to nothing.[52]

Lambert replied on the same day that nothing could be done until there was a government policy decision and a Combined Chiefs of Staff directive. He refused to have a war crimes coordinating official in the War Office. Investigations, he thought, would be the responsibility of G2, the Intelligence Branch.[53] Nothing could be done until a decision had been taken as to whether military courts would hold the trials, making war crimes a military responsibility.

Lambert's answer to Barnes cannot be seen other than as a tactic to delay and obstruct. He must have known that the Cabinet had settled the question of military courts three weeks earlier. Moreover, six days previously, SHAEF had determined that war crimes would be the responsibility of its military government section (G1) rather than its intelligence section (G2).[54] The effect of Barnes' intervention and Lambert's reaction was to provoke a crisis between the War Office and the Foreign Office which could only be resolved by the Cabinet.

In preparing his paper for the Cabinet discussion Dean found that Lambert remained obstructive. He commented on 2 November that Lambert's draft 'rather sketches over the important point that it is essential to any progress that the War Office should set its own house in order and establish a proper organization for collecting and dealing with alleged war crimes against British subjects (and for passing on any information to the Allied governments which may be of any interest to them). Mr Lambert has, however, promised that the War Office will not be obstructive as soon as they have obtained a definite direction from the Cabinet that crimes committed against British subjects or in British territory . . . are to be regarded as a military matter.'[55] The emphasis on 'British' was to be crucial.

The Paper[56] that finally came before the Cabinet on 21 November recited the need for a proper organization and pointed out that the Allies, interested in catching the Germans responsible for war crimes against their own nationals, would have to rely on the British and American armies for help: 'It will often be difficult for them to carry out the necessary criminal investigations without the assistance of the British and American military authorities in the respective areas.' Yet the Cabinet only agreed that the War Office should 'give effect to any measures required to carry out the above recommendations particularly in so far as war crimes alleged to have been committed against British subjects are concerned.'[57]

The Cabinet's decision was a defeat for the War Office. It now had a firm directive making it responsible for war crimes work. But Bovenschen and Lambert had jointly succeeded in limiting the damage. Crimes against British nationals made up a tiny proportion of the potential cases. Though the military would now, apparently, have to investigate these, there was absolutely no obligation for them to help the newly-liberated European countries to track down and arrest the far greater number of criminals they would want to put on trial. Lambert still believed that, in any case, the army's responsibilities would end with the war and that there was no need to plan for a continuing involvement.

Grateful at having succeeded in passing the responsibility for immediate action to the War Office, the Foreign Office became almost insouciant. Dean had already assured Lambert, on 18 November, that catching the war criminals would not be too difficult, as most of them would be among the mass of prisoners. It would, he explained, only be a matter of identification. A few weeks later, when Bovenschen inquired how many criminals the army would be expected to catch, Malkin told him that the total would be between one and two hundred. It was to be expected, he wrote disarmingly, that only a minority of those wanted would be caught. Thankfully, the Foreign Office felt, it was somebody else's problem now. To make sure that there could be no argument about responsibilities, Malkin wrote to Bovenschen in mid-December that, in the field of war crimes, the Commander in Chief would be acting under international law and would be responsible directly to the War Office and not, via the Control Commission, to the Foreign Office.[58]

Bovenschen sought to duck this last blow from the Foreign Office by sending a long list of questions of intricate complexity to Barnes. He wanted to know about the establishment of the war crimes organization, the powers of the military, the nature of the trials and relations with other countries.[59] He knew perfectly well that Barnes would not be able to provide the answers, though he perhaps felt that forcing him to seek them out would repay the damage the Treasury Solicitor had inflicted on the War Office by agreeing to Dean's request for his intervention. Barnes' office had only been appointed as the National Office for War Crimes because it was a convenient institution within the British legal system and could be presumed capable of keeping a list. Kent, who had been dragged out of retirement to keep it, had not officiously striven to make it a long one.

At the Foreign Office, which remained responsible for war crimes policy as opposed to its implementation, either paralysis or apathy prevented officials pressing Bovenschen into action. Even in areas where they could have helped, they held back. In October, in the aftermath of the upheaval caused by Simon's intervention, Wardrop had asked the Commission to submit their first war crimes list because so many Germans were being captured. When the six-hundred-name list arrived six weeks later, Wardrop instantly ordered the Commission not to send a copy to the War Office because 'it would avoid complication'.[60] On 29 January, still clutching the list, Wardrop minuted: 'I am not quite certain how we proceed from here . . . but no action seems required.'[61]

Nor would Dennis Allen agree to the lists being sent to the military in Europe, because he was uncertain whether the Commission's judgement could be trusted. Both he and Cadogan feared 'grave embarrassment' because the Czechs and Poles wanted to include Field Marshal von Brauchitsch on the lists.[62] Many of the atrocities committed in the East were carried out by units under his command. Cadogan insisted there had to first be direct documentary evidence before a senior officer could be listed. Even the one list that was ready was withheld from the military in Europe. A Foreign Office telegram to Washington on 29 July, asking how the lists should be distributed, remained unanswered.[63]

It was at this stage that Roger Allen finally decided that it was safe for him to hand over the Foreign Office's own list of crimes involving Allied nationals, because as he belatedly minuted, it now seemed that the Commission was, 'anxious to obtain all available evidence'. Allen added: 'I do not, so far as I can see, perform any useful function.'[64]

The fact that some names were actually given to the War Office at the end of the year did not advance matters. Lambert's only response was to inquire what he was supposed to do with them.[65] In fact the War Office's lackadaisical attitude made little difference.

Though the Cabinet's decision of 21 November might have been expected to result in something happening, this did not follow in the arcane world of inter-Allied diplomacy which the Foreign Office negotiated with such caution. The only immediate result was the production by the Foreign Office of a short description of the proposed Allied Criminals Investigation Department, ACID. It envisaged a para-police organization staffed by former Allied officers who had worked with the resistance movements. 'The initial staffing should not present great difficulty,' the circular said. Both their training and experience of Europe, it was believed, would be ideal qualifications for the investigatory work. The plan remained where it was, on paper.[66] ACID never materialized.

One reason was the almost mystical belief of the British, and especially the Foreign Office, in the importance of consultation and agreement with the Allies. This was especially so when the subject concerned involved policy towards Europe. Thus the British had put great energy and much effort into preparing papers and plans for the European Advisory Committee. The Americans and the Russians, in contrast, looked upon it as a minor concern which their ambassadors in London could fit into an already crowded schedule without the help of senior officials and staff. Where war crimes were concerned, the Foreign Office, believing that it was definitely not a British problem, saw no alternative but to draft and redraft papers and proposals, only to be frustrated when these elicited no response from Washington. The Foreign Office assumed that the long silence from the State Department on the UN Commission's proposals, or the draft of the SHAEF war crimes directive, concealed nothing more sinister than that these questions were being given the same careful and leisurely consideration that they had themselves devoted to them. They had no warning of the storm that was gathering force in the Department of War, and no grasp of the fact that in Washington these issues were about to be resolved with an unseemly haste and a total lack of regard for the niceties of inter-Allied consultation.

On 23 September 1944 Dean had noted that the only differences between London and Washington on war crimes concerned trial procedures, and asked whether this should be left in abeyance until the end of the war.[67] In fact, that same day, the assistant secretary of war, John McCloy, had decided it was time to break through the tangle of red tape for which he held the British responsible,[68] and to get something done. He telephoned Brigadier-General Weir, the US army's Deputy Judge Advocate-General and asked him if he had any ideas about building a war crimes agency.

Weir had. Delighted by the call he immediately rushed to McCloy's office carrying a plan which he had been drafting over the previous weeks. Considering the Department's internal politicking, its proposals were revolutionary. Weir proposed that twenty-five different departments and agencies, each involved in some aspect of war crimes, would hand over their powers to the JAG. Against General Staff opposition, McCloy announced two days later that the plan was approved and that the JAG was to be the sole war crimes agency. Blessing its creation, Stimson described its task as 'momentous'.

Encouraged and enthusiastic, Weir submitted a plan to expand his staff from four to 125. Getting no reply from the Manpower Agency, Weir phoned and asked for approval, only to be told that nothing could be done without hearings. Weir exploded: 'For God's sake approve something and let's get started. If you keep it over there much longer the war is going to be over.' He was allocated just twenty-nine people.[69]

But even Weir at the time did not envisage the reality or the scale of the problem. His blueprint envisaged directing the whole European programme from Washington. Having consulted the FBI, he ordered card-index machines, special maps to trace the movements of individual German divisions, and a statistical punch card system; he created a branch to collect all evidentiary film and stills, another branch to collect newspaper clippings and another to collect oral and written evidence.

A year later, a sadder and wiser man, Weir was to claim that his task was impossible without a staff of two thousand five hundred.[70] But for the moment it was clear that from a standing start, the Department of War had overtaken every other Allied institution involved. It apparently had a war crimes organization ready to go. It was late in the day but no one else in London or Washington had got even that far.

Once it had decided to take war crimes seriously, the Department of War did not rest on its laurels. Having created an organization to find the war criminals, it now moved on to the question of what should be done with them. It was, as the Foreign Office had never ceased to stress, a matter which involved the most delicate and difficult questions of law. But in Washington there were lawyers who believed that extraordinary cases merited extraordinary solutions; the law to them was not an obstacle course that made progress slow and compromise essential, rather it was an instrument that could be used positively. If it wouldn't work in its existing form then it must be reshaped.

One such lawyer was Colonel Murray Bernays, head of the 'Special Projects Branch' at the War Department. In September 1944 he had presented McCloy with the blueprint for a radical new approach to war crimes.[71] On 9 November sixteen representatives of the State, War and Navy Departments had met in McCloy's office to consider Bernays' plan.[72] A six-page document, called 'Trial of European War Criminals', proposed the prosecution at an international tribunal of not only the Nazi leaders, but also of figures representing each of the Nazi organizations, the party, the SS, the SA, the Gestapo and others.[73] On conviction of the organization, each of the individual members of the organizations would become automatically convicted as criminal co-conspirators. The conspiracy theory, as suggested by Bernays, overrode all foreseeable appeals by SS and Gestapo agents that they had only obeyed German law. By inventing new international crimes such as 'crimes against humanity'[74] and 'waging aggressive war', national law would not be a defence against conviction under international law. The tribunal would simply declare a national law unlawful, and those acting under the national law would be guilty as conspirators.

McCloy accepted the plan, with a few minor suggestions for improvements. His department's lawyers had become angered by the State Department's collusion with the British in denying Jewish refugees entry to Palestine, and they had been pressing him to accept an ambitious war crimes programme to avenge the atrocities in Eastern Europe. They particularly despised the British emphasis on limiting prosecutions to cases involving British nationals and leaving other crimes to be dealt with by the liberated nations. McCloy agreed; American policy, he told the meeting, was for a 'broad programme of prosecution'.

Hackworth from the State Department was present at the meeting on 9 November, and two days later formally approved the Bernays plan. Whether he grasped the implications of McCloy's 'broad programme' is not clear, but on 4 December the War Department spelled it out in a revised draft of the memorandum which it proposed to submit to the President.[75] On page one, quite explicitly, the War Department stated that American policy was to prosecute all crimes committed in Germany since 1933, including atrocities committed on racial, political and religious grounds against Germans.

A wide gulf was opening up between London and Washington. On 9 November, Hurst finally received Eden's answer to his proposals of 31 May, an answer which explicitly ruled out the prosecutions to which the War Department was proposing the US government should commit itself.[76] The British soon heard of the War Department's plans, but they found themselves powerless to resist the impetus that was sweeping their ally towards the kind, of disastrous commitment, as they saw it, which they had for so long tried to avert. They did however make a final, even desperate effort.

On 15 December Somervell and Simon, hearing that the War Department's proposals were winning ground, sent Churchill a memorandum urging that an Allied court, where the result was a foregone conclusion, would make the 'machinery of justice a facade and a farce', and lead to endless delays.[77] Five days later Roberts cabled Halifax that he should intervene and strengthen Hackworth's hand against Bernays.[78] But Hackworth had already, albeit reluctantly, agreed to the plan on 11 November.

Any influence the diplomats might have had was dissolved after Pell's arrival back in Washington. His accusations against the Foreign Office, and his insistence that the British were being aided and abetted in their efforts to let Nazi criminals go free by officials of the State and War Departments, added fuel to the already widespread public indignation. On top of that came news which settled the outcome of any inter-Allied dispute and made departmental reluctance irrelevant.

On 18 December a short signal from the US 1st Army in the Ardennes forest on the Belgian-German border arrived at SHAEF headquarters in Paris: 'SS troops vicinity L8199 captured US soldier, traffic MP with about two hundred other US soldiers. American prisoners searched. When finished, Germans lined up Americans and shot them with machine pistols and machineguns. Wounded informant who escaped and more details follow later.'[79] The murders were later to be known as 'the Malmédy Massacre'.

It was the beginning of the bitter Ardennes offensive, Hitler's desperate counter-attack in the Battle of the Bulge. The elite 1st SS Panzer group under the overall command of Sepp Dietrich, one of Hitler's favourite generals, had raced through the thick forests and for a short time made astonishing progress. The Panzer group *Leibstandarte SS Adolf Hitler*, under the immediate tactical command of Jochen Peiper, a tough, dedicated and committed Nazi, had led the break through the Allied lines. For two days their dash for the River Meuse had taken the American command by surprise, but without fuel supplies it began to grind to a halt by 17 December. What then followed is subject to little dispute.

Ingloriously, many American soldiers had surrendered rather than fight, and the advancing German armies had taken huge numbers of prisoners. Now that the Germans were forced to manoeuvre, the prisoners became an enormous burden. According to evidence at the later trial, Peiper had been left in no doubt by Dietrich that prisoners were not to be taken and he had passed on the order in a pre-attack briefing. Every SS man understood. At a field on the Baugnez crossroads, 102, not two hundred, American soldiers were herded into a field by Peiper's men. Machineguns from armoured carriers suddenly opened fire. There was panic. About thirty men escaped or feigned death while the machineguns, machine pistols and single shots shattered the air. It was not the only shooting of unarmed prisoners during those days – others were seen and reported – but it was definitely the largest.

American investigators, from the 1st Army's Inspector General's section, only arrived at the field on 14 January. Until then the area had been behind German lines. Snow had fallen, and after digging they began to find the bodies, all in good condition, preserved by the cold. Autopsies were carried out in a nearby building once the bodies thawed. Most had bullet wounds in the temple, forehead or behind the ear. The inspector's report concluded that there was definite evidence of deliberate murder of 'approximately 120 American POWs'. A war crime.

Inquiries in the area from captured Germans and Belgian civilians quickly revealed that *Kampfgruppe Peiper* had been in the area. There was even documentary evidence. One brave Belgian had complained to a tank commander that his vehicle had damaged a farm building. The SS NCO politely handed over a signed note authorizing payment of compensation. The inspector then forwarded his report to the newly established SHAEF Court of Inquiry. That inquiry held its first official hearing at a military hospital in Harrogate, Yorkshire in northern England.

Three officers, a Britain, a Canadian and an American, questioned Staff
Sergeant Henry Zach, who had feigned death in the field, and many of
the other survivors. The court's report, submitted in March, concluded
that 'beyond question' seventy-two unarmed POWs had been murdered.
It had been 'unprovoked, deliberate and brutal'.[80]

The fear of reprisals prevented the US War Department from openly
responding to the public uproar provoked by the Malmédy Massacre and
Pell's allegations by publishing their proposals. But the outcry was
enough to galvanize Stettinius, Stimson and the Attorney-General,
Francis Biddle, into hastily agreeing a memorandum on war crimes and
submitting it to the President on 22 January.[81] It included a commitment
to an international trial and to prosecuting prewar atrocities going back
to 1933, which they admitted were neither war crimes in the technical
sense, nor crimes against international law, but justified because: 'The
declared policy of the United Nations is that these crimes, too, shall be
punished; and the interests of postwar security and a necessary rehabilitation of the German people, as well as the demands of justice require
that this be done.'

The Foreign Office still did not know that Roosevelt had agreed the
plan when the minister of state, Richard Law, rose in the House on 31
January to answer a question which the Labour MP George Strauss had
asked for the first time three months earlier, but which had remained
unanswered. Strauss wanted a firm government commitment to
prosecute those responsible for the murder of German democrats, anti-
Nazis gypsies and clergy. At least one million non-Jewish Germans had
been murdered since 1933. Following Dennis Allen's suggestion that
the reply should be 'somewhat general and evasive',[82] Law gave an
answer based on a policy discarded by the War Department nine days
earlier:

> Crimes committed by Germans against Germans are in a different category
> from war crimes and cannot be dealt with under the same procedure. But in
> spite of this I can assure my honourable friend that His Majesty's Govern-
> ment will do their utmost to ensure that these crimes do not go unpunished.
> It is the desire of His Majesty's Government that the authorities in postwar
> Germany shall mete out to the perpetrators of these crimes, the punishment
> they deserve.

Pressed by Strauss to explain which authorities in Germany would be
responsible for prosecuting German crimes, Law's ambiguous answer
delighted Foreign Office officials:

1. *The Fight for the UN Commission*
Sir Cecil Hurst *(above left)* was the first British
representative on the United Nations War
Crimes Commission; together with his
American counterpart, Hubert Pell *(above
right)*, and Lord Simon, the Lord Chancellor
(right), Hurst fought with increasing
desperation to convince the British and
American governments that they should take
their committment to a war crimes
programme seriously.

2. Lack of enthusiasm at the War Office
John Lawson (*above left*), Atlee's first Secretary of State for War, was too weak to override the opposition of his senior officials, especially Sir Frederick Bovenschen (*above right*), to the army's involvement in war crimes. The Judge Advocate General, Sir Harry McGeagh (*below left*), was unenthusiastic while the Deputy Adjutant General in charge of war crimes work at the War Office, Viscount Bridgeman (*below right*), followed Bovenschen's instructions to keep the programme limited.

3. *Two who tried*
The two men who
fought the losing battle
within Whitehall for an
aggressive British war
crimes effort: Sir Hartley
Shawcross, the Attorney
General *(right)*, and
Patrick Dean of the
Foreign Office *(below)*.

4. *Belsen*
Scenes in the camp shortly after its liberation by the British. There was at first great reluctance in the War Office to accept responsibility for prosecuting the camp guards, and the eventual trial ended in humiliation for the British.

The authorities to which I refer are the authorities who will be in control in Germany when the war comes to an end. I think I can leave it to my honourable and learned friend to imagine who those authorities will be.[83]

The dam broke the very next day in Washington. Public opinion, it was clear, could only be satisfied by an announcement. A definite commitment to prosecute those responsible for the murder of Axis nationals in Germany was seen by lobbyists as symbolic of Allied policy for postwar justice. On 1 February 1945 Joseph Grew, the under-secretary of state, held a press conference and reluctantly unveiled the plan which was now the official policy of the United States. Asked whether crimes against Axis nationals would also be prosecuted, Grew said that he could only give an assurance that they would be, off the record. Journalists refused to accept the answer on that basis. Grew left the room and phoned Hackworth. Fifteen minutes later he returned and announced that the Germans would be punished for their crimes 'wherever committed'.[84]

The urgent telegram from the British embassy reporting the news was read with both surprise and cynicism at the Foreign Office. Even now, the officials did not realize to what extent thinking in Washington differed from their own. Initially, most thought that this was another meaningless commitment that could be easily ignored. P.S. Falla cynically took it at its face value: 'It is to be doubted whether we shall get very far by putting pressure on successor governments in Germany and elsewhere to punish the perpetrators of Nazi atrocities. Such governments will be unpopular enough already without having to appear as champions and avengers of the Jews and other more or less disliked minority groups.'[85]

Views within the department were divided. The lawyers were convinced that it would be wrong to impose retrospective laws. Andrew Clark, the chief of the Control Commission's Legal Division, was emphatic: 'Surely at a time when we are endeavouring to restore the rule of law in Germany we should not deliberately tar ourselves with the same brush.' Moreover, he was also convinced that: it would be disastrous to attempt to bring pressure on the Germans to do something which we ultimately found ourselves incapable of compelling them to do.' It was also a problem of drawing the line and deciding at what date to begin. Only John Ward seemed sure why the Americans were right: 'From a recent report I saw on Buchenwald . . . it is clear that war crimes and atrocities v. Germans are hopelessly mixed up . . . I suggest there would be an outcry here and in the USA if in the trial of an individual our military court drew a fine distinction based on the nationality of the victims.'

105

But by March 1945, the British were resigned to the fact that they had no choice but to accept the American initiative while trying to limit the damage as best they could.

On 12 March the UN Commission's responsibility was broadened to include any person responsible for or authorizing an act of violence committed since 30 January 1933.[86] Eight days later, Simon interrupted a debate in the House of Lords to insist that the cases would be tried by Allied and not German judges.[87] Hackworth agreed four days later. Neither had considered where all the judges were to be recruited. Until then no more than a small handful had been appointed for the Military Government courts which were to try offences committed by Germans against Allied laws and regulations. Now the courts were committed to try over one million murders and an indefinite number of physical attacks and property offences.

While the War Department was blindly prepared to accept the unlimited commitment, Troutbeck at the Foreign Office suggested that the initial commitment be two hundred serious cases and hastily wrote the inevitable draft directive for the EAC (European Advisory Committee) which would order the military to compile lists of Germans responsible for murder, torture and serious maltreatment.[88] Two hundred names were quickly pulled out of the German 'Who's Who'. Inevitably the draft was considered and rejected. Bovenschen was the first, and by no means last, to reject it out of hand because it placed on 'intolerable burden' on the military. He told Troutbeck that he would only agree if the directive specifically limited the commitment to one hundred cases. Troutbeck could not reply.[89] The Foreign Office had after all never wanted to accept the commitment. It had been forced upon them by the politicians.

To the war-weary British in March 1945, their towns badly scarred by bomb damage, and their economy in ruins, American pressure and willingness to hand out seemingly open-ended commitments like confetti seemed outright madness. When Judge Sam Rosenman arrived from Washington, it seemed to be yet another example of American foolhardiness. The President's speechwriter had brought the proposal for the international trial of Germany's leaders. Sitting beside him in the Lord Chancellor's room in the House of Lords was General Weir. Opposite them were Simon, Somervell, Malkin, Dean, Barnes and MacGeagh. Over several sessions, Rosenman spent hours describing the American plan for an international trial of Germany's leaders based on Bernays' plan. He was met by solid and uncompromising opposition. British policy was stuck at Churchill's suggestion, already discredited, of execution after six hours. Simon suggested as a half-hearted compromise a short trial on the basis of a document of arraignment which would list the charges with details but would allow no oral evidence to be called. Rosenman rejected the idea, as did the Cabinet later. To the relief of many in London, the stalemate, was broken by Roosevelt's sudden death and Rosenman's hurried return to Washington.[90] The continuing British resolve to see the commitment limited was officially confirmed in the House of Lords by Lord Wright on 23 March. He announced that the Commission's target was to prosecute just ten per cent of the war criminals. If those who were actually in favour of prosecution were so unambitious, there could be little hope of moving those who were opposed to greater efforts.

At the War Office, Bovenschen had spent the first three months of the year fighting a proposal by Cadogan to form an interdepartmental committee under Britain's new UNWCC representative, Lord Finlay. Its purpose was to coordinate British war crimes policy. Bovenschen launched what became another round of interdepartmental pingpong. He openly feared the beginnings of a war crimes industry, and truculently asked Cadogan why, if war crimes was a War Office responsibility, the committee's chairman was a Foreign Office nominee. Cadogan responded with a recapitulation of previous disputes.[91]

In the middle of the futile exchanges of veiled recrimination, Bovenschen confided his true feelings and intentions to Barnes: 'I am quite sure that before we know where we are we shall find ourselves landed with all sorts of demands by the Committee for the War Office or SHAEF to do this, that or the other in the way of chasing criminals on behalf of Allies, or trying them on behalf of Allies, and our capacity for finding sleuths, prosecutors and hangmen is not unlimited.'[92] The dispute continued until March, when Bovenschen gracefully conceded that the Committee could be formed, so long as it had no powers.[93]

On 9 March, the War Office took the first practical step towards discharging its responsibility. Lambert arranged a meeting at 20 Eaton Square to explain to representatives of Military Intelligence and Prisoner of War Interrogation (PWI) the responsibilities of a newly created section of the Adjutant-General's Department, AG3, which would coordinate war crimes work. Grouped around the table were men without any knowledge of the past negotiations or commitments. As Lieutenant-Colonel D. MacLeod, the chairman, told them, it was not a meeting which would take decisions, but was just intended to acquaint him with what had happened in the past. Their combined answer was very little. War crimes had been reported to Kent, and nothing else had happened. MacLeod, thinking out loud, surmised that some sort of investigating body might need to be created 'before the allegations could be disposed of'. That did not seem important at the moment, said Lieutenant-Colonel H.J. Phillimore of PWI, because it was little use to investigate 'until it was clear that there was a case for trial.' and both 21 Army Group and SHAEF had facilities for investigation.[94] In fact, the SHAEF facility closed down four days later[95] and 21 Army Group had never received orders to form investigation teams.

Satisfied on that, MacLeod asked whether existing records would be valuable. MI1 said they had 1300 names. PW2 said they also had some names, indexed, and Major V.A.R. Isham assured MacLeod that when the very 'limited' index cards which were available were centralized, 'it would be possible to link up the culprits with particular incidents by cross-reference.' On that note, MacLeod thanked everyone and reported to Lambert that everything was in hand.

Five days later Lambert arrived with MacGeagh, at the Foreign Office to discuss at an interdepartmental meeting the drafting of a directive on the 'investigation, apprehension and eventual surrender to justice' of war criminals. One of the subjects under discussion was handing over the army's existing war crimes investigation machinery and records to the Legal Division of the Control Commission after the surrender. (Another was the handing over of war criminals arrested by the army to the countries who wanted to put them on trial.) Lambert did not say a word. He listened silently as MacGeagh and Ivonne Kirkpatrick from the Control Commission argued in perpetual circles until it was finally realized that it had been a mistake to contemplate handing over war crimes to the small handful of lawyers in the Legal Division who would have no 'policemen' to carry out the investigations. At the end, less than two months before Germany's final defeat, Lambert was appointed chairman of a subcommittee, which included Dean, to examine and report on the necessary machinery to bring war criminals to justice.[96]

It had been an unequal fight for Dean, who had to suffer what he called 'JAG's and Lambert's general triviality in dealing with war crimes issues.'[97] Lambert obstinately refused to do anything, including sending the lists to the army in Europe, until the Combined Chiefs' directive had been issued. He well knew that it had literally 'got lost' somewhere between the State, War and Navy departments.[98] Dean now feared the 'possibility of a real fiasco with serious political consequences'. He found Lambert's role sinister. An urgent telegram was sent to the US Chiefs of Staff asking them to approve the directive. On 23 April, two weeks before the end of the war, they refused.[99] The directive, for them, had become entangled with the Rosenman negotiations. All that could be agreed was that the Commission's lists be sent to Germany and those named arrested. That limited directive was finally sent on 12 May. Dean's distrust of Lambert's apparent policy of deliberate inactivity soon intensified.

The liberation of Belsen on 15 April by British troops from the 2nd Army had not, as in the case of the American liberation of Buchenwald, been followed by press visits and newsreels showing the atrocities. The film shot of the army bulldozers pushing thousands of emaciated corpses in vast pits was not immediately released. Journalists were forbidden into the area. Dean soon suspected that the typhoid outbreak in the camps was not the real reason for denying access, because the journalists, like the troops, could be innoculated. To his shock, Lambert had rejected his suggestions of press visits, 'and blandly denied that any war crimes had been committed at Belsen'.[100] Dean urged him, to no avail, to encourage the British army to provide facilities for pictures like those which the American army had produced of Eisenhower and General Omar Bradley at Buchenwald.

Law even wrote to the War Office protesting about the British army's failure, and repeated a complaint from Lord Finlay, the British representative on the UN Commission, that the British army, unlike the Americans, was so badly organized that it had allowed the evidence to slip away. The Commission had also been barred from the camp.[101] J.G. Ward minuted Dean: 'The War Office are a contrary-cussed Dept. and I daresay Sir F.B. would go to pains to prove there were no war crimes at Belsen to keep out inconvenient visitors.' He suggested that one way to overcome the War Office's 'suspicious shut down on Belsen' would be to use the good services of Colonel Mocatta inside the War Office, 'who is racially much interested [and] might tweak Mr Lambert's tail.'[102]

Lambert rejected all the criticisms. The Belsen victims, he told Dean, were not British nationals, therefore the British army was not responsible. He was formally supported on 5 May when the Secretary of State for war, Sir John Grigg, wrote to Simon restating the principle that only the ally who suffered the crime should deal with the case.[103] On 14 May Grigg replied to Law that everything necessary was being done, including the collection of evidence − 'I feel sure therefore that we can safely leave this matter in the competent hands of 21 Army Group.' Such misplaced complacency was the consequence of the 'detached attitude' the British had stuck to for so long.

The American army had done better than their British counterparts. Acting unilaterally to meet the need, they had created twelve organized investigation teams which were at work in Germany, in contrast to the single British 'scratch' team at Belsen. But all was not well with the US programme either. By December 1944 Weir's war crimes agency was in a state of collapse. Its creators' enthusiasm had been transferred to the

Bernays plan. With Weir spending much of his time in interminable discussions with Bernays and Judge Robert Jackson, who persuaded him that his own programme should take second place to the international tribunal, the agency was, in effect, stillborn.

One of the consequences of this failure was that, three months after the Malmédy Massacre had occurred, no concerted effort was being made to track down the SS men responsible. When the report of the court of inquiry finally reached SHAEF in Paris in the middle of March it was simply filed, not for security reasons but because no one knew what to do with it. Although the arrest of war criminals featured in the SHAEF handbook as the fifth most important objective in the occupation of Germany, for the army it still remained the lowest priority.

It was an attitude instilled in part from Washington. The SHAEF directive had still not materialized. Little effort was made by the State Department to respond to London's pleas for assistance. On the contrary, Hackworth had rejected a suggestion from his own Department that the silence about war crimes, originally imposed for fear of reprisals, should be lifted.[104] Archibald MacLeish, a Department officer, wrote that the war criminals already knew from a succession of Presidential declarations that they would be punished. The silence, he argued, suggested an unwillingness to act rather than a fear for security. Hackworth ignored the memo. Detached to the end, as late as 24 March he ordered Fletcher Warren not even to send copies of the War Crimes Commission lists to the Department's own visa control section, because they had a 'top secret classification'.[105]

6

'A SUBSTANTIAL LACK
OF NATIONAL
POLICY'

In the spring of 1945 Germany was in chaos. Everything had collapsed. Roads, bridges, houses, water and telephone services were destroyed. Amidst the rubble, a seething mass of humanity was moving in every direction, attempting to return to their old homes, or to find a new home. Released concentration camp inmates, liberated slave workers, demobilized soldiers, refugees and the Allied armies were clogging what remained of the roads. Yet, amid this appalling confusion, an unprecedented nationwide manhunt had been launched by the British and Americans. It was, however, not a hunt for war criminals.

The operation, codenamed 'Project Paperclip', showed just what could be achieved, even amid the ruins of a defeated nation, given careful planning, well-researched information, resources and a sense of urgency.[1] Beginning in the autumn of 1944, nearly three thousand specialists had been selected and trained. They were given top priority classification, with authority to commandeer planes, ships, trains, motor transport, finance, even military units, if their mission required it. They were formed into units known as 'T Forces' – their helmets bore a distinctive red 'T' – and were supervised and directed to their targets by a 230-man Anglo-American mobile headquarters. Their targets were nine thousand of Germany's top scientists and technologists.

The operation was an almost complete success. Weeks before VE day, groups of specialists were dropped behind the enemy lines to find individual scientists and bring them back, while other groups found their families and escorted them to safety. Once in Allied hands, the Germans were taken to specially prepared interrogation centres. The result was a vast haul of expertise on torpedoes, tanks, ballistics, poison gases, bomb sights, anti-tank weapons, biological and chemical warfare, rockets and aircraft design. It was put to use immediately.

Professor Herbert Wagner, a missile designer, was found by an American 'T Force' in Oberammergau in the Bavarian Alps on 1 May. After rapid but tense negotiations, Wagner showed the specialists where he had hidden crates of blueprints of his wartime work. Fifteen days later he was at work designing glide bombs in a requisitioned Washington hotel. In Cuxhaven, a scuttled Walter submarine was salvaged and immediately shipped across the Atlantic alongside a revolutionary 2500 horsepower turbine found in Kiel. An entire IG Farben pilot plant for the production of synthetic fuels was crated and sent west. Whole laboratories were carefully packed for reassembly in England. Within five months over two hundred tons of documents had been shipped to London for examination. In requisitioned castles and mansions throughout the British and American zones prototypes of radar, air photography and communications systems were minutely scrutinized on one floor, while the teams of scientists who had built them were debriefed on another. Nazi Germany's finest scientific establishment, including the seventy laboratories of the Hermann Goering Aeronautical Research Institute and its revolutionary wind tunnels, was plundered and shared out between the British and Americans.

'Paperclip' was officially described as a 'denial and exploitation programme': exploitation by the Western powers of Germany's wartime scientific programme and its denial to the Russians. At five minutes' notice, an American 'T Force' moved forty-nine chemists and their families, at gunpoint, from their homes in Leuna in the Russian zone into the American one.[2] The Russians were just as eager; their equivalent of Paperclip, 'Operation Osavakim', was responsible for forcibly shipping a whole trainload of German scientists to Russia, where they were offered a choice between working for their hosts, albeit at double the salaries paid to their new Soviet colleagues, or signing a document which read: 'The undersigned herewith declares his unwillingness to assist in the reconstruction of the Soviet Union.'[3] No one who had spent the past twelve years in a totalitarian state can have had much difficulty in imagining the fate of those rash enough to opt for the second alternative.

The crowning achievement of 'Paperclip' was the arrest of over four hundred scientists who had been employed in developing the V2 rocket at Peenemünde under Wernher von Braun. The initial 'T Force' target was Nordhausen, a small town in the Harz mountains, which had become the centre for rocket development after heavy British bombing of the former centre on the Baltic coast in 1943. To ensure protection from future attacks, the SS, under the direction of the scientists, had transported tens of thousands of concentration camp inmates to the site to dig out vast caves inside the mountains and then service the whole operation. When the US 3rd Armoured Division arrived at Nordhausen on 11 April, there were twenty-three thousand survivors in Camp Dora where the inmates lived, many dying of tuberculosis. Three thousand bodies, rotting and unburied, were just stacked inside the buildings.

Thirty thousand others had already been cremated, having died of brutality, starvation and disease. The troops who seized Nordhausen were accompanied by a large 'T Force'. According to their report, they were overwhelmed by the 'magician's cave'.[4] Within hours of arrival, they had commandeered the healthier slave workers to clear a mile of the main tunnel, damaged by bombing, and brought the equipment out of the mountains. Meanwhile a fleet of trucks were requisitioned from as far away as Cherbourg in France, several trains were brought to a nearby depot, and a US combat engineer group rapidly rebuilt a damaged bridge. Over eight days, four hundred tons of equipment was moved to Antwerp for shipment to New Orleans.

There was no war crimes equivalent of a 'T Force' with the 3rd Armoured Division when it reached Nordhausen, although it was well known to the intelligence agencies that the factory depended on concentration camp labour. No one was interested in the hundreds of SS officers and men who ran the camp. Only thirty-nine of them were later tracked down and tried by the Americans.[5]

In contrast to Project Paperclip, the operation to hunt down the murderers of twelve million people did not even boast a codename. It had no trained staff, no headquarters, no plans and no priority. SHAEF, the operational headquarters in charge of the American and British armies which occupied more than half of Germany, had still only received a vague directive on its war crimes responsibilities. The 'Overlord' orders to Eisenhower on the invasion of Europe merely said that one of his objectives was the arrest of the Nazi leaders and those mentioned in the War Crimes Commission's lists.[6] Specifically, the order exclusively applied to the Allied army's duties once inside Germany. The first apparently investigative agency, the SHAEF standing court of inquiry, had only been established on 24 August 1944. But it was deliberately restricted to collecting and preserving evidence 'only in cases involving Allied personnel'. It was also specifically not allowed to seek out evidence. Affidavits were not accepted, witnesses had to be brought to the court in person.[7]

By the end of 1944, with the joint directive on war crimes drawn up by the British still literally 'lost' in Washington, the Department of the Army issued its own directive to Eisenhower to establish a war crimes office just for the American army in Europe, but it was only to be concerned with crimes involving American servicemen.[8] The instruction had not been the result of any sudden interest in implementing the politician's promises, but was the direct result of the Malmédy Massacre, and the growing determination within the War Department for Allied approval of their proposal for an international trial of Germany's leaders.

That plan would, in outline, be approved on 5 May in San Francisco by Eden and Molotov, the Russian Foreign Minister. Eden's approval was endorsed by a Cabinet committee on 18 May, although all the details of the trial remained unresolved.[9]

The emphasis on an international trial had left the military in Europe without new instructions. Eisenhower had formally implemented the Department of War's December directive on 24 February. After consultation with Weir at the Judge Advocate-General's office he issued a directive to all US army groups ordering them to establish war crimes investigation groups which would be responsible to the JAG.[10] The order stated that the new groups' primary function would be the 'investigation of alleged war crimes against members of the armed forces of the United States. . . Action by members of the United States forces in cases involving only nationals of other United Nations will normally be only limited to cooperation with the appropriate national agencies investigating such cases.' A subsequent circular, 'Eclipse memorandum No. 18', issued soon afterwards to explain the procedure for the arrest of war criminals, added: 'It is worthy of note that the majority of war crimes have been committed outside of Germany and therefore investigation will take place for the most part outside Germany. . . It is not anticipated that there will be a very large number of war criminals wanted for war crimes against British or US persons.' Read together, the directive and circular could only produce complacency and lack of interest. Wardrop in the Foreign Office minuted on reading the document: 'This is admirable. We have suspected that SHAEF were getting on with the job without waiting for formal instructions from the CCS; now we have the proof.'[11]

Nineteen groups were initially authorized, including one for each of the six US armies in Northern Europe. Each team was to consist of four officers and five NCOs. There were a further twenty-eight staff from JAG at the US army's European headquarters.[12] However only seven teams were formed before the end of the war.[13] None were with the combat troops when they liberated the concentration camps.[14]

The man selected at first to run the prosecution, and later the whole operation, was Colonel Clio E. Straight. Before the war Straight had practised law in Waterloo, a small town in Iowa. His expertise was arranging loans for local farmers and traders. He rarely got involved in criminal law. On call-up, he was assigned to the Quartermaster General's office, where he negotiated contracts with corporations for army war supplies and construction. Today, he says that he was excited by newspaper accounts of Patton's victories in Italy and frustrated that he was stuck in the mid-West not seeing the real war.[15]

In autumn 1943, Straight was eating at Washington's Army and Navy Club when a friend pointed out General Craemer, the JAG for the US army, sitting at a nearby table. By nature not impulsive, Straight nevertheless seized the opportunity and asked Craemer for a posting to Europe. After brief training, he arrived in Paris in January 1945.

Straight was in Lille on 10 March when he was telephoned by General Betts of SHAEF's Legal Division and the American army's JAG Department and told to return to Paris immediately and set up the war crimes section. Today, he admits that in April 1945 neither he nor Betts had any understanding of war crimes or of the scale on which they had been committed in Europe. He did not even have a list of the known concentration camps. He particularly remembers meeting, during that month, a group of American journalists who had been specially flown over to Europe by Eisenhower to see Buchenwald. He was struck by their apparent belief that the atrocity stories were a mere propaganda ruse. Significantly, while the journalists flew on the next day to see the camp, the head of war crimes remained in Paris.

Had Straight seen a War Department memorandum[16] when circulating in Washington stating that this was to be 'an aggressive investigation programme,' he might have spared himself a sorrowful smile. His repeated messages to the Department asking for the staff ostensibly allocated to him under the 24 February directive were never answered. Nor were his inquiries to Germany. But he admits that in April he still felt there was little cause for concern. The experts at SHAEF were quite reassuring. Major-General Barker, the assistant chief of staff in the Legal Division, wrote to Dean in London on 10 April, reporting that 'a large amount of war crimes material' had been accumulated, crimes were being investigated, and despite the absence of the directive, 'present arrangements will work out satisfactorily. . . . The new procedure for investigating war crimes has not yet been satisfactorily tried out. . . [But] it is not thought that, at the moment, there are any points which particularly want clearing up.'[17] It is not at all clear what Barker's confidence was based on, nor what the 'new procedure' was.

On 8 May, the day Germany surrendered, Colonel Straight was still in Paris, at the Hotel Majestic. He had no contact with his opposite number in the British army nor with the American teams operating in Germany. Yet this was the moment, if ever there was one, when careful preparation and organization would have paid off. In the first few weeks after the surrender, finding the war criminals would have been as relatively successful as discovering the scientists. New SHAEF directives in March[18] had considerably extended the list of Germans who were to be automatically arrested on security grounds. Literally millions were under arrest in internment camps. Disoriented and depressed as they were, skilful handling would have persuaded many of them to betray the criminals among them. In the course of their internment, each man was supposed to be questioned on his identity and, despite the enormity of the numbers, the evidence suggests that where the interrogators knew what they were looking for, they were often successful. But very few had any idea of what they were seeking.

Gustav Wagner, the 'Angel of Death' in Sohibor, was in an intern-ment camp in Bavaria. No one questioned him and he was released at the end of May. Ernst Heinrichsohn, who supervised the trains leaving Drancy, was also under arrest in Bavaria. He languished unquestioned and was released a year later. Baron von Schroeder, the Nazi banker, was found disguised as an SS corporal in a POW camp in France. An American 'T Force' agent had taken the trouble to search for him, and a few ques-tions in Cologne had revealed his whereabouts. Adolf Eichmann stayed unrecognized in an American POW camp until he saw his name in an Allied newspaper. With just a little trouble, he escaped.

There were also hundreds of thousands of former camp inmates and slave workers, the surviving victims of the atrocities, waiting in DP camps for their future to be unravelled. All of them were potential eye-witnesses. All of them could have pointed out former tormentors. It only needed a prepared system to tap the source.

A wholly unjustified complacency was encouraged by the daily reports of the arrests of the Nazi leadership, names whose very mention, until recently, caused fear. Himmler was arrested on Lüneburg Heath disguised as a private; Goering had actually surrendered to an American colonel of the 7th Army. He was only arrested after a chicken and champagne feast. Dr Robert Ley, the former Labour leader was found in a mountain hut, while the former foreign minister, Joachim von Ribbentrop, was arrested living quite openly in an old Hamburg apart-ment. Julius Streicher was found painting on a veranda, by an unwitting intelligence officer. When asked who he was, he calmly revealed his identity.[19] Many others, especially the military leaders, gave themselves up. 'Ashcan', an internment camp and interrogation centre for impor-tant Nazi personalities established in Spa, Belgium and later moved to Luxemburg, was soon crowded. Understandably, for the first few weeks there was a feeling of euphoria.

Finding men whose names and faces were less well known, and who were anxious to conceal their identities, was not so easy. Though by this point, in theory, a means of finding them existed. CROWCASS, the

Central Registry of War Criminals and Security Suspects, had been suggested to Eisenhower in November 1944 and was approved two months later.[20] Based in Paris, and utilizing the experience of Scotland Yard and the FBI, it was to be the world's biggest register of criminals. Under the plan there would be three lists: one for the wanted men, another for those detained for specific crimes, and a third of all POWs and the camp where they were held. Forms sent out to all the internment camps were to be returned with each man's photo and fingerprints. Using a Hollerith IBM card-index machine, all the information would be punched onto tabulated cards and produced on demand. Punching the names of an eight-million-strong army was, to say the least, ambitious. It had no precedent. Not even the German military command ever had the advantage of such information.[21]

CROWCASS had primarily been created to meet the need for an accurate list of those Germans who might pose a threat to the occupation forces. Bitter resistance was anticipated from diehard Nazi fanatics, and SHAEF had devoted much thought to forestalling it. Lists of those to be automatically arrested were issued to the armies and there was a 'personality black list' of potentially dangerous Germans. But CROWCASS was also intended to be a key ingredient in the war crimes effort. Confidence in its effectiveness ran high. At a meeting on 16 May,[22] Brigadier Henry Shapcott, from the Judge Advocate-General's department at the War Office, asked how he would find a wanted German and was assured by Colonel Brooks of SHAEF that CROWCASS would deliver the answer. Brooks was supported by Major Isham, of the newly created AG3, who had just returned from Paris. 'It is,' he told the meeting, 'the hub for information.'

Although it was an American idea, the job of creating and running CROWCASS was given to a British officer, Lieutenant-Colonel Palfrey. Like so many appointments connected with war crimes, Palfrey lacked suitable experience and qualifications. He took three months to find the three floors in the Rue Mathurins to house CROWCASS, complaining later that no one had given him any help. Most of the Hollerith machines that arrived were damaged and he failed to get them repaired. Amongst the undamaged ones were some requiring a type of electricity supply not available in Paris. Spasmodic power cuts frequently halted those that were otherwise serviceable.[23]

CROWCASS's first list in May 1945 was an amalgamation of the UNWCC list and eighty thousand names in SHAEF's 'Personality Black List'. Those listed by SHAEF were invariably merely suspected of being Nazis or Nazi collaborators. There was rarely any concrete evidence of them having committed a crime. The importance of this ommission had been commented on as early as October 1944. Lieutenant-General F.E.

Morgan, SHAEF's Deputy Chief of Staff had written to the British and American political officers attached to SHAEF warning them that only a few of those listed from the Intelligence viewpoint would also be war criminals. Morgan concluded, 'It would be a pity if the cessation of hostilities were to find us in a state of complete unpreparedness in this matter of war crimes.'[24]

When Dean saw CROWCASS's first list, he minuted: 'misleading and unreliable'.[25] Inevitably, Allied officers running the POW camps soon inferred that anyone not on the list could be released. Moreover, many of the SHAEF list had by then either disappeared or changed identities. A copy had actually been seized by German intelligence and the names listed given wide publicity before the end of the war.[26]

Palfrey tried to produce a second list in June based on the completed forms arriving from the internment camps. A visitor to Rue Mathurins at the time was appalled. Forty thousand completed forms were arriving daily, and instead of processing the expected thirty thousand per day, the staff could only manage ten thousand. The offices were so overcrowded that, if the machines were running, some of the three hundred staff had to stand on the streets outside. Unable to find printers in Paris, Palfrey sent his list to a London printer, but the five hundred copies were only due back in Paris at the end of September. Even he admitted the list was worthless.[27] The Russians were not members of CROWCASS, which ruled out the inclusion of thirty-five per cent of all the POWs, and the British POW camps were not even returning their forms. Even those pouring in were redundant because the POWs had invariably been moved. Asking for fingerprints had proved a wasted effort. No one had the prints of the wanted men. Tension between Palfrey and the American staff resulted in power struggles and not in an attempt to improve the organization.[28]

In the absence of proper lists the methods used to search for the wanted men sometimes became near-farcical. At the small Ascot POW camp in north-west England, Captain Morgan of the camp's record section summoned all the internees and read out a 3,308-name list of wanted war criminals. He was constantly interrupted with questions because of duplications, the lack of Christian names, faulty spelling, uncertainty over ranks, and his peculiar pronunciation. When he called out Hitler, Himmler and Goebbels, he was drowned by derisive laughter. After two days, red-faced and with a sore throat, Morgan promised himself not to repeat the exercise.[29]

Even more ambitious than CROWCASS was a proposal by the Office of Strategic Services (OSS: the American intelligence agency) to fingerprint the entire twenty-three million population of the American zone. After careful consideration, doubts arose when it was realized that between three thousand and four thousand American experts would be needed. But that was just a 'difficulty' and not an 'overwhelming one'.[30] Senior security officers clung on to the idea for some months even after a further impracticality was discovered, namely that people were moving from one zone into another. 'Doesn't matter, it'll have a salutary psychological effect on the German population,' said Colonel Keith Wilson, the Head of Public Safety.[31]

The head of the OSS, General William Donovan, also disputed a suggestion by Straight and Leon Jaworski, a JAG prosecutor (later the special prosecutor investigating the Watergate Affair), that lawyers should be recruited to take evidence on the spot. Donovan proposed hiring one hundred and fifty FBI men instead. Each party dismissed the other's idea out of hand and neither was put into effect. At a further meeting in Paris on 2 June between Donovan and JAG's war crimes group, to which Straight was not invited, Donovan, who had been appointed as Deputy to Judge Robert Jackson for the international trial, explained America's war crimes policy in outline.[32] It was to be an ambitious, wide-ranging programme, including trials not only of Germany's leaders, but also of the perpetrators of the atrocities.

All that remained, said Donovan, was to negotiate an agreement with the three other powers. His apparent self-confidence was soon to be shattered when the American prosecution team arrived in London. All were victims of exaggerated optimism about the volume and quality of evidence which was readily available for a trial. Infected by Jackson's euphoria and energy, Donovan was convinced that the trial would be a great American success for which he naturally wanted full publicity. For the JAG, traditionally a quiet backwater dealing with disciplinary courts martial, the proposition of basking in the limelight was definitely unappealing. General E.C. Betts protested that publicity was exactly what his department did not want. Sweeping aside Betts' protests by arguing that there was no longer any fear about reprisals, Donovan asked the group whether they agreed that the war crimes investigation personnel could be rapidly disbanded 'as the need for investigation dwindles'. No one saw any reason for disagree. Betts mentioned that Straight would quite like to get to Germany. Donovan saw no reason why he shouldn't go, but could not provide a plane to get him there. That only left one problem, and Donovan said he would see to it: it was to remind the Combined Chiefs that they still had not issued a directive for the army to start any trials.

In fact, on the same day, Eisenhower had sent a telegram from Frankfurt to the Combined Chiefs pointing out that there were still no directives to cover the prosecution of German concentration camp commandments and guards who had murdered and maltreated United Nations nationals in camps in Germany itself. These were not covered by the Moscow Declaration. 'It is believed immediate trial of such persons by military tribunal . . . would have a salutary effect upon public opinion both in Germany and in Allied countries. . . May immediate authority be given to set up these courts.'[33]

A month after the conference of 2 June, Straight did, finally, get to the scenes of the crimes. 'I had to force my way onto those planes,' he recollects, 'to get myself and my files to Germany.' He and his small staff arrived in Wiesbaden and were overwhelmed by the chaos. Installed in the requisitioned offices of the Deutsche Bank, Straight found himself isolated and friendless. He could not get transport, Intelligence Corps rarely handed on any information, the provost marshall and military police, responsible for internment camps, refused to escort suspected war criminals, while army command refused to give the facilities needed for a major investigation centre. An attempt to create an Anglo-American records centre in Wiesbaden collapsed within two weeks through lack of cooperation and staff.[34] Nevertheless, truckloads of records, often with vital evidence, were dumped haphazardly outside the Deutsche Bank's offices, although there was no one to sift through it. Enormous amounts of film and stills, a lot taken by the army in the concentration camps on the day of liberation, were amassed to identify the criminals; but there was no organization to look for the eyewitnesses who could be brought to identify and name the wanted men. Alternatively the film was too general to be of value. Thousands of returning American POWs (ninety thousand returned in all) were individually questioned as they disembarked in New York, while others were questioned before they boarded their ships in Europe, yet all their statements, according to Straight, were worthless.[35]

Looking back over the early stages, Straight was later to comment that they were 'marked by a substantial lack of national policy as to punishment of those who committed war crimes, broad restrictions on trials of war criminals and almost a complete lack of appreciation of the magnitude of the impending problem. . . . During most of this phase it was still not appreciated that war crimes had been committed on an extremely vast scale.'[36]

By July, Straight at least had no illusions about the scope of the problems. Including the quite separate team preparing for the international tribunal at Nuremberg, there were now a total of 211 officers and 345 men working on war crimes in the American zone. On paper it seemed impressive, but the effort was totally uncoordinated. There was barely any contact between the Nuremberg team and Straight's organization. Similarly, Straight had little contact with the investigation groups, now grown to seventeen, because they worked in splendid isolation within their own army groups, only sending their cases to the JAG when they considered the case complete. Too often, says Straight, the case was not complete and the statements worthless, but it was too late to get better evidence. Acting on their own self-made priorities, each team had its own system of work and what it believed to be a records centre, but which did not amount to more than a card index of names and files filled with accusations. Straight had no control over the investigations, only the prosecutions, and for a time was even handicapped in providing lawyers because JAG was overwhelmed by an avalanche of court materials against American soldiers.

Looking back over those early months, Straight says: 'It does not appear that steps were taken by the Commands to implement even the directives to arrest war criminals. Responsibility for apprehension and detention was just assigned indiscriminately to one or more agencies in addition to their normal function.'[37] The investigation teams were hamstrung by a ruling that when they find the wanted criminal, only a CIC (Counter Intelligence Corps) agent could carry out the arrest. But as Straight very soon discovered, the CIC agents just did not think it was their job. 'Sending the directive to soldiers in fighting units, who had a war to fight and then an uneasy peace to maintain, just couldn't produce any results,' he says.[38]

When the long-awaited directive arrived, the problem increased. Directive 1023/10 dated 8 July, ordered the US army to investigate not only crimes against US nationals and mass atrocities in concentration camps irrespective of nationality, but also 'atrocities and other offences, including atrocities and persecutions on racial, political and religious grounds, committed since 30 January 1933'. Pell had finally won, but at this stage it was a pointless victory. Seven months earlier the public row had proved the government's lack of commitment. The results of that shortcoming were now evident. There were no staff available to obey and implement the directive. Unashamedly, Straight tried to order the investigators to ignore all cases which did not involve American or concentration camp victims. 'It was not possible to try all those crimes, there was no useful purpose,' he recalls. But to his irritation, many of the investigators were European refugees, and ignored his directive. There was little he could do because they were not under his command. 'I just sent the cases back and said there was insufficient evidence for a prosecution. Eventually they understood.'[39] It was a considerable waste of precious time.

Reluctantly, Straight will also admit that he had a problem with his superiors, a problem which grew as the war crimes programme became controversial and then explosive. Unlike Straight, Brigadier-General Betts, his successor, Brigadier James Harbough, and his deputy, Colonel

Claude Micklewaite, were all professional soldiers who had served in the JAG throughout their long careers. While courts martial were a natural aspect of their work, searching for criminals, especially in a foreign country, was alien to both their training and, unequivocally, to their interests. It was sordid, unmilitary and unwelcome work. None of them had any experience of preparing big criminal trials nor of criminal investigation. Yet they were quite prepared to leave the work to Straight, the draftee, although he himself had no criminal or investigatory experience, and lacked the military background to be able to assert his interests and demands within the army. If there was ever a case of a small fish in an enormous ocean, that was Colonel Clio Straight in July 1945.

If things did not look good from Straight's position, as the effective head of the US army's programme in Germany, they were, if possible, worse for the men at the grass roots, in the investigating teams. SHAEF had done very little to smooth the way for the soldiers who, overnight, found themselves expected to become detectives. In an effort to combat the army's indifference, War Crimes Bulletins were issued from headquarters with horrific accounts of German atrocities. Bulletin No. 3, issued by the 12th Army, was about civilians attacking US airmen who had parachuted to safety. It contained an alleged quotation 'from the sworn statement of a very reputable person who actually witnessed the act of violence described':

. . . . I went over to where the American plane had fallen . . . I noticed four American soldiers; three seemed to be dead and one was still moving. He indicated to me that both of his legs were broken . . . blood was flowing from his nose and he appeared to be suffering great pain . . . five or six women jumped upon this wounded aviator. One of them punched him in the face several times with her fist and tore his hair, shaking his head from side to side, throwing much blood out of his mouth and nose. Another woman jumped upon his chest and started jumping up and down. The others grabbed his arms and legs and literally seemed to be tearing him apart. While two of the women pulled his broken legs apart I saw another woman kick him several times in the testicles. . . During all this the aviator groaned and seemed to be suffering excruciating pain. While these women were performing these acts to the wounded aviator, a great crowd gathered and lent encouragement by shouting: 'Give it to him. Tear him apart.'[40]

The bulletin ended: 'One of these women was described as being young and having black wavy hair and big black eyes. WHO WERE THEY?' No date, time, or place for the alleged attack was given.

Such worthless efforts were all the help men like Lieutenant-Colonel Paul Rigby got from the staff at Eisenhower's headquarters. Rigby had been given the job of forming the US 7th Army's war crimes group on 10 April.[41] His commanding officer gave him Eisenhower's February directive and ordered him to recruit whoever he could as fast as possible because units were suddenly reporting the discovery of many atrocities. Seventeen days later Rigby reported that he had found twenty-two men, mostly by looking through the record cards. He thought he had chosen men with legal, investigative or administrative experience, plus an interpreter and a clerk. Rigby remembers that it was nearly the end of May before he had found a typewriter, got some of his recruits together, negotiated for some jeeps and found an office. 'Then I had to tell everyone we were here.'

Within the first four weeks of work, Rigby's team had collected 120 cases, potentially implicating hundreds of Germans and others, but most of the cases involved slave labour or concentration camps – crimes which he was expressly excluded from investigating. Although the victims' governments had not sent their own investigating teams, he ignored the non-American cases and began searching for the murderers of some American airmen.

Even that was frustrating. Several of Rigby's team never materialized; when his jeeps broke down, he could not get them repaired; he had no priority status for anything from food to phone calls; he even had trouble arranging secure and separate internment for the people he arrested. Without special credentials he could not convince the different army commands that he needed special facilities, nor could he draw funds or goods to 'buy' information. Worst of all, many of the depositions taken from witnesses and victims in those early days were worthless because, as the interrogators were not lawyers, the wrong questions had been asked and the answers did not provide sufficient or appropriate evidence. By the time the errors were discovered, the witnesses had disappeared.

By August it was evident to the men at the top that the easy confidence of the spring had been disastrously misplaced. The American public was beginning to query the fact that not a single German had yet been put on trial in the US zone. Officers in the Military Government which was now in charge of the zone were also becoming worried. General Clay, the deputy military governor, ordered an immediate investigation. The report by Colonel M. Purvis, submitted on 7 September, listed the absence of any organization, the lack of equipment and trained staff as the major reason for failure.[42] Although there were 184 people distributed throughout the seventeen investigation teams, reported Purvis, 'only a small percentage of these are actually investigators . . . very few speak German. . . . The groups need an extra 750 staff. CIC personnel had to be doubled to three thousand.' But demobilization and postings to the Far East made realization of that possibility remote.

Purvis's description of the mechanics of investigation, the result of the division of labour between investigating and arresting, pointed Clay at the cause of the failure:

> Frequently CIC arrests an individual known to be a war criminal. . .the suspect is then placed in some enclosure. . .an arrest report is then sent off to the War Crimes Branch in Wiesbaden. The arrest report generally makes no statement or reference as to what war crimes the suspect is involved in or where he might be wanted. Frequently, these arrest reports arrive in Wiesbaden three weeks to one month after the arrest has been made. The War Crimes Branch searches its records to determine if and in what connection the suspect is wanted. In some cases it has been determined that the man is actually wanted and an effort is then made to locate him. In a good many cases it has been found that the individual wanted has been moved from the original place of incarceration or that no record can be found indicating his present location. This results in confusion and futility.

It was an appalling indictment, but not of the men on the ground who were trying to do an immensely difficult task amidst conflicting and confusing orders, without any training or preparation and with no help or facilities. The blame must lie with the politicians who had made such sweeping promises and made no efforts to assure themselves that the necessary effort and preparations were made to put them into effect; with the bureaucrats and staff officers who had delayed action to the eleventh hour and then issued orders which were impracticable and vague.

The international tribunal, whose opening in Nuremberg was already seriously delayed because of repeated and acrimonious disagreements between the Allies and the slow pace of preparation, had taken up such time and attention as was available in Washington and London. Jackson's blustering 'take-it-or-leave-it' presentation of the American trial plan had upset the Russians.[43] Methodically; they and the French exposed weaknesses which in turn upset Jackson's self-confidence.

Negotiating agreement for the trial became a full-time occupation. But it was, after all, a much more interesting and glamorous business than the dispiriting task of combing the internment camps and bombed out cities of Germany for obscure figures whose crimes had been committed far from the public eye.

Whereas the men at the top of the War Department in Washington had at least seized upon their responsibility for war crimes with some enthusiasm and vigour once they had finally taken an interest in them, the War Office in London had been dragged down the road of involvement resisting every inch of the way. Only in March had AG3 been created and given the responsibility for providing the minimum organizational help and essential food supplies for the military personnel involved in war crimes. Dean had found it difficult even to persuade the War Office to establish a separate department. Sir Ronald Adam, the Adjutant-General, while interested in the army's medical and educational services, had never hidden his violent dislike for all the disciplinary chores. War-crimes work was doubly distasteful to him.

Adams' prejudice was shared by Bovenschen and Lambert, both of whom continued to play an increasingly obstructive role. Following the meeting on 9 March at which the creation of AG3 was announced,[44] Lieutenant-Colonel Barraclough was appointed head of 21st Army Group's war crimes programme, the British counterpart to Straight. Barraclough was in Brussels, marginally nearer to Germany than Straight in Paris, but in all other respects his position was much the same. His first opportunity to learn about his new job came on 26 April, eight days after his appointment, when Major Isham of AG3 flew in to brief him.[45]

Barraclough was still bewildered and at a loss to understand why he had been appointed. Isham replied that AG3 had only been created six weeks earlier and still had no departmental head. 'But the War Office have given us no guidance on what we are meant to do,' complained Barraclough. Isham could give little help. No organization or establishment for personnel had yet been agreed, he told Barraclough, nor could trials begin until the Royal Warrant was published. MacGeagh had started work on that in July 1944, but had still not finished. Barraclough remained confused, and explained to Isham that until they knew how far down the scale Germans were to be held responsible, and what the nature of the trials would be, he could do very little. Isham left, having raised questions but given few answers. Barraclough stayed in Brussels.

In Germany, Montgomery's headquarters had just announced the formation of three war crimes investigation teams, each of four men.[46] It was little more than a formal announcement to legitimize the 'scratch' team which had been working at Belsen since its liberation. By 8 May, only three men had been recruited, compared with nearly one hundred in the American forces, who had a smaller population to cover. The three were described in a telegram sent from army headquarters on 16 May to the War Office as part of a 'proper investigation team' which would take over from the 'scratch' team in Belsen.[47]

Belsen's Camp Number One measured one mile by four hundred yards. Inside it British troops had found twenty-eight thousand women, twelve thousand men and thirteen thousand unburied corpses. Another thirteen thousand died within days of liberation, either from starvation or typhus. Probably another forty thousand had been cremated since the typhoid outbreak started in February. Two miles away, in the stores of a Panzer training school, were eight hundred tons of food, neatly stacked in warehouses, and a bakery capable of producing sixty thousand loaves a day.[48] Josef Kramer, Belsen's commandant, had come out to meet the British troops and asked for their help. Many British officers thereafter believed that Kramer, who had been trained at Auschwitz, had done his best to help the inmates.

Because of the typhoid, the army did not enter the camp for three days, but even after British troops were inside the camp, SS guards continued to hit and even kill inmates for taking what food was in the kitchen. According to Harold Osmond Le Druillenec, a Jersey schoolmaster, an inmate at the camp, many had survived the last days by eating the flesh cut from the thighs of those that died.[49]

Colonel Gerald Draper, a lawyer, was a member of JAG working on the Belsen case. He realized immediately that JAG was inadequately prepared to cope with war crimes:

> The evidence flowed in like a deluge and we were submerged by it. . . . Our efforts then and later were like a man standing at the edge of the sea dropping lumps of sugar into it, and saying: 'Behold it it sweet.' We were failing because the wave of criminality was so great and our resources were so inadequate. When Belsen was discovered it was decided in a hurried manner that the Judge Advocate-General's office should handle war crimes. We were not geared, or trained or qualified or had enough resources to do the job. It was a makeshift, hurried and ad hoc decision and we had to do the best we could.[50]

The decision that the Judge Advocate-General, the head of the army's legal department, should be responsible for preparing the evidence and charges in war crimes cases had merely added another department in Whitehall to the list of twenty or so which had be come involved in one way or another.[51] The JAG was to prove no more vigorous or effective than the others. The Judge Advocate-General himself, Sir Harry

MacGeagh, was old, pedantic and conservative, tired out by the war and totally oblivious to conditions in Europe. He had in fact never crossed the Channel.

When Bovenschen offered extra staff for the war crimes work, MacGeagh rejected the offer, blindly hoping that without staff there would be less work.[52] MacGeagh's deputy responsible for war crimes work, Brigadier Henry Shapcott, was more concerned but was dwarfed both intellectually and personally by MacGeagh. Shapcott was by nature more a cutter rather than a creator of red tape, but his department's bureaucratic inertia and self-interest was to prevail.

Brigadier Richard Halse, a member of the JAG since 1935, remembers the air of unreality at the Spring Gardens headquarters in the first part of 1945: 'I took over from Kent, the Treasury Solicitor. He gave me a file filled with his own lists of war criminals. Each one started "Hitler A., Bormann M., Goering H.", we really had nothing and knew nothing at the beginning. But everyone was tired at the end of the war and both JAG and the War Office felt that war crimes was not going to produce glory for anyone.'[53] War crimes work came as an unwelcome intrusion into the life of JAG, which, like army legal sections the world over, was a traditionally quiet military backwater.

The department was not eager to do anything about war crimes, but it was quite ready to devote its legal and bureaucratic skills to preventing anyone else encroaching on its territory in order to get something done. In the same fashion Sir Donald Somervell, the Attorney-General, was to further complicate matters by insisting that his office had to approve cases involving British victims before they went forward for trial, a stipulation later seized on by MacGeagh to further delay all prosecutions.[54]

The discovery of Belsen, and the inadequacies of the army in coping with it, had disturbed the War Office. On 16 May 1945 Major Isham reported on his trip to Europe the previous month.[55] He had collected a questionnaire compiled by the units at the camp which showed that, as far as they could establish, no British subjects were among the victims. That seemed to rule out any need for British involvement in preparing cases. When Isham asked whether the British would try those arrested at Belsen, Shapcott replied that he was still unsure because the Royal Warrant would need amendment if concentration camp officials were to be prosecuted by British courts.

It also emerged that the Joint Chiefs of Staff were still undecided whether military courts or Military Government courts should try the cases. Public pressure however demanded immediate trials and it was now obvious that the smaller countries were too involved in their own internal affairs to start trials for the murder of their own nationals in Germany. Yet, once again, the British felt that they could not take the initiative without American agreement. Dutifully the Foreign Office cabled the Washington embassy to get an agreement.[56] The affirmative reply took seven days,[57] but the trials could still not start. The Royal Warrant was still not ready, and the War Department told the embassy that it could not agree on a common set of procedures because there was still disagreement within the department.[58]

By the end of May, at least the head of AG3 had been appointed. He was forty-nine-year-old Viscount Bridgeman, whose wartime service had been in the Home Guard. Today, Bridgeman says that on his appointment he was candidly briefed that he was to ensure that the British commitment to war crimes was 'not to be bigger than absolutely necessary'.[59] The reasons, he says, were obvious. 'Everyone in the War Office felt that war crimes would be expensive, unrewarding work, which would not be popular with the public. We remembered the problems of the ''Hang the Kaiser'' campaign after the last war and how the public turned against it. We didn't want to have a repeat performance.' Bridgeman says his policy guidelines were explicit, namely to let the Americans make the running. 'We expected most war criminals to be in American zone. So we just sat and waited to see what would happen, and waited for orders from the politicians.'

In the House of Lords on 14 June, Simon and Somervell briefed journalists on the future programme. 'A great mass of material had been collected,' Simon told them, 'a large amount of work has already been done and the trials will begin very soon.'[60]

Both undoubtedly believed what they said to be true. Somervell had told Shapcott earlier in the month that trials should start in the first week of July. By the end of that week, Shapcott was obviously worried. He had the names of one hundred Germans whom he wanted to put on trial, but in not one case had he been told whether the wanted men had been arrested. He confided to Gurney, the war office's director of Personnel Services,: 'I don't know what can be done in this matter, which is causing me considerable anxiety.'[61] Equally frustrating, the most important case on his list, said Shapcott, was the shooting of a German officer by another German after the former had surrendered, and an assortment of ill-treatment of POW cases.

On the Belsen trial, Shapcott said that he hoped, having now discovered that at least one of the victims was a British national – a seaman from the Norwegian expedition – that everything would be ready 'in the not too distant future'. Yet at the beginning of August the opening of the trial seemed as far away as ever. MacGeagh and Shapcott had insisted that each potential witness had to make a sworn, typed and signed statement which would be sent to London. Former inmates were expected to stay near the Belsen camp while Shapcott decided whether their evidence would be needed in the trial. The refusal to delegate the decision to the JAG's office in Germany had not been challenged when MacGeagh announced it at the first meeting on 9 March, but now the British army unit at Belsen was losing patience.[62] Shapcott was sending endless requests for statements and replies to his queries. The former inmates, after years of suffering did not want to wait around any longer. Officers, looking for them in the DP camps with questions from Shapcott, found that many of them had disappeared. Major-General Chilton the deputy Adjutant-General at Montgomery's headquarters, wrote to Bridgeman that he had decided he could no longer ask witnesses to remain in the area and wait for the trial.[63] Vital witnesses were officially allowed to disappear.

The deliberately constructed delays in London were indeed absurd. After a slow journey from Germany, each document was, after scrutiny by Shapcott, passed to the Treasury Solicitor, to the UNWCC, and then to the Attorney-General, before being sent back to Germany via Shapcott. The round trip was taking two months. Brigadier Scott-Barrett, the head of JAG in Germany, telegraphed Shapcott that he had five cases ready for trial but 'considerable delay is inevitable' if the decision to prosecute could not be taken in Germany. 'There is a need for rapid action before there is any weakening of the present determination on the part of the public that war criminals be brought to justice.'[64] Even the Germans, recruited by 21 Army Group to help prepare the case, were telling Scott-Barrett and Draper that they were worried about the delays. Had the accused been British soldiers facing court martial, the whole trial, including execution of the sentence, would have been carried out in Germany without reference to London.

Bridgeman called a meeting to remove the obstacles. Outraged, MacGeagh wrote to him hours before the meeting began that any discussion to remove the authority of JAG in London was 'astonishing . . . ill considered and should be rejected in no uncertain terms'.[65] The meeting inevitably ended in failure[66] Item 1(c) on the agenda remained undiscussed – a request from 21 Army Group for more men if they were to investigate non-British war crimes.

Five days later MacGeagh wrote to Bridgeman: 'I take the view that. . . I am responsible for the collection of evidence against and the prosecution of war criminals . . . the decision as to the best means by which that can be effected is for me. . . I have yet to be persuaded that the present system is not efficient or that it causes or is likely to cause unnecessary delay.'[67] In a parting shot he announced that, while he would be happy to discuss the problem, which he thought only a Cabinet decision would resolve, any solution would have to await his return from leave.

British war crimes headquarters in Germany was based in Bad Oeynhausen, an undamaged spa town which had been forcibly evacuated on Montgomery's orders to house the British army's administrative staff. Heading the JAG in their Bahnhofstrasse HQ was Brigadier Scott-Barrett. The investigators worked as a separate group in Louisienstrasse under the overall command of Group Captain Tony Somerhough. Barraclough had never arrived in Germany.

One of the worst problems they faced was the almost total absence of trained interrogators, either on their own staff or in the internment camps. The idea of employing SOE operatives which had been mooted in November 1944 apparently disappeared from sight when ACID failed to materialize.[68] The intelligence services refused to help, though 21 Army Group's chief of Counter Intelligence did manage to get six interrogators from MI5 after creating a fuss when it came to Montgomery's attention that there was not a single trained interrogator in the entire army group.[69] After the war they were not available for war crimes work.

There was in fact an ideal source of such expertise in an elegant mansion in Kensington Palace Gardens known as the London Cage. Throughout the war the most stubborn and potentially valuable captured Germans and Italians had been sent to the Cage if less experienced interrogators had failed. There they were subjected to the methods developed by Lieutenant-Colonel Alexander Scotland. Scotland's methods were time-tried and tested. Having established an apparently respectful and confidential relationship with the prisoner, Scotland would suggest that as everyone else had admitted the truth or betrayed Germany, it would be best for this German too, to save himself. He had built an enviable reputation.[70]

Scotland was invited to the first AG3 meeting on 9 March.[71] The deputy AG3, Lieutenant-Colonel D. MacLeod, as acting chairman, explained that the meeting had been called to help him to understand what had been done about war crimes up to then. Scotland immediately answered that his own records were of little value, because he had rarely asked questions about war crimes. Other representatives of Military Intelligence and departments responsible for British and German POWs all confessed that while they had various index card collections, none were specifically relevant for war crimes.

Lord Finlay, chairman of the UNWCC, had tried to arrange that

Scotland or the POW departments should interrogate Germans about war crimes, but his request had been blocked by Dean,[72] a refusal which Dean even maintained in June 1945, on the grounds that it would breach the Geneva Convention to ask a soldier more than his name, rank and service number. Finlay protested, but Dean was adamant that a German could not be questioned, even if he wanted to give evidence. No such restriction had been applied to interrogations for military intelligence purposes. Until Dean's opposition was overcome, it effectively cut off a valuable source of information. At the meeting MacLeod had contented himself with concluding that AG3 would probably have to start its own index system 'and that some investigating body would need to be formed before the allegations could be disposed of.'

Among the many people whose job might have been both easier and more effective had there been such an index system or investigating body were those responsible for interrogating the hundreds of thousands of men in the internment camps.

In the absence of help from the intelligence services, Scotland's London Cage and the Field Security Services, the army had reluctantly begun recruiting German refugees for the task. Roger Elliot, an Austrian Jew and former SOE agent, was recruited, nominally as an interpreter, in June 1945, and after four weeks training sent to the Paderborn internment camp. Within an hour of arriving, he discovered that he and a Dutch recruit had been made responsible for the interrogation of no less than twenty-five thousand internees. 'They just left us amateurs all alone. We could have loafed or done anything we liked. Although they sent a few so-called interrogators later on, most of them were just waiting to be demobbed. I took the job seriously, but for all I know, the biggest war criminals could have got through our fingers. My only criteria was whether the German was a danger to security or of interest to intelligence. I never had anything to do with war crimes or JAG.'[73]

The question of interrogation was not the only one in which London seemed to find a perverse satisfaction in hampering the men in Germany. Every initiative or suggestion was relentlessly scrutinized, not for its efficacy or efficiency, but for its implications for the fine game of inter-departmental wrangling that still continued. On 21 July, the JAG's office in London wrote to the Legal Aid Division of the Control Office: 'In practically every village in Germany there was a minor form of con-centration camp. Now that the workers have been released they are making complaints to the military government detachments that they were ill-treated either by the camp staff or by the farmers who were their masters.'[74] Shapcott wanted to know the German law on employment of slave labour. American courts were already prosecuting German farmers and employers for war crimes but Shapcott hoped, as he told Gurney, to avoid that, because there would be insufficient lawyers in Germany. Perhaps, he wondered, the slave labourers' 'late German employers' could be all sent to their victims' countries to stand trial.

The most fanciful solutions were preferable to Britain holding the trials. MacGeagh was quite obdurate on the issue and told Bridgeman that British military courts would not prosecute Germans for slave labour offences.[75] – 'I do not consider that the Royal Warrant and Regulations were designed to deal with that type of case.' Defeated at a meeting on 20 August, when Bridgeman finally proved that the cases were not excluded by the Royal Warrant, the JAG shifted his argument to who could make the final decision on the trial.[76] Shapcott had telegraphed Scott-Barrett in Bad Oeynhausen not to send the non-British, non-concentration camp cases back to Britain.[77] Could the decision, Scott-Barrett asked, be therefore taken in Germany? No, replied Shapcott, all decisions had to be taken in London.

The War Office was not the only department eagerly shrugging off the responsibility for trials. At the Foreign Office, at the beginning of June, Dean was still faced with the unwelcome commitment to prosecute Germans for crimes against Germans, which had followed the American policy reversal in February 1945. Feeling that, if all the SS and Gestapo agents were to be tried after the Nuremberg trial, most of the offences would be covered, he was quite happy just to forget the whole subject. According to Mocatta in the War Office: 'Nothing further has happened and Mr Dean at the FO is not unhappy about it being left where it is for the time being.'[78]

On 31 July Richard Wilberforce, working at the Control Commission, asked Dean for guidance. Two watertight cases were ready for trial, the first against a German woman responsible for gassing two thousand partly deformed children; the second, against an SS NCO who had mown down two hundred German prisoners with a machinegun and then buried them, still half alive, with their heads sticking out of the earth. Wilberforce's predicament was simple. He feared that 'the publicity which would be given to the trials of Germans responsible for crimes of this particularly revolting character would lead to a flood of denunciations with which the Legal Division, with its present staff, would have some difficulty in coping.'[79]

Dean could not quite decide what to do. At the outset, he and his colleague Con O'Neil could not agree whether the cases were covered by the Nuremberg Charter. Dean was convinced, probably erroneously, that the acts were not covered by 'crimes against humanity'.[80] He delayed sending a reply until September. Yet on the 13th, General Robertson wrote, about the German crimes, that there was an 'urgent need for a policy regarding atrocities'.[81]

Reluctantly, Dean agreed that the British should prosecute the two cases and sent a list of another 186 Germans who could be prosecuted, adding: 'But of course we are not suggesting that you should seek to track them down and string up all 186 of them.' Fourteen months earlier, when Pell first raised the issue, Con O'Neil had minuted that the murderers 'would be better out of the way than left running round free in Germany.'[82]

What Draper calls 'the usual bureaucratic failure to coordinate different policies'[83] reduced the small British war crimes headquarters at Bad Oeynhausen to a feeling of frustrated hopelessness. Says Draper: 'We were hindered in our work because we were always running against the clock. Thousands were being released to bring in the harvest and dig the coal.' Amongst those released were three Gestapo officers wanted for the murder of the escapees from Stalag Luft III.[84]

It was only on 3 September that two former British police officers flew from Northolt airport to Bückeburg in Germany to begin the search for those responsible for the fifty Stalag Luft murders. Scotland's interrogation of the former camp commandant, Colonel von Lindeiner-Wildau, in the London Cage had produced the names of three Gestapo officers responsible for a few of the murders; MI9 had discovered three others. It was to take six officers and six NCO's three years to get the first convictions. Scotland had been deputed directly by the War Office and Air Ministry to supervise the investigation. It is remarkable that, throughout that and other investigations by Scotland, neither he nor his staff ever worked, other than in a perfunctory fashion, with the war crimes group in Bad Oeynhausen.[85] It was ignored, scornfully dismissed for what it was, a group of temporary would-be sleuths. At Christmas, its newly appointed head, Group Captain Somerhough, complained to the War Office; 'We have nothing, not even a typewriter.'[86]

The American investigators were both more numerous and less liable to find themselves up against an impenetrable barrier of red tape than their British counterparts. The investigation of the Malmédy Massacre thus finally got under way a little faster than the hunt for the murderers of the British airmen. But it was, ultimately, to be a very much more troublesome case.

At the end of June, Lieutenant-Colonel Martin Otto, chief of the JAG investigation section, had handed the thin SHAEF file on the Malmédy Massacre to Major Dwight Fanton and asked him to solve the biggest crime committed against American soldiers in Europe.[87] The file contained just a bare statement of the facts and the names of forty-two known members of *Kampfgruppe Peiper*. Fanton, then aged thirty, had five years' legal experience before he had been drafted into the Quartermaster Corps. He had been rushed to Europe in response to one of Straight's many pleas for more staff. Speaking no German, and without investigative experience, Fanton is the first to admit that he was not the best qualified man for the job.[88]

For the first four weeks he did very little. His team amounted to himself and a translator with whom he drove haphazardly from one internment camp to another looking for members of the *Kampfgruppe*. Each enclosure looked very much the same. Thousands of anonymous and dispirited soldiers stood behind barbed-wire fences waiting for their fate to be decided. At nearly every camp, Fanton's request was answered by the same exasperation: 'Hell, we don't know who we've got in here.' Few of the prisoners had been screened, any camp records were invariably out of date, and often, because of a serious food shortage, prisoners were actually being released as Fanton arrived.

For the first few weeks Fanton was not too worried by his failure. He and Otto had decided to rely on CROWCASS. He had sent a telex saying who he was looking for and confidently expected that a list would soon arrive with the whereabouts of all the *Leibstandarte SS Adolf Hitler*. It would then be just a matter of flipping through the pages, ticking off the wanted men. To his surprise and disappointment, the CROWCASS lists only produced the whereabouts of a small handful of the wanted men.

Fanton had his first break in mid-August. With a mixture of gall and relief, he read in the US army newspaper *Stars and Stripes* that Jochen Peiper was being held in a POW camp at Treising, near Munich. None of the American staff had thought of informing the JAG. Fanton's two-day interrogation of Peiper revealed a lot about the German's tank tactics, his courage and his impeccable English, and nothing about Malmédy. Fanton had an equally fruitless session with General Sepp Dietrich, who was discovered in another camp. At the end of October, Enclosure No. 78 at Zuffenhausen, specially selected to house the Malmédy suspects, still looked discouragingly empty. The interrogations were failing because the interrogators were dutifully warning the Germans that they should beware of saying anything that might be incriminating.

It was a sad fact that the American army, like the British, lacked trained staff. To remedy his plight, in October Fanton was assigned two new interrogators, William Perl and Harry Thon. Perl, a Czech-born psychologist trained in Vienna, had learned interrogation techniques in Maryland and Amersham, Britain, during the war. Thon, a German refugee, was excitable and untrained. Fanton was nevertheless glad that both had arrived. At Otto's direction, he had started a crash programme of telexes and messages to every internment camp in the western zones. Within a month a thousand had been collected in Enclosure 78. But now he faced a wall of silence, alternating with collusion. After each interrogation, the SS men would compare their alibis, stonewalling any progress. To break the resistance, Lieutenant-Colonel Burton Ellis, a Californian tax lawyer, also a newcomer to the investigation, suggested after talking to Perl that the five hundred most suspected SS men be moved to a purpose-built prison where they could be isolated from one another, and properly interrogated. In early December, they were moved to the Schwäbisch Hall, Heilbronn.

Perl was the first to get results. On 28 December, Georg Fleps, an ordnance sergeant, signed a sworn statement that he had taken a wounded US soldier, suffering from exposure, frostbite and hunger to Peiper's command post in a castle. After Peiper had unsuccessfully tried to cross-examine the soldier, Fleps asked whether he should take the soldier to the medical room. The regimental surgeon, Karl Schiff, in the room throughout the episode, pointed towards the door and said: 'Get the swine out and bump him off.' Fleps then described how he took the American to a field and shot him dead with his Luger.

Although the statement had nothing to do with the Malmédy Massacre, it was the first confirmation that Peiper was unwilling to take prisoners. Perl's success then gathered momentum as one after another of the lower ranks, taken from their isolation cells to an interrogation room, admitted that they had orders not to take prisoners and had witnessed American prisoners being shot; sometimes when they were waving white flags, on another occasion after they were captured and being marched in a column.

According to Perl his technique of telling the SS men: 'the war is over so why not start with a clean slate?' finally produced the desired result on 5 January when Sergeant Siptrott, an assistant gunner in a Panther tank, admitted his own involvement in the shooting at the Baugnez crossroads, and implicated others in the prison. Siptrott claimed that he had heard an officer give the orders to fight 'recklessly and cruelly' and to take no prisoners. Similar statements soon followed, describing the whole massacre. Confronted by Perl with the sworn statements and four of their signatories, Peiper finally admitted in his own sworn statement that orders did exist allowing prisoners of war to be shot, although he did not need to expressly give the order at the pre-attack briefing 'because those present were all experienced officers to whom this was obvious.' In his statement Peiper also confirmed Fleps' account of the wounded soldier being shot at his headquarters.

Straight was very satisfied. The confessions, he thought, would ensure that the trial was swift and decisive. Such optimism was misplaced. Perl's methods were to be the subject of no less than eleven separate inquiries. The Malmédy case was to degenerate into a bitter travesty of justice and a political weapon effectively used by those intent on denying that Nazi Germany had committed any atrocities whatsoever.

7

'WHAT KIND OF
GERMANY WE WANT'

Five weeks after Germany's defeat, Sir Ivor Pink, a deputy under-secretary, wrote to his Foreign Office colleague Jack Troutbeck: 'I understand that the News Department are having some difficulty in convincing the press that we really have a policy towards Germany.' The problem, wrote Pink, was how to make up lost ground. 'At the moment there is a political vacuum in Germany, which in many ways makes our task easier. Now is the moment when, if we choose, we can direct the unformed and chaotic political impulses in our zone into channels which will prove useful to us later on.' Pink's colleagues reacted with an equal measure of resigned agreement and forlorn bewilderment in the face of the problems of what should be done. Exhausted by five years of war, the task of deciding Germany's future was not an undertaking which they faced with any enthusiasm.

The victors of 1945 were in a position unprecedented in modern European history. No previous war had ended like this, with the unconditional surrender of the enemy, the occupation of his entire territory, and the destruction of all the institutions of his state. Authority over Germany and the Germans was entirely in the hands of the conquerors of the Reich; they were free to reshape the greatest European power in whatever fashion they chose.

There was however little agreement between the three major Allies on how the opportunity, won at such terrible cost, should be used. American and British views on both the immediate and the long-term future of Germany, in so far as they existed at all, were almost as divergent as from each other as they were from those of the Soviets. All were agreed that the ghost of National Socialism must be exorcised, but there was little agreement as to how that could best be done, or what political institutions should replace it.

The Foreign Office had opened a file on the treatment of Germany after the war during the dark days of 1940,[2] but serious work only began in July 1942, when the prospect became more than a pipedream. At first the Foreign Office was deliberately excluded from leading any interdepartmental policy committees. Bovenschen at the War Office had set up the Administration of Territories (Europe) Committee, of which he was chairman, while the Chiefs of Staff set up the Post Hostilities Planning Sub-Committee, responsible directly to themselves, from which the Foreign Office was at first completely excluded. By the time the Foreign Office's paramount interest was acknowledged, Bovenschen had set up his own Armistice Terms and Civil Administration Committee, which he dominated and jealously guarded against encroachments by other departments. The result was that Britain's policies towards postwar Germany were discussed in two parallel committees.

It could not even be resolved whether the government of Germany should be civil or military; in August 1943 it was thought that it should be civil, and therefore a Foreign Office responsibility; a month later the decision was reversed and it was decided that the army, who would obviously be in charge of the actual administration, should take their orders direct from the War Office. Rapidly, the War Office realized that it would require civilians to manage many aspects of the government, and so a Directorate of Civil Affairs was established by Bovenschen within the department. When Bovenschen prevented a Foreign Office bid to take this over, the Foreign Office created its own organization, called the Control Commission (British Element).

It was this last entity which finally emerged, in August 1944, as the Control Commission. But the interdepartmental wrangle was not finished. An argument raged right up to the spring of 1945 over who should control the Control Commission. At that point both sides suddenly realized that they might be struggling for possession of something they did not really want. The War Office belatedly recognized that it was not equipped to control many essentially non-military policy-making aspects; and the Foreign Office awoke to the fact that the job was going to involve far more than merely nominal supervision and decided that the management of Germany was clearly a military matter. Both sides reversed their positions and tried to thrust the poisoned chalice on the other.

The upshot was that, until October 1945, no single department in Whitehall was actually responsible for the Control Commission, which by then consisted of a staff of some twenty-four thousand people. As a compromise, a completely new ministry, the Control Office, was created. Its two thousand five hundred staff were chiefly distinguished by their almost complete ignorance of Germany. The Control Office only remained autonomous until April 1947, when it was put firmly under Foreign Office control.

If the British government could not satisfactorily coordinate the work of two of its own departments, it was no more successful in cooperating with its closest ally. Bovenschen's original Administration of Territories (Europe) Committee had tried to get American participation but was rebuffed. Washington was suspicious and unwilling to allow policies to be made in London. In Moscow, in October 1943, Eden tried again and proposed the tripartite European Advisory Commission. Again Washington rejected the idea, but was later forced to join when the Russians agreed to it. However neither the Russians nor the US took the EAC seriously, and Washington's participation was only token: the Americans had established their own interdepartmental committee to which the British were invited, an invitation which, in turn, was firmly rejected by Whitehall.

John McCloy explained to Kirby, the first head of the British Control Commission, that anti-British feeling was still strong in America and, for appearance's sake, the American public had to believe that the policy was made in Washington.[3] The mutual distrust even prevented agreement in early 1944 as to whether the military governments in the zones should be called 'Control Councils' or 'Control Commissions'. In fact there was no chance of agreement on what the overall policy should be. Britain had learnt the lessons of Versailles in 1919 and wanted to avoid the re-creation of dissatisfaction in the heart of the continent. Whitehall's policy was to demilitarize and denazify Germany, but to leave the country as intact as possible. Bankrupted by war, Britain had no taste for more than a limited commitment to appoint a few civilians who would supervise the German government running the country. Massive and extraordinarily comprehensive digests and descriptions of every aspect of German life – the economy, individual industries, government, the police force and transport – were compiled to help the future British administrators, but theirs was to be just an indirect role.[4]

In contrast, until 1944 policy-making in Washington had been sacrificed to a series of power struggles about who would implement the policies once they had been decided. The weakness was at the top. Roosevelt had no consistent German policy. He believed Germany should be weak and punished, but alternated about who should be weak and who should be punished.[5] He refused to recognize the German resistance movement and rejected all negotiations with any Germans, believing they were a degenerate race. Then, to Churchill's horror, he said he was willing to see Russia dominating the whole of Germany. Later, he wrote to the Secretary of State: 'I dislike making detailed plans for a country which we do not yet occupy,' and climaxed his indecision by memoing the Joint Chiefs of Staff: 'Please note that I am not willing at this time to say that we do not intend to destroy the whole German nation.'[6]

Neither Hull nor Stimson could argue. Both were old and sick. Hull was consistently ignored, while Stimson's department was badly organized and inadequately staffed. Into the vacuum stepped the Joint Chiefs of Staff and the newly created Civil Affairs Division. On his appointment in 1943 to head the CAD, General John Hilldring was asked by George Marshall: 'Do you know what your duties are?' Hilldring replied: 'Yes, sir.' Marshall: 'Well I don't think you really do. Your mission is to start planning from the day you go into business, how you're going to get out of it as fast as possible.'[7]

True to his orders, Hilldring excluded civilians from policy planning and consistently obstructed State Department policy towards the EAC in London. Hilldring's replies to Ambassador Winant's requests for instructions about the Committee were either pleas to be patient, or were so cryptic that they were valueless.[8]

Faced with Washington's indecision, the SHAEF planners in the 'German Country Unit' in London began drafting a series of orders for the occupation forces which partially reflected British policy. Only the war industries would be demolished, the rest would remain. To prevent the disease and starvation that followed the 1918 defeat, the Allied armies were instructed to provide enough to keep the Germans alive and healthy, but then leave the country to its own resources. The draft handbook, which very few and only very junior officers were likely to read, listed the military's duties to restore water and telephone services and to supervise the reopening of the schools, churches and government offices. The British opposed the issue of any handbook because it implied that SHAEF would continue after the surrender, which they opposed; they wanted Germany to return immediately to civilian rule.[9] Whitehall agreed to it being written in the interests of wartime unity and on the understanding that the British would not implement it in their zone when SHAEF was disbanded; consequently few paid it much attention.

But for Henry Morgenthau, the US Secretary of the Treasury, Roosevelt's neighbour and friend, the handbook was dynamite. In London, in August 1944, he was given a copy of the draft by Bernard Bernstein, the head of the American team on the German Country Unit. Bernstein was virulently anti-German, and it is not an exaggeration to say that Morgenthau and Roosevelt shared a hatred for Germany. They were obsessed by their personal experiences after the First World War, especially the President's own experiences in Germany itself. They had watched with seething fury as large numbers of Germans had been beguiled by Hitler into believing that Germany had not lost the First World War, but had been betrayed, stabbed in the back, by Jewish Bolsheviks.[10]

When he got back to Washington, Morgenthau gave the handbook to Roosevelt, suggesting that it seemed to point the way towards the rebuilding of Germany rather than its perpetual destruction. Morgenthau's influence was at its peak, and the President responded by immediately endorsing his neighbour's view. Just days before US troops crossed into Germany, Roosevelt ordered Stimson to withdraw the handbook: 'This so-called Handbook is very bad. I should like to know how it came to be written and who approved it down the line. . .It gives the impression that Germany is to be restored.' The opposite was the truth, wrote the President; every German had to recognize this time that Germany was defeated and that 'the whole nation had been engaged in a lawless conspiracy against the decencies of modern civilization.'[11]

On 2 September, at a special meeting of all departments in Harry Hopkins' office in the White House, Morgenthau unveiled his own solution to the German problem. To prevent any repetition of history, the sinews of German militarism were to be destroyed, the country was to be de-industrialized, its factories demolished, its mines flooded and millions of its people sent to Russia as labourers. What remained would be a nation of peasants and cuckoo clock manufacturers, which could pose no threat to the peace of the Continent. Everyone in the room was aghast but momentarily impotent.[12] Morgenthau had Roosevelt's support.

Eleven days later, Roosevelt met Churchill in Quebec. Behind the scenes, Morgenthau told the British that American money to save Britain from bankruptcy was conditional on support for his plan. Churchill and Roosevelt initialled an agreement after dinner. Days later, both men began to beat a rapid retreat and disclaim support for the draconian measures. Postwar policy was plunged into further confusion. After a series of indecisive committee meetings following Quebec, Stimson wrote to the President on 29 September: 'The fundamental question is what kind of Germany we want.'[13] It was a bit late to ask that particular question.

Three weeks later, at noon on 21 October, Colonel Gerhard Wilck surrendered what remained of the devastated city of Aachen to the American 1st Army.[14] Of its one hundred and sixty thousand population, only five thousand remained. The rest were either dead or had been forced by Nazi party officials to evacuate the town. Nevertheless, a temporary German administration had to be organized, and the first requirement was a mayor. The town's records had all been destroyed, so it seemed only natural for FIG2, the Military Government detachment, to ask the advice of the local Catholic bishop, who had remained behind. They did not know that the bishop, like the vast majority of German clergy, had not opposed Hitler and was a committed conservative and outright opponent of the Social Democrats.

The bishop recommended a 'good man', a devout Catholic, an outstanding citizen, Franz Oppenhoff. No, said the bishop, Oppenhoff had never joined the party; but don't be swayed by party membership, most who joined were never committed. It was an 'irrelevant encumbrance'. The Military Government detachment left the bishop's house satisfied that Oppenhoff, a local businessman, should be their choice. When they located him, he indeed looked ideal. Clean, intelligent, well-dressed, apparently respectable, he accepted the offer and appointed fellow businessmen to help him.

At first no American queried his authoritarian and anti-democratic views, or the fact that he and his fellow businessmen had prospered during the Nazi era. He was not, after all, a Nazi party member, and by definition was suitable. A non-Nazi, for soldiers, was automatically an anti-Nazi. It was the same at the mines. The local manager, Herr Aschke, seemed to be very reasonable and competent. Coal was needed, so he was kept on. No one thought about Aschke's use of slave labour to keep production going during the war, nor suspected that he had been an ardent Nazi; although no one was too keen about his ideas on incentives to increase production, namely cutting wages, he was the only man, they thought, who could maintain the vital coal supplies.[15]

Saul Padover, an American member of the SHAEF Psychological Warfare Division, arrived in Aachen two months after the takeover. He had heard that German trade unionists, especially the miners, were very critical of the appointments, but could not believe what he discovered. The Military Government officers, he reported, were 'politically ignorant and morally indifferent' and had made a 'thorough political mess' by appointing Oppenhoff and Aschke, who were 'as compact a clique of ultra-reactionaries and fascists as could be found anywhere in Germany'.[16]

Padover's report caused a sensation. Was this what all the fighting had been for, to put Nazis and opportunists straight back into office? There was no easy answer. The Military Government officers had been briefed to appoint a mayor and then leave everything to the Germans. Technical competence, respectability, and the ability to speak English were easier qualifications to grasp than political purity. The man who had done the job for the previous twelve years was the ideal choice if the alternative was chaos. Choosing socialists, communists and trade unionists, men who were less well-dressed, who after twelve years of dictatorship did not have the arrogant swagger and self-confidence of those who had profited by supporting the Nazis, would, many thought, actually hinder government and military operations.

The immediate problem of Oppenhoff was solved on 26 March. His crumpled body was found inside his hallway. A Werwolf[17] assassin had shot him through the head as a warning to those who cooperated with the Allies. But by then the lack of political directives and, more importantly, the complete absence of trained men to implement them, made it inevitable that the Western zones would not be denazified.

For Aachen was only the first product of the deep confusions over how the Allies should deal with the cities and towns which were now falling into their hands daily as they advanced across Germany in the winter of 1944 – 5. Even if the first SHAEF handbook had not been withdrawn, it would not have prevented disarray. The first handbook ordered that: 'Under no circumstances shall active Nazis or ardent sympathizers be retained in office for administrative convenience or expediency. The Nazi party and all subsidiary organizations shall be dissolved.' But it then added: 'The administrative machinery of certain dissolved Nazi organizations may be used when necessary to provide certain essential functions, such as relief, health and sanitation, with denazified personnel and facilities.'[18] The last sentence left enough flexibility to comfortably employ Aschke, Oppenhoff and many other sympathizers.

JCS Directive 1067, issued from Washington on 11 November 1944, was intended to remove the confusion. It stated:

> The entire Nazi leadership will be removed from posts of authority and no member of the German General Staff or Nazi hierarchy should occupy any important governmental or civil position. You will not permit the employment of active Nazis or ardent sympathizers, and no exception will be made to this policy on grounds of administrative convenience or expediency. You will remove and exclude from office any persons who act, or whom you deem likely to act, contrary to Allied interests and principles.

It was a sweeping order, followed a month later by another directive which forbade the use, 'without exception', of dissolved Nazi organizations for relief purposes;[19] and a little later still by the inclusion of many more categories of officials who were subject to automatic arrest just because they held a certain position. Every school, university, courthouse and newspaper was to be closed and all those employed by them were to be arrested.

The British were openly horrified by the American policies. Where, for a start, were the arrested people to be kept? McCloy sanguinely replied that the German concentration camps could hold two million, and that a further million would have died during the war.[20]

Reviewing the new directives, which directed that every symbol of Nazism, including street signs, should be removed, O'Neil commented: 'Is it really necessary that we should seize monuments . . . even if the Nazis put them up. . . It is a disastrous policy certain to lead to total chaos. If it means we do what we can, but accept no responsibility for the results, it is merely a clumsy attempt to escape criticism although we cannot escape control.'[21] But the sharp differences were to get worse. By February 1945, the absolute ban on employing Nazis was causing immense military problems. Armies rely on water, electricity and other civilian services. The temporary employment of Nazis had to be allowed, if only until the end of the war. An amending directive was issued allowing Nazis to be retained 'if military necessity so requires', but each individual exception had to be reported in writing.[22] Bernstein objected and claimed that too many detachments were taking advantage of the 'exception' clause. He blamed the British for the watering down of the directives.[23]

A month later an ideological war broke out within the American army. The 12th Army, under Bernstein's influence, issued its own, unique, directive overriding the exceptions and forbidding the employment of any Nazi, including non-party sympathizers. A sympathizer was defined as anyone who had financially or otherwise profited under the Nazis, had been promoted at work or been a member of a business that had given money or help to the Nazis.[24]

Added to the new directive was a 'clarification', which defined 'militarists', 'ardent sympathizers' and 'persons likely to act contrary to Allied interests and principles'. Prussian Junkers and landowners were to be arrested as militarists; sympathizers included anyone who, since 1933, had acted in a way which supported the government regardless of whether they belonged to the Nazi party – anyone who had profited by denunciation, aryanization, spoliation, rapid promotion, contributions to the party, membership of a company that had contributed to the party, or had escaped military duty because of Nazi influence. It meant, in effect, that there was no scope for making use of any individual German who was in a position to help, however reluctantly. On 23 March, the 12th Army's directive was modified by a directive issued from the White House. The latest directive permitted purely 'nominal' Nazis to be employed. Bernstein, in a letter to Clay, openly blamed the 'serious softening of our denazification programme,' on the British. But he could do no more than protest: 'It is my judgement, based on experience in the field, that this provision will be used as a wholesale excuse for retention.'[25]

It was all quite clearly a recipe for chaos. There were now no less than four different directives on the employment of Nazis and over forty different subsidiary regulations. As not all the changes had reached the individual detachments, each unit chose the directive which suited its particular political prejudice and answered their immediate practical problems. To increase the confusion, the British army refused to apply any of the American-drafted amendments. When Aachen was handed over to the British, Brigadier-General Frank McSherry, chief of SHAEF's G5 Operation Branch, suggested to the British commanding officer that Aschke be removed from managing the mines, as the miners had proved that he had been a fanatical Nazi supporter. The British officer refused. It would be 'suicidal' he told McSherry.[26] Producing coal was more important than punishment for political beliefs.

An exchange of letters between 15 February and 4 May between McSherry and Robert Murphy, the American political adviser in SHAEF command, highlights the almost total chaos which prevailed. McSherry wrote to Murphy that the intelligence reports, including that from Aachen, showed that:

Military Government cannot escape responsibility for the political situation in Germany merely by 'leaving things to the Germans.' Since we have no political directive from CCS (other than denazification and the negative directive to prohibit political activity and to avoid commitments to or negotiations with political elements), we are greatly in need of any assistance which you and your staff, as political advisers, can give us. . . I am making every effort to re-educate Military Government officers respecting our policy in Germany since there is evidence that some of them are concerned with 'efficient' administration without regard to some of the implications of Military Government in Germany.[27]

Murphy, whose political 'expertise' and judgement had in the past been seen to be, at best, flawed and uncertain, sent a vague reply. 'In my view,' he wrote on 4 May, 'we shall have to approach the problem gradually and experimentally.' In selecting Germans to help the Allies, he wrote: 'No label from twelve years ago is conclusive. . . It is highly important to make every effort to select people who are not only anti-Nazi but who are reasonably liberal and pro-democratic in their outlook.' The problem for McSherry was where to find any such people who had survived twelve years of Nazism. Murphy warned against taking advice from the Church, whose record had been 'exceedingly spotty', nor from the former Centre party, who were nationalist and militarist, while the left and trade unionists might have been anti-Nazi but not always liberal and democratic. Murphy concluded: 'No absolute rule can be laid down and the Military Government officer must rely on his own judgement.' McSherry did not try to turn Murphy's ambivalent political essay into a directive. But neither of them could have, in all honesty, believed in the judgement of their Military Government officers, who with some exceptions, were at best well-intentioned but untrained, and at worst, lazy and corrupt.[28]

Both British and American armies had given some thought to preparing men for the task of running the occupation of Germany.

A 'School for Gauleiters' had been opened in Charlottesville, Virginia, in April 1942. The same criterion was applied to recruitment as had governed the choice of candidates for the War Crimes Commission – they should be men who were unuseable for any other war purpose.[29] Mostly middle-aged, infirm and overweight, the first 416 arrived in Shrivenham, England, on 27 January 1944. The two-mile walk in the rain from the station to the camp decimated their numbers. Within two weeks, more than half were too sick to attend classes. The remainder suffered extreme boredom, an assault on their self-esteem, and finally succumbed to a variety of illnesses. None of the first arrivals ever reached in Germany.

The majority of those that did eventually arrive were either the same sort of person, recruited later and sent direct to continental Europe, or, when it came to staffing the central departments of the Military Government, specially selected experts from government departments, industry and the professions, who had the skills needed to manage the divisions from Berlin or Frankfurt.

Even the man to whom the Military Government officers were ultimately responsible in the American zone was scarcely, on paper, an ideal choice in terms of background and training. General Lucius Clay admits to having been 'amazed' at his appointment to the post of deputy military governor under Eisenhower, in which post he was to be in charge of administering government affairs inside the American zone.[30] He was apparently selected as a result of successfully clearing a bottleneck that was holding up supplies in Cherbourg harbour shortly after D-Day. After a spell in Washington, he found himself in Germany briefed to implement the 'Four D's' – demilitarization, denazification, decartelization and democratization. All admirable aims, but ones that would require political understanding as well as administrative skills. Clay's political education was to be a painful process.

As seasoned colonialists the British might have been expected to manage better. A training programme, started at the Cambridge Intelligence Centre in 1941, was expanded in 1943 to include a specially created school in Wimbledon. Once trained, the future Military Government officers returned to their regular units to await the time when they would be needed. Few ever found an opportunity to put their training to use. Those who did reach Germany were usually ignored. As General Alec Bishop put it: 'Monty wouldn't have any non-campaigners in Germany's postwar government. You had to have sand in your shoes before he would look at you.'[31]

In the event the vast majority of Military Government officers in both zones were recruited on the spot from the front-line troops who captured the town or village. The choice normally fell upon the man who was the nearest, and most dispensable to the commanding officer. His qualifications for the job were never queried or tested. Overnight, he was transformed from cannon fodder to a pro-consul with enormous powers. At best he was given an hour's training in his duties, but there was no test to see whether he had understood what he had been told. Usually unable to speak German and overwhelmingly anti-socialist, the officers quickly sought out the English-speaking, respectable-looking Germans; predictably, these were usually nationalists and Nazis.[32]

The level of political sophistication expected of the men who were to implement policy at grassroots level is illustrated by a guide to the 'German Character' widely circulated by the British Control Commission to the Military Government officers.[33] The 'average German' was described as 'primitive' because of his admiration for medieval cruelties, as having an inferiority complex, a guilt complex, a dual personality, lacking balance, inconsistent, highly emotional and wallowing in self-pity.

> The ordinary German, the husband and father, will derive pleasure in carrying out orders involving the infliction of torture and suffering. Yet in between he will take out the photo of his wife and children and slobber over it. . . It must be affirmed that the Germans are not divided into two classes, good and bad Germans: there are only good and bad elements in the German character, the latter of which generally predominate. But it may be said with a good deal of truth that the Germans can be divided into two other classes, namely the leaders who plot and plan, and the led which blindly follow, and that those two are equally dangerous and make up the great majority of all Germans.

Nor could the ill-equipped and unprepared officers look to their superiors for help or advice. Reading through all the reports on Allied government in Germany arriving at SHAEF Intelligence, Michael Balfour concluded in a report to the Foreign Office that no one even knew what was happening after the Military Government officers had been appointed: 'As a result of lack of communications and lack of staff, higher headquarters are lamentably ignorant of what is going on in the field.'[34]

As a consequance of the long sparring match between the Foreign Office and the War Office, things were no better organized when the Control Commission arrived in the British zone to take over the ad hoc arrangements which the army had made as it advanced across Germany.

When Major-General Kirby was appointed head of the Control Commission in August 1944, both Whitehall and Washington optimistically believed that Germany would surrender by the first week of November. His orders were to have the Control Commission machinery and two thousand five hundred personnel standing by to be flown to Germany by 31 October.[35] For his efforts, Kirby's nose was squashed by every department in Whitehall. The only personnel available were the same men who in North Africa, according to Ward at the Foreign Office, had proved to be 'duds appointed off a roster without much effort as assessing their suitability'.[36] Caught between Foreign Office demands and Bovenschen's insistence that 'we've got to take what we've got',[37] Kirby appealed for Treasury funds to recruit from outside the government service. To get support, he wrote to Oliver Harvey that, unless someone gave his work priority, the inevitable cost would be another peace lost by just 'paying lip service . . . in the usual British fashion'.[38] Kirby's plea failed. There were too many uncertainties and hypothetical questions, Harvey felt, for any minister to take a decision. The only policy they would support was to keep the duds out.

By November Kirby confessed to be 'at my wits' end'.[39] Only eighteen per cent of the recruits had been found, most of them of poor quality. Three departmental chiefs had been bribed into service by flattering letters personally signed by Eden, but very few of the recruits spoke German and most of them were unsuitable.[40] It was no better by the end of March. Only four and a half per cent of the interpreters, six per cent of the political division and nine per cent of the local government administration had been found. Overall, there was a seventy per cent deficiency.[41] Among those recruited, there was a heavy contingent from the old Empire. The Legal Division, for example, submitted a long, reasoned request to send someone to Egypt to research the nineteenth-century British records to see how the colonial service controlled the Egyptian courts. This, it was explained, would be useful experience for Germany.[42]

Deliberately excluded from both the American and the British recruitment programmes were the thousands of refugees who had left Germany before 1939. With the exception of the very few who were used for research or intelligence missions, they were all grouped as suspect and unusable. It was only as late as February 1945 that the Foreign Office made a half-hearted attempt at compiling as list of 'white Germans' who could be trusted. Inevitably it was useless.[43] The State Department made a similar attempt, which also failed, in April.[44]

Summarizing British opinion, John Wheeler-Bennett, the Foreign Office's official historian, wrote in April 1944: 'We cannot trust any Germans after the close of hostilities. . . From the refugees who were good Germans in the pre-Nazi days, there is little to be obtained but confusion.'[45] But the Americans, in sharp contrast to the British, were prepared to use many of the European refugees who during the war had become naturalized American citizens.

Strangely, the universal hatred of Germans seemed to extend more to those who had left Germany than to those who remained behind. Somehow, the act of leaving was seen as a weakness, a failure to stay behind and fight. It reflected the disbelief of the reports of the concentration camps and extermination policies. Nowhere are the baser motives for rejection shown than in the minuted reaction to a letter from a Mr S. Sass to Churchill in May 1944. Writing from Colombia, Sass explained that until 1939 he had been the managing director of a leading steel factory in the Rhineland and wanted to offer his expertise to reorganize the steel industry after the war. Although the Control Commission badly needed just that expertise, Dwight Chaplin of the Foreign Office's Enemy Branch wrote:[46]

> From Africa's shore, from Colomb's sunscorched strand,
> Urgent there streams an eager Hebrew band,
> Imbued with our desire to serve the aims
> Of Allied justice, see them stake their claims
> To jobs in Germany. *They* know the ropes,
> And *their* control will answer all our hopes.
> 'Let us but serve, and we will prove our worth.
> 'Till Hitler came and rudely thrust us forth
> 'We helped the men who laid the powder train.
> 'So you can trust us not to help again.
> 'Good Germans we? Perhaps, but all the same
> 'Profit or loss we'll play the Allies' game.'
> Such altruistic offers shall we spurn,
> Nor rather trusting to these helpers turn.

Loose them like vultures on the German scene
And hope they will not pick the carcass clean
Or, worse, revert to type and aid the Hun
To germanize the world with tank and gun?
Prudence invites we leave them where they are
And hitch our wagon not to David's star.
Paris we know, well worth a mass,
Berlin not less by Bellow-Fellow Sass.

For the British especially, the outright rejection of Germans was an extraordinary contradiction. If denazification was to be a limited exercise, why should those Germans who faithfully served the regime in the previous twelve years be more trusted than the refugees? The Foreign Office seemed to believe that no one could be trusted. In the very week of victory, Christopher 'Kit' Steele, a British political officer at SHAEF, complained to Troutbeck that everyone was annoyed at Richard Crossman's broadcasts from the Political Warfare Department which were 'prematurely boosting . . . dubiously repentant Huns [by] trying to find "good" Germans and publicize them'.[47] Taking the contradiction to its ultimate absurdity, the Cabinet decided on 18 May that the 'white' Germans should stay in Britain as cheap labour, while the 'black' Germans, those who could not be trusted, should return to Germany.[48] It was the bewildering result of having no policy. The British were deliberately excluding the very kind of people their army in Germany was searching for. On the American side, as late as 6 June, McSherry, then in Germany, outrightly rejected any use of political refugees, although he was prepared to accept one hundred carefully selected anti-Nazis with professional qualifications to be picked from the POW camps in America.[49]

The appalling results of the failure of the Allies to form a coherent policy for their occupation of Germany soon became apparent when the American Military Government set about finding Germans who could be appointed to administer their zone in the summer of 1945. In theory, the division of Germany into three, and then, later, four, zones, was intended only as a temporary arrangement. The four-power military occupation was not intended to imply that Germany would be permanently divided and run by four different governments.

According to the three-power Potsdam agreement, signed in Berlin on 2 August, Germany was to be temporarily governed by the Allied Control Council based in Berlin. The Potsdam agreement established, in broad and vague outlines, Germany's future restricted economy.

Beyond that, further and more detailed directives were to be agreed by the Control Council. Each of the four powers would be represented by its military commander. Policy directives could only be effective if there was a unanimous decision. Each of the powers was to establish divisions to run the economy, transport, education, courts and security and every other aspect of life in their own zone. They were to implement the directives unanimously agreed by the four powers in Berlin.

The American equivalent of the British Control Commission was OMGUS, the 'Office of Military Government for Germany, United States'. OMGUS was responsible for the government of the American zone in Germany, initially just to implement the Potsdam Agreement, but later becoming itself the policy-making agency for the zone. Its voluminous records show that, with few notable exceptions, the various divisions set up within OMGUS were staffed by American specialists whose expertise sadly did not extend to recent German history. Reasonably, they searched around for Germans whose knowledge and background equipped them for the task of getting the basic machinery of the country running again, but their curiosity about such men's politics and recent activities was strictly limited.

Theodor Ganzenmüller had taken part in Hitler's beer hall putsch in 1923, and had been distinguished by being personally presented by Hitler with the *Blutorden* decoration. As *Staatssekretär* in the ministry of transport during the war, he had efficiently organized train services to Auschwitz, Treblinka and all the other Polish extermination camps. If there was a hold-up, Himmler would personally telephone him to sort out the problem. There was even written confirmation of Himmler's gratitude. On 13 August 1942, his personal adjutant Karl Wolff wrote on his behalf to Ganzenmüller: 'With particular joy I noted your assurance that for two weeks now a train has been carrying, every day, five thousand members of the chosen people to Treblinka . . . I thank you again for your efforts in this matter and, at the same time, I would be grateful if you would continue to give these things your continued personal attention.'[50]

Seeking someone with the expertise to begin to rebuild the railways in the American zone, the US Transport Division unashamedly proposed that the former SA Brigadeführer would be the ideal choice.[51] Seven of their other nominations were also men in the automatic arrest categories. Ganzenmüller's nomination was only rejected after an urgent telegram from the State Department in Washington.[52] Some were surprised that he was removed: Dr Dorpmüller, Hitler's minister of transport, had actually been appointed.[53]

The British Transport Division had no such qualms. Dr Fritz Busch was appointed general manager of the railways because of his wartime experience in the ministry (as *Ministerialdirigent*). Despite attempts to block the appointment because of his membership of the SS and his categorization for compulsory removal, the British Transport Division obstinately protected their 'discovery' as the only man who could run the rail system.[54]

Over fifty per cent of those nominated by the American Legal Division for appointments to the new Ministry of Justice were former Nazi party members and were in mandatory arrest categories.[55] Nearly every German nominated for the Agricultural Division was in an automatic arrest category,[56] as were those in the Communications Division.

Only Bernard Bernstein, now head of the Finance Division, reported that he had found no one suitable to recommend.[57] There was special pleading for Dr Hermann Geisz to be appointed as head of the Communications Division by General Bickelhaupt, a vice-president of the American Telephone and Telegraph company, who was on temporary duty in Germany. Bickelhaupt insisted that Geisz was 'indispensable'.[58] Geisz had been head of the German telephone company before and during the war, and had bought a lot of AT&T equipment. His appointment was blocked at the very last moment by Clay because 'he occupied a high office in close association with Nazi leaders and gave to those leaders utmost loyalty and maximum capacity.' But that was an exceptional and relatively unimportant intervention.

Clay did not, to some people's surprise, immediately intervene in the American appointment of the new Bavarian minister president, Dr Fritz Schäffer. Born in 1888 in Munich, Schäffer had joined the right-wing Bavarian Freikorps which in 1919 revolted against the Berlin government and bloodily suppressed the socialist revolt in Bavaria. Appointed Bavarian minister of culture in 1920, he rejected a proposal by the Social Democrats two years later to outlaw the Nazi party's newly formed paramilitary units. 'Why should the Bavarian government protect the Social Democrats from their political enemies?' he asked.[59] In 1932 he told President Hindenburg that he and his party 'were not in principle opposed to Hitler becoming Chancellor' and told the then Prime Minister, Franz von Papen, that he was 'absolutely available to become a member of any future Hitler government'. Although his party was disbanded during the Nazi period, he pledged his support to Hitler until the cause was clearly lost; he was briefly arrested after the 20 July 1944 attempt on Hitler's life. Whether he was then an anti-Nazi is irrelevant. He did not have sufficient democratic credentials to govern Bavaria in 1945.

Schäffer filled his administration with men who had at best compromised with the Nazis, or at worst were in the mandatory removal class. Karl August Fischer, head of the Interior Ministry, was a former

Nazi official in Czechoslovakia and should have been arrested; another, Otto Hipp, the new minister of education, refused to denazify the schools, while the head of the Ministry of Economics, Karl Lange, had made enormous profits during the war with the help of his close Nazi contacts.

One man who was never slow to set at rest any over-scrupulous curiosity which the occupation authorities might harbour was Cardinal Faulhaber, the head of the Roman Catholic Church in Bavaria. It was on his recommendation that Schäffer was appointed,[60] and he was always ready to come to the protection of any member of his flock whose employment might be threatened by a Nazi past.

The cardinal found a sympathetic ear in Colonel Charles Keegan, the fun-loving and brash staff officer in George Patton's 3rd Army. Keegan, like most other officers, was trained for war but not to mastermind a political revolution. Denazification for him, as for others, meant arrests and the removal of swastikas, street signs and statues. Any offer to help organize the chaos was gratefully accepted. To base decisions about appointments purely on party membership, and not on the individual's activities, was for him patently unworkable. Moreover he had only one political adviser, and even fewer German speakers.

Not even those who (unlike Keegan and his commander, Patton) had some political sophistication, could offer an answer to the question of how to govern Germany. But they were not helped by the simplicities of the fighting soldiers who too often set the tone and made the decisions. At his Bad Tölz headquarters on 22 September, during an impromptu press conference, Patton was asked about his attitude towards denazification. 'This Nazi thing is just like a Democratic and Republican election fight,' he replied.

Patton's throwaway aside caused a sensation. It symbolized the blinkered apathy of the American army about Germany's history. Eisenhower, then still in command of the American zone, demanded an immediate inquiry. According to an eyewitness at the meeting between Eisenhower and Patton six days later in Frankfurt, the commander-in-chief shouted: 'What in the devil is the American army doing in Germany, if not to denazify the German government and administration? The Russians killed their Nazis; the Americans put them in office.' Schäffer and some of his Nazi ministers were summarily removed a week later. Patton was dismissed three days after that.[61]

Cardinal Faulhaber was not alone among his fellow clerics in publicly disapproving of denazification. The removal of 'good Germans' with whom he had coexisted since 1933 was unacceptable. It would have only been a step closer to accepting the 'collective guilt' of all the German people for Nazi crimes, which the Allies wanted the Germans to endorse. The Catholics, like the Protestant Church, had openly supported Hitler after his appointment as chancellor in 1933. Despite their exact knowledge of Nazi crimes, they never withdrew support, although they occasionally protested against some of the excesses.

In May 1945, the country's spiritual leaders had quickly to decide whether they would accept the consequences of that support and admit that they, like the rest of the German population, shared the guilt for Germany's crimes, in the knowledge that to admit the mistake was dangerous not only spiritually, but also politically. It was a risk which the Catholic Church was quite unprepared to take.[62] The German cardinals immediately and unashamedly reaffirmed the validity of the 1933 Concordat between Hitler and the Vatican as justification of their own uncritical support of Nazism. If there was any fault, they announced, it was among the individual clergymen and not the Church itself.

In their first joint pastoral message from Fulda in June 1945, the bishops praised the clergy for having resisted National Socialism, thanked Catholic parents for having clung to Catholic schools, and emphasized how the Church had successfully resisted attempts by the Nazis to interfere in Church affairs. Maintaining Catholic schools was an act, according to the bishops, of supreme resistance, an achievement recognized by the Pope in a letter to Cardinal Faulhaber on 1 November 1945. 'We know very well,' wrote Pope Pius XII, who himself had willingly collaborated with Hitler, 'that in dutiful observance of your office you withstood and resisted with complete conviction the unhealthy teachings and methods of unbridled National Socialism.'[63]

It was only one step more to deny the whole notion of collective guilt. If the Catholic Church, which had, up to the highest office, collaborated with Hitler, denied any guilt, then clearly no one else could be guilty either. Bishop von Galen told his flock: 'If anyone says that the entire German population and each of us is implicated in the crimes committed in foreign countries and especially in the concentration camps, that is an untrue and unjust accusation against many of us.'[64] Theological support for the recipe of political survival was also easily available. The Catholic Church denied the possibility of collective guilt, because guilt was an individual matter to be settled with God rather than man. For the Catholic Church it was an unchallengeable doctrine because the Pope himself said: 'It is meddling in the prerogatives of God to attribute collective guilt to a whole people and to treat it accordingly.'[65] The final step was to pray forgiveness for all those who had gone astray and forget the past.

The Protestant Church did not come quite so rapidly to the same self-serving solution. Initially, it was divided on the issue: Pastor Niemöller, an outstanding and rare opponent of the Nazis, isolated himself from his fellow Christians when he publicly and unconditionally accepted 'collective guilt'. Other Protestant leaders were more hesitant. Bishop Wurm, who was to become a persistent critic of Allied policy, at first accepted Germany's collective guilt; then in September, realizing how unpopular it was amongst the German people, he complained that the Allied programme exposing Nazi war crimes was 'seriously demoralizing and hampering Church cooperation with Military Government'.[66] When Clay and other Allied leaders lashed out at the German clergy for their prejudicial refusal to face the consequences of their actions, the Catholics remained stonefaced. But the Protestant bishops meeting in Stuttgart in December 1946 had second thoughts. Wurm told the meeting that Germany must accept responsibility for the war and the atrocities. But, other than dividing the Church, it was of no consequence. Accepting collective guilt also implied accepting collective and mutual forgiveness, since a nation could not punish itself.

By different routes the Churches, the only surviving leaders of Germany, had arrived at the same position: collective opposition to the Allies.

Where the Churches led, the people were not slow to follow. When British troops questioned the inhabitants of the area around Belsen they blandly denied any knowledge, or indeed curiosity, about what had been going on behind the fences where their fields abutted.

Nearly all the townsfolk of Dachau had lived and openly profited by trading with the nearby concentration camp since 1933. The trains of cattle trucks bringing the inmates to Dachau actually passed through the town. Ragged columns of starving inmates would march daily through the town to build nearby roads. The stench from the crematorium had been noticeable for years. Yet when the townsfolk were asked by a US 7th Army investigator for their reactions to the discoveries of horrors inside the camp, they shrugged their shoulders and rhetorically asked: 'What could we do?'[67] The investigator concluded that most 'did not give a damn', but generously added that: 'It should be pointed out in justice that there were no people who could seclude themselves from the community without harming their sources of income.' Efforts to change this attitude were to remain unsuccessful.

Based on the advice of SHAEF's Psychological Warfare Division, Allied propaganda and broadcasts after the final victory harped on Germany's total defeat and the Germans' common responsibility for the atrocities. The PWD believed that repetition of the message would crush any German resistance movement at birth, and compel the German population to obey Allied orders and recognized Allied superiority.[68] With the exception of isolated attacks on Allied soldiers, the intimidation of some Germans and the cutting of a few telephone lines, there was no meaningful German resistance movement. The broadcasts probably contributed to that success. Politically, however, the propaganda was counterproductive, especially that revealing the full horror of Nazi atrocities.

Soon after the surrender, PWD teams went through Germany's cities showing inhabitants photographs, booklets and films of concentration camp horrors. Confronted with the evidence, those questioned invariably blamed the Nazis and proclaimed their own innocence. They rejected the Allied policy that the Germans share collective guilt and defiantly challenged the questioners to justify the Allies' own bombing of German cities and their alliance with Stalin's Russia. Opinion polls compiled by the American army's Information Control Division in November 1945 showed that fifty per cent of those polled believed that 'National Socialism was a good idea badly carried out.' Only forty per cent thought National Socialism a 'bad idea', and while just twenty per cent accepted that Germany was responsible for the war, a massive seventy per cent rejected any responsibility.[69] To Allied surprise, the same pollsters discovered that, in January 1948, the percentages had barely changed. Allied propaganda had totally failed to convince the German people.

The Germans were puzzled or offended rather than ashamed by Allied efforts to bring home to them the revulsion which the Nazis inspired. At Roosevelt's behest, the Allied armies had adopted a policy of non-fraternization, in the hope that ostracizing the Germans would make them realize the contempt which was felt for them. In fact, an outbreak of venereal disease of near-epidemic proportions in all ranks rapidly revealed that, as might have been expected, there were some sacrifices the armies were not prepared to make. Here, surprisingly, the Germans simply failed to take the point. A SHAEF survey in March of 150 Germans recorded more than twenty reasons why the Germans thought they were being ignored.[70] Less than a dozen realized the true purpose. Most thought it was as a security measure, to help or hinder the soldiers looting, or to prevent them catching VD.

The worst effect of non-fraternization was on the few genuine anti-Nazis. They tried to personally welcome the Allied troops as 'liberators' but were often humiliatingly rejected, thrown into the same basket as fanatical Nazis. It was depressing for Germans who had waited years for the Nazis to be overthrown to see Allied soldiers consulting Nazis over the repair and reorganization of local community services. Even worse was to hear that the first Allied appointed mayors in Hamburg, Wuppertal, Bremen, Hanover, Kiel and many towns and villages throughout the country were either former party members or sympathizers and, as the spring, and peace, came, to realize that they were just the tip of the iceberg.

Touring the country for the Foreign Office in July 1945, Ritchie Calder found that the German people lacked what he called a 'moral acceptance of defeat'.[71] Calder's report, reflecting surveys by British and American intelligence, attributed the German reaction to something worse than just defiance. The Germans believed that the Nazi era had been beneficial. They had for much of the time lived off the plunder of Europe: they had food, raw materials, industrial goods and slave labour. As a result, Germans had been better fed and clothed than any other European nation. Those questioned refused to believe that, during the war, the British had been rationed to one egg per week.[72] In the aftermath of defeat Germans openly criticized the Allied failure to repair the damage of war, reorganize the disrupted administration and provide food. They interpreted that failure, according to Calder, as proof that the Allies 'could not run things as well as the Nazis did in the Golden Age when there were many guns and some butter.'

The expectation that they would find Germany humbled and contrite in the spring of 1945 was a gross miscalculation on the part of the Allies. The people of Belsen and Dachau were not exceptions. Their denials of knowledge or responsibility looked more outrageous than most, but their attitudes were shared by their countrymen as a whole. They were defiant rather than ashamed. If pressed they put the blame for the worst excesses on 'the Nazis'; but, in truth, many felt regret rather than repentance at the passing of the Nazi era. For they understood at base what the Allies found it so hard to understand, that the Nazi party had not been a minority imposing its will by force, but the activist element in what had very quickly become a national consensus.

Hitler's assumption of power was not a coup d'état but a social counter-revolution against the system and values of the Weimar experiment, a reassertion of the kind of political order which Germany was accustomed to and appreciated. Although the highest proportion of the popular vote ever secured by the Nazis was 37.3 per cent, in the July 1932 Reichstag elections, the Nazi party in March 1933, with 288 seats out of 647, was still by far the largest of the eleven parties in Parliament. In the Parliamentary vote on 23 March, which granted Hitler dictatorial powers, the conservative parties, which had 158 seats, voted nearly unanimously for Hitler. The conservatives, like the Nazis, were weary of the perpetual political and economic crisis which had dominated Weimar Germany. Hitler promised the security and authority which was Germany's customary government. It was an attractive alternative to the six million unemployed, especially to those who despaired of perpetual political crisis.

The left wing was viewed by the conservatives as disruptive of the necessary discipline and subservience which alone could guarantee the strength of the state. Hitler's support after March 1933 was drawn from all those who viewed political disagreement as a weakness in society, and not a strength. Predominant amongst those were the Church, the civil service, the professions and the army. Hitler's racism and promises of national glory were probably of comparatively little, if any, importance for the conservative non-Nazis compared to the promise of a return to a strong, authoritarian state, as Germany had been before 1918.

The motives of those millions of ordinary working-class people who joined the party after March 1933 are examined later. It is enough here to understand that many joined and remained purely 'nominal members' because they were insecure, both economically and socially. But, with few exceptions, the Establishment not only tolerated but even supported the violence and authoritarianism which followed after March 1933, because it believed that the alternative was chaos. What followed for those Germans who were not politically or racially persecuted was a period of economic achievement and stunning national pride. The six million unemployed were all at work by 1936. It was a real economic miracle. Germany's army, one of Europe's weakest in 1933, was the Continent's strongest by 1938. The Versailles Treaty, which had deliberately crippled Germany, was torn up by Hitler and all Europe's Germanic peoples were, to their satisfaction, united under one leader. For many in Germany, the six years until the outbreak of war were a period of excitement and prosperity.

By September 1939 the majority of Germans accepted the evidence of Nazi success at its face value; they believed in the war and in Goebbels' propaganda because it seemed to promise further triumph. Six years later, many of those who were ready to acknowledge the existence of Nazi evil could only plead that they had not known, that they were victims of Nazi propaganda. There were some, but not many, active anti-Nazis left in Germany by 1945. Those who had not fled before 1939 had been murdered in the camps. What remained was a population whose attitude towards the regime had ranged from fanatical support to passive acceptance; wherever an individual German stood in the spectrum between those extremes, he was not easily converted to the belief that the society he had lived in for the past twelve years was a monstrous perversion of humanity.

Least of all were the Germans likely to be persuaded by an army of occupation representing an enemy who had bombed German cities into ruins and who had been allied with the Russian Bolsheviks. All the elements in his own society which he had been taught to respect and imitate – the Church, the teachers, the business and professional men, the army – had, by word and example, encouraged support of Hitler's government. They might now be belatedly discovering that they had, all along, disapproved of National Socialism, but their somersault had little influence on those who had been encouraged from the pulpit and in the classroom to obey and admire the Führer, and who had seen local businesses prosper from the sweat of imported slave labour, while lawyers implemented Nazi law and doctors dispatched imperfect patients to the euthanasia centres.

Nevertheless, there is sufficient evidence[73] to suggest that a significant minority had survived the war who had been consistently opposed to Hitler, although they had been powerless to influence events. Invariably and inevitably they had not been in positions of authority, but they were nevertheless technically competent to administer a bureaucracy and manage essential service. It was these people who were ignored by the Military Government officers, discriminated against by the non-fraternization rules, and condemned by the theories of collective guilt.

The performance of the British and the Americans, their lack of a policy and their treatment of the German population, made a very striking contrast with what was happening further east. The Russians had always sharply distinguished between the Nazi leadership and the German people. They had given strong support to an anti-Nazi German army fighting with them under General von Paulus. Newspaper and intelligence reports from Berlin now exposed those differences to the West's disadvantage.[74] Instead of banning fraternization and closing everything down, the Russians had swiftly reopened cinemas and cafes, were publishing newspapers and even promoting football matches between Red army soldiers and German workers.

The Germans who had spent the war in Moscow were organizing the zone, encouraging political meetings and creation of trade unions, and promising a bright future. It was a gloomy contrast to the West's negativism and deliberate rejection of the anti-Nazi Germans who were bluntly told by Allied officials like Sir William Strang, Montgomery's political adviser, that: 'the occupation's prime purpose was not to foster an Anglo-German friendship pact nor to quickly rebuild the country.'[75] Commenting on reports about the losing battle for the hearts and minds of the German people, O'Neil wrote: '[I am] very pessimistic as to the success of the Western powers in any such struggle, because I think the Russians hold most of the cards.'[76]

At least the Russians seemed to know what they believed in and what they were about. In contrast, as a SHAEF officer put it in early 1945: 'It will take a quarter of a century to eliminate the theories on which Nazism came to power. This can only be done by the education of the next generation, for which we have made no preparations and have no plan. We are proposing to cast out Nazism-militarism, but we have nothing to put in its place. We offer no hope, no ideals of democracy or world citizenship, and no prospect of an economic future.'[77]

Certainly the damage that had been done to a nation's moral perception and political consciousness by thirteen years of Nazism was not easily cured, as a discovery two months after the surrender made clear. During a routine visit to a lunatic asylum in Kaufbeuren in Bavaria on 2 July 1945, American medical inspectors discovered to their horror that the institution was nothing less than a mini-extermination centre and that, two months after the surrender, it was still operating.[78]

A matter of hours before the Americans arrived, German adults and children were still being murdered either by intramuscular injections or slow starvation. In the mortuary lay bodies of men and women, none weighing more than seventy-five pounds, who had died within the last few hours. It was never possible to determine how many had died in the institution. The records had been destroyed. Among the survivors was a ten-year-old boy weighing twenty-two pounds. The chief nurse, who admitted to having murdered 'about two hundred and ten children over the past two years,' asked on being arrested: 'Will anything happen to me?'

But the greater shock was to come. Inquiries in the village revealed that Kaufbeuren's inhabitants had known that the asylum was involved in 'experiments on improvements in the race,' had known that the 'experiments' were still going on, and felt no sense of guilt whatsoever.

8

'SYSTEMATIC AND
METICULOUS IMBECILITY'

The purpose of denazification, in theory at least, was to eradicate every symptom and symbol of National Socialism, root and branch; to prevent any threat to Allied control of Germany and, in the longer term, to build a society which was immune against any recrudescence of fascism. To be effective, the denazification system had to recognize that the Nazi cancer was a complex and insidious disease which had infected each and every aspect of the state. Everything had to be microscopically scrutinized for any sign of a malignancy which might one day sprout anew.

Perhaps only the Russians, of all the Allies, could grasp, from personal experience, how to treat such a condition; for theirs too was a totalitarian system, with a single ruling party which was not superimposed or grafted onto the apparatus of the state, but was organically linked with it.

To dismantle such a monster was a daunting task. It was unreasonable to expect that the appropriate skill in political and social surgery could be found in the ranks of a victorious army, whose mind was principally set upon such spoils of victory as Germany had to offer and upon the prospect of demobilization. Even among his peers, General George Patton was not renowned for sensitivity, but he exemplified the military's level of political literacy by his quip at his headquarters comparing the fate of the Nazis to the fortunes of any other political party.

Yet it was largely the soldiers who had the task of denazifying Germany. As they soon discovered, it was a job to which the simple precepts of military organization did not apply. What test was there, to start with, to decide who were the real Nazis?[1]

Membership of the party was a poor criterion. Many had joined out of conformism, fear or necessity; a lot of petty officials, for example, had joined simply because membership was a condition of employment. Such people were often guilty of no more than weakness and certainly posed no threat for the future. Even the ranks of the Waffen-SS included thousands of men who had simply been conscripted into its fighting divisions in the last two years of the war.

On the other hand, there were many who had not joined the party, but had collaborated in, and profited from, some of its worst excesses.

Among the professional middle class in particular there had been an eager and subservient acceptance and implementation of Nazi policies which made many of its members unworthy of holding any position of power or respect. If denazification was to achieve anything, it had to identify and remove such men. This involved not only the dissolution of the armed forces and the arrest of their senior officers on security grounds, but the positive vetting of the teaching, legal and medical professions, removal of most of the officers in the police forces, removal and pauperization of those bankers and industrialists who had owned and managed the economy to serve the needs of the Third Reich, and the screening of the decision-makers in the civil service. As parts of the German establishments, all those people had not only served but actually supported the Nazis; often, as will be seen, by committing some of the worst atrocities.

Middle-class Establishment professionals are invariably harder to convict as murderers than their working-class equivalents. It gets even harder when they are several steps removed from the actual commission of the act of killing. The Judge who ordered the execution of a Pole for touching an Aryan girl; the doctor who knowingly sent a patient to a euthanasia institution; the civil servant who organized the arrest and transport of innocent people to the extermination camps from his desk in Berlin; or the industrialist who employed slave labour; all were equally guilty of murder. Yet as *'Schreibtischtäter'* those who gave the orders for murder while sitting behind desks, they were usually sufficiently removed from the final act to plead ignorance and innocence.

Only a few of those who had fervently supported the Nazis politically had committed a criminal act. Schoolteachers who taught the glories of Nazism were not criminals. Nor were the university professors who threw whole libraries onto bonfires, arranged for the dismissal of liberal colleagues and invented courses on racial purity. It would be hard to prove that the legal profession, ninety per cent of whom joined a Nazi party affiliate and who for twelve years acted out a parody of justice, were criminal. Equally the clergy, who with few exceptions, taught their flock to obey the Nazi state without fear of conscience, were not breaking any written law.

Germany was ruled by Hitler without a constitution. It had been suspended. The civil servants, however, claimed that, as loyal servants of the state, they were just applying the new laws. The fact that these were in fact just decrees, enforceable through fear and terror, did not make the civil servants actual criminals, yet they had all broken moral laws which in the Western tradition are more important than man-made laws. They were all enemies of that liberal democracy which the Allies wistfully hoped could be built in Germany in the distant future.

In the American zone, at least, the machinery that would perform the task of winnowing the human chaff from a population of twenty-three million people had been designed. It was the brainchild of Franz Neumann, a Marxist working in the Central European section of the OSS in Washington. In 1943 Neumann analyzed power in Nazi Germany as being divided between the Nazis, the military, the industrialists and the higher civil servants. He suggested that only the complete and mandatory removal from public and private office of those groups would eradicate Nazi influence.

On the basis of his analysis, members of the American OSS detachment in London attached to SHAEF formulated the first denazification directives.[2] Every adult in the American zone would complete a 131-point questionnaire, or *Fragebogen*, which was designed to elicit full details of their career under the Third Reich – dates of joining the party or affiliated organizations, dates of promotion and increases in pay during the period, and any changes in social and economic status.

With the *Fragebogen* in their hands, American Public Safety Branch officers would in theory be easily able to identify those who had supported, or benefited from, the Nazi regime and who should be removed from positions of influence or power or denied re-employment. Any appeals against such decisions would be heard by tribunals staffed by the occupation authorities.

When it was asked what would prevent the answers to the *Fragebogen* being falsified, it was suggested that the only way was to 'send a few hundred offenders to prison initially,' – as a result the majority would 'see the light'. The architects of the scheme believed that by making the submission of a *Fragebogen* a condition for obtaining food coupons, travel permits and, most importantly, work, they would make it impossible for anyone to avoid scrutiny. They failed to foresee that conditions in Germany in the aftermath of the surrender would be such as to make evasion all too easy. This was not a settled, law-abiding and orderly suburb in Virginia, but a country where disorder, corruption and confusion were commonplace; and of course, the people who found it easiest to avoid or delay the submission of the *Fragebogen* were those with money and influence. All too often they were the same people who, if they had not joined the party, had intimate and profitable relationships with the Nazi regime.

As a bureaucratic solution to a political problem, and one which took no account of the inevitable practical difficulties, it had little chance of success. Nonetheless, the British were persuaded to adopt a similar system, though they never backed it with either the faith or the energy which the Americans devoted to it. The British, unlike the Americans, had paused to consider the consequences of removing a large proportion of the administration of a modern state, even if only temporarily. Unlike Washington, Whitehall was not deeply immersed in an interdeparmental ideological battle provoked by Morgenthau's protest about the leniency of Germany's postwar treatment. The British were convinced that there were few anti-Nazis to fill the void. The records do not suggest that Washington gave even passing consideration to the problem. The odds against success were lengthened to near-infinity by entrusting the programme to untrained, politically uneducated and unenthusiastic soldiers. Moreover, there were never more than five hundred of the Public Safety officers, whose responsibility it was to oversee the programme, in either the US or the British zones.

Neumann's scheme was allegedly put into effect on the capture of Aachen in October 1944. It was the failure to denazify that city which prompted more draconian directives to be issued and applied as more German towns were captured during 1945. By 25 August 1945 Robert Murphy was reporting to the State Department: 'The immediate objectives of denazification have been achieved.'[3] It is unlikely that even Murphy could have believed that. All the reports on denazification in his file were contradictory, as was his own report. In consecutive paragraphs he wrote that 31,200 Nazis had been removed, and, later, that 'approximately seventy thousand' had been removed. In truth, three months into the peace, the denazification programme had proved to be an embarrassing disaster. Indeed, so concerned were Clay and Eisenhower at the failure, that two days later, on 27 August, they attended, along with Murphy, a special one-day conference in Frankfurt for all senior Military Government officers to impress on them the importance of denazification.[4] All the reasons for the failure were in the speeches. Colonel Keith Wilson, head of Public Safety, gave details of his wildly impractical scheme to fingerprint no less than three million Nazis in the American zone; Murphy warned everyone not to trust even anti-Nazis because they might just be rejected applicants for party membership; whilst Lieutenant Elmer Plischke, a Public Safety officer, reported that the worst offender was the American army, which was itself employing a lot of people who had been dismissed from their normal employment for being party members. Wilson underlined that discovery by revealing that Nazis were being employed by Americans in return for bribes, women, hunting facilities and black market goods.[5]

Not all the high-ranking officers in the occupation governments would have been dismayed by this evidence of failure. Not only had many of them come to like the Germans with whom their jobs brought them into contact, and to feel that it was unnecessarily vengeful to dig up their recent pasts, but they had a vested interest in encouraging respect rather than contempt for their conquered foe. Ritchie Calder explained in his report to the Foreign Office in July 1945: 'The War Lords are running Germany as a military and not a political operation, and are motivated by a soldier's natural characteristics – tough to his adversary in battle, he must be magnanimous in victory. The measure of the success of a General in battle is the greatness of the adversary he defeated. Therefore the Germans must be a great people because the Generals' achievement is that they defeated them.'[6] By August, that feeling was widespread amongst both American and British soldiers and Military Government officers. When faced in a dispute involving conflicting stories from a protesting German citizen and a group of liberated slave workers, desperate to reassert their dignity and wreak vengeance, Allied soldiers increasingly forgot what had brought them to Germany and sided with the Germans to 'slap down the DP irritant.'[7]

One soldier who did not share this feeling was Lucius Clay. A fair, honest and hard-working man, he had a genuine loathing of Nazism and all it stood for. Unlike many of his colleagues, he never forgot why the American army was in Germany and he never lost his sense of outrage at what had happened there. Clay believed in denazification, but all his training and experience had predisposed him to favour administrative rather than political solutions. Confronted with the evidence for the widespread failure of the programme to denazify his zone by the use of bureaucratic means, his instinct was to press on regardless. Unable and unwilling to alter policies when faced with unpleasant realities, he believed that the task could be accomplished by directives from the centre, and was utterly determined that it should be accomplished. These two convictions were to involve him in difficulties which a more subtly attuned and politically experienced man would, perhaps, have avoided.

Twelve days before the Frankfurt conference Clay had visited Augsburg. Over lunch, he had heard that the butcher who had supplied the meat was a former Nazi and still gave party members preference for the supplies available. Clay exploded, and hysterically committed the US administration to measures which would prove to the Germans that he was tough on denazification. The American Military Government issued yet another denazification directive. Law No. 8, published on 26 September, ordered the dismissal of any party member or sympathizer from all employment other than as a common labourer. Ironically the butcher in Augsburg was not affected. He was self-employed, and Law 8 only applied to employees. Thirty thousand others were arrested and interned without a hearing, unable to communicate with anyone outside the internment camps.[8]

Law 8 was not only draconian, but also unenforceable. Moreover, the Americans wanted all four occupying powers to apply it. When Con O'Neil read the directive in London he wrote: 'As an example of systematic and meticulous imbecility, it would be hard to beat. . .I hope that we shall be under no illusion that a policy of this kind is the sheerest madness.'[9] Nevertheless the British agreed, to please the Americans, and to avoid giving the Russians ammunition to show that the British were weak on denazification. But it was never enforced in the British zone. Politically, Law 8 was an appalling mistake. Colonel B.B. McMahon, the chief of American Information, summed it up to a British official a year later: 'We have done a good job of kicking in the teeth of everyone who could have been helpful.'[10] The indiscriminate punishment of those that had joined the party to keep their jobs, or because they were too weak to resist social pressures, made enemies out of potential allies. But it did more: it gave both respectability and massive support to the opponents of denazification, who were almost invariably Nazis themselves, and to those that opposed the prosecution of war criminals.

Leading the campaign, and lending it a cloak of sanctimoniousness, was Bishop Wurm, the Evangelical bishop of Württemberg. For a period, towards the end of the Third Reich, Wurm had openly criticized the Nazi regime. His conversion was late and relatively ineffectual, but he repeatedly exploited it to justify his criticisms of the Allies' denazification policies by drawing parallels between the arbitrary terror of the Third Reich and the indiscriminate removal of what he called 'persecuted of Nazi Party members and their sympathizers'.[11]

In the political vacuum immediately after Germany's defeat, the Church assumed enormous importance. No other German body possessed its organization and self-confidence. Regardless of the response of the Allies to the Church's increasing protests, the Church quickly won more influence over the German people than the Allies themselves. The arbitrariness of Law 8, Wurm protested to Clay on 3 October, was nothing less than 'a question of life and death of the German people'.[12] The Church, he claimed, had a right to intervene and 'speak in the interests of truth and justice', because only the Church understood 'what corresponds with the will and commandment of God'. It was a questionable proposition in view of the Church's comparative silence since 1933.

The immediate pretext for Wurm's protest was what he alleged to be the unjust dismissal of thousands of 'innocent' civil servants who had been members of the party. Without pay, they were now destitute. German civil servants, Wurm claimed, were unpolitical and incorruptible, always anxious only to fulfil their duty. Their dismissal was contrary to all the German constitutions which guaranteed their security of employment. A distinction should be made between leaders and the led. The latter, the vast majority, were just nominal members, unfortunate victims of 'extremely skilful propaganda', who had joined the party thinking first about public welfare rather than furthering party ends. They did not accept or identify themselves with the regime. Their dismissal, when they had 'already suffered so much', was an injustice because, while the 'civil service as a whole is co-responsible for the grievous offence our nation committed by not revolting against the outrages of the Nazi terror,' they had been intimidated by the fear of loss of income and position, and even worse, by terror. Germany, he claimed, could not be rebuilt by excluding the help of 'the very numerous excellent men among the party members who belonged to the party merely in name. . . A true peace can only be restored on the basis of justice.'

There was much truth, and some justice, in Wurm's criticism. But, it must be added, the bishop seemed to have been given to belated conversions. Hitler, recognizing that the civil service could sabotage his government, had promulgated a Law for the Restoration of the Professional Civil Service on 7 April 1933, which completely removed the very security of tenure which Wurm alleged was traditional in Germany. In Prussia 12.5 per cent of civil servants were rapidly eliminated for political or racial reasons and 15.5 per cent for lack of qualifications. Most of the victims were either Jews or socialists. Neither the Protestant nor the Catholic Church protested.[13]

Moreover, Wurm had admitted to Clay that many clergy, including himself, had joined the Nazis and supported Hitler in good faith, believing that 'it might produce a religious revival.' Wurm even referred Clay to *Mein Kampf*, where Hitler had written that National Socialism and Christianity could work together. He justified his belief, and that of many others, in Hitler by referring to the Concordat with the Vatican and the agreements signed between Hitler and Britain, which for the Germans, he claimed, were more than acts of recognition, showed actual approval of the regime. Even if Clay accepted those arguments, and his replies to Wurm prove that he did not, it was the Church's attitude to the Nazis in its own ranks which cast doubt upon Wurm's motives for the protest.

Protestant clergymen had joined not only the Brown Shirts, but even the SS. The American Religious Affairs Division listed 351 active Nazi clergymen in the American zone alone. While former Nazi Catholic priests were hidden in monasteries, the Protestant Church resolutely refused to remove its Nazi priests from their parishes. Even by October 1946, only three of the 351 had been dismissed.[14] Those who joined were defended by their bishops because 'he joined the party from the noblest of motives;' 'he did not realize the true objectives of the party'; or 'he stayed in the party to fight the party from within.'[15]

The most important of Wurm's demands was that Clay should appoint two Germans who had not been members of the party onto a panel which would investigate each individual case. Then, and later, the Churches were to allege that denazification could only have worked if the Germans had been allowed to denazify themselves. Wurm's demand and arguments are questionable. There was no evidence whatsoever that the Germans were at all committed to self-cleansing. Everything pointed to the opposite being the truth.[16] Clay rejected Wurm's suggestions and arguments outright.

Yet, by Christmas 1945, the Americans' denazification offices were submerged by no less than thirteen million *Fragebogen*. Over eighty thousand civilians were imprisoned in the American zone and fifty thousand in the British zone. Demobilization had sharply reduced the numbers of personnel who could vet the *Fragebogen* and man the tribunals. There seemed to be little alternative: if denazification was to depend on questionnaires and tribunals, then only the Germans could supply the manpower to manage the programme. As the politicians and Church had demanded the responsibility for self-cleansing, there was, it seemed, little to be lost by handing the whole problem over to them.

Negotiations with representatives of the four German *Länder*, or regions, which made up the US zone started in January. The American negotiators had been given a detailed programme to sell to the Germans. Page one established its purpose:

> Political and economic authority must be shifted from those who dominated German society under the Nazis to others who will establish a free and peaceful society. Denazification is a means for assisting in this shift of authority from those who usurped and abused it. Every person who exercised leadership and power in support of the Nazi regime should be deprived of influence or power, whether or not he was formally affiliated with the Party or any other Nazi organization.'[17]

The removal of the 'fascistic and militaristic elements' was a guarantee, said the brief, of a peaceful Germany. Within days David Robinson, one of the American negotiators, reported to Clay that the Germans' arguments and counterproposals 'revealed a complete absence of any intention to apply a vigorous programme of denazification to Germany.'[18] Clay was surprised by the report. Only four weeks earlier, Robinson himself had been urging him to hand denazification over to the Germans.[19]

The Americans proposed that thirteen million adults in the zone should complete new questionnaires, *Meldebogen*, and that each questionnaire be vetted by specially appointed officials of newly created Ministries for Political Liberation. Each individual would be categorized in one of five groups, ranging from war criminal to non-Nazi, on the basis of his own answers.[20] Any that fell into one of 136 categories of militarists, Nazis, profiteers and sympathizers was to be mandatorily removed if he was working in the public service. Everyone would be liable to punishments of imprisonment, fines and confiscation of property for having committed crimes against people and property, or having used party membership or contributions to the party to profit by aryanization, spoliation, denunciation, or just promotion. Serious cases and appeals against the initial categorization were to be heard by community denazification tribunals staffed by local 'democrats and long-standing anti-Nazis'.

The most important disagreement between the Americans, led by Charles Fahy, and the four minister presidents was the arbitrary American decision to discriminate only against those who joined the party before 1937. Those that joined afterwards were presumed not to be opportunists and committed followers. The date had been chosen because after the 1933 election the party, deluged with applications for membership, had temporarily suspended further enrolment. That suspension ended in 1937 and American experts decided that the civil servants, teachers and others who joined in 1937 and after had done so out of genuine fear of otherwise losing their jobs, often because of straightforward blackmail. The Americans argued that it was those who joined in or before 1933 who were the real Nazis. The Germans disagreed. They claimed that the early members were 'the dumb idealists', and usually decent. Those who joined before 1933, even more so. It was just those that joined in 1937 who were the opportunists, they argued, because by that time it was obvious that the Nazis were criminal; while those that joined after 1939 could have been in no doubt about the real intentions of National Socialism.[21]

Robinson was ordered by Clay, from the outset, to refuse to change any of the details of the American plan. Clay minuted on 2 February: 'I don't understand all this apprehension about a programme which has still not been inaugurated. . . If the Germans don't do the job, we will.'[22] Either Clay was being naive or playing tough. Probably both. It is hard to believe that either he or his advisers had any realistic hopes of the Germans finding the means or the will to properly implement an American plan which they opposed.

A secret Public Safety Branch report issued in January estimated that less than one per cent of the German population were committed anti-Nazis.[23] Robinson reported in the same month that; 'German political leaders admit that a "free" election held in Germany today would bring a modified Nazi government to power.'[24]

Clay's adviser on denazification, Dr Walter Dorn, was already concerned about where the members of the tribunals were going to be found. Dr Anton Pfeiffer, the new Bavarian minister for liberation, assured Dorn and Robinson that he only expected thirty thousand appeals at most.[25] Both recognized it as a two-edged guarantee. Either the denazification panels would put Nazis in such a very low category that no one would feel the need to appeal, or alternatively the German panels would just not function at all, so there would again be no reason for anyone to appeal.

With a few amendments to his plan, and after long and frequently acrimonious negotiations, Clay handed denazification over to the Germans on 5 March, under the 'Law for Liberation from National Socialism and Militarism'.

Four months later, the inevitable was confirmed. Reporting to Clay after touring the zone, Dorn described how the whole programme was plagued by problems despite the attempts of a handful of dedicated enthusiasts in the Ministries of Liberation:

> Weariness and lethargy have seized wide sections of the democratic public at large. There is an all-but-overwhelming tendency to forget the unpleasant past which sometimes solidifies into a conspiracy of silence. Even in centres where anti-Nazi groups do exist, one hears it said that Major Offenders should be hanged and all others left undisturbed. In some Landkreise where the will to denazify is lacking, the chairman of the tribunal is regarded as a leper and the public prosecutor is himself the accused.[26]

Nor, according to Dorn, were German politicians supporting the programme. Kurt Schumacher, the leader of the Social Democrats, rarely spoke about it, while conservative politicians publicly criticized denazification as an instrument of the Communists. Only the small Communist party itself saw anything to be gained by supporting the programme; and that was, for the majority, reason enough for condemning it.

As one of the architects of the scheme, Dorn cautioned Clay against undue pessimism by arguing that it was a valuable exercise in democracy for the Germans and that improvements would follow 'as soon as the work of the tribunals reaches its full momentum'. But Dorn was glossing over the reports coming in from the Public Safety Branch special agents who were inspecting the tribunals. At best, their reports showed that, in unheated and sparsely furnished rooms, often without transport and vital records, the handful of staff was failing to cope. At worst, the inspectors reported that the panels were systematically ignoring the law, accepting bribes and whitewashing defendants.

In fact, the programme could never reach 'full momentum', because it collapsed. In Bavaria, instead of thirty thousand appeals, the tribunals were overwhelmed with what finally amounted to no fewer than four hundred thousand appeals. With so little German political support, derided by the large number of Nazis who had a vested interest in destroying the programme, and debilitated by the bleak conditions in postwar Germany, it was sheer madness to expect to find ten thousand tribunal staff with the intellect, courage and stamina to investigate a minimum of one million five hundred thousand offenders. More so, because the system was based on alien laws, imposed by the victor.

Bishop Wurm and other German leaders had pleaded that the Germans should be allowed to cleanse their own society, albeit using their own system. The inspectors saw what that might have meant in practice. Special Agent Charles Hick could not believe what he discovered when he went to the pretty village of Marktheidenfeld, near Aschaffenburg, in early September. He had heard rumours that the local denazification panel was dubbed by locals 'the Nazi Welfare Organization'. He reported to Dorn that it was worse than he had imagined.[27] The case against the wartime mayor, Wilhelm Siebenlist, had collapsed because, while there were fourteen witnesses prepared to speak in his favour, ten of whom were his employees, only one witness appeared for the prosecution, and he was suspected of being a party member. Siebenlist, described by Hick as 'one of the worst Nazis' in the area, had made a fortune through his office and long party membership and should have been convicted as a profiteer. Yet he was allowed to keep his fortune and released on the panel's findings that 'no activity in the National Socialist sense could be proven.'

Hick discovered that the failure to get adequate proof was probably the fault of the prosecutor, Horst Schütze, who had been jailed three times in three months for embezzlement, once for falsifying his *Fragebogen*, and was himself a former member of the Nazi party. If it was not Schütze's fault, then Hick thought it might have been the fault of Heinrich Müller, the second prosecutor. Müller had also been a party member and had nine convictions for fraud. Confusingly, the credit for Siebenlist's acquittal had been publicly claimed by Julius Listmann, the panel's investigator. He gave Hick a sworn statement that he had not questioned Siebenlist properly, and then drove away in a car given to him by a grateful Siebenlist.

The Siebenlist case, Hick reported, was not exceptional. 'The panel is inefficient, incompetent, laughable and corrupt.' Hick blamed the local Catholic Church for encouraging abuse. Local priests had made it a sin to give damaging testimony while presenting themselves as witnesses for nearly every accused, testifying that they were good churchgoers and not active Nazis. These testimonies soon became known as a '*Persilschein*' – a certificate pledging that the accused was 'whiter than white'. Brown stains were removed. Depressingly, the wealthy men in the area had all produced at least one concentration camp victim, or even a Jew, to testify in their defence. Not one wealthy man had yet been deprived of his fortune, although many of them had become rich by the benefits of aryanization or by buying the business or home of someone who was racially or politically prosecuted for a ridiculously low price.

Hick's was by no means the only report to Dorn to confirm that the Germans had no intention of denazifying themselves. Agent Wallach reported from Hoffheim that the prosecutor refused to appeal when decisions were clearly wrong and that the tribunal in Gerolzhofen – 'the best tribunal so far' – was letting the 'Nazi big shots get off scot-free'.[28] In the districts of Unterfranken and Mittelfranken, witnesses refused to testify or changed their evidence in the courtroom.[29] In Dingolfing, the brewery owner, Hans Glas, a former member of the SS with an annual income of half a million marks, was fined just two thousand marks.[30] In the same tribunal, Xavier Lang, an 'outstanding Nazi', the owner of twenty-six hotels, fifteen of which he bought after the Nazis came to power, and with an annual income of seven hundred thousand marks, was also fined just two thousand marks for profiteering and support for the Nazis.

In Uffenheim, the anti-Nazi Landrat (the district commissioner responsible for government) was replaced by a former member of the SA, who then stopped recruiting and appointing members to the tribunal.[31] Uffenheim's local priest warned his parishioners not to speak to the prosecutor, a Jew, who had just returned from Auschwitz. The priest in Steinach went one stage further. He convinced the 'practically illiterate panel', that even the most fervent Nazis were 'mere followers' and they were then put in the lowest categories and not punished. The priest himself had joined the party in 1925 and had obtained no less than forty golden party badges for his devoted congregation.

Even Clay had to be told about the agent's report from Bremen, where officials had sold the prosecution's evidence to the defence, while the prosecutor, Mark Oberdorf, 'defends instead of prosecuting.'[32] The tribunal in Riedenburg was at least original in its deception. It 'officially' recognized a local resistance movement composed entirely of the town's leading Nazis, whose sole act of resistance was to have surrendered Riedenburg to the American army without a fight. Evidence proving the existence of the movement and its 'heroic' achievements was submitted by the movement itself and by the chairman of the town's new socialist party, a man with convictions for fraud.[33]

Even those tribunal staff and prosecutors who were determined to enforce the law, but were intimidated, and even attacked, by the Nazis, often got little encouragement from the American inspectorate. Many of the inspectors, according to US Adjutant-General, Lieutenant-Colonel G.H. Garde, were indifferent, sceptical and pessimistic about any chance of success.[34] Even the most fervent denazifiers began to fear for their livelihoods after the hearings were over.

If the failures in the American zone were caused by an over-ambitious and ill-considered programme, at least the intentions of its supporters were good, if naive. The British had never suffered from the sort of hubris that persuaded the Americans that it would be possible to completely purge the political and social life of the country. Instead, the British settled for a rather half-hearted realism, disguised behind a mask of idealism which they were forced to don by the example of the Americans and the criticisms of the Russians.

The real aims and intentions of the denazification programme in the British zone were described accurately in early 1947 by General Brian Robertson, the deputy military governor. Commenting upon recent German criticism of the failure of the British denazification programme in the zone, Robertson explained his views of British policy in Germany to the Foreign Office.

> Our interest in denazification is quite different from that of the Germans. Apart from war criminals, we are chiefly concerned with security, i.e. we wish the German administration and German industry to be staffed with people who are not dangerous to the aims of the occupation. For the Germans however, the question is largely one of justice and retribution upon individuals who have oppressed and persecuted their fellow citizens and brought disaster upon their country. Criticism of our denazification measures is scarcely ever now based on security considerations but emanates from political opponents of the Nazis, i.e. the left-wing parties both in Germany and outside it.[35]

A handful of left-wing officers on the staff of the Control Commission hoped for something more ambitious than the policy Robertson outlined; but most of those concerned, in London and Germany, simply wished to dispose of the whole business as quickly and painlessly as possible. In January 1946 the British set themselves a target of completing the whole programme within nine months. They had, from the start, rejected the idea of handing the task over to the Germans.

Strang, the political adviser to the military governor (at first Montgomery and later Air Marshal Sholto Douglas) and Christopher 'Kit' Steele, the head of the Political Division of the Control Commission, together with other civil servants in the zone, reported that: 'it is difficult to find Germans with the necessary anti-Nazi enthusiasm.'[36] Their finding was hardly surprising when it is understood that they also felt that: 'National Socialism did represent the German outlook and it is very doubtful if the Germans have it in them to change it.' Frank and realistic such feelings may have been, but they also begged a large question. For the majority of civil servants resolutely refused to consider employing those categories of Germans who might have found it in themselves to change their country's outlook.

The Labour government in London had ordered the employment of socialists and trade unionists on the denazification panels; in a report to Bevin, the Labour Foreign Secretary, in October 1945, Strang had written: 'Among the more intelligent sections of the community, however, there are many who wish to lend a hand. The Communists lead the field in promoting anti-fascist organizations which prepared lists of bad Nazis. Local advisory committees have been set up in some areas to deal with denazification, while in others, local officials pursue the matter. . . Much information comes from informants who are usually enthusiastic anti-Nazis such as Jews, Communists, Social Democrats or ex KL [concentration camp] inmates.'[37] Curiously Strang had prefaced this apparently encouraging description by telling the Foreign Secretary that 'all sources are unanimous that the majority of Germans do not regard this responsibility for denazifying the community as their own although it is clear that all are immensely interested in the subject. . . Their attitude is therefore, "Leave it to the British".'

The truth was that the officials distrusted the minority that was interested in playing a part in the process of denazification. They were likely to be socialists, if not communists. Since they were also the very people who had been persecuted by the Nazis, an obvious and often-quoted rationale for ignoring them was to hand: they would be liable to bias and might use the opportunity to victimize their opponents.

Strang's own bias was unmistakeable and undoubtedly set the tone for the whole Zone. In his July 1945 report to the Foreign Secretary he wrote that Dr Petersen, newly appointed by the British as Mayor of Hamburg, with whom he had recently had dinner, '. . . is a member of an old Hamburg family which has produced more than one burgomaster (sic) in the past. He talks excellent English, is a man of culture, widely travelled and possessed of a strong sense of public duty. If there are "good" Germans, this should be one of them. He is, and has been, sincerely anti-Nazi. Though he has much support in the city, he is thought by some to be reactionary.'[38]

The opposition to Petersen was in fact so strong, that the embarrassed British were soon forced to replace him with someone who had not willingly cooperated with the Nazis. In the same report Strang had voiced his reservations about using the 'Antifa', the German anti-fascist organizations, in the denazification committees. His reluctance was questioned in London by Oliver Harvey: 'There seems to be a demand for a clearer and swifter denazification among the Germans than our present procedure is carrying out. I cannot quite understand the doubts about "Antifa". The anti-Nazi movement should be fostered and encouraged surely more vigorously than this support seems to indicate.' In his letter to Strang, Harvey directed the British Political Advisor that, 'the purge of Nazis from office and posts of influence will be vigorously pursued. There should be no room for doubt as to our policy in this direction or as to our aim to encourage all genuinely anti-totalitarian movements. Whether "Antifa" qualified under this heading I am of course unable to judge.' Strang and most of his officials were in no doubt that the 'Antifa' members were unsuitable. Deliberately, and against instructions from London, the German contribution to the country's denazification was limited.[39]

But by April 1946 it was becoming obvious that with its limited resources, the Control Commission could not possibly meet its deadline six months hence. A preliminary report by Brigadier Heyman to the Control Commission and for the minister recommended that the programme be handed over to the Germans.[40]

After touring the Zone in May, 'Kit' Steele directed all regional commissioners to speed up the programme. He complained that Germans were not being allowed enough responsibility and asked the commissioners to only oversee the German panels rather than continue British supervision of individual cases. Typical of the replies was that from Air Vice Marshal H.V. Champion de Crespigny, the regional commissioner for Schleswig-Holstein. He wrote:

Admittedly all this is slow, but the only alternative would be to give the Germans complete executive authority for denazification. While greater speed would undoubtedly be obtained, I personally would view the results with grave misgivings, unless you are prepared to accept the consequences. Experience has shown that Panels, Committees and Review Boards are not entirely objective in their findings. They are apt either to 'whitewash' cases which would not pass, or, even worse, to allow personal feelings to influence their decisions and to raise the very grave suspicion of victimization.[41]

All four regional commissioners shared de Crespigny's views. They either naively believed that denazification could be an impartial judicial process or they realized that it was a political process and were unwilling to entrust it to the Left. In either case, they were influenced by what they considered to be the failure of German-managed denazification in the American zone, although they had no first-hand information and only relied for information on prejudiced German reports.[42] Faced with united resistance to handing over denazification to the Germans, both the Control and Foreign Offices believed that they were left with only one solution, to wind up the whole programme.

Control Office officials prepared a paper for the Cabinet at the end of 1946 which stated: 'We can, without being complacent, claim to have achieved substantial and satisfactory results. Working through the German advisory panels and committees we have examined some one million two hundred thousand cases: some one hundred and fifty thousand Nazis have been removed from office and a further eighty-six thousand have been refused employment in positions of responsibility.'[43] It is now impossible to check the accuracy of those statistics, because the records have either been destroyed or are not available. But, considering what was to follow a few weeks later, it is more than likely that they were a product of political requirements rather than reality.

Cabinet approval of the Control Office's recommendations seems to have been a foregone conclusion. Commenting in the previous October on the minutes of a meeting in Germany of the Standing Committee on Denazification, N. Reddaway, an official in the Foreign Office's Central Department wrote: 'This paper illustrates the dreary incompetence of denazification. . . Should we not agree on a date for ending the denazification process?'[44] Bernard Burrows, a more senior official replied: 'I think it is intended to do this.'

Before the recommendation was presented to the Cabinet's Overseas Reconstruction Committee, Gilmour Jenkins in the Control Office cabled Robertson on 3 January 1947 telling him, explicitly, what London wanted:

We have been considering with some concern the question of denazification with particular reference to the need for assessment and proximate termination of our programme. Public opinion here is likely to become increasingly insistent on bringing this to an end. We know that you have this problem very much in mind.

The target to be aimed at is to terminate the main process of denazification (as opposed to categorization) by the spring. We should like to be able then to announce the end of the period of destruction (although some military disarmament remains to be carried out) and the inauguration of a policy of reconstruction. There is a further point that we should like to be able to report to the CFM [the Council of Foreign Ministers] in March that denazification in the British Zone is complete or on the point of completion.[45]

Tempted by the plan, Robertson nevertheless replied two months later that, 'as much as we should like to', it was politically too dangerous because: 'it would expose us to damaging attacks whenever (as is bound to happen) new cases come to light.'[46]

The insurmountable political problem was the inevitable and embarrassing criticism from the Soviets. Moscow Radio and Russian newspapers consistently quoted examples of important Nazis being employed by the Control Commission or remaining in their positions with British connivance. Broadcasts monitored in London were often followed by cables to Germany asking for an immediate investigation so that Russian charges could be answered. Regularly, the allegations were embarrassingly accurate. Occasionally, a former Nazi was removed. More often, the British officers in Germany ignored London's inquiries and even directions.

The one British attempt to retaliate was a fiasco. Foreign Office researchers and British intelligence tried to discover former Nazis employed in the Russian zone whom Bevin could quote to embarrass the Russians at the London Council of Foreign Ministers meeting in November 1947. They only discovered a few scientists and technicians, none of whom had any political or economic power. At one stage in the search, Ivor Pink became quite excited about the discovery of a former Siemens director, who had been dismissed by the British for killing a Jewish worker, being re-employed by the Russians. This case, he wrote to Dean, would be ideal for counterpropaganda against the Russians. His ardour rapidly dampened, however, when he discovered that the director had been planted by British intelligence in the Russian zone. When the Russians discovered his real identity, he was dismissed.[47]

The Russians consistently condemned the American and British denazification programme for being too broad.[48] Denazification, the Russians claimed, should only be applied to the Nazi policy-makers and officials. The nominal members, they insisted, should not be penalized. As in the case of war criminals, the Russians firmly distinguished between Nazis and Germans. Where former Nazi scientists, technicians and police officers were employed, the Russians claimed, and the evidence suggests, that though their expertise was exploited, they were carefully controlled by political agents to ensure that they made no adverse policy decisions. It was the Allied failure to remove Nazis from policy-making positions which provoked left-wing criticism.

Nevertheless, General Bishop still announced at a press conference on 12 February 1947 that 'a large part of the administration and industry in the British zone had been purged of Nazis.'[49] The truth of that statement was questionable, but politically the British wanted to reassure the Germans in their zone that they had little to fear. As Bishop himself said: 'The German people must be relieved of the feeling of continued anxiety caused by denazification which hangs over their heads like the "Sword of Damocles".' Yet there is evidence, from the few British reports which still exist, that where individual Military Government officers did allow German Social Democrats and Communists to run the denazification panels, as, for example, in Soest and part of Hamburg, they swiftly removed the incriminated Nazis.[50] There were similar examples in the American zone. But the removals were always followed by an outcry, charges of victimization and allegations that it was 'destructive' of any hopes for Germany's future.[51]

Inevitably, one must query whether it was not, in fact, the British who prevented more German Social Democrats and Communists denazifying their own communities.

In autumn 1946, Germany faced a severe food and fuel shortage. The previous daily allowance of one thousand five hundred calories per person had been cut by Clay in July to one thousand two hundred and fifty. In the British zone, it was even lower, one thousand and forty calories. Many Germans in the towns were only getting seven hundred calories. It was slow starvation. Foraging for food became the major preoccupation. Without food, the miners, despite extra rations, were unwilling and unable to produce more coal. The reichsmark had lost most of its value. The major currency was cigarettes. A carton was worth two thousand reichsmarks, or five hundred dollars at the prewar exchange rate, if anyone even wanted the money.

Trade was done by barter and everything, including women, was exchangeable for food and cigarettes. Most of industry was at a standstill, the destroyed bridges remained unrepaired, there were few trains, no telephones for private use, and an erratic postal service. Reconstruction of the devastated cities had hardly begun. Large numbers of city dwellers lived in damp, unheated cellars. Schools had reopened but there were few books, even less paper and little chance of getting any coal to keep the classrooms warm in winter. No less than a third of all babies born did not survive their first year.

Politically the situation was equally depressing. The British were unwilling, and increasingly unable, to subsidize their zone. Eighty million pounds had been spent in the first year and more was needed. The Labour Government had been forced to introduce bread rationing so that wheat could be diverted to Germany. Bread had not even been rationed in wartime. American support already amounted to three hundred million pounds and was increasing faster than British aid diminished. All the problems were exacerbated by a flood of seven million ethnic Germans who had been expelled from Poland and Czechoslovakia and had fled from the Russian zone.

Clay and Robertson blamed the economic crisis on Moscow. They alleged that the Russians had broken the Potsdam Agreement by which Germany was to be treated as an economic whole. West Germany's food had traditionally come from the East, but Russians were taking the food for themselves. Nevertheless the Russians were demanding that Britain and America fulfil their obligations and export coal to the eastern zone together with one billion dollars worth of industrial reparations. Four-power talks between the generals in Berlin or the foreign ministers in Paris and Moscow resulted in futile deadlock. Yet the West had no alternative strategy other than to try and make the wartime and Potsdam agreements with the Russians work. Talks were started to merge the British and American zones economically, but for Germany it was only a slight modification to what still seemed to be a continued commitment to a future that was coming to looking very like the one Morgenthau had planned.

By this time, the failure of denazification was an open secret, and not just in Germany. The Russians were quick to point out that the British and Americans were re-employing notorious Nazis, and as a result of publicity in the American papers, Clay was under pressure from Washington to reconsider the whole programme. As it became obvious to the Germans that, not only were the Allies failing to get the country moving, but the process of denazification was falling into disrepute in the eyes of the occupying powers themselves, they became bolder in their criticisms. German politicians started to vie with one another, each trying to outbid the other for support by more and more outspoken attacks on the governments of occupation. Among the first into the field were the Churches. They now perceived a new threat, the modest success that had been achieved had persuaded them that denazification was a tool of the revolutionary, atheistic Left.

At first they based their criticism on the iniquities of the system itself. Having been given the chance for self-cleansing, the Protestant and Catholic bishops complained that the broad-based system was still unjust. Writing to Clay, Wurm said it was impossible to educate the

German people to understand democracy and justice if they were to be prosecuted and convicted on the basis of a retrospective law outlawing their party membership, which had been legal at the time.[52] To solemnize their protest, the bishops passed a resolution that 'the Christian Church' found that the law 'could not be squared with the conscience of the German people,' and the Protestant leaders were therefore 'not in a position to tell the German people that this law and its procedures are in all respects consistent with divine justice and truth.' The Catholic Church echoed these sentiments and even ordered its members not to work in the tribunals. Although the very scale of the operation offered itself as a proper butt for criticism, the Churches never properly explained how they would plan Germany's denazification, nor did they explain how any programme could have operated without retrospective laws.

In truth, the main reason for their opposition was fear of the Left, and in particular Communism. For the Church, working and seeking its own spiritual and political regeneration, the threat of Russian Communism was too real for it not to be very conscious of the danger to its own survival. As the anti-denazification campaign strengthened, and East-West tension became more apparent, Wurm no longer hid the basis for his objections. In an interview with the *New York Times* on 28 July 1946, he complained that: 'extreme Left-wing elements are using the denazification laws to destroy Germany's leading classes of educated men. . . There is something Bolshevistic about it.'[53]

The best ally the critics had was the denazification programme itself. Instead of driving a wedge between the leaders of National Socialism and the led, it consolidated them. The millions of nominal Nazis, the public servants, who while awaiting their denazification hearings were unemployed and destitute, watched in their communities as the real Nazis, especially those that had made their fortune by allegiance to the Third Reich, were either acquitted or able to delay their hearing. The nominal members therefore became the real victims of the denazification programme and, not surprisingly, joined the real Nazis in campaigning against it.

Touring Germany, both Strang and Steele reported that the Nazis remained a privileged class, often overtly discriminating against those who were not party members. The failure to remove the Nazi shop-keepers and tradesmen, and the Nazi foremen in the factories, meant that it was still the same people who determined the facts of daily life. The chances of the non-Nazis taking over seemed very slight. With the exception of the Communists, reported Strang, the anti-Nazis had neither the interest nor the strength to challenge the old order. The best amongst them had been wiped out by the Nazis and 'we are left too often with docile, ineffective material . . . who after twelve years of obedience had no concept of taking part in challenging the very authority they have for so long obeyed.'[54]

The British were fast losing interest in denazification. Only the fear of Russian and American criticism prevented them winding up their programme. Clay, however, was not only determined to make the system succeed, but actually believed that, despite the reports, it *was* working. If it was just a question of being overwhelmed by numbers, he was quite prepared to propose amnesties to remove hundreds of thousands from the process. A June youth amnesty had removed all those born after 1919 on the grounds that they would have been incapable of resisting Nazi indoctrination. He was already considering another amnesty to remove the aged, poor and wounded. But he believed in the need for denazification and that the tribunal system was the only method by which it could be achieved.

Opposition to denazification, however, had by now become as strong among Americans on both sides of the Atlantic as among the Germans. Clay had to prove his determination to everyone. At a regular meeting with the Länderrat in Stuttgart of 5 November 1946 he contrived a controlled explosion against the Germans sitting opposite him. He told them: 'We are sorely disappointed with the results and we have yet to find the political will and determination to punish those who deserve to be punished. . . I do not see how you can demonstrate your ability for self-government nor your will for democracy if you are going to evade or shirk the first unpleasant task that falls upon you.'[55]

Newspaper reports at the time claimed that the German politicians were shocked by Clay's outburst. Colonel Orlando Wilson's report to Clay three weeks later suggests the opposite: 'In almost every case the criticism expressed in General Clay's speech was believed to have been directed against the neighbouring *Spruchkammern* [denazification tribunals] and the Ministry for Political Liberation, rather than against themselves. This attitude was found among the personnel of those *Spruchkammern* who had been doing a satisfactory job as well as those who had been responsible for continuous whitewash decisions.'[56]

Politicians also found the courage to take more direct action. American CIC agents planted inside the Ministries of Political Liberation were reporting that the ministers themselves were deliberately lying to the Americans. Anton Pfeiffer, according to the CIC agent in the Bavarian Ministry, was actually shocked by some of the severe sentences given by the few Communist-dominated tribunals and was reported to be deliberately snubbing tribunal members who complained of lack of support.[57] In Baden-Württemberg, the minister, Reinhold Maier, was reported to have deceived the American authorities about the number of tribunals

181

established. There were considerably fewer than he had reported.[58]

Clay's trust in Pfeiffer's and Maier's willingness to denazify Germany is hard to understand. Both had voted in the Reichstag in 1933 to grant Hitler his dictatorial powers. Maier had said at the time: 'We feel ourselves at one with the views expressed by Hitler here today.'[59] Yet Clay, despite his criticism, did believe the assurances the Germans gave him in private. It was a trust which US intelligence was not prepared to endorse. General Burress, the G2 Assistant Chief of Staff, sent General McNarney, the military governor and the commander of American Forces in Europe, a classified report soon after Clay's 5 November outburst, claiming that no less than ninety-four per cent of the Germans that American agencies had labelled as dangerous had been effectively acquitted by German tribunals.[60] He further claimed that the denazification programme was so plagued by corruption and contempt that: 'it constitutes a ready-made basis for the organization of subversive or resistance movements.' The programme, Burress claimed, was actually undermining the American occupation. Intelligence reports proved that the most efficient underground groups were not fighting the American occupation, but were aiding comrades to escape from internment camps, or arranging for their cases at tribunals to be 'fixed'. Very few escapees, Burress reported, were actually leaving Germany. Instead, the underground groups were giving them false papers and new identities so that they could submerge themselves into communities in Germany itself.

Clay rejected the whole report. He claimed that reports of corruption were mere 'hearsay', that the Germans supported the programme, as did German politicians, that the sentences were severe compared to other zones, and that it was too early to judge the programme's success. 'His criticism,' Clay said of Burress, 'is largely destructive . . . in attacking the *Spruchkammern*, [and he] is perhaps unwittingly taking the same viewpoint as the Nazis who would like to see the programme destroyed.'[61]

Why Clay was still so obstinate in December 1946 is hard to understand. Out of the 41,782 cases completed by the German denazification tribunals up to 30 September, only 116 Germans were held to be major offenders, while 29,582 were classed as just 'followers', which implied no punishment. To a considerable extent the tribunals were only hearing the unimportant cases, deliberately avoiding the unpleasantnes of confronting the powerful and rich in their localities. But even where the Establishment was categorized, the results were humiliating for the Americans. Of 8,182 people categorized by the American Public Safety Branch as mandatory removal cases, no less than 6,363, or 77.8 per cent, were placed in the lowest categories by the German panels. The Public Safety Branch had ordered most of the cases to be retried; but after 21

September American control was almost totally relinquished, confined to cumbersome indirect supervision which was hardly ever exercised.[62]

Clay had told John Hilldring at the Department of War in March 1946 that effective denazification needed an irreducible minimum of ten thousand American personnel and that even then he could not guarantee that Germany would remain denazified.[63] By December there were just under two hundred Public Safety officers involved in denazification work, and thirty-five per cent were specially seconded German nationals.[64]

The results of Clay's abdurate faith, in the face of all the evidence that denazification was floundering, and of the lack of faith which prevented the British from even trying to make it work in their zone, were in the end the same. Failure. The beneficiaries were those who had most to lose by the proclaimed policies of the Allies: as denazification fell into disrepute they became bolder, and their resistance to attempts to remove them became more audacious. The victims of the failure were those institutions upon which hopes of a democratic Germany would rest: the universities, the police, the law.

In education, the reports of field agents visiting universities and technical colleges stated that, without exception, the rectors were employing staff contrary to the denazification laws. Professors, former members of the party, who should have been removed were demoted to common labourers on the staff payroll (labourers were not subject to the denazification laws), but in fact allowed to teach.

In July 1946, Dr E. Hartshorne, an American universities officer, investigated reports that students and staff at Erlangen University in Bavaria were actively discussing the virtues of Nazism.[65] He discovered that professors were denigrating democracy, criticism of Jews continued, Auschwitz was said in one lecture to be a 'paradise' compared to plans for the future, while the few anti-Nazi lecturers were systematically interrupted. Amongst those staff that had been reinstated were members who had joined the SS and the SA and were leaders of the Hitler Youth.

The dean of the Theology faculty was, Hartshorne discovered, a fervent Nazi who in January 1933 had publicly given 'grateful affirmation' for Hitler's success. Another about to be reinstated was Dr Preuss, who in 1933 had personally organized the burning of the library's Marxist books and books by Jewish authors. Erlangen's rector had deliberately made the university a refuge for former Nazis. Many of those who had been dismissed at other universities were rehired by Erlangen. Among them was Dr Walter Resch, the former head surgeon in Munich

University's gynaecological clinic. Resch's former colleagues had demanded his dismissal because he had squalidly divorced his Jewish wife in 1933, despite the possibility, soon realised, that she would later be sent with their daughter to a concentration camp.

Hartshorne's investigations at Erlangen were brief. He was accidentally killed on his second trip to the university. But he had by then completed his investigations at Würzburg University.[66] The first reports by the American Education Branch stated that the unversity was properly denazified. Hartshorne discovered that no fewer than 112 of Würzburg's staff, including many professors, should have been dismissed. Not only was the medical faculty and library totally staffed by active Nazis, but in the liberal arts faculty one member of staff was still teaching 'Germanics', a science of mysticism which formed the basis of the 'Superior Race' theory. He had taught the same course during the Third Reich.

The centre of resistance, Hartshorne discovered, was the Ministry of Education in Munich. Dismissals had little effect. The universities simply refused to employ any of the unnumerable and well-qualified anti-Nazi teachers who applied for the vacant jobs from all around Germany. After reading the reports, Dorn commented to General Gailey, Clay's Chief of Staff: 'We are merely playing marbles with the tightest clique in German society next to the civil servants, i.e. the "Guild" of German university professors.'[67]

When Hartshorne asked the rector of Würzburg why he had failed to dismiss the Nazi teachers, he replied that they would only be instantly rehired in the British or French zones. The rector was probably right. Although the British regarded the rebuilding of the zone's education system as one of their few successes in postwar Germany, their refusal to follow Clay's example sabotaged whatever successes were gained in the American zone.

On 16 October 1945 the Control Commission's Standing Committee on Denazification reported to London that they were: 'Satisfied that nearly all the prominent Nazis have been removed from the German administration and that some progress is being made in removing the smaller fry. Denazification has been carried out particularly thoroughly in the legal and education branches of the administration . . . [and] particularly good progress has been made in purging the police . . . Financial institutions have also been purged.'[68]

There is little that can be said other than the report was an outright lie. Whether it was deliberate, or the result of false reports from the inspectors and divisions, is hard to say. Representatives of all the divisions sat on the committee which made the report. The financial institutions, as has been seen in Chapter 1, were deliberately staffed by Nazis and those that worked with the regime. In the other sections, renazification was not as deliberate, but happened because officials believed that denazification prevented Germany's rapid recovery.

The British Education Branch, on their own admission, had less idea of any positive policy than their counterparts in the other three zones. In their book, *The British in Germany*[69], the educationalists admit that they remained as neutral as possible, unwilling to impose themselves on the German educationalists. Textbooks were rewritten and Nazi headteachers removed, but otherwise the Branch unilaterally decided to stay well in the background, just giving advice. According to George Murray, one of the founders of the Education Branch in 1944: 'It would be the height of arrogance to assume that victory somehow gave us the moral right to impose our way of life. . . In any case how could one educate an already civilized nation that had produced some of the greatest geniuses and benefactors of mankind.'[70]

The results of such timidity became plain at Göttingen University. Geoffrey Bird, who clearly enjoyed his stay, said that appointing non-Nazi staff was difficult. He wrote in the same book that the flood of denunciations did not make it easier, but 'if the appointment of everyone who had technically been a member of a Nazi organization had been disallowed, there would have been few qualified teachers left.'[71] That, of course, may have been true; but he did not explain the results of failing to remove Nazi teachers. In November 1945, at the time Bird arrived, four hundred students at Göttingen stormed out of a lecture hall to demonstrate their disapproval of a lecturer's attack on Hitler.[72] Avoiding similar incidents was easy. Staff alleged to be merely nominal Nazis were allowed to remain. The students would then not complain.

But, above all, the book shows a remarkable naivety and susceptibility to the charm and explanations of former Nazis on the part of intelligent men. It is the simplicity one might expect from the third-raters and duds recruited during the war, but not from academics. Even Dr Robert Birley, the distinguished former headmaster of Eton, who worked at Göttingen, alleges that the only charge against the professors at Göttingen was, not that they were Nazis, but that they were prepared to accept a regime which they knew 'to be based on academic nonsense'.[73] In other words, because after the defeat they sat round a table with their British supervisors and agreed that in retrospect Nazi doctrines indeed scientifically unsound, Birley assumed that they were genuinely convinced non-Nazis. Hartshorne and Dorn, who actually investigated the records of university teachers in the American zone, found the opposite to be true. The Englishmen's admitted 'neutrality' precluded them from undertaking such investigations.

The direct result of that failure to denazify German universities were the student revolts in 1968. The West German postwar generation had until then been kept in ignorance, both in schools and universities, about most of the history of the Third Reich. Critical studies were practically non-existent. Inevitably those that had accepted and taught Nazi doctrines for twelve years were unable to deliver a critical assessment of their own failures. More importantly, by dominating the universities' governing boards, the former Nazis successfully prevented their critics challenging them.

The Standing Committee on Denazification's report of 16 October 1945 also stated that: 'particularly good progress had been made in purging the police.' The true situation inside the police force was probably worse than in the universities.

On 15 May 1946 Kurt Schumacher, the leader of the West German Social Democrats, arrived in Hanover in the British zone for a political meeting. He was immediately given a five-man police guard. That night, Schumacher, who had been cruelly crippled during the twelve years he had spent in concentration camps, heard the police guards talking amongst themselves and was shocked at what he heard. Investigations the following day revealed that four of the five were former SS men, one of them a former major, another a former captain. The local Public Safety Branch had reported to the Control Commission headquarters that the Hanover police had been 'cleared of Nazis'.[74]

Schumacher complained and the Control Commission immediately investigated the police force, focusing first on the town's police chief, Lieutenant-Colonel Adolf Schult. Schult had been chosen by the British to be Hanover's chief of police after being vetted twice. The Public Safety Branch officers knew that Schult had been a member of the Nazi party since May 1933 and as an SS officer, was the chief of personnel of the German police in Nazi-occupied Holland. His record was clearly documented in his SS file, which they possessed. Schult had been fired from the SS when his black marketeering operations became too notorious. That was also in his file.

Schult, with British approval, had selected the remainder of the Hanover police. His criterion for recruitment seems to have been faithful service to the Third Reich. His principal assistants were Major Bez and Captain Frenzel, both long-standing members of the party and former SS officers in Berlin. Other officers were former members of the *Befehlshaber der Ordnungspolizei*, the most politically trusted of the Nazi police. The new chief of the Hanover police school, Major Distelmeyer, a former SS man, had actually been arrested by the British security services as a danger to security, but had been released on Schult's intervention. All Distelmeyer's staff were former SS officers; all of them had joined the SS voluntarily and were not members by virtue of the automatic enrolments of 1943 and 1944.

The director of the Hanover School for Detectives, Pius Wagner, had distinguised himself as an original old campaigner in Hitler's *Sternweckerbräu* group. Although Wagner's record file showed that he had been a party member as early as 1923, a British officer had written a large red 'R', recommended for appointment, on his file. Later investigations showed that local trade unionists had actually complained to the British authorities in late 1945 about the appointments, but they had been ignored. In early 1946 there was another complaint from Hanover to the Control Commission in London that the British were tolerating the removal by Schult of the non-Nazis; it resulted in an order from London that the whole police force be re-vetted. That order had been also ignored.

According to Fritz Kneipe, a career policeman who recently retired as Hanover's chief of police, the Schult saga was not exceptional.[75] Kneipe was drafted into Hanover in May 1946 to clear up the mess. He claims that the Nazis had been deliberately recruited and protected by British officers who enjoyed hunting and socializing and were 'vague about police matters'. In Hanover, the police provided the British officers with their pleasures. Kneipe himself joined the Brunswick police in 1924 but resigned in 1933 rather than join the Nazi party, as demanded by his then police chief. Nothing happened to him other than a fall in his standard of living while he worked as a textile worker until 1945. Soon after the German defeat, he was recruited by the British to help rebuild the German police force. He claims there were two major problems: finding suitable recruits and rebuilding the police to a blueprint which had been drafted in London.

The architect of the postwar police force in the British zone was Gerald Halland. Appointed in 1944 as head of the British Public Safety Branch, he had been one of the Home Office's Inspectors of the Constabulary, and was one of Britain's most distinguished policemen. Traditionally, the German police had been politically partisan, subject to centralized government control, and easily employed for political ends. Instead of being the friendly neighbourhood Bobby, German police officers were normally recruited direct from the army, were heavily armed, and part of a force based on military tradition.

After two months study in London, Halland, who had no knowledge or experience of Germany, submitted detailed proposals which, he said, would make the new German police force 'the servants rather than the masters of the state'.[76] Completely modelled on the British system, control would be decentralized, promotion would be from within the ranks, and the independent forces would be protected from political control. The programme, he submitted, would need ten years to implement, and eight hundred British policemen should be recruited to supervise the operation.

Halland arrived in Germany in May 1945 with just twenty former policemen, few of whom could speak German. With the exception of the creation of a new police training school, his plan collapsed within days of his arrival. Today he blames the failure on his late realization that there was not even a remnant of the old German police force to build on, and on the fact that he had too little time.[77] He denies that it was a mistake to suggest the transplantation of a purely British institution to Germany and that he failed to adequately supervise his officers. But that was the conclusion the Foreign Office in London came to in autumn 1947 after another series of exposures and scandals.[78]

Schumacher's complaint in May 1946 had been just one of many from Germany that the Public Safety Branch was deliberately recruiting Nazis into the police force. In February 1946, Kriminalkommisar Schülter, stationed at Göttingen, wrote secretly to the Foreign Office alleging that senior officials were protecting the 'old gang'. He claimed that the Nazi officers 'were astonished to find that they were not dismissed after the German defeat, and some have become quite arrogant', especially as they had actually been promoted by the British.[79]

There were even secret complaints to the Control Office in London from British officers in Germany. Lieutenant Arthur wrote from Schleswig-Holstein in April 1946 that British officers were recruiting former SS officers who had served in Poland and Russia and whose names appeared as security suspects on CROWCASS lists.[80] There were also substantiated complaints from Hamburg, Kiel, Oldenburg and Westphalia.[81]

For eighteen months the Foreign Office avoided taking any action other than asking Halland to investigate the complaints. Franklin commented on 11 April 1946:

It is fairly clear that if denazification of the police is carried to extremes there would be no police force left. With conditions in our zone as they are, it would perhaps seem that the essential is to have a reliable police force and this cannot be achieved without some sense of security. The C-in-C's latest directive makes a point of stressing the need at some stage to terminate the process of denazification just for these reasons. . . At this stage we surely still need the police as an instrument of Military Government.[82]

The Control Office's policy of allowing former Nazis to run the police force was even concealed from the Cabinet's Overseas Reconstruction Committee which was responsible for coordinating German policy. On 28 June 1946, John Hynd, the minister responsible for the Control Office, presented a paper to the Committee entitled 'Progress in Germany'.[83] Under 'Denazification', he reported: 'the police force and civil administration have been thoroughly denazified.' Yet on that very same day, Wilberforce, one of the Control Office's top officials, wrote to Major-General P.M. Balfour, the military governor's deputy chief of staff: 'Subject: Denazification of the Hanover Police. . . The Chancellor feels, however, that all may still not be well . . . if the matter became publicly known, it might well cause a scandal.'[84]

The scandal broke in September 1947, when workers at Kiel demonstrated against British dismantling of an arms factory. There were strikes, and the police refused outright to go onto the streets to keep the peace. Foreign Office officials were both embarrassed and shocked. It proved that the British attempt to depoliticize the police had failed. Worse still, the new, British-trained German policemen appointed to the force, who were considered to be among the most efficient and independent, had been dismissed by German politicians in the town hall. Reviewing the failure, Richard Chaput de Saintonge, the Control Office's under-secretary and one of the few officials in London to possess some sensitive understanding of the problems commented: 'it is clear . . . that it was a mistake for us to have sought to transplant a British institution in Germany, contrary to their whole tradition.'[85] No further attempt was made to democratize the police force, although it did remain decentralized. Halland remains unrepentant and blames the failure of Whitehall to give him the time and manpower he needed for success.

Not surprisingly, Jack Rathbone, the deputy chief of the British Legal Division, is also unrepentant about his Division's failure to denazify the German legal profession in the British zone. The record shows that, after a minimal attempt, they were forced to give up the attempt or face what he believed to be the only alternative, chaos.

Rathbone, a solicitor, had been appointed to the post by chance. Walking along London's Pall Mall, the centre of gentleman's clubland in 1944, he met an old acquaintance who was nervously searching for Control Commission recruits. Rathbone, who at night was in charge of an anti-aircraft battery, eagerly seized the chance of more interesting work. The Legal Division chief was Nicholas Macaskie, an elderly and undistinguished former county court judge. Rathbone says that both arrived in Germany with a brief to get a legal system operational as soon as possible. Faced with the insurmountable problem that ninety per cent of the German legal profession had joined a Nazi party affiliated organization, the *Rechtswahrerbund*, he immediately proposed that, to avoid an imminent breakdown in the work of the courts, fifty per cent of those readmitted as lawyers and judges could be nominal Nazis.[86]

Lawyers hold a special position in Germany and its government. More than fifty per cent of German civil servants, and nearly as many politicians, are lawyers. Unlike Anglo-American legal training, the education of German lawyers instils respect for conservative, traditional 'legal correctness'. German lawyers are not taught to be either sceptical or tolerant of any innovation, nor that they are the protectors of the citizen's rights against the state. According to Ralf Dahrendorf: 'There is an authoritarian bent in the attitude of German lawyers. . . If the regime is democratic in tendency, they do not hesitate to adduce natural law to remind it of its lack of authority; if the authority of the state is absolute, lawyers become its obedient servants.'[87]

During the Weimar Republic, German judges openly criticized the constitution, ignored its provisions and deliberately mocked the law, giving judgements against the liberals and the Left in favour of the Right. In contrast, during the Hitler regime, German judges and lawyers unquestioningly obeyed the Nazis' phoney laws, claiming a duty of obedience to the state. Their obedience was more than theoretical. After the massacre of Hitler's opponents on the 'Night of the Long Knives' on 30 June 1934, magistrates and civil servants swore an oath of allegiance to their Führer after he had declared himself Germany's 'supreme judge'.[88] Thereafter German judges and lawyers became the protector of the state against the citizens.

In their defence today, German lawyers plead that they had no alternative but to obey the legality of the state, the '*Rechtsstaat*'. There was of course an alternative, but they chose not to use it. Instead, they gave the Hitler regime a veneer of legality. It is significant that the decisions of Nazi courts are still respected by German courts today. Not one of those lawyers who refused to join the *Rechtswahrerbund* was ever punished for that refusal. Not one judge was ever punished for refusing to join the party, or even for his outright resignation. On the contrary, those that did resign could sit out the regime with the benefit of a full pension.[89] Yet ninety per cent of the profession voluntarily aligned themselves with the regime.

They remained to hand out no less than forty-five thousand death sentences in twelve years, the overwhelming majority for non-capital offences.[90] Death sentences were given for sexual relations between Jews and Christians, for petty theft of towels or a pair of trousers, even black-out offences where the statutory sentence was only ten years imprisonment.[91]

In the Special People's Courts, the judges did not even pretend to administer justice. They just dispensed terror and judicial murder in the name of the Third Reich. In March 1942, Judge Oswald Rothaug 'heard' the case against a Jewish shoe wholesaler named Katzenberger, accused of sexual intercourse with an Aryan girl. The thirty-two-year-old girl herself denied that there had been intercourse and explained that she had known Katzenberger for the past ten years, had been employed by him and received only help from him. She admitted that he kissed her cheek, but it was an act of kindness. Rothaug had ordered Dr Armin Baur, the court-appointed doctor, to examine Katzenberger and produce evidence that there had been intercourse. Baur disputed that the sixty-eight-year-old man man was capable of intercourse. Rothaug cut his protest short, shouting: 'It is enough for me that the swine said that a German girl sat on his lap.' He ordered Katzenberger's execution. It was carried out. The girl was convicted of perjury.[92]

Judges like Rothaug and the screaming Roland Freisler in Berlin could be trusted to fix the right penalty. Other judges had to be told. It became quite common for defendants to hear the outcome of their case being discussed between the judge and the prosecutor even before the hearing had begun. Defence lawyers invariably felt it their duty to help the court rather than their client. Justice ceased to exist because the legal profession willingly cooperated with the Nazi state. Yet by 1948, with very few exceptions, German lawyers had been allowed to resume their normal work. Not one judge was ever to be prosecuted for judicial murder.

Referring to the denazification of the legal profession in its October 16th report, the Control Commission's Standing Committee on Denazification stated: 'denazification has been carried out particularly thoroughly in the legal branch of the administration.' Yet, a month later, Rathbone admitted in a report to that very committee that he had already allowed the reinstatement of thirty per cent of former prose-cutors and judges, who were not just members of the *Rechtswahrerbund*, but actually members of the party and even officers in the SA. It was a clear breach of the stipulation that recruitment of former Nazis should be limited to just fifty per cent of purely 'nominal members'. Rathbone argued that their continued removal would be 'a serious handicap to the administration of justice in the British zone.'[93]

After appointing a handful of the top officials, Rathbone had stood back and allowed the vetting of those lawyers who were to be read-mitted to be delegated entirely to German lawyers, with predictable results. In Hamburg, the panel was composed entirely of lawyers who had practised during the Nazi period, not one of whom was an anti-Nazi. All the judges reappointed were former Nazi party members; those who had served on the Panel Senate and were reappointed were by definition active Nazis.[94]

The Hamburg appointments were immediately criticized by Senator Heitgres, himself a victim of Nazi judges. He alleged that the worst of the Nazi judges were being reappointed. Rathbone seemed unconcerned. His sympathies lay instead with the judges who, he felt, had no alternative but to cooperate because 'none of the judges was promoted unless they joined the NSDAP. They were given unenviable jobs in the criminal courts or they were spied upon, supervised or blackmailed. The result was that they either resigned or, in order to maintain some decent standards in the administration of justice, many of them perforce joined the NSDAP.'[95] Like the educationalists, Rathbone chose to believe the lawyers rather than their victims; he even praised the 'spirit of freemasonry' amongst lawyers who arranged collections for those colleagues who had been dismissed.'

Rathbone defends his decisions by arguing that the courts had an enormous backlog of cases and it would have been impossible to wait several years while a new generation of lawyers was trained. There was, however, a source of trained lawyers which the Control Commission deliberately excluded – the several hundred German refugee lawyers in London, many of whom had requested permission to return, only to be denied by the British authorities. The ban was lifted in March 1946. In May 1946, Rathbone spoke in London to a hundred who still wanted to return, but painted a dismal picture and was unable to offer any special facilities. Most were dissuaded. Further pressure by the German Association of Democratic Lawyers forced the British authorities to allow a representative to make an inspection trip in December 1946. His pessimistic report[96] and explanation that the British were unwilling to allow returning refugees to take extra clothing, send letters or money to their families remaining in Britain, or guarantee that re-entry visas would be issued, was enough to deter all but a handful.

The ban on most refugee judges returning was not lifted until even later. The Legal Division unashamedly defended their ban by quoting a unanimous resolution by the German judges who had stayed in Germany that 'it might unfavourably influence the attitude of the German population to other repatriated lawyers'.[97] Like many Germans' attitude towards the future German Chancellor Willy Brandt, who had spent the war in exile in Norway, there was a feeling that those who did not stay in Nazi Germany were traitors. The refugees protested that it was just those who refused to stay who believed in justice.

Cut off from any alternative source of lawyers, even if only to supervise the vetting of those who were being reappointed, the Legal Division's fifty per cent rule was bound to be short-lived. On 23 May 1946, Rathbone successfully argued that it be abolished. Excluding nominal Nazis was, he said, 'uneconomical, inequitable and politically unwise'.[98] The last restraint was removed. Anti-Nazi Germans were appalled and demanded that the judges at least be re-vetted by anti-Nazis. Rathbone could have none of it. He told Macaskie that even the demands themselves were 'undermining the independence of the judiciary', and demanded that the German press be censored to prevent seeing 'the administration of justice reduced to a farce'. Clearly for him the reappointment of Nazis did not have that same effect. 'We must bring this ghastly witchhunt to an immediate conclusion,' he wrote.[99]

Reviewing the results of Rathbone's denazification of German justice in November 1947, Hans Weigert, an American civilian working in the OMGUS Legal Division's 'German Courts Section', wrote:

During the discussion with Mr Rathbone it was brought out that the German Administration of Justice in the British zone employs many more former party members in key positions than is the case in our zone. According to statistics requested from the Central Legal Office by Mr Rathbone during our conference, of 121 key positions, thirty-eight or thirty per cent are occupied by former members of the party or the SA. The figure would be much higher if all key positions, according to our definition, would be considered. It may be noted that Mr Rathbone was rather surprised and shocked by these figures and he expressed himself strongly in favour of cleaning up the key positions to match our statistics. This goes to show that the British apparently have loosened their supervision of the German Administration of Justice to an extent by which they have more or less control of what is going on in their German courts. The situation is even more aggravated by the fact that the majority of the thirty-eight former Nazis in key positions have even now not yet been denazified.[100]

'Nominal Nazi' lawyers in the American zone had been readmitted even earlier than in the British zone. In March 1946 the American Legal Division admitted to itself that it was incapable of managing courts using the unfamiliar Roman system of law, and, rather than face chaos, removed the ban on Nazi lawyers. Preventing the renazification of the legal system theseafter depended, firstly on controlling the 180 key positions in the justice ministries in the Länder, which approved all appointments, and, secondly, on preventing, by persuasion and not by law, former

Nazis sitting as judges in trials of Nazi crimes.

The 1947 file of Hans Weigert chronicles the depressing failure of the Legal Division to prevent the appointment of Nazi judges to try Nazi crimes.[101] In Bremen, he watched helplessly as the state's judiciary did not even make a pretence of hiding the reappointment of Nazi judges. Not one of the fifty-nine judges and prosecutors was even summoned to a denazification tribunal. Cases involving Nazi crimes were for two years simply not prosecuted. When, after intense pressure, the first was finally brought to trial in January 1948, the prosecutor, Dr Heinrich Hollmann, protested that both the judges and the jury included men who had not been denazified. In reply, the presiding judge immediately stopped the trial. Shortly afterwards Hollmann was dismissed. The Bremen lawyers had always realized that the risks were minimal. The American inspector in the state could neither speak nor understand German.

Touring the zone in the summer of 1947, Weigert tried to plug the breaches in the dam. In Baden, one of the senior judges reappointed to the bench, Dr Sietz, had served eleven years on a notorious special court; in Mannheim, two former special court judges had convicted a Nazi policeman for the murder of three civilians who had hoisted white flags as the Allies approached, but sentenced him to just two years imprisonment. The third judge, a former concentration camp inmate, had wanted to impose a life sentence but had been outvoted. In Munich, the justice minister justified to Weigert the selection of former Nazis to try Nazi offences by explaining that the judges had told him that they did not feel prejudiced; while in the small Bavarian village of Schwanenkirchen, the school's headmistress, Maria Nothaft, helplessly pleaded with Weigert to force the local authorities to prosecute officials who had arrested and executed her sister for listening to an Allied broadcast.[102]

In all these, and many other cases, Weigert was powerless to influence events. Neither the British nor the Americans ever removed one German judge because of a Nazi past or as a result of his judgements. The French intervened once, in 1946, unceremoniously removing the judge in Offenburg who had acquitted the Nazi fanatic who had murdered Matthias Erzberger, the German signatory of the 1918 armistice.

Like Rathbone, the head of the American Legal Division, Alvin Rockwell, resisted demands from his staff that the Nazi appointments be purged. 'It would, be an injustice,' he said, 'and also greatly weaken the morale of the German judiciary as an attack against the independence of the judiciary.'[103]

The passionate defence by Rathbone and Rockwell of the independence of the German judiciary reveals that they were both either unable or unwilling to recognize the truth about the German judiciary. It had never been independent, and had never made any pretence of being anything other than an agent of the state. The more authoritarian the state, the more anxious was the profession to enforce its policies. As will be seen later, the collapse of the 'key positions' policy in 1948 was to result in miscarriages of justice to the present day. The immediate effect of allowing the reappointment of Nazis in 1946 was to confirm the cynical realization that the Allies had not restored untainted justice in postwar Germany.

There were two entirely different judicial systems operated by the two western Allies in their zones. While the armies directly ran the war crimes trials, both the Control Commission and OMGUS had created Military Government Courts to enforce the statutes and controls promulgated by the Military Governors. These laws governed every aspect of the daily life and business of all Germans. Effective enforcement was vital to maintaining control over occupied Germany. While the British recruited lawyers from Britain as judges in their courts, OMGUS appointed low-ranking army offices, usually without any legal training or experience. As the British records either do not exist or are unavailable, it is impossible to judge the credibility and performance of the British courts. The few American records available, however, confirm beyond doubt that for both Germans and interested Americans, there was often little to choose between the arbitrariness of the OMGUS Military Government courts and their immediate German predecessors.

Reviewing OMGUS court decisions in Bavaria in February 1947, Garret Houman, an American lawyer, reported to Haven Parker, the chief of Administration of the Justice Branch in the Legal Division: 'Our courts are sitting daily dispensing a brand of justice which is often bad. I am ashamed of it as an American and I see a serious danger to our policy of 'selling' democracy to the German people in its continuance.'[102] Houman had been appointed to review the 'Death Sentence' cases and advise on clemency. Many of those convicted were DP's and Germans allegedly involved in black marketeering, breaking curfew regulations, smuggling and attacks on former 'employers'. Houman characterized the attitude of the judges by quoting the chief of personnel recruitment as saying: 'It is better that a hundred innocent accused be found guilty than that one be acquitted.' Houman claimed that the same officer even ' "bragged" of the number of death sentences he was able to impose.' The result, claimed Houman, was that while, 'at least ten percent of the prisoners sentenced to long terms. . .in the Military Government courts were illegally sentenced. . .at least an additional twenty-five per cent of the prisoners now confined were given sentences so grossly excessive as to shock the conscience of any impartial court or Board which might review them.' Houman and his clemency board 'substantially' reduced the sentences of sixty-six percent of the cases they reviewed.

According to Houman, the cause was obvious. The prosecutors, he wrote, were 'prejudiced, lazy or overworked,' the judges accepted as evidence, 'rumour, theory, and imagination,' while the interpreters for the defence were 'poor'. 'Many men found themselves on the bench. . .who not only were not lawyers, but had never been in a court-room.' Houman's report was filed. Neither Parker nor Rockwell, the director of the Legal Division, took any action. Two years later the Military Government courts collapsed in discredit.

Faced in March 1949 with the simple decision as to whether American military personnel were subject to German law, the courts and the Military Government gave, on the same day, contradictory opinions. The cause, wrote William Clark, the chief judge, was that 'in my judgement many of the (judges) are in no way qualified. Some of their opinions childish, and many of their decisions are unfortunate.'[103]

In response to protests from other American lawyers reviewing cases and complaining that there were 'so many mistakes in jail' and that many Germans had an 'unjustified criminal record', Colonel John Raymond, the new director of the Legal Division replied that 'I am satisfied of the abuses,' but refused to take any action.[104]

The Military Government Courts and the army's war crimes trials were intended to show the Germans the meaning of true, impartial and democratic justice. Not only would justice be done, it would be seen to be done. It was the collapse of that programme which paved the way for the war criminals to benefit from a blind eye to murder.

9

'UNTIL THE
CRACK OF DOOM'

The trial of the commandant and forty-four of the staff of Belsen finally
began on 17 September 1945 at Lüneburg in the British zone. It was the
first major set-piece war crimes trial, and for the newspapers and public
of the world a dramatic curtain-raiser to the international tribunal that
was due to begin its proceedings in Nuremberg the following month.

Unlike the Nuremberg tribunal, which was designedly an attempt at
legal innovation on an international scale and had been prepared by large
teams of lawyers who were entirely separate from the rest of the war
crimes programme, Belsen and the zonal trials which followed it were an
effort to adapt established judicial procedures to serve an unprecedented
purpose. But, as has been described, the army's existing legal machinery
in the Judge Advocate-General's department had not proved either able
or willing to adopt new ideas or methods in preparing for the trial. The
traditional forum of military justice, the court martial, was to prove just
as inadequate when it came to the trial itself.

Expressly, from the outset, the British looked upon the war crimes
trials as an attempt, not only to punish the guilty, but also to show the
German people just what had been done in their name, and to provide
them with an example of efficient and impartial justice. All three ambitions were to be frustrated, and the Belsen trial revealed most of the
factors that were to lead to the failure of the whole programme. From
the press conference on the eve of the trial, at which Shapcott, the
Deputy Judge Advocate-General responsible for War Crimes, refused to
answer any questions, to the final verdicts, the proceedings left virtually
everyone dissatisfied.

On the opening day the four-hundred-seat public gallery was packed.
Over one hundred journalists were crammed into another side of the
brightly lit hall. In the middle sat the accused, twenty-one women and
twenty-four men. Attention was mostly focused on Josef Kramer, the
last commandant of Belsen, who, with ten other of the accused, had
arrived in Belsen in December from Auschwitz. Putting the eleven from
Auschwitz on trial with the remainder who had lived and worked at
Belsen for much longer was the first fundamental mistake.

Whereas Auschwitz had been an extermination centre, where

Kramer had been the commandant of Camp Two, otherwise known as Birkenau, Belsen was originally specially constructed for the so-called 'exchange-Jews'; those who were, on Himmler's orders, to be handed over to the Allies in return for the many German nationals interned in America.[1] Himmler had invented this special class of Jews because there were so few American and neutral nationals in Germany for whom the interned Germans could be exchanged. The first arrivals in August 1943, Spaniards from Salonika, found a well-constructed brick block building. There were no gas chambers, though inmates were severely beaten, tortured and badly fed. It was the arrival of evacuees from Auschwitz at the end of 1944, when the camp population rapidly increased from ten thousand to forty-two thousand, that turned the camp into a cesspit of typhus, systematic brutality and mass death. The witnesses would testify that inmates at Belsen had suffered a daily round of beatings, floggings and whippings. Some were shot dead for stealing a carrot; all were subjected to innumerable perverted savageries on the part of the camp guards.

Kramer consistently maintained that he had desperately tried to prevent the tens of thousands of deaths at Belsen. He produced the copy of a letter he had written to Richard Glücks, the Inspector of Concentration Camps, on 1 March 1945, urging him not to send any more Jews to the camp because of the typhus outbreak which was causing two hundred and fifty to three hundred deaths per day. Many British officers were impressed by that letter and by Kramer's behaviour when he surrendered the camp to the British. He asked them for desperately needed medicines and food, pleading that he had been abandoned in the closing stages of the war without supplies. His supporters chose to ignore the fact that two miles away was a Wehrmacht store containing no less than eight hundred tons of food. Kramer had not asked for the food because it would have meant 'special indents'.[2] Mass deaths was in any case nothing new for Kramer. He had directed it for some years at Birkenau, often making the daily selection of those to go to the gas chambers.

Yet neither Kramer nor any of the other defendants was charged with murder. Instead the charges alleged that 'members of the staff at Bergen-Belsen/Auschwitz concentration camp responsible for the well-being of the persons interned there, in violation of the laws and usages of war were together concerned as parties to the ill-treatment of certain persons causing the deaths. . .' There followed the names of a few people known to have died in the two camps.[3]

As the charges were read out, the use of the phrases 'well-being' and 'ill-treatment' struck many of the non-British spectators as peculiar. Concentration camps like Auschwitz were after all not designed for 'well-being' but for murder. Those who died at Belsen did so as a result of deliberate savagery and neglect on the part of men and women who knew full well what the results would be. The British seemed to be treating the deaths as an administrative failure rather than the planned outcome of the Final Solution policy. By lunchtime, some of the observers in the court were feeling uneasy; during the afternoon, more joined their ranks.

Each of the accused had been provided with British lawyers, nearly all of them serving army officers. The defence began trying to score procedural points before the trial even got under way. In the Anglo-American legal system it is a traditional art, but a seemingly interminable dispute between the lawyers about the definition of the word 'concert', using *The Little Oxford Dictionary*, was not a good omen for those who hoped they were about to witness exemplary justice.

Critical reports began appearing in Russian and American newspapers in the third week of the trial. In cross-examining the survivors who appeared as witnesses, the defence tried to dispute their accounts of the horrors of the camps. Witnesses testifying that they had seen someone beaten to the ground were unable to prove to the defence's satisfaction that the victim had actually died of the wounds. They were unable to give dates and times for the assaults. Their explanation, that there was no sense of time in a concentration camp, did not seem to be understood. When they added facts which were not included in their original affidavits, or omitted to repeat what they had written months before, the lawyers seemed to regard that as something important, which discredited them. Contradictions in the evidence, for example when one witness alleged that a murder had been committed by shooting in the head and another testified it had been the stomach; or uncertainty as to whether the victim was a man or a woman, were seized upon as proof that witnesses were concocting stories. When a witness explained that sexual differences were not so easy to distinguish when someone was emaciated and their head was shaven, it did not seem to carry much weight.

Criticism of the trial began to intensify when the defence opened their case. Kramer's lawyer, Major T.C.M. Winwood, and his colleagues for the defence began mysteriously referring to House of Lords decisions on the international law about shipwrecks, a fishing dispute in Scotland and the decision of an American court over the validity of a treaty. It emerged that the British officers were actually arguing that concentration camps were legal in Germany and that therefore those who worked in them could not be punished for obeying orders. They were also suggesting that murder in a concentration camp was not a war crime.

As the weeks wore on, and the audience in the public gallery thinned to just a handful of people, stories about 'British softness' and lack of sympathy for the victims were suddenly overtaken by reports of Winwood's closing speech. According to Winwood, the rollcalls, which sometimes continued twelve hours, while inmates died of exposure, exhaustion or systematic beatings, were 'a part of concentration camp life and it was the only way of being able to make out a strength return for rations'. The beatings, Winwood said, were only necessary when food became scarce. 'The internees had to be restrained.'[4]

Explaining the behaviour of Kramer, a man who had devoted his life since 1934 to the murder of innocents, Winwood said that his misfortune had been that he had dealt with 'the dregs of the ghettos of Eastern Europe'.

Major L.S.W. Canfield, defending Ilse Grese, who whipped her unfortunate victims in Auschwitz to death and who continued to do the same in Belsen, described his client as not the beast but the scapegoat of Belsen.[5] He told the court that corporal punishment, even when inflicted on women, was perfectly acceptable in a prison, because it was 'reasonable conduct in the circumstances'. The continual use of the word 'prison' seemed to imply that there were justifiable legal grounds for the inmates' confinement.

The international reaction was predictable. The daily reports of the trial in the Russian newspapers became attacks on the British, rather than accounts of the evidence. According to Sir Thomas Brimelow, in the Foreign Office's Northern Department, responsible for Soviet affairs: 'The publicity given to this trial in the USSR has been most damaging.'[6]

For a few days, Dean and other officials believed that the Russians were deliberately misunderstanding the role of defence counsel in Western countries. An explanatory answer, he thought, could be written up in the British Ally, a small-circulation British government publication.[7] The idea was dropped when reports reached London of the summing-up delivered to the five officers who were judging the case by Carl L. Sterling, the Judge Advocate-General. Sterling told the officers that the affidavits on which much of the prosecution case rested, because witnesses had been unwilling to wait in DP camps for five months in order to give evidence in person, 'were dangerous material.' Too much of the evidence he said, was 'vague'. The court should ignore witnesses who just said: 'She threw people to the ground and cruelly beat them and many died.' It was too unspecific. There had to be certainty of death.[8]

But it was one of Sterling's closing remarks which brought the criticism to a crescendo, because it seemed to confirm the worst suspicions of British lack of commitment. 'The court,' said Sterling, 'would have to be satisfied that a person on the staff of Auschwitz or Belsen concentration camp was guilty of deliberately committing a war crime; just being a member of the staff itself was not enough to justify conviction.'

At the Old Bailey, the scrupulous fairness would undoubtedly not have even been noticed. It would have been expected. At Lüneburg it caused a sensation which was only eclipsed by the actual verdicts. Thirty convicted, fifteen acquitted. Eleven were sentenced to death, one to life imprisonment, the remainder to terms of from one to fifteen years. Overlooked in the flood of criticism was the fact that most of those acquitted, or given a low sentence, were not SS personnel, but camp inmates who had become 'Kapos', the trusties who seized on the chance to supervise their fellow inmates as a possible chance of survival. The court felt that the distinction was important. Those who had survived the camps had clearly failed to convince the British officers that the Kapos, in order to prove their worth, were usually more brutal than the Germans.

Some of the strongest reaction to the verdicts came from France. Protest meetings and letters to the British embassy complained about the 'derisory sentences'. According to a British embassy official who went to a meeting in the Salle de la Mutualité in Paris: 'the sincerity of the protests can hardly be called into question . . . the degree of publicity which the proceedings received has had an effect which is exactly the reverse of that which it was presumably intended to produce.'[9] The French government asked the British to hand over the fourteen acquitted so they could be retried. The Foreign Office insisted there would have to be other charges, based on new evidence. The French asked for a transcript of the trial. The War Office refused.[10] Paris announced that new evidence had been found. They were told that the fourteen had been released soon after the verdicts.[11]

Only the British army seemed pleased with its performance. 'I am bound to say,' Lambert told the under-secretary of state at the Foreign Office, 'that the Army Council is satisfied that the trial was carried out with the best tradition of British justice.'[12]

In fact, the Belsen trial revealed almost all the flaws that were to dog the British war crimes programmes. The preparation of the case had been agonizingly slow; in the absence of witnesses much evidence had to be in the form of affidavits; the court was asked to resolve intricate matters of law and principle instead of deciding on the facts within an agreed framework. The officers who made up the court were inexperienced and often unable and unwilling to grasp that the scruffy, undernourished figures, straight from the DP camps, could really be telling the truth about the apparently respectable men and women who faced them from the dock. The niceties of procedure and the points of law, the to and fro of cross-examination on events that had occurred months before, would have seemed proper and dignified when a single murder in an orderly community was being tried; as a means of uncovering the monstrousness of a system designed and dedicated to murder they looked absurd.

The verdicts undoubtedly comforted the Nazis and dismayed their enemies within Germany; not that many Germans had the opportunity to learn from this example of British justice in action, for the public gallery was soon denuded of all but a handful of spectators, and in the absence of newspapers and radio the German public heard little more than the bare facts of the verdicts.

Unlike the War Office, some drew lessons from the experience. The American army's trial of those responsible for running Dachau, which started shortly after the Belsen trial, lasted just one month and resulted in the conviction of all forty of the accused, twenty-six of whom were sentenced to death.

Comparing the two trials, both Clement Attlee, the Prime Minister, and Sir Hartley Shawcross, the Attorney-General, were angered. Attlee sent a memo to John Lawson, the Secretary of State for War:

I am concerned at the delays which have occurred with regard to the prosecution of war criminals particularly in the Belsen trial. It is essential that in BAOR [British Army of the Rhine] . . . the person on whom rests responsibility for the investigation of war crimes and the bringing to trial of their authors should be officers with drive and energy and that the high priority to be accorded to war crimes matters should be fully understood. I hope that you will see that this is done.[13]

Lawson asked his department for an explanation. Colonel George Bradshaw, the deputy director of Personnel Services, suggested that these were just 'teething troubles which have now been remedied'.[14] Lawson readily accepted the explanation and replied to Attlee that the fault was the excessive number of defendants and the language barrier. 'Since however the whole procedure was new, I do not feel surprised that the machinery did not work well in the early stages. I think however that proper action has now been taken to overcome the defects which have appeared.'[15]

Lawson's reply satisfied Shawcross no more than Lambert's self-congratulation impressed Ernest Bevin at the Foreign Office. Both men were convinced of the need for an effective war crimes programme, and, as the British Chief Prosecutor at Nuremberg, Shawcross was in a better position than most of his ministerial colleagues to see that things were going awry.

He had his first suspicions in August. 'Progress is slow,' he wrote to Attlee on 24 August.[16] For the next four weeks, together with Dean, he was involved in the negotiations to agree who was to stand trial at Nuremberg. Neither paid much attention to the minor war criminals. But during that month Shawcross did hear from Dean about his past problems in forcing the War Office to accept their responsibilities and about Lambert and Shapcott's indifference.

Shawcross was sufficiently concerned to speak to Bevin. Unlike Eden, the Labour Foreign Secretary was both interested in war crimes and determined that there should be trials. Both ministers recognized that their immediate problem was the new Secretary of State for War, John Lawson, a timid and ineffectual trade unionist whom Attlee had appointed as a reward for past services rather than because of any recognizable talent.

Shawcross agreed to keep a watching brief and began to make some inquiries. From a friend returning from Germany he heard that while there were thirty-eight Belsen-like concentration camps in the British zone alone, only three were being investigated. There were, he was told, an estimated twenty thousand officials who could have been involved in those camps over the past seven years.[17] Yet only three of the camps and at most fifty of the former staff were being investigated. His informant was mistaken. There were in fact eighty-one Belsen-like concentration camps in the British zone. It is indicative of the state of the war crimes investigation organization and the JAG that forty-three of them had still not been discovered.

Investigation was now the formal responsibility of the recently formed British War Crimes Group based at Bad Oeynhausen, but with just five investigators it was still little more than a name. Its newly appointed commander, Group Captain Tony Somerhough, a charming, intelligent and charismatic man, had already discovered that his group had the lowest priority for manpower and equipment. More than half his time was spent, not in organizing the hunt for war criminals, but in fighting to get more staff from Ronnie Hoare, responsible for the War Establishment, and with all the other divisional heads to get transport, desks, typewriters and radios.

The root of Somerhough's problems lay in the fact that only recently had it been agreed between BAOR and the War Office that the army in Germany would be responsible for investigating crimes other than those committed against British forces. Major-General Maurice Chilton, the Deputy Adjutant-General in BAOR, had made the acceptance of that responsibility conditional on more staff being sent out from Britain.

Somerhough could not understand why that was necessary. There were countless combat soldiers and officers now under-employed in Germany who could, he felt, have been seconded to war crimes investigation. But neither Chilton nor Hoare would accept that solution. Nor did they seem prepared to take any initiative. There was already considerable resentment at BAOR headquarters about the War Office's refusal to recognize the consequences of the delays in bringing the Belsen case to trial. A result of JAG's obstinate insistence on keeping control of the prosecutions in London had been a rapid loss of interest at BAOR headquarters and a refusal to believe that war crimes investigation was any more important than it had been before the surrender.[18]

Somerhough had no allies in Whitehall. In August he had met Bridgeman who, as the head of AG3, was supposed to deal with exactly this kind of problem of providing staff and facilities for the investigations, but the Viscount seemed neither interested nor inclined to overly exert himself on Somerhough's behalf. Bovenschen and Lambert had after all made it quite plain to Bridgeman that the War Office's commitment was to be kept as limited as possible.[19]

Nor were the investigators alone in their frustration. There were now 780 men and women under arrest on suspicion of having committed war crimes, but Shapcott at JAG had not given his approval for any of them to be brought to trial. Like Somerhough, the JAG officer at Bad Oeynhausen, Scott-Barrett, had to admit that he was powerless in the face of Whitehall's inertia.[20]

By the end of September Shawcross had, as a result of his own efforts, discovered the stalemate that existed in Germany. He and Bevin agreed that the cause was Lawson's inability to move his civil servants into action, and they decided that Shawcross should, in effect, read the Riot Act to the bureaucrats. He wrote to Lawson on 10 October that he was arranging an interdepartmental meeting to solve the problem, a meeting to which Lawson was not invited.[21] The letter showed that Shawcross was fully aware of the reasons for the failure. Mentioning that the work in Germany 'is in a way police work,' he continued: 'I believe that over a year ago the War Crimes Commission itself recommended the establishment in Germany of some such organization, but I cannot find that anything was done.' On the War Office's organization he commented: 'it is far too cumbersome and circuitous to achieve its purpose expeditiously. . . What is needed is that someone possessing high rank and real driving power should be made available to devote the whole of his time to organizing and coordinating the machinery for investigation and prosecution of war crimes.'

Although, in writing to Lawson, Shawcross stressed the contrary, his investigation could not have left him with much confidence in

Bridgeman and Shapcott. When he actually confronted the two of them, together with MacGeagh, the JAG, Dean from the Foreign Office and Colonel Bradshaw from the War Office's Department of Personnel Services two days later on 12 October, he did not mince his words.

In retrospect, that Friday's meeting can be seen as a perfect example of a minister explaining in clear and detailed terms exactly what he and the Cabinet expected the civil service to do, and of the civil servants agreeing to accept the instructions without demur and then proceeding to ignore them almost totally.

Shawcross told the officials[22] that the Cabinet was seriously concerned about the lack of progress and wanted an 'accelerated war crimes programme'. He went on:

> There are tens of thousands of Germans responsible for millions of murders. We must set ourselves an absolute minimum of prosecuting at least ten per cent of those criminals in the British zone. That is about two thousand people. I am setting as an irreducible minimum that we try five hundred cases by 30 April 1946. To achieve that, personnel must be provided as the first priority. Montgomery must be told that it is his responsibility to achieve the five-hundred-case target and to allocate the War Crimes Group the facilities and personnel he needs. JAG should set up six courts to sit simultaneously and if there is any shortage of lawyers, then dispense with lawyers.

'I also think,' Shawcross told Shapcott and MacGeagh, 'that the whole operation, including JAG's work, should be centralized in Germany.'[23]

Neither of them protested. Nor did Viscount Bridgeman; on the contrary, he said he would ring Major-General Chilton the following Monday to ensure that Shawcross's orders were carried out.

Five days later Lawson wrote to both Bevin and Shawcross confirming that the target was five hundred cases by 30 April 1946 and that the priority was to recruit the qualified staff.[24] All agreed that, after that date, the British would no longer investigate non-British crimes.

Attlee remained unsatisfied. After reading the report of Shawcross's meeting he wrote to Bevin complaining that the 30 April deadline 'would surely have the effect of leaving a large number of criminals unpunished and at large.'[25] Bevin did not reply. But there did now seem some guarantee that at least a measure of success would be achieved.

A week after the meeting, on 19 October, a cipher telegram was sent to the commander of British forces in South-East Asia informing him of the target of five hundred cases in his area of command by 30 April.[26] No telegram went to BAOR at Bad Oeynhausen. Instead Bradshaw went to Germany to explain the government's wishes in person. It is not recorded whether Chilton had already been told of them by Bridgeman over the telephone as Shawcross had been promised, but in any case Bradshaw took a copy of the minutes of the 12 October meeting with him.[27]

The result of Bradshaw's mission was curious to say the least. He had to report to Bridgeman that, in effect, BAOR refused to obey the Cabinet's instructions.[28] They disputed the notion that it was their responsibility to investigate crimes against non-British nationals, since they had not been provided with the additional staff they had insisted were required for the task. No one, it seemed was prepared to order Hoare or even Montgomery to make the staff available. They rejected outright Shawcross's suggestion that they should dispense with lawyers. In general, BAOR told Bradshaw, there were too many other priorities.

Faced with this pointblank refusal to even try and follow the clearly expressed wish of the government, Bradshaw seems to have decided to do nothing. But, while Lawson inquired no further of his officials after he had, on behalf of his department, accepted the job of meeting the target, Attlee and Bevin were more wordly-wise. They both sent memos inquiring about progress.[29] As a result on 3 November Bradshaw confirmed the Cabinet's instructions in Cipher 83002 to Bad Oeynhausen.[30]

Or at least he apparently did so. In fact the wording of the telegram subtly, but very significantly, changed the effect of those orders. Shawcross had made it perfectly clear at the meeting. He had set a target of prosecuting five hundred cases in the British zone, which he estimated would involve some two thousand individual defendants. But while paragraph one of Bradshaw's telegram read: 'HM Government have decided that early trial of German minor war criminals will be treated as matter of great urgency', paragraph three read: 'Target for BAOR is minimum repeat minimum five hundred repeat five hundred *individuals* will be tried for war crimes by 30 April 46.' Paragraph five read: 'C-in-C will be responsible for ensuring the completion of their target number of trials within the stated time limit.'

Looking at the undispatched cipher it is clear that Bradshaw had thought about the key word very carefully. The word 'trials' had only been added after the whole cipher had been typed. He was clearly thinking of an alternative word to 'cases'. It was what it seemed. A deliberate distortion. In the meantime, MacGeagh had not obeyed Shawcross's orders to delegate the decision on prosecutions to the JAG in Germany.

Despite the fact that the telegram was given a dispatch number by the War Office, it was allegedly never received by Chilton, to whom it was addressed.[31] Whether it was sent or not remains a mystery, but Chilton was in any case well aware of the target that had been set – after all, Bradshaw had come from London in order to tell him about it. Nonetheless, he chose to use the non-receipt of Bradshaw's message as an excuse for continued inaction for a further month.

Nor did Bridgeman go out of his way to see what action was being taken to meet the target, even at the level to which it had now been reduced. However, on 25 November Scott-Barrett returned to Bad Oeynhausen from London carrying a copy of the cipher. He showed it to Montgomery's staff and asked them what action they were taking. They pleaded ignorance, but nevertheless wrote to Bridgeman the following day that Headquarters could not agree to any targets without knowing what prosecutions were being planned by Shapcott in London.[32] It was just another tactic for delay, albeit short-term. The message arrived in London when pressure on Lawson from Attlee, Bevin and Shawcross after the Belsen trial débâcle was at its height.

The War Office's response was to send, on 3 December, a personal letter from General Sir Ronald F. Adam, the Adjutant-General of all the forces, to Montgomery about the 'high priority' to be given to war crimes.[33] But as Adam admitted that 'a good deal of delay has been due to initial difficulties at this end,' it did not carry much conviction.

By the time the letter reached Germany, Shawcross had written again to Lawson complaining that only ten cases had so far been tried. 'I am by no means happy about the progress,' he said. 'The five-hundred-case target probably only touches the fringe of the problem.' Also it seemed that the result of Attlee's directive for Montgomery to be told that he was personally responsible for ensuring the target be met 'as of the first priority' was 'most disappointing'.[34]

Shawcross's rebuke had no effect. Lawson was unable or unwilling to force his department into action and they remained unimpressed by this ministerial importunity. 'You cannot have your bun and eat it,' Shapcott commented to Bradshaw. 'I got the JAG [MacGeagh] to write to the Attorney-General and say that he was perfectly satisfied that everyone engaged in the preparation of cases was giving of his best. With that I am in complete accord. I think it is very disturbing to those engaged in this work to be constantly pressed on this matter. Time must be given to the preparation of these cases if we are to do the job properly and to carry out the trials in accordance with the best traditions of British justice.'[35]

The 'best traditions of British justice' were to provide an alibi for the army throughout the next two years; it never occurred to them that speed and efficiency were not the least important elements in those traditions.

Chilton wrote to Bridgeman on 16 December explaining his difficulties in meeting the target.[36] He started by suggesting that it could be only be achieved if 'you agree that it is preferable to try a large number of trivial cases rather than a few involving more serious charges.' It was, he must have known, an offer even Bridgeman could not accept. He then went on to elaborate: 'unless cases are carefully prepared and presented for trial, Military Courts will not convict and an undue number of acquittals will result.' He dismissed Shawcross's suggestion that lawyers might be dispensed with: 'the standard of prosecutors and defending officers must be maintained if the German public is to be suitably impressed with the merits of the British judicial procedure and the justice of the trial.'

Lawyers were not only needed to argue the case but also, according to the Royal Warrant, to act as the judge advocates who sat with the officers trying the case to advise them on the law. As demobilization gained pace, the number of available lawyers in BAOR was falling from just over five hundred to less than twenty.[37] Chilton was at least not overstating this aspect of the situation when he wrote that the 'shortage of legally qualified officers is acute and increasing.' It was to relieve that bottleneck that Shawcross had suggested in October holding trials without lawyers arguing the cases.

The military courts consisted of either three or five serving officers, chosen at random and at the very last moment, often because their services were more dispensable to the army than those of their colleagues. They had to perform a role for which they had no training, little disposition and, increasingly, much distaste.

There was a justifiable belief that a summary court, staffed by amateurs, facing professional advocacy, needed the presence and advice of a trained lawyer. It was only in 1947, after the event, that it was recognized that an alternative had existed. It would have been possible to recruit magistrates or county court judges from England who were experienced in swiftly and fairly dealing with what were not legally complicated cases but essentially disputes about facts. It was the solution chosen for the Military Government courts in Germany used for judging the cases of offences committed by Germans against Military Government laws. In fact many of the judges for these courts were recruited from BAOR itself, so reducing yet further the number of lawyers available for the war crimes trials.

The nub of Chilton's message to Bridgeman was that the number of trials held would depend on how many more lawyers the War Office sent over from England. Recruitment however was a problem, especially when it came to defence counsel. Shawcross had tried to convince a packed meeting of the Bar that barristers should be prepared, in their traditional manner, to accept briefs for both the prosecution and defence in the war crimes trials. The meeting voted against his suggestion, a defeat which some believe resulted more from political bias against the new Labour government than a distaste for defending mass murderers. The alternative was to recruit lawyers just as prosecutors and judge advocates. The obstacle was the low five-guinea fee permitted by the Treasury. Surprisingly, neither Shawcross nor Bevin thought of challenging that limit. Lord Jowitt, the Lord Chancellor, suggested an increase in June 1947 when the shortage had reached a crisis.[38] The fee was doubled and the crisis was temporarily relieved, although new problems were created.

The American programme did not suffer as badly. As Shawcross ruefully says: 'There are more lawyers in New York alone than in the whole of Britain.' That fact was reflected in the number of lawyers available in the American army. Moreover, Straight had made sure that never less than forty officers were permanently assigned to the war crimes division as judges. He acknowledges that it was an unwelcome posting for the officers. It inevitably implied that they were unemployable in other army work. But it did mean that they became experienced in judging cases. Lack of such experience was to seriously undermine any benefits that might have resulted from the British trials, as the Belsen trial proved.

For the moment, Chilton succeeded with his ploy of, in effect, putting the responsibility for successfully reaching the five hundred target onto the War Office. It was supported by Montgomery in his reply to Adam: 'I must point out,' wrote the Field-Marshal on 30 December, 'that it is unlikely that the target figure will be reached unless I receive the extra assistance for which I have asked.'[39] After drawing breath, Gurney, the director of Personnel Services, accepted the responsibility and replied that recruits were being sought in London.[40]

It left the situation at the end of 1945 worse than Shawcross or Bevin could have imagined. No war crimes supremo had been appointed; MacGeagh had refused both to delegate decision making to Germany or amend the Royal Warrant to allow faster trials; no extra lawyers had been sent to Germany; Ronnie Hoare, responsible for the all-important War Establishment on which the size of the staff of the War Crimes Group depended, had still not increased its allocation; and, most important of all, neither Montgomery nor his headquarters had yet accepted responsibility for prosecuting even five hundred individuals by 30 April.

Bridgeman's explanation of the failure is simple. He claims that Bovenschen had quite explicitly given orders that he was not interested in the War Office becoming involved in war crimes, and did not want British soldiers tied up guarding Germans long into the peace. Lambert was a 'negative man', overshadowed by Bovenschen, constantly denying responsibility for everything, especially expensive, unrewarding work which would not, in his view, be popular with the public. Sir Ronald Adam, the Adjutant-General, was surprisingly quite uninterested in anything concerning discipline. In Germany, Chilton was apparently insufficiently persuasive to convince Montgomery to undertake anything as distasteful as trials.

Pincered between these two immovable forces, Bridgeman believes that Bradshaw, who had the more intimate daily control over the war crimes programme, was powerless to do any more than he accomplished. Clearly there are many scapegoats, nearly all of whom are now dead. Yet the results of their prejudices are clear, especially in the recruitment of staff. Bradshaw, having promised Chilton that he would send fifty SAS soldiers as investigators to Germany, sent only eight by December, all of whom then searched exclusively for Germans responsible for the murder of SAS men. As compensation, thirteen bilingual, ex-SOE officers arrived, who although enthusiastic, had no investigative experience. A request in September for twenty-eight Polish officers to investigate the crimes against Poles was left 'pending' for three months – twelve finally arrived.

According to Alan Nightingale, Somerhough's deputy responsible for the 'Haystack' search branch, the War Crimes Group was considered so lowly by the War Office and army hierarchy that; 'I had to scrape the barrel and still kick out those I could recruit.'[41] Many of those who wanted to join were more attracted by the free travel ticket throughout Europe than by the work itself. Those who were attracted by the work were invariably former refugees, whose motives were considered suspect, and who therefore were often not recruited.

Surprisingly, the War Office was nevertheless critical of Somerhough's efforts. On 6 December Bradshaw wrote criticizing the War Crimes Group for failing to catch more wanted Germans and for being too 'static minded'. Understandably Somerhough's reply lacked his customary politeness. 'We have found twenty-four wanted men, taken over one thousand statements. A check on correspondence emanating from this team with regard to vehicles, the need for mechanics and policemen, will show that for months past we have been screaming for facilities to make us less "static minded". We cannot move if we have no transport.'[42] It was at this time according to Draper, that, one officer told Somerhough that the War Crimes Group did not need jeeps, they should make do with the railways.

On 8 January Somerhough, in order to try and improve matters, started discussions on the creation of an integrated War Crimes Group where the investigators and lawyers would work together. His negotiations with Hoare and the War Office were to take exactly one year.

There is no documentary evidence that Bradshaw or anyone else in AG3 gave him any help whatsoever during that year.

At the end of it, on 23 December 1946, AG3 was unceremoniously closed down and all responsibility for war crimes was handed to the JAG. Shapcott's comment in March 1947 on the removal of duplication was that: 'smoother running . . . and concentration will save much time.'[43] It was an ironic obituary for a department that had been brought into being simply and solely to try and achieve such smooth running and concentration.

In January 1946 Shawcross managed to extract from the War Office, JAG and BAOR the bare facts of the progress, or lack of it, which had been made. He had also received a few informal reports from friends over the Christmas holidays. All together it was obvious that, three months after he had made the Cabinet's instructions crystal clear, and when the deadline of 30 April was hardly more than three months away, the statistics would reveal an outright refusal to implement those instructions.

By the first week of January 1946 only twenty cases involving ninety-one criminals had been tried. Whereas in October fifty cases had been awaiting trial, now no fewer than 241 cases involving offences against British and Allied nationals were awaiting trial, while 306 cases involving offences against British nationals alone could have been tried but for the not unimportant fact that the accused had not been found. The number of known crimes, many involving innumerable people, had risen to 3,678. The War Crimes Group had 1,281 prisoners in custody on suspicion of having committed war crimes, but the cases against them were still incomplete. Investigations into no less than thirty-nine concentration camps had been summarily ended because, according to Bridgeman; 'No evidence is at present held to justify investigation.'

Shawcross wrote to Attlee on 17 January:

> The general position seems to be very far from satisfactory. At the present rate the trial of war criminals will go on until the crack of doom. The information I have leaves no doubt that the Commands have completely failed to treat this matter as one of the highest priority, or indeed of any urgency at all. I must again emphasize that this matter ought not to be left to be dealt with by inexperienced people at Corps level, but . . . is a Command responsibility not to be delegated, and that it is for Commands, perhaps by transferring some of their not inconsiderable staff personnel, to ensure that the whole process is speeded up by increasing the number of investigating teams.[44]

A more able war minister and a less obstructive ministry might have been moved into action by the clear evidence of their failure. The opposite was the case. Shawcross's report of 14 December on what he called 'the unsatisfactory position' had not even been acknowledged, whilst the replies to the two reports in January just produced a series of excuses, contradictions, and even a challenge to Shawcross to show specific evidence for his suggestion that 'a lack of energy had been displayed'.[45]

Lawson's formal explanations to Shawcross, Bevin and Attlee written over the next four weeks made no mention of the fact that Montgomery had rejected the target, but on the contrary insisted that the Field-Marshal accepted the high priority for the trials. The biggest problem, Lawson claimed, was the shortage of lawyers, which might be solved, he hoped, by holding trials without lawyers or allowing German lawyers as defence counsel[46] – the solution Shawcross had suggested four months previously. On paper, the War Office officials might well have felt pleased with their reply. They had protected BAOR from any blame and suggested that the causes were a shortage which was beyond their personal control. But they did not explain why the American army had seventeen investigation teams employing over 150 full-time investigators, while the British army had only three teams and thirty investigators.

A franker account of the reasons for the failure is contained in a letter which Brigadier P.G. Turpin, Montgomery's chief of staff, wrote to Bradshaw on 15 March denying that the programme was in any way hindered by 'a pile-up of cases awaiting trial'.[47] Turpin explained:

> War Crimes trials cannot always be given top priority. We do not, for instance, give them a higher priority than Release, nor in December and January could they come before the Disbandment of the Wehrmacht. . .
> We do our best to urge the importance of War Crimes Trials, but a Brigade Commander has his own sense of proportion and makes up his own mind about the relative importance of many of the tasks he is ordered to carry out with insufficient manpower and insufficient time. The impatience of a Cabinet Minister will not influence him greatly or make him change his mind. You can fool him sometimes, but not all of the time. . . I don't think anyone will gain anything by throwing mud at us.

The letter was, to say the least, an interesting display of military independence. Turpin even frankly admitted that the vital War Establishment ceiling for manpower had not been altered, as directed, to divert more people into the war crimes programme. Every ministerial directive had been disobeyed. According to Henry Cleaver, a lawyer at War Crimes Group headquarters: 'Ministerial inquiries were treated as a ritual dance. Somerhough was pleased when they came, but their effect was imperceptible.'[48]

Turpin's denial that there was a backlog of cases taxed even the patience of Shapcott, who was, some might have thought, not in the best position to complain. Writing to Bradshaw on 5 April he said: 'I am seriously concerned with the delay in bringing Germans accused of war crimes to trial. . .'[49] He had given the go-ahead for sixteen trials in the previous month but only eight had been heard. Lawyers hired in London to go to Germany were stood down at the last moment because the JAG in Germany did not have all the witnesses and evidence prepared.

Bradshaw did not follow up a suggestion from Shapcott that Turpin should be prodded into setting up an inquiry. He had just returned from Bad Oeynhausen with the progress report until 30 April. A total of 199 people had been tried, in seventy-seven cases. Ninety-three had been sentenced to imprisonment, forty-nine condemned to death and no less than fifty-two acquitted.[50] The inevitable failure to reach even the reduced target of 500 individuals had long been expected, so there was little to say.

The Foreign Office, among others, were struck by the high rate of acquittal and the leniency of the sentences passed on those who were convicted. Dean's experience in preparing for and attending the Nuremberg Tribunal had demonstrably influenced his attitudes. Perhaps it was that the actual documentary evidence of a bureaucratic machine which had been monstrously perverted impressed him in a way which, during the war, unproven evidence and second-hand accounts by foreigners could not equal. He was openly aghast at the results of the trials which were coming from Bad Oeynhausen:

> The position as regards German minor war criminals is most unsatisfactory. Almost all the trials have been for murder, often with horrible additional circumstances, and the JAG had managed to obtain death sentences in twenty-five per cent of the cases, complete acquittals in twenty-five per cent and sentences of imprisonment, often for ridiculously small periods, in fifty per cent. As the Germans are fully aware of these trials, and the crimes for which the accused are indicted, the effect can only be very bad. . . One of the difficulties is that . . . the JAG insists on trying to prove in concentration camp cases that each of the accused was personally responsible for at least one murder. This is a ridiculous method of procedure, since the victims or potential victims who could have proved the necessary facts are themselves dead or vanished long ago. It seems worse than ridiculous to anyone who had any knowledge whatever of the calculated cruelty with which the

concentration camp staffs carried out millions of murders all over Europe.[51]

Unknown to Dean, MacGeagh had refused outrightly, in August 1945, to give any advice to the army on sentencing policy, a refusal he reaffirmed a month later when specifically asked for advice by BAOR.[52] Not everyone agreed with Dean's uncharacteristically passionate outburst, but then only he had been to Nuremberg to hear and even see the evidence at first hand. Those, like his colleague Basil Newton, who remained in England, took a more sanguine view: 'If sentences err on the side of leniency that is a fault on the right side and if they vary from death to acquittal that also should help to prove the care and sincerity with which justice was done.'[53]

Newton, like many others, believed that revealing the magnitude of the crimes to the Germans was more important than establishing individual guilt. There were however three serious flaws in that argument. The first misconception was that the Germans actually believed that proper justice was being administered in the military courts; secondly that the Germans would respect the courts' disclosure of the atrocities more than all the other attempts to convince them; thirdly, that an acquittal of anyone who had worked as a concentration camp guard or in the Gestapo could favourably impress any German at all. The contrary was the case.

Moreover it was surely unreasonable to expect the Germans to accept the evidence for the scale and degree of criminality when, apparently there were many in London and Washington, as well as in the Allied armies of occupation, who refused to accept it. As will be seen, by the end of 1946 an increasingly influential and vocal minority in Britain and America was openly opposing the continuation of the trials. Much of the opposition took the form or criticism of the variations from traditional legal procedures which were permitted. Bridgeman himself opposed the waiving of rules against the admissibility of hearsay evidence, and the fact that evidence was admitted by means of affidavits which were not subject to cross-examination.

For many, such views could only be sustained by those who had not heard at first hand and in detail, the irrefutable and nauseating evidence that was coming before the courts from Nuremberg downwards. Interestingly, three weeks after his defence of the verdicts produced by the British courts, Newton did go to Nuremberg. As a result he wrote to Dean on 24 June: 'While at Nuremberg last week I had the impression that we were not being very successful in using the trials to educate German public opinion . . . the accounts [of the trial] were not widely read or treated by Germans as anything more than a kind of

Allied propaganda.'[54]

In the officers' messes, from which the staff of the courts martial had to be drawn, the feeling was, according to Draper, that the army should give up its responsibilities as soon as possible. Surprisingly, the judges did not seem to feel strongly even when the victims had been fellow servicemen.

In May a series of trials in Wuppertal resulted in verdicts so astounding that Dean commented: 'It will merely confirm the view held by so many Germans that the British are fools and not that they are the living embodiments of justice.'[55]

The first series of verdicts were announced on 21 May.[56] Fourteen Germans, part of the Kommando Ernst, under the command of Captain Karl Golkel, were accused of shooting eight members of the British No. 2 Special Air Service Regiment who had been captured in uniform in France. After interrogation, the eight servicemen had been taken to a forest at La Grande Fosse, ordered to undress so that the Germans would always be able to allege that they had been spies, and were then shot and buried. There was no doubt about the events or who had been responsible. Interrogations of those arrested early in the investigation had quickly revealed the names of the others involved. Most of them gave written statements confirming their admissions.

Yet, in court, all of the defendants withdrew their statements, explaining that they had been excited at the time of their arrest and had consequently been mistaken. According to their German lawyer: 'They were unprepared. They were arrested after they had returned to civilian life and were confronted with facts and questions for which they were not prepared. Names had been read out to them and in the general excitement they just became confused.' The lawyer did not even attempt to make the customary accusation that the statements had been made under threats of violence.

For Brigadier J.B.G. Hennessey, the president of the court, it had seemed to be a routine case. The previous week, with four other judges, he had judged a similar case involving the shooting of six SAS soldiers. Karl Buck, the organizer of the executions, and four others had been sentenced to death; five others were imprisoned for two and three years – sentences which Hennessey believed were too low for murder, especially as there was evidence that some German soldiers had refused to take part in the executions. But in the Golkel case he was shocked. Discussing the case with four officers, none of whom had sat on a trial before, he discovered that they believed the recantations. Nor could he change their minds. As a result, six were acquitted, and the remainder, although found guilty of murder, were sentenced to between two and ten years. The latter sentence was for Golkel, who had organized the

215

whole execution.[57]

Hennessy immediately protested to the War Office. He complained that the British officers judging the Golkel case were just the latest in a series of men who lacked the temperament, experience and intelligence to cope with a murder trial. Some were so young that they had not actually served in the war, but their unsuitability was only discovered after the damage was done. Many arrived not even knowing what they had been detailed for. But they were not, in Hennessy's view, the only ones to blame for what had been a long series of acquittals for men who in his opinion were obvious murderers. He claimed that the legal advice given to them by the Judge Advocate-General was misguided.

Gestapo and SS officers had seen that the defence of superior orders had not been accepted. They had now switched their defence and pleaded that the victims had been lawfully executed after a proper trial. The JAG was instructing the officers that the prosecution had the burden of proving that there had not been a legal trial, something which in the chaotic circumstances of postwar Germany, was nearly impossible to establish. The Gestapo's records had invariably been destroyed.

Hennessey's reasoned and balanced letter also contains other damaging criticism, substantiated by many other British officers, especially those from the War Crimes Group, who attended trials throughout the British zone. Some interpreters, he claimed, were 'quite inadequate . . . and were not of the mental calibre necessary to comprehend the gist of the remarks of the prosecuting and defending counsel and then to interpret them intelligibly.' The administration of the trials was so inadequate, he claimed, that the lack of arrangements to bring witnesses to the trial, rather than the trial itself, were the topic of news stories written by foreign journalists. Moreover, while seating for four hundred had been provided in the courtroom, the system of admittance was so rigid 'that after the first day or two of the first trial, the court-room was practically empty'.

Captain Harry Schweiger, an investigator in the War Crimes Group, was also angry about the trials.[58] A former member of the Austrian SOE, Schweiger arrived at Bad Oeynhausen in January 1946 and worked under Nightingale. His most notable success, which took more than a year, was the discovery and arrest of Oswald Pohl, Himmler's deputy and the head of Section D, which ran the SS slave labour programme and economic enterprises.

Schweiger is bitter at the JAG's failure to get more convictions. Too often, he claims, the officers acting as judges were swayed by the poor physical appearance of the witnesses who had survived concentration camps and lived in DP camps; alternatively, they were impatient that testimony was not given in English. He also criticizes the poor quality of the prosecutors. Very few of them were lawyers. The best qualified amongst the prosecutors was a former British prisoner of war who had taken a postal course on law from his German prison camp. In contrast the defendant was represented by a qualified lawyer and the court was advised by a member of the JAG.

Newly recruited prosecutors were given a two-page duplicated sheet called 'Hints to New Prosecutors in War Crimes Trials'. It listed laws which should be read, suggested that the new prosecutors should read the transcripts of 'a couple of trials' to get familiar with what might be expected. 'Make sure,' the 'Hints' advised, 'that half an hour before the court is due to open that all the accused and your witnesses are available (they generally aren't).' Page two was a child's diagramatic guide to the German police force. The Gestapo was described as 'roughly corresponding to our Special Branch'.

The result of the amateurism, says Schweiger, was acquittals. 'I spent weeks tracking down a German medical orderly who had given lethal injections to women at Ravensbrück concentration camp. The eyewitness testimony from former inmates was conclusive. The orderly naturally claimed that I had maltreated him. I definitely hadn't. The prosecutor was so timid and unimpressive that he could not cope with the challenge. The orderly was acquitted.'

The British courts did not seem to be displaying the 'best traditions of British justice' which Shapcott and Turpin had in mind.

Reviewing the results of all the trials and sentences, Dean wrote: 'It is quite fantastic to go to all the trouble to try and convict these Germans (many of whom are the worst form of SS thug) and then impose sentences of imprisonment which in some cases run down to periods of a few months only.'[59]

Sir Richard Beaumont, an Arabist temporarily working in the German Section of the Foreing Office, read Hennessy's report and commented: 'US courts do manage to award more drastic sentences and I confess I find it difficult to follow how, in cases where the issue is whether or not a man is guilty of murder, a British military court can find grounds for the award of a mild sentence of imprisonment rather than give a verdict of death or acquittal.'[60] It was a comparison which Dean seized on:

> The JAG appears to work on the curious principle that the court should start sentences for the most serious offences and that if a man is convicted of having been implicated in the murder of more than, say, a hundred persons, he is worthy of death, while if he has only murdered two, three or four, he should get off with a prison sentence. . . From the point of view of the Germans there is nothing to be gained in acquitting or imprisoning for short

terms these terrible murderers. Those that are imprisoned will only be released just when the Allied control of Germany begins to relax, and the type of German who committed this sort of crime is of no value whatever to the future of Germany.[61]

A letter in *The Times* from the Conservative MP Anthony Marlowe defended the sentences, asserting that the German lawyers and public were 'deeply impressed' by seeing British justice at work.[62] Dean, who had just returned from Nuremberg, was scathing about Marlowe's assertion, especially about those lawyers who had supported the Nazis: 'The moment they think they can do so with impunity, they show the old intolerance and impertinence which characterized Nazis and Nazi courts.'[63]

Dean's was a fairly isolated voice at the Foreign Office. War crimes was no longer a prime concern to the department since it had become a War Office responsibility. It was possible to stir up some indignation over the War Office failures. Newton had been among those who criticized the attempt to avoid the commitment to the target of five hundred cases in November 1945 – 'Our good name and our reputation for the efficient administration of justice are at stake,' he wrote[64] – but, perhaps with some justification, given the history of war crimes policy, the War Office paid no heed to the opinions of the Foreign Office. Dean's criticisms of Lambert in the spring of 1945 had soured relations, and each letter that Bevin wrote to Lawson had the effect of getting the War Office officials more deeply entrenched.

Moreover, the day-to-day responsibility for war crimes, apart from Dean, who was by then involved in many other activities, had been handed over to two officials who today admit to having been uninterested in the subject.

Sir David Scott-Fox had, with Dean, negotiated over arrangements for the Nuremberg trial. As head of the British War Crimes Executive, he had travelled frequently between London and Nuremberg representing the Foreign Office and reporting back to London on the trial. As that work began to dwindle, attempts were made to involve him in the trials being held in the British zone. Besides replying to Shawcross's complaints about the War Office, the work included relations with the UNWCC and deciding on requests by other countries for the extradition of wanted war criminals held in the British zone. Scott-Fox, however, was obviously uninterested. In 1978 he said that he believed that the public was 'soon bored by the trials' and that they should have been ended much sooner than they were.[65] He moved to the Egyptian Department.

The position was inherited by Frederick Garner, who remained responsible for war crimes for the next twelve months, until October 1947. Today Garner does not disguise the fact that his indifference amounted to a determination to get his department closed down as fast as possible.

Garner had been the prewar British consul in Shanghai. He was caught by the Japanese while trying to escape after the invasion. After his wartime captivity he returned to England at the end of 1945.

The Foreign Office said to me: 'You've been a prisoner of the Japanese, therefore you are an expert on Japanese war crimes, go and work in the War Crimes Department.' I explained that I knew nothing about Japan, and nothing about war crimes. The Japanese had in fact treated us rather well. I was a China expert. They weren't interested. For me it was all a chore. I had never been to Germany, knew nothing about the country and just wasn't enthusiastic. When Scott-Fox moved, I became the whole department and I didn't even have a typewriter. All I wanted was to get back to the East, so I spent a lot of my time trying to convince other departments to take the responsibility. Thank God someone finally did.[66]

The battle for those who cared, like Dean, Bevin and Shawcross, was first to keep a war crimes programme going. When he received the reports from Bad Oeynhausen showing just how far short the results had fallen by the deadline of 30 April, even Shawcross could not hide a tone of resignation in his report to the Prime Minister. Rather than diminishing, the number of crimes that had been reported was increasing. No fewer than 5,937 cases, more than double the January figure, were now listed by the War Crimes Group. Three thousand eight hundred Germans and others were under arrest as suspected war criminals, one third of them former concentration camp staff. The War Crimes Group had a further one thousand four hundred on their wanted list. Yet the number of British staff available was falling. Even Turpin's position, described by Bradshaw as a 'key man', was about to be deleted by the War Establishment Committee.[67] Only a fraction of the cases were being investigated.

'In the circumstances,' wrote Shawcross, 'I can only suggest that the trials should continue until the end of the year and that we should then review the situation with a view to bringing them to an end except in the case of the most serious offences.'[68]

It was a decision taken after the event. A year into the peace, BAOR had already stopped investigating any newly reported non-British crimes and had decided to hand over all the concentration camp cases to the countries those nationals had been murdered. But there was, despite protests to the contrary, a curious reluctance on the part of European countries to carry out the trials themselves.

10

'WE JUST PLAIN TURNED THEM LOOSE'

In the early hours of a June morning in 1946 a convoy of three-ton British military trucks left the Recklinghausen internment camp. Inside the trucks were forty-six Germans, all former guards and officers at the Sachsenhausen concentration camp. They had been told by their British escort that they were being moved to the Hamburg internment camp as part of rountine procedure. There was no reason for the Germans to doubt the British, and the security precautions were normal. The flaps at the back of the lorries were fastened, and jeeps filled with armed soldiers were positioned between each truck. In fact the convoy's destination was Helmstadt, the border crossing between the British and Russian zones. Sachsenhausen had been in the Russian zone. For Alan Nightingale, the Russian-speaking chief of the War Crimes Group's 'Haystack' section, the handover represented a hard-won success.

Since the end of the war, neither the British nor the Americans had been able to break through the Russian bureaucracy and establish any joint machinery to investigate war crimes, exchange information about criminals wanted or held, or even hand over Germans responsible for the murder of Russians. Sacha Smith, a Russian-speaking liaison officer of the War Crimes Group based in Berlin, remembers the first twelve months as a 'civil service madhouse'. Every time he tried to arrange something it would collapse as if nothing had been agreed. Smith now believes that: 'the Russians were so disorganized, with inadequate lines of communication, that the problems were never put to the man who made the decisions.' The Russian government had refused to join the War Crimes Commission, refused to cooperate with CROWCASS, and only once allowed an Allied war crimes investigation team to enter their zone.

Smith and Nightingale had for some months tried to convince the Russians that they should accept the Sachsenhausen guards, but, despite Russian accusations that the British were failing to honour the Moscow Declaration of 1943 whereby war criminals would be returned to the country where they committed their crime, the Englishmen were met by a blank refusal. 'It was very odd,' remembers Nightingale. 'After all, thousands of Russians had been murdered at Sachsenhausen.'

For no apparent reason there was a short-lived change of heart in May 1946. Asleep at his Bad Oeynhausen headquarters, Nightingale was woken at 4 am and told to report five hours later to Colonel-General I.A. Serov, the commander of the Russian garrison in Berlin. Finally, at three in the afternoon, Nightingale presented Serov with the list of Germans the British were prepared to hand over and another list of Germans wanted for their involvement in the Neuengamme concentration camp. Serov agreed to the exchange but refused all requests for British teams to investigate crimes in the Russian zone. 'He kept on chuckling,' remembers Nightingale, 'and calling me an intelligence agent, which of course I denied.'

For Nightingale, the chuckling ended when he watched the exchange at Helmstadt. The lorries had been driven without stopping a few hundred yards into the Russian zone. When the back flaps were opened and the first Germans who jumped down saw Russian soldiers, panic spread throughout the convoy. 'They pleaded with us not to hand them over,' remembers Nightingale. 'They were sure it was certain death.' After being methodically checked against the list, they were led away, screaming abuse at the British. Joe Lenewski, a Polish-born war crimes investigator, also at Helmstadt, had other regrets about the exchange: 'It might not have been pleasant, but we wanted to get rid of them. The annoying thing was that the Russians never gave us the men we wanted in exchange.'[1]

The Americans had been equally frustrated. Clay had initially written to General Sokolovsky on 30 August 1945, asking for three witnesses to be sent for a trial. There was no reply. In a memorandum to Clay on 18 December 1945, Charles Fahy, the director of the Legal Division, wrote: 'This division has sent the Soviet Legal Division a large number of reports of investigations of war crimes involving Soviet nationals [Fahy wrote eleven letters between 22 September and 26 November] but has received no acknowledgement. In many of these cases a suspected war criminal is being held in custody in the US zone and his further detention or release will be affected by the intentions of the Soviet authorities with respect to his trial.'[2] Clay ordered Fahy to continue trying.

Negotiations for a handover of 265 Germans, all former guards and officers at the Buchenwald and Nordhausen concentration camps, lasted until September 1946. On the 3rd the Germans were driven to the Hunsfeld border crossing. The plan was for them to be met by a Russian escort party. But the Russians did not arrive. The American convoy left but returned two days later, this time waiting for three days. Again the Russians failed to arrive.[3]

On 10 September, two Russian officers arrived at the Wiesbaden headquarters to discuss the handover. By this time the Americans were suspicious and made a written transcript of the discussion. Asked repeatedly by the Americans what evidence they had gathered about the two concentration camps and whether they would like to look through the American evidence, the two Russians replied, according to the transcript, as if they did not understand what the Americans were talking about.[4] By the end of the discussion the Americans were obviously nervous about the Russian understanding of a trial. After looking over the transcript, Straight decided not to go ahead with the handover. Instead, he decided, the Americans would prosecute the two cases; but wherever the evidence against an accused was not cast-iron, the suspect was to be released. About 150 of that group became the first of many war criminals to benefit from those early intimations of Cold War.[5]

It was not just mistrust of Russian intentions which frustrated the implementation of the Moscow Declaration. In the chaos of the newly liberated countries, which were desperately trying to organize national governments after war, occupation and devastation, the prosecution of Germans for committing atrocities was not even on the list of priorities. It was only when the British and American armies realized in the summer of 1945 that the expected national war crimes investigation teams from former occupied countries would not materialize, that Eisenhower asked the Combined Chiefs for permission to prosecute those responsible for running the concentration camps in the American zone. But it was understood to be a strictly limited responsibility, born directly out of the immediate horror of discovering the camps themselves.

Churchill had not proposed the Declaration as an empty gesture to please Stalin. He intuitively realized that the British would not have the stomach or interest to continue prosecuting war criminals for very long after the war. Their comparative lack of suffering would, he felt, limit their appetite for revenge; moreover there seemed little reason for the British to prosecute Germans for the murder of Russians and Poles when those countries would presumably have both the motive and the means to mount their own trials.

But it was only in the spring of 1945 that the Foreign Office and State Department began to seriously consider the implications of the Declaration. The newly liberated countries, while not demanding the immediate return of Germans for trial, did want the return of their own countrymen who had been collaborators, Quislings and traitors. Throughout the war there had never been any doubt that 'those vile creatures', as Churchill called them, would be judged by their own countrymen, and the ones that came most readily to mind were Frenchmen, Belgians and Dutch. But in March, the Foreign Office and State Department became seriously concerned about what they saw as a critical distinction between atrocities in Eastern Europe which were straightforward 'war crimes' and those which were 'politically motivated'.[6]

Distinguishing the motives for the crime could never be easy, especially because information in the West was very sparse. After the invasion of Russia, the German army had discovered that many people in the Baltic states of Latvia, Lithuania and Estonia welcomed their arrival. In the Ukraine the nationalism and the ferocity of anti-Soviet feeling was sometimes even an embarrassment to the Germans. Many of the Balts and Ukrainians joined one of the eleven specially formed non-German SS units to fight alongside the Germans, and not only against the Russians. There had been antisemitic pogroms in that area for the past one hundred years. Grateful for any 'natural' assistance, the *Einsatzgruppen* and the SS recruited Ukrainians and Balts into their ranks to participate in the Final Solution. Many joined the execution squads for the mass shootings, but even more went to the extermination and concentration camps in Poland as guards and officers. At Sobibor, the sixty Germans were outnumbered three to one by Latvian SS units which manned the perimeter fences. In Treblinka and other camps the Balts and Ukrainians played an active role in the daily atrocities and brutalities. It was the Ukrainian SS which cleared the last Jews out of the Warsaw ghetto.

But even after May 1945, the crimes committed by the Baltic SS were unknown in the West. Primarily because the Russians had not given the Western Allies any details – traitors were an embarrassment – but also because there were no means of communication, nor survivors in Western Europe to give the Allied armies any information. The Baltic SS had retreated with the German army into Germany and naturally continued westwards to avoid capture by the Russians. Some were arrested in uniform, but others had stolen civilian clothes and pretended that they were liberated slave workers. Naturally, for some time no one could tell the difference. They all blended into the mass of humanity in the DP camps. Linguistic difficulties made it hard for Anglo-American soldiers to distinguish between names and even to understand informants anxious to denounce the murderers who they eventually discovered in the camps. This class of murderers, definitely numbering tens of thousands, had barely been considered during the war.

Building on the Moscow Declaration, the War Crimes Commission had suggested in September 1944 that the extradition of war criminals between countries should be formalized by treaty.[7] The State Department rejected the recommendation because it would impair America's sovereignty. In its reply, which was delivered as late as August 1945, it insisted that: 'in view of the rigid control exercised over the entry of aliens into the United States, the entry of war criminals and traitors into the United States . . . is most unlikely.'[8] It was an empty boast. In 1979 the US Department of Justice established a bureau to trace and prosecute several hundred Balts and East Europeans known to be responsible for participating in mass murders, who entered the United States from DP camps and obtained US citizenship even after disclosing their true names, which by then were listed by CROWCASS together with a description of their crimes.

The British rejection of the Commission's proposals, delivered in March 1945, arose more out of direct anticipation of postwar problems. Not only the Foreign Office but also officials from the Air Ministry and Ministry of Production suspected that the Russians would demand Germans in huge numbers, using the label 'war criminals' as a blank cheque to obtain cheap labour, or worse, valuable German scientists and industrialists.[9] Even more important was the growing realization that the term 'war criminal' would be used to cover collaborators, traitors and Quislings, who if from Rumania, Hungary and, especially, Yugoslavia might not be enemies of Britain, but just anti-communist.

Many Yugoslavs had fought with the Germans and Italians against Tito. Often they had selected the hostages to be shot, rounded up civilians for forced labour in the mines, and committed gruesome tortures against fellow citizens in the name of the Third Reich. But there were other Yugoslavs who had not collaborated with the Germans, but were loyal to the prewar monarchy and, by definition, enemies of Tito. To protect such political opponents, the Foreign Office asked the War Office on 9 March 1945 to instruct the army in Europe not to hand over any war criminal without *prima facie* evidence being produced by the demanding country to establish that he or she had committed a genuine war crime.

It was a suggestion that Bovenschen rejected outright.[10] He argued that it would limit the military's discretion and involve the creation of cumbersome machinery to vet every implication. But, more important, he pointed to a dramatic inconsistency in the Foreign Office's attitude towards returning East Europeans to their own countries. Despite the War Office's opposition, the Foreign Office had insisted that, in conformity with the agreement at Yalta, the British army should immediately return the captured Russians who had been fighting for the Germans.

Thousands of Russians had been drafted into the German army, either voluntarily or as an alternative to perishing in concentration camps. At Yalta, Churchill and Roosevelt had agreed that they would be automatically repatriated. Now, as Bovenschen pointed out with some satisfaction, while Russians, regardless of their degree of choice or political motive for joining the Germans, and 'disregarding the possibility that in some cases they might well be executed after their repatriation', were to be returned just because they wore German uniforms, those who had murdered Russians or Yugoslavs and were clearly criminal were to be given protection.[11] By his silence, Orme Sargeant conceded that it was an inexplicable contradiction.

For the moment the Foreign Office had to be content with a stipulation that *prima facie* evidence must be produced only for the extradition of wanted war criminals held as POWs in Britain. The Cabinet agreed that they alone were protected by British law.[12] It was a decision which in 1947 saved several thousand Yugoslav and Ukrainian SS soldiers from facing their fellow countrymen.

As an immediate compromise, Sargeant suggested in June that extradition in Europe should be conditional on the criminal's name appearing on a UNWCC list.[13] It was, however, an unsatisfactory arrangement. Both Allied enemies were already handing over criminals and Quislings on demand, without referring to the lists. The Americans had not submitted one single name for inclusion on the lists. No one was in more despair than Lord Wright, who had become chairman of the UNWCC on Hurst's resignation. He complained to Dean that the Commission's work had been made 'superfluous and nugatory'. Dean however, had little sympathy with Wright or the Commission. The latest lists, numbers seven and nine, contained the names of people against whom, according to Dean, there could not be 'a serious *prima facie* case even of complicity'.[14] He refused to authorize sending the lists to Europe.

As expected, in the middle of June the Foreign Office was faced with a demand from the Yugoslav government to Churchill asking for the extradition of a long list of people interned in Austria by British forces under Field-Marshal Alexander. All were accused of 'treason against the Yugoslav nation'. It was the first demand by a communist country, other than Russia, for the return of soldiers who had fought with the Germans. Yet, although they were by definition also Britain's enemies, the Foreign Office ordered Alexander not to hand over the Yugoslavs, although many were known to have committed terrible crimes.[15] Paradoxically, at that very moment thousands of Cossacks and other Russians were being forcibly repatriated by Alexander's troops, amidst scenes of brutality and bloodshed, under the Yalta Agreement.[16]

The Yugoslav request prompted Sargeant to write to Bovenschen on 2 July suggesting that an agreement had to be made on the extradition of collaborators.[17] He made no attempt to define the difference between a collaborator and a war criminal, but nevertheless suggested that the army should only hand over wanted persons if there was *prima facie* evidence of them having committed war crimes. Bovenschen clearly recognized the legal quagmire, but agreed to an order which would restrict extradition to those countries where 'it is difficult to be satisfied that persons who we hand over will receive a reasonably fair trial.'[18] It was a formula which had already been laid down by the State Department. On Bovenschen's insistence, the requirement covered not only East and South-East Europe, but also Russia.

The orders issued to Eisenhower on 11 July instructed him to hand over all Germans wanted for war crimes against Allied nationals or Italians on the basis of receiving a plain statement of the facts, but without demanding a *prima facie* case. It was left to the unit on the spot to decide whether the statement was made in good faith. But a special proviso was added to the effect that no Germans were to be handed over who were wanted by more than one country, or 'whose cases involve special political or other unusual considerations, which cases should be given careful study in consultation with your political advisers.' Additionally, for the moment, no Yugoslavs, Poles or Baltic nationals were to be handed over in any circumstances. The proviso soon became a charter of liberty for murderers.[19]

The first to benefit were Germans who had committed murders in Austria and Hungary, wartime allies of Germany. At the Foreign Office, Troutbeck believed that Austria had 'no moral right' to try Germans for war crimes against its citizens – 'we would refuse to hand over those Germans to Austria. We might even demand that Austria return any Germans they hold.'[20] As Britain did not intend to try them either, the decision effectively meant that murderers went free because of the nationality of their victims.

For the remainder of 1945 there was little trade in war criminals. Although approximately eight million Germans were interned, only 134 war criminals were extradited from the American zone during the remainder of the year. The overwhelming majority went to Czechoslovakia and Hungary, not yet communist countries.[21] Poland and Russia had asked for the extradition of eleven people but had been granted none, while Yugoslavia had asked for 289 and received just three. A Yugoslav request to Wiesbaden in November for 274 members of General Mihailovich's army, which had fought with the Germans against Tito, was rejected outright.[22]

Yugoslavia's chances of getting anyone handed back distinctly worsened in February 1946 when the Americans handed a Yugoslav over as a witness on the understanding that he would be allowed to return after the trial, but on arrival in Belgrade he was immediately charged with war crimes and not seen again.[23]

The British were adopting a similarly cautious, but less rigid, line. In February Bevin personally intervened and ordered three Ustachi ministers to be handed over, arguing that there was little to gain by irritating the Yugoslavs by protecting former collaborators.[24] Until September 1946 the only problem was where to keep all the wanted collaborators pending the investigation of the evidence against them. 'The whole problem is most tiresome,' the Foreign Office told the embassy in Washington in a telegram which suggested that the State Department should be convinced that there was little advantage in not cooperating with the Yugoslavs.[25] Other countries were getting the criminals they wanted, although it seemed they wanted very few. Throughout 1945, repeated offers to Poland of forty-one German concentration camp staff were rejected; the Poles asked the British to stage the trials.[26]

Until summer 1946, France, Holland and Belgium did not even have proper investigation teams in Germany. At the end of that year, the Belgian and Dutch governments returned a group of Germans responsible for the murder of thousands of Dutch and Belgian nationals at the Lahde-Weser and Schandelah concentration camps to the British, asking them to stage the trials.[27] Belgian and Dutch courts did not have jurisdiction over crimes which were not committed in their own countries, a problem which Hurst had warned Simon about in 1943, but which had been ignored.[28]

But Russians indifference was the most puzzling. Repeated offers of Germans suspected of murdering Russians remained unanswered. In February 1946 Somerhough received a request from Major-General Malkoff, the chief of the civil administration division of the Soviet Military Government, to investigate the deaths of Russians at the Hunswinkel concentration camp and the shooting of thirty Russians by the Gestapo at Wuppertal in March 1945.[29] With a feeling of some pride, some of those Germans responsible were handed over at Helmstadt a few months later. In exchange Somerhough immediately asked for eight Germans who had been responsible for shooting British POWs. Malkoff refused. For seven months the Russians also refused to reply to Colonel Scotland's inquiry as to whether they had arrested Wilhelm Scharfwinkel, the former chief of the Breslau Gestapo, who was responsible for the executions of many of the Stalag Luft III escapees.[30] A British interrogator finally questioned Scharfwinkel in a Moscow prison in August.

In May Somerhough had suggested to the War Office that the War Crimes Group stop investigating cases involving Russians.[31] On 13 May the War Office agreed to the suggestion, but Shawcross, in the interests of justice, and 'despite Russia's curious reluctance', asked the Foreign Office to intervene and insist that trials of those arrested continue. Garner and others at the Foreign Office were unsure. Putting Germans on trial for shooting Russians and not sentencing them to death, was, they felt, inviting trouble. Releasing them quietly seemed the best solution.[32] It was decided that, until the end of the Nuremberg trial, it would be best to do and say nothing.

Sacha Smith believes that the reason for Russian lack of interest in the minor war criminals could be their belief that they had just obeyed orders as every good commissar would be expected to do.[33] As a parallel with the Russians' denazification policy of only removing the leadership but not penalizing the nominal members, the theory does have its attractions. An alternative explanation, apart from lack of organization, is pure suspicion of the West. During two years in Berlin, Smith only secured the extradition of one war criminal, Gerde Quernheim. A former concentration camp guard, she was reputed to have made lampshades out of human skin. Her trial ended in acquittal on a 'technicality'. Released, she was last heard of teaching in a West German school. Combined with the sentences at the Belsen trial, it would have convinced the Russians of British 'softness'.

The people the Russians did want, according to Smith, were the collaborators, the very people whom the Foreign Office and State Departments had decided to protect. Indeed, it was a Russian attempt to sidestep that restriction which hastened the end of the extradition of war criminals from Germany. It followed that once extradition ended, trials in the Western zones would also have to be brought to an end, lest the British and Americans found the task of trying all the alleged criminals thrust upon them.

At the beginning of September 1946, the Czech liaison mission in Wiesbaden submitted a request for the extradition of Kajun-Chan-Veli and Julian Reway, both being held in an American internment camp. Czechoslovakia's government at the time, although containing a strong communist element, was still regarded as pro-West. A total of 354 war criminals had been handed over to the Czech mission in Wiesbaden, which was respected by Straight for its hard work and honesty. Yet investigations by British intelligence into Veli's past revealed that he was a violent anti-communist and influential Muslim leader, who was really wanted by the Russians.[34] Reway was discovered to be a Ukrainian social democrat and also passionately anti-Soviet.[35] The Czechs were formally told that no more extraditions would be granted.

In retaliation, on 11 October the Czech government ordered the closure of the US War Crimes Commission in Prague, which had been established in May 1945 to gather evidence for the Nuremberg trial. The Czechs alleged that it had become a front for the OSS. It was a charge vehemently denied at the time, though, according to a letter marked 'secret', dated 15 October, from Commander Edward Green, deputy chief of the Strategic Services Unit in Germany to G2 Intelligence at Army Headquarters, the Prague office was in fact being used for the 'establishment of an effective undercover organization.'[36]

The revelation that the Eastern European countries were misusing extradition in order to try and lay their hands on political opponents was but one of the reasons that the British Control Commission and the British army advanced for bringing the entire war crimes effort to a swift end. Neither the British military governor, Sholto Douglas, nor his deputy, Brian Robertson, shared Clay's moral commitment to the war crimes programme, any more than they shared his belief in denazification.[37] Moreover, all the practical problems on the spot in Germany seemed to point to the benefits of as rapid an end to war crimes work as could be contrived without loss of dignity.

Unfortunately for the two military men, they found political opinion in the British government strongly opposed to them. Even Lawson at the War Office, whose apparent inability to override his officials' lack of enthusiasm amounted to support by inaction, had resigned. He was briefly replaced by Fred Bellenger, who was both more energetic and less sympathetic to the views of the Military Government and BAOR. Shawcross remained as emphatic as ever that the trials should continue despite the 'slow' progress. 'People who are known to have committed crimes should not be allowed to go free,' he told the War Office.[38] Bevin was equally adamant: 'War criminals should not escape scot-free sinces apart from other considerations, such a policy will not lighten our task in Germany.'[39]

Neither was in any doubt where the blame for the failure to reach the five-hundred-case target lay. It was, Shawcross told Attlee, the fault of the War Office, and more particularly of the Rhine Army Command, who failed 'to treat the matter as being the highest priority'.[40] Some consolation for the failure in Europe was provided by even worse reports from the war crimes trials in Japan. There, according to Shawcross, the American prosecutor, Joseph B. Keenan, 'was incapable even when sober' of giving coherent instructions to anyone. 'Confusion frequently arises because of his apparent inability to distinguish between black and white unless blended in the same bottle.'

Unfortunately for Robertson, even officials in the War Office and servicemen's organizations were complaining that the murders of over eight hundred British airmen were still unsolved, as was the massacre of Le Paradis and a newly discovered one at Wormhoudt.

Attempts to investigate many of the murders of British POWs had already been abandoned. Most of the cases had occurred in camps which were now in the Russian zone, and the Russians had maintained their refusal to allow British investigators to cross the border.[41]

Suggestions from BAOR that the programme should be brought to an end were countered by quoting Eden's words on 23 June 1944 when he announced the murders of the Stalag Luft III escapees: 'HMG is firmly resolved that these foul criminals shall be tracked down to the last man.' So far only eighteen of the fifty known Gestapo agents involved had been found.

The War Office and BAOR did however seriously consider another way around Shawcross's and Bevin's insistence that the trials continue. Both men had been convinced that the priority should be the serious cases. The War Office now drafted a letter suggesting that the definition of a 'serious case' should be 'arrived at by assessing the number of "serious cases" which can be dealt with . . . in the span of life which we decide to allot to them. The balance . . . will then constitute "less serious" cases for our purpose.'[42] Without ever putting the novel suggestion to either minister, the War Office sent orders to BAOR only to investigate serious cases, and to release the minor offenders.[43]

The target of trying five hundred individual criminals, originally set for completion by 30 April 1946, was finally achieved in December, and still fell far short of Shawcross's original aim of five hundred *cases*. Ministers decided that investigation should continue until the end of 1947, when the programme would again be reviewed.[44] This was despite a Cabinet minute of 4 November, when ministers apparently agreed that Britain should 'advocate a policy for discontinuing trials for war crimes'. Curiously, this decision seems to have been ignored in London, although it gave heart to BAOR Command.[45]

On 25 November Robertson tried to get a government commitment to end extradition and suggested a final date of July 1948 as an opening shot.[46] While his letter remained unanswered for four months, Bellenger decided, on 1 January, that the trials should continue for at least one more year.[47] In the meantime Robertson's antagonism, shared by most British officers in Berlin and at Bad Oeynhausen, grew.

Contrary to Attlee's instructions, Somerhough's War Crimes Group was still deprived of the staff and facilities they needed. He had only eleven legal officers who were described as being 'not necessarily qualified'.[48] Although on 1 January it was finally agreed that the Group should be organized as one cohesive investigatory organization, directly responsible to JAG in London, its authorized quota of staff was never filled. Instead of forty investigators there were never more than twenty-eight. The raw statistics of their results revealed as gloomy a picture as ever.

On 17 January 1947, 447 cases involving 1,341 people were ready for trial, but not one of the accused had yet been arrested. In contrast 4,200 men and women were being held as suspected war criminals, but lack of identification or proper evidence prevented them being brought to trial. 'Progress has been disappointing,' Shawcross commented. The Group had not devised any system of photographing the internees and circulating the photographs around the DP camps.

CROWCASS had collapsed in May 1946, the victim of a deluge of millions of unprocessed forms, a leadership crisis after the removal of Palfrey following the revolt of the American staff at the headquarters and, finally, of growing East-West hostility. The Russians insisted that the whole organization be physically moved to Berlin so that it become genuinely a Four-Power responsibility. After the convoys with all the equipment arrived, the funds were cut off and it never reopened.[50] It claimed to have been responsible for the discovery of 145 war criminals. It is unlikely that even half that number were found through the agency. By mid-1946 there were over two hundred separate lists and sub-lists of war criminals in circulation. Instead of being an aid to investigation, they had become an object of investigation themselves.

Faced with one of the coldest winters on record and a chronic food shortage, Robertson ordered Somerhough to reduce the numbers of suspects as fast and as drastically as possible. 'Operation Fleacombe' resulted in 2,500 suspects being released within eight weeks on the grounds that there was no chance of prosecution, or because they would not be extradited. A complementary 'Operation Ferret', a search for wanted men among the 30,000 Germans still interned, produced just eight men. Somerhough was also instructed to hand over to the Control Commission any of the 2,000 interned concentration camp guards who had not been claimed by another country and against whom there was no evidence of a specific crime for trial by a German tribunal.[51]

But Robertson was not pacified, nor was the army. Officers in BAOR were irritated by the army's role in the stream of executions which continued throughout 1946. By March 1947 there was a persistent rumour that the prison burial grounds were full, which was nearly true, and that some of the executions had gone wrong, which was completely true. The Royal Warrant had stipulated that death should be by hanging. Shooting, it was felt, might have been seen as an honourable death. Judicial hanging, however, is a skilled craft. Instantaneous unconsciousness results only from an accurate calculation based on the combination of the victim's weight, the length of rope and the depth of the fall. The distasteful problem for the British army in Germany was that, by March 1947, 110 people had been executed, but there was only one gallows and only one experienced hangman, Albert Pierrepoint, who had to be brought specially from Britain for each series of executions. The British Treasury, for economy reasons, would only allow him one day for up to thirteen executions.[52]

Normally bodies should hang for half an hour to ensure death; but to overcome the time problem the executions were done in pairs and immediately afterwards chloroform was injected.[53] Some time in February Pierrepoint was unable to come to Germany and his assistant carried out a series of executions, which, according to a Foreign Office report, were 'inefficient on one unfortunate occasion'.[54]

For subsequent executions, the army decided to use a firing squad. The results were an unforeseen calamity. Inexperienced young soldiers without battle experience were drafted to shoot a condemned woman. The woman was only wounded, not killed. The cause was either a deliberate intention to shoot off target or plain bad aiming. In the event, the officer in charge was forced to deliver the *coup de grâce*.

The mishaps occurred at the same time as the trial started in Venice, in front of a British court, of Field-Marshal Kesselring. He was accused of ordering the execution of 335 Italians in Rome in March 1944 and the unlawful killing of civilians during anti-partisan operations in Italy.[55] Kesselring's trial followed the convictions by a British court on 30 November 1946 of Generals von Mackensen and Maelzer, both accused of ordering the same executions, which were reprisals, ordered by Hitler, after a bomb had killed thirty-three German policemen marching through Via Rasella, Rome. The 335 men, women and children had been selected by Colonel Hubert Kappler, the SD chief in Rome, at the rate of ten dead Italians for one dead German, taken to the Ardeatine caves and individually shot. In his zeal, Kappler had exceeded his orders and executed five more than necessary.

There was no doubt that all three officers knew about and agreed to the reprisals. The only element of doubt is whether their agreement was irrelevant because the order to Kappler had been given from Himmler's office, and therefore it was an SS and not a Wehrmacht murder. But, in the event, even that distinction became irrelevant, because Kesselring had given Scotland at the London Cage a full confession, accepting responsibility.[56]

But it is one of the peculiarities of that postwar period that Allied officers felt an admiration for their German counterparts regardless of their criminal and unmilitary activities, so long as the victims were not British or American. So it was that the officer's messes in BAOR were displeased that Kesselring should be prosecuted. Indeed, even the prosecutor himself, Colonel Richard Halse, admits to sympathizing with Kesselring during the trial, and to secretly smuggling tins of tobacco to him.[57]

Sympathy for the German generals increased in direct proportion to the growing antagonism towards the Russians. That, and Kesselring's trial, provoked questions in both Houses of Parliament about the fate of 156 other German generals being held without trial as security risks; their only defence, according to the politicians, was that they had done their duty. Sourly Dean remarked, 'Many of them seem to have personal friends in the House.'[58]

At the end of March 1947, the protests in Parliament and the rancour in BAOR coincided with the meeting of the foreign ministers in Moscow. The difficulties with the Russians seemed insurmountable. Molotov used the occasion to launch a bitter attack on the West, particularly Britain. He reeled off the names of important Nazis, key supporters of Hitler, who had been reinstated by the British, and accused Bevin of secretly rebuilding a German army.

Because of their partial accuracy, particularly in the case of the Nazi appointments, Molotov's charges were all the more embarrassing. There were in fact 70,000 uniformed Germans and other nationals, members of the *Dienstgruppen*, employed in mine clearing and other postwar operations in Schleswig-Holstein.[59] Whether they were part of a secret army is disputable. To Sholto Douglas it seemed to be the right time to unilaterally declare to the Foreign Office that BAOR was no longer prepared or able to search for criminals wanted by Russia and Yugoslavia.

Douglas complained that the British army was severely undermanned and those few who had the proper training for finding wanted war criminals, the Intelligence Division, were 'fully engaged on this vital work'. Moreover, he complained, the Russians and Yugoslavs gave inadequate details of the wanted men, who had probably not only changed their names but also their facial features. 'It seems to me,' wrote Douglas, 'that any odium we may have incurred as a result of the non-apprehension of these war criminals will be swallowed up in the fury which the intended transfer of the Chetniks from Italy to Germany will create. If HMG are prepared for this latter, the other rather stale grievance will surely pale into insignificance.'[60]

No direct reply from London to Douglas is filed, but it was clearly analysed at the Control Office as an attempt to hamper the policy of extradition and the continuation of trials. The letter provoked a swift and, perhaps, unexpected, reply to Robertson's letter of the previous November. Lord Pakenham, the minister responsible for the Control

Office, declared that there could be no limitation on extradition from the British zone, not only because it would be unfair to Britain's allies, but also because it would make the British zone into a sanctuary for war criminals.[61] As new evidence of hitherto unknown crimes was constantly being produced, there seemed to be no end to the trials in sight.

Douglas and Robertson therefore decided to force the issue. During May, Jowitt, the Lord Chancellor, toured the British zone for the Cabinet to see how to speed the war crimes investigations and trials. The commitment was not weakening but the problem was increasing. Three hundred and thirty people were still awaiting trial and a further thousand had been arrested during the year as suspects.[62] Not only Robertson but also the Foreign Office were criticizing the iniquity of keeping men imprisoned for up to two years without trial. It was a characteristic of the Nazi regime, a parallel frequently drawn on by the opponents of the trials. In the army messes Jowitt was lobbied by the War Crimes Group to continue the trials and by the regular officers to end them as fast as possible.

The mood of the army at that time should not be underestimated. According to Draper, it was venomous: 'The office of the prosecutors of war criminals was not the most popular part of the military headquarters.' The unpopularity intensified while Jowitt was actually in Germany. The Venice court found Kesselring guilty and sentenced him to death. British anger was not confined to the military. Even Churchill phoned 10 Downing Street and threatened to publicly attack the sentence if the Field-Marshal was not quickly reprieved. In a letter to Attlee the following day, Churchill wrote: 'the process of killing the leaders of the defeated enemy has now exhausted any usefulness it may have had.'[63] The decision on Kesselring's fate was ultimately taken by the British commander in Italy, General Harding, who commuted the sentence to imprisonment: Kesselring was released in 1952.

According to Draper, the JAG prosecutors immediately felt the impact of the army's resentment: 'I have known what it is to be ostracized for being the prosecutor of a German Field-Marshal. The army seemed to have forgotten what all these Germans had done. There was a great deal of talk about the stories of Auschwitz being exaggerated communist propaganda. They queried whether the stories about the gassing, the sheds of clothes, artificial limbs, gold teeth and children's toys were all just propaganda.' According to General Sir Alec Bishop, most British officers felt sorry for their German colleagues: 'I knew what they'd done, but I felt that they had had just obeyed orders. I used to take magazines to Werl prison, where a lot of them were held. I felt "suppose we had lost the war. . ." '

Seeing that Jowitt was not about to break ranks with his colleagues,

Douglas and Robertson brought to his attention a surprising account of an American protest to Douglas against BAOR's intention to extradite a Yugoslav called Bergmann to Belgrade to answer charges of economic war crimes. Jowitt's report to the Cabinet did not support the commanders' pleas for an end to the trials, but it did include an account of the Bergmann case and an explanation that Douglas was forced to intervene because Bergmann would otherwise have been murdered.[64] Just after Jowitt's report was circulated to all the Cabinet, Douglas announced that all extraditions from the British zone would be temporarily halted.[65]

Until that decision, over 3,000 war criminals had been extradited from the British zone and only two cases, including Bergmann's, had ever been referred to the military governor. Extradition was a War Crimes Group and JAG responsibility. It was scarcely a coincidence that the Bergmann case, in itself totally unimportant, should arise just as Jowitt met Robertson, and that it was followed by a temporary ban.

But it was a coincidence, when the Cabinet committee met on 18 June to consider Jowitt's report and to review the ban, that a Foreign Office attempt to close the War Crimes Commission had just been humiliatingly defeated, with Britain finding itself in a minority of one against the nineteen other countries. Even Bevin was by then embarrassed by the constant Yugoslav demands for Italian generals accused of atrocities in Yugoslavia. But the smaller powers had argued that they were only just starting their hunt for war criminals and Wright argued that the British public still demanded that the war criminals be prosecuted.[66] To avenge that defeat, the Foreign Office agreed at the 18 June meeting that the military governor in Germany should be responsible for extraditions and that all interned war crimes suspects should be released by 1 October 1947, unless they were previously claimed.[67]

Building on his victory, Douglas announced that new arrests would only be carried out after the demanding nation had presented its case in writing and been granted a warrant.[68] In the intervening thirty hours, as many countries were to discover, the wanted men were normally able to escape. Even the Foreign Office protested that Douglas' new rules were excessively restrictive; but, having finally won control, he ignored their letter and started the countdown to releasing 2,700 men and women.[69]

The British decision was followed six weeks later by Clay, who went even further. On 30 July he announced that extradition from the American zone would cease altogether after 1 November.[70] Exceptions would only be made where the demanding nation could convincingly explain why the request could not have been made before. More importantly, three weeks earlier, he had ordered the JAG to end all war crimes trials by the end of the year.[71] Considering that there were at least seven hundred murders of American airmen still univestigated, it might have seemed surprising; but, as is explained later, the American war crimes programme had in mid-1947 become entirely discredited, the victim of an extraordinary and vicious political campaign.

Poland's apart, the international protests against Clay's announcements were the loudest from those countries who had done the least. The French government claimed that their list of 20,000 wanted criminals was growing daily, that they had only just started investigating German war crimes and that Clay had no right unilaterally to break an international obligation.[72] But it was the vehement Russian protest which was the most persistent and, in the light of past events, the most unconvincing. On 29 October, on the eve of the deadline, the Russians held the first and only public war crimes trial in their zone. Fourteen Germans were charged with 'countless atrocities' at the Sachsenhausen camp. Among the defendants was the camp commander, senior officers and the camp's hangman.

Under the glare of lights specially installed for newsreel cameras, the defendants were brought into a courtroom packed with journalists specially flown in from all over Eastern Europe and military officers in full dress uniform. Each German, defended by a lawyer specially brought from Moscow, faced the death penalty. Nevertheless, each pleaded guilty and gave detailed confessions of tortures inflicted on helpless prisoners. All were then sentenced to periods of imprisonment. The following day, Clay received a hand-delivered letter from Sokolovsky demanding the extradition of thirty-one named Germans 'all guilty of the mass killing of peaceful Soviet citizens, the wanton destruction and plunder of Soviet property, and of other war crimes'.[73] Besides two field-marshals, the remainder were senior SS officers.

It was a curious request, and goes a long way towards proving that the Russian refusal to cooperate on war crimes with the West was not so much the product of political suspicion as of hopeless disorganization. Three of the thirty-one names were in fact held by the British, while all of the remaining twenty-eight were at that moment actually being tried by the Americans at their own zonal trials in Nuremberg. The probable explanation is that Sokolovsky needed names of criminals and a member of his staff, lacking a war crimes bureau to supply the necessary information, simply listed the easiest names to hand.

The Sokolovsky letter episode reveals a surprising lack of interest. The Russians claimed to have lost twenty million people in the war, many of them murdered in concentration camps and mass shootings; captured Russian soldiers had been mercilessly treated. Yet the Russians seemed curiously unconcerned with avenging their people. The total of criminals extradited to Russia from the US zone was forty-five out of a total of 3,914 extraditions.[74] Straight now proudly claims that all the forty-five must have been Russians or Balts because he never agreed to Germans being handed over to the Russians. He claims he was just obeying orders. 'I was told by the War Department not to hand over anyone where there was a chance of there not being a fair trial. Would you want to be tried by the Russians? Anglo-American decency is not turning people over to Russian roulette.'

The first beneficiaries of Clay's decision to end extradition were seven Wehrmacht and SS generals responsible for the destruction of Warsaw in 1944 and the murder of tens of thousands of Poles during the German retreat. The Poles had demanded their extradition at the beginning of 1946, but it was only on 30 August 1947 that Telford Taylor wrote to Straight recommending that five of the seven should be extradited to Poland.[75] Unlike those in the other East European countries, Poland's trials had been as fair as any in the West. One thousand one hundred and seventy-two men and women had been extradited from the American zone to Poland to stand trial. Forty-two had actually been returned after acquittal.[76]

Amongst the five generals the Poles wanted was SS General Heinz Reinefarth, the so-called 'Butcher of Warsaw'. A German soldier standing near to him as he watched a column of Poles being marched out of the burning city of Warsaw, had quoted his remark: 'See, that's our greatest problem; we don't have enough ammunition to take care of them all.'[77] In fact the SS soldiers under Reinefarth's orders were shooting Poles at the rate of fifteen thousand a day. Straight automatically referred the request for the extradition to the State Department in Washington. At the time all five were working on the US army's 'Eastern Project', a historical analysis of the German army's campaign in Russia during the war. SS General Rode was describing the organization and function of the SS division's field HQs and the SS's anti-partisan tactics. Reinefarth was describing his anti-partisan activities. The Wehrmacht generals von Lüttwitz, von Vormann and Guderian were being debriefed by US intelligence on conducting a military campaign against Russia.

At the request of the director of intelligence, Clay ordered that the Poles be told that all five were being held as 'material witnesses' and could not be released.[78] None were ever returned to Poland or stood trial.

The sequel, by no means unusual, was distasteful. Reinefarth, released in 1949, became mayor of Wastermand, a small island in the North Sea, and a high-ranking official in the Ministry of the Interior. In 1951 he stood for election as representative of an extreme right-wing party. Protesters quoted his complaint about lack of ammunition to shoot all the Poles. He was unabashed. 'Even if I did say that. . .what about it? That wasn't violating any law was it? It may have been nasty and shameful, but we didn't take care of them after all. That's what counts.' He won the election. Polish attempts to pressure the West German government to prosecute Reinefarth failed. All charges against him were withdrawn in 1965.[79]

Straight cannot remember the Reinefarth case. Winding up the war crimes programme was a hectic period. At the time literally thousands of war crimes suspects were being set free without even being tried.

Straight had been given the first order to bring the trials to a quick end by Colonel Claude Micklewaite, the deputy JAG in Germany, as early as June 1946.[80] Straight had originally thought that the trials would continue until 1948. Now he was increasingly anxious to oblige the abolitionists. Constant demobilization had reduced his staff to fifty per cent of his authorized quota and the investigative effort was all but destroyed. With rare exceptions, members of the team were 'not well qualified', according to Straight. The group's work was repeatedly interrupted over the next twelve months, as it was compelled to move its headquarters and records from Wiesbaden to Augsburg, to Friesing and finally to Munich.

Micklewaite saw, according to Straight, no glory for his service record in continuing the trials, and because the trials were unpopular in the army, Micklewaite refused to persuade Headquarters to allocate more and better staff. The only obstacle in Micklewaite's path was a report sent from JAG in Washington on 24 June 1946 written by Damon Gunn.[81] Gunn had toured the zone in May and had been disappointed that while there were more than 15,000 war crimes suspects in the Dachau enclosure, there had been only sixty-three trials involving less than five hundred people. Gunn recommended that a further 1,500 trials, involving a minimum of 3,000 people, be held. The recommendation was scotched the day after it arrived in Germany. On Micklewaite's suggestion, it was turned down by Clay personally.[82]

Not interested in questioning orders – 'Headquarters was always ordering me to "Hurry up" ' – Straight cut the number of reported atrocities to be investigated from 3,603 to 793. Within a year, the number of war crimes suspects at Dachau was reduced to 2,000.

Among those listed for release was Dr Karl Brandt, at one time

Hitler's personal physician and later responsible for the fatal medical experiments on hospital and concentration camp inmates. His release was stopped at the last moment when Dr Baer, the Belgian member of the War Crimes Commission, just happened to be at Dachau and saw Brandt's name on a list for release 'because of "lack of evidence" '. Baer told the American commander that Brandt was named on the Commission lists. According to Baer, the commander claimed he had never heard of or seen the Commission lists.[83] Brandt was later tried at Nuremberg and executed.[84]

Wilhelm Hamman was released however, although three former Buchenwald inmates had identified him as a sadistic Kapo in charge of the camp's children's block.[85] In the bid to clear out the enclosure, the inmates were just told by the War Crimes Group that their evidence was not good enough. Anton Winek was another release, although he had been a Kapo at Dachau for four years and there was eyewitness evidence that he had murdered inmates. His file was marked: 'Release. No satisfactory evidence available.'[86]

Today, as in 1947, Straight is unconcerned about these and all the other releases: 'I was ambivalent whether we should carry on or quit. We had established the principle and to carry on and try thousands would have been expensive. So when I got the orders, I set the production line going. No special effort was made. There was no method, no discussion about handing cases or bodies over to the Germans. We just plain turned them loose.' His War Crime Group files had evidence against at least another 2,500 people who had never been caught.

On 12 December 1947 the last case was completed. A total of 1,672 men and women had been tried and 1,306 convicted in 489 trials. For Straight it was like the end of school. 'I had been in charge of war crimes from womb to tomb and I was glad it was over.'[87]

It was an end with a series of unfortunate postscripts, not least that the US zone did become a sanctuary for war criminals. Three examples from the period immediately before the Berlin blockade reveal how justice had become tempered by political expediency.

On 28 March 1948, Lieutenant-General M. Dratvin, the deputy commander of the Soviet military mission, wrote to Major-General G.P. Hays, Clay's deputy, enclosing a list of seventeen Russians who had either collaborated with the Germans in shooting partisans and burning whole families alive in their houses, or worked for German intelligence. Remarkably, Dratvin supplied the addresses in the American zone where each man could be found. Hays curtly rejected the request for extradition.[88]

On 31 March, the US Legal Division approved the extradition of four German officers to Yugoslavia. The evidence presented proved conclusively that each of them had committed a series of murders. Their extradition was halted on political grounds by the director of intelligence. All four were released.[89]

On 15 June, Army Headquarters replied to a detailed denunciation from a Lett refugee in a DP camp naming five former Lett SS and SD officers responsible for countless atrocities in Warsaw and Riga whom he had recognized living in the same camp under false names, or working for American units as civil guards. The reply, in its formal blandness, sums up the change that had come over the armies that had liberated Dachau and Belsen in the three years since the surrender:

> With the exception of atrocities committed in concentration camps which were located in the US area of control or overrun by US troops, the war crimes activities of this headquarters do not entail prosecutions of criminals who committed offences against the civilian populations of other countries. . .We thank you for bringing this matter to the attention of this headquarters.[90]

11

'WE'VE TRIED THE CORPORALS, NOW THE GENERALS MUST BE TRIED TOO'

On 22 November 1947, General Robertson arrived in London for the fourth meeting of the four foreign ministers to negotiate an agreement for the postwar settlement of Germany. Clay describes the meeting as 'chilly and tense'.[1] It amounted to little more than unusually acrimonious exchanges of recrimination. From the beginning Molotov snubbed Bevin, and he launched into a tirade of invective against Western policies. For the first time, the three Western Allies were united, but that only tended to confirm the deadlock between East and West. Britain and America had already drawn up contingency plans in case of a breakdown; the plans abandoned the Potsdam pretence that the Four Powers were jointly managing a united Germany. Preparations had already been made to introduce a separate West zone currency and both Clay and Robertson had started talking to German politicians about the nature of an eventual West German state. Clay, expecting the worst, had ordered the American army in Germany to begin a series of manoeuvres to test their readiness for an emergency, or even war.

On 13 December, two days before the conference finally collapsed, Robertson met the new British Secretary of State for War, Emanuel Shinwell, at the War Office. Shapcott and Michael O'Grady from the Foreign Office were also there.[2] Robertson had arrived in London determined to convince Whitehall to end the war crimes trials at the end of the year and to cease extraditions after 1 June 1948. In his own mind he was convinced that after two years, they were no longer serving any useful purpose and were indeed counterproductive. He had been easily swayed by those German leaders who told him that their support for the West was inhibited by the continuing prosecution of German soldiers. There was, he felt, no reason why Britain should not follow America's example, especially because winning German support for the West was not a foregone conclusion. Many Germans in the Western zones were still attracted by the Russian offer to allow the zones to be reunited and were suspicious of the West's policy. What better time, Robertson felt, with the breakdown of the conference in sight, to get the final decision. But it was not just a matter of closing down the War Crimes Group. Both he and Douglas had for the previous four months tried to prevent a prosecution which would, in their view, be little less than disastrous.

On 19 August 1947 Clay had written to Douglas enclosing an eighty-page memorandum compiled by American lawyers at Nuremberg under Telford Taylor; it contained evidence against three German field-marshals and one general.[3] All four, von Rundstedt, von Brauchitsch, von Manstein and General Strauss, had commanded armies during the Russian campaign and were currently under arrest in Britain. The documents collected by Taylor's team strongly suggested that all four had given orders for the mass execution of civilians and the murder of Russian prisoners of war, and for the Wehrmacht to help the *Einsatzgruppen* in their activities. Clay's letter to Douglas opened on a challenging note. He quoted verbatim the Judgement of the International Court at Nuremberg that the criminality of the German military leaders had been 'clear and convincing':

> They have been responsible in large measure for the miseries and suffering that have fallen on millions of men, women and children. Without their military guidance, the aggressive intentions of Hitler and his fellow Nazis would have been academic and sterile. Although they were not a group falling within the words of the Charter, they were certainly a ruthless military caste. The contemporary German militarism flourished briefly with its recent ally, National Socialism, as well as, or better than, it had in generations past.
>
> Many of these men have made a mockery of the soldier's oath of obedience to military orders. When it suits their defence, they say they had to obey; when confronted with Hitler's brutal crimes, they say they disobeyed. The truth is that they actively participated in all these crimes, or sat silent and acquiescent, witnessing the commission of crimes on a scale larger and more shocking than the world has ever had the misfortune to know. This must be said.
>
> Where the facts warrant it, these men should be brought to trial so that those amongst them who are guilty of these crimes should not escape punishment.

All four officers were in the classic Prussian mould, the sort of soldiers that Douglas and other British officers had come to respect. Gerd von Rundstedt had been in overall command of the German invasion of France in May 1940 and then, in succession, commanded the army for the invasion of Russia and in Western Europe. Dismissed by Hitler for failing to repel the Normandy landings, he was later recalled to command the brilliant but futile Ardennes offensive in December 1944. Rundstedt, like all the Prussian officer class, was devoted to military service. Soldiering was more a religious calling, passed on from father to son, than merely an honourable profession. Authoritarian and anti-democratic, they prided themselves on their unswerving loyalty to the German government, regardless of its politics – except, that is, when they did not like the politics. The officer corps hid neither its dislike of the successive liberal governments during the Weimar period, nor its support for Hitler's suppression of civil liberties.

Von Rundstedt's loyalty was greater than many of his fellow officers. During the intensive investigations into the July plot on Hitler's life, he willingly cooperated with the Gestapo and 'convicted' many of his former colleagues for participating in the intrigue on the basis of documentary evidence which the Gestapo provided for him.

Erich von Manstein was a charming and arrogant man, and probably Germany's most brilliant commander during the war. He based his plans for the tank offensive which effectively destroyed the French army in May 1940 on his reading of the English strategist Captain Basil Liddell Hart. His suggestions had been scorned by the General Staff but were accepted by Hitler. He had been the chief of staff of Army Group East during the Polish invasion and was a corps commander in Russia until September 1941, when he was promoted to commander of the 11th Army. A year later he was appointed commander of Army Group South, fighting in the Crimea.

According to his admirer Reginald Paget, the British Labour MP, Manstein was the only German general ever to argue with Hitler in person.[4] For six hours on 6 February 1943, Manstein and Hitler discussed the perilous situation of the German army outside Stalingrad. According to Manstein, he told the Führer to his face that he, Hitler, was an inadequate military leader and that the supreme command should be handed over to a professional soldier. It was strong stuff, but Manstein survived for another similar argument on 14 November about the need for an orderly retreat. A week later, Manstein was retired by Hitler.

Manstein's own evidence of his criticism of Hitler is important because it implies that what he did not criticize, he presumably accepted. The evidence against him suggested that among the things he agreed to were the extermination policies and his army's active support of the mass executions. After his dismissal he retired to his family home and, until he surrendered to Montgomery, lived on a comfortable pension.

Rundstedt had offered his resignation no fewer than four times between 1938 and 1945; twice it had been accepted, yet he had been recalled. He too was not penalized. Both were physically courageous, but at the very best, moral cowards.

Field-Marshal Walther von Brauchitsch was appointed by Hitler in 1938 as the Wehrmacht's commander-in-chief. He commanded the army's operations during the Polish invasion; it was during the two following years, until he retired on grounds of ill health, that he negotiated the army's role in the liquidations, firstly in Poland, and then in Russia, after discussions with Hitler and with the SS.

Colonel-General Adolf Strauss was a lesser figure. He commanded the 9th Army during the invasion of Russia, but was withdrawn from frontline fighting in 1942. Nevertheless, his signature, like that of the other three, was at the bottom of documents which ordered and approved of the deaths of tens of thousands.

The memorandum which Clay sent to Douglas was a collection of just a few of those documents. None of them had been found before or during the Nuremberg trial, but now, taken together, they proved that when the three field-marshals gave evidence at the trial they had all blatantly lied in professing ignorance of the mass executions and atrocities.

The 'Commissar Order', dated 8 June 1941, was sent by Brauchitsch to Rundstedt and Strauss. It dealt with the action to be taken when a commissar, the communist political officer attached to each Russian fighting unit, was captured. Explicitly, the Order set out that, if captured in battle, he was to be executed immediately. Those captured outside actual combat were to be either shot, held pending orders, or handed over to the SD. The latter provision, proof that the army was cooperating with the SD, a branch of Himmler's organization, is important, since the Wehrmacht had always insisted that it had kept its distance and was therefore ignorant of the SS's activities.

The equivalent on the Western front was Rundstedt's 'Commando Order' issued on 21 July 1942, preceding Hitler's own similar order of 18 October 1942. Army units were ordered to execute Allied commandos and parachutists as spies, even if they were dressed in uniform and therefore protected by the Geneva Convention. The documents in Clay's dossier showed that Rundstedt had personally ordered specific executions of British commandos.

But the most damaging evidence was documentary proof that the *Einsatzkommandos* in Russia had not only reported their activities to the headquarters of all four generals, but had also received total cooperation, not only by way of transport, supplies and manpower, but also intelligence and general propaganda to the army. An order entitled 'Treatment of Enemy Civilians and Russian Prisoners of War in Army Group Rear Areas' distributed by Brauchitsch on 25 July 1941 was found in the files of Manstein and Rundstedt. The introduction to the orders read that the country could be pacified if 'every threatening attitude by the hostile civilian population is ruthlessly suppressed.' It then continued: 'Suspected elements who cannot be proved to have committed a serious crime, but who appear to be dangerous on account of their conviction and attitude, have to be transferred to the *Einsatzgruppe* or command of the SD.' Furthermore German soldiers who committed 'criminal acts out of *indignation at atrocities* or the *destructive work* of the emissaries of the *Jewish-Bolshevist* system are not to be prosecuted' (emphasis in the original). It was a barely disguised invitation to pillage and murder. According to the Russians, approximately three million of their prisoners of war died after capture, as did hundreds of thousands of Jews and other civilians in areas occupied by the German army.

Similar directives were issued to army commanders at regular intervals, all of which expressly ordered the army to hand over all suspects to either the SD or the *Einsatzgruppen*. It was after the receipt of one of those, the 'Reichenau Order', that Manstein, then commander of the 11th Army, issued his own order on 20 November 1941. Part of it read: 'The Jewish-Bolshevist system must be exterminated once and for all. Never again must it encroach on our living space. . . The soldier must appreciate the necessity for the harsh punishment of Jewry, the spiritual bearer of the Bolshevist terror.' Other parts of the directive ordered the soldiers not to have a 'misguided sense of humanity' and to appreciate that he was in Russia 'as the bearer of a racial concept'.

In isolation, Manstein's order might be read as just rousing propaganda, intended to stir the troops to great acts of bravery – the type of material that all commanders issue to their armies on the eve of battle. But in the context of all the other evidence, it was nothing less than an acceptance of the Nazi racial theories, and what it implied was their inevitable consequence.

At his trial at Nuremberg, Otto Ohlendorf, the commander of *Einsatzgruppe D*, who admitted murdering at least 90,000 civilians in Russia, described his working relationship with Manstein's headquarters. Ohlendorf, aged thirty-four in 1941, had studied at three universities, held a doctor's degree in jurisprudence and, before the war, held a research directorship in the Institute for World Economy and Maritime Transport in Kiel.[5] These apparently strange qualifications for the leadership of a battalion of murderers were not unique. Commanders of other *Einsatzgruppen* included a former minister of the Church (Ernst Biberstein), a physician (Weinmann), a professional opera singer (Klingelhöfer) and a number of lawyers. At his trial by an American court Ohlendorf did not minimize his role; instead he explained it.[6] According to Ohlendorf, Manstein's headquarters at Nicolaiev and

Simferopol had directed where the liquidations should take place in relation to the headquarters themselves and had also requested a number of
Einsatzgruppe commanders to hasten the liquidations to prevent the
worst effects of an impending famine and housing shortage.

Ohlendorf's reports to Manstein's headquarters were equally incriminating. A report dated 16 April 1942 concerned the 'freeing of Crimea of
Jews' and another reported that: 'the Jewish question in this vicinity has
been solved.' Other directives showed quite clearly that Manstein had
ordered the *Einsatzgruppen* to work closely with, and sometimes under,
Wehrmacht officers.

At the end of his letter to Douglas, Clay wrote: 'This material is forwarded for your information and for whatever action you deem appropriate.' Douglas' initial reaction was to do nothing. The four generals
had after all been held in England for the past two years, and had anyone
wanted to prosecute there would have been ample opportunity. It is
indicative of the attitude of Whitehall and JAG that no one had even considered them as war criminals. Two weeks after he received Clay's letter,
Douglas wrote to the War Office giving the gist of Clay's message, but
did not send the memorandum.[7] The initial reaction in London was one
of surprise. Some officials felt that the four could be tried by a routine
denazification tribunal. Dean was concerned that here was an example of
a British failure to exploit their German generals, as the Americans had
done, by ordering them to write a history of their exploits. At least here
was a field where the American monopoly could be broken, he wrote,
because it was too late for a trial.[8]

Taylor's memorandum arrived in London at the beginning of September. He had sent a copy to Shawcross. After reading it Bellenger wrote
to Bevin on 3 October that the evidence showed that there was a *prima
facie* case which, unfortunately, could not be ignored, although 'we
were all hoping that there would be no more of these trials of German
generals.'[9] However, he told Bevin, the army could not mount the trial
because: 'I shall have no officer possessing the background, experience
and linguistic qualifications necessary to interrogate accused of the
standing and ability of Brauchitsch or Rundstedt.' Nor would he have
the qualified staff to sift through the 'vast quantities of captured German
documents' by then transported to Washington.

'For these reasons,' concluded Bellenger, 'I do not recommend that
we should take on the trials.' The best solution was to hand the four
over to the Poles or the Russians, whose nationals they had murdered, or
alternatively to ask the Americans to include them in their own zonal
trial of other members of the German High Command which they were
then preparing at Nuremberg. The Foreign Office telegraphed Douglas
on 15 October instructing him to ask Clay whether the Americans

would be prepared to include the four in the forthcoming trial of Field-Marshal Wilhelm von Leeb and thirteen other generals accused of similar offences.[10]

For eight days Douglas did nothing. There was no doubting his anger that a trial should even be contemplated. The army's revolt against the Kesselring verdict had resulted in a swift reprieve. Field-Marshal Alexander had been just one of many British officers who had written to the Prime Minister about Kesselring's fine record, explaining the reprisals as something unfortunate, but understandable in the heat of battle. Douglas was sure that there would be a similar, if not greater, protest if more generals were tried. After discussing Whitehall's suggestion with Robertson, he cabled Lord Pakenham:

> Before Clay is approached by Robertson or myself on this matter, I should like to be satisfied that the equity of our proposed action has been carefully considered. We apparently do not wish to be concerned in these trials because we know that public opinion in England will be revolted. We know that the Americans will make use of a lot of evidence of a very dubious character. Yet we are apparently prepared to send these men, including one who is seventy-three, to trial by the Americans. I frankly do not like this. I feel that if the Americans wish to be critical about our inaction in trying war criminals, I should prefer that they should continue to criticize rather than we should commit an injustice in order to avoid their criticism.[11]

One must assume that Douglas had read Taylor's memorandum and that his description of its evidence as having a 'very dubious character' was little more than a reflection of the commander-in-chief's unashamed prejudice. The ages of the four in 1947 were; Brauchitsch sixty-six, Rundstedt seventy-two, Manstein sixty and Strauss sixty-nine. They were elderly no doubt, but all four had, within the last six years, commanded armies in battle – itself more strenuous than standing trial. America's criticism of Britain's inaction was justified, however. Taylor and over 1,500 American and German staff were in the midst of twelve major trials in Nuremberg, which involved 185 Germans representing every aspect of the German Establishment – the banks, the army command, the legal and medical professions, the civil service and the industrialists. It was an ambitious, purely American, programme, which, although limited to a comparative handful of defendants, was establishing a more detailed indictment of the German Establishment's eager and active participation in the atrocities committed than the international trial had achieved.

Pleading poverty and lack of manpower, the British had refused to participate in any of the trials. With the exception of the trials of industrialists, which are described later, the Americans did not pressure the British to change their minds. On the contrary, Taylor had originally wanted to ask the British to hand over the four generals to him to include in his own trial. Clay had rejected the proposal, saying that he wanted the British to share some of the work and that he did not want it to be thought that only the Americans were prosecuting war criminals.[12] Others suggested that Clay rejected Taylor's request because he frankly opposed the prosecution of professional soldiers. There is no documentary evidence to support that view.

At the end of September, hearing about Douglas' opposition to the trial, Taylor invited the Labour MP Elwyn Jones, a British prosecutor at the International Trial and Shawcross's Parliamentary private secretary, to come to Nuremberg and see the evidence at first hand. Jones was impressed, but could not give Taylor any idea what the British decision would be.[13]

Ironically, Douglas' silence led Clay to a conclusion which frustrated British intentions before they had ever been stated. On 18 October, two months after he had sent Douglas the memorandum and, significantly, during the eight days when Douglas failed to pass on the Foreign Office's inquiry to the Americans, Clay cabled Taylor:

> Do not wish to ask Britain to return Rundstedt *et al.* British have accepted custody which is valid in view of SHAEF Command. We have presented evidence to British to justify charges and have no indication from British of unwillingness to accept responsibility. We do not wish to suggest joint trial particularly in view of our original decision to proceed unilaterally. . . At Nuremberg we are establishing precedent for future and not aiming at specific individuals. History will make no distinction between a von Rundstedt and a von Leeb.[14]

Had Douglas approached Clay immediately, a joint trial might have been possible. Two months later, it had been ruled out. On 29 October the Foreign Office impatiently replied to Douglas' protest: 'The final decision on these four generals will be taken by the Cabinet and your views will be considered when the case is presented.'[15] It continued by instructing Douglas to quickly ask Clay whether the Americans would include the four generals in the von Leeb trial.

The request was sent to Clay the same day, but the reply was delayed while Clay ostensibly consulted Taylor.[16] The American prosecutor had by then become irritated by the British attitude. The head of the British Legal Division in Berlin, Macaskie, had offered unathorized help for the Nuremberg prosecutions, only to withdraw the offer later. He had also agreed to extradite Otto Thierack, the former minister of justice, to

5. *Nazi-hunters*
The men in charge of hunting down the war criminals in Germany. Colonel Clio Straight, of the US Army (*top left*) and Group Captain Tony Somerhough (*top right*) in charge of the British War Crimes Group (*below*).

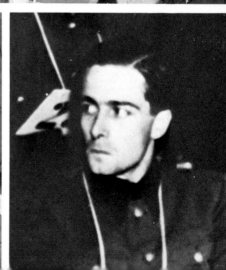

6. The Malmedy Massacre

(facing page, top) The scene shortly after the discovery of the murdered American soldiers in January 1945. *(centre)* Inside the courtroom at Dachau when seventy-seven former SS men were brought to trial in 1946. *(bottom left)* Sepp Dietrich, reportedly Hitler's favourite general, who commanded the *Leibstandarte SS Adolf Hitler*, and *(bottom right)* Jochen Peiper who ordered the murders.

WAGNER, Gustav (German)	Oberscharführer, Commander of the camp.	May 1942 – Nov.1943. Sobibor Extermination camp, Włodawa district, Lublin province, Poland.	Murder, massacres and other crimes.	A. Poland.
WAGNER, Hans (German)	Major	-do-	-do-	A. Poland.
WAGNER – SPIESS, (German)	SS-man	-do-	-do-	A. Poland.
WALTER, Emil (German)	Member of the Medical corps in camp 7.	1939 – 1945. Poland – Germany.	Ill-treatment.	S. Poland.
WALTER, Ludwig (German)	Ortsbauernführer at Weinoldsheim.	-do-	-do-	A. Poland.
WARLEOH, (German)	Politischer Leiter.	-do-	-do-	S. Poland.
WATZ, Karl Johan (German)	"Hopman" in the N.A.D. (Nederlands Arbeidsdienst)	11th September 1944. Drierbergen.	Murder.	A. Nether-

7. The fate of two wanted men

Gustav Wagner, the deputy commandment of Sobibor, appeared on the UN Commission's list of wanted men *(above)*, but despite this he was released from internment by the US Army and made his way to South American where he lived in comfort *(left)*. Oswald Pohl was less fortunate, convicted for his part in running the concentration camps, he was among the last war criminals to be executed by the Americans *(right)*.

8. *British successes*
(*top*) Colonel Gerald Draper of the British War Crimes Group photographed as he finally secured the confession of Rudolph Hoess the commandant of Auschwitz to the murder of three million people. (*below*) Josef Kramer, the commandant of Belsen, and Irma Grese, an overseer at the camp. Both were hanged by the British.

stand trial at Nuremberg. When an American prosecutor and escort party arrived at the British internment camp to collect Thierack, he was told that the German had committed suicide two months previously.[17]

The Americans had also agreed to hand over, for trial by the British, SS Obergruppenführer Karl Wolff, Himmler's personal adjutant, who headed the German SS and police organization in Italy during the latter part of the war. Instead of trying him, the British proposed to hand him over to the generous mercies of a denazification tribunal. Wolff treated the exercise with contempt and was released four years after the war. (In 1964 he was sentenced by a West German court to life imprisonment for the murder of 300,000 Jews, but was released after serving only seven years.)

In that context, Taylor was, not surprisingly, reluctant to help the British, and Clay accordingly told Robertson on 7 November that the Americans could regretfully not include the four generals in their trial.[18]

Whitehall swiftly realized that it could not win whatever solution it now adopted. If it chose to do nothing, then once the American evidence leaked out there would inevitably be international uproar criticizing Britain for harbouring the men who gave the orders for mass murder. The next possibility was that they should be handed over to Russia or Poland. With the exception of only one official, that was ruled out near-unanimously as politically unacceptable. The exception was A.G. Gilchrist, who cogently argued that only two fates awaited the four generals in Russia. Either they would be executed or used by the Russians. If the Russians did the former, did it really matter because: 'they are not very nice people.' If, however, Gilchrist suggested, the Russians used them, it would be good propaganda for the West.[19] Unfortunately his argument was never even read. Instead Bevin decided on 3 December that whatever the problems of cost, the British had no alternative but to try them.[20]

Bevin's reasons for accepting the responsibility were characteristically blunt: 'We've tried the corporals, now the generals must be tried too.' How, he asked, could one execute the subordinates who pleaded superior orders and not even try the men who had given those orders? Jowitt immediately opposed that decision. He wrote to Bevin that he had spoken to Robertson, who was in London for the November Council of Ministers meeting, and that the general had told him that: 'the evidence against these men is decidedly shaky.'[2] Bevin and Shawcross met Jowitt and showed him the memoranda, and Jowitt agreed that there was a *prima facie* case against all four.[22]

Robertson still hoped to convince Emanuel Shinwell, who had succeeded Bellenger as Secretary of State for War in 1947, that not only the trial of the generals, but all war crimes trials and extraditions, should be

ended. At the War Office on 13 December he told Shinwell and
Shapcott that it was ridiculous to be prosecuting crimes that had been
committed two years previously in the heat of battle. These were not
ordinary crimes, he said, and reconciliation was more important than
continuously stoking up recrimination. Any beneficial effects had long
been outweighed by keeping suspects imprisoned for long periods
without trial, and by holding trials whose procedures were an insult to
any recognized standard of justice. The whole programme, he claimed,
was doing more harm than good.[23]

But to Robertson's surprise, Shapcott not only proved to be
unpleasantly stubborn, but, annoyingly, seemed to be influencing the
new minister. 'We are investigating very few battle crimes any more,'
replied Shapcott. 'These are cold-blooded murders, and murder is
murder. Are we to let murderers go free and not even extradite them
from the zone?' 'For every person that asks why we are still continuing
these trials,' said Michael O'Grady of the Foreign Office, 'another asks
why we have still not found his son's murderer.'

Only a few weeks earlier, fourteen former Gestapo men had been
executed for their part in the Stalag Luft III murders, but the hunt still
continued for over thirty others known to be involved. There was still
no progress in the Wormhoudt massacre. Encouragingly, however,
Captain Fritz Knöchlein, the SS officer responsible for the massacre at Le
Paradis, had been arrested, tried, and executed in Hamburg. Yet over
four hundred named Germans were still being sought for other crimes
against British servicemen. At the end Shinwell was unyielding. The
trials had to continue for at least another three months and then there
would be another review. There was, at the time, little purpose in discussing the trial of the four generals. Gracefully, Robertson bowed to
the opposition and returned to Berlin.

Soon after he arrived, he set out his arguments in writing to Shinwell,
only to have them again rejected.[24] From Berlin, he clearly thought the
ministers were struck by some madness. On the day his letter to
Shinwell arrived in London, Bevin told him in an urgent telegram that
the Cabinet, after hearing intelligence reports about a communist
sabotage plot in the Ruhr, had decided to launch an offensive against the
communists which would include 'repressive measures to hamper their
activities by administrative and obstructive measures'.[25] In those circumstances it seemed extraordinary to annoy the Germans unnecessarily.

Robertson responded with untypical impetuosity. The normally cold
and aloof soldier wrote to Shinwell again, urging the end of the extraditions and trials, this time adopting in some respects the very same arguments used by the Nazis themselves. The majority of crimes were com-

mitted not for gain but on superior orders, he said. Those who committed them were dominated by a terrible fear of the consequences of disobeying the Nazis. Punishment should be a deterrent, he said, and so long after the event the trials were purely for revenge.

The Foreign Office, faced with Shinwell's adamant opposition to any compromise, was at first tempted to send a curt rejection. The counter-arguments to Robertson were not only obvious, but were the basis of the whole Allied war crimes policy since the first declaration in 1940. Officials argued that there was no evidence whatsoever that the mass atrocities were ever committed by men in fear of their lives if they disobeyed. Furthermore, if those who had actually committed the murders were not Nazis, and should be excused, then at least those who gave the orders and were Nazis should be punished. Finally, no country put a time limit on the punishment of murder, and the punishment/revenge argument could equally be, but was not, applied to any peacetime crime.[26]

Kirkpatrick, however, convinced other officials that a showdown had to be avoided.[27] As a compromise, the Foreign Office agreed that an extradition would only be allowed after a proper hearing of the evidence, with the accused present, in front of a tribunal. The trials however were, somewhat reluctantly, to be allowed to continue.

It is possible that Robertson's latest letter had been sent when he heard from London that, in Shapcott's words, the trial of the four generals 'was rather in the melting pot.'[28] Three army doctors under Brigadier A. Torrie had, after a medical examination, unanimously declared that all four were unfit to stand trial. Shinwell told Bevin:

> The doctors are of the opinion that it would adversely affect the health of these four generals if they were to be tried as war criminals. Each of them is suffering from a hardening of the arteries and is not unlikely to collapse either before or during the trial, which would be bound to be of a protracted nature. In addition Brauchitsch is likely to remain bedridden. It would be a most unfortunate occurrence should any of them collapse during a trial, and the risk is one which in the face of medical opinion I am not prepared to take.[29]

Shinwell suggested that the four should therefore be repatriated to Germany.

Everyone in the Foreign Office, from Bevin down, was immediately suspicious that this was a crude army and War Office ruse. After all, three were in their sixties and Rundstedt, aged seventy-two, had apparently been fit enough to travel to Germany recently to visit his dying son. Bevin minuted to his officials: 'We shall be accused of not being straight about this. Using the health reason to release them. I'm afraid it won't do. The small fry has [sic] been tried.'[30] The suspicions were confirmed when the army medical report was sent to the Director of Public Prosecutions for advice as to whether civil murder trials would still go ahead despite the medical evidence. 'Unhesitatingly,' he replied, and pointed out that the question the army doctors had been asked was self-serving and begged the negative reply. Trials will invariably affect a defendant's health and all men over sixty suffer from hardening of the arteries.[31]

To solve the interdepartmental clash of interests, the Home Office was asked in March for a medical report on the four men's health. Three were declared fit, while Brauchitsch was said to be too ill. Immediately the War Office argued that either all four were to be tried or none at all.[32] It was a novel argument, further complicated by a timely demand from Sokolovsky to Robertson that all four be extradited to stand trial in Russia.[33] Robertson immediately cabled Pakenham not to allow the four to return to Germany, so that he could tell the Russians that they were not in his custody. But the Russian demand compelled the British to undertake the trial regardless of any other consideration.

It was now the end of March. Officials realized that only the full Cabinet could resolve the Foreign and War Office disagreement. Technically, it was for the War Office to prepare a paper for the Cabinet describing the problem and stating the options. The Foreign Office waited for it to arrive. It was to take three full months, suspiciously long.

In the meantime, opposition to the continuation of the trials in Germany became a national controversy. Leading the opponents in the House of Lords was Bishop Bell, the bishop of Chichester, who during the war had been a vocal opponent of the bombing of Germany. Supporting him were Viscount De L'Isle, Lord Hankey, the former Cabinet secretary, Viscount Maugham, who until 1945 had been a passionate critic of the government's failure to prepare for the investigation and trial of war crimes, and a host of Conservative peers, among them many former appeasers.

In the House of Commons, the campaign was led by Reginald Paget and Richard Stokes, dubbed the MP for Hamburg because of his persistent criticism of the Allies' negative German policy. He too had waged a lonely campaign during the war against the indiscriminate bombing of German towns and civilian populations, arguing that it was a war crime, serving no military purpose.[34]

Outside Parliament the leading campaigner was the Jewish publisher Victor Gollancz, who argued that reconciliation was all-important. Together, they believed that justice was degraded by the victor's vengeance and that the collective guilt theory was false because the Germans had not supported Hitler knowing that there would be war. As a result of their mistake, Germans had both suffered enough and more than anyone else. The most controversial argument was that, in a total war, there can be no such concept as a war crime.

Although the group never remotely approached the size of a mass movement – both during and after the war they continued to meet at Hankey's Westminster home – their influence increased in direct proportion to the rising tension in Europe. German scorn for the moral validity of the trials and the Nuremberg Judgement in the light of the Allies' association with Stalin's Russia was no longer as easy to ignore after the murder of Masaryk and the communist coup in Czechoslovakia in February 1948.

By the time the Cabinet's Overseas Reconstruction Committee met on 12 April to take what became the final decision on the continuation of the trials, the Russians were manoeuvring towards the blockade of Berlin. Passenger trains between the Western zones and Berlin had been halted by armed Russian soldiers who had tried to inspect them, contrary to the postwar agreements. A British passenger aircraft flying to Berlin through the air corridor had crashed after being buzzed by Russian fighters. Clay, feeling that the West had to make a stand against communism, had sent a top secret cable to the director of intelligence of the army General Staff in Washington, saying that he had revised his opinion that war was unlikely in the next ten years.[35] The start of 'Operation Bird Dog', the issuing of the new deutschmark in the Western zones which would automatically divide Germany, was delayed only by the need to go through the political motions of pretending that an agreement with Russia had been attempted.

The ORC meeting had been given Robertson's latest estimate that the War Crimes Group were holding 208 Germans charged with murder, who had been awaiting trial for nearly three years.[36] Everyone agreed that it was a cause for 'great concern' and 'intolerable'. That statistic and the general political situation were sufficient for the Foreign Office to press for modifying Shinwell's uncompromising insistence that the trials continue indefinitely.[37] Extraditions were left to the discretion of Robertson, and a deadline of September was set for the trials of those imprisoned. Robertson immediately announced the end of all extraditions,[38] while Bevin distorted the Committee's decision to imply that all war criminal trials, even of those who were not yet caught, would end on 1 September.[39]

Bevin explained his unilateral decision to a protesting Shinwell on the grounds that he expected the first steps towards the creation of a West German government in September and that: 'the threat of the gallows

overhanging Germany had to be withdrawn by then.'⁴⁰ 'Even,' as
Foreign Office Officials explained, 'at the expense of a small number of
atrocious murderers escaping justice.'⁴¹ Bevin was even unwilling to
extend the trials until the end of September so that British lawyers, sent
out during the summer vacation, could be used.

In fact, the information Robertson provided for the Cabinet Committee was incomplete and misleading. War crimes trials would not
come to an end with the trial or release of the remaining cases held by the
War Crimes Group; what would come to an end was the army's role in
them.

On Robertson's behalf it must be said that continuing extradition
seemed of limited practical value, while the political cost of antagonizing
the Germans was considerable. Of the 1,080 names printed as being
available for extradition in September 1947, only 156 had been claimed,
although the great majority were believed to have committed murders.
The remainder had been released, amongst them Herbert Hagen, the SS
officer in Paris who had been placed on the CROWCASS lists by the
French. Among the many other criminals rejected by the French were
twenty-one former officers and guards at the Ravensbrück concentration camp, where many French women died. Having refused to try the
twenty-one themselves, the French Ministry of Justice even failed to find
vital witnesses for the prosecution which the British undertook.⁴²

Many of those who had been demanded by the French, and then surrendered, had not even been tried. Among them were Oberg and
Knochen, the Gestapo and SS chiefs in Paris. Both had been condemned
to death by the British for ordering the murder of British servicemen,
but were then, strangely, handed over to the French for further trial.⁴³
They remained untried until 1954; after being sentenced to life
imprisonment, they were released in 1962. Knochen is now comfortably
retired in Baden-Baden, living on a West German government pension.
Many others were released by the British at the Belgian and Dutch
governments' request. Some fifty-five Germans suspected of committing murder who had been extradited to Belgium were returned to
Germany untried and released.

Robertson was right in arguing that Britain's responsibility to look
after other nations' wanted men had worn very thin. As a final compromise, Robertson agreed to allow extradition on murder charges as
defined by the German Penal Code, if it was proved that the murder had
been committed by the accused of his own free will and not under the
duress of superior orders.⁴⁴

But if it was the Committee's belief, based on Robertson's brief, that
the ending of the British trials would give the Germans the finality they

wanted, that was untrue. Robertson had not mentioned that the Germans would continue their own war crimes trials under Control Council Law No. 10. In April 1948 no fewer than 2,129 Germans, most of whom has been arrested in May and June 1945, were still awaiting trial, charged with committing crimes against humanity, as defined in the Judgement of the International Court at Nuremberg.[45]

Robertson's argument to the government that it was unjust to hold the 208 War Crimes Group suspects for three years without trial seemed what it was, a questionable political manoeuvre. But it had been successful. While the British, in a series of trials labelled 'Operation Grand Slam', rushed through the motions of trying 124 men and women, and were then compelled to release the remaining eighty-four suspected murderers, the Germans continued trials for lesser offences. The only British trial started after 1 September was against three more Gestapo officers responsible for the murders of the Stalag Luft III escapees. Two were convicted and condemned to death but later reprieved. Of the remaining thirty-eight wanted men believed to be alive, four were eventually tried in West Germany. Two were acquitted and two sentenced to two years imprisonment each.

One of the less predictable effects of Bevin's decision to end the trials regardless of the consequences was Shinwell's conversion to wholehearted opposition to the trial of the four generals. At the Cabinet meeting on 5 July, eleven months after Clay first wrote to Douglas, he insistd that all four should be released because of the delays, the cost of a trial and because there had been so few British victims involved.[46] But the Cabinet minutes suggest that Shinwell was unbriefed on the War Office's part in the war crimes saga.

The War Office was itself to blame for the delays, a point which Shawcross immediately picked on. 'I am myself thoroughly sick of these war crime trials,' he told the Cabinet, 'but the inexcusably long delays which are now being used as an excuse for doing nothing, are the fault of the army and War Office.' Stung by the military's sabotage of the war crimes programme, Shawcross even saw the issue as a trial of strength between the government and those British army officers who were reluctant to see 'highly placed members of the profession of arms be submitted to such indignities, owing to the fact that for the most part the victims were, after all, only Russians or Poles.' But it was Bevin's argument that the failure to prosecute would provoke excessive international criticism that finally committed Britain to undertake another trial. Only two months previously, for political reasons, he had insisted that they had to be ended. In the first weeks of the full Berlin blockade, that argument was, if anything, stronger.

There is little evidence that British prestige would have suffered had the four not been prosecuted. The other West European governments had themselves a lot of failures to answer for. Russian and Polish criticism might, in the circumstances, not have been taken seriously. But at that time Bevin, to Clay's irritation, was still hoping to get a negotiated settlement with the Russians over Berlin, and he felt that it was better not to annoy Moscow more than necessary. The Cabinet therefore decided that the trials should be held at Hamburg as soon as the case had been prepared. Five weeks later, Strauss and Brauchitsch flew to Hamburg; and Rundstedt and Manstein went to Nuremberg to give evidence at the trial of von Leeb and other members of the High Command.

It was on Rundstedt's journey from Nuremberg to Hamburg in August that a most curious incident occurred: an event which more than any other indicates the attitude of the British army towards war crimes. Rundstedt stopped overnight at Bad Oeynhausen. According to Nightingale, then rapidly closing down the war crimes operation, the officers of the War Crimes Group were assembled and gave a dinner in the Field-Marshal's honour. 'It was a full-dress affair,' says Nightingale, who organized it. 'A person of his calibre deserved the honour and he was very touched. As far as we were concerned, he was not a criminal.' Shortly afterwards, the War Crimes Group officers, with a few exceptions, notably Gerald Draper, resigned en masse rather than accept the offer of helping the prosecution prepare the case for the forthcoming trial. Paradoxically the Group had just completed another series of trials of Germans who had executed SAS commandos in France on direct orders from von Rundstedt. The incongruity does not seem to have occurred to them.

The Cabinet decision and the transfer of the four to Munster Lager Hospital in Hamburg was shrouded in such secrecy that not even Robertson knew about it until he heard in a roundabout way from his staff. He immediately sent a strong protest to Bevin:

> I am most surprised that a decision should have been taken after this lapse of time without consulting me and that I should not have been notified of the decision reached . . . I wish to record my conviction that to bring these old men to trial three years after the end of hostilities will have an exactly contrary effect in Germany from that for which war crimes were instituted. All sympathies will be on their side and instead of holding them up to opprobium as criminals the trials will turn them into martyrs. I have long been conscious that the public is sick of and wishes to see an end of such trials. Each death warrant that comes before me brings with it a bundle of petitions from religious and political leaders and I have no doubt that these prosecutions will excite widespread indignation and resentment against us. . . I

can see no reason why we should accept the odium of holding this trial ourselves while we have relatively little direct interest in the alleged crimes. . .
These men are a spent force in Germany. The only asset which they retain is
their dignity, which will only be enhanced if we bring them to trial. . . I
therefore appeal to you most earnestly to have the matter reconsidered before
it is too late.[47]

Bevin predictably rejected Robertson's protest, saying that not to try
them would be 'indefensible'.

Robertson had also complained about the conditions under which the
four were being held in the hospital. Fearing an outcry in Britain from
Bishop Bell and others, Whitehall had decided not to even tell the three
that they were to be tried as war criminals. All four had suddenly been
placed under close twenty-four-hour guard, which meant that they
could not even go to the toilets unsupervised. Brauchitsch immediately
threatened to go on hunger strike in protest, which the War Office
countered by suggesting that he be forcibly fed. The draconian conditions were humiliating and invidious, Robertson said. The story soon
became public.

Deliberately, Manstein was allowed to write to his new English friend
Basil Liddell Hart, with whom he had spent a lot of time discussing tank
tactics while in captivity in Britain. His letter, later published in *The
Manchester Guardian* was a heart-rending account of his suffering,
describing what he called his 'torment and torture'. His wife could only
visit him for an hour each day, while his children could not come at all.
Kept in ignorance about his future, he complained of endless humilia-
tions: 'We are being confined like criminals.'[48]

The published letter had its desired effect. There was a tidal wave of
protest and sympathy and the British Establishment seemed to be
unanimously appalled. Bevin was unrepentant. When Churchill
threatened to publicly protest in the Commons if an annoucement was
made that the three were to be tried, Bevin scribbled caustically: 'I don't
mind what he does. Most of the others under them have been tried.
After all he started this business.'[49] To his officials, who queried whether
in the light of the outcry it might not be better to pull back, Bevin
retorted: 'We owe it to the German people as a whole, particularly the
workers in the Ruhr. We've tried the corporals, now the generals must
be tried too.'[50]

But the ferocity of the protest had clearly surprised Bevin who, in the
light of Shinwell's refusal to make the Commons announcement that
the trial would be held, insisted on another Cabinet meeting to reaffirm
their previous decision and unanimously approve the statement which
he agreed to read out to the Commons on 22 September.[51]

Bevin's statement had been carefully vetted by Shawcross. As the Attorney General somewhat mournfully pointed out, 'It is only when really high ranking officers are involved that sympathy seems to be stirred up.'[52] He therefore suggested that the Foreign Secretary emphasize that Britain was under an international obligation either to surrender the four to an eastern power, or to put them on trial. He listed, in five pages, a summary of their crimes: the gruesome murders of hundreds of thousands of civilians and the deliberate destruction of Eastern Europe and Russia.

Yet, mindful of the probable reaction to the announcement, Shawcross diligently removed as many dates as possible. 'I think the less we say about dates the better because quite frankly I still feel that we shall have great difficulty in justifying the delay which has occurred. The War Office knew when these Generals were captured that they were already on the list of war criminals and I think that, immediately, after the judgement of the Nuremberg Tribunal in October 1946 . . . they should have taken steps to ascertain what evidence was available at Nuremberg.'

Despite Shawcross's efforts, the reaction to Bevin's statement in the Commons was decidedly hostile. Not one voice was raised to support the Government's decision. Not only did the regular critics like Richard Stokes and Reginald Paget immediately pounce, only to be swiftly rebuffed, but in the ensuing foreign affairs debate, even MP's who had suffered during the war complained that it was wrong after a three year delay, to prosecute these 'broken old men.'

'There is nobody in this country who attaches more importance than I do to swift justice,' Lord Simon told the House of Lords on 2 November when they debated the Government's decision to hold the trial. 'I feel most deeply grave doubts as to whether the carrying on of this process is going to do any good.' As one of the champions of the war crimes programme during the war, his opposition to the trial confirmed the government's vulnerability. Ministers who were convinced that mass murderers should not escape justice were facing accusations of acting contrary to all the best traditions of British justice as a result of deliberate sabotage by their civil servants.

The apparent injustice of trying the four generals after so long a delay offered those who opposed the principle of war crimes trials an ideal opportunity to mount a large scale public campaign. Since so many of the protesters attested to the honour and honesty of the German generals, it is worth examining just one aspect of Manstein's published letter. He claimed to Liddell Hart that, having been taken to Nuremberg to give evidence for the defence, he had been denied that opportunity and was told that he was not needed. On the surface it seemed suspiciously as if the Americans, whose war crimes programme, as will be seen, had become severely discredited, had once again been suppressing the truth. In fact Manstein had himself decided not to give evidence, after being advised privately by the court that he had the right to protect himself from self-incrimination – an important consideration, if he was to be tried himself. In itself, it is a minor point, but it remains indicative of the 'honesty' of the developing German campaign against the Allied trials. Among others, it clearly convinced Churchill, who in the Commons debate on the government's decision on 28 October said: 'Retributive persecution is of all policies the most pernicious. . . British policy should henceforth be to draw a sponge over the past – hard as that may be – and look for the sake of our salvation to our future.'

The government ignored the criticism and launched 'Operation Marco', the preparation for the trial. The Foreign Office gave it a six-month deadline for completion. There were known to be 6,000 relevant documents at Nuremberg, 2,000 in Washington and an unknown number among fifteen tons of documents packed in US army containers stored outside Washington. A team of linguistic experts had to be recruited not only to sift the documents but also to search for evidence and witnesses in Brussels, Paris, Belgrade, Warsaw and Moscow. The War Office was responsible for recruiting the research team. Shawcross was aware that the War Office was again dragging its feet. Writing from Paris, he warned Shinwell, 'I am not satisfied that the question of staffing has been given the first priority that it deserves by the War Office or that the Treasury appreciate that the matter is not one in which they should be too concerned to secure economies. . . I have the clear impression that those who are immediately responsible for the preparation of the case are meeting, if not with lack of cooperation, at least with a lack of interest from the various departments concerned.'[53] Once again, his warning had barely any effect. By the end of the year, the six month target had receded into dim memory. Little work had been done; and though the Poles were cooperative, the Russians had officially refused to help the British prosecutors. In view of the fact that the majority of the victims had been Russians, the irony of the situation was inescapable, even to the most fervent supporters of the trials.

Meanwhile, conflicting reports began arriving in London about the health of the three remaining German officers – Brauchitsch had died the previous October. On 10 February 1949 Shinwell wrote to Bevin: 'I am seriously disquieted about reports . . . about the health of von Rundstedt and Strauss.'[54] Five days later, a four-man joint Home Office and army panel of doctors was appointed to re-examine the three officers. But before they arrived, the army doctors at Munster Lager sent their own report, saying that both Manstein and Rundstedt were fit to stand trial, while Strauss was likely to suffer a fatal heart attack if exposed to a sudden emotional strain.[55] Yet when Shinwell reported the joint panel's findings to the Cabinet on 31 March,[56] he wrote that they had unanimously concluded that both Rundstedt and Strauss were unfit to stand trial and the Munster Lager doctors agreed that their original diagnosis was wrong.

Shawcross was inevitably suspicious, but the situation was complicated by a formal demand from the Russians that the three be extradited to stand trial in Moscow. All concerned agreed that if any of the accused collapsed while on trial the consequences would be little short of catastrophic; but it was by then equally impossible to consider handing over Manstein to the Russians because of the inevitable Parliamentary criticism and what were called 'security considerations'.[57]

On 1 May in the lord chancellor's office in the Houses of Parliament, during what Draper describes as an 'extraordinary afternoon', Jowitt, Shawcross and Professor Sir Henry Cohen, then one of Britain's most eminent physicians, put the joint medical panel through what Draper calls 'a thorough grilling'. The electrocardiograms and X-rays were minutedly inspected, while doctors were, literally, interrogated about their individual findings. At the end the three unanimously agreed that only Manstein was fit to stand trial.

The decision was endorsed by the Cabinet on 3 May.[58] At the same meeting they also agreed that Straus and von Rundstedt should not be extradited to Russia, although extraditions of other war criminals could continue where there was *prima facie* evidence of murder which was acceptable under the German legal code.[59] The announcement to the House of Lords on 5 May was greeted with derision.

The Manchester Guardian described the government's announcement as 'an inglorious decision'. Its editorial continued: 'Heaven is weary of the hollow words, which States and Kingdoms utter, when they talk of truth and justice'

Faced by protests from all sides in the House of Commons, Shinwell insisted that the government's decision to try Manstein alone had not been taken because of fear of the Russians. 'Justice cannot be set aside,' he said.[60]

The groundswell of sympathy for Manstein in Britain rapidly increased. To an extent, it was the product of that British quirk, 'love for the underdog'. Some had always disliked the philosophy underlying the prosecution of war criminals. Others, in the midst of the Berlin blockade, just did not think it was necessary for Britain to prosecute Germans for murdering Russians and Poles.

It was a situation which was brilliantly exploited by Dr Paul Leverkühn and Dr Hans Laternser, the two German lawyers appointed to defend Manstein. For some months they had been trying to convince the

Foreign Office that Manstein should have a British lawyer to defend him, who should be paid from British government funds, as the Field-Marshal had no funds in Britain. The Foreign Office rejected the idea.[61] On 11 July, Leverkühn, with De L'Isle's help, wrote to *The Times* appealing for a British lawyer to defend his client, claiming that German lawyers were at a disadvantage linguistically and in their ignorance of the alien law and of Anglo-American courtroom techniques. Both German lawyers had, in fact, spent the previous four years ably pleading in front of American and British judges in Nuremberg, Dachau, Hamburg and Venice. Nevertheless, the letter was an immediate success. Two days later, Viscount Bridgeman, late of AG3, and De L'Isle opened a public subscription for the defence fund for 'the belated trial of an aged German general'. Churchill was among the first to contribute, he gave £25 towards the £2,000 collected.[62]

The Germans, while clearly delighted about Churchill's support, were to be for ever puzzled by the great affection which sections of the British public had for Manstein. His supporters included T.S. Eliot. Many interpreted it not as a gesture to make amends, or the result of deeply felt philosophical convictions that it was wrong to prosecute war criminals, but as overwhelming proof that the British wanted the help of the German officer class against the Russians. Moscow interpreted British sympathy for Manstein in the same way and accused Churchill of being 'Warmonger No 1'.[63] Attempts by the British embassy in Moscow to negotiate even a modicum of help were now formally rejected.[64]

Churchill's open support presented Viscount De L'Isle with just one problem. Leverkühn had already approached Sam Silkin, a Labour MP and barrister, to defend Manstein. He now feared that if Churchill discovered that his money was to finance a socialist, he would withdrew his contribution. Some quiet behind-the-scenes work by Bridgeman ensured that solicitors were found who could 'brief' Silkin. German propagandists were not slow to mention that Silkin, who agreed to work for no fee, was Jewish. Leading the defence, also for no fee, was Reginald Paget, another Labour MP and a King's Counsel.

The trial opened on 24 August in the Curio House in Hamburg. The courtroom walls were covered with maps showing where Manstein's armies were positioned at relevant dates in their campaigns across thousands of miles of eastern Russia. Manstein was charged with seventeen offences, involving complicity in both general and specified murders and ill-treatment of civilians and soldiers in disregard of international laws and conventions. Prosecuting was Sir Arthur Comyns Carr, leader of the British prosecutors in Tokyo, helped by Elwyn Jones and Draper. But in Hamburg, Carr was both tired and outwitted by Paget's bullying tactics, as was Judge Advocate-General Mr Justice Collingwood, a shy county court judge.

Paget opened his defence with an attack on the prosecution lawyers, especially Elwyn Jones: 'The prosecution, which has not hesitated to cast gibes and slurs upon Manstein's honour [which Paget had previously described as 'immaculate'] would do well to look to the honour of their own profession.' It was the first of many attacks which were to lead on one occasion to the temporary suspension of the trial to allow tempers to cool.

Paget argued Manstein's case on two entirely different premises. Firstly, that the facts alleged were untrue; and, secondly, that the legality of the trial itself was questionable.

On the facts, Manstein claimed, and Paget apparently believed him, that he had cared for the Russian POWs as well as possible.[65] Whenever he heard that German soldiers had broken his strict ruling of adherence to the Geneva Convention, Manstein claimed that he had ordered them to be disciplined. He also claimed that while the death rate amongst Russian POWs under his command had been a mere two per cent, no less than seventy per cent of Germans taken prisoners by the Russians perished. The atrocities were not committed by the Germans, but by the Russians. His whole Army Group, he claimed, had only executed forty-nine Russians, not the tens of thousands alleged, and those were justifiable reprisals for commander fighting a vicious partisan war behind the lines.

Manstein further argued that, while he was aware of the persecution of the Jews, he believed it was only 'religious' and had never heard of the concentration camps or the atrocities. He had either amended or not passed on Hitler's many orders against the Jews which were found in his files. Some he had been forced to pass on because he had no alternative but to obey orders. Ohlendorf's reports submitted to his headquarters, Paget argued on Manstein's behalf, were wildly exaggerated. Instead of the 90,000 whom Ohlendorf claimed to have murdered, it was more likely to be 3,000. The figures were inflated to impress Himmler in Berlin.

Paget went to some lengths to prove, using a method remarkably similar to that of the present-day Nazi publication *Did Six Million Really Die?*, that there were not even 90,000 Jews living in the area where Ohlendorf's *Einsatzgruppe* operated. In other words, even at his trial for his life, Ohlendorf, who was trying to atone for his sins, was still wildly boasting. In testimony, Manstein even claimed not to have heard of the 3,000 alleged deaths. He explained that his staff had not passed Ohlendorf's reports on to him because they knew how upset he would have been. Indeed, this most punctilious of field-marshals, who, Paget claims in his account of the trial, never ceased to visit every section and unit of his massive army, testified that he had, at most, only heard of five per cent of the events for which he was charged with responsibility.

Manstein's ignorance was matched by Paget's assertive disbelief of all the evidence of atrocities uncovered since the German defeat. He gave both credibility and respectability to the popular German argument that the atrocities, and the Wehrmacht's alleged complicity in them, were products of communist propaganda. Paget asserts that: 'the German Army in Poland behaved well . . . some synagogues burned, occasional indignities were imposed on the Jewish population,'[66] while Manstein's 'Jewish-Bolshevist' order was 'no different from the Allied non-fraternization rule'. He consistently ignored the fact that Germany was the aggressor against Russia.

When Paget advanced these arguments in court, the president of the trial, Lieutenant-General Sir Frank Simpson, asked him, after the murmurs in the public gallery had been silenced: 'Are you being funny?' 'Not at all,' replied Paget.[67] Throughout the case he revealed a political rather than a legal interest, which was clearly not hindered by having a Jewish fellow lawyer and politician on his side.

For Major B. Acht, the official Polish observer at the trial, Paget's behaviour was just too outrageous. On 10 November he wrote to Sir Frank Simpson that he was withdrawing from the trial:

> The trial is tending to change its meaning and is developing into a trial of the millions of fighters against Nazi fascism [and the] glorification of Nazism. . . The defence is advancing the thesis that it is not the murderer but the murdered who is guilty. The defence is daring to plead openly the justification for the moral and legal reasons of the murder itself. . . Unquestionable crimes are being glorified by counsel for the defence who are attempting to camouflage crimes by quoting military discipline.[68]

Paget and Silkin were undeterred and continued the same line of defence.

Paget's unedifying arguments obscure his more valid legal challenges to the trial. The practical ones were, to some extent, well founded and a constant source of ammunition for the sincere and non-Nazi German critics of all the trials. The defence, they claimed, were disadvantaged in terms of time, facilities and manpower by comparison with the prosecution. Whether Manstein's defence team was at a greater disadvantage than the defence normally is in Britain and America is debatable. Paget's complaints definitely secured for Manstein conditions superior to those that had been offered to his German predecessors.

Legally, Paget's arguments do however have merit. The British court's unquestioning acceptance that the Geneva Convention on the Treatment of Prisoners of War and the 1907 Hague Convention on

Land Warfare were international laws which were binding on Germany, was suspect. The Germans and Paget argued that, as Russia was not a signatory of those agreements, she was therefore not entitled to the benefits just because Germany was bound. The British replied, as in Nuremberg, that countries were bound regardless of whether they were signatories, to which Paget retorted that retrospective laws were repugnant to justice and the rule of law. War, he said, was by definition an abandonment of all order and there could be no binding rules. Punishment after the war was equally irrelevant because its purpose was to deter, and after such a crushing defeat the trial was revenge, not justice. The murderers, he claimed, should have been left for the Germans to deal with.

Paget also argued that Britain and America, in their treatment of POWs and the war criminals, had themselves broken the Geneva Convention. Manstein was charged with the illegal use of Russian POW's as labour to build barricades and anti-tank trenches, an offence under the Convention. But Britain's employment of the *Dienstgruppen* for mine clearance was very similar. The Convention also stipulated that POWs should be released as soon as hostilities ceased. In 1948 Britain was still using German POWs as low-paid agricultural workers to bring in the harvest.

Prisoners of war were, under the Convention, not expected to give more information than their name, rank and serial number. Yet the Allies had subjected the suspected German war criminals to long interrogations. To overcome that legal inconvenience, the Allied courts had held that once a soldier commits a war crime, or is alleged to have committed one, he automatically becomes demilitarized and has no rights or protection. It satisfied the Allies, but obviously not the Germans. It looked very much like the victor rewriting the rules to suit the situation.

For the few transgressions which he admitted and could not explain as forced on him for operational reasons, Manstein defended himself as being bound by the duty to obey superior orders. It was just the defence which the Nuremberg Judgement so roundly condemned and which, coming from a Field-Marshal who prided himself on his unique challenge to Hitler, seemed a poor advertisement for a great Prussian hero. If accepted, it would have meant that, besides Hitler, there would have been very few Germans out of the sixty million population who could have been responsible for anything.

Manstein's use of the defence is more remarkable because while, as Paget rightly points out, the British had at the outbreak of the war accepted it as a defence, the Germans had not.

During the First World War the British, American and German military manuals expressly stated that a soldier could not be punished if he obeyed his commander's orders. That rule remained unaltered in the revised British military manual published in 1940 and in the American equivalent. Chapter XIV para 443 of the British manual stated: 'Members of the armed forces who commit such violations of the recognized rules of warfare as are ordered by their government or their commander, are not war criminals and cannot therefore be punished by the enemy.'

The German manual, however, was changed following a decision at the otherwise farcical trial at Leipzig in 1921 of two German submarine crewmen charged with shooting helpless survivors of a torpedoed British hospital ship. The German court held that the crewmen could not plead superior orders and convicted them. Accordingly Section 47 of the revised German Military Criminal Code stated that superior orders were not a defence if the person obeying the order knew that the order related to the carrying out of a crime. Goebbels expressly condemned the plea of superior orders in a newspaper article on 18 May 1944, when he justified the German shooting of captured Allied airmen who claimed that they had been sent to Germany by their superior officers.[69]

It was only at the beginning of 1942, after Roosevelt and Churchill had publicly condemned German atrocities, that the British Law Officers examined the superior orders defence. Confusion and uncertainty mark their report to the Cabinet in April 1942.[70] At one point they wrote that it *was* a *prima facie* defence, while later they say: 'we are not quite sure whether we accept the view that it is a *prima facie* defence.' Later, they wrote: 'no person should be punished for the commission of an act which he did not know to be forbidden, or which he could not reasonably be expected to know to be unlawful,' but there followed detailed examples of how the defence was unavailable to those who must have realized that their act was excessive and contrary to humanity, or where knowledge of illegality could be imputed. The lawyers concluded: 'It would be contrary to all our principles to proceed after hostilities are over against a subordinate acting under orders in circumstances in which he clearly had no option but to obey. To take an obvious example. If there had been an illegal shooting, no one would think of proceeding against the firing squad, they would proceed against the officer who had ordered the man to be shot.'

When the Cabinet met on 6 July 1942, it agreed that superior orders should be a *prima facie* defence, since it was the only practical solution if war crimes trials were to be avoided altogether.[71] Cavendish–Bentinck had put it less delicately in November 1941, when confronted with the reports of massacres in Poland. Accepting the plea, he wrote, would prevent Britain being put in the 'same grotesque position as we [were] after the last war of punishing men who were merely carrying out orders from superior authorities.'[72]

Yet on 18 February 1943, seven months after that Cabinet decision, Lord Simon, who had been at that Cabinet meeting, said in a public speech about war crimes at the Stephens Club in Westminster: 'We have never in this country recognized that the defence of superior orders is a sufficient excuse or a proof of innocence when blackguardly deeds are done which the perpetrators must know to be infamous.'[73] Simon was then speaking exclusively about Germany's leaders. The law apparently changed to suit the size of the crime.

It was at the end of 1943, after Allied politicians had proclaimed the most binding pledges of postwar justice, that the Law Officers realized that if the Allies were to punish German subordinates for war crimes, then the British and American military manuals would have to be altered. No announcement of the change was made; it was quietly introduced in spring 1944. The amended regulation stated that: 'members of the armed forces are bound to obey lawful orders only and they cannot therefore escape liability if in obedience to a command, they commit acts which both violate unchallenged rules of warfare and outrage the general sentiment of humanity.'[74]

Justifying the suspicious timing of that alteration, Draper claims today that its omission from the previous manual in 1940 had been an unfortunate oversight by the JAG in both countries, who had not read the new edition of Oppenheim-Lauterpacht, the standard international law textbook. Oppenheim had reported the 1921 Leipzig Court decision, but its mere report hardly made it binding on Britain and America.

Mr Justice Jackson, the American prosecutor at Nuremberg, clearly did not think it was binding when he wrote a progress report on the preparations for the trial to the President on 7 June 1945.[75] The defence, he wrote, would not apply where the accused 'had discretion because of rank or latitude of his orders.' 'Enlisted or conscripted soldiers on a firing squad,' he wrote, could claim the defence. But both the Nuremberg Judgement and Law No 10 unequivocally stated that it was not a defence.

To confuse matters further, German courts after 1945, in applying German law to cases involving crimes against Germans, had accepted the defence although it was explicitly denied by German law.

Manstein's defence of superior orders was therefore invalid under German law, and, as Paget explained, dubiously valid under British law. The obscurity, contradictions and political atmosphere resulted in the court acquitting Manstein on eight charges and convicting him on the remaining nine after seven of them had been amended. The acquittals were on the most serious charges of responsibility for the reprisals and atrocities to the Jews, but he was found guilty of neglecting to protect civilian life. He was sentenced to eighteen years.

Paget hailed the verdict as a vindication for a German who was only 'vicariously responsible' for Hitler's orders. It was condemned by Liddell Hart as a 'glaring example either of gross ignorance or gross hypocrisy' by the British court because Manstein had opposed, ignored or mitigated Hitler's orders. The prosecution was satisfied that Manstein was at least not acquitted.

Manstein was imprisoned in a fortress with his family and a secretary to help him write his memoirs. In 1952 he was released and soon afterwards consulted in the rebuilding of the German army. It is noteworthy that not one of the 632 war criminals executed after conviction by British and American military courts were generals. Those executed were all subordinates who had pleaded superior orders.

It was not only Manstein who benefited from Paget's courtroom performance. More importantly, it was the Nazis themselves who seized on his utterances as vindications of their own arguments. If a reputable British politician supported their contention that the handful of deaths in Russia were justified, and were in any case only carried out in the best military tradition of 'an honourable soldier just obeying orders', it was only a small step to justify a lot more, and even to argue that the Allied trials were themselves not only immoral and illegal, but tainted with the very crimes of which the Allies accused the Nazis. Paget himself gave substance to those Nazi allegations. Both in court and in his book,[76] Paget claims that the interrogation techniques used by the American investigators of the Malmédy Massacre left 137 of the 139 German suspects with 'their testicles permanently destroyed by kicks received from the American war crimes investigation team'. It was a complete lie, a fabrication produced by the Nazis themselves to discredit the trials. Not one defendant was found by the many subsequent investigations to have suffered any permanent physical harm whatsoever, with the possible exception of the loss of one tooth. Paget had effectively endorsed, for whatever motive, the Nazis' campaign to pass a sponge over their crimes.

12

'THE MEN
OF 39'

It was the news of the Malmédy Massacre which had dramatically cata-
pulted the United States into its commitment to hold war crimes trials in
postwar Germany. Given the circumstances, the motives of those concerned were indisputably honourable. Reporting to Truman on the
preparations for the Nuremberg trial on 7 June 1945, Justice Jackson
concluded: 'We must see that it is fair and deliberative and not discredited in times to come by any mob spirit. Those who have regard for
the United States as a symbol of justice under the law would not have me
proceed otherwise.'[1]

Most Germans did not feel that the trial, when it finished on 1
October 1946, had enhanced the good name of the United States; they
were uniformly critical. The social democrats and communists attacked
the acquittal of Schacht and Franz von Papen, the former Chancellor
who had played a key role in smoothing Hitler's road to power. The
conservatives, like the archbishop of Cologne, Cardinal Frings, condemned the trial for failing to include amongst the accused those who
had ordered the bombing of German cities, while others criticized the
absence of a German judge.[2] Yet, even if the trial did not enhance
America's reputation, it did not offer even its most fervent critics the
opportunity and the weapons to dismiss and cast doubt on the evidence
of German atrocities and individual guilt. There might be justifiable
criticism of details of the trial, but only convinced Nazis could doubt the
guilt of Goering, Kaltenbrunner, Frank or Streicher.

The Malmédy trial at Dachau and its aftermath did, however, give
those critics the ammunition they needed to undo and further discredit
what Roosevelt had called 'the necessary rehabilitation of the German
people'. The Malmédy trial, the American army's biggest war crimes
trial, was also the biggest calamity to befall the attempt to punish the
individual murderers and, more importantly, the effort to demonstrate
to the Germans the fact that their countrymen had committed appalling
crimes. The last attempts to keep Germany denazified collapsed in the
wake of the débâcle.

Brigadier-General Josiah T. Dalby formally retired with the seven
other judges and Colonel Abraham Rosenfeld, their legal adviser, to

consider the verdict on the seventy-three accused (one had been extradited to France) at 2 pm on 11 July 1946.[3] The last submission had been made by Colonel Willis Everett, Georgia lawyer assigned to defend Peiper and several other defendants. Everett asked the judges to consider the case objectively and not be motivated by 'vengeance and retaliation among a victimized people'.

To everyone's surprise, two hours and twenty minutes later, the bell rang and the judges filed into the courtroom to deliver their verdicts. After allowing just under two minutes to consider the case against each defendant, Dalby announced that all seventy-three were guilty. All the accused were then allowed to make statements in mitigation. There was little tension in the room as forty of the accused stepped forward to make garbled pleas, which, after translation, did not sound very impressive. Some admitted that they had shot prisoners but pleaded superior orders. Others denied having shot anyone. The remainder just pleaded for their lives. Five days later, Dalby read out the sentences. Forty-three were to be hung, twenty-two were sentenced to life imprisonment, the remainder were sentenced from ten to twenty years. All seventy-three were then taken in a convoy of trucks to Landsberg prison.

Everett left Dachau dissatisfied. He was surprised, not only by the speed with which the court had come to the decision, but also by the sentences. Sepp Dietrich, who had allegedly given the order that prisoners were not to be taken, was sentenced to life imprisonment; while Peiper, who had passed on the order, was sentenced to death. But Everett's dissatisfaction was more deep-rooted. The judges had refused to split up the defendants and run separate trials. He felt it must have been humanly impossible for them to distinguish the evidence concerning seventy-three different men involved in several incidents at different times and places. The numbers painted on cardboard hung around the necks of the Germans might have helped, but it was marginal. He did not doubt that there had been a general smear effect – the evidence against one harming the remainder.

The court's procedural decisions had also been openly biased against the defence. Rosenfeld's rulings had, he felt, always favoured the prosecution. Everett, whose letters written in the months after the trial show him to have been antisemitic, was antagonistic not only towards Rosenfeld, who was a Jew, but also towards the War Crimes Group investigators, especially Perl, Thon and Kirschbaum. All three were refugees and did not, he felt, understand the traditional protections afforded to the defence in an American trial. Perl had actually been caught prying into defence papers of one of the defendants temporarily absent from his cell. Others had been actually interrogating various defendants right up to the time the trial started. Not only the refugees, but the whole prosecution and the court, had seemed too smug and self-congratulatory when the sentences were read out. But there was nothing Everett intended to do at that time. After getting free dental treatment, he was demobilized and returned to his native Georgia.

Straight remembers that when he heard the trial's outcome he was not surprised. 'I didn't see how they could have come to any other conclusion. Not after that terrible crime.'

All verdicts were automatically subject to review, and Straight passed the Malmédy case to one of his staff, Maximilian Kössler, hoping to get a report within two months. By January 1947, Kössler had made only slow and painful progress. Straight relieved him and completed it himself. By early spring, he had read enough to agree with Kössler's preliminary criticisms of the way the trial was conducted, and both the questionable admissibility and the nature of the sworn statements by the accused which had formed the bulk of the prosecution case. Straight suggested to Harbough, Micklewaite's successor as Deputy Judge Advocate-General in Germany, that there were grounds for doubting whether all forty-three should be executed. On 22 July Harbough got Clay's authority to grant temporary stays of execution wherever necessary. At the time, Straight had an awesome 389 death sentences to review.

Straight sent his completed review to Harbough on 20 October recommending that only twenty-five of the forty-three death sentences should be confirmed. Some might have seen that as a clear indictment of the trial, but Straight denies that interpretation: 'The Malmédy judges were faced with a heinous crime and imposed heavy sentences because of emotion. It was my job to be benevolent.' His criterion was simple: the younger the accused, the greater the leniency – 'They had to obey orders.' But all the convictions were upheld. Basing a reprieve on the age of the accused had not been used as a criterion before. Its sudden use was indicative of something serious. Quite simply, after reading the transcript, Straight had realized that in many cases there was insufficient evidence to support the conviction. But he did not reveal that discovery in his final report.[4]

There was little satisfaction about the commutations in any quarter. For some time there had been rumours and criticism not only of the trials, but also of the personal behaviour of the Americans involved in the whole programme. Allegations by Germans of intimidation and brutality were expected and not new. But whereas the complaints in the British zone were, with very few exceptions,[5] easily refutable, the complaints about the events in Dachau seemed to be more specific. Moreover, they were actually being repeated, as if believed, by American officers at Army Headquarters. Harbough, who had until then shown little interest in the trials, became suddenly alarmed because it was his department which was the focus of the criticism.

The immediate cause of the rumours was the discovery by guards at Dachau of documents being smuggled out by visitors leaving the compound. All of them contained complaints by inmates of ill-treatment, intimidation and abuses by the interrogators, and of unnecessary delays in hearing the cases. Both at the time and later it seemed curious that so many people should be caught on one day attempting to smuggle out written allegations when previous searches had never revealed any hidden messages. It looked as if it was part of a new, orchestrated campaign which the Nazis and the German clergy were beginning to mount. The bishop of Munich had already complained to Clay about the Malmédy defendants being beaten, but the complaint had been brushed aside.

The complaints were now becoming more persistent and Gailey, Clay's Chief of Staff, ordered Harbough to investigate them quickly. Straight was surprised however when Harbough arrived at the War Crimes Group's headquarters in Munich on 6 September to discuss what Harbough's memorandum of their two-day discussion called 'alleged irregularities in the operation at Dachau'.[6] For Harbough to even put an otherwise normal conversation between a chief and his deputy into writing was proof of his anxiety. The subject headings confirm that concern: professional witnesses; time detainees are held in confinement; tardy designation of defence counsel; intimidation of witnesses and accused by threats such as surrender to Eastern powers for 'trial'; promises of favour and prolonged interrogation; inaccurate statements presented to witnesses and accused for signature; poor interpreters.

On intimidation and threats, the minutes of their conversation record:

> Colonel Straight stated that for the past fifteen months there had been very definite orders against any mistreatment of detainees and witnesses. Recently, three additional orders have been issued and Colonel Straight has personally talked with the interrogators. Considerable discussion took place regarding more adequate supervision of interrogators while interrogating witnesses. . .In this connection I suggested the use of inspectors to be present at line ups and from time to time during interrogations.

Straight told Harbough that he was unaware of any specific irregularities but that he would not be surprised if, in dealing with hard-bitten Nazi murderers, the kid gloves were sometimes taken off, but only to the extent of verbal abuse. Putting restrictions on interrogations in September 1947 with the trials ending in December would be an unnecessary encumbrance and might even be interpreted as an admission of guilt. Harbough accepted Straight's assurances and told Gailey that the situation at Dachau was under control.

Gailey, however, was dissatisfied and telephoned the army's inspector general to send an investigator immediately to Dachau. When Major Arthur Hanna arrived no one at Dachau knew why he had come and who had sent him. It was one of the conditions which Gailey had stipulated for the investigation.[7] As Hanna's department was not involved in war crimes and he was investigating on the direct orders of the Chief of Staff, there is no reason to believe that he personally had any interest in covering up the truth.

His report, sent direct to Gailey, concluded that there was no evidence of mistreatment of detainees at Dachau. Not one detainee had been admitted to the hospital for injuries and not one of the detainees with whom he had spoken complained about ill-treatment. His only recommendation was that Joseph Kirschbaum was too excitable, and as he was named in many of the complaints, it would be best to remove him. But Hanna did report that he had found evidence of an organized movement outside Dachau whose objective was to discredit the war crimes programme using any evidence available, including information from the detainees. For the moment that dampened any concern at Army Headquarters. The last trial was due to start shortly and Harbough had estimated that all the reviews of the verdicts and sentences should be completed by mid-1948.

No one therefore at first paid much attention to a short telegram from the Department of the Army in Washington which arrived on 5 November.[8] It seemed a routine piece of information, although it did have some novelty interest. Lawyers representing the American relatives of Stefan Krech, awaiting execution at Landsberg, had given notice that they intended to petition a local American court to set aside the conviction on the grounds that Krech's trial was unfair.

Krech, a Rumanian, had been convicted for committing numerous atrocities while employed as a guard at Dachau between 1942 and 1945. His sentence had been approved by the JAG, the Review Board and by Clay. Harbough instinctively ordered an indefinite stay of execution while the petition was heard. It was a tactic which had not yet been considered by German lawyers. The Royal Warrant expressly forbade appeals to British courts. Appeals went only as far as the Commander in Chief and executions were invariably carried out within two weeks of his rejection.

But the German newspaper reports of Krech's petition led enterprising German lawyers to realize that there was still another possibility of appeal for the American cases. The first petition to get to the Supreme Court, on 8 January, was that of Willie Rieke, convicted for the murder of American POWs. Two days later, Clay ordered all executions to be temporarily halted to allow all 238 condemned men the opportunity to appeal.[9]

The programme was now in limbo. Had the operation been finally closed at the beginning of 1948 and the executions carried out, posterity might only have recorded that, in less excited and emotional times, some of those condemned might have been reprieved. Instead, having rushed through the trials as fast as possible, taking as many short cuts as was permissible for expediency, the army began to scrutinize some transcripts as if the trials had been conducted under the most ideal conditions. A second review of the Malmédy trial was delivered to Harbough on 8 February by a newly formed Review Branch.

Harbough had suggested to Clay in July 1947 that a separate review board be established, 'not because of any lack of confidence in the fairness or impartiality of the Deputy Judge-Advocate for War Crimes,' but because it was invidious that the prosecutor should also be the reviewer. The Malmédy case had been re-reviewed by Colonel Howard Bresee, the head of the Review Branch. Some might have thought his impartiality somewhat suspect, since he had previously been the chief prosecutor inside the Dachau enclosure; but, perhaps with that in mind, Harbough had appointed John Dwinell to help Bresee. Dwinell had been a defence lawyer at the original Malmédy trial and shared Everett's critical views. Harbough later explained the appointment by saying that Bresee needed someone to guide him through the transcript.

Bresee's review[10] was more than Harbough had bargained for. It unhesitatingly exposed Straight's review for actually misstating crucial testimony in his analysis and then listed the gaping holes in the evidence on which the court had ostensibly based its decision. He recommended that twenty-nine of the defendants, including Sepp Dietrich, be immediately released because of lack of evidence, and that only twelve of the death sentences, including Peiper's, be confirmed. The recommendations, combined with his critical description of the court's pro-prosecution bias, amounted to a shattering condemnation of the army's most important trial.

Harbough spent several weeks considering the indictment of his department before recommending to Clay that only thirteen accused, not including Dietrich, he released, and thirteen be executed. With one exception, Clay accepted Harbough's recommendations and confirmed the sentences on 20 March, twenty months after the verdicts had been announced.

But Bresee's review had also reported that he had found 'much evidence' of improper pre-trial investigation, including 'mock trials' which had led to 'confessions' which had been written by the interrogators. It was these confessions which the court had wrongly used as evidence against defendants other than the men who had allegedly made them. The methods by which these confessions were obtained now became the central issue not only in the Malmédy trial but in the whole campaign, which spread from Germany to Congress in Washington and throughout the United States, to denigrate the war crimes trials and rehabilitate the Germans involved as honourable soldiers.

The first suggestions that improper methods were used to get the confessions had been made by Everett to Straight two weeks before the trial started. He claimed that some of the accused had complained that their statements were extracted under duress. Straight immediately ordered an investigation, the first of thirteen separate inquiries into the treatment of the Malmédy prisoners before the trial. Lieutenant-Colonel Edwin Carpenter interviewed between twenty and thirty of those who, according to Everett, had made the most serious charges. To his surprise he found that only four actually claimed they had been attacked, not by the interrogators, but by the Polish guards in the prison as they were moved from the cells. Carpenter's account was later corroborated by the interpreter he used when questioning the SS men. The attacks amounted to blows to the head or body or being pushed down a flight of stairs.

The use of 'mock trials' had never been kept secret and had been approved by Ellis, in charge of the investigation, on Perl's recommendation. It purposely had all the trappings of an Inquisition. Two or three interrogators sat behind a table. In front of them was a crucifix and two lighted candles. The prisoner was brought from his cell with a black hood covering his face. According to the interrogators, the hood was necessary so that the other prisoners, all of whom were kept in isolation, remained unaware of who was being questioned. When the hood was removed, the prisoner was told that he was about to be tried for the shootings. While one interrogator pretended to be the tough prosecutor, another acted as the defending lawyer, the 'soft guy', urging the prisoner that his confession would count in his favour. Perl and Kirschbaum usually played the dual act, with Kirschbaum acting the SS man's friend trying to quieten the screaming Perl.

To avoid the embarrassment of 'sensational revelations' at the trial, the prosecution and the interrogators admitted at the outset that many of the confessions had been obtained by the mock trials. They were passed off as 'legitimate ruses and tricks', necessary to break the tight conspiracy of silence imposed by Peiper on pain of death. Perl admitted that, in getting Peiper's own confession, he had told the tank commander that his life was ruined and he would never be released. In his testimony at the trial, Peiper admitted that he had heard reports of American prisoners being shot which had been described as a 'mix-up, and agreed that the wounded American prisoner had been shot on the surgeon's orders. He had not retracted his confession. Nor did he or any other defendant say in court that their confessions had been extracted by force. The interrogators naturally also denied that they had used any 'harsh, cruel or inhuman treatment' to get the confessions.

Bresee's report on 'mock trials' therefore contained nothing new. His review had merely confirmed a badly run trial and repeated what was known about the methods used for extracting confessions; which, although more dramatic, amounted to nothing more than what occurred daily in police precincts in every major American city. Yet that admission, combined with Clay's drastic reduction in the numbers to be executed, fuelled the rumours of American atrocities put out by the SS organizations.

At Army Headquarters, the same type of officers as those in the British messes who opposed the trials seized on the rumours as evidence that the good name of American justice was being besmirched. If there was truth in even one of the stories circulating of how the confessions were extracted at Schwabisch Hall prison, where the suspects had been interrogated, then the American army had created nothing less than a bloody inferno. The SS men had allegedly been starved into submission, frozen in their cells, nearly suffocated by intense heat; bullet holes had been found in cell walls with human hair and flesh clinging to the brickwork, the black hood had been found and was covered with dry blood (some said it was still damp with blood), there was a death cell with gallows outside; and, most notoriously of all, the testicles of each of the defendants had been crushed.

However fanciful the stories, they became more credible when the JAG conceded that there had been mistakes in the trials. In January 1948 it announced that the evidence of Karl Kramer, who had testified in 24 different Dachau cases, was being given 'little credence' in the reviews because it revealed 'substantial inconsistencies'.[11] It was a clear admission that the army had used professional witnesses.

The impact of that announcement was eclipsed by a stunning outburst in Nuremberg on 21 February by Judge Charles Wennerstrum from Iowa. The judge had just completed the Hostages case, the trial of eleven Germans accused of ordering and executing large numbers of innocent civilians throughout Europe as reprisals for the shooting or kidnapping of individual German officers. Hours before he left Nuremberg,

Wennerstrum gave an interview to the *Chicago Tribune* a Mid-western, staunchly conservative newspaper, in which he accused the American prosecutors of being 'vindictive' and pursuing 'personal ambitions'. He further alleged that the prosecution had deliberately withheld documents from the defence and that the only value the trials had was to teach the Germans that they had been defeated by tough conquerors. Within hours of the *Tribune*'s article reaching Nuremberg, Taylor published his reply, accusing Wennerstrum of a 'baseless and malicious attack'. He continued: 'I would use stronger language if it did not appear that your behaviour arises out of a warped, psychopathic mental attitude.'[12]

The exchange did little good for the reputation of American justice in Germany, or the army's reputation in America. The *Tribune* was the first, but not the last, to seize upon Wennerstrum's attack as confirmation that all the other rumours and stories were true. 'The moral degradation of the Army of Occupation in Germany has advanced so far that all sense of distinction between honourable and dishonourable conduct has been lost. . . The standards of American justice have been degraded. The pretence that the full historic record was to be exposed was fraudulent from the start.'

The trials were just as unpopular in the Department of the Army in Washington as at the headquarters in Germany. No one was more critical than the Secretary of the Army himself, Kenneth Royall. Royall made no secret of his opposition to denazification and his belief that Germany should be allowed to rapidly reindustrialize itself. In secret testimony to the House of Representatives Appropriations Committee in April 1948, he told congressmen that he had wanted to end the war crimes programme much earlier because it was weakening the government's prime objective of building up a strong Germany.[13] His major obstacle was Clay, who had resisted Royall's pressure for a change of policy in their nightly teleconferences. But on 24 May, through an unfortunate misunderstanding, Clay put himself in Royall's hands.[14]

Regardless of the political situation, Clay had always insisted on examining the evidence against each condemned man before confirming the sentence. Lawrence Wilkinson, the deputy head of the Economics Division, remembers seeing Clay ashen-faced at their 8 am conferences after he had spent the night reading a trial transcript.[15] The seriousness with which he took the duty is evidenced by an exchange between himself and Gailey. Clay had decided to commute the sentences on Max Anerswald, who had been convicted of murdering three men. Gailey memoed Clay: 'Personally, I don't get the recommendation. . . I wonder what the dead men think of it.' Clay replied: 'I don't think the evidence warrants death – there is not strong enough testimony – a life sentence can be corrected, a death sentence cannot. If there is the slightest doubt, much less a reasonable doubt, a death sentence should never be administered.'[16]

Everett had watched as all the internal army reviews had failed to reprieve his client, and then followed the by now well-trodden route to the Supreme Court in Washington. Besides reasoned legal challenges to the Dachau court's decision, the Georgia lawyer included in his petition each and every one of the allegations of violence to extract confessions which were circulating in Germany, as grounds for the Supreme Court to overrule the army's verdict. The court gave its judement on 18 May. The judges divided equally, four to four, on whether they had jurisdiction, and therefore Everett's motion to set aside the Dachau verdict was rejected. It was however, not a coincidence that four days later Royall had usurped Clay's exclusive authority over the fate of the condemned men.

While in Washington, Everett met and briefed Royall on the case. He also repeated the lurid allegations of the interrogator's treatment of the defendants at Schwabisch Hall. Anyone less anxious to find a reason to intervene in the trials would have recognized the prejudice which underlay Everett's hysterical and unsubstantiated allegations, but Royall sat spellbound as Everett described the mass trials by candlelight, how the testicles of all the seventy-four defendants had been crushed and how the accused had been tortured in their cells by Jewish refugees intent on revenge. Immediately after Everett had left, Royall cabled Clay, ordering him to halt all executions. It was an unnecessary instruction because Clay had already ordered a temporary halt, pending the Supreme Court's decision,[17] but Royall wanted to get control over the trials as fast as possible.

Four days later, Clay was told by Harbough that there were 550 executions still awaiting review.[18] He cabled Royall: 'I find it difficult to adjust my own mental processes to requiring what looks to be almost a mass execution . . . it gives an appearance of cruelty to the United States even though there is no question in my mind that the crimes committed fully justify the death sentence.'[19] To avoid the problem, Clay suggested that a clemency board be established so that a substantial number of the cases could be commuted. Clay had in fact been wrongly briefed. There were only 150 men awaiting execution. When he discovered the mistake he cabled Royall that he could handle that number.[20] It was too late. Royall seized Clay's invitation to intervene directly.

By halting all executions, and not just those of the men involved in the Malmédy Massacre, Royall had consciously handed the pro-German lobby in America and the Nazis in Germany an official licence to attack the whole war crimes programme. The tortures which allegedly occurred at Schwabisch Hall were now said to have been a daily routine at Dachau as well.

Before Pearl Harbour the pro-German lobby in America had been a major factor in limiting support for Britain's lone fight against Hitler. Ethnic German communities were unwilling to believe stories about gas chambers in Poland. Rather, in 1948, they were convinced that the Kirschbaums and Perls, Jewish refugees, possibly with leftist ideas, were members of the Zionist conspiracy still intent on destroying Germany. They were 'Avenging Angels' or 'the men of 39', the remnants of the bacillus which was even infecting America. The news that one of the Jewish members of the court in the Malmédy trial had named his dog 'Peiper' only confirmed that the foreigners had deliberately denigrated American justice and honour for their own purpose. Writing to the JAG in Washington, Everett sarcastically referred to the 'underhand methods used by *our* American prosecution' (emphasis in the original).[21]

The anti-war crimes protest was just part of a much wider pro-German lobby in America intent on reforging the valuable commercial, banking and industrial partnerships with Germany which had officially been broken in December 1941 and which had remained paralysed since the war. Focusing on the harm allegedly caused to apparently innocent Germans naturally helped the argument that Germany should be rebuilt.

It was that sectarianism which underlay Wennerstrum's attack on the trials in the *Chicago Tribune*. Wennerstrum had also condemned Allied 'whitewashing of their own crimes' and vindictiveness towards Germans. Those responsible, he claimed, were American officers 'who became Americans only in recent years and whose background and prejudices were imbedded in Europe's hatreds and prejudices. It was they, he claimed, who had used duress and intimidation to deny Germans true justice.

The impact of Wennerstrum's outburst had hardly subsided when, in the same court at Nuremberg, an account of a pre-trial interrogation seemed to confirm the worst of his allegations. Dr Robert Kempner was prosecuting in the 'Ministries case', a trial of twenty-one defendants who were individually charged under eight counts with planning the war and conspiring to commit atrocities against civilians and employ slave labour. Giving evidence was Dr Friedrich Gaus, a former senior official in the Foreign Ministry who, to the prosecution's satisfaction, was giving evidence against his former colleagues. On 10 May, a defence lawyer dramatically read out in the courtroom a transcript of Gaus' pre-trial interrogation. It had taken place after Gaus had been held for four weeks in solitary confinement, an experience which he admitted had been extremely unsettling. The interrogator had been Kempner himself.

Kempner: 'Well, things aren't as simple as that. The Russians are interested in you. Do you know that?'
Gaus: 'The Russians?'
Kempner: 'Yes as a professional violator of treaties.'
Gaus: 'No, that is not correct in the least. My God.'

The interrogation ended, according to the transcript:

Kempner: 'Well, let's finish for today. I'll tell you something. . .'
Gaus(interrupting): 'Don't extradite me to the Russians.'[22]

Despite Gaus' and Kempner's claims that the written record did not accurately reflect the atmosphere of the moment, the outside world interpreted the exchange on its face value. Namely that it was exactly the intimidation which the trial's critics had complained was commonplace. Gaus, it seemed, had given evidence for the prosecution rather than be handed over to the Russians. Making it all much worse, Kempner was a Jewish refugee who had fled from Berlin to America in 1933. Charles LaFollete, an American lawyer at Nuremberg, remembers how sickened the Americans at Nuremberg were. He later wrote to Clay: 'His [Kempner's] foolish, unlawyer-like method of interrogation was common knowledge in Nuremberg all the time I was there and protested by those of us who anticipated the arising of the day, just as we have now, when the Germans would attempt to make martyrs out of common criminals on trial at Nuremberg.'[23]

LaFollete was commenting on a petition to Clay from Bishop Wurm, also signed by Pastor Niemöller, complaining about the denial of justice by the army at Nuremberg.[24] Seizing on Wennerstrum's complaints and Kempner's alleged threats, the clergy complained that the American prosecutors had unlimited funds, privileged access to documents and the ability to search the world for witnesses. In contrast the defence could not get witnesses, worked in cramped offices, was poorly paid, had inadequate telephones and had to speak to their clients 'sitting in a cage'.

Referring to the imprisonment of witnesses, all of them former Nazis, at Nuremberg until they had testified for fear that they would otherwise disappear, Wurm complained: 'The confinement of witnesses [is] a practice foreign to German legal customs.' The use of civilian judges instead of military personnel, Wurm complained, had 'its last historic precedent in the treatment of the German officers of the 20 July by Adolf Hitler.' To compare Roland Freisler's show trials with the Nuremberg trials and to refer to German legal customs as if they were blessed with an international reputation for fairness was, in Clay's view, just more of the same old impudence, now sharpened by the army's exposure to criticism from America.

Wurm was not interested in Clay's reply. He already knew that there were 190 German defence lawyers in Nuremberg as against seventy American prosecutors, that the German lawyers at Nuremberg earned much more than other German lawyers, and that the separation of an accused from outsiders by a metal grille was common practice.[25]

Clay's justification for the trials was that the Germans had broken internationally recognized laws and morality, but that argument began to look very thin after the 'true meaning' of America justice had been exposed. He was, however, in the political circumstances and especially when compared to Robertson, courageously unrepentant about the trials and unwilling to compromise even with those whose support he needed. Responding to Wurm's allegations of brutality, he wrote:

> I regret indeed to find that the allegations contained in your letter and the resulting charges are based largely on unverified reports rather than on information within your own knowledge or supported by factual evidence. . . Of course there have been irregularities – procedures of which I do not approve. These occur in all law cases and obviously would be of greater frequency in a new court operating without precedent. . . It is difficult to understand how any review of the evidence of those yet to be sentenced could provide a basis for sentimental sympathy for those who brought suffering and anguish to untold millions.

Clay's replies, however reasoned, never even temporarily stemmed the rising level of criticism. But the evidence of his papers and files suggests that he was contemptuous of the complainants' motives and ignored their criticisms. For those who had been sentenced to death, Clay again had no sympathy. Irritated by Royall's continuing block on the executions, he had cabled the Army Department on 9 June that he wanted to start them immediately unless Royall sent the promised clemency board.[26] To forestall that, Royall appointed a three-man commission to investigate the whole war crimes programme, and in particular the Malmédy trial.

On 30 July Gordon Simpson of the Texas Supreme Court, Judge LeRoy van Roden of the Orphans Court of Delaware County, Pennsylvania, and Lieutenant-Colonel Charles W. Lawrence of the JAG arrived in Frankfurt. For the next six weeks, the three men pulled out random files, concerning the Malmédy case and sixty-five others. They then returned to Washington to write their report. What they had hoped to achieve in that short time is not quite clear. The transcripts of the big concentration camps cases, some involving forty defendants, are 5,000 pages long. It would take six weeks just to examine one of them properly. Yet another separate review of the Malmédy case, ordered by Clay, which was then under way, took seven full months on just the one case.[27]

Yet in their initially classified and unpublished report to Royall on 14 September the Simpson Commission made sweeping recommendations, as if they had carefully weighed all the available evidence.[28] The report suggested that the twelve Malmédy death sentences and another seventeen death sentences should be commuted, while the remaining 110 condemned men should be executed. (Eleven had in the meantime been reprieved.) Amongst the seventeen was Anton Bertheimer, the deputy commandant at Buchenwald, who had confessed to everything, except to deny that he had personally murdered anyone. Simpson recommended commutation because 'the evidence is sufficiently doubtful.'

Significantly the Malmédy commutations were not recommended by the Commission on the grounds of inadequate evidence. On the contrary, Simpson reported: 'The record of the trial, however, sufficiently manifests the guilt of the accused to warrant the findings of guilt.' The commutations were proposed in order to atone for any injustices that might have been committed.

On the Dachau cases generally, Simpson reported that there was no evidence of systematic intimidation and that the trials were 'essentially fair' although some of the methods of getting the sworn statements were 'questionable'. It was the evidence upon which that conclusion was based that discredited an otherwise politically acceptable review. Throughout their six-week visit to Germany the Commission took evidence from German critics of the trials, but none from alleged victims of assaults. Nor was one American interviewed, either from JAG or Dachau. The only American evidence was in a written statement from Bresee, who seven months earlier had recommended the first commutations. He wrote that, having spent three years in Dachau: 'I feel that I am in a position to know and do definitely state that every possible effort was made to ensure that each accused had a fair trial. At no time during my period of association with war crimes was the mistreatment of war crimes suspects permitted or condoned. . . There have been no instances of intimidation of witnesses at Dachau within my personal knowledge.'[29]

Without any eyewitness evidence, the Commission concluded that the allegations of physical ill-treatment were unfounded. They could do little else without the evidence. But by not even trying to look, they gave their report the appearance of a whitewashing exercise.

Clay seized upon the occasion of the report to decide that the executions of those not recommended for clemency would be carried out immediately.[30] Royall reluctantly agreed, just two days before Clay had ordered the first ten men to hang.[31] Every Friday from 15 October 1948 until 2 February 1949 there were executions at Landsberg, sometimes fifteen on one day.[32] The total was 104.

News of the impending executions leaked out of Landsberg, and on the eve of the first hangings the anti-trials campaign developed a new twist. Judge LeRoy van Roden, one of the members of the Simpson Commission, was persuaded to make a series of sensational public speeches claiming that he had been prevented by Simpson from publishing the truth. He claimed that he had independently secured statements from those who had suffered at Schwabisch Hall which proved that the interrogators had indeed abused, beaten and tortured the Germans to extract their confessions. 'Never has American justice sunk to the degradation depicted by Judge van Roden,' claimed the *Chicago Tribune*, one of many papers grateful for new and seemingly authoritative confirmation of their old and still unproven allegations.[33] Van Roden's dramatic 'revelations' did not halt the executions, but did raise the whole anti-trials campaign to new heights.

What was not known at the time was that van Roden had shared a room after the war in Frankfurt with Everett and, while back in Germany as a member of the Commission, received a stream of letters from the Georgia lawyer.[34] The letters contained all of Everett's most extreme allegations. Van Roden shared his bias and prejudice: he was both antisemitic and convinced that the Jewish refugees were using their new American nationality as a cloak for vengeance against the Germans.

The damage done by van Roden's 'disclosures' to the army's already tattered image was suddenly, but only temporarily, eclipsed by the disclosure in a German newspaper that same week that three months earlier Clay had 'secretly' reduced the life sentence on Ilse Koch to just four years.[35] Koch, the wife of the former commandant of Buchenwald, had lived in the concentration camp from 1937 until 1943, two years longer than her husband, who was removed in 1941 after SS investigations into his corruption.

'Mrs Kommandant', as she was known to inmates and staff alike, had become infamous for her manufacture of lampshades and gloves made out of the tattooed skin of dead inmates. Many stories had been printed of how she had personally selected and then ordered the death of inmates with interesting tattoos. After their murder, the skin would be skilfully removed, scraped, tanned and dried in the camp's pathology department. Other accounts detailed her sadism while walking or riding through the camp, ordering SS guards to beat or whip individual inmates who displeased her. Reputedly, she and her husband would select an inmate for a night's sexual perversion which ended with the inmate's death in the morning lest he reveal the details.

The victims of Buchenwald included 51,000 who had perished not from gassing but as a result of straight physical torture and starvation. Inmates were hung on iron hooks, some taking forty minutes to die. Hundreds died from the injection of typhus and other diseases. Thousands of Russian prisoners of war had been murdered by the infamous *Genickschuss*. They were led into a large hall believing they were to be medically examined. Germans walked around in white coats telling them to strip to the waist to have their weight taken and their height measured. As they stood against the wall, a small-calibre pistol was aimed at their head through a hole. The trigger was pulled by a man standing on the other side of the wall. Loud recorded music drowned the shot. There was no blood because the special small-calibre bullet did not exit through the other side of the skull. Specially sealed lorries transported the bodies to the crematorium without leaving a trail of blood.

Through all this Ilse Koch lived quite voluntarily. She had no military rank, so there was no suggestion of compulsion or fear of death should she refuse to remain. On the contrary, all the evidence suggested that she enjoyed living at Buchenwald. After all, she even stayed on after her husband's dismissal as camp commandant.

'Maybe the army reduced her sentence . . . so she could go back into the lampshade business,' wrote Ed Sullivan in the *New York News*.[36] 'Isn't it a shame seeing them put Frau Koch on a train back home rather than a lampshade,' commented the *New York Mirror*.[37] Aside from the wit, Sullivan and others who, in the face of the German lobby's campaign, had supported the trials, were at first uncertain whether the army had lost its nerve or had really been running an improper trials programme. Neither supposition was accurate. The truth was that the reviews, like the trials, were being conducted by second- and third-rate lawyers.

Despite all the stories about Ilse Koch and the undisputed facts of the torture and murder at the camp, the actual testimony at the Buchenwald trial only contained one solitary eyewitness account of her physically beating an inmate. There was also testimony that inmates had been beaten on her orders, and of tattooed lampshades, photo albums and gloves in her house. But there was no evidence of her personally killing anyone.

None of the thirty-one accused at the Buchenwald trial were charged with particular murders. All were charged with participating in a common criminal plan of encouraging, aiding, abetting and participating in the atrocities in the camp. Twenty-two accused had been sentenced to death. Ilse Koch had never denied that she knew what was happening in the camp, but she denied the evidence of her own part in the camp administration and her activities.

When Straight got the trial transcript for review in September 1947, it was just one of 220 other cases on his desk. Each transcript was accompanied by bundles of petitions from the accused and their families pleading for mercy and alleging that the court had misunderstood the evidence or not admitted proper evidence. The complaints about the Malmédy trials – the convictions based on uncorroborated and hearsay evidence – had already unnerved the former prairie lawyer, whose disenchantment with the trials was only eclipsed by that of Harbough, who had not been associated with the trials in the immediate postwar months. Straight immediately handed the Buchenwald case over to two newly recruited civilian lawyers for their review. Both were unfamiliar with the problems of the postwar prosecutions and advised on the basis of the transcript that there was insufficient evidence that she had participated in running the camp and she should therefore be acquitted. Straight rejected that advice. His recommendation to Harbough was emphatic but legally unsound. Although Koch was guilty, the evidence of her beating only one inmate was insufficient to convict her of participating in the common plan. Therefore the sentence should be reduced to four years. Harbough agreed. 'As a general rule,' he wrote to Straight, 'we [only] hang the top leaders and the underlings against whom we have definite evidence of personal participation in killings or evidence that they ordered killings against others.'[38]

The legal mistake was elementary. Either she was guilty of the charge of participating in the common plan, in which case her sentence would be a measure of the extent of her own participation, or alternatively she did not participate and therefore should have been released. There was no middle way. It is most unlikely that either Himmler or Eichmann personally murdered anyone, but that did not absolve them from guilt for their participation in a common plan to murder. The JAG lawyers' concern for the evidence of the one beating proved that the very essence of any just legal system – certainty – was absent.

Explaining his decision later, Straight said that he did not believe some of the prosecution witnesses. Yet their evidence had been oral, subject to cross-examination, and corroborated by other oral testimony. Moreover it had been believed by the eight judges and their legal adviser. It was a strange contrast to his Malmédy review, where he had accepted a lot of sworn confessions which were not even repeated in court. There was much more evidence against Koch, who had spent five years in a concentration camp, than against Peiper!

Clay accepted Harbough's recommendation for the reduction on 8 June 1948. Harbough said later that they had not discussed the recommendation. In reply to the criticism three months later, Clay accepted both responsibility for the decision and the failure of the JAG or the press offfice to announce the reduction. 'My judgement may have been wrong,' he told a press conference on 21 October, 'but it is a judgement for which I am responsible to my own conscience and I acted in the sincere belief that in years to come those who read the history of that evidence would not find the sentence [of that court] conformed to American justice and it would leave our war trials themselves on a record not of complete justice as we would want them to be left for future history.'[39] It was a brave attempt to accept responsibility for his subordinates' mistakes, as well as to rescue some credibility for the trials.

Despite the pious explanation, he ordered American lawyers to sift the sixty volumes of the trial's evidence to see whether there were any other charges. There were not. In a face-saving deal with the Bavarian minister of justice, Koch was handed over to the Germans for trial.[40] She later died in a mental asylum.

It is significant that throughout this sensational affair, which was fully covered in the American press and radio, the *Chicago Tribune* and newspapers with similarly pro-German views did not write one editorial about the Koch decision and gave it the barest of coverage. When Royall was asked to intervene to reverse Clay's decision, he rejected any possibility of his personal interference in the army's clemency decisions.[41] Somehow it seemed that the murderers of Poles, Russians and Jews were not such bad people. To many Germans it appeared as if there were official American support for their campaign. The American connection took on a new dimension.

At Christmas 1948, sixty-four men at Landsberg prison were still awaiting execution. Each wore a distinctive red jacket. With few exceptions, all were mass murderers. Yet they were the object of sympathy and support throughout Germany. Athough they were better fed and warmer than most Germans outside the fortress, the German Church monitored their individual conditions with passionate consideration. When the prison director took down an Advent wreath which had been hung by the prisoners, claiming it was a fire hazard, Bishop Johannes Neuhäusler wrote self-righteously to Clay: 'I am personally surprised at the brutal proceedings of the prison director, all the more because I never saw such a thing even in a concentration camp. During the four years, when I was there [in a concentration camp], neither Advent wreath nor Christmas tree was forbidden.'[42]

Clay found it impossible to answer Neuhäusler's complaint satisfactorily. The victim of a concentration camp had a moral advantage.

Regardless of their individual records or the past, by 1949 most Germans were identifying themselves with their fellow countrymen at Landsberg regardless of their crimes. Whatever they had done, they had done for Germany, and the revelations of malpractices in the American trials, recognized by American judges and politicians, demolished any moral justification for the Americans to execute patriotic Germans.

The American consul in Hamburg, Edward Groth, reporting to the Secretary of State at that time, was emphatic that: 'the German public as a whole has been renazified.'[43] He continued:

> The German people have never been sufficiently aware, and they have no desire to know, the outrageous crimes which the Nazi regime perpetrated, and they will never admit their own guilt in supporting that regime. They are told by Nazi underground propagandists that the concentration camp horrors and other Nazi atrocities are only exaggerations and lies which have been spread by the Allies. They believe this new Nazi propaganda because it fits their new pattern of mind and they also believe that its they who have been victimized – pitiful victims of the cruel oppression of their conquerors.

It was those Nazi propagandists who were supplying Everett and other sympathizers in America with the material to continue their campaign. Prominent amongst them was Dr Rudolph Aschenauer, a former party member and lawyer from Munich who had unsuccessfully defended Ohlendorf. Another was Dr Georg Fröschmann who represented over three thousand Landsberg inmates. His allegations that they were dying through 'heat exhaustion' were sent to Bishop Wurm, who automatically forwarded them to Clay with his endorsement. As usual, he did not check whether the information was true.[44] Their stories became increasingly more fanciful and outrageous. The *Neue Ruhr Zeitung* ran a series under the title 'Justice or Revenge' quoting sympathetic stories from American lawyers about how the 'Avenging Angels' had run identification parades at Dachau. Inmates, according to the paper, had competed in inventing stories about former camp guards while they were paraded on a stage in front of men who only 'acquired' American citizenship as late as 1939.' What the 'Angels' apparently did not realize, said the article, was that: 'the majority of concentration camp inmates were convicted criminals.' The series ended on the poignant question: 'Why, if Ilse Koch had committed such terrible crimes, was her sentence reduced? Was it not proof that she had not committed the crimes?'[45]

It was the type of material which appealed to sympathetic congressmen, increasingly keen to compete with one another in championing the rights of the victims of the 'Men of 39'. Neat bundles of petitions for mercy crisscrossed the Atlantic from German lawyers and clergymen to congressmen, who endorsed them and sent them on to Clay. Joseph McCarthy, the brash young senator from Wisconsin, a state with a large German population, demanded to know why Clay had not commuted the sentence on Hans Schmidt, the former adjutant of the guard battalion at Buchenwald. McCarthy endorsed the allegations made by Schmidt's wife that her husband had been denied a proper trial, had been severely tortured during his interrogation, and had been intimidated into making a damaging confession.[46] In fact Schmidt had not made a statement in the prison where the alleged torture occurred, had not given evidence at his trial but had frequently consulted his lawyer. McCarthy ignored the fact that Schmidt had officiated every day for four years at the executions in Buchenwald.

When Clay rejected the pleas, duplicate bundles of the petitions went to the White House. The case of Martin Sandberger, a member of the *Einsatzgruppe D* responsible for murdering at least 90,000 people, included a photograph of the SS officer with his wife and three children. The message to Truman read: 'Just as you were in World War One an officer in a field artillery unit, so Martin Sandberger was an officer in a German army unit, fighting in Russia during World War Two. By order of a higher authority, he had many unpleasant things to do including some executions. Some of his decisions must have cost him as much soul torture as your decision to drop the atomic bomb.'[47]

Just after Christmas, Everett received a letter from Clay stating that after reading the latest review of the Malmédy trial, he had decided to confirm the twelve death sentences.[48] The report, following the seven-month investigation by the Administration of Justice Review Board, which had thoroughly cross-examined practically everyone involved in the pre-trial interrogations and had scrutinized the trial transcript, confirmed that unorthodox interrogation methods had been used but reported there had been no violence. The methods used, it said were 'justified by the difficulty of cracking the case'. Moreover, it confirmed there was substantial evidence against the twelve condemned men. Clay however agreed to delay the executions until after 3 March, when Everett was due to appeal to the International Court at the Hague – an appeal which everyone knew to be meaningless because it was a court to judge disputes between nations and not individuals. It was a desperate gesture which revealed how Everett's campaign seemed to have faltered in the face of Clay's rock-like determination.

Help for Everett arrived on 6 January, when Royall sanctioned the release of the hitherto classified Simpson report. The release could only have been agreed to either counter van Roden's allegations or to help

Everett's campaign. In the event the release helped Everett and also, naturally, van Roden. Ignoring Simpson's conclusion that the twelve were guilty, Everett and a host of congressmen seized on the report's acknowledgement that the methods of getting sworn statements were 'questionable' and that the twelve should therefore be granted a reprieve.

Representative James Davis of Georgia, a friend of Everett, was the first to phone the Department of the Army demanding to see Royall because there was new evidence favouring the twelve.[49] When he arrived he admitted that he had no new evidence but used the occasion to bully the Department to overrule Clay. He failed.

The campaign's antisemitism and pro-Germanism now became entangled in pure internal American politics. The war crimes trials were the product of a Democrat administration and it was natural for Republicans to seize on an issue which, if exploited properly, could embarrass their political opponents. On 27 January the Republican Senator William Langer of North Dakota introduced a resolution for an inquiry into the Malmédy trials by the Senate Committee on the Judiciary. That resolution was quickly countered by Senator Raymond Baldwin's resolution that the inquiry should be conducted by the Committee on the Armed Services. Either way, the army was about to be embarrassed and even humiliated.

Hoping that Clay would be intimidated by the prospect of an inquiry, Congressman Davis immediately sent off a demand for reprieve to Clay saying that: 'it sickens me to the core of my being . . . that Americans have engaged in these brutal and unjustified acts.'[50] Unintimidated, Clay replied to Davis that he was sickened by the political exploitation of the 'cold-blooded crime which has been perpetrated in the murder of unarmed American soldiers who had surrendered as prisoners of war.' He continued: 'When it is realized that these defendants were the most fanatical and cruel of Nazi adherents, it is difficult indeed to give the same weight to their affidavits as it is to the affidavits of the American personnel engaged in the prosecution.'[51]

While the letter was on its way to Washington, Clay telegraphed the reasons why he intended to confirm six of the twelve executions.[52] In each case he explained why the evidence of guilt was overwhelming:

Ss Staff Sergeant Hubert Huber: even admitted after repudiating his sworn statement that he shot one American soldier who jumped up in the field armed with a small gun. But three other unrepudiated statements claim that Huber shot the American in cold blood and then stole the dead man's watch and some clothing. – Death sentence approved.

Ss Sergeant Paul Zweigart: after repudiating his first sworn statement which admitted shooting American POWs, [he] claimed that he had shot them acting on orders, then repudiated that statement and claimed that both statements had been made under duress, then claimed that the first account of shooting the Americans without orders was the truth. Three statements by other German soldiers, all unrepudiated, corroborated Zweigart's original story. – Death sentence approved.

Ss Sergeant Friedel Bode: admitted walking among prostrate bodies of thirty American soldiers and shooting them with a pistol. Later repudiated, but repudiations inconsistent and unbelievable. Unrepudiated eyewitnesses confirm his original account. – Death sentence confirmed.

Ss Colonel Peiper: originally seventeen statements that Peiper had ordered and was present at various shootings. Even if the repudiated ones are ignored, there still remained unrepudiated statements that Peiper was present at one deliberate shooting, which happened at his approval. Little doubt that as the senior officer, he was the principal in the case. – Death sentence confirmed.

The arrival of the confirmations and the letter to Davis coincided with the Senate's approval of Baldwin's resolutions. It was another victory for Everett, because Royall had already ordered Clay to postpone the executions until after the Baldwin Committee had reported.[53]

The Committee's first meeting took place in room 212 in the Senate Office Building on 18 April 1949. McCarthy was a member of the Committee and arrived briefed by both Aschenauer[54] and the National Council for the Prevention of War, a pro-German organization. In retrospect it is unlikely that he ever intended to stay the full course. At the time he was still unknown and probably saw the issue as a fast route to national prominence. Some have suggested that he might have wanted to use the hearings to distract attention from his impending conviction by the Wisconsin Supreme Court for unethical conduct in a local trial.[55]

The eyewitnesses McCarthy introduced were invariably inconsistent, contradictory and not telling the whole truth. They gave accounts of events they could not have witnessed and embellished things they had seen to a point of absurdity. Although he made many references to 'testicles being ruptured' and men 'crippled for life,' he produced no evidence to substantiate the allegations. The absence of proof did not prevent him reciting all the old claims and adding some more, including the account of a dentist who practised in the town of Schwabisch Hall who claimed to have heard screams of pain from the prison. He claimed that he had repaired the teeth of nearly twenty of those who had been attacked by the interrogators.

McCarthy also attacked the foreign-born Jews who had maliciously abused the procedures and protections afforded by American justice. It was still another year before he started his own investigations into so-called Un-American Activities, when those same procedures seemed to provide little protection.

McCarthy's harangues lasted just one month. As if on cue, he challenged Perl to take a lie detector test. Perl agreed, but after consideration Baldwin predictably rejected the idea. McCarthy had already prepared his resignation speech. To a packed news conference on 20 May he announced that he was resigning rather than remain part of an inquiry which was intentionally whitewashing the men who had extracted confessions under torture using 'brutalities greater than we have ever accused either the Russians or Hitler's Germany of employing'.

He walked out just in time to miss the collapse of his allegations. The assistant of Dr Edouard Knorr, the Schwabisch Hall dentist, claimed that Knorr's testimony had been written by a group of German lawyers who had come to the surgery, and that the records of prisoners' treatment were mysteriously missing. An American dentist sent to Landsberg to examine all the prisoners' teeth testified that just one prisoner claimed to have been treated by a German dentist. The others had been treated by American personnel.

McCarthy also missed the evidence of Dietrich Schnell, a medical student working in the prison hospital, who claimed in meticulous detail to have watched from a window while Perl hit a prisoner with the back of his hand and then kicked him. In the time-honoured fashion, Schnell was taken back to the window and shown that, because of the height of the window and the angle, it would have been impossible for him to have seen Perl. During the war, Schnell had been a party *Blockleiter* and had a reputation as a fanatical Nazi.

Judge van Roden's allegations were shattered when it was proven that his informant Friedrich Ebble, who had claimed to have been scarred by the interrogators when they inserted burning matches under his fingernails, had no scars whatsoever. Ebble, who had a criminal record, was medically declared to be mentally disturbed. Van Roden publicly admitted his mistakes, but McCarthy had already gone.

The senator had however walked straight into Senator's Hoey's Committee on Expenditure in Executive Departments. Unlike the Baldwin Committee, which was staffed by politicians sympathetic to Clay and the army, Hoey's members were Mid-Western conservatives. On 16 June Hoey wrote to Gordon Gray, the new Secretary of the Army, that his committee wanted the army's inspector-general to investigate every one of the 489 war crimes trials, including the pre-trial investigations. It was a straight political manoeuvre to keep the issue boiling regardless of the consequences in Germany.

In an overt bid to get juicy new allegations, or even old ones resuscitated, Senator Karl Mundt of South Dakota actually wrote to Joseph Unrecht, a prisoner at Landsberg, asking him to 'confer with your fellow prisoners to determine if there are any notorious cases of injustice involving any of them so that you will be able to call such cases to the attention of the representatives of the Inspector-General when they arrive.'[56] The letter had its intended effect. Within days of its arrival at Landsberg, Bishop Neuhäusler sent the National Council for the Prevention of War a long list of allegations of ill-treatment and bad conditions at Landsberg.[57] Investigations by the inspector-general and a representative of the American prison service showed that not only were the allegations untrue but conditions inside the fortress were as good if not better than most prisons in America.[58]

Hoey's giant probe never started. Asked by the army whether his committee was prepared to sanction the finance for twenty researchers to sift through 12½ tons of records and the retyping of 5,000-page trial transcripts, the senator backed down.[59] The Committee settled on an investigation just into the cases of seven other Germans condemned to death at Dachau for offences other than the Malmédy massacre.

While that was under way, the Baldwin Committee reported.[60] It dismissed the allegations of violence and blamed their acceptance on the work of an organized campaign by Nazis and their American sympathizers to discredit the trials. The initial cause of the problem, said the Committee, was the personnel used for the investigations and interrogations:

> It was found that many of the persons engaged in this work had no prior criminal investigative experience whatsoever, and had been former grocery clerks, salesmen or engaged in other unrelated trades or professions. It was also found that a surprisingly high percentage of these persons were recently naturalized American citizens. This sub-committee . . . does feel that it is unfortunate that more native-born, trained American citizens were not available to carry out this most important function.

Although Baldwin did not propose that the six remaining death sentences should be commuted, the inspector-general did suggest to the Hoey Committee on 13 December that the seven cases he investigated should be reconsidered. But for the movement in Germany, mere reprieves were no longer sufficient: the stakes had been raised.

On 15 December Thomas Dehler, the new West German minister of justice, asked Clay's successor, John McCloy, the new American high commissioner, to grant nothing less than an amnesty to all war criminals.[61] Dehler was not a former Nazi, but an anti-Nazi. Yet he was seriously demanding that the gates of Landsberg be immediately opened and all 500 inmates released. Among these were Ohlendorf, Pohl, still awaiting execution, and many others of the highest rank who had been intimately involved in the planning and implementation of the Final Solution.

There were few Germans who did not agree with Dehler's demand and his reasoning that as the trials no longer held any credibility, their verdicts should be set aside. It was a convenient conclusion for those Germans who wanted to believe that those inside Landsberg were merely unfortunates who had served their Fatherland and obeyed orders. Domestically, there was political capital to be won by demanding, and hopefully securing, their release. So Dehler and others argued that, of course, if Germans had been allowed to try the criminals from the outset, none of the criticisms and problems would have arisen: proper justice would have been done, and seen to be done.

13

'IT WOULD BE
JOLLY GOOD
FOR THEM'

The idea that the release of murderers would serve the interests of justice seemed as astonishing to McCloy as Dehler's assertion that if only the Allies had left the prosecution of war criminals to the Germans, the results would have been the same but more credible. The real but unpleasant truth was that most German lawyers and courts had done their utmost to sabotage all the opportunities given to them by the Allies to punish the profiteers, sadists and murderers who appeared in front of them. The tiny handful of American and British legal officers who tried to reverse the injustices had been humiliatingly rebuffed, first by the Germans, and later by their own superiors, anxious not to insult their new Allies.

No one had tried harder to build and protect a non-Nazi legal system in the American zone than Hans Weigert, an American civilian employee attached to the Legal Division. But on 25 May 1948 he knew that he had lost. On that day Dr Andreas Holzbauer was appointed chief prosecutor of Wurzburg by the Bavarian minister of justice, Dr Josef Müller. Holzbauer's appointment had been blocked for a year by Weigert threatening that he would be physically removed from office by American soldiers. For Müller and the Germans, Holzbauer's appointment was a test case.[1]

The new prosecutor had joined the Nazi party in 1940. At the time he was a member of four affiliated Nazi organizations. In his local party he held the senior rank of *Blockleiter*. His late membership did not harm, but rather helped, his promotion prospects. In consecutive years, his salary as a state prosecutor increased and the president of the Bavarian Supreme Court wrote on his annual report: 'He is capable of taking a leading part in the administration of justice as an adherent of Nazi ideology.'

It was the sort of testimonial which, after 1945, should have guaranteed his non-employment as a state prosecutor. Yet Holzbauer's appearance at the Kronach denazification tribunal produced a verdict which granted him ticket back to employment. The panel decided that not only had Holzbauer 'exerted active resistance' against the Hitler regime, but that this 'outstanding man . . . cannot have acted as *Blockleiter* because he was never a party member.' The party records and the personnel file at the Ministry of Justice were clearly erroneous.

Holzbauer's appointment was, as intended, an open challenge by the Nazis to the Americans and German non-Nazis. Weigert's department had issued no fewer than nine separate warnings against the reappointment of Nazis to the so-called five per cent key positions. By then, seventy-six per cent of the Bavarian junior prosecutors were former Nazis and even SS men. As in the British zone, attempts to prevent their re-employment had been half-hearted. But Weigert believed that if at least the top policy-making positions were kept politically clean, then there was a chance the injustices would be kept to a minimum. Holzbauer's appointment was, as his division chief Juan Sedillo commented: 'the tip of an ominous iceberg'.

Weigert drove to Munich on 15 July to order Müller to obey the 'key positions policy'. Müller, one of the founders of the modern Christian Socialist party (CSU), was at the time in the centre of as many notorious scandals as any men in Germany. He had packed the Bavarian Supreme Court with more Nazis than non-party members, and was just holding back the remaining nominations until he saw how the Americans would respond to the Holzbauer appointment.

His reply to Weigert's threats was to himself threaten resignation rather than implement the ban on Nazi appointments. Weigert left and memoed Sedillo that only personal intervention by Clay could prevent 'a complete breakdown of our efforts to keep at least the few key positions totalling slightly over 100 [people] free from former Nazis'.[2]

Weigert might have hoped for some positive response. Only three months earlier Clay's office had scathingly rejected the British nominations for the Bizonal High Court. Amongst those selected by the British were former members of the right wing, paramilitary Freikorps Severein (1922), pre-1934 SA officers, and one former judge whose personal record included the comment: 'has done outstanding work in the dissemination of national socialistic ideology in the legal profession.'[3] But now, in the midst of the Berlin airlift, Gailey took the opposite line.[4] He bluntly refused to intervene. Keeping Nazis out of office had proved an embarrassing failure. The statistics for April 1948 showed that out of the 12.7 million people who had registered for denazification in the American zone, a mere 1,046, or 0.2 per cent, had been classed as Major Offenders, while 15,389 (2 per cent) were officially 'offenders'.[5] The majority, like Holzbauer, had either been acquitted or amnestied, or if they were serious cases had held out until the end, when the sentences were sure to be merely nominal. Weigert swallowed his anger and humiliation.

No one could be blind to the unpleasant reality after Holzbauer's appointment was confirmed. German lawyers and judges were delighted to realize that, regardless of their verdicts, the American Legal Division was powerless to interfere.

Soon afterwards, German judges at the Frankfurt trial of five directors of DEGESCH, an IG Farben subsidiary, the manufacturers of odourless Zyklon B gas, acquitted the accused because they decided they could not have known that the specially ordered gas was for. In 1943 alone, seventy per cent of DEGESCH's business was Zyklon B gas supplied to Auschwitz.[6] Yet the judge told the court that: 'Millions of people had been saved by Zyklon B gas from typhus and other epidemics.' The judge added that: 'Very few in Germany or abroad believed in the Final Solution.'[7] A British military court, on the same evidence, had found no difficulty in condemning to death Dr Bruno Tesch, who had bought the gas from DEGESCH, and supplied it to the SS.

A Munich court sentenced Philomena Mussgeller, a former Auschwitz Kapo, to just four years, although there was abundant eyewitness evidence that her brutal assaults on inmates had caused innumerable deaths.[8]

Franz Rademacher, the Foreign Office official who smoothed the path for the Final Solution in Allied and occupied countries, was charged in Nuremberg, given bail by the court and promptly disappeared.[9] Even the murder of Germans by Germans was hardly prosecuted in German courts in those postwar years. Of 5,228 prosecutions for offences against Germans prosecuted in the German courts, just under one hundred were for murder and only eighty-three men were convicted. Fourteen were sentenced to death, and three were executed.[10] The bulk of the prosecutions were for comparatively trivial offences. Yet at least one million Germans were murdered by the Gestapo, or by the SS in concentration camps. Not only Jews, but also socialists, communists, trade unionists, Jehovah's Witnesses and gypsies. German courts turned a blind eye to the murders even of their own countrymen.

Leonard J. Ganse, the American chief of the Bavarian Legal Affairs Division, probably made the last attempt to save the now renazified German courts from reducing the whole of postwar justice in Germany to a farce. German prosecutors in Nuremberg and Augsburg had charged several doctors and nurses in their areas as accomplices to manslaughter for their work at the Hartheim and Sonnenstein 'euthanasia institutions'. Thousands of Germans, either elderly or mentally sick, had been sent to these so-called hospitals, allegedly to be cured but in fact to be murdered. Materially, it removed a drain on the Reich's scarce resources, while spiritually it countered the suggestion that the Aryan race was other than perfect. The charges mentioned that each of the doctors and nurses had been involved in anything from 100 to 899 deaths. Ganse had tried to force the prosecutions to change the charges to ones of murder. He failed. None of those convicted were sentenced to more than one year's imprisonment. On release, the convicted doctors either went back into practice or were retired on full pensions.

Ganse also tried to intervene in the case of Hans Eisele, a doctor whose medical practice amounted to injecting inmates at the Natzweiler concentratiom camp with typhus and sending his private patients to Hartheim. The German prosecutor responsible had decided to drop the case before it came to court. He told Ganse that he felt he could not prove that Eisele's typhus injections had not been administered with the intention of saving the inmates from a worse death, or that Eisele would have known that patients sent to Hartheim would be murdered.[11]

Dr Bernard Werner, the chief prosecutor at Regensburg, explained to Ganse that all the prosecutions were bound to fail because the doctors were just obeying orders issued in Berlin that untreatable cases had to be sent to the institutions. After all, said Werner, the doctors even got reports back from the institutions about their patients' progress. Ganse pointed out that some of the doctors accused had actually admitted in their defence that they had held patients back because they felt 'uneasy'. That proved that they knew. Moreover, all of the doctors must have heard of the Church's open attack on the euthanasia campaign. It had made a powerful impression on prewar Germany.

Ganse did not convince Werner, and the case was dropped. His report concluded: 'It is extremely deplorable in that it seems to reflect a general reluctance to deal with the perpetrators of Nazi crimes in an appropriate manner.'

It was with these and many similar cases and reports in mind that McCloy rejected Dehler's demand to release the mass murderers in the interests of justice.[12] How, he asked the new minister of justice, could he justify the German courts' record? The problem, replied the German, was the Allied insistence that German courts prosecute Germans on the basis of Allied and not German law. German prosecutors and judges had been reluctant to convict men who defended themselves by arguing that their only crime was to have dutifully obeyed Nazi laws. He felt that the Allies should have taken heed of the resolution of the minister presidents of the German Länder passed on 26 March 1946, which had asked the Allies to recognize the mistake of allowing not the Germans, but an international court, to judge German crimes. In the words of the resolution: 'It would stifle at birth the legend that the war criminals were found guilty by an international court of justice, but not by the German people.'[13]

To blame the Nuremberg Judgement for the failure of German justice was convenient. But the truth was that German judges claimed that they too had just faithfully followed Nazi laws. They were therefore in no position to reject the same explanation from others in defence of their alleged crimes. Yet murder, with some exceptions, always remained an offence throughout the Third Reich, and in the American zone, unlike the British and French, German courts were ordered to use the German penal code and not the Allied Law. No. 10. The US Legal Division's decision not to use Law No. 10, which had been drafted by American lawyers, was intended specifically to prevent the Germans from accusing the Allies of imposing on them retrospective laws, which they vehemently condemned as a Nazi practice. It seemed to many Americans as though the Germans were looking for any excuse not to prosecute. Their feelings and suspicions were reinforced by the recent finale of 'Operation Old Lace' in the British zone. That had been an attempt to compel German lawyers to try declared war criminals; it ended in ignominious failure.

The Bernays plan to prosecute the criminal organizations had been hailed by Stimson as 'an expression of civilization's condemnation of the Nazi philosophy and aggression which have relentlessly plunged the world into war'.[14] Bernays believed that by convicting the SS, SA, SD, Gestapo, and the Nazi party and its affiliated organizations of criminal conspiracy, the individual members of those organizations could be automatically convicted as co-conspirators.

Lord Simon had been attracted by the deft legal theory behind the plan, but Bovenschen had been appalled by the practical problems. Just after Rosenman left London in the spring of 1945, Bovenschen warned Dean that the American plan would create liabilities far beyond anything previously contemplated.[15] Including the Waffen-SS, the Americans were proposing to prosecute no less than five million Germans. The prosecution was only one problem. Finding the members of the organizations was an allegedly overwhelming prospect. Army intelligence had reported that tens of thousands of SS and Gestapo officers had shed their uniforms. Piles of black tunics, some buried, others half-burnt, had been discovered in fields and houses throughout Germany. The members of the organizations being arrested by Allied troops were not SS and Gestapo agents, but *Blockleiters* and other civilian Nazi party officials who had been found sitting in their homes. Rosenman's ideas, advised Bovenschen, were best ignored. Dean agreed.

British policy, even after the Nuremberg trial had started, was to prosecute only the equivalent of lieutenant-colonels and above in all the organizations, and to release the rest.[16] For a few weeks there was no pressure from the Department of War or the American Army Headquarters to plan anything else. At the time, General E.C. Betts, the American JAG, was himself uncertain what to do. One solution, he wrote to Clay's office, would be to include the SS and other members in the proposed reparation labour shipments for France and Russia.[17] But that possibility disappeared when reports arrived from France about the appalling conditions under which German prisoners were being forced to work. Reparations labour stopped overnight. It was too reminiscent of the Nazis' slave labour. American policy reverted to mass trials and a proposal that the Four Powers should adopt their draft for Law 10 which would include a positive commitment to try the members of the criminal organizations.

The British felt hustled, and hesitated in the face of what Troutbeck described as 'an immense and indeed impossible task'.[18] Facing an impatient Clay at the Control Council meeting on 20 November 1945, Robertson suggested that an acceptable compromise would be for the American draft to be approved on condition that each zonal commander had discretion about the number of the trials and that their individual decisions could await the verdict at Nuremberg.[19]

Clay, in front of Sokolovsky and to Robertson's great embarrassment, angrily accused the British general of having a 'half-hearted approach to the implementation of the law'. Robertson, supported by a Foreign Office terrified by the 'intolerable burden' of Clay's suggestion, refused to budge.

It was not only Whitehall that was alarmed by the American plan. American and British judges at Nuremberg had also become concerned about the consequences of a verdict that the organizations were criminal. In any circumstances, for judges and prosecutors to meet outside the court to discuss the implications of a verdict before the end of a trial violates basic legal ethics. Yet the judges' concern was such that, on 6 December, Norman Birkett, the alternate British judge, secretly met both Dean and Sir Hartley Shawcross, the chief British prosecutor at the trial, to confide in them the judges' fears. Dean and Shawcross suggested that Biddle and Lawrence, the American and British judges, should confront and cross-examine the chief American prosecutor, Justice Robert Jackson, personally.[20] Six days later, Jackson tried but failed, to answer the judges' questions. Why, asked one judge, should the SA, which had lost a lot of its power after the 'Night of the Long Knives' in 1934, be convicted? Did Jackson mean that a cleaner at Gestapo headquarters or an SS telephonist should be prosecuted? As the proposed charge would be restricted to those who were members after 1939, did that mean that those who fought with Hitler in the Twenties were to remain untouched? Last but not least, were those many German soldiers who had been drafted without choice into the Waffen-SS, fighting as an elite but otherwise normal unit, to be treated like the truly criminal SS?[21]

Jackson's unsatisfactory answers strengthened Robertson's position when the Control Council next met on 20 December. Without rancour, it was agreed that zonal commanders would have discretion how to implement the Judgement. More importantly, the Council also agreed that the trials, both for membership of a criminal organization and crimes against humanity (where the victims were Germans or stateless persons), could be delegated to German courts.

Jackson still tried, two months later, to rescue his proposition that the members of all the organizations should be properly tried in formal courts, but his thirty-page memorandum was rejected not only by the Department of War but later by Clay himself.[22] Instead of formal trials, Clay decided that all the hearings should be handed over to the denazification tribunals. It effectively absolved his command of directly responsibility.[23]

Clay's clear-cut decision was not copied by the British. On the contrary, the British, who had constantly warned the Americans about the lessons of Leipzig and were convinced that the Germans would never prosecute German war criminals properly, committed themselves to the exact opposite of what they had intended. They ordered German lawyers to prosecute 27,000 members of the criminal organizations in the German courts.

The lurch towards the unforeseen and unintended started on 4 March 1946. A massive document entitled 'disposal of War Criminals, Militarists and Potentially Dangerous Persons' emerged after Four-Power discussions in Berlin. It extensively listed and categorized the Germans who were liable for prosecution and what were the agreed recommended punishments. It further established that trials could be by German courts.

'All this may lead us into very deep water,' concluded one Foreign Office official. 'Far from satisfactory.' commented another.[24]

Robertson had already told the Foreign Office that the army did not have the staff to run any trials, so the responsibility was transferred to Macaskie and Rathbone of the Control Commission's Legal Division. The Commission's joint policy at that stage, as agreed at a meeting of the Standing Committee on Denazification on 4 March, was that: 'The final solution must be to build up a German state with a political life capable of digesting these elements.' Prison sentences, it also hoped, would be kept to an absolute minimum because there were not enough prison guards; the commitment was best fulfilled by 'administrative means'.[25]

In April, Brigadier D.G. Heyman arrived in Germany to find the best 'administrative means' which would absolve Britain of any responsibility for mounting the trials. At Lübeck he met Jack Rathbone, who now describes his role at that time as 'the minister of justice dressed up in a colonel's uniform'. Rathbone convinced Heyman that the Germans should try the members of the organizations in ordinary German courts and not denazification tribunals. Rathbone now says: 'They had created the mess so I thought they should clear it up. It would be jolly good for them.' At the time there were 72,000 internees in the British and American zones who were former members of the indicted organizations. But after further discussions between Jackson and the Nuremberg judges, both sides agreed that the SA would be acquitted and only the more senior ranks of the Nazi party would be convicted. That reduced the numbers to be tried in the British zone to 27,000.

By accepting and, later, endorsing Rathbone's suggestion for ordinary trials, Heyman defeated the purpose for which he had been sent out to Germany. Indeed, he seems to have come back from Germany completely confused about why he had been sent out in the first place. Not only did he suggest that the 27,000 should be tried, but he also reported that there were at least another 45,000 party officials and an estimated 200,000 SS and Gestapo agents liable for trial who had still not been arrested. They would have to be found, he wrote, but his suggestion that the Public Safety Branch could be responsible was totally unrealistic. Public Safety had even refused to arrest known war criminals, claiming that they were understaffed. [26]

Heyman had also become confused about what would happen to those convicted. Robertson had demanded that 10,000 of the lower ranks of the party and Waffen-SS be immediately discharged because of supply shortages and camp conditions. They were 'not in themselves criminal,' he said. Dean vigorously rejected this suggestion, on the grounds that the evidence at Nuremberg had proved the Waffen-SS responsible for some of the worst atrocities in Eastern Europe and Russia; while the lower party officials had been the bedrock of the tyranny on which the regime had relied. Rather than be released, he wrote, they should all be tried. According to Heyman, the Control Commission secretariat agreed with Dean. Most of the 27,000 were expected to be sentenced to long terms of imprisonment. [27] Some British officials seemed to have forgotten their desire for a 'detached attitude' policy. It had drowned in the reaction to the mass of evidence of German atrocities.

British officials were also so strongly agreed that the internees were dangerous and convinced Nazis that a British policy statement about their conditions of imprisonment was rewritten to deliberately exclude any reference about their re-education. According to Walmsley, a

Foreign Office research officer; 'Experience has shown that it is unlikely that the outlook of internees would be sufficiently improved by re-education.'[28] Attempts at re-education had in fact proved an outright failure.

The confusion, contradictions and reversals of policy were not remedied, or even recognized, when the Nuremberg verdict was delivered on 1 October. As expected, the whole SS, the Gestapo and the Nazi party leadership corps were convicted. The SA was acquitted. Conviction, according to the Judgement, was based on proof of guilty knowledge of the organization's illegal activities, gained either before or after joining the organization. But the judges, at Biddle's persuasion, had left ambiguous the crucial decision on whether there should be an absolute presumption of guilt. Jackson had urged that there should be, but Biddle had been reluctant to totally reverse the traditional Anglo-American presumption of innocence.[29]

Within a week, the American Command, after consulting Jackson, issued an ordinance interpreting the Judgement in the way that suited them – namely that 30,000 internees in the American zone would have to prove their own innocence.[30] It neatly acknowledged the warning of the oldest of legal sayings: 'The devil himself knoweth that the thought of man is not triable.'

On 6 November the British Control Commission in Berlin, after consulting Robertson, cabled the Control Office in London that the British trials would also be held on a presumption of guilt. The alternative was trials lasting for the next five years. Foreign Office lawyers later thought that estimate conservative. They feared trials on a presumption of innocence lasting thirty years.[31]

The curtain now rose on Act Two of the blunder into an unwanted commitment. The majority of officials in the London Control Office for Germany were young, inexperienced and ignorant, not only about Germany generally, but also about the specific problems on which they were expected to give advice. Divisional chiefs in Germany had quickly learnt to ignore the civil servants in London and make policy decisions on the spot. But this latest telegram, presenting a *fait accompli*, was simple enough for the Control Office lawyers to understand. It would give them an opportunity to show their mettle.

Without consulting ministers, the Foreign Office or the Law Officers, they bluntly rejected Berlin's proposal the following day. To dispense with the presumption of innocence would, they telegraphed, 'violate the judgement'.[32] Richard Wilberforce, one of the Control Office lawyers, commented on the idea of reversing the burden of proof; '[It] appeared to me to indicate a lack of energy in approaching the problem, which view I communicated to Berlin by telephone.'[33] But to reduce the burden of 27,000 trials the Control Office suggested another violation of the Judgement. Wherever evidence was not easily obtainable to prove an individual's guilty knowledge, they suggested the internee should be simply downgraded so that he would not have to be tried, but could instead be sent to a denazification tribunal or be released.

Wilberforce was quite certain that it was just the form and not the substance of the trials that mattered. In a few words he suggested that the officers in Germany set up a hundred special courts and complete those trials where there was evidence within no more than one year. To simplify the commitment he hoped that the majority of the estimated 40,000 SS soldiers held as POWs in Britain and the Middle East, 'which represent a substantial and awkward commitment . . . could be graded as harmless before return to Germany.' Wilberforce even admitted in the same paragraph that the majority of the 40,000 were 'blacks', fanatical Nazis who were so unreliable that their return to Germany had been delayed.[34] He did not mention the other members who were free inside the British zone, conservatively estimated at 200,000.

Explaining their suggested tactics, John Simpson, another Control Office lawyer, wrote to Macaskie: 'We see no reason why individuals, particularly of lower grades, should not be downgraded without trial if on examination there appears to be no evidence of knowledge or personal participation.' Not only did that confuse the membership question with that of war crimes, but it still left 27,000 people to be individually investigated.[35]

At a press conference at the end of January 1947, Robertson twice emphasized that the operation had the highest priority and that he had given an order that the trials had to be completed by the end of the year. Six months later only one case had been tried. Five thousand low-ranking members had been released untried, but another 5,000 had arrived for trial from the American zone because they lived in the British zone. Legal Division officials had calculated that operation 'Old Lace' would need 3,496 staff and a daily consumption of 3,122,700 calories. Not only would food have to be found but also transport, furniture, buildings, coal for heating, typewriters, paper and even ink. Despite the 'high priority' classification, none of the necessary supplies materialized. It was reminiscent of Turpin's quip to Bradshaw nine months earlier: 'A Brigade Commander . . . makes up his own mind about the relative importance of the many tasks he is ordered to carry out . . . The impatience of a Cabinet Minister will not influence him greatly or make him change his mind.' Robertson clearly had just as little influence.

Jowitt's report to the Cabinet on his tour of the zone in May 1947 contained a stinging rebuke against the Control Office lawyers who had rejected Berlin's suggestion that the trials be run on a presumption of guilt: 'I am apprehensive about the whole thing and fear that the experiment may lead to discredit and chaos.'[36] Control Office officials tried to cover up their mistake and briefed the minister, John Hynd, that it had never been intended to try more than 7,000 members. The plan, Hynd was told, had been to release the remainder.[37] The documents suggest this was untrue.

But the immediate cause of the impending chaos was neither the presumption question, nor the enormous numbers involved, but Rathbone's assumption that the German legal profession would be not only prepared, but keen, to accept the responsibility for trying German SS officers and party officials. He was mistaken. Moreover it was a mistake which he had realized, but did nothing to remedy, shortly after the Heyman report was circulated in the spring of 1946.

At the ninth meeting of the Standing Committee on Denazification on 2 July 1946, Rathbone reported that the German legal profession had flatly refused to cooperate in the trials.[38] Membership had not been a crime when the members had joined, said the lawyers, and retrospective legislation like the anticipated Nuremberg Judgement and Law 10 was one of the more repulsive aspects of the Nazi regime. Rathbone told the committee that he was undeterred. Two anti-Nazi lawyers would be appointed to write a law which would establish special courts and instruct those courts to apply the Nuremberg Judgement retrospectively. No one, apparently, discussed Heyman's comment that the trials could only succeed if the courts were thoroughly anti-Nazi. By then the fifty per cent rule on the non-admittance of nominal Nazis had been effectively breached.

As director of 'Old Lace', Rathbone had one strength and several weaknesses. He was probably correct in thinking that, if Germans could be made to properly enforce the Nuremberg Judgement, the verdicts would be more acceptable to the German people. It was with that belief in mind that he, unlike Macaskie, had agreed that there should be a presumption of innocence. But his weaknesses were considerable. He knew hardly anything about German law or the history of Germany's courts, nor was he a talented enough lawyer in his own right to overcome the obstacles which the German lawyers threw in his path. If the operation was to succeed and German courts were to accept the Allied interpretation of German criminality, Rathbone had to be able to foresee the inevitable challenges, both practical and theoretical. In the contest of intellect, he lost the initiative.

It was only at the end of February 1947 that Rathbone was told that the German lawyers wanted to see the detailed evidence on which the

Nuremberg Judgement was based. Until then he had assumed that the trial transcript and the Judgement itself would be enough. Dr Meyer Abich, appointed as the inspector-General responsible for supervising the courts, gave Rathbone a list of 144 documents which the lawyers wanted to read: the 'Commando Order', evidence of the 'Night and Fog' decree, the regulations for the treatment of Russian POWs, and the telegrams and orders on slave labour and the extermination of the Jews.

Predictably, the lawyers refused to take anything for granted. As they started investigating the individual cases, the prosecutors and judges also demanded the personal files of each of the accused, so as to be able to challenge the member's own account of his activities in the Nazi era on his *Fragebogen*.

Getting the documents and then reprinting them for circulation delayed the trials for two months. Finding sufficiently detailed personal records proved near-impossible. The Berlin Document Centre, under American control, was still disorganized and understaffed. A lot of the party records had still not been found. According to Rathbone, only one per cent of the replies from Berlin were helpful. Internees, realizing that their trials were based on their own invariably incomplete *Fragebogen*, at first denied knowledge of any criminal activities; they even professed ignorance that Jews in Germany had to wear yellow stars.

The practical obstacles could probably have been overcome if the German lawyers' theoretical arguments had been refuted as they arose. At the beginning of March 1947 German lawyers told Rathbone that they could not envisage any convictions at all because all the defendants would plead *Notstand*, compulsion: that is, that they were ordered to join the organization and there had been no alternative but to obey superior orders. The alternative, the accused would argue, was a concentration camp and death.

For some time Rathbone and Macaskie tried to argue with the Germans that the defence was precluded by Article 8 of the Nuremberg Charter, the Nuremberg Judgement itself, and Article 2 (4b) of Law 10. Unfortunately, and to the Germans' confusion, the Allied laws were contradictory. Article 2 (4b) of Law 10 stated: 'The fact that any person acted pursuant to the order of his government or to a superior does not free him from responsibility for a crime, but may be considered in mitigation.' Law 10 however conflicted with the Nuremberg Judgement, which stated that superior orders was a complete defence where the person was drafted into the organization by the state or the Nazi party 'in such a way as to give them no choice in the matter'.

The Germans brushed Rathbone's defensive arguments aside. As the trials were, according to the British Ordinance 69, to be run on the basis of German law and procedure, they argued that Section 54 of the

German Penal Code applied.[39] It explicitly allowed *Notstand* as a defence. Allied laws had no relevance.[40] German courts had by then interpreted Section 54 so widely that defendants did not even need to prove compulsion. They normally just had to mention it for it to be accepted by the judges. Rathbone despaired. Control Office lawyers recognized that giving in to the Germans would reduce 'Old Lace' to 'mere farce and cause a feeling of triumph among the Nazis.'[41]

German lawyers were convinced they had won. In May, they thrust what they called their 'definitive argument', an article by Freiherr von Hodenberg, the president of a state court, into the hands of an increasingly alarmed Rathbone. Having read it, British lawyers told Rathbone that the article was nothing less than 'a serious danger threatening the administration of justice from political bias'.[42] According to Hodenberg, German judges should ignore all the Allied laws because they conflicted with the honoured and just legal principle *nulla poena sine lege* – literally, 'no punishment without law', which implied that retrospective legislation was not law.

To meet the challenge, Macaskie and Rathbone organized a special conference on 5 June for Macaskie to explain why the Nuremberg Judgement was binding and how guilty knowledge could be proved.[43] According to E.D. Renwick, a Foreign Office official sent to Germany to check on Dr Meyer Abich, even those avowedly anti-Nazi prosecutors who attended were untrustworthy.[44] They found the whole operation distasteful and believed that the vast majority of the lower ranks should be acquitted. Former Nazi prosecutors in Macaskie's audience were at that very time being re-vetted by British intelligence because they had been improperly denazified. In those circumstances, Macaskie would have had a hard battle, regardless of his arguments. Not surprisingly, at the end of the day he had clearly lost.

He had told the prosecutors that the Nuremberg Judgement had to be unconditionally accepted because the Allies and the court had stated that their Judgement 'cannot be challenged'. It was a weak argument, too similar to victor's justice to be acceptable. Proof of guilty knowledge, said Macaskie, was no problem. Every member of the organization must have known what was happening, and their pleas of ignorance should not be accepted. For the German lawyers, that was too much like shifting the presumption to one of guilt. They felt that it was an inadequate reply. Von Hodenberg and his fellows could feel confident that, as in Weimar times, they had successfully interpreted the law to suit their political feelings.

Only in September did the British present conclusive counter-arguments to the German lawyers. First, that German law had always allowed the *nulla poena* rule to be overridden by *lex posterior derogat legi priori* (the later law takes precedence over previous law). Von Hodenberg's claim that there was a traditional rule against retrospective law in Germany under any circumstances was pure fiction. Secondly, and more important, the British lawyers suddenly realized that if an SS officer pleaded *Notstand* or superior orders, he would first have to admit to the guilty knowledge. It was a plea of mitigation after a confession of guilt. But by September, when the prosecutors and judges realized that *Notstand* was ineffective, the fortnightly reports on the trials showed that the outcome of 'Old Lace' was very similar to that of the denazification tribunals. According to the 22 October report of K. Ronau, a German-speaking British legal officer, over thirty per cent of SS men were being acquitted, usually on the advice of prosecutors who told the court that they had insufficient evidence to go ahead with the case.[45] Ronau reported that 'rabid Nazis', senior members of the party and the SS, were being acquitted although they had been members of execution squads and special courts; or even where they had mercilessly denounced anti-Nazis, well knowing what the inevitable consequences would be.

Liberius Schäffer, a SS NCO from 1933 until 1945, would have been one of those to benefit had Ronau not intervened. Although Schäffer himself admitted that he knew from personal experience about Buchenwald and Orianenburg, and actually lived near the Wevelsberg concentration camp, the prosecutor recommended that Schäffer be acquitted because his health was poor and he had eleven children. His eventual sentence amounted to immediate release. Just under six per cent of all sentences were over one year. The model sentence, passed on the second case of the operation, against a former SS guard at Belsen and Orianenburg concentration camps, was just two years. Although the maximum sentence was ten years, the highest sentence passed in all the trials was five years, against a single defendant.[46] Offenders like the nobleman Erbprinz Ernst Zurlippe benefited from the timidity of the prosecutors and the bias of the judges. Zurlippe, a *Sturmbannführer* in the SS, had joined the Nazi party in 1928 and worked as an assistant to Darré, the minister of food. Darré had been sentenced to seven years imprisonment by the Americans at Nuremberg for, among other crimes, ordering atrocities against civilians. Zurlippe proudly admitted at his trial in Bergedorf that he knew Jews were deported to concentration camps and were guarded by the SS. 'I was proud to wear the black uniform,' he told the court. The prosecutor asked for a nine-month sentence, yet the court acquitted Zurlippe on the grounds that despite his admission, he really did not know that the SS were committing crimes.

Both judges and prosecutors were refusing to implement the law. It was a solution of the problem by 'administrative means', but in a different fashion from that originally intended. It satisfied not only

Germans, but also British politicians like Richard Stokes and publisher Victor Gollancz, who claimed that those interned were unimportant unfortunates with nothing to hide. Their misfortune was that they were among the few who were arrested, Stokes said. He insisted that the Germans being detained were either innocent or not given sufficient privileges. He wanted them re-educated to appreciate 'British fair play', but refused to listen to those British education officers who had tried and failed to re-educate the Germans.

Nevertheless Stokes' pressure, combined with the obvious failure of the trials, convinced Pakenham to commit the government to releasing 7,500 internees without trial as part of a youth amnesty before Christmas. But as only 2,500 of the interned members fell into that category, Control Office officials in London insisted that a further 5,000 be released, 'we feel that the need to make good the Chancellor's undertaking in the House of Lords outweighs the possible political repercussions.' – senior SS, Gestapo and Nazi officials were released en masse.

The last progress report filed by Rathbone was on 8 April 1948.[51] It claimed that eighty per cent of those prosecuted were convicted (against less than fifty per cent in the US zone). But that was eighty per cent of the 7,000 who had been actually tried. At that stage, 19,500 members had been either released, remained untried or had accepted a procedural conviction, which in effect meant immediate release.

The trials continued until early 1949. Only 400 of the 40,000 SS soldiers who were prisoners of war were returned to Germany for trial. At the request of a small group of German prosecutors, Rathbone had agreed that trials should also start of the very large number of serious offenders who had escaped arrest in 1945. On Pakenham's orders, he had to revoke that permission within a few days. The minister wanted the trials to end regardless of what a minority of Germans felt.

The disillusioning postscript for those prosecutors who had taken their task seriously was that, like the few dedicated denazification officials, they were the only real victims of the trials. German government ministries stubbornly refused to re-employ many of them because they had collaborated with the Allies against the Germans. Those who had prosecuted the Nazis were classed as traitors.

14

'THEY WERE NOT NAZIS, THEY WERE BUSINESSMEN'

No one in Germany has ever described Baron Herr Direktor Doctor von Schnitzler as a traitor. Known to his fellow directors on the IG Farben board as 'IG's salesman', von Schnitzler was the chemical giant's representative at the secret and historic meeting on 20 February 1933 when twenty-five of Germany's leading industrialists and bankers pledged financial support for the Nazi party. The twenty-five were invited by Schacht to Hermann Goering's Berlin home, where the future Reich Marshal assured them that the forthcoming elections on 5 March would be the last for the next ten or even one hundred years. His honest description of the methods the party intended to use to achieve that aim clearly did not dismay his handpicked audience. The opposition, said Goering, would be simply wiped out and the Wehrmacht's power restored.

When at the end Schacht appealed for three million reichsmarks to finance the Party's campaign, von Schnitzler pledged four hundred thousand reichsmarks, over one million dollars at today's values – more than anyone else in the room. It was the beginning of a very close and criminal relationship between the Nazis and the company.

From the outset of the Nazi regime, IG Farben's worldwide activities were monitored in Washington.[1] Intent on breaking up cartel agreements between international companies which had secretly agreed on price fixing and the 'ownership' of countries to exclusively sell their products, the Anti-Trust Division of the US Department of Justice began a series of unsuccessful probes into IG's activities. But it was only at the outbreak of the Pacific war that Justice officials got a real taste of the company's astute subterfuges over the previous six years.

Cut off from their traditional supply of rubber in South-East Asia, the American government discovered to its horror that the American chemical industry did not have the technical knowledge to make artificial rubber. The cause was not scientific incompetence but the result of a deliberate strategy by IG Farben executives to prevent their American competitors carrying out their own research.

IG Farben and Standard Oil had developed secret understandings in the late Twenties. The result was an agreement, in August 1928, that IG would stay out of the oil business and Standard would keep out of chemicals.[2] Under the agreement, both sides would exchange scientific research which involved the other's exclusive field. Standard kept to its side of the agreement, while IG, on the Nazi government's instructions, did not. IG developed the technology of Buna (artificial rubber) production, but then during the two years prior to the war used every ruse imaginable to successfully prevent the knowledge crossing the Atlantic. American executives both at Standard and in the American rubber tyre industry, believing IG's final excuses that the Nazi government was preventing the immediate handover and not realizing that it was the result of an agreement between IG and the government, held back from undertaking their own costly research. The ensuing rubber shortage in America throughout the war was severe.

Masterminding that particular deception from the outset was Carl Krauch, an IG board member. Krauch however was destined for greater achievements. IG had already made a secret agreement with Hitler to develop synthetic fuel out of coal, although it contravened the 1928 agreement with Standard. Krauch, on behalf of IG, now offered the Nazi government not only the benefits of a whole range of technical expertise but also proposed himself as the regime's natural co-ordinator of army ordnance. In 1937 he suggested to Goering's office that the incumbent General Loeb, responsible for army ordnance, had seriously miscalculated the amounts of chemicals needed in the event of war. Rebuffed several times, he finally outmanoeuvred Loeb in a humiliating session in front of Goering.

The rewards were immediate. Krauch was appointed by Goering to be responsible for the planned expansion of the chemical industry to meet the army's wartime needs. Production of nitrates for gunpowder, explosives, poison gas, synthetics and a thousand other military requirements immediately increased.

What IG could not produce themselves, they obtained by subterfuge. Exploiting their close relationship with Standard Oil, Krauch met representatives of the Ethyl Export Corporation, a Standard affiliate, in London in early 1938. At the request of the Air Ministry he was trying to obtain tetraethyl lead, a crucial additive for aviation fuel. The Air Ministry feared that Hitler's Czechoslovakian bluff would turn to war and Germany's own plants would not be ready until 1939. Krauch told the American negotiators they needed the additive only temporarily, as a 'loan'. Five hundred tons of it arrived just before Chamberlain met

Hitler at Munich, despite protests in Washington, by Du Pont among others, that it was a dangerous agreement in view of Germany's bid for rearmament. But Krauch was not working just in Germany's interests. When it came to producing chemicals for war, what was good for Germany was profitable for IG Farben, and the company's profits multiplied. Duping Standard Oil was made easier by the American company's own conspiracy with IG to deceive the Anti-Trust Division of the US Department of Justice about their cartel agreements. By 1940, those agreements had become an international scandal.

German industry's experience after the First World War had rightly convinced Hermann Schmitz, the chairman of the IG Farben board, that IG's assets in America and other hostile countries would be confiscated in the event of war by the Custodians of Enemy Property. At stake were not only factories but, more importantly, patent rights over very valuable scientific processes. To avoid that seizure, IG Farben had established, latterly with the help of Standard Oil, the companies IG Chemie in Switzerland and IG America in the USA. Until the outbreak of war the directors of those two companies had consistently lied to the Anti-Trust Division that IG Farben of Germany was not connected to either company. In an attempt to reinforce that lie, IG and Standard Oil directors embarked on a series of intensive negotiations in the Hague, London and New York between 1 September and 23 September 1939. Under the final agreement, IG transferred all its non-German rights and property to Standard for just twenty thousand dollars. When the agreement was finally scrutinized by the Justice Department, it was clearly seen to be worthless. It was an ineffective transfer.

But the web of camouflage which had been constructed – using American nominee shareholders, the creation of IG Chemie as an allegedly independent company in Switzerland, and alternating pleas of commercial secrecy and ignorance by the American directors – was so tight that the cases about the company's true ownership continued in American courts until 1967. The immediate effect during the war, however, was to commit those radical officials in the Anti-Trust Division who were preoccupied full-time in unravelling IG's ingenuity to destroying the company when Germany was finally defeated.

Two of those officials were Russel Nixon and James Martin, both assigned to the US Military Government's Cartels Section. They arrived in Frankfurt at the end of April 1945 to discover that while IG Farben's giant headquarters had miraculously escaped any bomb damage, four hundred tons of IG's documents which had been carefully filed over the years were being unceremoniously tipped out of the windows and burnt in the courtyard. A lot of what had not been burned was being used as bedding by liberated slave workers. SHAEF commanders had decided to use the building as their headquarters, and ordered it to be 'cleared of refuse'.[3]

Before they could destroy IG Farben, Nixon and Martin had to understand it. They really knew very little about the company, and few Germans outside its *Vorstand*, or managing board, had an overall insight into IG's activities. The documentary evidence was clearly vital, but what survived the war took nearly two years to assemble and examine. Interrogating the directors and senior officials was clearly the second source of information; from the beginning, the Americans were convinced that two directors – Hermann Schmitz, the chairman, and von Schnitzler – were more responsible than the others:

By the time Martin and Nixon had found von Schnitzler on 8 May, they knew enough about him to realize that the 'salesman' tag was misleading. Von Schnitzler was the company's plunderer. He had negotiated the forced acquisition of the Polish, Austrian, Czech and French chemical industries. He had also prepared plans for the absorption of the British industry into the IG empire.

Russel Nixon had discovered that von Schnitzler was last seen in Frankfurt on 28 March and was probably living in his country home in Oberursel, comfortably removed from the devastation of the cities. There are several versions of von Schnitzler's arrest. Indeed, with the omission of his name, it has become the legendary account of how all German industrialists reacted when they first met Allied troops.

According to a SHAEF intelligence report: 'Schnitzler received the Americans dressed in fine Scottish tweeds, cashmere sweater and English brogue shoes. On the wall of his sitting room was a Renoir painting from the Louvre in Paris. So far he had managed to have eggs, poultry, milk and plenty of butter; all things most Europeans have not seen for a long time.'[4] James Martin tells another version: 'He looked every inch a baron, from his black homburg, velvet collar and grey spats, to the young and beautiful baroness on his arm. One would never have guessed that von Schnitzler was a criminal, one of the financial mainstays of the Nazi regime and a mastermind of the IG Farben foreign organization.'[5]

Both versions agree, however, that von Schnitzler was effusively polite and welcoming. He offered Nixon brandy and then immediately withdrew the offer, murmuring, with a regretful gesture, that it was clearly forbidden by the non-fraternization order. Sitting down, von Schnitzler told Nixon that he was glad that 'all this unpleasantness is over' and how he looked forward to seeing all his old friends at ICI and Du Pont again. 'My friends and I,' he said, 'must pick up from where we left off and build for the future.' Nixon, who had agreed with Martin that Schnitzler be brought back for questioning, remained stony-faced.

According to the SHAEF report: 'When the Americans demanded to see the records of IG Farbenindustrie, he [Schnitzler] said he regretted deeply but the records had been destroyed. The Americans asked him to come along to his old office, but he replied that he was unable to do so as the way was so long and he was so old. The next invitation came from a sergeant with a tommy gun in the jeep. This time the Herr Direktor did come.'

Schnitzler's first interrogation lasted three days. Martin claims that his first question, 'What is IG Farben?' was designed to lull the director into a sense of false security. But in reality, Schnitzler, like the other industrialists, was convinced that the Americans would never discover the truth. Firstly, they did not believe that their colleagues would speak, and secondly they were convinced that the incriminating documentary evidence was either destroyed or well hidden. Huge bonfires of IG documents had been burning for some days before the Americans captured Frankfurt. Other documents had been hidden in forests, mines and farmyard barns, stored in cupboards and even sewn into clothes. IG had rented a monastery's refectory to store 'personal effects of bombed-out employees'. The sixty-eight packing cases were crammed with agreements between IG and French, British and American companies.

Investigators did not even realize until late 1945 that the nerve centre for Krauch's work was the IG office in Berlin known as 'Northwest 7'. It took another year to discover that many of the missing office files had not been destroyed but had been packed and shipped to the Alexandria archives outside Washington. At the beginning of Martin's interrogation, Schnitzler even denied that he was a member of the party; he had in fact joined in 1937, along with all the other board directors who had not joined in 1933. His denial, and all the other hundreds of thousands of denials of party membership, were only refutable once the party's eleven million card index files were discovered at a paper pulp mill outside Munich. The mill owner tipped the Americans off as an insurance policy against future problems.

Schnitzler's first admission of responsibility for IG's crimes came after Martin confronted him with the evidence of his contribution on IG's behalf to the Nazi party. 'Through this course of action,' conceded Schnitzler, 'IG took on a great responsibility and gave, in the chemical sector, substantial and even decisive aid for Hitler's foreign policy which led to war and the ruination of Germany. Therefore I must come to the conclusion that IG is largely responsible for the policies of Hitler.'[6]

This and many other very incriminating confessions made over the next two years by Schnitzler would be ignored at his eventual trial, when Judge Curtis Shake asserted: 'Von Schnitzler was seriously disturbed and no doubt somewhat mentally confused by the calamities that had befallen Germany, his firm of Farben, and himself personally. His eagerness to tell his interrogators what he thought they wanted to hear is apparent throughout.'[7]

It was the fearsome relationship between Germany industry and the government which the Anti-Trust Division wanted to destroy. In their estimate, one hundred industrialists and the six major banks controlled two thirds of the German economy. It was that concentration of power, they believed, which had made it so easy for the Nazis to mobilize Germany for war. Martin wrote to Clay that the industrialists were: 'convinced chauvinists, racially conscious, greedy and ruthless . . . all of them were monopoly oriented and anti-democratic and many, if not most, openly supported Hitler . . . There is no force within Germany, private or public, capable of purging the will of the German monopolists.'[8]

Martin's assessment was controversial. British and American politicians and Military Government officials were divided about the nature of the marriage between Germany's industrialists and the Nazi government. Largely influenced by their own political prejudices, the Allies disagreed amongst themselves whether the marriage was forced by circumstances or voluntary. The evidence now available suggests that the industrialists and bankers were initially divided and hesitant about their support, but that once they had identified their own self-interest with the Nazis, they were enthusiastic about the new relationship. Indeed, some allege, on the basis of the timing of the marriage, that it was only when Hitler won the industrialists' support that he was in a position to demand and be granted, the dictatorial powers he sought.

Throughout the Twenties the majority of industrialists and bankers considered the Nazis unreliable, suspect and even dangerous. The Ruhrlade, the industrialists' club, refused attempts by Alfred Hugenberg and Fritz Thyssen, the steel manufacturer, to get them to listen to Nazi politicians. There were however some notable exceptions. One was Friedrich Flick, a steel manufacturer, coalmine owner and a director of the Dresdener Bank. Others were Wilhelm Zangen, a member of the Deutsche Bank board (*Aufsichtsrat*) and the bank's nominated chairman of the Mannesmann group; Robert Bosch, the electrical manufacturer; and Otto Wolff, Hugo Stinnes and Ernst Pönsegn, owners of Ruhr coalmines and steel plants. But even some of these, according to Walter Funk, the wartime president of the Reichsbank, were hedging their bets by contributing to other political parties.[9]

It was Funk who in 1931 made the first approaches to the industrialists for financial support to the Nazi party. Until then the Nazis, who saw themselves as a revolutionary workers party, were suspicious of the industrialists. But the party needed money and respectability.

The approach was three-pronged. On 11 December, Funk met Baron Kurt von Schröder, the owner of the Cologne bank, I.S. Stein. He asked von Schröder to arrange for Hitler to meet industrialists who might be potential supporters. Simultaneously, Wilhelm Keppler, a small industrialist and early party supporter, was charged with collecting a small group of businessmen who could advise Hitler on what to offer the industrialists in order to win their support, and who would later be at his disposal when he got into power. It was the beginning of the so-called *Keppler Kreis*, the Keppler Circle, which later became the Himmler circle. Amongst the early members were representatives of Flick, the giant United Steel and the Dresdener Bank.

The third approach was made on 27 January 1932. Six hundred members of the Industrie Klub, representing the cream of German industry, were invited by Fritz Thyssen to Düsseldorf's Park Hotel. Suddenly there was a shout from behind: 'Everyone stand up.' There was some fumbling, some confusion. Some stood, others did not. But the effect was dramatic. Through the industrial elite marched twenty Brown Shirts. Behind them marched Adolf Hitler, the master of dramatic theatre. It was the first time he had spoken to the leaders of the German economy. They had come because unemployment had just reached six million, there was open warfare on the streets between all political factions, and Hitler had just won some impressive election victories. The threat of anarchy was bad for business and he offered a solution.

Hitler told his audience that they faced a stark choice – a brown or a red Germany. Democracy, he told them, was dangerous, the communists even more so. The violence on the streets, the political stalemate and Germany's economic crisis could only be solved, he said, by abolishing the trade unions and electing a Nazi government.

There is little doubt that many in the audience were impressed. Contributions to the party increased. Discreetly, they were paid into 'Sonderkonto S' (Special Account S) at von Schröder's bank. Amongst the largest contributors in 1932 were Flick, United Steel, Siemens, Bosch and the Dresdener Bank.

On 6 November the Nazis suffered an election setback and they were again in financial difficulties. Thyssen and Keppler quickly persuaded thirty-eight industrialists to underwrite the party's debts at von Schröder's bank. Amongst those thirty-eight were Krupp, Vögler, a steel manufacturer, and Wilhelm Tengelmann, a mine owner.

It was three months later, at Goering's home, that the Deutsche Bank committed itself to supporting Hitler. Gustav Krupp was also among those invited by Schacht. Two days later, the armaments manufacturer wrote to Hitler and thanked him for addressing the meeting. Krupp wrote again to Hitler on 25 April after the new Chancellor had been granted dictatorial powers by the Reichstag: 'The turn of political events is in line with the wishes which I myself and the board of directors have cherished for a long time.'[10] Thereafter Krupp, like the other industrialists, increased his contributions to Sonderkonto S. He and the other industrialists had a lot to be grateful for. Their pre-1933 losses quickly turned to profits.

As those profits increased, criticisms disappeared. Attempts were made by industrialists and bankers to protect their Jewish colleagues, but few resigned in protest when they were finally removed. The wiser and more far-sighted non-Jews made sure that their Jewish colleagues and competitors left feeling indebted for their help. Either the amount paid out for the enforced aryanization of a bank was a little more than strictly necessary, or a lump sum was sent to London or New York so that the refugee would be able to live in comfort. There were few leading industrialists and bankers who, in 1945, after twelve years of profitable support and allegiance to the Nazi cause, were not able to produce a sworn affidavit from a Jew that they had done their best to mitigate the worst aspects of Nazism for that one person. There were many other Jews, invariably by then gassed and cremated, who could have sworn the opposite.

But in 1933 these were minor considerations. For most of the industrialists in the years to come the only problem was how to divide the spoils, which included not only the results of aryanizing their competitors in Germany and the later plunder of their foreign competitors in occupied Europe, but also the profits of the partnership in government which the Nazis offered. None of them resisted, and to their satisfaction, industrialists and bankers in other western countries were more than prepared to continue trading with them on the same basis as before, namely under the same cartel agreements.

It was the international powers of the cartels which Martin wanted to attack. There was ample evidence that even British and American industrialists had ignored national interests during both world wars, even to the detriment of their countries' own war effort, just to protect business agreements. During the First World War, Farben had successfully restricted the Bayer Chemical Corporation in the USA from expanding production. In the 1939 war the Bendix Corporation of America had signed an agreement with Siemens which restricted Zenith in Britain from expanding its wartime production of aircraft equipment.[11] Karl Zeiss of Jena, the manufacturers of optical instruments, were more ingenious. To avoid the Versailles Treaty ban on the production of periscopes, bomb-sights and range-finders, Zeiss made an agreement with Bausch & Lomb of Rochester N.Y. giving them all their scientific expertise. Zeiss calculated that the handover would save them from confiscation during a future war. Bausch & Lomb continued production throughout the war for the American army, but faithfully submitted to Germany accurate and detailed monthly production returns for licence payments. From those returns, Zeiss could easily tell German intelligence what sort of tanks, aircraft and submarines the Americans were producing.[12] Paying licence fees to an enemy was not unusual. After the First World War, Krupps sued Vickers, the British armaments manufacturers, for £1.6 million in payment for the use of the patent in their manufacture of fuses for hand grenades. Vickers settled the action by giving Krupps a steel mill in Spain.

In theory, the anti-cartel section should have not found much trouble in breaking up the German cartels. Both JCS 1067, the American policy document for Germany, and the three-power Potsdam Agreement, uncompromisingly laid it down that the concentration of German industrial power was to be destroyed for ever. Any last-ditch opposition from the German industrialists could easily be smothered. What Martin and the anti-cartel section did not reckon with, however, was the strength of the opposition from their own side. The British and American bankers and industrialists who had worked with their German partners until 1939 and, in some cases, until 1941, saw little reason why their business relations should not be picked up where they left off. The advantages were clear, especially as before 1939 American industry held controlling interests worth $420 million in German industry, and its total investment was much greater.

The anti-cartel section was part of the Economics Division which was headed by William Draper. Describing their first discussion on the problems ahead in April 1945, Martin wrote about Draper: 'The investment banker's view was uppermost.' Draper was on secondment from the long-established New York bankers, Dillon, Read & Co., who had a history of long and profitable relations with German industry. Working with Draper was Captain Norbert Bogdan, a vice president of J. Henry Schroeder Banking Corporation of New York. Schroeder had close links with Germany, even with the I.S. Stein Bank owned by Baron Kurt von Schröder, who had not only channelled the German industrialists' funds to the Nazi party but had also, at a historic meeting in his bank, introduced Hitler to von Papen, so paving the way for an agreement between Hitler and the conservatives in the Reichstag. Schroeders of New York had continued trading with Nazi Germany until the declaration of war in 1941.

A former Schroeder's director was Allen Dulles, the OSS representative in Switzerland. Dulles' law firm, Sullivan and Cornwall, had its own strong German contacts. His brother, John Foster Dulles, also a partner in the firm, had personally represented IG Farben's American company, General Analine and Film Corporation, in the early stages of IG's attempt to prove in the American courts that GAF was not German-owned. His methods in handling that case to protect IG Farben were described by a state prosecutor as being those of a 'scoundrel who should be disbarred'.[13]

Section heads under Draper were also committed men. Rufus Wysor, president of the Republic Steel Corporation, and Fred Devereux, the retired vice president of AT&T, acting as Draper's deputy, were both singled out by the Kilgore Committee report to the Senate in 1945 as representative of the many Allied officials serving in Germany who believed that: 'no effort should be made to penalize German industry or prevent it from recapturing its prewar position in world markets . . . They look forward to resuming commercial relationships with a rehabilitated German industry whose leading figures are well known to them.'[14]

Martin and Draper's first meeting resulted in an immediate and unpleasant confrontation. Draper refused to announce the tough deconcentration and decartelization measures that Martin demanded. Unlike Martin, who decided to stay and fight, Nixon resigned in December 1945 in protest at Draper's refusal to implement American policy. Bernard Bernstein of the banking section had also left by then, on the same grounds.

In September 1945 Bernstein had reported to Clay that flying visits by his ten-man investigation team to banks throughout the zone had removed 9,500 employees who were proven active Nazis. It was proof, he claimed, of the culpability of German finance.

But he demanded even stricter measures, and the removal of US officials who were refusing to implement the denazification regulations properly. Too many incriminated Nazis, even pre-1933 members, he claimed, were being allowed to remain in control of banks. Clay, who had already approved the draconian Law No. 8 which removed all former Nazis from public employment other than as common labourers, refused to do any more.

Nixon and Bernstein's departure undoubtedly weakened Martin's position in the American command, but his greatest strength still remained. Clay himself was determined to break up the power of German industry in accordance with JCS 1067 and the Potsdam Agreement. Until mid-1946, Martin could have still defeated Draper had two conditions been satisfied: firstly, if the anti-cartel section had possessed the information about German industry necessary to actually organize the break-up; secondly, had the Americans and not the British had physical control over German industry. The Ruhr, in which the steel and coal industries were situated, was beyond Martin's control, in the British zone. The head of the British Military Government's Economics Division, Sir Percy Mills, made Draper look and sound like a liberal socialist.

Unlike the other appointments to the Control Commission, finding Mills had been comparatively easy. In retrospect it seems that British industry wanted 'their man' in control. Mills' last prewar visit to Germany had been to Düsseldorf on 15 March 1939. He had been a member of a delegation of the Federation of British Industries which met representatives of the Reichsgruppe Industrie headed by Wilhelm Zangen. For two days the British and German industrialists had discussed how to improve the cartel arrangements between their two countries. According to the confidential FBI minutes of the meeting, the two sides concluded that: 'The two organizations agree that it is their objective to ensure that as a result of an agreement between their industries, unhealthy competition shall be removed.' Another paragraph recorded that the two sides agreed to remove 'destructive competition . . . to the mutual benefit of Great Britain and Germany'. The meeting ended on an optimistic note, looking forward to further meetings and even closer cooperation.[15]

In the Whitehall interdepartmental meetings during late 1944 and 1945, it was Edward Playfair from the Treasury who prevented acceptance of the Americans' strong denazification policies and gave considerable support to Percy Mills. One result of Playfair's efforts, was that Mills arrived in Germany totally unencumbered by any formal directive to remove Nazi businessmen. Indeed, Military Government Officers were rightly convinced as late as July 1945 that they did not have the authority to remove Nazi businessmen, however strongly they had supported Hitler's regime. Protesting against the absence of any directive, Brigadier A.E. Hodgkin wrote to Mills at the Control Commission's headquarters, 'very many prominent Nazis are untouched by the present regulations, and their continuance at liberty in positions of unofficial influence is not consonant with our general policy.'[16]

Mills ignored the protest. He was not only a full-blooded opponent of decartelization and deconcentration, but also appeared to be convinced that the German industrialists were innocent of any wrong going. Not surprisingly, his first list of Germans appointed to control industries in the Ruhr was selected from those industrialists he had last met in 1939. According to the SHAEF directives they should all have been under arrest.

Wilhelm Zangen, a party member since 1927 and an employer of slave labour at Mannesmann, was reappointed to continue the same work, but without slave labour.[17] Ernst Pönsgen of the steel industry, decorated in 1941 by Hitler with the Eagle Shield, the Reich's highest award for economic services, was employed to revive the Ruhr steel industry.[18] The citation on Pönsgen's award quoted his 'extraordinary services in arming Germany'. Pönsgen's successor was Heinrich Dinkelbach, another committed Nazi supporter, who with British approval immediately recruited twenty-seven steel experts who had held senior positions in the Third Reich.[19]

Herbert Tengelmann, son of the Wilhelm Tengelmann who became a notorious mine owner during the Nazi period, was appointed as textile adviser.[20] His qualifications for the post should have resulted in his immediate arrest. Before 1933 he acted as a confidential liaison between Goering and the small industrialists in the Ruhr. As a reward, he was appointed president of the national textile organization in Berlin. Within weeks, he and his friends began to systematically take over first the Jewish and then the other textile companies so that the industry could be reorganized to produce uniforms. It was straightforward confiscation, for which Tengelmann was given a series of decorations. His appointment provoked uproar even in Britain. He was replaced by Ernst Vits, a *Wehrwirtschaftsführer* (leader of the war economy) under the Nazis. In 1940 Vits had been appointed by Hermann Abs to run the Dutch textile giant AKU, after the banker had negotiated its Germanization on behalf of the Deutsche Bank.[21]

Mills' policy for the appointment of German industry's new leaders was automatically reflected in the failure of British Military Government officers to denazify individual industries. But the blame for their failure was not placed on Mills. At the eighth meeting of the Standing Committee on Denazification on 4 December 1945, it was laid on 'the officers of the Economic Division in the field [who] were technicians and made no pretence of familiarity with the Nazi hierarchy. They [are] hardly fitted to take a leading part in denazification.'[22]

Ignorance was not the only reason for the British failure to denazify. Calculated blindness, based on self-interest, was the more important cause. It was the standard argument of both British and German industrialists that only the Nazis had the expertise to run the industries and that their removal, merely to satisfy a political objective, was in the circumstances an unaffordable luxury. With very few exceptions, the claim was false, but it was rarely put to the test.

Immediately after the war German miners in the Ruhr protested about the British refusal to denazify their industry by refusing to work. During the war, mine managers had recklessly caused the deaths of countless slave workers and even of German miners, by employing overseers to force them to increase their production. Flick, Stinnes, Tengelmann and others had not hesitated to force the miners, most of whom were not Nazis, to comply with the orders of the overseers who were trusted party officials.

It was those same overseers who Henry Collins, the British Military Government's deputy controller for North German Coal, refused to dismiss. Reporting to London on that refusal, Strang wrote that, of the twenty-two dismissals recommended in one mine on 27 July 1945, only one had been carried out by 21 September. He added: 'Many of the overseers whose harsh treatment of foreign workers is frequently reported, are quite unnecessary to the maintenance of production.'[23] Yet Collins, a British Coal Board official, told both the miners and Whitehall that only the overseers had the technical knowledge to guarantee that the coal, which was desperately needed throughout Europe, would be produced. The miners stayed away and coal production slumped, crippling any hope of an early economic recovery in Europe.

British prejudice was reflected in their refusal to arrest the mine owners who had been whole-hearted Nazi supporters. It was only in October 1945 that the leaders of the Rhine Coal Syndicate were interned, more for their own protection than because the British intended to prosecute them. According to Kellam, Stinnes enjoyed champagne parties in his prison cell.[24]

In early 1946 two mining accidents, in which over four hundred miners died, were used by Collins to prove that only the Nazis had the technical skills to prevent disasters. At the Monpol Grimberg mine the rescue operation was directed by a Nazi official who had earlier been dismissed after a series of protests by the miners. At first sight, Collins' arguments were convincing, but an official inquiry by General Erskine revealed that the accidents had not happened because of denazification removals, but because of poor discipline.[25] Collins countered that there was a lack of discipline because the overseer's leadership had been removed. The miners replied that there was poor discipline because too many Nazi overseers, whom the miners resented, remained.[26]

Until June 1946, Collins won, but coal production slumped even further and Robertson finally agreed that the miners should be responsible for the appointment of denazification committees to vet all mine officials. When the committees reported at the end of November 1946, only eleven officials had been removed.[27] The Nazi overseers had not reapplied for their jobs. After that, production rapidly increased.

No other German industry was denazified like the coal industry. Europe's need for coal was too great to allow British and German resistance to denazification to succeed. The dramatic increase in coal production during and after 1947 proved that the industry was not dependent on the expertise of former Nazis. It also proved that where, as in all the other industries, the German workers were not united and determined enough to enforce their demands, British Military Government officers could easily ignore the denazification regulations. Neither Mills and the Control Commission in Lübeck, nor the political officers in Berlin, had either the time or apparently the motive to investigate their failures effectively. The only risk was that the continued presence of Nazis would be exposed in London and the minister demand an explanation. Even then, Military Government officers tended to ignore London's demands.

In autumn 1946, German trade unionists complained to British trade unions that IG Farben factories remained Nazi-run. It was not the first time that the Control Office had heard indirectly that IG was still managed by incriminated Germans. In August 1946, John Churchill in the Control Office had sent the Commission a report on Martin's discovery that the 'notorious Dr Carl Peters' was trying to 'resuscitate the cartel with the assistance of Du Ponts of America and ICI in this country'. The Americans, he wrote, 'were sore however about the position in the British zone':

> I saw a confidential list of those in control of the Farben establishment in our area. The first four important posts were avowed Nazis; the next five were professedly ex-Nazis and undoubtedly are Nazi sympathizers. It is not until one gets low down in the list that anti-Nazis are found. But the absolute control is in the hands of the Nazis. It was suggested to me that ICI representatives dealing with chemicals are possibly following the same rules as that of Dr Peters.[28]

Unable to ignore the situation any longer, Commission officers started a slow investigation into staffing at IG's factory at Huls.

Special Branch in Germany admitted that a survey in January 1946 showed that there were ninety-nine employees at Huls who were classed as mandatory removals.[29] None of them were removed by March 1947, despite repeated demands from London.[30] On the contrary, the numbers of committed Nazis employed at the factory actually increased. Nazis removed from IG Farben factories in the US zone were guaranteed work by the management at Huls in the British zone; with British connivance, it became a repository for removed Nazis. Critical messages from the

Control Office about 'unsatisfactory and slow progress' were ignored. Even the minister's complaints were ignored by the British officers. The German workers who had originally protested became timid. They feared victimization from the management.[31] Significantly, the British had resisted allowing workers in the factories to set up their own denazification committees because, as Sir William Strang reported to Bevin: 'this would result in a good deal of irresponsibility and victimization.'[32]

The farming and food industries should also have been denazified, but the division representative, R. Hollins, halted the removal of Nazis from the sugar industry and the ownership of farms 'in view of the critical food situation'.[33] Hollins argued that the dispossession of the Nazi farmers 'would cause great hardship and discontent'. Undoubtedly it would have – amongst the Nazi farmers.

Hollins chose to ignore the huge number of non-Nazi German farmers who had been dispossessed by their Nazi neighbours after 1933, and were experienced and qualified to produce food. At the committee meetings he used the arguments of Playfair and Mills, that efficiency could not be sacrificed just for retribution. It is noteworthy that the arguments against removals could even be used to protect those who had employed slave labour. Although pressure by the dispossessed farmers finally forced both the British and Americans to produce a scheme to remove the Nazi farm owners, it was never implemented. The Nazi farmers remained; those who had opposed the Nazis lost. The extent of that failure was reported to Washington in April 1949. Exactly six hectares had been confiscated and redistributed.[34]

The denazification of the oil industry was also delayed indefinitely. L. W. Harford, the British officer responsible, explained throughout 1945 and 1946 that he had neither the qualified staff, nor proper instructions. He claimed that there was 'little known' about the Germans employed in the industry, and that with insufficient evidence it would be wrong to dismiss them.[35] Yet Harford had not even visited the installations for which he was responsible, nor apparently did he ever find the industry's records.[36]

Appointments to Kontinental Öl, the German oil company managed by Karl Blessing, were always carefully screened by the Gestapo and government ministries to guard against anyone but the most committed Nazi discovering the state of Germany's vital oil supplies. Yet Harford reported in December 1945 that as far as he had discovered, the Germans in the oil business were able to 'stand with their feet planted firmly in two camps'.[37]

The Denazification Committee actually rejected Harford's excuses but was unable to undertake the denazification itself. Unknown to its members, British and American oil company representatives working for Anglo-Iranian Oil and Shell were at that very time secretly investigating the German oil industry and examining its drilling logs to evaluate how they could increase their own share of the market.[38] When Murphy criticized what were by then the blatant attempts of the Anglo-American oil companies to take over the German oil market in June 1947, he was momentarily reassured that they would be stopped. They were not.[39]

British self-interest could also result in the destruction rather than the protection of an industry. The shipbuilding section within Mills' Economics Division was intent not on denazifying but on completely dismantling the German shipbuilding yards on the North Sea coast. It would have effectively removed British shipbuilders' most aggressive competitors. Only a Cabinet decision prevented their total success.[40] In stark contrast, there were serious complaints that the same section had allowed the Hamburg shipowners associations, whose leaders started contributing to the Nazi party as early as 1931, to distribute the few merchant ships that survived the war amongst themselves, at the expense of the smaller, anti-Nazi shipowners.[41]

Mills supervised not only the failure to denazify German industry, but also its plunder in the interests of British industry. It earned him the title amongst senior staff in Berlin of 'Robber Mills'. On 12 November 1947, Bevin told the House of Commons that 2,066 items had been taken from Germany as unilateral reparations. But the official figures were just the tip of the iceberg. Not only black marketeering but thefts on an enormous scale were quite commonplace. There are innumerable accounts of senior Control Commission officers seizing, without authorization, industrial machinery, patents and even the silver from requisitioned homes and shipping them back to Britain. After leaving Germany, they were immune from prosecution because there was no extradition treaty between Britain and Germany, and the British army command preferred to suppress its discoveries rather than face embarrassment and humiliation in front of the Germans.[42]

Some of the more ham-fisted attempts were investigated by a special team of forty Scotland Yard detectives sent out to Germany exclusively to investigate corruption amongst Control Commission staff.[43] One team investigated attempts by Courtaulds, then a large British textile company, to get Control Commission officers to 'look after their interests'.[44] Another team investigated an attempt by Britain officers to force the owner of the '4711' eau-de-cologne scent to hand over the formula for its preparation as a 'reparation'. The British officers were in fact directors of a British company also manufacturing scent.[45] The investigations did not result in prosecutions but revealed that the corruption was more widespread than previously imagined, and definitely not confined to the British officers.

'Operation Sparkler' exposed the fact that the corruption and black market in Germany was worth one billion pounds at 1946 prices. Whole factories had been packed and shipped to Belgium and France on the orders of individual British and American officers and for their own profit. Trainloads of minerals and suitcases packed with precious gems were seized on the pretence of orders from the Economics Division, and then sold on the black market.

Reading through the official records, it is hard to feel other than critical of many of those who worked for the Control Commission. Their 'spineless indifference' and 'horrid examples of carnal lust' were quoted by the Reverend Geoffrey Druit in a public denunciation from his pulpit in Germany. The assistant chaplain general condemned the British officers' morals and claimed that they were making Germany 'the cesspool of Europe'.[46]

In more orthodox language, every Labour minister and MP who returned from Germany reported that the quality of the staff of the Control Commission was so low that the British administration should be ended as soon as possible.[47]

The British, however, prided themselves that conditions were even worse in the American zone, and the boast was probably justified. Corruption amongst the American military was not confined to the Military Government officers, but was spread amongst the officers and men of the regular army. The court martial of the American commander of Bremen revealed that he had run the town like an Arabian fiefdom. Cars, valuables and women had to be handed over to him in return for any privileges. Similar cases in southern Germany never even came to trial. According to Harold Zink, an American Military Government officer in Germany; 'their sexual antics . . . must have served to reduce the respect of some Germans for the American Military Government personnel almost to the point of ridicule.'[48]

The Allied policy, set in May 1945, was the denazification, deconcentration and decartelization of German industry. Blocking its implementation were corruption, incompetence, political prejudice, personal self-interest, and irreconcilable antagonism, not only between British and American Military Government officials, but among the Americans themselves.

According to James Martin, the lines were already drawn towards the end of May 1945. Mills arrived for breakfast at the Villa Hugel, the

Krupp family mansion outside Essen, requisitioned by the Allies. Over breakfast, an American Public Safety officer complained loudly about how ridiculous it was to be vetting the villa's laundress because of her party membership, while the British allowed notorious Nazi industrialists to remain free. In fury, Mills swung round and shouted: 'What's wrong with them? They were not Nazis, they were businessmen.' Draper, sitting next to Martin, silenced the American, making it clear that his sympathies were with Mills.[49]

The cause of the friction was the form and extent of the decartelization laws which the Allies were to impose. The official forum for the arguments was the Four Power Economic Directorate in Berlin. The American trust busters argued that the laws should break up German industries and only after this was achieved should the industrialists have a chance of pleading their innocence. Mills argued that the American plans were dangerous and unworkable. The break-up should only happen, he said, if, after investigation, there was a proven 'excessive concentration of power'. There followed an interminable argument about the definition of 'monopoly' and 'excessive concentrations'.

Britain was in a minority of one, but that did not deter Mills who, pompous and outspoken, argued word by word through the American-drafted law. 'Is it a crime to be big?' Mills asked Martin. The Americans were divided about the answer. On the same day Mills suggested that it was not for the Economic Directorate to be drafting laws, which was the work of the Legal Directorate. By 27 November all Mills' stalling tactics and excuses had been exhausted, and it came to the vote. Mills vetoed the draft law.[50]

Draper's sympathetic support for Mills and the British was not based purely on self-interest and prejudice. Sitting in Berlin, a vast expanse of rubble and desolation, it was quite easy to believe Mills' argument that Germany's industrial power in the Ruhr had been destroyed by Allied bombing. It was an opinion shared by a report for President Truman and Congress written by Dr Don Humphrey and former President Herbert Hoover. After a dislocated tour through Germany's destroyed cities the two men recommended that the German economy needed to be revitalized rather than further destroyed.[51]

The fallacy was that what their eyes saw did not tell them the truth. German industry had not been destroyed by Allied bombing. The US Strategic Bombing Survey showed that at most only twenty per cent of Germany's *extended* wartime industrial capacity had been destroyed. The country's peacetime needs were far smaller. Allied bombing had in fact been a miserable failure. While large sections of residential and city centre areas had been destroyed, the bombers had wildly missed their industrial targets outside the towns. Only the destruction of the oil refineries and the rail network had finally crippled German production. Krupp was producing more tanks in early 1945 than ever before, but had to stop production because there were no trains to transport the tanks to the front.

The myth of the bombers' success had been created during the war by Bomber Command. From aerial reconnaisance photographs taken the day after the bombing of a German city, Bomber Command blindly asserted that Germany had suffered terrible losses.[52] The myth was kept alive into the peace by Mills.

The truth, obvious to those who sought it, was only realized in London in 1948 after the currency reform produced an enormous industrial boom. A report to the Foreign Office on 5 February 1948 described the amount of damage to IG Farben factories as 'greatly exaggerated'.[53] Most of the buildings which had been officially listed as 'destroyed' were not factories but small offices, salesrooms and shops. Each 'destroyed' shop on the list got the same status as a 'destroyed' factory. In the British zone, there were just two IG Farben factories destroyed. Even in those factories, as in many others in the Ruhr, once the rubble of what was previously the roof had been removed, the machinery was found to be intact.

John Kellam, attached to the Banking Section in Hamburg, was also responsible for decartelization in the British zone. He remembers Martin as a 'rabid trust buster' who was ignorant about the structure of German industry. 'As far as I was concerned, Monty ordered us to get Germany going, and Americans like Martin wanted to put all of them [German industrialists] in a room and shoot them. I just told Martin that I wasn't interested in trust busting.'[54]

The British decartelization branch numbered four officers. The American section had a staff of forty lawyers plus one hundred researchers and others.[55] Every attempt by the Americans to base themselves in the British section's Düsseldorf offices was flatly refused. Kellam insists that their initial refusal was not based on specific orders from Mills – 'because we had no instructions one way or the other' – but just because he did not agree with American policy. He did not need specific instructions. British policy was clear enough. Foster Adams, an American investigator at the Nuremberg trials, who several times went to Düsseldorf in an attempt to negotiate access to a German industrialist or banker, vividly remembers the effect of Kellam's policy: 'The British in Düsseldorf were more interested in protecting than cleaning out. It meant there was always conflict.'[56]

Captain Irving Roth, an American lawyer in the anti-cartels section, was one of the three Americans who worked for a short time in the Düsseldorf office. His protests were rarely committed to paper because he, like the other American officers, knew it would have no effect. But the appointment of Dr Schafhausen was one of those rare occasions when he could not keep silent. Schafhausen had been sought out because one of the British officers had known him before the war when they had worked together for Price Waterhouse, the international firm of accountants. A few days after the German arrived, Roth discovered that the British had secured his release from an internment camp where he had been correctly labelled as as automatic arrestee because of his high party rank. Roth's written protest against the employment of someone who was in the mandatory removal category was naturally ignored.[57]

The protest only made British officers more cautious about revealing their intentions to the Americans and hardened their opposition to allowing more Americans into the British zone. The British resisted more than a token American presence in Düsseldorf until Germany became a sovereign nation in 1949.

British policy never changed; but, eager to get a change in American policy, British officials in Berlin and diplomats in London and Washington slowly began to exploit the disagreements in the American camp. The change in American policy was slow. It is not an exaggeration to describe the process as a vicious battle which rankles even today in the memories of those who participated in it. Draper and Martin's battlefield was Berlin and Washington. Both had their allies in Congress and both fought to influence the numerous fact-finding delegations to Germany. The ultimate cause of Martin's eventual defeat was the changing political situation in Europe, which favoured the traditional German Establishment.

There are arguably many dates when the Cold War can be said to have started, and 29 December 1945 is as good as most of the others. On the presidential yacht, the *Williamsburg*, on the Potomac River in Washington, President Truman had a bitter argument with Secretary of State James Byrnes. Byrnes had just returned from a disastrous foreign ministers meeting in Moscow. On his own initiative, he had tried to pacify the Russians and break the deadlock between the wartime allies. Purposely, he had ignored Bevin and sided with the Russians against the British. Bevin had felt betrayed and British diplomats in Washington had quickly explained to the State Department that the Americans had failed to understand communist tactics. Communist penetration in Eastern Europe, the Balkans and the Middle East could not be halted by being conciliatory. After he had read Byrnes' report of the meeting, Truman agreed with Bevin. 'I'm sick of babying the Soviets,' Truman jabbed at Byrnes. 'No more compromises.'[58]

During the previous weeks in Berlin, Robertson, to Clay's open anger, had refused to compromise with the Russians about industrial reparations. By 3 May 1946, Clay had accepted the new hard-line policy and announced the suspension of any new dismantling of German factories for reparations to the Russians. But Clay still believed in decartelization.

In June, Draper returned from Washington having recruited a new team for the Economics Division. All of them were 'recovery men', critical of the old punitive policies. Among them was Lawrence Wilkinson, the new head of the industry branch. Wilkinson is one of those former officers whose resentment of Martin has not diminished with time. 'A horrible little bastard. Didn't he go to Czechoslovakia?' was his reaction when Martin's name was mentioned to him thirty-three years after his appointment. (Martin did not go to Czechoslovakia.) According to Wilkinson, 'Martin wanted to pull everything down.' According to Martin, Wilkinson told the visiting American delegations that while 'we are pulling the man up by the hand, Martin is keeping one foot down on his neck.'[59]

Decartelization, claimed Wilkinson, would hamper German economic recovery and so automatically add to America's already enormous costs in Europe. Like denazification, it achieved nothing except to cause resentment and weaken the Allies. So Wilkinson happily worked with the British against Martin. With British help, and dressed in civilian clothes, he met Abs on several occasions for consultation and advice. Martin alleges that both Wilkinson and Draper actually asked Sir Cecil Weir, Mills' successor, to raise certain issues in the Four-Power discussions which would give Draper a suitable pretext for seeking Washington's agreement to change in American policy.[60]

Treasury, trade and Control Office officials in Whitehall, wanting to help Wilkinson and Draper, devoted a lot of time and energy to convincing visiting American officials and politicians that the decartelization programme was mistaken. 'Take the line,' said one Control Office briefing, 'that we are in Germany to make laws for the Germans and not for ourselves, and that we did not come to Germany to liquidate Allied interests, but rather to liquidate German war potential.'[61] It was an argument which appealed especially to American industrialists, anxious either to buy up German factories at bargain prices or to resume production in their own factories.

It was during a session at the Control Office in London on 9 August 1946 that an urgent message came from Berlin that Clay, on Martin's suggestion, had declared that America would decartelize industry in its own zone unilaterally because the draft law had still not been approved.[62] Clay made the surprise announcement just after leaving a meeting with Draper, Robertson and Mills where they had finally agreed on an economic merger of the American and British zones. Martin hoped that the announcement would force the British into line. William Ritchie, in the Control Office, handed the message to Terrell of the State Department without hiding his pleasure that it was evident that Terrell was as surprised by Clay's announcement as the British were.[63] Ritchie had in fact been about to make some concessions in the interest of building a joint front against the Russians, but he sezied on Terrell's sudden vulnerability to ask him, in the classic style of British understatement: 'Do you think that the Russians understand what Clay means by trust busting? I would have thought that the Russians have their own inimitable methods of trust busting.' Terrell replied: 'My hands are tied. Clay has something like one hundred Department of Justice representatives in Berlin itching to get to work.'

Days later, Draper flew to Washington. He returned to Berlin on 13 September and telephoned Martin to meet him at Tempelhof Airport. On State Department instructions, said Draper, American policy had changed. The Economics Division would now seek a compromise with the British.[64]

Martin played his last trump, General Clay's own support. After hearing Martin's account of Draper's instructions, Clay memoed Draper, criticizing him for telling visiting American delegations that denazification and decartelization were to blame for Germany's dire economic conditions. 'Our economic program has not progressed sufficiently as yet to have any real effect on the German economy. . . I am certain that the revival of democracy in Germany is dependent on our ability to develop an economy which is not controlled by a handful of banks and holding companies.'[65]

Clay's reprimand had no effect. On 13 November, Sir Cecil Weir, soon to replace Mills as Division chief, cabled the American embassy in Washington that Draper had promised him that it was just a matter of time before American policy fell into line with the British.[66] One month later Willard Thorp, an assistant secretary of state at the State Department, promised the British embassy that the Department was doing its best 'to keep the wild men in check'.[67] In the meantime the Republicans had won the Congressional elections, tilting America's policy in Germany towards helping business.

The Four-Power law against cartels which was finally approved in January 1947[68] suited British demands perfectly. The status quo was to be maintained unless the need to intervene was proven. As the British resisted American attempts to investigate, the law was unenforceable from the outset. Mills returned to Britain shortly afterwards, to be rewarded with political honours when the new Conservative government took office in 1951. Martin held off resigning until May. His successor was Philip Hawkins, Draper's son-in-law, and a relative of the Du Ponts, owners of the giant chemical company.

Back in Washington, Martin did not stop his campaign. He and some of the remaining members of the decartelization branch testified to the Fergusson Committee which was investigating American policy in Germany. Ranged against the decartelizers were those who produced innumerable statistics to prove that while German industry remained unused, the American taxpayer was heavily and increasingly subsidizing the German economy. To break it up further would only cost America more money. Fergusson's report however ignored the easy option and blamed Hawkins and Wilkinson for deliberately sabotaging the decartelization policy. The report recommended that they be fired. It was a bitter-sweet victory for Martin against Wilkinson.

In retaliation, Wilkinson, fired two members of the remaining decartelization team who had given evidence against him to the Fergusson Committee. One of them, Alexander Sacks, had said: 'They have done whatever they could, by innuendo and misstatement, to discredit a programme which they did not understand and they did not like.'[69] Joining Sacks in the exodus from Germany were 120 of the section's staff. Just twenty-five remained.

Until the very last moment in 1949 when the Allies returned partial sovereignty to the Germans, the twenty-five still pathetically tried to break down the restrictive practices and power of the German cartels. They still had Clay's support, but General Robertson stood firmly in their way. In one last desperate manoeuvre, Clay thought he had convinced the British that the decartelization office should be situated in Frankfurt alongside the other bizonal offices managing the merged economy of the zones. On 11 January 1948, in a personal phone call to Robertson, in front of his staff, Clay reminded Robertson of their agreement. Robertson reneged on the agreement and again refused to allow Americans to come to Düsseldorf.[70]

It was a rebuff that was followed four months later by a letter from the British decartelization branch formally announcing that the British refused to cooperate in any way with American plans.[71] Brigadier Oxborrow told Richard Bronson, the last chief of the decartelization branch, that the British refused to put any limitations on Germany, which was 'desperately short of enterprising, efficient men'. In his final report to McCloy before leaving Germany in July 1949, Richard Bronson, wrote: 'British indifference and antagonism defeated the American programme.'[72]

In retrospect it would be possible to understand Britain sabotaging America's policy of eradicating the political power of German industrialists and bankers if it could be viewed as pure expediency. If Germany's recovery really had depended on Nazi industrialists and the alternative was the impoverishment of Britain and Europe, then there was a case for some unpleasant compromises. But there is no proof that the steel, coal and industrial barons were vital to that recovery. The myth that is perpetuated, that they were the only people with the expertise, has only been accepted in the past because no alternatives were ever sought. Germany's economic boom started because of the currency reform in June 1948; because of large amounts of American aid poured into Germany under the Marshall Plan; and because, with the exception of 159 plants dismantled for reparations (instead of the orginal 682 agreed),[73] Germany still had an enormous amount of industrial capacity and expertise available to sell to an insatiable world market. There is no evidence that the Nazi economic leaders were vital to Germany's economic recovery, yet they were made the king-pins by British policy.

Mills, Chambers and Playfair went even further than just allowing the Nazis to regain power. They allowed them to return with their enormous wealth intact. None of the industrialists or bankers were forced, or even asked, to hand over the billions of dollars worth of materials, industrial plant, patent secrets and gold which they had stolen from the European countries and brought back to Germany. Even within Germany, the spoils of aryanization were rarely confiscated.

The plans for confiscation were sent to London from Berlin and Washington on 29 March 1946.[74] They were part of the massive programme for the 'Disposal of militarists, Nazis and war criminals'. It was estimated that there were at least two hundred and fifty thousand 'profiteers' in the British zone and the same number in the American. The suggestion was that a proportion of their assets should be confiscated 'where it can be proved that an individual has profited from his allegiance to the Nazi party. The object will be to prevent him and his dependents, heirs and nominees retaining wealth sufficient to command influence or authority in German life.'

The disposal document was discussed on 8 April at a Whitehall interdepartmental committee meeting.[75] Of the whole massive document, the profiteers section was the only one to provoke any lengthy discussion. The main objector was Playfair. He claimed that it was 'administratively impossible to deal with ill-gotten gains' and reported that Sir Paul Chambers, head of the Finance Section, agreed with him and had suggested that the confiscations should be limited to 12,000 people. The minutes of the meeting reveal that Playfair's objections divided the nineteen-man committee between those who believed that confiscation was politically important and should not be limited to only a few people, and those who just agreed that 'there was a problem'. Playfair, with Richard Wilberforce's support, insisted to the end that it was impossible to implement even a limited part of the proposal, if only because of the vast problem of actually investigating the value and whereabouts of each individual's property – problem which would be further complicated by the zonal boundaries, Playfair claimed.

In the end, the committee compromised and agreed to Chambers' suggestion that initially 12,000 profiteers be penalized. The Control Office cabled Chambers a new definition of profiteer: 'anyone who during the Nazi regime gained or possessed substantial economic resources and used those resources for the advancement or maintenance of the Nazi regime.'

Having won his case for limitation, Chambers declared three weeks later that it was impossible to find even 12,000 profiteers because the value of their possessions would have to first be proven, and: 'carefully to examine up to thirty thousand estates in order to assess their exact content and worth would involve years of work.'[76] The Finance Section therefore recommended that the only practicable solution was to confiscate all of the declared profiteers' wealth.

The objections to the proposal were obvious. Firstly it would cause untold injustices; but more importantly the investigators would still have to search for the profiteer's wealth before it could be confiscated. It did not reduce the workload.

On 16 May, Robertson intervened and offered what he called a compromise solution.[77] A distinction had to be made between 'profiteers pure and simple, and criminal profiteers, because profiteering by itself is not a criminal activity.' Robertson was clearly not proposing a solution, but was gratuitously complicating the issue even further. Proving a profiteer to be a criminal would be very difficult and time-consuming. The record of the denazification tribunals and war crimes trials showed how difficult it was to find evidence of criminal behaviour. In the case of profiteers, it would be even more difficult. In any trial the only witnesses who would have been in a position to know how an industrialist or businessman got a contract, a factory or machinery, would be other Nazis.

Together, Robertson, Chambers and Playfair had created an unnecessarily complicated solution which inevitably led in only one direction: inaction. The result of doing nothing was reported on 17 September 1946 by Major-General Long of the Intelligence Division: 'There is abundant evidence that many such persons [profiteers] are escaping the net. Among them are some who materially assisted the Nazi party in its struggle for power and/or were intimately connected with the building up of the war machine. The British authorities are letting the big men escape.'[78]

15

'MASTERLY INACTIVITY'

Under the original plan, the conviction of Baron Alfried Krupp at the main Nuremberg trial should have established the criminality of German industrialists. As an armaments manufacturer, in Allied eyes Krupp, more than any other German industrialist, represented the conspiracy between German industrialists and Hitler. The plan came unstuck on 27 August 1945 when Judge Jackson, unnoticed and for no apparent reason, wrote Gustav instead of Alfried on a list of possible defendants. Gustav was Alfried's father, and although it was he who had supported Hitler in the Thirties, it was Alfried who had managed the company during the war. Gustav had retired from the business, a sick man.[1]

Lawyers representing Gustav had tried as early as September to warn the Allied prosecutors that their client was not fit to stand trial, but it had sounded like the old excuse, and they had been ignored. It was only on the eve of the opening of the trial, on 6 November, that six eminent physicians, representing the four Allies, examined Gustav. On the same day the prosecutors realized that they had mistakingly charged the senile father who could control neither his thoughts nor his bladder. Jackson immediately tried to correct his error and suggested that Alfried be substituted for Gustav. The French and Russian prosecutors agreed. All three felt that, without Krupp, there was no representative of German industry in the trial.

Shawcross opposed the idea. At the prosecutors' meeting he argued that the trial was already badly delayed and any further delay would be too serious to contemplate.[2] Opposing Jackson's proposal in court, Shawcross told the judges: 'This is a court of justice, not a game in which you can play a substitute if one member of the team falls sick.' The court agreed with Shawcross. But between the prosecutors' first discussion and the court decision, Shawcross had successfully won the support of Charles Dubost, the French prosecutor. The price of Dubost's support was Shawcross's promise that Britain would agree to a second international trial, to follow the main trial, in which only industrialists and bankers would be prosecuted. It was a commitment which the Foreign Office spent the next twelve months trying to evade.

The Foreign Office had always opposed the idea of prosecuting industrialists and bankers as war criminals. Eden's first list of war criminals who could be shot on sight did not name one industrialist. Attlee, the

Labour deputy prime minister, immediately submitted a written protest: 'I think it is wrong that the big businessmen of Germany who financed Hitler should escape. The group of men in the heavy industries sought to use the Nazis for their own nefarious ends. Some should be executed as an example to others. All should be deprived of their property.'[3]

His protest made no impression. When Eden was asked in parliament in October 1944 whether the industrialists were to be prosecuted, Dean commented: 'It is not a war crime for anyone to have financed and assisted the growth of Hitlerite power, and the industrialists and others who may have done this cannot be indicted as war criminals.'[4] James Wardrop agreed with Dean. 'A line will have to be drawn somewhere,' he wrote, 'unless the entire race is exterminated.' Eden's Parliamentary reply was evasive. At that time, the Foreign Office lawyers were equally opposed to depriving the industrialists of their property. International law, they believed, prevented an occupying power interfering with private enterprise, except for security reasons. Property was sacrosanct.[5]

It was the French and Russian prosecutors who had pressed for the inclusion of Krupp amongst the defendants. At first the British and Americans had resisted the idea, but had then conceded once they saw the strength of Franco-Russian feeling.[6] It is probable that even in summer 1945 the Anglo-American lawyers in London still did not realize the real crimes of Krupp and the industrialists. While British and American lawyers seemed to be only interested in establishing political responsibility at an international trial, the French and Russians wanted also to punish Krupp for his employment of slave labour, if only because many of their nationals had worked and died in his factories.

In the earliest days of the war, the Krupp management decided that production could only be expanded to meet the army's demands if they could obtain a constant supply of labour. At first Heinrich Lehmann, a Krupp manager responsible for labour procurement, toured occupied Western Europe, organizing the selection, arrest and shipment of thousands of workers to the Ruhr. But the problems and delays and the comparatively irregular arrivals convinced the Krupp management that the labour supply had to be better organized.

New possibilities were opened up for satisfying what was to become an insatiable appetite when Germany invaded Russia. Soon afterwards Russian soldiers were delivered by the Wehrmacht, and Sauckel, the minister of labour, who had begun an enormous programme of kidnapping whole communities in Eastern Europe, delivered yet more workers to Germany's factories. But even then, Krupp's demands were unsatisfied. Increasingly, German workers were recruited into the army and Krupp management had once again to consider where replacement workers could be found.

It was Alfried Krupp who personally approached both Hitler and Himmler about this shortage in May 1942. After explaining his company's predicament, he proposed a solution. He wanted a contract between Krupp and the SS to supply concentration camp inmates to the Krupp factories in the Ruhr and elsewhere. In return, Krupp would pay a daily rate to the SS. Himmler agreed.

The results of all these methods of recruiting labour were described by an Essen railway worker in a sworn deposition to a British investigator after the war:

> In the middle of 1941, the first workers arrived from Poland, Galacia and Polish Ukraine. They came to Essen in goods wagons in which potatoes, building materials and cattle had been transported; they were brought to perform work at Krupp. The cars were jammed full with people. . . The people were squashed closely together and they had no room for free movement. The Krupp overseers laid special value on the speed the slave workers got in and out of the train . . . the people were beaten and kicked and generally maltreated in a brutal manner . . . I could see with my own eyes that sick people who could scarcely walk . . . were taken to work. One could see that it was sometimes difficult for them to move themselves. The same can be said for the Eastern workers and POWs who came to Essen in the middle of 1942.[7]

But the supply of workers was still too small. On 31 October 1942 the Krupp board of directors, with Himmler's agreement, approached Rudolf Hoess, the commandant of Auschwitz, to get an agreement to build a Krupp factory to produce detonators inside the extermination camp. After two million reichsmarks had been invested, the board quickly reconsidered their decision. Despite his promises, Hoess had not supplied all the labour that Krupp managers had expected. The SS, it seemed, were more interested in gassing the inmates than in getting them to work for Germany's victory.

Krupp and Hoess agreed to reverse their plan. The planned factory was to be scrapped and instead suitable inmates were to be sent to already established Krupp factories throughout Europe. But even that was unsatisfactory for Krupp.

Alfried's personal files contain dozens of letters and agreements on slave labour supplies with the SS, Gestapo and Wehrmacht. Most of the letters are complaints from Alfried that the organizations are failing to fulfill their obligations.[8] One of the last agreements, only partially fulfilled, between Alfried and Himmler called for Hungarian Jewish women, newly arrived in Buchenwald, to be sent straight to the Ruhr.

The fate of the estimated hundred thousand Krupp slave workers was unadulterated misery. Peter Hubert, a German employee of Krupp in Essen, testified that he had seen fourteen-year-olds weighing less than ninety pounds pushing massive loads that he himself found impossible to handle. Other German employees testified to seeing six-year-olds forced to do the work of adults. Krupp policy was not to discriminate between ages and sexes. Everyone who worked for Krupp, according to Adolf Trockel, a Krupp official, was expected to carry huge amounts of bricks or corrugated iron, because as their SS guards would repeatedly shout: 'No work, no food.'[9]

'Food' was not the word used by either the slave workers or the Krupp official to describe the infamous *Bunkersuppe* which was handed out once a day. On 26 March 1942 Adolf Thiele, the Krupp manager responsible for the boiler construction shop of the locomotive works at Essen, complained that the management-approved 350-calorie soup was having a negative effect. His letter to the head office explained that less than fifty per cent of the Russian workers at the plant were 'capable of even the slightest work. . . The reasons why the Russians are not capable of production is in my opinion that the food which they are given will never give them the strength for doing the amount of work you want. The food one day, for instance, consisted of watery soup with cabbage and a few pieces of turnip.' Even the Wehrmacht complained that the Krupp management's policy of deliberate slow starvation was unacceptable. One army medical inspector's report stated: 'they have never met with such a bad state of affairs in the case of Russians as in the Krupp camps.'[10] Even the army High Command protested. Not only did Alfried Krupp and his directors not reply, but conditions during 1944 constantly worsened.

To this day, no one knows exactly how many concentration camps Krupp organized either in his factories in Germany or elsewhere in Europe. Living conditions, however, seem to have been uniform. The inmates were plagued by rampant disease – tuberculosis, typhus, dysentery – and malnutrition, and were brutally treated by the SS guards. Conditions were so shocking that even Dr Wilhelm Jäger, a Krupp doctor, complained after visiting the Humboldtstrasse camp in Essen:

Upon my visit I found these females suffering from open festering wounds and other diseases. . . They had no shoes and went about in their bare feet. Their only clothing was a sack with holes for head and arms. Their hair was cut off. . . A person could not enter the prisoners' quarters without being attacked by fleas. . . . I myself left with huge boils from them on my arms and the rest of my body.[11]

Those fortunate to survive the camp conditions were often killed by the torrent of Allied bombs falling on Essen. Krupp inmates were expressly forbidden, on pain of death, to take cover in bomb shelters even if there was space. They died on the open ground. When their barracks were destroyed, the inmates had either no shelter at all at night or lived in waterlogged basements.

Daily, the inmates were marched by Krupp overseers and SS personnel through the streets of Essen, directly under the windows of Alfried Krupp's own office, to the factories. After twelve hours work, they were marched back again. Both inmates and the Germans working alongside them knew that those too weak for work would be automatically sent to be gassed. Medical help was nearly non-existent. According to Dr Apolinary Gotowicki, a Polish army doctor and himself an inmate:

> Every day at least ten people were brought to me whose bodies were covered with bruises on account of the continual beatings with rubber tubes, steel switches or sticks. The people were often writhing in agony. Dead people often lay for two or three days on their palliasses until their bodies stank so badly that their fellow prisoners took them outside and buried them somewhere.[12]

There were scores of eyewitnesses who could testify that it was not only the SS but also German workers who beat the inmates. Even the SS were on the Krupp payroll. Some of the SS women had been recruited by Krupp and sent by the company for a three-week training course at Ravensbrück concentration camp to learn their trade. Alfried Krupp did nothing in half-measures. Even his torture chamber in the basement of the main administrative office was said both by the victims that survived and the Krupp staff who heard their screams to be truly unbearable, but ingenious. It was a cupboard-sized cage into which water was poured when the temperature fell below freezing. A Krupp secretary was later to admit that the screams could be heard on the fifth floor of the building.

Even at the end, Krupp did not mitigate his brutality. As the Allied armies pushed towards the Ruhr, Alfried became uneasy lest the slaves survived as witnesses to his labour policies. When he raised the problem with the rest of the Krupp board in February 1945, Max Ihn, a senior director, mentioned that Heinrich Lehmann, the labour manager, had told him a frightening story. It seemed that the SS guards had constantly taunted the workers not to eagerly await the Allies 'because the last five minutes will be saved for us.' According to Lehmann, the guards intended to carry out their threat and carry out their mass murders. In normal times, the regular flow of bodies through murder and death had been manageable. Routinely, the cadavers had been taken to the crematoria. But it would have been impossible to cope with the disposal of hundreds of bodies in the midst of the chaos before the collapse. According to the unrefuted documentary evidence of a February board meeting in which Alfried took part, the Krupp board decided to move the problem elsewhere.

On 17 March, 520 women from the Humboldtstrasse camp were marched to the Bochum railway station. Lehmann, after a lot of work, had arranged 'for transportation of the women to Buchenwald'. One thousand five hundred men were already on that train when it arrived, but only 515 women got on to it at Bochum. Five had escaped and testified at Krupp's trial. To Alfried's undisguised distress another 300 suddenly appeared in 1959 to claim compensation from the company for their suffering.[13] The train had arrived at Buchenwald but the camp commandant said it was too late to murder 2,000 extra people. After some quick thinking, the train sped northwards towards Belsen, but just twenty-four hours after its arrival, the camp was liberated by the British. None of the passengers had been executed yet.[14]

Alfried Krupp's use of slave labour fitted into his and the company's overall support for Hitler's policies. His personal files found in Essen – the few that had been overlooked in the mass destruction of Krupp records in the last days before the American capture of the city – revealed a constant flow of congratulatory messages to Hitler, the leaders of the SS and leaders of Nazi organizations. The experience of all Europeans from the Atlantic to Russia convinced the subjugated populations that the greediest of all the German industrialists in their countries was Krupp. Krupp devoured whole factories, shipyards and mines with the same insatiable appetite and speed that burnt up those who became his unwilling labour force. Yet when the Foreign Office reviewed the evidence against Krupp in January 1946, the researcher concluded that it was 'relatively weak'.[15]

But curiously the strength or the weakness of the evidence against Krupp, or any other industrialist, seemed to be of no consequence whatsoever when the Foreign Office's German department started to consider its policy towards a trial of the industrialists.

Shawcross, who felt personally committed to holding a second trial because of his promise to Dubost, told Scott-Fox in January 1946 that negotiations would have to start soon. Scott-Fox clearly wanted to discover what the Department's views were on a second trial and set out the background to the problem 'to clear our minds.'[16]

The other Allies, he explained, were 'anxious that the public should not get the impression that we are letting German industrialists get off more lightly than they deserve.' The best would be a 'shortlist of eight to ten names', he thought, but he foresaw two problems. Recruiting staff and a Russian demand that the trial be held either in Berlin or Moscow. The minute then went to Con O'Neil, who was clearly disturbed by the idea:

> I understand that we are committed to try the industrialists and therefore, though I think the idea absurd, it is no use arguing against it. . . In general I hope that we shall leave it to our Allies to make the running over these new trials and not hasten too much to keep up with them. I feel that the Nuremberg trial . . . and the minor but many trials which should be its direct consequence, will be enough not only for justice, but also for public opinion, both here and in Allied countries and even in Germany. We don't want war crimes trials to become a universal bore.

To his already powerful distaste and indifference, O'Neil added a heavy dose of ignorance. Looking down the list of possible defendants, he wrote: 'I fear I don't know who Ohlendorf is.'

Foreign Office policy had now been agreed. It was neatly summarized by Oliver Harvey after he had read O'Neil's minute: 'I would favour going slow.' On the list of industrialists who could be tried were Pönsgen and Zangen, both of them employed by Sir Percy Mills, and Hugo Stinnes, who had only just been arrested. The remainder were Alfried Krupp, Albert Vögler, (the steel manufacturer), Baron von Schröder (who had been discovered disguised as an SS corporal in a POW camp in France), Paul Pleiger, a very committed Nazi industrialist who had managed the Hermann Goering factories, and 'some representative of the IG Farben concern'.

Maxwell Fyfe, the deputy British prosecutor at Nuremberg, started the negotiations towards the end of January. They seemed to be awkward from the outset. The French, it seemed, only wanted to try the German industrialists because it would strengthen their own government's hand against those many French industrialists who had willingly collaborated with the Germans.[17]

Turning to the Americans, Fyfe discovered not only hesitation but also confusion. The original euphoria for the main trial in the American camp had turned into sour bitterness. Disillusioned by the slow pace of a Four-Power trial and the effects of Jackson's intemperate personality, nearly all the American staff had declared that they were unwilling to stay for a second trial. Jackson himself had announced in January that he would not run any second trial because he too wanted to return to America. Telford Taylor, Jackson's deputy, was put in charge of all negotiations, but Taylor discovered that 'the obstacles to a second international proceeding are certainly substantial.'[18] There were, he discovered, at least another hundred non-industrialist major war criminals who should be tried. They could not all be tried at once, or grouped with the industrialists. There was no immediately apparent solution. But more important was what he felt to be his own vulnerable position. He told Jackson that he did not have 'the experience, reputation or rank to handle the assignment adequately' and that Jackson should seriously think of 'finding someone of greater ability to take over'.[19] With that, he left Nuremberg and returned to America, leaving the American team temporarily leaderless in the negotiations.

It was Shawcross who approached the Russians. On 15 February, Andrei Vyshinsky, a deputy foreign minister, was visiting London. He had clearly not even thought about the problem, but seized the opportunity to lay down Russia's two non-negotiable conditions for any trial: that it would have to be held in Berlin, and that the president of the court would have to be a Russian.[20]

Putting a Russian in charge of a trial of capitalists was enough to send shudders down the Foreign Office's collective spine. Dean and O'Neil were convinced that the trial had now to be avoided at any cost. Fortunately the news from Nuremberg seemed good. Dean reported that the French now appeared uncertain whether the evidence was adequate in any case, and he positively distrusted the enthusiasm of Drexel Sprecher, the senior American prosecutor, for a second trial. Dean wrote to London: 'I think [Sprecher] sees a good job for himself if there is a second trial.' Ignoring Sprecher's support for the trial as being self-interested and not representative of the American position, Dean concluded: 'I cannot help feeling that there is much to be said for going very slow on this matter. . . I should recommend that no further steps be taken at present.'[21] 'Masterly inactivity' was how Scott-Fox described Foreign Office policy. It was decided to leave any initiative to the Americans.

With Taylor still in Washington, it was Jackson who, despite his earlier stated lack of interest, gave his unsolicited opinion to Washington. His advice on 9 April was to remain sitting on the fence.[22] Shawcross, he told the War Department, was against a trial, but the French appeared to be genuinely in favour. The British objections on the grounds of cost seemed valid, he thought, but it was best to wait and see what happened at the end of the first trial.

Patterson at the War Department misinterpreted Jackson's advice as outright rejection and by his reply showed that he had completely misunderstood the situation:

> We hold a second trial to be highly undesirable and hope that you will resist all efforts in that direction. At the same time we recognize it may be hard to resist strong pressure of other three powers, and concur . . . for proceeding now with preparations before final decision since we desire, should second international trial be necessary, to conclude it rapidly. We are further of the opinion that if there is to be a second international trial, US should not act as host and should not continue to bear principal burden for planning, preparation and administrative arrangements.[23]

Three weeks later, on 13 May, Jackson sent another memorandum of his views to Patterson, this time fiercely opposing any suggestion for a second trial. 'I see little to be gained from our American point of view, and a good deal to be risked,' he wrote, and concluded: 'At the present time I would not recommend United States participation in another trial.'[24]

There were two reasons why Jackson suddenly jumped off the fence. He had already been humiliated by his personal failure to expose Goering's crimes in his cross-examination of the Reich Marshal. Reconciling himself to Goering's victory in the courtroom had not been easy and he had barely recovered from the depression when the same happened again. His recent cross-examination of Hjalmar Schacht, the former president of the Reichsbank and minister of economics, had also been a miserable event. Birkett was later to describe it as 'perfectly futile' while Biddle noted that it was 'weak' because Schacht was 'too clever' for Jackson.[25]

Outwitted and outmatched for the second time, Jackson was in despair not only because of his wounded ego, but because there were strong rumours around the Palace of Justice that the judges would now acquit Schacht. In his depression he wrongly, but willingly, interpreted that possibility as an acquittal of all German bankers and industrialists. 'The acquittal of Schacht,' he wrote to Patterson, 'would be a precedent nearly as fatal to the less convincing cases against industrial and financial figures. Few businessman had such close relations with the regime, or held offices which imply knowledge of the political plans and aggressive intentions behind rearmament, as did Schacht.'[26] This was arguable, of course, because Schacht had been dismissed as minister of economics in 1937.

During the preliminary negotiations in London to agree a list of defendants the British lawyers had argued that the evidence against

Schacht was too weak. But the American lawyers insisted that he symbolized the criminal support of German financiers for the Nazis. His quip in 1936 to Dr Max Hershfield that 'to achieve rearmament, I will ally myself to the Devil' neatly summarized, they felt, his deception of the Western world. Why, other than in preparation for war, would he have secretly ordered eighty million ration cards to be printed? Newsreel film of the crowds greeting Hitler at Berlin's Westbahnhof in May 1940 on his triumphant return from France showed Schacht, arm outstretched, amongst the first to reach the Führer to congratulate him. Schacht's defence that he had resigned in 1939 as president of the Reichsbank in protest against Hitler's policy was dismissed as ridiculous. He had really resigned, said the Americans, in a fit of egoistic pique because Goering, and not he, had been appointed economic supremo.

Schacht's fate at the trial, however, had no legal bearing on a case against the industrialists. Schacht was charged only with the *planning* of an aggressive war, while the industrialists would be charged also with *participation* in the aggressive waging of war, and that was much easier to prove.

But Jackson also had political reasons for deliberately blurring the distinction. By May he had become outspokenly anti-Russian, and believed that the communists were intent on overthrowing capitalism. He now argued:

A trial in which industrialists are singled out may give the impression that they are being prosecuted merely because they are industrialists. This is more likely since we would be associated in prosecuting them with the Soviet communists and the French leftists. . . I have also some misgivings as to whether a long public attack concentrated on private industry would not tend to discourage industrial cooperation with our government in maintaining its defence in the future while not at all weakening the Soviet position, since they do not rely upon private enterprise. . . If we prosecute industrialists who provided Germany with tanks to invade Poland, what about the Commissars who built tanks for Russia at the same time to invade Poland? Industrialists in their defence, would have the experience of this case to go by and they are likely to be better defended and to strike back more stridently than has yet been done in the present trial.[1]

In Washington, Jackson's legal arguments were ignored, but the political argument made some sense. His alternative solution was also attractive – namely that the industrialists could be prosecuted in American zonal courts. It was definitely a solution which appealed to Dean because it avoided the risk of a Russian or French president, saved money and would probably satisfy public opinion.

But Dean, who was the Foreign Office's legal expert, went even further than Jackson in scorning the possibility of a successful trial against the industrialists. International trials, he wrote, were for fixing political responsibility, not common criminality. He even doubted whether there was enough evidence to prove that the industrialists were 'fully aware of and in agreement with the Nazis' plan to wage an aggressive war and commit numberless murders and other crimes. There are some documents in the files which go to prove this but there is little to show that any of the industrialists were in the inner counsels of Hitler to anything like the extent of people like Himmler, Goering or Goebbels.'[28]

Dean, perhaps deliberately like Jackson, but more probably out of ignorance of the facts, was confusing two entirely different charges against the industrialists: their deliberate collusion in preparations for war, and their conduct during the war. The documentary evidence of a general conspiracy between the industrialists and politicians to start a war was meagre, although there was some evidence against the managers of Krupp, IG Farben and some steel manufacturers.

However there was ample evidence, which Dean for some reason had decided to ignore, to prove the industrialists' voluntary wartime participation with their government. When so many industries used concentration camp labour, Dean could only have written that the industrialists were not 'fully aware . . . of . . . the Nazis' plans . . . to commit numberless crimes'[29] as a product of wishful thinking, at best, or at worst as a means of justifying a decision not to put the industrialists on trial. It was just the same policy which caused the Foreign Office to conclude in February 1946 that the overall evidence against Krupp was 'relatively weak'. Ignoring the facts, naturally, went hand in hand with the 'masterly inactivity' policy.

A series of bizarre negotiations to resolve the matter started on 15 May. Dean, on Shawcross's behalf, announced that the British were keeping an 'open mind'.[30] Taylor, who had just returned from Washington with the promise of promotion to improve his status and a guarantee of extra staff for further trials, announced that he had already begun work on the second trial and named Krupp, von Schröder, Schmitz and Schnitzler of IG Farben, and Röchling, as a preliminary list. Dubost, saying that the trial should be just 'symbolic', suggested that only Krupp and Röchling should be tried. Röchling was a Saar industrialists with strong French connections; he had written to Hitler in 1936: 'War is inevitable . . . the German people must first be strengthened spiritually for battle . . . to a great extent through National Socialist education.'[31]

To everyone's surprise, the Russian representative, Zorya, said nothing at all. Shortly afterwards he committed suicide. No replacement with any authority was appointed. The Russian position remained that any trial would have to be in Berlin with a Russian president.

By the end of July, the negotiations had become ludicrously entangled. It had slowly and uncomfortably become clear that none of the three remaining national representatives in Nuremberg were negotiating from an agreed brief provided by their governments. British embassy inquiries in Paris revealed that Dubost had no authority to negotiate at all. The French government had not yet decided its policy.[32] Britain in contrast, had two different policies, depending on who was asked. Shawcross, who changed his opinion quite frequently and who felt honour-bound to Dubost, wrote to Jackson on 25 July that he now supported a second trial involving five defendants as long as it was held in Nuremberg. 'I feel little doubt, 'he wrote, 'that the British government will adopt this view.'[33] He was wrong.

Unknown to the Attorney-General, his political colleague, Ernest Bevin, on the advice of Dean and Orme Sargeant, had already decided to approach Byrnes secretly through Averell Harriman at the forthcoming foreign ministers' conference in Paris, to get an agreement with the Americans to prevent an international trial, and, as Newton said, exploit 'various ways of putting a spoke in the wheel.'[34] The Foreign Office hoped that the Americans could be manoeuvred in to making a unilateral announcement so that the British would not seem to be breaking a promise and Shawcross could be presented with an 'unavoidable' *fait accompli*.

The first time Shawcross heard of the Foreign Office's outright opposition was on 31 July. Orme Sargeant wrote: 'We are disagreeably impressed by the disadvantages and dangers of holding such a trial and we feel that we ought to make a final effort to persuade our allies of its inexpediency.' But Shawcross was not told about Bevin's secret approach to Byrnes.[35]

The American position was equally confused. While Jackson's opposition only solidified with time, Taylor, believing Shawcross's letter to Jackson, submitted a fourteen-page memorandum to Patterson recommending that the United States also support a second international trial.[36] Taylor's recommendation was ignored. In Patterson's view, there could be no question of letting the Russians prosecute industrialists 'in view of the many connections between the German and American economies before the war [because] there would be an excellent opportunity for the trial to embarrass the United States.'[37]

When Byrnes met Bevin in Paris on 3 September, the American had already been briefed against the trial by Jackson, who had flown especially from Germany. But Byrnes did not need much convincing. As he confided to Bevin, the clinching argument against the trial was the vehement opposition by American business leaders.[38] But Washington's willingness to cooperate did not extend to a promise that the Americans would take the initiative, nor did it resolve the thorny problem of Shawcross's commitment to putting industrialists on trial.

During the August negotiations between the Foreign Office and State Department to scuttle Shawcross's commitment behind his back, Scott-Fox had written: 'There is no suggestion that those industrialists should not be tried.' It was just a matter, he said, of deciding which would be the most suitable courts for the trials. Britain would only be 'too happy' to hand over any industrialists held in the British zones to its allies where there was a *prima facie* case to answer.[39] Those not demanded, but against whom there was *prima facie* evidence, would, by implication, be tried by British courts.

Elwyn Jones had found no difficulty in providing the Foreign Office with a list of twenty-six industrialists and bankers against whom there was, he believed, a *prima facie* case. At the top was Hermann Abs, at the bottom Wilhelm Zangen. Ominously, in between were other German industrialists who were employed in some capacity by the British Military Government.[40] Both Jones and Shawcross were in September committed to an industrialists' trial. But they were now to fall victim to the Foreign Office's 'masterly inactivity' policy. Stage one had started during the summer.

Shawcross had sent Bevin several letters warning him that, unless plans were made, the whole British prosecution team in Nuremberg would return to Britain and there would be no experienced staff available to replace them.[41] Both the War Office and Control Commission, he told Bevin, had refused to provide any replacements. The Foreign Office just did not reply. Accordingly, at the end of September there was no British prosecution team left.

Stage two was to welcome the American request for the extradition of six industrialists including Krupp, plus Field Marshal Milch and two ministers, Friedrich Gaus and Otto Thierack, to stand trial in the American zone. 'It seems to me,' Garner wrote, 'that this provides the simplest solution of this troublesome problem.'[42] Dean cynically agreed: 'If any of the trials do go wrong and the industrialists escape, the primary political criticism will rest on American shoulders and not ours.' The handover, he said, could be explained to the public as a desire to avoid wasteful duplication of effort.

Handing over the nine named Germans was the substance of the Bevin-Byrnes agreement. But what Dean and Garner implied as regards Foreign Office policy was that the handover of the nine satisfied whatever commitment the British had to the prosecution of German industrialists.

Schacht's acquittal on 1 October quickly started a new tide of rumours amongst the Americans at Nuremberg, to the effect that it was part of a British conspiracy to protect German industrialists and bankers. According to Foster Adams: 'There were strong rumours that Montagu Norman, who was after all a prewar friend of Schacht's, had got at Sir Geoffrey Lawrence, the British judge. We thought that Norman had convinced Lawrence that bankers can't be criminals.'

Adam's suspicions are partially confirmed in the diary of Francis Biddle, the American judge. He noted that, from the beginning of the four judges' secret discussions on the verdicts, Lawrence had argued that Schacht was innocent. According to Biddle, the British judge had said that Schacht was a 'man of character' while the other defendants were 'ruffians', men of lesser breed.[43] Lawrence's argument first staggered and then divided the other judges. At first he was outnumbered three to one, but Biddle was shocked to discover the following morning that the French judge, Donnedieu de Vabres, had been contacted by Lawrence and converted in favour of acquittal.

According to Biddle, it was British prejudice which also saved Albert Speer from the gallows. Speer, the minister of armaments, admitted at the trial his demands for, and use of, slave labour for German industry. None of the atrocities committed during the Third Reich had swayed his Nazi beliefs. Ruthlessly and immorally, he exploited every opportunity to get more slave labour to fulfil his production quotas for war materials. Biddle and the French and Russian judges all agreed that Speer be executed. Lawrence said Speer should be sentenced to just ten years. Lawrence had been clearly impressed by Speer's 'honesty' and 'intellect' and by the fact that he, too, was not a 'ruffian'. As a compromise and after a long argument, Speer was sentenced to twenty years.[44]

Lawrence did not however have the same scruples about the fate of Fritz Sauckel, the minister of labour. A crude and uneducated man, it was Sauckel's job to obey Speer's orders and find the slave labour in Europe. Speer impatiently criticized Sauckel for delivering too many women and children among the two million in 1942, and in September 1943 he demanded that the minister of labour find another 1.2 million to work in Germany's factories. Sauckel obeyed and was hanged.

Schacht's acquittal, Speer's lenient sentence and the failure to prosecute Krupp made nonsense of the original intention of condemning the industrial and financial section of the German Establishment. Murder in occupied Europe and in the gas chambers had been exposed and condemned, but murder in the factories and mines had gone unpunished.

The omission was all the worse for Shawcross and Jones since they had been so intimately involved with the trial from its birth. Determined to compensate for that failure, Jones wrote to Bevin on 17 October arguing that as the Ruhr was in the British zone and British investigators had collected a lot of the evidence against Krupp, the armaments manufacturer who symbolized the Ruhr barons should be tried by a British court:

> I do not think that it is enough simply to hand Krupp, Schröder, etc, who are in our custody, over to whichever of our Allies cares to try them. Quite apart from the fact that the acquittal of Schacht and the subsequent political agitation in Germany and elsewhere has underlined the need for HM Government to demonstrate its belief in the criminality of the Nazi industrialists, I think severe criticism will follow if the British zone, in which so much Nazi industry was concentrated, were to be the only zone in which industrialists were not to be tried.[45]

At that stage neither Shawcross nor Jones had yet been told that the Bevin-Byrnes understanding, reached six weeks earlier, included Bevin's assurance that the British would hand over whichever German industrialists the Americans demanded. Bevin clearly believed that his officials had consulted both men. The Foreign Secretary was surprised to receive the long letter from Jones, and to then be shown a six-day-old letter from Shawcross suggesting that the American request for Krupp be rejected 'until we get a clear decision whether there is to be either a second international trial or a trial of industrialists in the British zone'.[46]

Foreign Office officials had apparently not informed Shawcross of all the implications of the Bevin-Byrnes agreement. When he had read the letters from the two lawyers, Bevin memoed to Dean: 'I am confused about all this. I arranged for Sargeant to see all the parties. I made it clear.' Not informing Shawcross obviously saved a time-consuming argument. It was a neater way of arriving at the solution that the Foreign Office officials wanted.

But now, with Elwyn Jones' intervention and Bevin wanting Shawcross to be consulted, the issue had to be finally settled. Deftly, Sargeant arranged for that to be done while Shawcross was at the United Nations in New York. On Foreign Office advice, at a meeting on 24 October the Lord Chancellor told Frank Soskice, the Solicitor-General, who had no interest in or knowledge of the issue, that it would be impossible for him to spare even one single judge for an industrialists' trial.[47] Soskice then left to send a cable to Shawcross in New York saying that he was convinced that the industrialists should be handed over to the Americans. The cable was sent to the Foreign Office for transmission. The beginning of the final paragraph of the telegram Soskice sent to the Foreign Office read: 'This [i.e. the summary of the discussion] is for your general information and you may wish to discuss it with the Foreign Secretary.' That paragraph was removed by the Foreign Office, which inserted another substitute line telling Shawcross that, according to the Foreign Office, the Law Officers had no responsibility and therefore no power to influence or make the decision. It was a clever move and nearly worked,[48] except that Shawcross immediately cabled from New York insisting that any decision be made by Attlee personally.[49]

Rising to the challenge, Sargeant immediately sent a memorandum to the Prime Minister.[50] Anyone reading it without prior knowledge of the issues would have had no doubts that the case against prosecuting the industrialists was overwhelming. According to Sargeant, the only person in the whole world in favour of a trial was Shawcross. Yet Attlee might have been expected to reject Sargeant's advice. Two years before, he had argued in Churchill's Cabinet not only that the German industrialists should be deprived of their property, but that some should be executed as an example to their successors and other capitalists in the world. Now he was Prime Minister of Britain's first secure socialist government, which had embarked on a massive programme of nationalizing private industry. If Britain's own industrialists had grounds for fear, what immunity could their criminal German counterparts expect?

Surprisingly, whatever fears the Foreign Office might have had were soon dispelled. Attlee accepted Sargeant's arguments without question. Indeed the whole Cabinet was so convinced that, when it met on 4 November in Shawcross's absence to consider the problem, the minuted conclusions went even further than just rejecting an industrialists' trial, and stated that Britain should 'advocate a policy of discontinuing trials for war criminals'.[51] The trials were in fact to continue for another two years, but the Foreign Office had achieved its immediate objective by skilful manipulation.

The Cabinet added one rider to its rejection of a British industrialists trial. A British observer, they decided, should be present at the Krupp trial, as a token gesture of British interest. But that was to be the absolute limit of British involvement. When Taylor wrote to Elwyn Jones on 25 November suggesting that, as the British had done so much of the preparatory work on the Krupp case, they might like to take part in the prosecution, the Foreign Office declined the invitation. 'I understand', wrote Garner, 'that General Telford Taylor is not finding the going as easy as he thought. . . . I expect that General Taylor is feeling a bit uneasy as a result of the US elections. Senator Taft's views on economy and on the Nuremberg trial are well known and it is unlikely that the new Congress will favour these sixty-odd highly paid US lawyers [sic] running around conducting expensive subsequent proceedings in Nuremberg.'[52]

When Shawcross tried to protest a few days later, Sargeant slapped him down with equal vehemence. Only the Cabinet, the Foreign Office official told the Attorney-General, could authorize any help whatsoever, and the Foreign Office would strongly oppose any such proposal.[53]

Taylor's letter had also said that the Americans did not intend to ask for the extradition of von Schröder. It was a clear indication to the Foreign Office that his trial was a British responsibility. Von Schröder had always featured on the shortest of British lists of German industrialists and bankers who should be tried as war criminals. He was at the time being held in a British internment camp. Yet the Foreign Office ignored the implication in Taylor's letter and his name does not appear again in Foreign Office files until November 1948. A duplicated report of the Old Lace trials states that von Schröder, Himmler's secret banker, had been sentenced to three months imprisonment and fined one thousand five hundred reichsmarks, the equivalent of a carton of cigarettes on the black market. On appeal by the prosecution the fine had been increased to five hundred thousand reichsmarks, but after the currency reform the amount was trivial.[54]

How else could Taylor and the American lawyers who continued at Nuremberg interpret Foreign Office policy other than as being politically motivated? Hugo Stinnes and most of the other employers of slave labour in the Ruhr had been released in August 1946. The foreign minister's stock answer to MPs who irritatingly asked why Britain was not prosecuting the industrialists was to explain that British policy was to prosecute for the specific crime of slave labour. In fact only a handful of factory foremen and workers were prosecuted, never the managers or owners of the factories and mines.[55] Those MPs who pressed a little harder were referred to the conviction of Dr Bruno Tesch, the supplier of Zyklon B gas to Auschwitz, and the only company director ever to be convicted by a British court. His case was a minor exception to a consistent British policy.

16

'ALL GERMAN INDUSTRIALISTS WERE REALLY ON TRIAL'

Congressman John Rankin of Mississippi was one of many Americans who, in the course of 1947, believed that they had discovered not only a glaring but also a dangerous paradox. While socialist Britain had deliberately released and cooperated with German industrialists in its zone, the world's greatest capitalist power had recruited over 1,700 staff to investigate and prosecute, among others, industrialists, men of their own kind. Not one to hide his suspicions, Rankin spoke out on the floor of the House of Representatives on 27 November 1947: 'What is taking place in Nuremberg, Germany, is a disgrace to the United States. Every other country has now washed its hands and withdrawn from this Saturnalia of persecution. But a racial minority, two and a half years after the war closed, are in Nuremberg not only hanging German soldiers but trying German businessmen in the name of the United States.'[1]

Representative George A. Dondero of Michigan pinpointed the cause of the treachery as not only a Jewish but also a communist conspiracy. He particularly singled out ten lawyers involved in the IG Farben case, including the main prosecutor, Josiah Du Bois, whom he described as a 'known left-winger from the Treasury Department who had been a close student of the Communist party line'.[2] The Dow Chemical Company was based in Dondero's Congressional district. There was, thought Du Bois when he read about the attack, more than a chance that Dow were seriously concerned lest their prewar relations with IG Farben were exposed in the trial.[3] It was a natural fear.

The Foreign Office were also anxious that ICI's prewar cartel arrangements with IG should not be exposed. When aspects of their close relations were finally mentioned in court, the Foreign Office was gratified to note that: '*The Times* discreetly omits reference to ICI Ltd.'[4]

There were certainly Jews amongst the American staff at Nuremberg, and it probably contained a sprinkling of left-wingers. But control of the whole operation was firmly – too firmly, some said afterwards – in the hands of a Harvard Law School mafia. Young, inexperienced, wholly ignorant about Germany and faced with immense obstacles, they diligently tried to convert a group of undistinguished and conservative American judges to a radical theory: that educated, respected and otherwise normal businessman could be guilty of murder.

The initial weakness of the subsequent Nuremberg trials was that they started and finished so long after the war had ended. Little work had been done before October 1946. Jackson had sent the first memorandum about the importance of appointing Taylor and plans for further trials to Truman on 4 December 1945. 'I cannot emphasize too strongly,' he wrote, 'the proportions of the problem that lies ahead, or the importance of settling without delay upon the organization for further prosecutions.'[5]

It was also Jackson who, in the following February, wrote to Clay about his fears that the German industrialists would remain unprosecuted because no one had started to organize proper investigations of their activities.[6] Two weeks later Clay ordered the Intelligence Division to organize a four-man investigation team to produce a list of businessmen who could be considered for prosecution.[7] It was never appointed because of OMGUS economies and staff cuts, but the omission was only realized in June. As a poor substitute, counter-intelligence sent forms requesting information to four hundred Military Government sections that might be expected to possess either evidence or experts.[8] At the beginning of September, the Intelligence Division chief reported to Clay that just two out of the four hundred had bothered to reply.[9] Martin's decartelization division was amongst those that did not reply.

Explaining the failure to Clay, General Gailey reported: 'The war crimes investigation agency is not concerned with these investigations and has done nothing about them. They are responsible for the apprehension and extradition of *actual war criminals* and have no direct responsibility in connection with German business leaders, industrialists and so forth.'[10] It was the same blindness and prejudice which Taylor described in his final report on the trials written in 1949: 'It proved exceedingly difficult to 'get it across' to the Germans (and indeed to some others) that it was not the purpose of Nuremberg to try Nazis who might or might not also be criminals, but to try suspected criminals who might or might not also be Nazis.'[11]

The Subsequent Proceedings Division was formally established on 24 October 1946. Taylor was appointed as head of the office, chief of counsel for war crimes. Reviewing his achievements three years later, Taylor wrote that if there had been the time, money and personnel, he could have prosecuted and got convictions of between two thousand and twenty thousand Germans for war crimes.[12] His actual achievements, in numbers, were considerably smaller. His first proposal to Clay in August 1946 was to prosecute 266 Germans in thirty-six trials which he expected to be completed by the end of 1947.[13] By May 1947, the target had been reduced to sixteen trials. When the programme ended in November 1948, there had been twelve trials against 177 accused (eight of the accused had either committed suicide or were too ill to stand trial). Thirty-five were acquitted. The Division had no search parties or investigators out looking for wanted men. Only those already under arrest faced the possibility of trial: and, in the event, the majority were not prosecuted but set free. The criterion was whether there was any hope of getting enough evidence, and as the weeks passed the chances grew increasingly slim.

Lists of those under arrest and available for trial were constantly revised. Of the thirty-two industrialists named by Taylor on 20 May 1947 as major offenders who would definitely be prosecuted, only six finally stood trial. The three groups of industrialists who were finally tried, forty-two of the directors of Krupp, IG Farben and Flick, were selected because the prosecutors already had evidence against them. There was no time to find enough documents or convince enough accomplices to make incriminating sworn statements to move against the directors of Mannesmann, Siemens, Bosch and hundreds of other German companies.

Finding the documents in the Krupp case involved going deep into the mines at Hansa, searching through remote houses in the Harz mountains, and digging up canisters of microfilm in a forest. A few key documents in the IG Farben case were found in a bathroom cupboard, hidden there by the personal assistant of one of the defendants, Otto Ambros. For eighteen months after the war, Ambros, one of those who masterminded the development of IG Auschwitz, had been protected from American investigators by the French, while he worked at the IG factory in Ludwigshafen. He was only reluctantly handed over to stand trial after repeated demands, and even threats, from Clay.[14] Ambros had methodically destroyed bundles of incriminating files, but had hidden just a handful whose destruction even he could not contemplate. It was a fatal, but isolated, mistake. Their discovery, as in most cases, resulted from chance information from an informer.

Finding government documents should have been easier because only a few government officials had systematically destroyed their files and so many documents had been duplicated. According to a SHAEF plan, all government documents discovered throughout the Western zones were taken to a Ministerial Collecting Centre near Kassel. Reports during

1945 from the Allied officers responsible for those centres to their commanding officers describe two predominant problems. The German staff, all former ministry officials, recruited to sift through the documents, were being slowly starved because food supplies were inadequate; and the same officials were systematically destroying any incriminating documents they discovered. Having been very casually appointed in May 1945, it only slowly became apparent by the end of that year that the German officials had not been vetted and were usually former party members.[15] The benefits of their work to the prosecutors at Nuremberg were, not surprisingly, very limited.

Even Taylor admits that the early interrogations were invariably worthless.[16] Seated in a room with the suspect and the interrogator were an interpreter and a formal note-taker. It was not the atmosphere for producing confessions. The Harvard mafia had ruled at first against allowing any German refugees to conduct interrogations. It was all part of what Foster Adams describes as the 'vacuum-cleaner approach. We just didn't know what we were looking for, so we grabbed at everything.'

Karl Blessing's three interrogations provide perfect examples of the operation's weaknesses. The result of the first, by an OSS agent in August 1945, was a statement that the 'prominent businessman and financial expert . . . did not become a member of the Nazi party.'[17] On that basis he was recommended to Clay as a possible candidate for a government post. When interrogated again on 10 December 1946, he admitted his party activities but presented some colourful explanations about his innocence, despite being responsible for Germany's oil industry, and a dubious assessment of the Nazi government's real intentions. The interrogator did not challenge him on one of his many untrue answers, because he was ignorant of the truth. Blessing was confident enough, at his next interrogation on 1 January, to offer a succession of excuses about his appalling memory. He had even forgotten what he had said three weeks earlier. Asked about Hermann Abs, he could remember only that the two men had talked often together, but not what they had talked about.[18]

Taylor called a special conference at the beginning of May 1947 to decide whether to prosecute Abs or any other of the dozens of bankers who had been arrested. Present at that conference, among others, were Sprecher and Adams. A 324-page report on the Deutsche Bank and an equally large appendix of documentary evidence had been prepared by six special investigators.[19] The investigators had concluded that there was enough evidence to prosecute Abs and some of the other bank directors as war criminals. Reluctantly, Sprecher and Taylor had to disagree. All the report proved was how well the bank's directors had concealed their own activities. Taylor then turned to the Dresdener Bank. Here he felt the chances were better. The chairman, Karl Rasche, was not only a member of the SS but had been betrayed by von Schröder, and had consequently been forced to give incriminating answers in his own interrogations. Taylor later told Clay that he was hopeful that at least eight out of the sixteen Dresdener directors could be prosecuted.[20] Among them was Hans Walz, the managing technical director of Robert Bosche, electrical manufacturers in Stuttgart. Walz had joined the party in 1933, and after joining the SS in 1934 he had been regularly promoted. Before the end of the war, he had joined a further seven Nazi organizations. He had been an early member of the Friends of Himmler group, had visited Dachau with Himmler, and had regularly contributed substantial sums through von Schröder's bank. Twenty-five per cent of the employees at Bosche had been slave labour.[21]

Walz had written on his *Fragebogen* that he had not been a member of any Nazi organization. When confronted with evidence to the contrary by an American interrogator, he alleged that he had joined to protect his business and undermine the party from within. The interrogator told Walz that he thought it was a 'comfortable method of opposition'. Walz said nothing. Within a week, lawyers acting for Walz had presented dozens of affidavits that their client had been a well-known anti-Nazi and was an undiscovered conspirator in the 20 July plot against Hitler's life.

Faced with equally determined opposition from all the other bankers, Taylor could only rely on the judges' interpretation of the documentary evidence of the bank's activities. Any hope of a sympathetic response was shattered on 22 December 1947 when Judge Charles Sears read out his court's judgement in the case against Friedrich Flick and five of his co-directors.[22] It was the first postwar prosecution of an industrialist and was the crucial precedent for the remainder of the trials. Flick epitomized the worst of that group's greedy exploitation of what the Nazis offered. Unlike Krupp, he was not a hereditary industrialist and felt that he had to suckle the Nazis even more than the others. He had pledged a hefty contribution to Hitler's election fund at the February 1933 meeting in Goering's home, joined the Keppler Circle in 1935, paid regular amounts into von Schröder's bank for Himmler's benefit, and had been on the Dachau tour in 1937. He had willingly taken over those aryanized German competitors offered to him and had seized competitors' companies in occupied Europe.

In an unsworn statement in his defence, Flick explained away his close links with the SS as 'an insurance premium to insure personal safety' and justified his antisemitic activities and utterances as just 'howling with the wolves'. He even used the necessity argument to justify his use of slave labour. There had been, he insisted, no choice because the SS had forced him to accept the workers. All his defences would probably have been accepted by the judges had the prosecution not, by chance, discovered just one set of documents which proved that Bernard Weiss, one of the Flick directors, had, on Flick's initiative and instructions, started negotiations with the SS for the supply of more Russian prisoners of war to manufacture railway trucks. The documents disproved Flick's defence that he had been forced to accept all the slave workers as a 'necessity'.

Yet, according to the judges, it was an isolated incident which barely affected his defence. The court stated:

> The evidence clearly established that there was in the instant case 'clear and present danger' within the contemplation of that phrase. We have already discussed the Reich reign of terror. The defendants lived within the Reich. The Reich through its hordes of enforcement officials and secret police, was always 'present', ready to go into instant action and to mete out savage and immediate punishment against anyone doing anything that could be construed as obstructing or hindering the carrying out of governmental regulations or decrees.[23]

On the charges of economic plunder, the court refused to consider any pre-1939 activities, but could not ignore the evidence that Flick had tried to seize permanent ownership of a large steel plant in Lorraine. Yet according to the court, Flick's 'acts were not within his knowledge intended to contribute to a programme of "systematic plunder" conceived by the Hitler regime and for which many of the major war criminals have been punished. If they added anything to this programme of spoliation, it was in a very small degree.'

On the charges of using slave labour, spoliation and being an accessory to the crimes of the SS, Flick was sentenced to seven years. Taylor described the judgement as 'exceedingly (if not excessively) moderate and conciliatory'.[24] It effectively granted to industrialists the defence of superior orders, while the SS men who had supplied and supervised the slave workers on Flick's behalf were denied that same defence. When Flick was later asked in the IG Farben trial to name one German industrialist who had been punished for refusing to employ slave labour, he could not name one. Yet there had been many German companies which had continued work throughout the war without slave labour although their profits may not have been so high.

Taylor realized that if the judges refused to accept the evidence against Flick, there was no hope of convicting bankers. Walz and all the other Dresdener Bank directors were reluctantly released. Only Karl Rasche,

against whom there was overwhelming evidence that he had done everything in his power to exploit his close connections with the party and SS
was prosecuted. His eventual conviction was for his bank's plunder of
Europe, but he was acquitted on slave labour charges. A banker,
according to the American judges, could not be responsible for the way
his money was used, even if he knew it was to be used criminally:

> The real question is, is it a crime to make a loan, knowing or having good
> reason to believe that the borrower will use the funds in financing enterprises
> which are employed in using labour in violation of either national or inter-
> national law?. . . A bank sells money or credit in the same manner as the
> merchandiser of any other commodity. It does not become a partner in enter-
> prise. . . Loans or sales of commodities to be used in an unlawful enterprise
> may well be condemned from a moral standpoint and reflect no credit on the
> part of the lender or seller in either case, but the transaction can hardly be said
> to be a crime. Our duty is to try and punish those guilty of violating inter-
> national law, and we are not prepared to state that such loans constitute
> violations of that law.[25]

The three judges who came to that decision in the Rasche case came
from the conservative states of Minnesota, Iowa and Oregon. Had they
been judging a case in their home states where the 'commodity' was a
gun knowingly supplied for an intended murder, it is unlikely that the
supplier of the 'commodity' would have been acquitted as an accesory to
the murder. According to their judgement, Dr Bruno Tesch, the
supplier of Zyklon B gas to the SS, should also have been acquitted
because he was just selling 'merchandise'. Tesch had deliberately
removed the warning odour from the gas supplied to the SS, so that the
victims in the gas chambers would not be immediately alarmed. The
American judges seemed to be suggesting that the British had been
unjust in executing Tesch.

Taylor had realized quite early that the quality of the judges who had
arrived from America would cause problems;[26] to his surprise, Chief
Justice Vinson had ruled that no Federal judges could accept invitations
to Nuremberg. Instead the thirty trial judges had been recruited from
state courts where by definition they had considerably less experience of
the issues raised at Nuremberg and were wholly ignorant of international law. Some of them, like Wennerstrum, were also prejudiced.
Taylor's misfortune was that in the IG Farben case, where there was
sufficient evidence to establish beyond any doubt that the directors were
murderers, one of the judges, Judge James Morris, from North Dakota,
a centre of opposition to the war crimes trials, was, like Wennerstrum,
outspokenly prejudiced. Within days of the trial opening the prosecu-

tion staff began to feel that it was they, and not the IG Farben directors, who were on trial.

According to Du Bois, Morris had said to him over lunch on the first day of the trial: 'We have to worry about the Russians now; it wouldn't surprise me if they overran the courtroom before we get through.'[27] It was Du Bois who was to be accused of being a communist.[28] Morris' wife often invited the wives of the IG Farben directors on trial for drinks, especially Baroness von Schnitzler. Drexel Sprecher, an American prosecutor, claims that he was publicly attacked at the bar of the Grand Hotel in Nuremberg by the assistant of one of the trial judges for being 'anti-German'.[29] Increasingly Morris and the presiding judge, Curtis Shake, became impatient with the prosecution's presentation of the case, insensitive about the evidence and, according to the prosecutors, noticeably biased in favour of the defence in their decisions during the trial. German newspaper reports about Shake's hospitality to the German defence lawyers at the Nuremberg Grand Hotel, where Germans were normally not admitted, and the lawyers' own accounts of Shake's deep and genuine understanding of the German case, hardened the prosecution's suspicions.[30]

The IG Farben trial started on 27 August 1947. Twenty-four directors and four officials were charged with offences under three main headings: Planning, Preparation, Initiation and Waging of Wars of Agression, and Invasions of other countries; Plunder and Spoliation; and Slavery and Mass Murder.

Carl Krauch was the one executive director whom the prosecution was confident of convicting on the charge of planning and preparation of the war. It was not only his activities in mobilizing the chemical industry to Goering's specifications which incriminated him, but a chance discovery of an undestroyed letter from Krauch to Goering. Krauch wrote, in April 1939:

It is essential for Germany to strengthen its own war potential as well as that of its Allies to such an extent that the coalition is equal to the efforts of practically the rest of the world. This can be achieved only by new, strong and combined efforts by all of the allies, and by expanding and improving the greater economic domain corresponding to the improved raw material basis of the coalition, peaceably at first, to the Balkans and Spain.
If action does not follow upon these thoughts with the greatest possible speed, all sacrifices of blood in the next war will not spare us the bitter end which once before we brought upon ourselves owing to the lack of foresight and fixed purposes.[31]

Krauch's defence had a logic which appealed to the judges. 'Replace

IG,' his lawyers asked the judges, 'by ICI for England, or Du Pont for America or Montecatini for Italy, and at once the similarity will become clear to you.' Krauch, his lawyer claimed, like any other businessman, feared communism and worked for his government in the honest defence of his country. Despite the evidence of Krauch's work on the Four-Year Plan after 1936, his close cooperation with Field Marshal Keitel, and his own letter, the three judges acquitted him of the charge, stating: 'The prosecution is confronted with the difficulty of establishing knowledge on the part of the defendant, not only of the rearmament of Germany but also that the purpose of rearmament was to wage aggressive war. In this sphere, the evidence denigrates from proof to mere conjecture.'[32] The very assumptions which were made by the international court at Nuremberg two years previously, in the cases of the politicians and soldiers, were rejected by the IG court when applied to an industrialist.

The acquittal of Krauch on that charge only stirred the ranks of the prosecutors awaiting the whole judgement. The real shock was still to come. Mistakenly, they had spent the first weeks of the ten-month trial trying to prove the complicated and less sensational charges of participation in the preparation of war, and of IG's plunder. It was only later that Du Bois realized that the judges might have been won over at the outset had the case started on the mass murder charges. The evidence seemed to him nevertheless to be quite convincing.

IG's decision to build IG Auschwitz had been taken on 6 February 1941.[33] Dr Otto Ambros, the company's Buna expert, and Dr Fritz Ter Meer, IG's top scientist and chairman of the company's technical committee, had been called to the Ministry of Economics and told that the government needed an expansion of Buna production. Ambros had investigated the possible locations for a plant, and after some discussion with Krauch it was decided that Auschwitz, rather than Norway, was the best site. Both Ambros and Krauch had been told that the SS had ambitious plans for expanding the number of inmates at the camp, and the prospect of disciplined cheap labour was the deciding factor. IG's *Vorstand* decided to make Ambros responsible for the Buna plant and Heinrich Bütefisch responsible for the parallel synthetic fuel plant.

To ensure that the promised labour supply for the 900-million-reichsmark investment was fulfilled, Krauch used his, by then, excellent relations with Goering and Himmler and asked the Reichsmarschall and the SS Reichsführer to send written orders to Rudolf Hoess at the camp, ordering him to guarantee that there would always be between 8,000 and 12,000 construction workers on the site. Himmler's adjutant, Karl Wolff, was appointed as liaison man between IG and the SS. As with the Krupp contract, IG agreed to pay the SS three reichsmarks for unskilled, and four reichsmarks for skilled labour. Children cost IG one and a half reichsmarks per day.

Walter Dürrfeld was selected as IG's director of construction at Auschwitz. In reporting back to Ambros and Bütefisch about keeping the workers disciplined, he wrote that Hoess had promised him that IG would get the most sadistic Kapos available. 'These Kapos,' wrote Dürrfeld, 'are being selected from among the professional criminals and are to be transferred from other concentration camps to Auschwitz.' The IG directors looked forward optimistically to fast results. Ambros wrote to Ter Meer: 'Our new friendship with the SS is proving very profitable.'

Problems, however, set in very soon. The inmates, unfed by either the SS or IG, were unable to work hard enough. The Kapos did not stop hitting them. Dürrfeld reported to Frankfurt that the physical violence was 'unpleasant', although some months later he became reconciled to its value and reported that it seemed to be the only way to get the inmates to work. But the building programme was slipping far behind schedule. The project was too important to allow extra time for construction. The IG board therefore decided in July 1942 to build its own concentration camp adjacent to the building site so that inmates, usually exhausted by the long march from Auschwitz to the site, could start fresh in the morning. It only cost another five million reichsmarks.

Thereafter, the fittest of the new arrivals at Auschwitz were selected by the SS soon after they jumped down from the cattle trucks, to go to IG's own camp at Monowitz, rather than be immediately gassed in Birkenau. Conditions at Monowitz were as bad as at the main Auschwitz camp. Three inmates slept on each bunk, which meant that sleep was impossible. Unheated in winter, the barracks had no latrine facilities and were disease-ridden and infectious. Food was so inadequate that prisoners survived on the fat of their own bodies, losing up to nine pounds of their weight per week. Within three months even the fittest became skeletons. Once unable to work, they were immediately transferred to Birkenau for gassing. Even IG's hospital was a place to fear. Whenever IG's self-imposed capacity was reached, the sickest would automatically be sent to the gas chambers. In short, it was an extermination camp, managed by the SS in partnership with Europe's largest industrial corporation.

The eyewitness evidence at the trial seemed to be conclusive. Rudolf Vitek, a physician and inmate, described the conditions to the court:

> The prisoners were pushed in their work by the Kapos, foremen and the overseers of IG in an inhuman way. No mercy was shown. Thrashings, ill-treatment of the worst kind, even direct killings were the fashion.

The murderous working speed was responsible for the fact that while working, many prisoners suddenly stretched out flat, turned blue, gasped for breath and died like beasts. . . It was no rare occurrence that detachments of four hundred to five hundred men brought back with them in the evening five to twenty corpses. The dead were brought to the place of rollcall and counted as being present.

Other eyewitnesses described how men who had been hanged as punishment by IG were just left on the gallows as a warning to those that passed by. All the witnesses, including those called by the defence, agreed that the stench of burning flesh from the Birkenau crematoria always polluted the air. When the smoke cleared, one could often see the flames. Every visitor to the camp knew what was happening, especially the IG directors involved with the project. Even those directors who did not travel to Poland were fully aware. Weekly reports on progress and problems were provided to the whole executive board, and as the project was IG's largest investment, there were regular discussions about the financial aspects.

The prosecution was able to prove from the documents that were found that Ambros, Ter Meer, Krauch and Bütefisch had visited the camp. Dürrfeld had lived on the site throughout IG's operation. Three other senior executives directly involved in the project were also proved to have been to the camp: they were Friedrich Jähne, August von Knierem and Christian Schneider, IG's so-called 'director of welfare'. Twenty-three defendants were accused of involvement; in unison they all pleaded compulsion and necessity. The star witness on the necessity defence was Flick, who had set the precedent in the same court.

In their verdict read on 29 July 1948, Morris and Shake breezily told the stunned prosecution that they did not believe the evidence against most of the defendants. Eighteen out of the twenty-three directors charged with using slave labour were acquitted of the charge, including Schmitz, the company's chairman, and Jähne, Knierem and Schneider, who had all been proved to have visited the camp. The criterion for guilt, said Shake, was whether the defendants had used their own 'initiative' in asking for slave labour. There had to be a 'real and moral choice' to prove responsibility. The mere participant, said the judge, had a proper defence of necessity or superior orders. Quoting the Flick judgement, the judges repeated that those directors who had not complied in the use of slave labour would have been subject to severe penalties. Yet, even on their own evidence, the IG directors had admitted that neither the government nor the SS had forced them to build their factory at Auschwitz. They had selected the site because the cheap labour seemed to guarantee higher profits. Evidence of that decision, and much similar evidence which had been obtained in the pre-trial interrogations, had been denied in court by the defendants and was then deliberately ignored by the judges, who put their own gloss on what they had heard.

At least one hundred thousand innocent people died building IG Auschwitz, yet Judges Shake and Morris described the conditions at the camp as if it was just a rather rigorous state prison:

> Camp Monowitz was not without inhumane incidents. Occasionally beatings occurred by plant police and supervisors who were in charge of the prisoners while they were at work. Sometimes workers collapsed. No doubt a condition of undernourishment and exhaustion from long hours of heavy labour was the cause of these incidents. . . While food was inadequate at Monowitz, as was the clothing especially in winter. . . Farben voluntarily and at its own expense provided hot soup for the workers on the site at noon. This was in addition to the regular rations.

The court's sentences matched their interpretation of the evidence. Dürrfeld, who had run the camp, was sentenced to eight years. Ambros was sentenced to eight years; Ter Meer to seven years; Krauch and Bütefisch to six years. On the plunder charges only, Schmitz and Schnitzler were sentenced to four and five years. For the defendants, the leniency of the sentences might have seemed poor consolation for their failure to actually complete the Auschwitz project. For, despite the cost and effort, IG Auschwitz never produced one ounce of Buna.

Five months after the verdict, the third judge, Paul Herbert, dean of the Louisiana State University Law School, delivered a dissenting opinion. It was a carefully reasoned, trenchant attack on the prejudice and distortions of his two colleagues. He dismissed Shake's differentiation of the directors' criminal responsibility between those who visited the camp and those who did not as 'without any sound precedent under the most elementary concepts of criminal law'. Herbert then continued:

> Far from establishing that the defendants acted under 'necessity' or 'coercion', I conclude that Farben frequently sought the forced workers. In fact the production quotas of Farben were largely fixed by Farben itself. I cannot agree with the assertion that these defendants had no other choice. In reality the defence is an afterthought, the validity of which is belied by Farben's entire course of action.
> The conditions at Auschwitz were so terrible that it is utterly incredible to conclude that they were unknown to the defendants, the principal corporate directors who were responsible for Farben's connection with the project. . .
> The extreme cold, the inadequacy of the food, the rigorous nature of the work, the cruel treatment of the workers by their supervisors, combine to

present a picture of horror, which I am convinced has not been overdrawn by the prosecution and which is fully sustained by the evidence. . . The defendants, members of the *Vorstand*, cannot in my opinion, avoid sharing a large part of the guilt for these numberless crimes against humanity.

Herbert's conclusions were only of historical interest.

The day after the IG Farben trial ended, on 30 June, Alfried Krupp and eleven Krupp directors stood to hear their sentences. The result was a sharp contrast to the IG trial.[34] Alfried and ten others were convicted on the slave labour charges. The judges made no attempt to construct a nice distinction about 'necessity' and 'initiative'. Their judgement, like Herbert's, stated quite firmly that those directors who remained on the board were criminally responsible. All three judges rejected Alfried's defence that he only complied because he feared the alternative would be to lose his factory and be sent to a concentration camp himself. After describing what he called the appalling conditions in Krupp's camps, Judge Wilkins referred to Alfried's defence of fears for his own safety:

. . .in all fairness it must be said that in any view of the evidence, the defendants, in a concentration camp, would not have been in a worse plight than the thousands of helpless victims whom they daily exposed to danger of death and great bodily harm from starvation and the relentless air raids upon the armaments plants, to say nothing of the involuntary servitude and the other indignities which they suffered. The disparity in the number of the actual and potential victims is also thought-provoking.

Throughout his trial, Krupp had remained impassive and seemingly unconcerned. Some might have misinterpreted his attitude as arrogance had they not seen the occasional wince in his face when a particularly sensitive document was produced, or a survivor of his concentration camp eloquently described the conditions that Alfried preferred to forget. As he stood to receive his sentence – twelve years for employing slave labour – he remained contemptuously impassive. Seconds later his face was as white as a sheet. Judge Anderson announced that the second part of his sentence was the forfeiture of his complete possessions. For a moment it seemed the dynasty was destroyed.

As the convicted Farben and Krupp directors were taken to Landsberg prison, they knew there was little prospect of them ever serving out their sentences. It was not only Germans but also Americans who believed that the industrialists were the unfortunate victims of an isolated and discredited group of left-wing fanatics. Daily events lent credibility to that smear. Berlin was blockaded and everyone was talking about the possibility of war. The day after the trials, the same lawyers and judges who had sat for endless months arguing about the crimes committed in the Second World War had hurriedly packed their belongings and fled to catch the next transatlantic liner home, hoping to miss the Third.

In Landsberg, the industrialists quickly established a comfortable routine. With the ordeal of the trial behind them, they soon discovered that Flick, who had arrived some months earlier, was managing to keep his interests under efficient control with the help of the weekly visit from his lawyer accompanied by whichever business associate was needed on that occasion. They also heard that Flick had chosen as a financial adviser Hermann Abs, who by the end of 1948 was effectively managing the recovery programme. Trusted by the Allies and trusted by the Nazis, Abs had become one of the keystones of Germany's recovery.

Although condemned to death by the Yugoslavs in his absence as a war criminal, Abs had found it easy to avoid prosecution at Nuremberg. When Forster Adams asked him to either give evidence against Rasche or face prosecution himself, he had called Adams' bluff. 'I told Adams,' says Abs, 'I was not educated by my father to be a hero or by my mother to be a donkey shot. I avoided both.'[35] In between the interrogation sessions, in which he managed to avoid incriminating anyone, Abs went to the public gallery of the IG Farben trial. 'I was giving the directors moral support,' he says, 'because all German industrialists were really on trial.'

There was no bravery in that gesture. Rather, it was just the banker, ever considerate about his clients, seeing them through the bad times as well as the good. He was to become the first chairman of BASF Chemicals, one of the successor companies of IG Farben. With evident self-satisfaction, he now says: 'I always thought IG was too big.'

On 1 March 1948 Abs had been appointed deputy head of the Reconstruction Loan Corporation, and president of the Bank Deutsche Länder, both of which decided which German industries should get a slice of the billions of dollars of Marshall aid. The appointment had not been made without some misgivings especially by Clay. According to Jacques Reinstein, one of the American economic advisers: 'we just didn't have a handle with which we could cut him off.'[36] Distributing money gave Abs influence, not only amongst German, but also with the Americans.

By mid-1949, the Americans were very anxious that German industry should expand to help the West resist communism. Naturally, the advice of the banker who was handing out American money could not be ignored by the Americans who entrusted him with that money. One key to German recovery and cooperation, Abs told McCloy, was the release of the industrialists in Landsberg. His friends Ludwig Erhard and Karl Blessing told the Americans the same. So did Konrad Adenauer. In fact, every German told every American who cared to listen that Germany's friendship and help against the communists would be easier to secure if the gates of Landsberg prison were opened not just to release the industrialists, but every one of the five hundred convicted men inside.[37]

17

'SHAKING THESE PEOPLE OUT AS FAST AS WE CAN'

At 10.30 on the morning of Monday, 8 January 1951, Dr Walter Strauss, West Germany's deputy minister of justice, arrived at the Heidelberg office of General Thomas Handy, commander in chief of the US European Command.[1] Handy already knew what Strauss wanted to talk about. Over the weekend, John McCloy, the American high commissioner, had phoned to warn him that the German government were making another attempt to save the lives of the twenty-eight convicted war criminals still awaiting execution at Landsberg prison. Handy had the power to commute fourteen of those sentences, all of whom had been convicted at the army's Dachau trials. Six of those condemned men, including Jochen Peiper, had been convicted for their part in the Malmédy Massacre, two had been condemned for murdering Allied airmen, and the remaining six had each been personally involved in thousands of murders at Dachau, Buchenwald and Mauthausen concentration camps.

It was a bad week for American prestige and morale. The East-West war had finally broken out, not in Europe, but in Korea, and the news from the Far East was bad. Seoul, southern Korea's major city, had just that week been captured by the communists. Western losses had been calamitous. The American chiefs of staff had finally convinced the politicians that West German rearmament was vital if the West was to be saved. The British and French governments had for some time resisted American pressure to allow their recent enemy to rearm, but were being reluctantly persuaded of its necessity. When Strauss arrived to see Handy, the American commander had just left a long briefing session on the military situation in Central Europe. His army was on constant alert, but their supplies of military hardware were perilously low. McCloy and the two other Western high commissioners had already agreed that German industry should be encouraged to expand to supply desperately needed steel and other necessities.

Strauss stayed for ninety minutes. It was a stiff and uncomfortable meeting. The two men had discussed the same issue several times before.

Handy knew that Strauss had come rather than his minister because the Americans had grown to distrust Thomas Dehler. His phone calls, letters and personal appeals had become counterproductive. Despite his anti-Nazi record and his suffering during the Third Reich, Dehler seemed, to some, astonishingly nationalistic, always advocating that agreements be made with former Nazis so that the government's wafer-thin Parliamentary majority could be improved. His party, the FDP Liberal party, had a large number of former Nazis amongst its members. As chief prosecutor and president of the *Oberlandesgericht* (Provincial Court of Appeal) in Bamberg, Bavaria, Dehler had, according to Hans Weigert, personally allowed the ranks of the judiciary to be filled by more than ninety per cent of former Nazis.[2] It made his pleas for clemency and justice seem suspect.

Strauss, probably the real power in the Ministry, disagreed with Dehler about appeasing the Nazis, but his explanation to the Americans of why clemency was vital was just a regurgitation of the old, and hitherto rejected, arguments. What made them more immediate were the rumours that the gallows had been once again set up inside Landsberg and that McCloy and Handy were about to announce the outcome of their reviews.

It had been four to five years since the sixteen men had been condemned to death, said Strauss. In Germany, executions normally followed the sentence within four weeks. But, as Handy well knew, the German Parliament had abolished the death penalty. Strauss reiterated his agreement that the men should be punished, but argued that their sentences should be commuted to life imprisonment.

If the executions went ahead, said the minister, the government would be unable to control the inevitable press outcry. Nor would it only be the Nazis who would protest. The ensuing sensation would be damaging to everyone. Certainly the Russians would exploit the situation and use the opportunity to reprieve or even release the hundreds of war criminals they held at the Volheim prison; it would be a propaganda gift for them. Many Germans were already impressed, Strauss said, by the accounts of alleged American war crimes in Korea. The congregation at the Church service he had attended the previous day, anti-Nazis to a man, had begged him to press on the American commander that the executions would be a 'tragic mistake'.

Then Strauss played what he thought would be his strongest card, the case of Jochen Peiper and the definite effect his execution would have on the chances that Germany would agree to rearm. Peiper, said the deputy minister of justice, was a fine soldier who could not possibly be guilty of the alleged crimes. All of the others might be guilty, but not Peiper.

Handy interrupted for the first time. He agreed that there was, of course, a difference between Peiper and the concentration camp cases, but the evidence in the Malmédy case had been reviewed and re-reviewed many times. There could be no doubt about his guilt.

With considerable emphasis, Strauss slowly explained the effect of Peiper's execution on Germany's contribution to Western defence. The army, he said, had always been anti-Hitler and anti-Nazi. Tactfully, Handy did not interrupt and tell the minister that Peiper had not only spoken repeatedly during and after the war of his personal devotion to Hitler, but had gone with Himmler for a private visit to see a group of concentration camp inmates being gassed.

According to Handy, Strauss was insistent right up to his departure. As he got up to leave, he passed Handy a piece of paper and asked him to read it after he had left. It was a quotation: 'To permit one sentenced to death to remain for months or even years, without knowledge of his reprieve and under intolerable anxiety and mental stress of not knowing whether the next day would be his last day on earth, is a trait typical of the sadism of the Nazi regime, and if anything could be considered a crime against humanity, such a practice is. . .' At the top was written the quotation's source: 'Case Eleven: The Judgement in the Ministries Case. American Military Tribunal, Nuremberg.'

Handy was unimpressed by the whole discussion. He felt that the Germans were themselves to blame for the delays in the executions. Ever since early 1947, American and German lawyers acting for the condemned men had been bombarding the District and Supreme Court in Washington with endless petitions for *habeas corpus*. Repeatedly, the two courts had said that they did not have jurisdiction over non-resident enemy aliens. Persistently, the same petitions were again refiled. Each time the petition had been submitted, the court had to order a stay of execution while the papers were studied. Both the lawyers and accused naturally thought it could only be advantageous to buy time. When the judges had become so familiar with the cases that the delays became uncomfortably short, the lawyers had discovered a new tactic. They had not paid the necessary court fee. The cases could neither be heard nor dismissed until the petitioner's money had been paid into court. Some of the executions had been postponed for nearly four years.[3]

There was no doubt that the fourteen men had committed murders, all of them quite appalling. Moreover in each instance other Germans condemned to death in the same cases had already been executed. Some of those executed had not even been the principal murderers, in contrast to those for whom Strauss was now pleading. Hans Schmidt and Gustav Heigel, former senior officers at Buchenwald, had committed countless murders and several of their subordinates had already been executed. But

Congressman Kenneth B. Keating and Senator Morse had both sent Handy telegrams asking him to review their cases yet again while their petitions were being heard in Washington.[4]

To meet the criticism that the sentences for the same crimes had been excessively varied, depending on which American officers had heard the case, an Army War Crimes Modification Board had already reviewed all the sentences and paroled, pardoned, released and reduced many of the convicted men. In the Bokum Island case, one of the worst examples of the torture and murder of American pilots by German civilians, Handy had even accepted the Board's recommendation to commute the death sentence of Kurt Göbell, although it was he who had organized the lynching party while three of those who had obeyed him had already been executed. Göbell survived because he had hired better lawyers.[5]

None of the fourteen remaining cases seemed to Handy worthy of commutation. But the best dates for the executions seemed to have already passed. Damon Gunn, the new Judge Advocate-General in Europe, had sent him a memoramdum at the beginning of November 1950 about the need for executing the unreprieved Germans as fast as possible as: 'We are desirous of getting military cooperation from Germany.'[6] Gunn had recommended either late November, when Congress was involved in elections, or the anniversary of the armistice day of the First World War, which he thought would be 'propitious for psychologically minimizing the shock effects'. The best days had come and gone, and the pressure for reprieves had increased.

A few days after Strauss had made his final plea, Dehler sent another letter, this time suggesting that the Americans allow a German judge to review all the cases to see whether there were not, after all, some mitigating factors. Handy had dictated two replies, one saying that he was quite prepared to allow the Germans to review the cases, while the second castigated Dehler for failing to recognize that the condemned men were war criminals and not decent citizens.[7] The decision on which one to send, or whether to reply at all, was not Handy's. Although the Department of War had fought six months earlier for the army's right to make the final decision, it would in fact be John McCloy's judgement that would finally count.

When he first arrived in Germany McCloy took much the same attitude as Clay had done towards the convicted men and their sympathizers. In December 1949, he wrote to Bishop Müchen of the Apostolic Nunciature in Germany about the 'numerous petitions for clemency I have received'; and the Bishop's demand for an amnesty for all war criminals:

I have been somewhat disturbed, however, in examining these petitions by what appears to be a persistent tendency to question the legal basis for the prosecutions and the judicial soundness of the judgements. I feel at it would be very unfortunate if any considerable body of responsible German should undertake to question the fundamental principals on which the war crimes prosecutions were based. . . I do not think that any German who sincerely believes in the future of Germany as a responsible and peaceful member of the community of nations can reasonably doubt the enormity of the crimes of which the war crimes prisoners have been convicted or the fundamental principles of international justice pursuant to which they were tried.

In that connection, I think that the term ''amnesty'' is perhaps unfortunate. I do not believe that world opinion is prepared to accept the proposition that those crimes have yet been sufficiently atoned for or that the German people should now be allowed to forget them. Anything approaching a general amnesty would, I fear, be taken as an abandonment of the principles established in the trials of the perpetrators of those crimes.[8]

McCloy had fourteen other death sentences to consider, all of them Germans condemned by American judges at Nuremberg. All fourteen were either, like Otto Ohlendorf, members of the *Einsatzgruppen* who had murdered hundreds of thousands in Eastern Europe, or officials, like Oswald Pohl, who had directed the Final Solution from Berlin. Since assuming office, McCloy had been the target of an even more intensive campaign than Handy. It seemed that every German he met, including Adenauer, had looked for the opportunity to mention the political need for reprieves.

Most of the Germans knew that nearly five months earlier, McCloy had received the report of a three-man advisory board which had reviewed all the Nuremberg sentences. Appointed in March 1950, its president was David Peck, a presiding judge of the Appellate Division of the New York Supreme Court.[9] The other two members were Federick Moran, chairman of the New York Board of Parole, and Brigadier-General Conrad B. Snow, the assistant legal adviser at the State Department. Meeting in Washington and Munich, the Peck Commission nearly surpassed the Simpson Commission in the speed of its review. Within less than four months it had allegedly read through twelve massive cases, involving 104 defendants, which had taken three and a half years to pass through the courts. Like their predecessors, the Peck Commission had deliberately sought out the help of the defendants (Moran went to Landsberg) and their lawyers, but ignored all offers of help from the prosecutors. According to Benjamin Ferencz, an assistant to Taylor, who had an especial interest in the Krupp case, the coffin-like boxes containing the evidence of that trial had remained sealed in the basement of the Munich house where the Peck Commission was meeting throughout their hearings.[10]

Peck recommended that McCloy make hefty reductions in nearly all of the sentences. Yet in the Foreword to the report, he set out an excellent, contradictory, argument for not reducing any of them. After speaking to the convicts or their lawyers, Peck wrote:

> [The] main impression given, and one that is most disappointing, is that the majority of the defendants still seem to feel that what they did was right, in that they were doing it under orders. This exaltation of orders is even more disappointing as an attitude than as a defence. . . Clemency, where any grounds can be found for exercising charitable instincts, may be a charitable example, but a mistaken tenderness towards the perpetrators of mass murder would be a mockery. It would undo what Nuremberg has accomplished.

Yet clemency was just what Peck recommended.

In 1947, Clay had felt strong enough to dismiss many of the Simpson recommendations. When he had followed them, it was not out of expediency, but because he felt there was genuine room for doubt; he had also tried to ensure that in exercising his powers of commutation he did not totally undo the effects of the original trial. Ilse Koch might not have been hanged, but she was not released from jail either.

By the end of 1950, McCloy faced political problems which, given the best will in the world, must have weighed heavily in his mind when he considered the recommendations of the Peck Commission. His decision, announced on 31 January 1951, resulted in the drastic reduction of the sentences in seventy-four out of the 104 cases, including commutations for ten of those sentenced to death.[11] Ten sentences, including five death sentences, were confirmed. The remaining twenty men had already completed their sentences. The five death sentences confirmed were all of men directly involved in mass murder. So were the ten who were reprieved. When Ohlendorf heard that he was to be executed, he complained of the injustice. There had been over ten thousand members of the *Einsatzgruppen*, he claimed, yet only thirty-three had been convicted and he was one of just fourteen who was to be executed.[12]

Justifying his decision, McCloy said that there had been a 'legitimate basis for clemency' in all seventy-four cases because the sentences were unequal to other sentences in similar cases. He explained that in many cases he had decided that the defence of superior orders was justified. New evidence had been provided that the accused had at some stage tried to resist the criminal orders, although on other occasions they had been obeyed. Even though Peck had recommended that all the death sentences for the members of the *Einsatzgruppen* were justified, McCloy announced that 'with difficulty' he had found grounds for reprieve, although they had been involved in what he called 'a programme of deliberate and calculated crime, of historic proportions'. Other reductions were prefaced with phrases like: 'though difficult to find room for clemency' or: 'I have had difficulty in finding a justification for clemency but. . .'

To answer the inevitable arguments in favour of mercy for the men whose death sentences were confirmed – four members of the *Einsatzgruppen* and Oswald Pohl – McCloy explained: 'These sentences reflect upon the individuals concerned, not upon the honour of the German military profession.'

Simultaneously, and with the same problems in mind, Handy announced the reprieve of the six remaining SS officers involved in the Malmédy Massacre and all but two (Hans Schmidt and Georg Schallermair) of the fourteen men held in Landsberg. The most significant and, to many, surprising part of McCloy's announcement was that which concerned Alfried Krupp and eight of his colleagues. Not only were they to be immediately released – McCloy argued that their guilt had been no greater than that of Flick and the Farben directors who had received lower sentences – but Krupp's property was to be restored.

One man who was not taken by surprise was Krupp himself; he had known for some time that he was to be released. A room had been set aside at Landsberg for the Krupp directors to discuss corporate business, and directors and officials would come from Essen with the necessary documents to plan the company's programme for rapid expansion to meet Western demands in Korea. Eating and drinking the best food and wines available, Alfried and his fellow convicts took pleasure in insulting the very people who put them there.

In justifying his decision, McCloy seemed to go beyond a straight explanation, producing what was almost an apology for the courts' harshness. About the slave labour charges he said:

> There is no doubt whatever that this labour was inhumanely treated, being constantly subjected to corporal punishment and other cruelties. There is likewise no doubt that the industrial concern and its management were not primarily responsible for this treatment. The judgement does indicate that several of the defendants were involved with certain of the illegalities but it is extremely difficult to allocate individual guilt among the respective defendants.

McCloy had clearly not read the evidence. Understandably, he had not had the time.

Even now, he staunchly defends all of his decisions, including the reprieve of the *Einsatzgruppen* officers, as if they were made on judicial and not political grounds. 'I did it,' he told the author, 'because I had to do it. I had to get down on my knees to do it. I tried to do it in accordance with my own conscience. I wasn't dickering with any – I wasn't manoeuvring in any connection with any – I wouldn't have permitted any manoeuvres to be made. I had to think through with my deepest form of conscience as to what the right thing was to do in a situation like this.'[13] To help him make those decisions, McCloy had even gone to Landsberg to meet the prisoners. But he had not met Krupp.

Explaining his decision on Alfried Krupp, he told William Manchester:

> We tried him reluctantly and the confiscation troubled me. I consulted my French and British colleagues, and they agreed with me. My feeling – it was a feeling – was that Alfried was a playboy, that he hadn't had much responsibility. I felt that he had expiated whatever he'd done by the time he'd already served in jail. Oh, I don't doubt that he'd supported the Nazis early; he was a weakling.[14]

Alfried did not look like a weakling when he walked out of Landsberg at 9 am on 3 February. According to the *New York Times* reporter, 'at his press conference, Krupp was greeted as a returning national hero.'[15] When Fritz Ter Meer was released, he was reported as saying: 'Now that they have Korea on their hands, the Americans are a lot more friendly.'[15] Behind them, they left seven others who had also pleaded superior orders but would hang because they had nothing to offer the West. After five more months of delaying tactics in the American courts, they were executed on 7 June. The last and 257th war criminal to fall through the trapdoor was Hans Schmidt, the Buchenwald adjutant. The American army spokesman afterwards neither confirmed nor denied that his last words were: 'Long Live Germany.'[17]

McCloy's and Handy's decision caused anger and protest in many quarters; ironically, nowhere was the reaction more ferocious than in Britain. In Parliament, both Attlee and Churchill condemned the release of Krupp in particular. The American embassy cabled McCloy that the Cabinet had held 'two very agitated sessions on the subject within the past few days and a third is scheduled for 12 February to consider statement regarding prisoners in their zone.'[18]

McCloy felt that British anger was pure hypocrisy. He had not only discussed his decision with Kirkpatrick, the British high commissioner, but also remembered that the British had been very keen to avoid any responsibility for trying Krupp.[19] Churchill had even contributed to

Manstein's defence fund. Loyal to McCloy, Kirkpatrick told the British press in Berlin that he saw no reason why all sentences of war criminals should not be reviewed. When he read the reports, Attlee was furious and immediately ordered Kirkpatrick to return to London and explain himself. Once in London, Kirkpatrick convinced Foreign Office officials that the alliance with Germany was too important to allow the past to get in the way. The Foreign Office agreed and immediately began their own review procedure.

Cases were referred from Germany to Sir Patrick Hancock in the Foreign Office's Western Department. Hancock was sympathetic to all appeals for leniency. 'It was a frightful bore to have these people in prison,' he now remembers. 'Most of them anyway were small-time rats.'[20] Giving him legal advice on each case was John Liddle Simpson, who admits that he, like all other Foreign Office officials, realized that the price for German cooperation was the removal of their grievances: 'I had mixed feelings. I didn't let real brutes out straight away just because of policy. But I accepted superior orders as grounds although the defence had been denied during the trials.'[21] The cases were then referred to what can only be called 'the old crowd'. Frank Roberts, advising the new foreign minister, Sir Anthony Eden, just reappointed after the Conservatives' election victory, remembers that one of his first discussions with the Foreign Office's new minister of state, Selwyn Lloyd, concerned the inauguration of a clemency programme. Roberts, surprisingly, insists that there was never any pressure from the Germans for releases. Gerald Draper, consulted by the Foreign Office about the legality of the clemencies, remembers otherwise. Eden, he now says, was so keen to get the convicted men freed, that he was asked whether the period before their conviction could not be deducted from their sentence. When Draper and Simpson told the minister's office that the deduction had already been taken into account, 'I knew,' says Draper, 'that they would just look around for another way.'

The creation of the Federal Republic was fraught with seemingly insurmountable problems and frustrating tensions. Many Germans were unwilling to agree to the division of their country. Others were unprepared to be reconciled with the permanent loss of their homes and land in the East. Some were still unable to admit that Germany had lost the war and was not in a position to make unconditional demands. Uniquely, the Bavarians wanted only a limited role in any future West German state.

Compounding the differences between the Germans were even more serious and fundamental differences between the three Western Allies.

France in particular wanted to severely limit the new state's sovereignty. Having effectively blackmailed the French into agreement with the American position, Clay suddenly discovered that the British favoured a centralized government while he and the French wanted a decentralized, federal system.

The fact that an agreed Basic Law emerged from the delegates to the Parliamentary Council in Bonn in January 1949 owed more to negative than positive forces. There was simply no alternative. The debate which led to the Basic Law had been dominated by an emotional dispute between Adenauer and Schumacher, the socialist leader. Both were vying for the eventual leadership of the new state and sought support by seeking to criticize the Allies more than the other. Adenauer's eventual victory by a single vote only perpetuated their differences and the insecurity of the new government. He felt compelled to cling on to whatever support he had won.

Adenauer immediately fell victim to substantial pressure from many groups, especially the veterans' organizations, to secure their members' early release. He was sympathetically responsive, although he was probably less interested in the injustice of the continued imprisonment of 'Our Boys in Landsberg' than in the humiliating political embarrassment. The very existence of German war criminals undermined his attempts to cultivate a new image of a sovereign and democratic Germany which had no links with the past. Landsberg represented a defeated, criminal nation.

Landsberg was also the major obstable to German rearmament. In 1950 pressure from the NATO allies to rearm Germany was thwarted by the German military's refusal to cooperate until their comrades in Landsberg were freed. The early release of convicted Wehrmacht generals had not solved the problem. Once free, they had demanded that the imprisoned SS officers also be released as a condition of their cooperation.[22]

Gustav Heinemann, the pacifist minister of the interior, was the only member of Adenauer's Cabinet opposed to rearmament. Adenauer himself had always been a fervent rearmer. His dismissal on 6 October 1945 by the British as mayor of Cologne had followed a press interview the previous day where he had spoken openly about the need for the three Western zones to ally themselves to the West against the Russians.[23] Heinemann, according to Dieter Possa, then his personal assistant, believed that German rearmament could only be prevented by campaigning outside Germany against releasing the Landsberg criminals.[24] Possa states that Heinemann realized he was fighting a lost cause when he discovered that even senior American and British military officers were lobbying their governments for the releases. When

Adenauer overruled his objections in September 1950, Heinemann resigned, and the German Cabinet agreed to German rearmament.

But for practical purposes, the German government's decision amounted to little more than the vetting and selection of some key officials and the slow development of plans for the infrastructure of the new military organization. Plans for recruitment were still severely hindered by the German military's demand that Landsberg be completely emptied. It was only in April 1953, when Adenauer visited Washington, that the obstacle was removed. Adenauer admits in his memoirs that he frankly told Eisenhower that German rearmament was prevented by this 'psychological problem. . . It would, however, put obstacles in the way of future recruitment if people against whom no war crimes have been proved continued to be held in gaol'.[25] Within weeks of Adenauer's return to Germany, the two governments announced the establishment of a joint parole board to reconsider again all the cases which had already been re-reviewed. It would replace the permanent American review board which had been working since the Simpson Committee reported. One hundred and forty convicted men had already been released before the completion of their sentence.

The announcement of the establishment of 'The Interim Mixed Parole and Clemency Board' was final proof, most German newspapers and politicians claimed, that even the Americans admitted that those convicted had from the outset been innocent men.[25] To the surprise of Damon Gunn of the JAG, the German government was quickly disillusioned. Their appointees to the Board reported that the Americans were rejecting their argument that all 160 remaining prisoners should be released because they were not criminals. The American members had tried to explain that parole could only be granted with conditions attached. The Germans replied that conditions cannot be placed on the release of innocent men.

The stalemate seems to have been resolved on 11 May 1954. According to the records, just after ten o'clock that morning, Steere from McCloy's office rang General Ferenbaugh at Army Command Headquarters (USAREUR). In a friendly manner Steere wanted to know what was happening at the Parole Board. Progress did not seem fast enough. Ferenbaugh agreed: 'I am not sure whether we are accomplishing our mission or ultimate objective, in shaking these people out as fast as we can in order to create as much as, I guess, goodwill with our erstwhile or future Allies . . . they [the Parole Board] have got one hundred and sixty more to go and these are the tough ones.' Ferenbaugh told Steere that the only solution was for Steere to have a quiet word with the American representative, Judge Shaddock.[27]

9. *Antagonists*
(top) General Lucius Clay, Deputy Military Governor of the American Zone, with his Russian counterpart, General Sokolovsky. Clay fiercely resisted criticisms of the American war crime trials and of the denazification programme by German churchmen, led by Bishop Wurm *(right)*.

10. *The Governments of Occupation*
(top) General Clay with Marshal of the RAF Sir Sholto Douglas, Military Governor of the British Zone. (below) Douglas' deputy, General Brian Robertson, with Clay's successor, John McCloy. Douglas and Robertson did not share Clay's committment to prosecute war crimes and to denazification, and by the time McCloy took over Washington had called a halt to denazification.

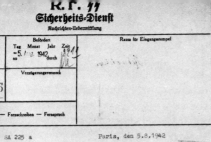

11. *The deportation of the French Jews*
One of the regular messages from Heinrichson to
Adolf Eichmann reporting the shipment of a
trainload of French Jews to Auschwitz. Part of
the evidence which, thirty-eight years later,
secured the conviction of Heinrichsen (*above right*),
his commander, Kurt Lischka, and Herbert
Hagen (*right*). The official who negotiated with
the French to ensure that the three got cooperation was Ernst Achenbach (*below*) — until
his retirement prominent in West German
politics.

12. *The New Germany — and the Old*
(*top*) Konrad Audenauer, first Chancellor of West Germany, with his State Secretary, Hans Globke. Globke had, before the war, drafted the Nuremberg Race Laws, his appointment symbolised the fact that a 'brown past' was no handicap in Audenauer's Germany. (*centre*) The I.G. Farben managing board in 1937. Four of the men were convicted of war crimes; second from the right is Hermann Abs (a member of the Supervisory, but not the Managing, Board), representing the Deutsche Bank, who was not prosecuted and today heads the bank which he rebuilt after the war. He is shown (*bottom*) with Franz Ulrich his war-time assistant and former SS member who now is the Bank's President.

Amongst those still imprisoned was Andreas Shilling, a former SS corporal at Mauthausen. At his trial there had been ample eyewitness evidence of how he had injected inmates in the camp hospital with motor oil. Then he sat back and watched with pleasure as his victim suffered a slow and agonizing death.[28]

Another inmate was Horst Dittrich, a self-confessed member of 'Kommando 99' at Buchenwald. His specific duty, for which he was rewarded with extra rations, was to shoot Russian POWs as they stood against the wall to be measured during the phoney medical examination. He confessed to having shot at least thirty-eight Russians, but at least 3,000 had died. He was not compelled to do the job. Dittrich's predecessor had asked to be moved from the job after one day and, without any trouble, had been redeployed.

These were just two of what Ferenbaugh called 'the tough ones', yet they were amongst the first to be released.[29]

Progress apparently improved after Steere's phone call. By August 1955 fifteen months later, only forty-one men remained at Landsberg. One of those was Sepp Dietrich, Peiper's commander. The JAG report on his morale application reads:

> Former Waffen-SS General, Nazi Party number from 1928 . . . an unscrupulous and aggressive opportunist . . . one of Hitler's most trusted adherents . . . the executioner who summarily exterminated the suspected leaders of the 20 July plot against Hitler . . . character of Dietrich not changed during incarceration . . . tried to smuggle political articles against the German Federal Republic out of prison just before the 1953 elections . . . third parole application should be rejected.[30]

Sepp Dietrich left Landsberg a week later. Jochen Peiper was released before Christmas 1956, among the last to leave the prison where Hitler had written *Mein Kampf* thirty-three years earlier.

Rehabilitation for those who had committed murder was swift and automatic. Dr Herte Oberhauser had been convicted and sentenced to twenty years imprisonment at Nuremberg for her role in conducting medical experiments on women inmates at Ravensbrück concentration camp. According to Professor Keith Mant, the British pathologist who investigated German medical experiments in concentration camps: 'Oberhauser can be described as little better than a sadist. She actually volunteered to work in Ravensbrück.' Inmates selected by her were infected with either tetanus or gangrene. She removed limbs and vital organs, and in the post-operative period rubbed ground glass or sawdust into the open wounds. Deliberately she allowed infections and diseases to spread on previously healthy women, to search for cures which might be used on German soldiers. An estimated one thousand women died from the Ravensbrück experiments. Despite her crimes, Oberhauser's sentence was reduced by McCloy and she was released in 1952. Six years later she was discovered working as a family doctor at Stocksee, in Schleswig-Holstein. The state's chamber of doctors, well aware that she had voluntarily gone to Ravensbrück, had treated her as a returning prisoner of war and given her a cash grant, an interest-free loan, and help to build up a practice.[31]

For Oberhauser, as for all the other criminals, whether convicted or not, and for most Germans, the past had been buried. It was the *Schlusstrich*, the final end.

18

'IF YOU'RE CONCERNED
ABOUT MORALITY,
GO TO CHURCH'

It was the government of Konrad Adenauer which ensured that, as the new decade of the 1950s opened, those citizens of the new Federal Republic who had 'a brown past' could not only sleep easily in their beds, but could rise in the morning to a future in which their influence and power would be restored. The men who had dedicated themselves to making sure that the wheels of National Socialism turned smoothly and profitably would not be denied the chance to do the same for the new political dispensation. The witch-hunt was nearly over, the hunters discomfited. It might still be necessary to throw them a morsel or two, but they could be restricted to that: the men of substance need not be afraid that they would be sacrificed. For they understood one another, they had kept their foothold on power, and now the time had come to climb back.

No one was more instrumental in ensuring that that reascent was smooth and painless than Dr Hans Maria Globke, state secretary in Adenauer's own office. Born in 1898 in Düsseldorf, Globke gained a doctorate of law and became a civil servant in the Prussian Ministry of the Interior. Whereas until 1933 his had been an unspectacular but steady career, his fortunes improved when the Nazis removed both Jews and socialists from the civil service. For those who remained, and were considered by the Nazis to be trustworthy, the rewards were considerable. Vacated posts had to be filled and Globke was among those favoured with rapid promotion.

His first major contribution to the Nazi cause was to draft the Nuremberg Race Laws, later described by Adolf Eichmann as 'basic for the Final Solution of the Jewish people'. Globke, on Bormann's orders, drafted a law which placed severely oppressive restrictions on all Jews living in the Reich. Half a million Germans suddenly found themselves the victims of a series of unique discriminatory regulations, governing their lives and profession. Even Jews married to non-Jews and the children of both so-called first- and second-degree mixed marriages, were forced to divorce, separate from their parents, and face confiscation of their property and dismissal from their work.

But administering an apartheid policy among people who usually did not appear physically different clearly had its problems. To overcome these, Bormann suggested that each of the half million should have the word 'Jew' added to their official names for easy identification. Globke's suggestion, which was accepted, was that instead of crudely adding 'Jew', their names should include 'Israel' or 'Sara'. It was a cosmetic touch, but Globke's defenders were to quote it after the war as proof of his attempt to mitigate the worst aspects of the law.

Delighted by his work, Dr Wilhelm Frick, the minister of the interior, praised Globke to Rudolf Hess. 'Dr Globke,' he wrote, 'is undoubtedly one of the most qualified and gifted officials in my Ministry.' The same laws were later used in Austria, Czechoslovakia and throughout Europe as the preliminaries to the Final Solution. Deeply involved in many of the discussions for the initial identification of the occupied countries' Jews, prior to their deportation, was the state secretary at the Interior Ministry, Wilhelm Stuckart. Assisting and often travelling with him was Globke. Both knew the fate of those deported once they arrived at Auschwitz, Sobibor or Treblinka.

Globke avoided prosecution after the war quite easily. Blaming everything either on the dead or the more incriminated, he was released in early 1946 and recommended to Adenauer in 1948 as the man who could best advise the relatively inexperienced former mayor of Cologne on the most suitable candidates for senior appointments to the new national civil service.

Globke's recommendations, which Adenauer accepted, reflected his own past. The new state secretary at the Ministry for German Affairs was Franz Thedieck, who in June 1933 had betrayed a group of left-wing opponents of Nazism to the Gestapo.[1] The state secretary of the Finance Ministry was Alfred Hartmann, who in 1942–3 supervised the confiscation of Jewish property in Globke's own ministry. Dr Günther Bergmann was appointed state secretary of the Ministry of Transport. During the war Bergmann had, as a government official, supervised the plunder of Serbia. The state secretary in the Ministry of Economics was Ludger Westerick, member of the Ohlendorf-Erhard *Arbeitskreis für Aussenwirtschaftsfragen*. As manager of Germany's wartime aluminium industry, Westerick employed a workforce which was eighty per cent slave labour. Rudolf Senteck was the departmental chief of the Ministry of Refugees. During the war as a senior SS officer, he had served in the RUSHA, the Race and Resettlement Main Office responsible for aryanizing Germany.

The official responsible for Foreign Affairs was Herbert Blankenhorn. Blankenhorn's career and attitudes were neither spectacular nor special, but just typical of most officials in the German foreign service. But, unlike other German civil servants, both his career and, more importantly his attitudes, are well chronicled because between 1935 and 1939 he served as second secretary in the German embassy in Washington.

On 20 April 1945, Stettinius, the American Secretary of State, sent Robert Murphy a secret and personal telegram warning him to beware of Blankenhorn:

> While in Washington, Blankenhorn is known to have been active and aggressive as a propagandist working through mainly social contacts, for the Nazi party and Hitler. Racialism was one of his favourite subjects. While professing great sympathy for the United States, he was yet an ardent and convinced member of the Nazi party and was also a member of the SS. . . Department believes . . . he is not to be trusted.[2]

Stettinius had sent the warning after receiving a report from Murphy on an OSS interrogation of Blankenhorn. The interrogator had summarily concluded that Blankenhorn 'was truly and actually strongly anti-Nazi' and 'was deeply involved in the July putsch to overthrow the Nazi regime.' According to the OSS, in May 1945 he was prepared to serve in any future German government so long as it was 'not a tool of the Allies'. Three weeks after Stettinius' cable, Grew sent another warning to Murphy against trusting Blankenhorn.[3]

Yet, until 1950, Blankenhorn was Adenauer's personal assistant and then he became head of the foreign affairs section in Adenauer's office. Adenauer had wanted to appoint Abs as Germany's first foreign minister, but bowed to a French veto.[4] The full effect of the Globke/Adenauer appointments might have been mitigated had a series of Anglo-American proposals for democratizing the civil service been implemented. The reforms presented by the Allies to the Consultative Assembly in 1948 were aimed at breaking both the dominating position of lawyers and the lifelong security of employment which civil servants enjoyed. Civil servants had become a class rather than just a profession, transferring their positions to their sons as if it was an inheritance. Conservative, unresponsive and intolerant towards minority views, they had also enjoyed the privilege of being able to retain their position in government service while simultaneously acting as members of a parliament or local government. It was a fundamental breach of the hallowed separation of powers, particularly offensive to American constitutional principles.[5]

German politicians in the Assembly, both socialist and conservative, united to oppose the Allied reforms. Many were themselves civil servants and had an interest in preserving both the traditions and the duopoly. Too embarrassed to oppose the proposals in principle, the Assembly deliberately procrastinated in their discussions, hoping that the occupation would end without them making a final decision. Infuriated, Clay summarily used his military powers in February 1949, and imposed the reforms.[6]

Within weeks of the handover of power, the new German Parliament reversed the Allied laws and adopted the 1937 civil service regulations in their entirety, with just the references to the Führer and Reich sensibly omitted. On 1 April 1951, the Parliament went one stage further. Globke, in cooperation with the newly appointed state secretaries, masterminded a vital change to the new constitution. Under Articles 131 and 132, those former civil servants who had been expressly removed by the Allies for their Nazi activities during the Third Reich were guaranteed the return of their positions, or even higher ones, if they had been due for promotion. Young, newly recruited civil servants were suddenly swamped by the old guard. Not only were their hopes of rapid promotion summarily terminated, but any chance of them having a liberalizing influence was mercilessly squashed.

Alarmed by the return of the Nazis, the Socialists in the Bundestag voted for an immediate investigation, pinpointing Blankenhorn's activities in the Foreign Affairs Department. The investigating committee reported that no less than 184 former party members had returned to the Department – just under fifty per cent of the total staff. Of these, 153 had previously worked in the old Foreign Ministry under Joachim von Ribbentrop, who had been executed after the Nuremberg trial. The Bundestag demanded that fifty per cent of the newly returned officials be compulsorily retired, but according to a senior present-day Foreign Office official who was one of those disappointed new recruits: 'Most of them were just shuffled around to take them out of the limelight.'[7] Within ten years many of them had re-emerged.

In the early Sixties, more than sixty West German ambassadors and Foreign Officials were former Nazi party members who, working with Rademacher, had helped organize the Final Solution. Graf von Mirbach had been involved in the operation to prevent the 5,000 Jewish children reaching Istanbul. Franz Krapf, a former SS officer, was appointed head of the new Eastern Department. Under Krapf was Hans Schirmer, a former SS officer working in Croatia. Hans Albers, formerly attached by Ribbentrop to Hans Frank in Warsaw, became ambassador in Nicaragua. Georg Vogel, another former SS officer, was German ambassador in Venezuela.

Similar, but less publicized, appointments were made in most of the other ministries, particularly the ministries of Refugees, Labour and Finance. But Adenauer's more public appointments could not be protected forever, despite some brave attempts. Theodor Oberländer, the minister of refugees, had been a senior officer in the SA, had participated in Hitler's 1923 putsch, and had been directly involved in Hitler's plans for absorbing Eastern Europe. As minister, he appointed officials who had been committed Nazis and stormtroopers, some of whom he had met on service in Eastern Europe. Few Germans working in Eastern Europe for the Nazi government had been unaware of the worst Nazi crimes. Defending his appointment, Adenauer told the Bundestag: 'It may well be that Minister Oberländer was brown, even dark brown, if you will. But he never did anything which was dishonourable, a misdemeanour or a crime.'[8] All the same, Oberländer was forced to resign.

For a time, Adenauer also publicly defended his appointment of Karl Vialon as an economic adviser and later state secretary at the Ministry for Economic Cooperation. During the war, Vialon was head of the Reich Finance Department in Riga, one of the most notorious centres for the extermination of Jews. Captured documents reveal that he was responsible for collecting the property of the murdered Jews and dispatching it by the trainload to Germany.

Management of the economy was handed over by Adenauer to the surviving members of the wartime *Kleine Arbeitskreis*, and the *Arbeitskreis für Aussenwirtschaftsfragen* – Erhard, Westerick, Blessing and Abs. The minister of finance was Fritz Schäffer, appointed by the Americans as minister president of Bavaria in 1945, but afterwards removed as a Nazi sympathizer.

The management and ownership of industry naturally belonged to the same industrialists who survived the Third Reich. Flick had been compelled to sell his coalmines; on Abs' advice and with his help, he bought Daimler-Benz and many other companies, and became Germany's wealthiest man. Not far behind was Alfried Krupp, determined to reassert himself as emperor of the Ruhr. The IG Farben directors involved in the company's Auschwitz project were snapped up on their release and appointed to the boards of the successor companies. Fritz Ter Meer became chairman of the board of Bayer Chemicals; Bütefisch became a member of the board of the government-owned Ruhrchemie AG; Walter Dürrfeld, who had managed the Monowitz concentration camp, became a member of the *Vorstand* of Scholven-Chemie and a director of many other companies; Otto Ambros was soon appointed onto several company boards and became an adviser to the government. The rewards went not only to the famous, but also to those who had faithfully served the Third Reich or were dependents of those who had. Generous pensions were paid out to every SS man or his widow, because they had been state employees. The widow of Reinhardt Heydrich got a pension, as did Field-Marshal Erhard Milch, convicted of war crimes by the Americans at Nuremberg. Notorious SS officers quite openly claimed, and received, compensation for the loss of personal effects which had been confiscated by the Allies for distribution to liberated slave workers.[9]

The less fortunate were those who had not served the Third Reich. A widow of seventy-six, whose husband had been liquidated in the Riga ghetto, was refused a pension because she could not prove that her husband had died there. A German worker's widow, whose husband had been executed in 1945 for collecting money for the widow of an executed communist, was denied a pension because his collection was for a supporter of a tyrannical regime. A claim for invalid insurance by a former concentration camp inmate was refused because 'the camp's low-fat diet must have been good for his health.' The SS officers who had run the camp, however, would have had no problems in getting a pension. They were former state employees.[10]

Adenauer's protection and even promotion of Nazis was at best pragmatic and politically opportunist. At worst, he was repeating the compromise which he had made with the Nazis in 1934. Adenauer had been dismissed as mayor of Cologne very soon after the Nazi election victory in 5 March 1933. His bank account and pension was blocked and he was forbidden to leave the Cologne area. He only avoided arrest by escaping just before the police arrived at his home. On 10 August 1934, after a period of bitter discomfort in hiding, he wrote to Frick, the Nazi minister of the interior, a long letter asking that the restrictions on himself and his family (he had seven children) be lifted because he had always been a faithful supporter of Germany against the Left. About his attitude towards the Nazis he wrote:

I have always treated the NSDAP properly although I acted contrary to the Ministerial instructions and the policies of the Centre Party in Cologne. For many years I also allowed the NSDAP to meet in the city sports ground although I was acting contrary to instructions from the Prussian Ministry of the Interior. Moreover I allowed the Party at those meetings to use the pulleys to hoist up the swastika. . . I always said that in my opinion it was wrong to exclude such a major party as the NSDAP from government.[11]

His plea was successful, and for the next ten years he led a peaceful and blameless life. It was brusquely shattered in the wake of the attempt on Hitler's life. Like many others uninvolved in the plot, Adenauer was caught in the Gestapo's massive dragnet. He was only saved from transportation to Buchenwald and certain death by help at the last moment from a communist fellow prisoner.

Adenauer's letter to Frick is either that of a desperate man prepared to compromise for the sake of comfort, or must be taken at face value. In 1949, Adenauer faced a similar political dilemma. Despite his tiny Parliamentary majority, he was determined to prevent the socialists having any influence on the future of Germany. Needing political allies, he turned to the only other cohesive political force in Germany, the Nazis. It naturally followed that he would not encourage the minister of justice to press the Länder governments and the police to investigate and prosecute Germans for crimes committed during the Third Reich. The reverse made better political sense.

The size of the problem facing Germany in 1950 was indisputable. Most informed sources agree that there were at least 150,000 Germans and people of other nationalities directly involved in the Nazi murders; it was probably 250,000. Of these, according to West German government statistics, 1,814 were convicted by the Americans at Dachau and Nuremberg, 1,085 by the British, 2,107 by the French, 75 by the Belgians, 10 by Denmark, 197 by the Netherlands, 92 by Norway and 5,452 by Poland. An estimated 25,000 were convicted by Yugoslavia, Russia and the East Germans. Together, the total is just over 35,000 convictions.

Traditionally, West German officials and politicians either proffer a series of explanations for the failure to continue investigations and prosecutions, or insist that the Republic has, with a few exceptions, actually prosecuted most of the surviving Nazis. Adalbert Rückerl, the present director of the Ludwigsburg Central Office for Investigation into Nazi Crimes and the government's expert on the subject, does both. In his official publication, *'The Investigation of Nazi War Crimes 1945 – 1978*,[12] Rückerl insists that few Nazi war criminals have escaped justice and then devotes one hundred pages to explaining why the Federal Republic is not responsible for the few who did.

The official statistics, quoted by successive ministers of justice in West Germany, show that since 1945 German courts have 'convicted over 6,000 Nazi war criminals'. Seventy per cent of those convictions resulted from the 5,228 indictments brought before the German courts in the years of Allied occupation between 1945 and 1949. The figure of 6,000 convictions is often quoted as evidence of German efforts to prosecute war criminals who remain at large, but it becomes less impressive when it is analysed. Even in the case of the 5,228 indictments which were brought by 1949, only one hundred were for serious crimes involving manslaughter or murder, and only fifteen involved murders in concentration camps.[13]

According to Rückerl, there are many reasons for the failure to do more in the immediate postwar years. Germany was devastated, and its judiciary and police disorganized not only by the aftermath of war but also by the division of the country into sovereign zones, the German public's dislike of 'victor's vengeance', and the public's equal revulsion against the iniquities of the denazification tribunals. Two further practical difficulties are advanced. Rückerl claims that the jurisdiction of the German courts was limited by the Allies and that German prosecutors and police were denied vital documentary evidence held by the Allies.

These are puzzling excuses because they ignore more than they explain. Considering that one million Germans had been murdered and countless others were victims of brutal attacks and torture, there would seem to have been more than enough crime for the German authorities to investigate which was within the German courts' jurisdiction, even if, until 1949, the courts only had jurisdiction over crimes against German nationals and stateless people, not against Allied nationals.

Rückerl and others have always complained, with justification, that after the war the Allies moved the vital documents either to America or beyond the reach of German prosecutors. They allege that after 1949 they were also unable to get access to the enormous quantities of documents seized by the East European countries. Today, they still complain that the Berlin Document Centre is under American and not German control. In all three cases, the reality is that the West German government has been reluctant to ask for documents whose absence provides a convenient excuse for the failure to prosecute. The present American director of the Berlin Document Centre, Daniel Simon, has repeatedly and publicly told the Bonn government that the Americans are prepared to hand over the Centre to Bonn. It is Bonn, anxious because it might be unable to deny access to the documents to antagonists, which has consistently refused the American offers.

The East European archives were always available except, briefly, at the height of the Cold War. Documents seized by the Americans have always been available on request. In both cases, West German prosecutors had to ask first, and until the late Fifties, on government orders, they deliberately did not do so.[14] That attitude is hardly surprising considering that the government, judiciary, civil service and police numbered many former Nazis among their senior staff.

Robert Kempner, the former prosecutor at Nuremberg, claims that when the subsequent trials ended in Nuremberg, the prosecution handed over most of their evidence to the representatives of the German Länder: 'Thousands of files were handed over. Documents with the signatures of the criminals; complete proof in many cases showing very clearly the responsibility of those criminals, their orders for murder, giving green lights to other agencies to murder. For example from the Foreign Office to an agency for deportation.' Asked what the German authorities did once they were given those files, Kempner replied: 'They put them in good order, in their filing cabinets.'[15]

Clay so distrusted the postwar German authorities that in December 1948 he ordered the release of thirty Germans involved in sending Russian POWs to extermination camps, rather than hand them over for an eventual trial in a German court.[16] He feared that the result would be embarrassing for the Allies. His decision followed the acquittal by Hamburg judges of the president of a naval court martial who had ordered the execution of three deserters some time after the surrender. The court had justified its decision by claiming that judges had to protect their freedom to act under law.

Anxious to defend both themselves and every other state official, all judges then asserted that, with few exceptions, acts committed on behalf of the Third Reich were legal. They accepted the defence of superior orders, despite the denial of that defence by Germany's own military laws, and demanded that the prosecution should prove that an accused voluntarily wanted to commit a murder and was not obeying orders. The inevitable result was that the few who were accused only faced charges of second-degree murder, or manslaughter, where the sentence, if convicted, could be minimal.

After 1949, there was a dramatic fall in prosecutions. Just over 500 indictments were laid in 1950, but five years later there were only twenty-one. Rückerl lists three main reasons for that sudden loss of interest: the continuing lack of evidence, ignorance on the part of the prosecutors about the background to the cases, and the prosecutors' total involvement in what he calls 'the investigation of everyday crime'.

He claims that the premature releases of criminals formerly condemned to death, but reprieved, 'created the impression in the public that the goal of "coming to terms with the past" had now been reached. The prevailing opinion among wide sections of the population was that those responsible for Nazi crimes and who had either not survived the war or had succeeded in disappearing abroad, had by then been tracked down and prosecuted by the Allies, the German courts or the denazification tribunals.'[17] Rückerl further claims that when German were denounced to the police by victims or their relatives, the investigating officer was so baffled by the Nazis' organizational set-up and chain of command that he stopped the investigations due to lack of evidence. 'Too often, too many of the accusations appeared to be so incredible that it was difficult for any right-minded person to believe that such things could possibly have happened.'[18]

It is a bizarre explanation, which ignores not only the background of the police and prosecutors who found the problems so great, but also the policies of the government. It was political pressure which demanded first the reprieve and then the releases of the criminals. For Rückerl to use 'public opinion' as the scapegoat is convenient but ignores the fact that it was the German politicians, and to some extent the Allies, who created that attitude. Instead of proclaiming how much there was still to be done, politicians and officials deliberately covered up how little had been achieved.

The Ministry of Justice was in the vanguard of that campaign. Dr Arthur Bülow, who became state secretary in the ministry after being first recruited by the British in 1945, says he cannot remember Dehler or other officials ever discussing the need to prosecute Germans for their crimes against other Germans.[19] Hermann Massen, Dehler's personal assistant, says he cannot remember Dehler ever initiating discussion about the need to prosecute Nazis at all. The problem was only discussed when the minister had to react to criticisms.[20]

The ministry's lack of initiative is today explained as the inevitable result of Germany's federal constitution.[21] Decisions on prosecutions, it is said, are exclusively reserved to the sovereign Länder governments, and the federal minister cannot interfere. Significantly, that constitutional inhibition did not prevent the creation in the Ministry of Justice of a secret department, later moved to the Ministry of Foreign Affairs, to care for the needs of German war criminals either serving sentences or facing prosecution for their crimes in other countries. Called the *Rechtschutzstelle*, it had an annual budget of up to three million deutschmarks to send officials and lawyers, usually to Eastern Europe, to help nationals prepare their defence or appeals, including the provision of documents.

In sharp contrast, those same officials, who occasionally also gave unofficial help to defendants charged in West German courts, were expressly forbidden by government order from asking the East European countries for evidence which could be used by the prosecution in West German trials. The order was based on the Hallstein Doctrine – a policy which excluded cooperation with countries which had accepted the permanent division of Germany.

But the standard public explanation by West German officials for the failure to ask for the documentary evidence in the Fifties is not the Hallstein Doctrine and the secret departmental memoranda forbidding requests for evidence. Instead the blame is firmly placed on the Allies for continuing to limit the jurisdiction of the German courts. The argument is that, until 1955, the courts' jurisdiction was so limited that it was pointless to even try to start proceedings. Rückerl goes even further and claims that the Allied-imposed 1955 Transition Agreement, under which Germany became a fully sovereign country, actually perpetuated the limitation on the German courts. Article 3(3)(b), he claims, 'had an immense psychological effect on Nazi trials held after 1955 in German courts.'[22] He places extraordinary emphasis on what is to all appearances a relatively innocuous provision.

Article 3 of the Transition Agreement gives German courts full and unrestricted jurisdiction over all criminal acts committed anywhere: '. . . unless investigation of the alleged offence was finally completed by the prosecuting authorities of the Power or Powers concerned, or unless such offence has been committed in the performance of duties or services for the Occupation authorities.'[23] Rückerl explains the 'immense psychological effect' as follows: 'High-ranking Nazi officials who had been investigated by the British, French or American prosecuting authorities for certain offences, but whose cases were dismissed due to lack of evidence, could not be brought to trial today even if one adduced proof of their guilt.' Because no one can be tried twice for the same offence, Rückerl claims that convicted SS men who were later pardoned by the Americans 'could no longer be brought to trial.'[24]

In fact there are probably less than 200 previously convicted SS men involved. Moreover, Rückerl misreads the context of Article 3. It is not only to protect the accused from a second trial, but to protect Germans who had helped and collaborated with the Allies after 1945 from persecution, prosecution and discrimination by the new German government. The Article did not prevent convicted SS men being retried on other offences; for example, after his premature release, Sepp Dietrich was re-arrested by German police and tried for directing 'The Night of the Long Knives', the mass murder in 1934 of Ernst Roehm and senior officers in the SA. Convicted in 1957, he was sentenced to eighteen months imprisonment.

Finally, Article 3 would not prevent the German prosecutors charging the remaining ninety-five per cent of SS men who were not tried by the Allies. The choice of former senior SS officers liable to prosecution was enormous, yet to take one example, August Heissmeyer, an SS general and close associate of Himmler, was only prosecuted for giving a false name after the war. He spent the rest of his postwar years as the West German director of a Coca-Cola subsidiary.[25]

The German prosecutors could still, if they did not feel themselves barred by the Statute of Limitations, charge Reinhard Höhn for his involvement in the Final Solution. A dedicated Nazi, Höhn was a Brigadeführer in the SS and a close collaborator with Wilhelm Stuckart in the Ministry of the Interior.

As a lawyer, Höhn advised both Stuckart and the SD on the implementation of Nazi laws in occupied Europe. As late as 1 October 1944,
Höhn wrote: 'Taking an oath to the Führer not only obliges him to allegiance and obedience to the national socialist idea as long as the Führer
lives, but also beyond his death and, therefore, to the new leader rising
out of the movement.' Today, Höhn is the director of the 'Academy for
Economic Leaders' in Bad Harzburg, a well-known institute used by
German industry, and for a time even by the German government, as a
centre for management studies.[26]

The universal complacency was disturbed by accident in 1956. Bernhard
Schweder, a former SS officer and German chief of police in Memel, had
after the war been employed under a false name to run a refugee camp in
Germany. When his real identity was discovered, he was dismissed.
Press reports of his court action for reinstatement were read by a former
victim in the Memel area who recognized Schweder as a member of an
Einsatzgruppe responsible for mass executions. Schweder's arrest and the
subsequent '*Ulm Einsatzgruppen*' trial of ten other members of the
murder group provoked, for the first time since 1945, some uncomfortable questions throughout the world about the failure to prosecute
Nazi war criminals. According to Rückerl, the trial 'revealed beyond
doubt that many of the gravest crimes, notably in the East, had not yet
been punished at all.' Unfairly, all the blame was heaped upon the West
German government.

Anxious to rebut international criticism, the eleven state ministers of
justice decided at their bi-annual meeting in October 1958 in Bad
Harzburg to create a centralized federal investigation agency for Nazi
war crimes. It was the first attempt by the West Germans to systematically search for the criminals, who had until then been left to the individual state prosecutors. The existence of the Central Office for the
Investigation of War Crimes in Ludwigsburg is now used as proof of
Bonn's determination to prosecute the criminals. Yet there are several
points to be made which cast doubt on some of the motives of the
ministers in creating it.

Chairing the meeting was Fritz Schäffer, the federal minister of
justice, who had been dismissed by the Americans for his Nazi sympathies. His ministry appointed Erwin Schüle as Ludwigsburg's first
director. In 1966, the Russians revealed that Schüle was a former
member of the Nazi party and the SA. Moscow also alleged that Schüle
had been a member of a special army group based around Leningrad
which had directed the 'scorched earth' operations. Schüle admitted his
party membership, but denied the allegations about his wartime service.
At that time, he insisted soon after the disclosures, he had been posted

somewhere else in Russia. He nevertheless resigned.

Schüle's successor, Adalbert Rückerl, is a passionate defender of his predecessor: 'You should not assume that every member of the NSDAP was a Nazi. Herr Schüle was never a Nazi. He was only a formal member of the NSDAP.'[27] Herr Rückerl felt that to question Schüle's suitability for the post showed, 'a lack of objectivity'.

Until 1964, Ludwigsburg never employed more than ten lawyers on its staff. Their work, despite the institution's name, was not to actually leave Ludwigsburg and 'investigate' crimes, but rather to research the documentary evidence. Once enough documents had been discovered to prove that a crime had been committed, the case was handed over to a state prosecutor in the area where one of the possible defendants lived. Invariably the file was thin, and a lot more work was needed before the prosecutor knew whether there was the possibility of a charge.

Under its charter, Ludwigsburg was restricted by the politicians to investigating crimes committed outside Germany. It could not investigate Nazi crimes committed inside Germany itself, including those committed inside German concentration camps against German and other nationalities. Superficially, it might have seemed a constitutional necessity that the power of the state prosecutors should be protected. In fact, it nearly sabotaged the very purpose of the new agency. Under the self-imposed rules of the Foreign Ministry and the Hallstein Doctrine, the Ludwigsburg investigators were forbidden to approach the East European countries for information and help. They were effectively prevented from getting access to their most important source of evidence and eyewitnesses.

Nevertheless, there were so many uninvestigated crimes and so much evidence that, in its first year, Ludwigsburg had started investigations into 400 separate crimes. Systematically, the handful of investigators sought out the evidence available in the West on all the known concentration camps in Eastern Europe.

Kurt Schwedersky, an examining judge in Düsseldorf, got the benefit of Ludwigsburg's work on the Treblinka extermination camp. It was, he remembers, a very thin file. Besides a short description of the camp and an estimate that 700,000 (the Poles claim it was 900,000) had been gassed on its forty-acre site within seventeen months, it told Schwedersky that Kurt Franz, one of the camp's former commandants, was alive and well and living in an apartment near Düsseldorf. His exact address was enclosed.

The file, little different from many others sent out over the following years, raised some controversial issues. Franz's whereabouts had never been a secret and legally there was no reason for not having prosecuted him in the previous ten years. Moreover, while Ludwigsburg suggested just prosecuting Franz, over the next four years Schwedersky single-handedly found another thirteen former SS officers living in West Germany, who had worked in the same camp. Many of them, he says, were quite easy to find.[28]

The files of the Central Military Pensions Office provided not only the addresses of former SS officers receiving pensions, but also details of their military service. Others were registered, under their own names, as refugees from the East Zone.

Asked why he had not looked for Franz and the others in the previous ten years, Schwedersky explained: 'Allied legal restrictions and the internal conditions in Germany prevented this kind of work. We were also greatly hindered by not getting any help or documents from Poland and other communist countries.'

Bonn's interpretation of the question of availability and access to Poland's vast archives is curious. Not only Rückerl, but also Hans-Jochen Vogel, the minister of justice, flatly blame the Polish government for refusing to hand over the documentary evidence. According to Vogel: 'Everyone was invited to give information, especially in the Sixties. Nobody was forbidden and nobody was hindered in giving any documents.' Asked why the West German authorities did not ask for the documents, Vogel replied: 'Well, it is very difficult to go around in the world and look for documents. I think it would have been in the interest of those people who had the documents, especially in territories occupied by German forces, to just deliver them to us. It wouldn't have made sense if we sent people round the world to look into archives.'[29]

Vogel's interpretation is not accepted in Poland. Czeslaw Pilichowski, the long-serving director of the Commission for the Investigation of Nazi Crimes in Poland, claims that the Poles were always willing to allow the West Germans access, although he admits there were problems in the early Fifties at the height of the Cold War.[30] Six million Poles were murdered by the Germans during the war – a population loss which has barely been replaced today. Pilichowski claims that his country suffered an inferiority complex for many years because of its failure to defeat the Germans. Faced with the devastation of the country and apparent German indifference to Polish losses and suffering, it was only in the mid-Fifties that he began to search for ways of forcing the German prosecutors to acknowledge that they were deliberately shunning the richest source of evidence.

In 1959, Pilichowski finally convinced Ludwigsburg to accept some documents surreptitiously delivered through the Polish military mission in Berlin. Fritz Bauer, Frankfurt's energetic prosecutor, pursued the breakthrough in Poland the following year while ostensibly on holiday. The Poles gave him enough information for his office to successfully prosecute in 1963 twenty former SS guards and officers who had worked at Auschwitz. Realizing that 1960 was also the first major Statute of Limitations barrier, after which all prosecutions other than for first-degree murder were barred, Pilichowski astutely exploited the tenuous link to West Germany and quickly and quietly supplied enough documents for charges to be listed against another 400 Germans. It was a desperate move to convince Bonn that the evidence was available for the asking.

Although Ludwigsburg accepted the documents from Poland its officials were conditioned to believe that prosecutions would end, as stipulated in the constitution, in 1965. At the time, charges for murder could not be made more than twenty years after the event. Suggestions by some that the constitution might be amended were roundly condemned. German lawyers and politicians were convinced that democracy could only be preserved if the constitution remained unamended. Changing a constitution was, they claimed, a Nazi practice. Any hopes that the Bundestag might reconsider its rigid attitude were seemingly scotched in March 1960. A socialist proposal to extend by four years time limit for the prosecution of murders committed before 1939 was decisively rejected, although the vast majority of the victims had been German citizens.

The event which disturbed Bonn's complacency was the kidnapping and trial in 1961 of Adolf Eichmann, the organizer of the Final Solution.

Isser Harel, the founder of Mossad, Israel's intelligence organization, had heard from Fritz Bauer that Eichmann was living in a Buenos Aires suburb. His military-style operation to seize Eichmann was unique in Israel's history. Contrary to popular belief, Israelis have done comparatively little to discover their people's murderers. Harel now claims that Eichmann was always the exception. During the Fifties, he says: 'Whenever I had a moment to spare, I told Ben Gurion that we had to find Eichmann.'[31] Harel admits however that until the Eichmann kidnap in 1960 Israel had 'very few successes' in getting war criminals: 'Until 1948 we were fighting to establish our country, and after that we were fighting to defend it.' During that time, a small number of Nazis were murdered by self-appointed freelance groups roaming Europe just seeking vengeance.[32] At most they killed a few dozen men.

In 1951, a Mossad officer was directed, as one of his many duties, to liaise with an official in the Foreign Ministry's research department about the proper filing of the information sent by sympathizers overseas. Harel describes it as little more than a 'letterbox' for information. A lot of it came from Israeli embassies and some from the maverick Nazihunter, Simon Wiesenthal. But Mossad had no orders to either act or not act on the information received. Invariably, whatever was received was just filed. The only operations deliberately mounted were those against Nazis who were working for Arab governments. 'We sent a few letter bombs,' says Harel somewhat mournfully, 'but we had very few successes.'

Israeli requests for extradition when Nazis were identified were rejected on the grounds that Israel was not a state when the crimes occurred. Requests for help to Interpol, the Paris-based international police force, were also rejected. Interpol members had decided that Nazi crimes were 'political' and therefore excluded under Interpol's charter. As no other government showed any interest in searching or trying Nazis, the Fifties had left those few Germans in exile secure in the knowledge that they were quite safe.

Even the Eichmann operation was only a fifty per cent success. A simultaneous operation to kidnap Josef Mengele, the infamous doctor at Auschwitz, failed. Further attempts to kidnap or assassinate Mengele cost, it is said, at least two lives. Harel denies any deaths.

His denials are not just a product of professional discretion. Politically, Israel was unwilling to infringe the sovereignty of South American countries whose votes it needed in the United Nations to defeat Arab motions of censure. In an attempt to act legally, Israel, according to folklore, formally asked the Paraguayan government for the extradition of Mengele to stand trial as a Nazi war criminal. President Stroessner, the country's dictator, allegedly replied: 'There is no war criminal Mengele in Paraguay. If you are referring to Josef Mengele, the President's friend, there are no grounds for extradition.'

In contrast to the remainder of the world, the revelations at the Eichmann trial had little immediate effect on the Ministry of Justice in Bonn. Ewald Bucher, minister of justice between 1963 and 1965, is quite categorical: 'I did nothing about improving the investigation of war crimes whilst I was minister. Everyone in the Ministry was sure that the trials would end after 1965.'[33] Bucher, who finally resigned over the issue, honestly admits that both he and, he believes, the public 'were not interested to continue the trials.'

Bucher believed that the German *Rechtstaat*, the state based on the rule of law, would be irreparably damaged by tampering with the constitution. Like Thomas Dehler, he felt that changing the constitution would be more damaging than leaving murderers unpunished. 'Morality has nothing to do with law. If you're concerned about morality, go to church.'

Against Bucher and those who were eager for the trials to end, stood a handful of prosecutors who, without Ludwigsburg's help, had suddenly begun to stage trials in German courts against former SS men who had committed murders in Sachsenhausen and Buchenwald, concentration camps located in Germany itself. When it was asked why it had taken so long to try the accused, there was no answer.

But there was another question. Some of the documentary evidence used at the Eichmann trial had been found among the records which Kempner and the American prosecutors had handed over to the German justice authorities in 1948. Why, some prosecutors asked, had the material not been used against others named in the same documents who were living in Germany? Surveying the postwar achievements of the Länder, the results seemed to be grotesquely inequal. In the Rhineland the Ministry of Justice had established no less than two offices, in Cologne and Dortmund, to investigate Nazi crimes. Other Länder barely kept one office properly staffed.

State prosecutors confided that their investigations, heavily dependent on the good will of the police who had to follow up information they provided, often faltered because replies to their requests arrived six months or even a year later, or not at all. Every prosecutor told the tale of his horror when he discovered that his request for information to the town's police chief had landed on the desk of a former Gestapo or SS officer.[34]

In Düsseldorf, the chief of the CID was Dr Bernard Wehner. During the Reich, Wehner was the police chief who investigated the plot on Hitler's life and led the SS investigation into the charges of murder against the commandant of Buchenwald, Standartenführer Koch. Clearly Wehner was a man trusted by the Nazis.

Requests to the police chief in Giessen were referred to Hans Hoffmann, previously convicted for killing 162 Jews in Poland. The CID chief in Kiel was Arno Besekow, a former SS captain in the SD and Gestapo agent in Magdeburg. In Hamburg, requests often went to Berthold Boldt, formerly in an SS police battalion in Lublin, Poland. Former SS Sturmbannführer and Berlin Gestapo agent Kurt Geissler was the CID chief in Cologne; while the former SS Hauptsturmführer Fritz Riedel, who had spent the war in Latvia, was the CID chief in Munich. Nearly every West German town's police force counted amongst its senior staff former SS or Gestapo officers involved in the atrocities in Eastern Europe.[35]

Prosecutors were not only denied help, but sometimes even typewriters and telephones, when they wanted to use police facilities. According to one prosecutor: 'I remember having dinner with one senior CID officer in Cologne who laughingly said to me: "I didn't know that people were shot without trial during the Third Reich." '

A handful of determined prosecutors also began analysing and comparing the sentences in those cases which they had finally squeezed through the sieve and brought to court. They were shocked by the results. Out of 309 murder cases tried between 1946 and 1965, the majority were sentenced to less than twelve years, while one third of those convicted were sentenced to five years imprisonment. Only eight out of sixty-eight members of the *Einsatzgruppen* tried, and forty-one out of 106 former SS concentration camp officers tried, were given life sentences.

Particularly galling for the prosecutor was the fate of Dr Otto Bradfisch, the former chief of *Einsatzgruppe 8*, who admitted to the murder of at least 15,000 people (the actual figure was much higher). Tried in Munich in 1961, Bradfisch was sentenced to ten years. Explaining his low sentence, the judge said that only Hitler, Heydrich and Himmler could be held fully responsible for the crimes. Bradfisch was found guilty only as an accomplice, since he had only passed on and obeyed the orders he received.[36]

The judge's opinion was not unusual. On the contrary, it followed the example of most of the decisions in West German courts. But the timing in the Bradfisch case was unfortunate for the German judges. For the previous five years, the East German-based 'Committee for German Unity' had been publicizing the Nazi background of the West German judiciary. Questions had been asked in the British House of Commons about the East German allegations in 1957 and 1958.[37] But the communist campaign had barely embarrassed either Bonn or the judges themselves.

In December 1959 a West German, Reinhard Strecker, had, with East German help, staged an exhibition in Karlsruhe, the site of the West German constitutional court. It exposed the names and backgrounds of judges and prosecutors who had been involved in the People's Courts and had demanded or passed death sentences for trivial offences. To win publicity for his campaign, Strecker privately prosecuted forty-three of those named for manslaughter. Again nothing had happened. But the Bradfisch decision in Munich forced the Ministry of Justice in Bonn to acknowledge the evidence. In June 1961, the Bundestag passed a law allowing judges and prosecutors 'who feel themselves morally implicated' by their activities in the Third Reich to volunteer for premature retirement on full pension. Yet by the end of the twelve month deadline, only 143 had 'volunteered to incriminate themselves'.[38]

According to East German and Czech records, sixteen of those who retired had been involved in no less than 931 death sentences awarded in special courts. Klaus Weiss, who voluntarily retired as court counsellor in Oldenburg, had, just on the evidence of his captured personal file, demanded 127 death sentences.[39]

Within weeks of the June 1962 deadline passing, the East Germans published the names of a further 791 judges and prosecutors in West Germany whose Nazi activities cast doubt on their qualifications for administering justice. For a time the West Germans resisted East German pressure. To counter East Berlin's publication of the 'Brown Book',[40] a documented catalogue of 2,300 known former Nazis then holding important positions in West Germany, the West Germans published their own list of Nazis serving in the East German government. Called *Ehemalige Nationalsozialisten in Pankows Diensten* ('Former Nazis Serving in Pankow'),[41] it was a sorry attempt to counter-attack. It proved that, at most, twelve low-ranking SS NCOs were employed in local government administration, and that 350 former Nazi party members, only a few of other than nominal rank, were employed in public institutes and industries. Hardly proof that former Nazis had in any way seriously influenced events in any sphere of East German politics, society or the economy.

East German claims that they removed the Nazis seemed to be justified. Their own methods of removal however, had often imitated those whom they were judging. In 1950 3,432 alleged Nazi criminals were processed through a series of twenty-minute show trials in Waldheim. It had solved the problem efficiently, but it was hardly an example for the West Germans.

Ewald Bucher never hid his distaste for the communists. Determined to resist pressure from his ideological enemies, he was equally determined to end the prosecutions after 8 May 1965. A dour, humourless Schwabian, Bucher, with the help of his officials, tried to prepare a watertight case for the finale. A fundamental part of his strategy was to deliver proof that West Germany had not only done as much as possible to convict the remaining criminals, but could be seen to have done its utmost.

On 20 November 1964, despite the Hallstein Doctrine, the Ministry sent letters to eighteen countries asking them to deliver any evidence of Nazi war crimes as soon as possible so that prosecutions could be started before the 8 May deadline. For Bucher and the Ministry officials the results were embarrassing. When researchers from Ludwigsburg searched through the archives in Warsaw in February 1965, according to Rückerl: 'The results confirmed the assumption that the Polish archives contained an enormous amount of evidence about crimes which had still not been prosecuted. Moreover, it reveal quite clearly that the government's plan to process all the material by 8 May was unrealistic.' Bucher was undeterred, however, and announced on 26 February that although some important crimes might remain unpunished, 'the great majority of crimes have by now been completely dealt with.'[42]

On 10 March, during the Bundestag debate on the continuation of prosecutions for another five years, Bucher went even further: 'Well over 80,000 Germans have already been convicted for both actual and alleged Nazi crimes.'[43] It still remains unclear how he reached that statistic. While he claimed that the Poles had convicted 17,000 Germans, the Poles themselves, who had generally staged very fair trials, claim to have convicted only 5,352 Germans.[44]

An official Ministry of Justice publication issued on 26 February 1965 claimed that West German prosecutors had started proceedings for Nazi crimes against an impressive 67,716 individuals.[45] But since Bucher claimed that, this far, only 6,115 had been convicted, the minister was asked to explain an embarrassing and obvious failure. The Ministry's publication was later suddenly withdrawn.

Shortly after quoting the figure of 80,000 convictions, Bucher unequivocally told the Bundestag: 'One can fairly conclude that the vast majority of crimes have been investigated and it is most unlikely [that the documents from Eastern Europe] will tell us anything we don't know already.'[46] The majority of the Bundestag members were unconvinced by his arguments and he lost the vote. He resigned soon afterwards.

The consequences of the vote were startling. Within four weeks, the staff at Ludwigsburg was increased to 121, including forty-eight lawyers – a five-fold increase. Investigations also increased, but convictions did not. The judges, again under suspicion, were now vetted by the government. In 1967 several hundred incriminated judges (the full number has never been disclosed) were forced to retire by Gustav Heinemann, the new Socialist minister of justice. But the judiciary, determined to protect themselves, had the final word. The Federal Supreme Court, fearful that the judges who had been forced to retire might themselves be prosecuted for murder, ruled on 20 May 1969 that an accessory to murder could only be convicted if there was proof that he shared the very same motives as the person who actually committed the murder. The judges and others would always insist that they were just applying and obeying the law.

In deliberately distorting a Parliamentary amendment to the Penal Code, the Court had effectively prevented any prosecutions of the *Schreibtischtäter* those who, like the judges, had sat behind desks and given the orders for murder. True to their historical tradition of interpreting the law to suit their political views, the Court further ruled that their decision was retrospectively effective back to 1945. With judicial slickness, they had also made 8 May 1960 the last date when prosecution of 'aiders and abetters' could have been started.[47]

Ludwigsburg immediately dropped its investigations into the survivors of Himmler's Reich Security Office (RSHA), which had run the Gestapo and SS. One prosecutor did not even bother to bring to court a case against former Reich officials who had ordered the execution of Polish intellectuals between September and December 1939. They had only 'aided and abetted' the murderers, and were not accomplices to the principals. Their decision was justified. Two participants at the 1941 Wannsee conference, where the decision to start the extermination phase of the Final Solution was taken, were acquitted soon afterwards. The two men were not, according to the judges, 'principals in the ensuing murders'.

Even those who had executed slave workers could not thereafter be convicted of murder. According to Rückerl: 'Many of the foreign slave workers were executed because they had broken rules or regulations [e.g. insulting or physically attacking German foremen or employers, indulging in illicit sexual intercourse with German women etc.] Those executions lacked the vital characteristics of murder [because there was, according to the court, no provable malicious intent] and could only be classed as manslaughter.'[48] Manslaughter could no longer be prosecuted because it was barred by the Statute of Limitations.

Despite the decision, there remained a large number of cases which could still be prosecuted, especially after the Bundestag voted in 1969 to continue prosecutions for another ten years. Yet the results, despite the unlimited funds available, were at best disappointing.

Pilichowski has no doubt that Ludwigsburg is to blame. He claims that, after 1969, the Polish government repeatedly invited Rückerl and the West German state prosecutors to search through the archives, but says that only a trickle of lawyers arrived and worked 'at a snail's pace'.

'I offered Rückerl our help,' says Pilichowski, 'but he never accepted it. His officials just came here to look through the papers for one case and then went away. We have thousands of uninvestigated cases here which he just doesn't want to look at.'

Relations between the two men are by now understandably sour. Those between Ludwigsburg and the Czech authorities are little better. According to one senior German prosecutor, relations had barely been established in 1966 before they became 'deep-frozen'.[49] The Czechs insisted that the two countries should cooperate on equal terms. Bonn however, according to the West German prosecutor, wanted to protect former Nazis who had hidden their past from an embarrassing attack. 'The stupid thing was,' says the prosecutor, 'that by not just throwing their documents at us, the Czechs protected the same sort of people.'

Valuable time was wasted before individual prosecutors realized that relations between Ludwigsburg and the East Europeans had broken down. Painfully, the more dedicated prosecutors began rebuilding the bridges. For those prosecutors, Ludwigsburg has been an unfortunate obstacle. They claim that it was obsessed by bureaucracy, uninterested in results, and always seemed to be more like a university than a criminal investigation department.[50]

Instead of the staff being made up of the best investigators, each Land nominated as its representatives those officials whose services would not be missed. More than one state prosecutor has told Rückerl: 'If you had five people less, you wouldn't notice it. But if I had five people extra, I could have done so much more.'

Speaking in Washington in March 1975, Martin Broszat, the internationally respected director of the Munich-based Institute for Contemporary History, said about Ludwigsburg:

> It is permissible to ask whether the effort put into investigations is commensurate with the results obtained. . . They worked on the principle of first reconstructing in every tiny detail the history of the most notorious crimes and only then began to look for the individuals responsible. Although logically compelling, it ran the risk of getting out of control because it took no account about who still survived to be prosecuted. This apparently happened after the protracted inquiries in Berlin into the RSHA. The research produced an unusually comprehensive mass of historically valuable documents but, as far as I know, did not produce a single conviction. . . In the overwhelming number of investigations – ninety-five to ninety-eight per cent in the last few years, according to the director of the Central Office – their inquiries ended without a conviction. . . This represents a very poor rate of success for criminal justice.[51]

Adalbert Rückerl staunchly refuses to concede that his agency has committed any errors, although he does admit to being surprised that the courts have given such low sentences. Since 1958, he claims that 556 persons have been convicted, out of 832 tried. He insists that the number of potential criminals is 'vastly exaggerated'.[52]

But Rückerl's confidence, like Bucher's, is contradicted by the statistics. The number of Germans indicted for war crimes on the basis of East European evidence rose at the beginning of 1979 to 85,802. Of the '6,440 Germans convicted' (the official statistics), only 156 were given life sentences. A discrepancy also exists between the Ministry of Justice's claim that 80,000 have been convicted and a further 85,802 remain indicted, and Rückerl's insistence that the numbers involved are 'vastly exaggerated'.[53] It lends credibility to those who insist that at least 250,000 Germans and others were involved in the murders.

Rückerl's explanation for the failure to convict more than 566 people since 1958 reveals more about Rückerl than the causes of the failure. He admits that the German atrocities committed against non-Jewish nationals in Yugoslavia, Greece, Hungary, Rumania and Bulgaria have not been investigated.[54] Similarly, he concedes that investigations of atrocities committed in Belgium, the Netherlands, Luxemburg, Denmark, Norway and Italy have been nominal.[55] No Nazi crimes committed in Czechoslovakia have been investigated.

Explaining why only one single crime in Russia has so far been investigated, Rückerl asserts that the information supplied by the Russians was unusable because it 'usually contained a phonetic spelling of the suspect's name or else such a garbled version as to render identification impossible'.[56] One is entitled to assume that had the Russians sent the 'phonetic spelling' of the location of, say, a Baader-Meinhof terrorist, someone in West Germany might have picked up a telephone to make further inquiries.

But remarkably, Rückerl goes further and challenges the accuracy of the documentary evidence established at the Nuremberg and subsequent trials. In explaining why other atrocities were not investigated, he simply says that 'the bulk' of the murders in Yugoslavia and Albania 'took place as a result of combating the resistance and partisan organizations by the police or German armed services.'[57]

About the murders in Russia, he writes: 'the brutal measures taken [in Russia] against certain categories of civilians were contrary to the interests and wishes of most military commanders.' He continues: 'One type of crime not thoroughly investigated was the killing of Soviet prisoners of war in compliance with the "commissar order". Since the Nuremberg trials, it is quite clear that many army commanders did not pass this order on to subordinate units, while other officers who received the order, refused to carry it out.'

Rückerl clearly does not believe the evidence of the subsequent Nuremberg trials and the Manstein trial. Instead, he seems to be relying entirely on German evidence. This argument probably explains why only one German has been convicted for crimes committed against the Russians.

Johansen Thummler, the former Gestapo chief of Katowice in Poland, is just one of many who have benefited from this curious self-deception. Now a works manager in the Karl Zeiss works at Oberkochen in Baden-Württemberg, Thummler was the president of the Auschwitz police court. The accused were condemned to death by him at the rate of one every two or three minutes. Thummler has justified the surprising speed of the conveyor-belt trials by insisting that the inmates had already signed confessions. According to Pery Brod, an eyewitness who gave his evidence to the Polish authorities, the Gestapo extracted the confessions by suspending the trussed-up victims on two poles which rested on tables. Then they were either whipped or suffered boiling water poured down the nostrils. Those waiting outside the building for their own 'trial' did not always hear screams. Often it seemed to be just a whine. A gas mask had been stuck by the SS over the victim's face.

Poland's demand for Thummler's extradition to stand trial was curtly rejected. Extradition of German nationals is barred by the German constitution. Pilichowski has sent bundles of sworn statements substantiating Thummler's crimes, and demanded that the West Germans prosecute him. The Baden-Württemberg prosecutor has rejected the demand. Under West German law, if Thummler's crimes were manslaughter the prosecution is barred by the statute of limitations. If it is murder, the decision by the Supreme Court in 1969 prevents a prosecution, because Thummler, as a judge, was not a principal murderer.[58]

Ernst Achenbach is another, albeit more prestigious, beneficiary of this self-imposed 'Catch-22'! The former Berlin Foreign Office official, who served at the German embassy in Paris, gave orders to Hagen about the deportation of Jews to Auschwitz. After the war, he befriended Robert Murphy, Clay's political adviser, and Murphy's German-born wife.

Protected by Murphy's magic signature, he ran a flourishing defence practice at the subsequent Nuremberg trials, then pressure for his arrest from Paris forced him suddenly to flee to the British zone. Ignoring American demands for his extradition, the British authorities quickly pushed him through a denazification tribunal and he established a law firm in Essen.[59]

French demands to the British for his extradition in 1948 were also ignored. In January 1953, Achenbach was one of many extreme right-wing members of the Liberal party (the FDP) who were suspected by British intelligence of being members of a plot to overthrow the Adenauer government. France again demanded his extradition, but it was again denied. Under a Franco-German agreement signed in 1954 Germany agreed, to allay French fears that any war crime trials in Germany would be a farce, not to prosecute Germans for crimes committed in France. Now safe, because he could not be extradited to France, Achenbach became a prominent politician in the Bundestag. When the Franco-German agreement of 1954 was revoked in 1971, it was a Bundestag committee under Achenbach's chairmanship which delayed ratification of the new treaty for four years.

The treaty was finally ratified in 1975. Three years later, Hagen,

IF YOU'RE CONCERNED ABOUT MORALITY.

Lischke and Heinrichsohn were charged as accomplices to murder for their part in the deportations to Auschwitz. Their trial in Cologne started in October 1979. According to the prosecutor they could not be charged with murder because it is impossible to prove that they possessed the malicious intent to kill. Achenbach, the prosecutor insisted, was too remote to be even considered as a criminal.

Existing documents suggest the contrary. It was Achenbach who had often given the orders to Hagen and Lischke. Heinrichsohn, then aged twenty-two, had simply obeyed Lischke's orders. Yet Heinrichsohn was imprisoned and Achenbach is enjoying his retirement.

Once Adenauer's republic was established, a firm limit was set on how far up the ladder of power blame could be attached. Many of those who had given the orders in the Third Reich were again giving the orders. If international pressure demanded justice, then it was those who obeyed the orders who were, in the last resort, expendable. Not those who had given orders, and who now gave them again.

19
'SCHLUSSTRICH'

In March 1964 the President of the Federal Republic honoured one of the country's leading industrialists with Germany's highest civilian award, the *Grosses Bundesverdienstkreuz*. For anyone who chose to cast their mind back twenty years, it was an event rich in irony. For the President was Heinrich Lübke and the industrialist was Heinrich Bütefisch, then on the board of one of West Germany's giant chemical companies.

Incontrovertible documentary evidence shows that, during the war years, Lübke had designed concentration camps and that he had organized slave labour from the Buchenwald camp to build facilities for the production of V-rockets at Peenemünde and at Peissen, near Bernburg. At the same time, Bütefisch had been a member of the IG Farben managing board and was to be convicted at Nuremberg for his part in the IG Auschwitz project.

Nothing could have more clearly symbolized the fact that the denazification programmes had not achieved that shift in 'political and economic authority' which Clay had demanded. Unable to agree among themselves upon an answer to that fundamental question of 'what kind of Germany we want,' the Allies had settled for a Germany in which power, influence and wealth remained in the hands of those who had held them under the Third Reich. With authority back in its own hands, one of the first acts of the German Establishment was to ensure that, for its members at least, there should be a *Schlusstrich* (literally, a bottom line), a closing of their account with the past. The result was a country in which both Lübke and Bütefisch could not only be powerful, but could also accept public positions and honours without any sense of incongruity.

It may, with reason, be argued that such things do not matter, may indeed be for the best. The Federal Republic has been outstandingly successful economically; it is a strong and staunch member of the NATO alliance; and it has remained stable and steadfastly democratic. Perhaps those who felt like Robertson, Mills and Gunston were right to resist Clay, Bernstein and their allies. Perhaps the kind of Germany the Allies needed, even if some of them felt qualms about it, was the kind of Germany they bequeathed to the world.

Leaving aside questions of justice, there are two reservations to be made before such a comfortable conclusion is accepted.

Firstly, the acceptance of a *Schlusstrich* has left in authority an Establishment whose assumptions have not been challenged; its members may have reconsidered the wisdom of their support of Hitler, but they have not been forced to reconsider their own moral position or their view of society. A democratic structure has been superimposed on the system, but men who felt no qualms about serving and prospering under the Nazis find no difficulty in serving and prospering under a democratic government. Their only condition is that their natural right to do so shall not be questioned.

In order to ensure that their authority is not questioned they have limited the spectrum of 'legitimate' politics in Germany. It is a narrow one – at least when it comes to the Left. Those who in many other democratic countries would be considered at best liberals, and at worst radicals for whom a niche could be found within the political system, have been effectively classified as outcasts and accused of threatening the whole basis of freedom and prosperity. The result is that there exists in Germany a large class of people who are denied a place in the broad consensus on which any democracy rests; instead of being the mavericks or even figures of fun which they might be elsewhere, they are bogeymen. Cast as dangerous villains, they are tempted to behave villainously.

It cannot be without significance that, with the exception of a patently corrupt and inadequate Italy, Germany is the only Western European country in which the dissension of the Sixties, especially among young people, turned to a vicious and perverse violence, whose perpetrators could not explain their motives save in the bankrupt and sterile rhetoric of Marxist revolution. They had no cause save their own frustrations with the bland, inflexible façade of the seemingly unreformed German Establishment.

The dissenters include a high proportion of young people, and that is at least partly because another corollary of the *Schlusstrich* was that, when it came to educating the postwar generation, recent history was forbidden territory. They could not be allowed to ask the collective question: 'What did you do in the war; Daddy?' It was not just that the question was embarrassing to individual parents; it would also open to undesirable debate the values and assumptions of the Establishment which stood *in loco parentis* to a new and fragile nation.

The second reservation to be made about the consequences of burying the Nazi past is that the Federal Republic has yet to face the test of prolonged adversity or internal dissension – adversity, say, on the scale which Britain's economic decline has created during the past decade, or the kind of dissension which shook America during the Vietnam War.

In short, the new Germany has not been tested by the kind of circumstances in which its democratic forebear, the Weimar Republic, failed. If the Eighties prove to be a decade of recession and unemployment, then the test may not be long delayed.

For anyone who is concerned as to whether the Germany which was the product of the failures of denazification, among many other things, is durable and flexible enough to cope with crisis, the events of September and October 1977 provided a test case; in the view of some, an ominous one.

Just after 5.25 on the afternoon of 5 September 1977 a blue Mercedes, closely followed by another, white, one, turned into Vincenz-Satz Strasse, a quiet, leafy one-way street in the Cologne suburb of Braunsfelder. In the first car, along with a chauffeur and two bodyguards, sat Hanns Martin Schleyer, the 'Boss of the Bosses', the tough, scar-faced president of the Federation of German Employers. A third guard followed in the other car. The guards were part of a twenty-four-hour protection system which the Cologne police had provided for Schleyer in view of the recent spate of murders carried out by the remnants of the Baader-Meinhof gang and their sympathizers. The latest victims had been the federal prosecutor, Dr Siegfried Buback, whose office had secured life sentences for the gang's leaders, Andreas Baader and Gunther Ensslin, and the chairman of the Dresdener Bank, Dr Jurgen Ponto, who had been shot by his own god-daughter.

Just as Schleyer's car passed a white Volkswagen van, a yellow Mercedes swerved in front of it, blocking the road, and a pram rolled out from the kerb. Schleyer's car screeched to a halt, and immediately, five sub-machineguns opened fire. The driver and guards were killed almost instantly, their bodies torn apart by the .223 calibre dum-dum bullets. Schleyer was dragged from his car and bundled into the Volkswagen van.

The police reaction to the kidnapping was quick and impressive. Within hours, 650 experts had been assembled at Cologne police headquarters. They were drawn from Army intelligence, the Federal Intelligence Agency, the Border Police and the Federal Criminal Agency. On the ground, at least 10,000 policemen were working exclusively on the task of finding Schleyer and his kidnappers. Roadblocks were set up and houses raided throughout the country, travellers were carefully scrutinized at the frontiers and, in Cologne itself 467 telephone booths were tapped in the hoped of intercepting a ransom call.

In Bonn an all-party crisis committee was formed by the Chancellor's office to organize the government's response to the crisis. Its members quickly and unanimously agreed on two fundamentals: firstly, there would be no surrender to the terrorists' demands; and, secondly, this was an unprecedented situation calling for extreme measures. It followed that they felt justified in invoking a state of emergency. The laws placed before the Bundestag gave the police and other government agencies virtually unlimited powers. Arrests and searches could be carried out without warrants; those arrested could be detained for what amounted to an indefinite period without access to anyone.

To an outsider, the surprise was not the scale of the police effort – though, as will be seen, this contrasted glaringly with the effort devoted to a different kind of crime – but the political reaction. The kidnapping of Schleyer was not a crime different in scale or in kind from the terrorist outrages which were, and are, relatively commonplace in Europe. The fact that a prominent man's life was at stake rather than already forfeit added drama, but such situations have become familiar in Italy and France. There was nothing in the nature of the crime or the status of its victim to make it qualitatively different from, say, an IRA bomb attack or assassination in Britain or the murder of a Fiat executive in Italy. Yet the German government made it clear that it regarded the kidnapping of Schleyer as nothing less than a threat to the very existence and integrity of the state.

Nor, when the terrorists made their demands known, two days after the kidnapping, was there anything unexpected about them: they wanted the release of their convicted and imprisoned comrades; there could be no question of giving in to them.

Those who felt the full force of the state's authority in the six weeks between the kidnapping and the discovery of Schleyer's mutilated body in the boot of a car in Mulhouse, France, on 19 October were not the criminals, but all those elements in German society which the Establishment, and the police, suspected of liberal of left-wing sympathies. The crisis provided a useful excuse for ransacking the lives of all those who were suspected of dissidence, whether or not there was any evidence that they had the remotest sympathies with the terrorist gangs.

One of the reasons that the Social Democratic government had found it necessary to involve the other parties in the management of the crisis was that they were all to well aware that it offered a fine opportunity for their right-wing opponents to argue that this was the inevitable outcome of left-wing softness and tolerance. This, the conservatives could claim, was the 'Red Götterdämmerung' so luridly forecast by politicians like Franz Josef Strauss, the leader of the Christian Social Union. With Strauss and his colleagues sitting in on the crisis committee, their teeth would be drawn in the Bundestag.

But the conservatives felt no constraints when they addressed the public. Only four members of the ruling Social Democratic party had opposed the emergency legislation on the floor of the Bundestag, and they were instantly labelled as terrorist sympathizers. Worse was reserved for those outside the legislature who questioned the government's motives or the need for such drastic steps. They were stigmatized as 'poisoners', 'gangsters', the 'carriers of moral epidemics', 'viruses who are blackmailing the state and must be exterminated'. Even respected figures, like the writers Heinrich Böll and Günther Grass, whose political stance was critical and unorthodox, were 'enemies of the state' and 'spiritual bombers'.[1] This was not the language of leaders eager to unite the country in the face of crisis; it was rhetoric in a German political tradition that went back at least to the night of the Reichstag fire.

The Schleyer kidnapping highlighted two sinister trends in German political life. The social democratic Left did not have the authority to stand up for its principles when it found itself in danger of being out-flanked by the Right; because it, too, understood the public appeal of the Right's simplistic solutions. And the Right did not hesitate to take advantage of a crisis to smear its opponents wholesale.

When it came to the point, the Right did not believe in the virtues and strengths of democracy and liberty; nor even in the rule of law to which it paid such lip service. Earlier in the year, Strauss had told an audience of party members in Munich: 'Those who are supposed to be fighting for the freedom of the people should be left to the people, then to the police, and the courts would not have to worry about them any more.'[2] Hans Filbinger, the minister president of Baden-Württemberg, another member of the crisis committee, went even further. He suggested that the imprisoned terrorists, Baader and Ensslin, should themselves be treated as hostages, and executed in retaliation.

The moral attitudes of both Strauss and Filbinger had undergone some changes in the previous thirty-five years. Under the Third Reich Strauss had held a position where his official duties included training the Nazi party's equivalent of the communist commissars, activists whose job it was to work within the Wehrmacht to ensure that the ordinary soldiers were properly conscious of Nazi ideological principles. According to the party's official job description, those who, like Strauss, taught the *Führerprinzip*, had to be 'absolutely and reliable fanatic' Nazis. It was, no doubt, a demanding job, especially if, again like Strauss, you claimed to have been a covert anti-Nazi.[3]

Shortly after the end of the Schleyer emergency, some embarrassing facts about Hans Filbinger's past came to the surface. Just before the end of the war he had sentenced two deserters from the German navy to death. Filbinger was unabashed: morality, he claimed, was not relevant, his decision had been correct and justified because he had acted in accordance with the law.

In trying to assess the motives of the terrorists who kidnapped Schleyer it would be possible to argue forever as to how great a part was played by the failure to denazify Germany and the consequent lacuna in the historical consciousness of the postwar generation. Those who support the German Establishment will deny to the bitter end that the retention of the industrialists, the lawyers, the teachers and the bureaucrats who had served Hitler contributed to the alienation of German youth. Those who fear or suspect the Establishment will maintain the opposite with equal determination. What is certain is that in their choice of Schleyer as a symbol, the terrorists had picked upon a figure who might well stand as a paradigm for all those members of the German middle class who had most to lose from an effective denazification programme, and most to gain from the declaration of a *Schlusstrich*.

Two days after the kidnapping, Daniel Simon, the American director of the Berlin Document Centre, received a telephone call from the Hamburg police. They explained that a journalist at a press conference had just asked whether Schleyer had been a member of the SS, and the police spokesman had publicly doubted the allegation. In the newspaper accounts of Schleyer's career, there was no mention of his wartime activities. The reports just said that he was born in May 1915, that he had studied to become a lawyer, getting a doctorate of law at Innsbruck University, and that he had joined Daimler-Benz in 1951. Nevertheless, the police spokesman had agreed to check. The police were among the privileged few with access to information in the Document Centre. Within ten minutes, Simon had the answer. Schleyer's bulging SS file had been lying on the open shelves.

He had joined the SS on 1 July 1935 and joined the Nazi party on 1 May 1937. Contrary to the account in the current German equivalent of *Who's who*, he had been sent to Innsbruck University in 1938 as the director of the Nazi party training school. On 9 November 1941 he had been posted to Prague to manage the Reich's Central Office for Industry, returning to Berlin on 1 January 1944 to work in Himmler's Reich Security Office.

Also inside the file was Schleyer's 1937 request to marry Waltraut Ketterer. Both had diligently completed their ancestral history back to the early eighteenth century to prove that they were of pure Aryan stock. Schleyer had found a priest who could confirm that his ancestor, Johann Schleir, born in 1733, was not Jewish. To speed the authorization for the wedding, because Schleyer was about to be posted to Innsbruck, his fiancée has asked her father, a general in the SA and a party member since 1923, to use his personal friendship with Himmler to order the Berlin Race Office to send their approval for the marriage by telegram.

Schleyer's file also contains long handwritten testimonials by himself and his fiancée describing their devotion to Adolf Hitler and the cause of the Third Reich. Schleyer had affirmed: 'I am a long-serving National Socialist and SS Leader.'

It was a background which served Schleyer well in the postwar era. There was a quip in Germany in the mid-fifties: 'Tell me which internment camp you were held in by the Allies after the war, and I'll tell you where you work.' Schleyer was interned in a camp with a large number of industrialists and bankers. It was one of those acquaintances who in 1951 recruited him to Daimler-Benz, then owned by Flick. The company, according to a *Stern* magazine analysis, only recruited from amongst those who, during the Nazi period, were the 'high and mighty in the economy'. As director of personnel, Schleyer ordained that only right-wing graduates could be recruited, and that as part of their training, they would be sent to Reinhard Höhn's 'Academy for Economic Leaders'. Schleyer clearly sympathized with Höhn's wartime theme that people should 'not be governed, but ordered and led'.

As an industrialist, Schleyer had put his principles into effect. In 1963 he organized a lock-out of 420,000 metal workers in Baden-Württemberg, which the moderate union leaders were to describe as 'an act of outright warfare'. He came to symbolize the hard and unrepentant face of the German Establishment; but it was not the image he presented of himself when, in one of his videotaped messages from captivity, he said: 'I've been locked up for five and a half weeks by these terrorists just because I've worked so hard to build a free and democratic society.'

Not all Germans shared Schleyer's view of what constituted a free and democratic society. Not that anything can excuse or mitigate the crime which led to his death, but nor can there be any excuse for using Schleyer's misfortune as an occasion to persecute and vilify those who did not share his opinions. For the Federal Republic prides itself on its status as a *Rechtstaat*, and the misuse of influence and authority is as much an offence against the rule of law in a democracy as is the breach of the law.

Those within Germany for whom the emergency following Schleyer's kidnapping came to be a new 'dark age' have some reason to fear that in another crisis the protection and privileges of the *Rechtstaat* will not extend to them. No one can doubt the commitment to democracy and liberty which Chancellor Schmidt and his colleagues have; but, equally, no one who knows Germany can doubt that in the political wings there wait men whose instinctive resort in times of danger is to intolerance and authoritarianism – and they are confident that they would have the support of the rich and powerful if and when their time should come.

Finally, to turn away from consideration of the practical and the prudent; though the Second World War was a conflict between nations, there was another motive in the minds of those who resisted Hitler's tyranny and aggression. The resistance fighters, the citizens of the occupied countries, the deportees, the slave labourers, those on their way to an obscure death in the concentration camps, the soldiers, sailors and airmen of the Allied forces, they had all been promised that, after victory, there would be justice.

If, on the morning after the kidnapping of Hanns Martin Schleyer, anyone had been concerned with how far that promise had been honoured, they might have found their way to Room L111 in the Düsseldorf court house. There they would have seen an example of law and order which was a million miles away in spirit and in intensity from the manhunt that was getting under way across Germany.

For 6 September 1977 was listed for the 187th sitting of the court which, for nearly two years, had been hearing the case against fifteen Germans accused of murdering a quarter of a million people in the Majdanek concentration camp. The government of Poland, where Majdanek was sited, has contended that the true total of those who died at Majdanek was well over a million: but in modern Germany there were some who, not content with dividing that number by a factor of four, were ready, eager and officially permitted to stand up in a court of law and argue that there had in fact been no Final Solution at all.

The fifteen defendants and their eight lawyers began arriving at about 8.45 in the morning. They shook hands with one another, smilingly greeted the two police attendants, and went to the same chairs which they had occupied for the previous two years. Slumped behind tables, casually talking to one another, it was hard to imagine that these elderly men and women, all of them on bail, stood accused of murder, let alone of murder on a massive scale. Without handcuffs or armed guards, the courtroom looked more like a school classroom; the occasion had the atmosphere of a big family reunion rather than a murder trial. Nine o'clock came and went. Judge Günther Bogen was late, delayed either by the morning traffic or because of another night's bad sleep. Some of the evidence he had recently heard had given him nightmares. Even a heavy bout of drinking did not always guarantee an undisturbed night.

No one in the room seemed to notice his unpunctuality. Hermann

'Jonny' Hackmann, the camp's deputy commandant, read, as he usually did, the tabloid *Bild Zeitung*. It was the second time he had faced trial for his SS activities. In 1947 an American court at Dachau had condemned him to death for committing innumerable murders at Buchenwald and Sachsenhausen concentration camps. German pressure forced the Americans first to reprieve him and then release him in 1955. It was only because of the change of German policy in 1960 that Ludwigsburg saw documentary evidence supplied by Poland which proved that the then furniture dealer had played a leading role in the murder of the Polish Jews at Majdanek. Hackmann, unabashed, told the interrogators before the trial: 'As far as I can remember, no inmates were killed unlawfully.'

Near Hackmann sat Hildergart Lächert, a fifty-seven-year-old mother of two, who, according to witnesses, was good-looking in her youthful days when she was SS overseer in the camp. Known to inmates as 'Bloody Brigitte', the prosecution allege that she was responsible for at least 1,196 deaths, but the survivors say that the real total ran into tens of thousands. Her victims were women who were whipped to death, hanged, or shot when she fired indiscriminately into crowds. Most of the eyewitnesses to her murders perished in the camp, but one survivor saw Lächert routinely separate mothers from their babies. The babies were left uncared for in a hut for up to three days, after which, under her supervision, they would be thrown into a truck to be taken direct to the crematoria. Another eyewitness has testified that she delighted in searching through the mothers' clothes in the changing room after they had walked into the gas chambers, eager to find children who had been hidden in the forlorn hope that they would escape death.

Again, this was Lächert's second trial. She was convicted in Poland after the war on assault charges and released in the early Fifties. The Poles only discovered the real evidence of her activities after she had been deported to Germany.

Sitting near Lächert was Hermine Ryan-Braunsteiner, another SS camp overseer accused of numerous equally horrific murders and of selecting inmates for gassing. After the war she had lived under a false name in a DP camp and had emigrated to the USA. For over twenty years she lived a married life, in Queens, New York, until neighbours became suspicious. After lengthy denaturalization proceedings, she was deported to Germany in 1973.

Behind the two women sat Emil Laurich, Majdanek's 'Angel of Death'. Amongst his many responsibilities was the execution of the prisoners delivered by the Gestapo. Efficiently, he always shot them right outside the crematoria.

Next to Laurich sat Johanna Zelle. Her quirk, according to a witness, was to give a child a sweet, and then seconds later shoot it dead.

SCHLUSSTRICH

A sixteenth defendant, Alice Orlowski, had already died. Still, she had not escaped imprisonment entirely. She had been jailed for eight months after she loudly complained in a Cologne bar that it took twice as long to serve a beer as to kill all the Jews.

The fifteen accused were only a tiny minority of the 10,000 Germans known to have worked in the camp. Of those 10,000, only 1,300 are known by name. The remainder have escaped detection because of incomplete or destroyed records. West German police have investigated 387 of the identifiable SS officers at Majdanek camp, but when Ludwigsburg sent its thin brief to the Cologne prosecutor's office in 1962, only twenty-nine former camp officers were named as suspects. Of those, only eight were ever charged. The other eight defendants were only included as a result of subsequent investigations.

For nine years one prosecutor, with an occasional assistant, struggled with the Majdanek investigation. After protests from Poland and Israel he was finally moved to less onerous work and replaced by apparently more energetic colleagues.

It was only on 26 November 1975 that the trial finally started. It was originally expected to last one year. Billed as the last of the great Nazi trials, the prosecutors believed the evidence to be incontrovertible. Over 1,000 survivors had been interviewed. Of those, 260 had been selected as having actually seen one of the defendants commit murder. The German courts insist that there must be an eyewitness to the act of murder. Hearsay or supposition is insufficient. Yet at the end of the first year only sixteen of the 260 witnesses had been heard. Judge Bogen was confronted by the obstructive tactics of the government-paid defence lawyers, intent on using the trial for their own purposes. He consistently refused to limit their attempts to disprove the existence of the Final Solution.

Exploiting the procedural rules which were drafted to prevent a repetition of the shotgun trials of the Third Reich, the defence lawyers embarked on a daily ritual, submitting endless challenges against the prosecution's introduction of evidence, and introducing evidence designed, not to clarify the issues or bolster their client's defence, but to rewrite the history of the Nazi era.

Hans Mundorf, defending Braunsteiner, seized every possible opportunity during the first eighteen months to challenge the evidence that human corpses had been burnt in the crematoria. Every witness was asked whether they knew the difference between the smell of burning human and animal flesh. Veterinary doctors were called to testify that those outside the crematoria would not know the difference.

Ludwig Bock, the thirty-eight-year-old lawyer defending Lächert, went even further and called witnesses, all of them neo-Nazi historians, to disprove that there had ever been a planned Final Solution. With a conviction that goes beyond purely professional duty to a client, he insisted that no one, including animals was gassed at Majdanek. 'Even if there were gas chambers at Majdanek,' he told the author, 'it doesn't mean that they were the reason for the death of a lot of people, because it is possible that the gas chambers were used to clean clothes.'[4] Bock, who claimed that Lächert went to Majdanek as if it was just another job, 'like being a cook in a kitchen', insisted that she had no idea that anyone was being gassed or killed in the camp. That defence did not prevent him demanding, when a former inmate explained how she had been forced by a defendant to carry Zyklon B gas to the gas chambers, that the witness be charged as an accomplice to murder.

Hermann Stolting, who defended another of the accused, Hermine Böttcher, has a Nazi record of his own to explain. As a wartime prosecutor in a special court in Bromberg, Poland, he 'persuaded' the court to give a series of death sentences for trivial offences like a farmer's illegal killing of six pigs. Today he unrepentantly justifies those sentences: 'If both the circumstances and the law were the same today, I would do the same again.'[5] He points to his chairmanship of the German Animal Welfare Society as proof of his humanitarianism.

When the lawyers were not rewriting history, they were cruelly denigrating the survivors and their testimony. Credibility is hard to establish at the best of times, but thirty-five years after the event it is often impossible to remember the exact details which the defence lawyers always demanded. Time, date, place, the exact words, the precise movements of every person in the drama, the position of the lorry in relation to the hut, or was it a cart, the final curse of the girl who was hanged by Lächert. 'How can you be sure that the girl did not push the stool away herself?' 'Did you see Lächert throw the children into the crematoria?'

These tactics have paid off handsomely. While the average trial in 1962 lasted 3.6 years, in 1978 the average had risen to 12.5 years.[6] As the trials grow longer, the witnesses' memories become feebler; not surprisingly, they are less robust than the accused. They are beginning to die off. In September 1977, enough survivors could still remember. But the court is also faced with the insolence of witnesses who could themselves be among the accused.

On 3 November 1943, 18,000 men, women and children died in what the SS organizers dubbed a 'Harvest Festival'. Starting at 5 o'clock in the morning, to the alternate sound of waltzes and foxtrot music blaring out across a field, a seemingly never-ending line of naked Jews shuffled towards an enormous trench in which they were ordered to lie down flat, to be machinegunned to death. Layer upon layer of dead bodies slowly filled the trench, as the SS men took their turn to either execute the victims or wander across to a table at the end of the field for the extra rations of food and vodka provided by the considerate camp commandant.

Jadwiga Wegrezecka, then a twenty-year-old student, watched the murders through a window in her barracks. She particularly remembers a macabre twist when suddenly a naked boy and girl left the line and literally danced towards the grave. 'They must have gone mad,' she now says, 'but they were amongst the dead when it all finished at 6 o'clock that night. We remembered the massacre for days afterwards. A thick yellow fog and the stench of burning flesh filled the air for days, and they still couldn't burn all of the bodies.'[7]

In the Düsseldorf courtroom Johann Barth, now living in Ingolstadt, found it harder to remember what happened, although he had a better view of the field. Barth had been one of the SS guards around the field. Called as a witness to trial, he was asked by Judge Bogen what he felt like when mothers holding their babies fell onto their knees begging him to save the lives of their children. Brusquely he replied: 'I didn't think about it at all. I had forgotten all about it the following day. I was only eighteen years old.' Franz Bauer, another SS officer standing in the field, told Judge Bogen that he didn't think about the massacre either. 'I just thought about my holidays, which were due on November the ninth.'[8]

It took nearly four months to sort, pack and dispatch to Germany the belongings of the 18,000 murdered that day. The sorting section was perpetually overworked. Even when the camp was liberated, there were still 820,000 pairs of shoes in the camp shed. According to the camp records, 730 kilos of human hair had already been forwarded to factories in Germany. It was on the basis of those discoveries and the unrefuted evidence that the crematoria burnt an average of 2,000 corpses every day, that the Poles and the judges at the Nuremberg tribunal concluded that one and a half million people had been murdered at Majdanek.

When Judge Bogen finally arrived for the 187th hearing, the prosecutor called Andrzey Stanislavski, who had been imprisoned in the camp for eighteen months when he was twenty-one years old. For five hours he withstood the hectoring of the defence and identified three of the defendants. The prosecution was satisfied. Some witnesses, thirty-five years later, could no longer associate the elderly men and women dressed normally and sitting calmly with the screaming, black-dressed tormentors who had the power of deciding life and death.

At the end of the day's hearing Stanislavski said: 'I feel and I see that the accused know me as well. One of them stuck his head behind a newspaper, another one put on a pair of big glasses, and another one was reading a book.' He is mistaken in thinking that such behaviour is evidence of embarrassment or shame. The defendants have behaved like that nearly every day. Ostensibly unmoved by the trial, they were, they say, only doing their duty and should not be tried for that. Putting the best interpretation on their excuses, it is Germany that is on trial and not those who just obeyed orders.

There was no hearing in the Majdanek trial on the day Schleyer's body was found. There was not one for another five days. The pace throughout has been deliberately unhurried. With two prosecutors facing the fifteen defendants and their twenty-eight defence lawyers, there are at most only three trial days per week and sometimes none at all. When the witnesses are too ill to travel to Düsseldorf, or refuse to come to Germany, the court flies to them. Few of the lawyers complain. At a daily cost of 1,000 deutschmarks each, they have flown, at state expense, first class, around Europe, to Israel and North America. Staying with them in 5-star hotels, journalists representing the more sensational German magazines have always been rewarded with colourful stories of one day's work being stretched out for a week, while the lawyers enjoy themselves drinking in a club bar or by a hotel swimming pool.

It is not only justice that has suffered. Judge Bogen has been struck by a heart attack, one of the lay judges has died, and another has retired through ill health; one of the defence lawyers has died and another retired because of illness. The trial should have ended in 1976; it is now scheduled to continue into 1981.

But now there are only nine defendants on trial. Two became ill, and on 19 April 1979 Judge Bogen ordered the acquittal of four others. The camp doctor, Heinrich Schmidt, who was responsible for the daily selection of who would go to the gas chamber and who would live ('You're not good enough for work, you're only good for heaven'), was acquitted. So were Rosa Süss, and Charlotte Mayer, who allegedly selected women for the gas chambers, and Hermine Böttcher, who did the same. In all four cases, the eyewitnesses had in the meantime become too ill or had died. Under German law, without their testimony the four had to be acquitted.

Buffeted by international criticism, Judge Bogen finally agreed with the prosecutors on 13 June 1979 that there was sufficient evidence against the four main defendants to warrant their bail being suspended. But whether 'Bloody Brigitte' or Hermann Hackmann remain imprisoned for one year or the rest of their lives makes little, if any, difference to justice. Few of those who gave the orders have ever been punished. The dead are beyond seeing their murderers punished. Only the handful of victims who survived can gain any solace. At least they are spared the chance of meeting one of their many tormentors shopping in their own neighbourhood, or holidaying in their favourite resort; but no one has asked them for an opinion about the *Schlusstrich*.

Perhaps the sad farce which will draw to an end in Düsseldorf some time in 1981 does not matter either. Perhaps the crimes of the Third Reich were too monstrous for human justice. If so, then the hopes and faith of countless men and women, many of whom paid for their beliefs with their lives, have been betrayed. Perhaps another generation will learn the lesson when they are invited to fight for justice and a better world, and realize that when victory is won they will not be asked what kind of justice was meant, or what kind of world they want. Those in London and Washington who, during the war, persistently argued the futility of giving any commitment to postwar justice have been proved right. Or was it just a self-fulfilling prophecy?

BIBLIOGRAPHY

Adenauer, Konrad. *Memoirs, 1945 – 1953.* Weidenfeld and Nicolson, 1966.

Andrews, Allen. *Exemplary Justice.* Harrap, 1976.

Avon, Lord. *The Eden Memoirs: The Reckoning.* Cassell, 1965

Bennett, Sir John Wheeler, and Nicholls, Anthony. *The Semblance of Peace.* Macmillan, 1972.

Biddle, Francis. *In Brief Authority.* Greenwood Press, 1962.

Blum, Howard. *Wanted! The Search for Nazis in America.* Fawcett Books, 1977.

Borkin, J. *The Crime and Punishment of I.G. Farben.* André Deutsch, 1979.

Borsdorf, U. and Neithammer, L. *Zwischen Befreiung und Besatzung.* Peter Hammer Verlag, 1976.

Brickhill, Paul. *The Great Escape.* Arrow Books, 1979.

Bundesjustizministerium. *Die Verfolgung Nationalsozialistischer Straftäten im Gebiet der Bundesrepublik Deutschland seit 1945.* Bundesjustizministerium, 1964.

Churchill, Winston S. *The Second World War.* Cassell, 1951.

Clay, L.D. *Decision in Germany.* Greenwood Press, 1970. *The Papers of General Lucius D. Clay,* ed. J.E. Smith. Vols I and II, Indiana University Press, 1974.

Cobler S. *Law, Order and Politics in West Germany.* Penguin 1978.

Craig, Gordon A. *Germany 1866 – 1945.* Clarendon Press, 1978.

Czichon, E. *Der Bankier und die Macht.* Pahl-Rugenstein Verlag, 1970.

Dahrendorf, R. *Society and Democracy in Germany.* Weidenfeld and Nicolson, 1965.

Davidson, E. *The Death and Life of Germany.* Jonathan Cape, 1959.

Delius, F.C. *Unsere Siemens-Welt.* Rotbuch Verlag, 1972.

Donnison, F.S.V. *Civil Affairs and Military Government: Central Organisation & Planning.* HMSO, 1966.

Dorn, Walter L. *Inspektionsreisen in der U.S. Zone.* Deutsche Verlagsanstalt, 1973.

Du Bois, Josiah E. *The Devil's Chemists.* Beacon Press, 1952.

Eggebrecht, Axel. *Die Zornigen Alten Männer.* Rowohlt, 1979.

Elkins, M. *Forged in Fury.* Ballantine Books, 1971.

Engelmann, Bernt. *Wie Wir Würden, Was Wir Sind.* C. Bertelsmann, 1980.

Das neue Schwarz Buch. Franz Josef Strauss. Kiepenheuer und Witsch, 1980.

Grosses Bundesverdienstkreuz. Rowohlt, 1976.

Ferencz, B.B. *Less Than Slaves.* Harvard University Press, 1979.

Fitzgibbon, C. *Denazification.* Michael Joseph, 1969.

Gimbel, John. *The American Occupation of Germany. Politics and the Military 1945–1949.* Stanford University Press, 1968.

Griffith, William *The Denazification Program in the U.S. Zone of Germany.* (Thesis) Harvard University 1950.

Grunberger, Richard. *A Social History of the Third Reich.* Penguin, 1974.

Haffner, Sebastian. *The Meaning Of Hitler.* Weidenfeld and Nicolson, 1979.

Harvey, John (ed.). *The War Diaries of Oliver Harvey.* Collins, 1978.

Hastings, M. *Bomber Command.* Michael Joseph, 1979.

Hausner, G. *Justice in Jerusalem.* Nielson, 1967.

Hearnden, Arthur (ed.). *The British in Germany.* Hamish Hamilton, 1978.

Hilberg, Raul. *The Destruction of the European Jews.* W.H. Allen, 1961.

Horne, Alistair. *Back Into Power.* Max Parrish, 1955.

International Russell Tribunal. Rotbuch Verlag, 1978.

Jaspers, Karl. *Wohin Treibt die Bundesrepublik.* Piper, 1966.

Jolly, C. *The Vengeance of Private Pooley.* Heinemann, 1956.

Kennan, George F. *Memoirs 1925–1950.* Little, Brown and Company, 1967.

Klarsfeld, Beate. *Wherever They May Be.* Vanguard Press, 1975.

Die Geschichte des P.G. 2633930 Kiesinger. Joseph Melzer Verlag, 1969.

Koch, P. and Hermann, K. *Assault At Mogadishu.* Corgi, 1977.

Koch, P. and Oltmanns, R. *S.O.S. Freiheit in Deutschland.* Stern, 1978.

Krausnick, H. et al. *Anatomy of the S.S. State.* Collins, 1968.

Kruse, Falko. *NS – Prozesse und Restauration.* Kritische Justiz Frankfurt, 1978.

Laqueur, Walter. *Weimar.* Capricorn Books, 1976.

The Terrible Secret. Weidenfeld and Nicolson, 1980

Lasby, C.G. *Project Paperclip.* Atheneum, 1971.

Litchfield, E.H. (editor). *Governing Post-War Germany.* Cornell, 1967.

Manchester, William. *The Arms of Krupp.* Bantam Books, 1970.

Martin, J. *All Honourable Men.* Little Brown and Company, 1950.

Maser, Werner. *Nuremberg, A Nation on Trial.* Allen Lane, 1979.

Merritt, A.J. and R.L. (ed.). *Public Opinion in Occupied Germany.* University of Illinois, 1970.

Michel, Jean. *Dora.* Weidenfeld and Nicolson, 1979.

Mitscherlich, A. and M. *The Inability to Mourn.* Grove Press, 1975.

Morse, A.D. *While Six Million Died.* Secker and Warburg, 1968.

Neave, Airey. *Nuremberg.* Hodder and Stoughton, 1978.

Ott, Erich. *Die Wirtschaftskonzeption der S.P.D. nach 1945.* Verlag Arbeiterbewegung und Gesellschaftswissenschaft, 1978.

Padover, S. *Experiment in Germany.* New York, 1946.

Paget, R.T. *Manstein.* Collins, 1951.

Peterson, E.N. *The American Occupation of Germany.* Wayne, 1978.

Pierrepoint, Albert. *Executioner Pierrepoint.* Hodder and Stoughton, 1977.

Poole, J. and S. *Who Financed Hitler.* McDonald and James, 1978.

Reitlinger, G. *The Final Solution.* Sphere Books, 1971.

Rose, Norman. *Vansittart – Study of a Diplomat.* Heinemann, 1978.

Rückerl A. *The Investigation of Nazi Crimes 1945–1978.* C.F. Müller, 1979.

N.S. Vermichtungslager. Deutscher Taschenbuch Verlag, 1977

Schmitt, H.A. (ed.). *U.S. Occupation in Europe After World War II.* The Regents Press of Kansas, 1976.

Scotland, Lt.-Col. A.P. *The London Cage.* George Mann, 1973.

Sereny, Gitta. *Into That Darkness.* André Deutsch, 1974.

Smith, B.F. *Reaching Judgment at Nuremberg.* André Deutsch, 1977.

Speer, A. *Inside the Third Reich.* Sphere, 1975.

Spott, F. *The Churches and Politics in Germany.* Wesleyan University, 1973.

Sullivan, Mathew Barry. *Thresholds of Peace.* Hamish Hamilton, 1979.

Tauber, K.P. *Beyond Eagle and Swastika.* Vols I and II, Wesleyan University, 1967.

Thomas, Hugh. *The Murder of Rudolph Hess.* Hodder and Stoughton, 1979.

United Nations International Law Commission. *The Chapter and Judgment of the Nürnberg Tribunal.* United Nations, 1949.

History of the United Nations War Crimes Commission and the Development of the Laws of War. HMSO, 1948.

Law Reports of Trials of War Criminals. Vols II–XV, HMSO, 1945–48.

Vinke, Hermann and Witt, Gabriele. *Die Anti-Terror Debatten im Parlament. Protokolle 1974–1978.* Rowohlt, 1978.

Vogel, R. *Ein Weg aus der Vergangenheit.* Ullstein, 1969.

The War Office. *The Law of War on Land: Manual of Military Law.* HMSO, 1958.

Wasserstein, Bernard. *Britain and the Jews of Europe 1939–1945.* Clarendon Press, 1979.

Weingartner, J.J. *Crossroads of Death.* University of California, 1979.

Wheeler-Bennett. *See Bennett, Sir John Wheeler.*

Ziemke, E.F. *The U.S. Army in the Occupation of Germany 1944–1946*. Centre of Military History, United States Army, 1975.

Zierer, Otto. *Franz Josef Strauss*. Herbig, 1978.

Zink, H. *The United States in Germany 1944–1955*. Greenwood Press, 1974.

NOTES

In the interests of brevity certain commonly occurring references have been abbreviated.

TB indicates material obtained in the course of the author's own interviews.

British documents from the Public Records office in London come under the following categories:

CAB   Cabinet meetings and papers
CP   Cabinet Minutes
CP   Cabinet Papers
FO   Foreign Office files
LCO   Lord Chancellor's Office
ORC   Overseas Reconstruction Committee files
PREM   Prime Minister's papers
TS   Treasury Solicitors files
WO   War Office papers
WP   War Papers
War Cab. War Cabinet papers

American documents denoted by abbreviations come into the following categories and are located as indicated:

EW The European War Papers 1939 – 45 at the National Archives, Washington OMGUS The papers of the Office of Military Government, United States, at the National Archives, Suitland, they include: the AG decimal File, the papers of the Office of the Political Advisor to the Military Governor (Polad), and of the Commander-in-Chief of the US Army, Europe (USAREUR).

CHAPTER 1

1   TB/Abs.
2   TB/Gunston.
3   NI 471 (Roll 128).
4   RS 238 War Crimes Interrogations.

5 Report on the Investigation of the Deutsche Bank, OMGUS Finance Division (hereafter OMGUS Report), November 1946, p. 15.
6 ibid. p. 49.
7 F.C. Delius, *Unsere Siemens-Welt;* OMGUS Report, p. 160.
8 OMGUS Report, p. 164.
9 Joseph Borkin, *The Crime and Punishment of I.G. Farben,* p. 111.
10 Deutsche Bank File — Abs, Deutsches Zentralarchiv, Potsdam 16682.
11 TS 36/111 25.4.44.
12 FO 942/306 20.3.45 and FO 371 46701/C1797 25.445; and cf. FO 371 46799/C1397 where Playfair protested that the American proposals to purge the Reichsbank were 'more sweeping than our own directives. . . and were likely to afford not a little embarrassment to the Treasury in their plans for the financial reorganisation of Germany.'
13 Chambers's memoirs (unpublished), period 7, p. 7.
14 *Financial and Property Control Manual,* p. 31.
15 Chambers, period 7, p. 13.
16 TB/Gunston; TB/Hellmuth; OMGUS Report, p. 280.
17 TB/Kellam; TB/Abs.
18 FO 371 46801/C9406.
19 FO 371 46800/C6223.

CHAPTER 2

1 *Treatment of German Nationals in Germany 1938 – 1939* Cmd. 6120, 1939.
2 The Americans refused to list anyone because they were opposed to the whole concept of prosecuting politicians or soldiers for acts committed during the war, which according to the American delegates were not crimes when actually committed. See *Violation of the Laws and Customs of War: Reports of Majority and Dissenting Reports of American and Japanese Members of the Commission of Responsibilities, Conference of Paris 1919*, published by Carnegie Endowment for International Peace, 1919; RG 153 War Crimes Division JAG Law Library 1944 – 49.
3 9.7.1921.
4 FO 371 24472/11/C5471 21.5.40.
5 FO 371 24422/C2544 17.2.40.
6 FO 371 24422/C2901 26.2.40.
7 FO 371 24422/C3646 28.2.40.

8 FO 371 26540/C7721.
9 FO 371 26540/C10982.
10 WP (41)233 and War Cabinet Conclusions 100(41) 5.10.41.
11 WP (41)235 8.10.41.
12 FO 371 26540.
13 FO 371 26540 16.10.41.
14 FO 371 26540/11518.
15 TB/Roberts.
16 John Harvey (ed.), *The War Diaries of Oliver Harvey,* p. 194.
17 FO 371 26540/11998.
18 *Punishment for War Crimes — the Inter-Allied Declaration signed at St James's Palace London on 13th January and Relative Documents,* HMSO. 1042, Vol I, p. 15.
19 FO 371 26540/11999.
20 FO 371 26540/11999 11.11.41, Roger Allen and Victor Cavendish-Bentinck, who added: 'The more I think about this business the less I like it. I fear that we may get involved in complications that will do us no good.' Roberts added: 'I fully share Mr Bentinck's qualms about this. . . . My own preference would therefore be to drop this question altogether. . . without giving undue encouragement to the Allies to think that we shall in fact draw up lists and carefully examine and punish individual cases after the war.'
21 The full text read:
Whereas Germany, since the beginning of the present conflict which arose out of her policy of aggression, has instituted in the Occupied countries a regime of terror characterised amongst other things by imprisonments, mass expulsions, the execution of hostages and massacres,
And whereas these acts of violence are being similarly committed by the Allies and Associates of the Reich and, in certain countries, by accomplices of the occupying Power,
And whereas international solidarity is necessary in order to avoid the repression of these acts of violence simply by acts of vengeance on the part of the general public, and in order to satisfy the sense of justice of the civilised world,
Recalling that no international law, and in particular the Convention signed at the Hague in 1907 regarding the laws and customs of land warfare, do not permit belligerents in Occupied countries to commit acts of violence against civilians, to disregard the laws in force, or to overthrow national institutions,
(1) affirm that acts of violence thus inflicted upon the civilian populations have nothing in common with the conceptions of an act

of war or of a political crime as understood by civilised nations,

(2) take note of the declarations made in this respect on 25th October 1941 by the President of the United States of America and by the British Prime Minister,

(3) place among their principal war aims the punishment, through the channel of organised justice, of those guilty of or responsible for these crimes, whether they have ordered them, perpetrated them or participated in them,

(4) resolve to see to it in a spirit of international solidarity that (a) those guilty or responsible, whatever their nationality, are sought out, handed over to justice and judged, (b) that the sentences pronounced are carried out.

22 FO 371 30914 9.1.42. Malkin complained that it breached the policy of a 'detached attitude'.

23 FO 371 26540/12746 12.12.41. The European signatories were quite keen at first to keep the Russians out of the ceremony, but were concerned as to why the US government did not want to participate. Eden asked the British embassy in Washington to discover the reasons.

24 FO 371 26540/14223 26.12.41. See also 26540/11839, 26.10.41 where Roberts commented; 'I am afraid that the Commonwealth Government are also wrong in supposing that there is no desire to utter vague threats.'

25 FO 371 30916/4049 15.4.42.

26 WO 32 10790.

27 WO 32 10790 18.5.42. Malkin had earlier (12.2.42) commented: 'If the Japanese atrocities are confirmed it will be more difficult for us to maintain the somewhat detached attitude which we have so far adopted' — FO 371 30914/C1510.

28 WP (42)264; FO 371 30916/6291 22.6.42.

29 WO 32 10790 29.6.42.

30 WO 32 10790 18.6.42.

31 PREM 4 110/10 6.7.42.

32 WP (42)277 1.7.42; PREM 4 110/10.

33 FO 371 30916/7182 4.7.42.

34 War Cab. 86(42)4.

35 War Cabinet, Committee on the Treatment of War Criminals, FO 371 30917/7573.

36 FO 371 30917 20.8.42.

37 *Punishment for War Crimes*, vol. II, p. 8. FO 371 30918/8472.

38 FO 371 30917/7853.

39 FO 371 30917/7877 12.8.42.

40   A.D. Morse, *While Six Million Died*, p. 8.

CHAPTER 3

1   Records of the meetings are in the possession of Serge Klarsfeld. See also Beate Klarsfeld, *Wherever They May Be*; Raul Hilberg, *The Destruction of the European Jews*, pp. 389ff.; G. Reitlinger, *The Final Solution*, p. 327.
    Quotations of German participants are from interviews with author.
2   Hagen, Lischke and Heinrichsohn were sentenced to twelve, ten and six years imprisonment respectively. Until their arrest, Heinrichsohn had been a lawyer and the mayor of Miltenberg, a small town near Frankfurt, while the other two were businessmen.
3   FRUS 1942, vol. I p. 48, 5.8.42, Winant to Roosevelt.
4   War Cabinet, Committee on the Treatment of War Criminals, FO 371 30918/C8569.
5   FO 371 30918/C8569.
6   ibid.
7   Dennis Allen minuted about the proposed declaration: 'This comes dangerously near to providing sanction for another "Hang the Kaiser" campaign which . . . should in the light of experience at the end of the last war, at all costs be avoided.' HMG strongly and successfully resisted Allied pressure to adhere to the Declaration.
8   FRUS 1942, vol. I pp. 54–5, 57, 20.9.42, Winant to Roosevelt.
9   FRUS 1942, vol. I p. 59. Winant was not told that Washington had agreed to Eden's other recommendations, principally that a list of wanted war criminals should be included in any armistice terms. He only learnt of that from the Foreign Office. For US agreement see FO 371 30918/C9596; also Morse, p. 26.
10 FRUS 1942, vol. I p. 59.
11 House of Lords 7.10.42.
12 FO 371 30916/C7877.
13 FO 371 30918/C8683. Allen minuted: 'We have not consulted Soviet Russia or China about the Commission idea. There seems however, no compelling reason why we should at this stage consult them.'
14 FO 371 30922/C11678. A Soviet Note dated 9 November to the Foreign Office listed three previous messages from Molotov to Eden between 25.11.41 and 29.4.42 on war crimes and several Russian declarations. On 15.11.41 at FO 371 26540, Roberts had successfully advised against detailed discussions with the Russians on

atrocities because it 'would raise serious difficulties'. But see the comment on 8.11.42 about the Soviet protest: 'The publication of this document was the first indication HMG had received of the Soviet Government's views on the whole question. They had hitherto received no indication from the Soviet Government of any desire to discuss the punishment of war criminals' (FO 371 30922/C11678).

15 FO 371 30920/C10718.
16 FO 371 30920 and 30922.
17 FO 371 30920/C10193.
18 FO 371 30920/C10718. Clark Kerr's telegram referred to 'prolonged bickering' and 'My expostulations, which were loud'. 'Stalin's prevarication irritated me,' he complained.
19 FO 371 30920/C10718.
20 ibid.
21 ibid.
22 FO 371 30922/C11700. But FO officials did admit that the threat of trials was having an effect on the Germans. Commenting on a speech by Ribbentrop in September 1942 which complained that the leaders of Britain 'are ceaselessly occupied with thoughts of revenge, punishment of Nazi leaders, punishment of fascists, of Japanese militarists, and so on,' both Roberts and Malkin noted that the 'Nazis are rather stung by the increasing references here and in the USA to war criminals and retribution.' Eden even commented: 'Good.' FO 371 30918 28.9.42.
23 FO 371 30921/C10830.
24 FO 371 30922 8.11.42.
25 FO 371 34363/C1010.
26 FO 371 34363/C580.
27 FO 371 30922 9.11.42.
28 FO 371 30921/C10833.
29 FO 371 30923/C11923.
30 ibid. Eden noted: 'I agree.'
31 ibid.
32 FO 371 30923/C11975.
33 740.00116 EW 1939–694 Reams memo to Hickerson 9.12.42.
34 Morse, p. 32.
35 Statement by Eden, House of Commons 17.12.42.
36 Lord Avon, *The Eden Memoirs: The Reckoning*, p. 358.
37 Hans Frank Diary, PS–2233. [National Archives, Washington].
38 TB/Wagner.
39 TB/Blatt.
40 FO 371 34365.

41 FO 371 34365/C3325.
42 740.00116 EW 1939– 813. Mathews to Secretary of State 5.3.43.
43 740.00116 EW 1939–1275. Roosevelt to Pell 14.6.43.
44 740.00116 EW 1939–1084.
45 740.00116 EW 1939–1079 10.9.43.
46 740.00116 EW 1939–1084.
47 740.00116 EW 1939–1143 29.10.43, 4.11.43.
48 740.00116 EW 1939–1178 9.11.43.
49 PREM 4 100/9 8.10.43.
50 PREM 4 100/9 9.10.43.
51 PREM 4 100/9 12.10.43.
52 PREM 4 100/9 and see FO 371 34374/C12028.
53 Churchill to Eden, 21.10.43: 'I attach great importance to the prin-
    ciple that the criminals will be taken back to be judged in the coun-
    tries or even in the districts where their crimes have been com-
    mitted. I should have thought this would appeal to U.J.' FO 371
    34376/C12428.
54 The Moscow Declaration.
55 FO 371 34378/C12957 and FO 371 34377.
56 FO 371 34375/C12253 and RG 218 CCS 000.5 War Criminals
    (10–18 –43) Sec. 1.
57 ibid.
58 RG 218 CCS 000.5 War Criminals 10–21–43. Sec. 1.
59 RG 218 CCS 000.5 War Criminals 10–28–43 Sec. 1.
60 FO 371 38990/C488 and C831; and see FO 371 38991/C1941,
    War Cabinet London Political Warfare Co-ordinating Committee
    (LPC (44)2) 'Kharkov Trials–Relation to Moscow Declaration'.
61 Department of State, The British Commonwealth, FRUS 1943 vol.
    3 (Washington DC 1963), p. 849; and see FO 371 34380 8.1.44,
    where D. Allen minuted: 'Mr Winant had warned Mr Pell . . . that
    this was not the moment at which we should offer provocation to
    the Germans.'

CHAPTER 4

1 FO 371 34368/C7943.
2 FO 371 26540/C14190.
3 ibid.
4 FO 371 30925/C12874. It was not passed on, although Cadogan
  minuted on the report about Buchenwald that: 'this ought to go
  some time to the Fact Finding Commission.' Also see FO 371
  39005/C14586, where Roberts minuted (18.11.44) on considering

an answer to a Parliamentary Question about whether the latest
Buchenwald list would be passed onto the UNWCC: 'This is
tricky.'
5 FO 371 39006/C15090.
6 FO 371 38998/C9346.
7 FO 371 30924/C12452 Gepp to Roberts.
8 For Pooley's account see Cyril Jolly, *The Vengeance of Private Pooley*.
9 Lt. Col. A. P. Scotland, *The London Cage*, p. 74.
10 Scotland, p. 94. Both killings were apparently claimed by the
Germans to be in retaliation for similar massacres by British troops;
see Nicholas Harman, *Dunkirk*, Hodder and Stoughton 1980, pp.
89, 97 ff.
11 WO 32 10790/27A para 2b.
12 FO 371 38994/C6819.
13 FO 371 34368/C7943.
14 FO 371 26540/C11999.
15 FO 371 34363/C774.
16 FO 371 38993. Memorandum by Sir Cecil Hurst.
17 740.00116 EW 1939–1304 15.2.44. The Americans had still not
established an office to collect evidence of war crimes against
American nationals.
18 RG 153 War Crimes JAG Law Library 1944–9 L–341.
19 ibid. But Stimson did also add: 'I think it desirable, when practicable, that US personnel on the spot assist in gathering evidence of
war crimes whether or not they primarily affect the United States.'
20 740.00116 EW 1939–2644. Hackworth memo 26.7.44.
21 RG 218 CCS 000.5 3.8.44. See also FO 371 38994/C6773 on
Hackworth's queries to the Foreign Office.
22 740.00116 EW 1939/1306.
23 740.00116 EW 1939/1299.
24 FO 371 38993/C4637.
25 WO 219/3586 1602/195 Malkin to John Foster.
26 FO 371 38993 1.4.44.
27 WP (44)294 United Nations War Crimes Commission. Memorandum by Lord Chancellor.
28 FO 371 38993/C4637.
29 ibid. But see Roberts to the FO's Political Intelligence Department,
16.7.44, assuring a 'discouraged' inquirer that the Commission was
truely established for 'more than "mere window-dressing" '. FO
371 38998/C8977.
30 FO 371 38994/C6745. Dennis Allen.
31 WP (44)294 para 6. Cadogan's view is at FO 371 38996/C8665.
'The Commission,' Cadogan wrote, 'are apt to produce wild and

unrealistic recommendations.' But in fact Simon was wrong. Continental European law does provide for the prosecution of groups.

32 FO 371 38998/C9748, the official request; and WO 219/3586 1602/298. See also C9888 for the official FO response that 'the question needs consideration'.

33 FO 371 38994/C6712.

34 WO 219/3586 1602/195. Roberts also used the argument that the Commission could not be involved in Europe, because Russia was not a member, FO 371 38998/C8982. For the same reason, the Commission was not allowed to ask permission to visit and investigate German war crimes in Russian-occupied Poland FO 371 39002/C12783. SHAEF was not expected to continue after Germany's surrender, and it still had no general mandate on war crimes. Communication had to remain through the governments.

35 FO 371 38900 1.4.44.

36 See for example WO 219/3586 1602/343. Ironically, in the House of Lords on 13 July 1944, during a debate about the Gestapo murders of the Stalag Luft 111 escapees, Lord Cranborne said on behalf of the government: 'We intend to root out utterly the whole devilish organization.'

37 FO 371 38998 18.7.44.

38 FO 371 30920/C10560.

39 ibid.

40 FO 371 34379/C14325.

41 740.00116 EW 1939–1340 16.2.44.

42 740.00116 EW 1939–2344 3.2.44. Preuss to Sandifer.

43 ibid.

44 As n. 41.

45 740.00116 EW 1939–1340 24.2.44.

46 ibid.

47 740.00116 EW 1939–1382.

48 740.00116 EW 1939–1456C.

49 740.00116 EW 1939–7–1544.

50 ibid.

51 FO 371 38994/C6744.

52 Hilberg, p. 509.

53 FO 371 38994 31.5.44.

54 War Cab. 83 (44).

55 WP (44)294.

56 PERM 4 100/10 2.6.44.

57 FO 371 38996/C665.

58 War Cab. 83 (44)(5).

59 WP (44)294.
60 Simon accused the Commission of being 'unenterprising in this matter' of collecting evidence.
61 War Cab. 84(44)(5).
62 FO 371 38998/C8982.
63 FO 371 38996/C8438.
64 FO 371 38999/C9971.
65 ibid.
66 FO 371 42809/115 and see Bernard Wasserstein, *Britain and the Jews of Europe 1939–1945*, p. 259.
67 FO 371 38998/C8982.
68 ibid.
69 FO 371 39180 30.8.44.
70 FO 371 38999/C10561. Simon suggested the need for a War Crimes Bill to give the British courts jurisdiction over those wholly non-British cases. See also the Admiralty circular on the *Peleus* case WP (44)388.
71 FO 371 38999/C9971; received on 17.8.44 as 740.00116 EW 19398–1544.
72 The Foreign Office reaffirmed the principle 'to exert pressure' on the successor government.
73 Wasserstein, p. 268.
74 740.00116 EW 1939/8–144.
75 740.00116 EW 1939/8–2644.
76 740.00116 EW 1939/7–2744.
77 FO 371 38999/C10371.
78 Morgenthau Diary (Germany) vol. 1 p. 612; E. F. Ziemke, *The U.S. Army in the Occupation of Germany 1944–1946*, p. 170.
79 740.00116 EW 1939/7–2744; at FO 371 38999/C10371, Pell was told that publicity would be regarded by the Axis powers as a pretext and encouragement for more atrocities.
80 *Daily Telegraph* 31.8.44.
81 FO 371 34380 8.1.44; and see the FO minute that the UNWCC has 'strayed beyond their proper functions' by discussing Hitler's inclusion.
82 WO 219/3586 1602/295.
83 FO 371 39003/C13615.
84 Hackworth also referred to the public declarations by politicians which, in his view, had not distinguished the nationality of the victims. 'It is believed that considerable disappointment would result if diplomatic pressure should fail and other ways were not found for dealing with these elements.'
85 Dean suggested at FO 371 39004/C13661 that the crimes could

only be prosecuted if the new German government passed the necessary laws. He wanted to leave everything until the Allies were in control of Germany.

86 FO 371 39004/C13661.

87 ibid.

88 FO 371 39005/C14744.

89 ibid.

90 740.00116 EW 1939/1–545 to 1–945.

91 See for example RG 84 Polad 810.80 1.2.45, Memorandum to Ambassador Murphy on War Crimes: 'The recent resignation of Sir Cecil Hurst was attributed to dissatisfaction with the response of the British government to the Commission's recommendations. This is not supported by the facts. While it is understood that he was annoyed at the tardiness of the Foreign Office, he actually resigned because of poor health.' But see Simon to Eden FO 371 39010/C17673 for the Australian suspicions about Russia.

92 LC02/2976 and FO 371 39010/C17673.

93 FO 371 39010/C17673, in which D. Allen surpisingly writes: 'We have always abeen in favour of the Commission taking a wide view of its functions.'

94 FO 371 51010/U517.

95 At FO 371 39010/C17673 Roberts criticized the Americans for their failure to reply to British proposals: 'To my mind the FO is neither equipped nor qualified to act as a centralising and initiating department in all these complicated matters. . .we have been left to do all the work.' He added: 'The fundamental weakness is the absence of the Russians.'

96 FO 371 39009/C168455.

97 FO 371 34378/C13455.

98 FO 371 34378/C13453; and Cadogan's reply PREM 4 110/10 p. 625.

99 War Cab. 52(43).

100 PREM 4 110/10 p. 616.

101 War Cab. 34(44).

102 FO 371 38992/C3770.

103 PREM 110/10 p. 606.

104 WP (44)330.

105 LC02/2976. Simon wrote: 'Russia has pressed us to "try" Hess (what for?)'

106 FO 371 38994/C7250.

107 WP (44)345.

108 WP (44)330. 'Those named,' wrote Eden, 'should rather be chosen because they personify the worst and most extreme features of

Nazism and Fascism than be guilty of specific war crimes.'
109 War Cab. 83(44).
110 PREM 4 100/10 p. 569.
111 US studies suggest that it was Morgenthau's original idea which
Churchill accepted. See for example B. F. Smith, *Reaching Judgment
at Nuremberg*, p. 24. But Morgenthau probably got the idea during
his August 1944 visit to London. See the draft telegram from
Churchill to Stalin, PREM 4 110/10 p. 559.
112 PREM 4 100/10 p. 539. Churchill had on 2.10.44 decided that the
time between identification and execution should be increased from
one to six hours, PREM 110/10 p. 546.

CHAPTER 5

1 WO 32 10790/14A.
2 FO 371 39002 23.9.44.
3 WO 219/3586 1602/220.
4 ibid.
5 WO 219/3586 1602/265.
6 WO 219/3586 1602/206 and FO 371 38998/C9748.
7 WO 219/3586 1602/284.
8 WO 219/3586 1602/277.
9 WO 219/3586 1602/285.
10 FO 371 39001 30.8.44.
11 WO 219/3586 1602/314, 315.
12 FO 371 38998/C8992.
13 FO 371 38998/C9346.
14 Allen Andrews, *Exemplary Justice*, is an account of the escape and
the subsequent investigation into the murders.
15 FO 371 39001/C12185.
16 WO 32 10790/27A.
17 WO 32 12210.
18 ibid.
19 FO 371 39001/C12185.
20 LCO2 2976 18.9.44.
21 FO 371 39002/C12425, and see 39003/C13428 and
39001/C12185.
22 WP (43)293, 'Warning to Neutrals not to grant asylum to Enemy
Leaders and War Criminals'.
23 FO 371 39007/C15543.
24 FO 371 38999/C10825; the Vatican even told the Allies that it
would give asylum to war criminals, 39001/C12185.

25 FO 371 38998/C9748.
26 FO 371 39002 12.9.44.
27 LC02 2976 16.9.44.
28 LC02 2976 20.9.44.
29 FO 371 39001/C12185.
30 FO 371 39000/C11109.
31 LC02 2976 18.9.44.
32 LC02 2976 21.9.44.
33 LC02 2976 22.9.44.
34 LC02 2976 20.9.44. The Allied requests and British prevarication continued until the end of the war. See the minutes of the Inter-Departmental Committee on War Crimes, CAB 78/31.
35 PREM 4 100/13 22.9.44 and 27.9.44.
36 FO 371 39003/C13209.
37 TB/Dean.
38 FO 371 39005/C14788.
39 FO 371 50101/U2710. On 7.4.45 Wardrop wrote: 'We are justified (but only just) in passing a copy to the UNWCC.'
40 LC02 2976; PM/44/631.
41 FO 371 39003/C13210.
42 FO 371 39002 23.9.44, and 39003/C13210.
43 FO 371 39004/C13734.
44 131st(44)meeting(3).
45 PREM 100/13.
46 FO 371 39004/C14255.
47 Dean's description, FO 371 39003/C13210.
48 FO 371 39003/C13575.
49 ibid.
50 WO 219/3586 1602/321; and see 39004/C14080 for invitation.
51 FO 371 39005/C14972 for results.
52 FO 371 39005/C14743.
53 ibid.
54 WO 219/3586 1602/325. Originally it had been decided that it should be a G2 Intelligence responsibility 1602/308 5.6.44.
55 FO 371 39007/C15505 and C15634.
56 WP (44)648.
57 CAB 66/53 and 65/44.
58 WO 32 12210 13.12.44; Malkin's assurances WO 32 12210/39A 22.9.45.
59 WO 32 12210 28.9.44.
60 FO 371 39010/C17544.
61 FO 371 51010/U664.
62 WO 32 11729 23.2.45.

63 FO 371 39008/C16344 (telegram is in C10188).
64 FO 371 39003 16.10.43. Allen also complained that someone should have been allowed to attend the interrogations of POWs to get evidence of war crimes. See 39008/C16363 for first British war crimes list.
65 WO 32 12210 25.1.45.
66 FO 39009/C17057.
67 FO 371 39005/C14788 and 39002 23.9.44.
68 RG 153 War Crimes Division JAG Law Library 1944–49 L–486.
69 ibid.
70 ibid.
71 RG 107 ASW 1940–47 000.51 War Crimes 1943–44.
72 RG 107 ASW 1940–47 000.51 War Crimes 1943–44.
73 Box 15 Ass.-Sec. (Jan. 43–Dec. 44 file) 27.10.44. [National Archives Washington.]
74 The term had already been used during the First World War.
75 Box 15 Ass.-Sec. (Jan 43–Dec. 44 file) 4.12.44.
76 FO 371 39005/C14744, and see 39010/C18103 for Eden's reply to Hurst on all the other proposals. Eden excused the Foreign Office's delay by explaining that the Foreign Office had to await replies from all the other Allies, but the reply hardly reflected his own officials, criticisms at C17673 of the Commission itself, their proposals and the Allies.
77 PREM 100/13 15.12.44.
78 FO 371 39010/C17674.
79 Report of SHAEF Court of Inquiry re Shooting of Allied Prisoners of War by the German Armed Forces Near Malmédy, Liège, Belgium, 17 December 1944, RG 319 National Archives.
80 SHAEF Report, 'Findings of Court'.
81 RG 107 1940–47 ASW 000.51 War Crimes Working file 'Trial and Punishment of Nazi War Criminals'. Significantly, James Forrestal, the Secretary for the Navy, refused to sign the memorandum. Both the American Navy Department and the British Admiralty resolutely refused whenever possible, both during and after the war, to be involved in any war crimes prosecutions. Some British JAG prosecutors believe it was the Admiralty's lack of cooperation in 1946 which resulted in the acquittal of Colonel Werner von Tippelskirch, charged with the murder of six captured British marine commandos, whose story was told in the book, *The Cockleshell Heroes*.
82 FO 371 39007/C15594.
83 House of Commons 31.1.45. O'Neil minuted on 6.2.45 at 46795/398 that the minister 'succeeded in maintaining an

ambiguity which in view of the difficulties now cropping up, may prove very useful.' But on 14.2.45, Somervell interpreted Law's statement as definitely committing the Allies and not the Germans, to prosecute (46795/C775).

84 FO 371 46795/U829 Telgram No. 835, and FO 371 51011/U832.

85 FO 371 51011/U832.

86 FO 371 46795/C755.

87 House of Lords 20.3.45 col. 656.

88 ACAO/P(45)22 in FO 942/311; discussed on 14.3.45, WO 32 11728. The draft also ordered the arrests to be carried out by the Germans at the risk of punishment if they failed, and provided that German law, significantly *not* retrospectively altered, should be applied.

89 FO 371 46796/C2121 69th Meeting of the ACAO Committee 2.5.45. Grigg, the Secretary of State for War, wrote to Simon on 5 May repeating that the politicians' public commitments would 'involve an almost intolerable burden' which should be left to the country whose nationals suffered. WO 32 11728/33A.

90 For the Roseman negotiations see Smith, pp. 36ff.

91 WO 32 11729/1A to 5B 17.1.45.

92 WO 32 11729 8.2.45.

93 WO 32 11729 16.3.45.

94 WO 32 11726 9.3.45.

95 WO 205/265. The orders to create investigatory groups were finally issued on 25.4.45.

96 WO 32 12197 14.3.45, ACAO/M(45)9.

97 FO 371 511017/U2994.

98 WO 32 12210 29.3.45.

99 WO 32 12197/15A.

100 FO 371 49796/C2230.

101 ibid. In his reply, Grigg denied that there had been any ban on journalists and insisted that investigations were going ahead.

102 FO 371 46796/C2230. Jews were not always considered useful. Basil Newton commented on the appointment of Lord Schuster as chief of the Legal Division for Austria: 'I doubt the wisdom of appointing a Jew in all the circumstances' FO 371 39183/C18191.

103 WO 32 11728.

104 740.00116 EW 1939/2–645.

105 740.00116 EW 1939/3–1945.

CHAPTER 6

1 C. Lasby, *Project Paperclip*, is the best available account of the operation, although it relies on very few of the archival documents now available. The Operation was originally called 'Project Overcoat', but the name was changed when it was noted that crates containing the scientists' luggage for shipment to the USA were openly covered with the word 'Overcoat'. RG 260 OMGUS HQ Ad.-Gen. 1945/6 370.2 and see RG 218 CCS Germany 5–1–45 Sec. 4 471.9.
2 RG 260 OMGUS HQ AG Decimal File 1945/6 231.2. The Russians asked for their return on 8 Sept., Sokolovsky to Clay.
3 RG 260 OMGUS HQ AG Decimal File 1945/6 231.2.
4 Lasby, p. 38.
5 The trial was held at Dachau.
6 CCS 551.
7 EUCOM Report, JAG Dept for War Crimes, June 1944 to July 1948, Ziemke, p. 170.
8 RG 260 OMGUS HQ AG Decimal File 1945/6 000.5, Nov 44; and Ziemke, p. 173, quoting War Dept, AG, to CG, ETOUSA, SHAEF G-1, 00.5–7 25.12.44.
9 Smith, pp. 40, 41.
10 RG 107 1940–47 ASW 000.51 War Crimes; and WO 32 11728.
11 RG 338 HG USAREUR JAG War Crimes case files 1945–55, War Crimes Organization 1945; and FO 371 46801/U2686G.
12 Ziemke, p. 219; RG 107 1940–47 ASW 000.51 War Crimes.
13 Report of the Deputy Judge Advocate for War Crimes European Command, June 1944 to July 1948, known hereafter as the Straight Report, p. 25.
14 Ziemke, p. 220.
15 TB/Straight.
16 G 153 War Crimes Division, JAG Law Library 1944–49 L-341.
17 FO 371 51017/U2686.
18 'Arrest and Detention in Germany', SHAEF G-5 000.52.
19 W. Maser, *Nuremberg, A Nation on Trial* p. 50.
20 RG 165 OPD 000.5 Sec. IV Cases 54.
21 RG 260 OMGUS HQ AG Decimal File 1945–46, 322.
22 WO 32 12197/25A.
23 WO 32 12200 6.12.45 and 17.12.45.
24 FO 371 39005.
25 FO 371 51033 21.6.45.
26 TB/McDermott.
27 WO 32 12200; Report on Bridgeman's visit WO 32 12197/57A.

28 WO 32 12200/7A.
29 FO 939/439 23.6.45.
30 RG 84 Polad 1945, 810 24.4.45.
31 ibid.
32 RG 260 OMGUS HQ, Box 1.
33 SCAF 431, WO 32 12197/38A. The first directive was JCS 1023/10 on 8.7.45.
34 WO 32 12197/57A (Bridgeman report), and see Straight Report p. 32 passim.
35 Weir claimed some success, RG 153 War Crimes JAG Law Library 1944–49 L-341. Col. Halse of the British JAG War Crimes told the author that the British did get some results using the Q-forms.
36 Straight Report, p. 3.
37 Straight Report, p. 17: 'It does not appear that steps were taken by Commands. . .to implement the directives.'
38 TB/Straight.
39 ibid.
40 RG 107 1940–47 ASW 000.51 War Crimes.
41 RG 338 HQ USAREUR JAG War Crimes Case Files 14.2.45.
42 RG 260 OMGUS HQ AG Decimal File 1945–6 000.3 Box 3.
43 Smith, p. 43 passim.
44 WO 32 11726.
45 WO 32 12202/10A.
46 WO 205/265.
47 ibid; and see WO 32 12202 4.4.45, where Barnes suggests to the War Office that the only way to keep the UNWCC investigating teams out of the concentration camps in the British zone would be for the 21 Army Group to set up their own teams.
48 The Belsen Trial, Transcript p. 53.
49 Reitlinger, p. 509.
50 TB/Draper.
51 WO 32 12197 2.8.45.
52 WO 32 12210 6.2.45.
53 TB/Halse.
54 WO 32 12197 1.8.45 referring to H. of C. 29.5.45, cols 35–7. Churchill was in fact referring to cases involving British servicemen, and not concentration camp cases.
55 WO 32 12197/25A.
56 WO 32 12202 6.6.45.
57 ibid. On 29.3.45 Nigel Roland described the delay to Maj.-Gen. Hollis at the War Cabinet Office as having the potential of creating 'a real fiasco with serious political consequences' WO 32 12210.
58 WO 32 12197/43A FACS 245 (and FAN 575) was the order from

the CCS to Eisenhower removing some of the restrictions on war crimes trials. Others remained until 8 July, removed by FAN 591/FACS 259 (WO 32 11728).
59 TB/Bridgeman.
60 WO 32 12197.
61 WO 32 12202/38A.
62 WO 32 12197.
63 WO 32 12202 9.8.45.
64 WO 32 12197.
65 WO 32 12197 1.8.45.
66 WO 32 12197 2.8.45.
67 WO 32 12197 7.8.45.
68 WO 32 12210 21.11.45.
69 TB/McDermott.
70 Scotland.
71 WO 32 11726.
72 FO 939/437 8.6.45.
73 TB/Elliot.
74 WO 32 12202 and FO 937/29.
75 WO 32 12197.
76 WO 32 12202 20.8.45.
77 ibid.
78 WO 32 11727 6.6.45.
79 FO 371 46797/C4573.
80 ibid.
81 ibid.
82 FO 371 38998/C8992.
83 TB/Draper.
84 Andrews, op. cit. p. 59.
85 Information given to author by members of both organizations.
86 WO 32 12202/84B.
87 J. J. Weingartner, *Crossroads of Death*, p. 72.
88 TB/Fanton.

CHAPTER 7

1 FO 371 46867/C3225.
2 Cf. F.S.V. Donnison, *Civil Affairs and Military Government: Central Organization and Planning*.
3 Ziemke, pp. 39, 91.
4 The author saw the digests belonging to former CCG officers. For Bovenschen's jealousy see FO 371 40801/U7062.

5 For Roosevelt's attitudes see Ziemke, pp. 85ff; E. N. Peterson, *The American Occupation of Germany*, p. 21, and books cited by Peterson.

6 Peterson, p. 21, quoting William McNeill, *America, Britain and Russia: Their Co-operation and Conflict, 1941–46*, London 1953.

7 Peterson, p. 33.

8 G. Kennan, *Memoirs 1925–1950*, p. 172.

9 FO 371 39180/C12938; and Kirby to Harvey FO 371 40801/U6923 11.8.44; also see Kirby to Harvey about staff shortages FO 371 40802/U7158, and Kirby to General Hildring, 'I am rather worried' about the differences between two Allies' policies, RG 260 OMGUS HQ AG Decimal File 1945–46 350.5.

10 Mathias Erzberger, a Jewish socialist, signed the armistice after the German military decided at the last moment not to go to Compiegne.

11 Ziemke, p. 86; Peterson, p. 38ff; and E. Davidson, *The Death and Life of Germany*, pp. 6ff.

12 TB/Riddleberger; Riddleberger was a State Department official in Europe.

13 General Records of the European Division 1944–53, Box 1. Stimson, while wanting to demilitarize and control Germany, opposed Morgenthau's harsh terms.

14 Ziemke, pp. 178ff; W. Griffith, 'The Denazification Program in the United States Zone of Germany', Thesis, Harvard University, 1950 (hereafter, Griffith), p. 38.

15 WO 219/3857 9373/295 and 9373/178 SHAEF report.

16 Griffith, p. 40; S. Padover, *Experiment in Germany*, p. 222.

17 The Nazi resistance movement was, with the exception of Oppenhoff's murder, singularly ineffective. See FO 371 64352/C3435, the FO brief for the March 1947 Council of Foreign Ministers meeting; FO 938/386 29.7.46 is a justification for keeping 40,000 interned on 'security grounds'; by 1.6.47 this was reduced to 6,000, FO 371 64712/C7782 Lord Chancellor's Report; RG 260 OMGUS AG Sec. Class, Decimal Files 1945–49 350.09 1.2.47, a list and analysis by the Director of US Intelligence of all the Nazi Underground Organizations. FO 371 46894/C2049 7.5.45, a SHAEF Intelligence Report describing the Werewolf movement as 'so far sterile, but potentially fertile'.

18 FACS 93 7.10.44.

19 SHAEF/G-5(Ops)/803 WO 219 3848 8983/580 23.2.45.

20 Peterson, p. 51, quoting FN 104, ASW 370.8 Germany McCloy to Chandler 12.10.44; for Plischke Report on how 'millions' of arrests were to be carried out, see RG 84 Polad 810 17.5.45; also see FO 371 46799/C1048.

21 FO 371 39180/C12938G.
22 SHAEF/G5/Ops/803/4.2.45 at WO 219 3857 8983/594.
23 RG 84 Polad 810 19.6.45.
24 WO 219 3857 9373/306 12th Army-G5 Operational Instructions.
25 WO 219 3857 9373/326; RG 250 USGCC 1944–45 383.6 Report from SHAEF G5 to Provost Marshal at War Department 16.5.45. Bernstein's protest, RG 84 Polad 810 19.6.45.
26 Peterson, p. 142.
27 RG 84 Polad 810 7.5.45.
28 Murphy's files (RG 84 810) are full of complaints of failures of MG officers refusing to obey directives; see also Griffith and H. Zink, *The United States in Germany 1944–1955*.
29 Ziemke, p. 8ff.
30 L. Clay, *Decision in Germany*, p. 2.
31 TB/Bishop.
32 RG 260 OMGUS HQ AG Decimal File 333.5; RG 260 OMGUS USGCC 1944–45 014.3 Murphy to Clay 4.7.45.
33 RG 260 OMGUS USGCC 1944–45 383.7 6.3.45.
34 FO 371 46975 10.8.45; Plischke reported the same to Headquarters — denazification was being 'pushed into the background'. RG 84 Polad 810 25.5.45.
35 FO 371 39182/C14580.
36 FO 371 40801/U6869.
37 ibid.
38 FO 371 40802/U7158 23.8.44.
39 FO 371 39183/C16092 19.11.44.
40 FO 371 40802/U7126. The low pay also meant that only 'people of insufficient calibre' would accept. Kirby was not allowed to advertise, FO 371 40802/U7158.
42 FO 371 39182/C14794. Calder later described the calibre of the staff as 'low', FO 371 46973. Throughout files 40801–2 are examples of how confused the British were about the Control Commission's task. Kirby insisted at U6894 that Germany could not be 'administered like a Crown Colony', while Troutbeak at U7156 was 'worried' about the confusion.
43 FO 371 46799/C482; and see FO 371 46865/C816: 'Our policy is not to employ enemy aliens at all at present,' 5.3.45; and see FO 39151/C4935, written 15.4.44: 'There is no White List of good Germans at the moment, although there are thoughts of compiling one.'
44 Murphy did however sanction the employment of Germans in non-executive positions RG 260 OMGUS HQ AG Sec. Class Decimal File 1945–49 340 1.3.45.

45 FO 371 46868/C3967: 'To imagine we will be received as liberators is illusory. . .Don't appease any German, "good" or "bad".' At FO 371 39183/C18193, there was a decision that in Germany Germans could be employed by the British in a non-executive capacity.
46 FO 371 40816/U5266 9.6.44.
47 FO 371 46894/C2049 7.5.45.
48 CAB 62(45)(3). See FO 939/439 7.6.45, where some British officials hope the Cabinet decision could be reversed; FO 371 46933/C4131 (27.7.45) is a directive from the Political Intelligence Department to BAOR not to even mention the possibility of the return of anti-Nazis from abroad; FO 371 46867/C2234 queries the 'danger of treating all Germans alike' and of not backing the 'good German'. Hynol explained the reasons for government policy in the House of Commons on 12.12.45. Yet in March 1947 the British still held 435,295 German POWs, a clear breach of the Geneva Convention, which stipulated the return of POWs at the end of hostilities and forbade their use as cheap labour. See FO 371 64453/C4515.
49 RG 84 Polad 810 6.6.45; for British attitude to American policy, see Balfour's report at FO 371 46975 10.8.45.
50 Hilberg, p. 313.
51 RG 260 USGCC General Correspondence AG Decimal File 014,12 8.7.45.
52 RG 84 Polad 810 28.7.45.
53 FO 371 55696/C7527 for British comment.
54 FO 371 64745/C9228 2.7.47, and see FO 371 64747/C152312 for an astonishing account of how the British Transport Division had deliberately protected its appointments despite their notorious Nazi records. The denazification panels were invariably comprised of only Nazis, or occasionally a nominal 'non-Nazi'. Robertson suggested that the FO should not investigate what he admitted seemed to be a conspiracy between the British and Nazi officials. Although on paper the FO rejected his advice, nothing was done. Proof that it was from the outset a common occurrence can be found in FO 371 46799 6.8.45 where Maj.-Gen. G. Templer wrote: 'It should be realised that there is considerable evidence. . .that the Nazis are being retained in office unnecessarily and that evidence against them is ignored'.
55 RG 260 USGCC General Correspondence AG Decimal File 014 12.7.45.
56 ibid.
57 ibid.
58 G OMGUS Chief of Staff file 250.3 11.9.45.

59 B. Engelmann, *Wie Wir Würden, Was Wir Sind*, p. 40ff.
60 Peterson, p. 214ff.
61 Peterson, p. 219, quoting from the many American books available on the subject.
62 Griffith, p. 115; Frederic Spott, *The Churches and Politics in Germany*, p. 89.
63 Spott, p. 90.
64 Spott, p. 91.
65 Spott, p. 92.
66 FO 371 46935/C6450.
67 Ziemke, p. 252.
68 FO 371 46933/C4131; FO 371 46838/C4032; FO 371 46796/C2865.
69 A.J. and R.L. Merritt, *Public Opinion in Occupied Germany*, p. 30ff.
70 FO 371 46894/C972.
71 FO 371 46973/C7624.
72 FO 371 46935 Calder Report 1.9.45.
73 For acknowledgement of the strength of the Antifa (Anti-Facist) groups, see Strang's report FO 371 46933/C3858 and comments; FO 371 46934, a report by Annan on how the British were sacking anti-Nazis because of mistrust; FO 371 46973/C7200, Strang on the coalminers' anti-Nazi feelings.
74 FO 371 46975/C9515; FO 371 46867/C2334; Davidson, p. 75ff.
75 FO 371 46933/C3858. Newton minuted: 'The British authorities are getting together with and building up the Germans much too successfully and much too fast.'
76 FO 371 46867/C3225.
77 Ziemke, p. 108. The despair was echoed even louder after Germany's defeat. Troutbeck wrote to Strang after visiting Germany: 'The worst of it is that genuine democracies have always started spontaneously as a revolt against established authority. But here the established authority has to try and impose free thinking on a people that greatly prefers not to think for itself' FO 371 46973/C5960.
78 *The Times*, 5.7.45.

CHAPTER 8

1 A British team of psychologists, appointed by the Control Office, tried to discover the answer but failed. PREM 8 520 ORC(46)9th Meeting.
2 Griffith, p. 8.

3 RG 84 Polad 810 25.8.45.
4 RG 84 Polad 810/820 16.10.45 Conference Report.
5 RG 84 Polad 810 16.10.45; and see OMGUS HQ AG Decimal File 1945–46 230.02 Intelligence Report to COS 26.10.45.
6 FO 371 46973 31.8.45 Calder Report.
7 FO 371 46973 31.8.45. Strang's early reports mention antagonism towards DPs. See also Ziemke and Davidson.
8 Griffith, p. 90; Peterson, p. 143.
9 FO 371 46801/C8985.
10 FO 945/16 75A.
11 Wurm protest to Clay 24.5.46 reported by DANA News Agency.
12 RG 84 Polad 810 3.10.45.
13 G.A. Craig, *Germany 1866–1945*, p. 578.
14 RG 260 OMGUS HQ AG Decimal File 1945–46 014.3 2.10.46.
15 Spott, p. 111.
16 FO 371 46975/C9515 Strang Report.
17 RG 260 OMGUS HQ Adj.-Gen. Decimal File 1945–46 014.3 15.1.46.
18 ibid. 2.2.46.
19 ibid. 3.1.46.
20 The categories were: war criminals; major offenders; activists, militarists and profiteers; followers; non-offenders.
21 FO 371 46805 'Reactions to Denazification'.
22 RG 260 OMGUS HQ Adj.-Gen. 1945–6 014.3 2.2.46.
23 Griffith, p. 149.
24 RG 260 OMGUS HQ Adj.-Gen. Decimal File 1945–46 014.3 3.1.46.
25 RG 260 OMGUS HQ 7885 162 1/17 22.7.46.
26 ibid. See also the Adj.-Gen.'s directive ordering American personnel to cease showing 'an attitude of scepticism and pessimism. . .Dissatisfaction expressed in spoken criticism. . .can only lead to demoralization of those charged with its enforcement and to the comfort of those whom the law was designed to punish' RG 260 OMGUS HQ Adj.-Gen. Decimal File 1945–46 014.3 6.9.46.
27 RG 260 OMGUS HQ AG Decimal File 1945–46 322 18.9.46.
28 RG 260 OMGUS HQ AG Decimal File 1945–46 014.3 17.8.46.
29 ibid. 17.8.46.
30 ibid. 26. 8.46.
31 ibid.
32 RG 260 OMGUS HQ AG Decimal File 1945–46 333.5 3.10.46.
33 RG 260 OMGUS HQ AG Decimal File 1945–46 014.3 2.12.46.
34 ibid. 6.9.46.

35 FO 371 64744/C8058.
36 FO 371 46973/C7200.
37 ibid.
38 FO 371 46933/C3858.
39 The Americans were no different. A report from Murphy to the State Department in Aug. 45 contained a report from an officer stating that the Antifa had 'presented the Military Government with something of a problem in their evident desire to play a part in the denazification activities' RG 84 Polad 810 25.8.45.
40 WO 32 12208/64B.
41 FO 371 55437 16.6.46.
42 FO 945/13 6A.
43 FO 371 64352/C1648.
44 FO 371 55438/C11071.
45 FO 371 64352/C223.
46 FO 371 64744/C8058. The mistake of associating Nazis and militarists seems only to have been realized at the end of 1946.
47 FO 371 64353/C16033.
48 FO 371 64352/C3435 Report to the CFM, Denazification.
49 FO 371 64352/C2278. Statistics available in Justus Fürtenau, *Entnazifizierung*, Berlin 1969, p. 159, state that the results in the British zone were that out of 2,041,454 people found to be incriminated, not a single German in the British zone was categorized either as a Grade One of Grade Two Nazi. More than half (1,191,930) were put in the bottom category and 600,319 were released altogether. Only 27,000 were classed in Grade Three as being 'slightly incriminated'.
50 FO 371 46801 Minutes of the 8th Meeting of Standing Committee on Denazification.
51 FO 371 64352/C1648. File also contains an account of the British removal of anti-Nazis in Hamburg.
52 Spott, p. 101.
53 Spott. p. 102.
54 FO 371 46973/C7200.
55 Peterson, p. 150; J. Gimbel, *The American Occupation of Germany*, p. 109.
56 RG 260 OMGUS HQ AG Decimal File 1945–46 014.3 2.12.46.
57 ibid. 27.8.46.
58 Quoted in RG 260 OMGUS HQ Adj.-Gen. 1947 013.3 24.2.47. See Pollock to Clay that Maier proved during the negotiations 'to be lacking. . .what Bismarck once referred to as "civil courage" ' RG 260 OMGUS HQ Adj.-Gen. 1945–46 014.3 23.2.46. For allegations of Maier's later (1950) $217^1/_{17}$ open sabotage of denazi-

fication programme, see RG 260 OMGUS 8010 217¹/₁₇, the Kase
case, involving payments of large bribes by Nazis seeking to avoid
incrimination. Reluctantly, McCloy was forced to intervene.

59 US House of Representatives 26.7.47 Rep. A.J. Sabbath.
60 RG 260 OMGUS Adj.-Gen. 1945–46 014.3 2.12.46.
61 ibid. 26.12.46.
62 ibid. 21.9.46.
63 Gimbel, p. 102.
64 RG 260 OMGUS HQ Adj.-Gen. 1945–46 014.3 26.12.46.
65 ibid. 20.9.46.
66 ibid. 31.8.46.
67 RG 260 OMGUS HQ AG Decimal File 1945–46 300.4 24.7.46.
68 FO 371 46800 16.10.46 Standing Committee on Denazification.
69 A. Hearnden (editor)k, *The British in Germany*.
70 Hearnden, p. 66.
71 Hearnden, p. 148.
72 RG 260 OMGUS HQ AG Decimal File 1945–46 014.3 9.1.46.
73 Hearnden, p. 55.
74 FO 945/95.
75 TB/Kneipe.
76 FO 945/100.
77 TB/Halland.
78 FO 371 64697/C12519.
79 FO 371 55837/C3974.
80 FO 945/98.
81 FO 945/98; FO 938/324 (Kiel police); FO 371 64647/C16020
   (Oldenberg).
82 FO 371 55837/C3974.
83 ORC (46)60.
84 FO 945/95 37C.
85 FO 371 64697/C12519.
86 FO 937/16.
87 R. Dahrendorf, *Society and Democracy in Germany*, p. 246.
88 Craig, p. 579.
89 K. Löwenstein, in E.H. Litchfield (ed.), *Governing Post-War
   Germany*, p. 246.
90 K.P. Tauber, *Beyond Eagle and Swastika*, p. 960.
91 R. Grunberger, *A Social History of the Third Reich*, p. 163.
92 Hilberg, p. 110.
93 FO 371 46801 17.11. 45.
94 FO 937/16.
95 ibid.
96 FO 937/13.

97 ibid.
98 FO 371 55436 23.5.46.
99 FO 371 55438 19.9.46.
100 RG 260 OMGUS 7964, 201²/₁₇ 18.11.47.
101 ibid.
102 RG 260 OMGUS 217²/₁₇ undated.
103 RG 260 OMGUS 8011 217³/₁₇ 4.6.47.
104 RG 260 OMGUS HQ Adj.-Gen. 1949 013.3 5.2.49.
105 ibid. 17.3.49.
106 ibid. 2.5.49.

CHAPTER 9
.

1 Reitlinger, p. 364ff.
2 Reitlinger, p. 506.
3 United Nations War Crimes Commission, *Law Reports of War Criminals* (hereafter UNWCC Report), vol. II p. 4.
4 UNWCC Report, p. 80; see Dean's comment FO 371 50989 21.10.45: 'This is not helpful. . .it seems to me a good deal more than need have been said'.
5 UNWCC Report, p. 83.
6 FO 371 50992/U8804.
7 ibid.
8 UNWCC Report, p. 117.
9 FO 371 57560/U154.
10 FO 371 57579/U4680.
11 FO 371 57579/U1664.
12 FO 371 57560 8.1.46.
13 WO 32 12197 21.11.45.
14 ibid.
15 WO 32 12202 30.11.45.
16 WO 32 12202/64A.
17 WO 32 12197/67A.
18 WO 32 12197 July.
19 TB/Bridgeman.
20 WO 32 12197 July.
21 WO 32 12640.
22 WO 32 12197.
23 On 12.2.1946 Newton estimated that only 'a fraction of the 50,000 [war criminals] will be tried' (FO 371 57612/U1832).
24 FO 371 46797/C7345.
25 FO 371 50991/U8558.

26 WO 32 12202 26.10.45.
27 WO 32 12197 29.11.45.
28 TB/Bridgeman and WO 32 12202 16.12.45.
29 FO 371 50991/U8558.
30 WO 32 12202 3.11.45.
31 ibid. 16.12.45.
32 ibid. 26.11.45.
33 WO 32 12197 3.12.45.
34 WO 32 12640 14.12.45.
35 WO 32 12202 28.12.45.
36 ibid. 16.12.45.
37 FO 371 57541/U2495.
38 FO 371 64713/U734.
39 WO 32 12197 30.12.45.
40 WO 32 12202 30.12.45. Gurney had clearly heard that the letter
    was on its way.
41 TB/Nightingale. See WO 32 12202/145A (July 1946), an officer
    writing to London: 'I have tried but it is impossible to find even
    two officers for attachment to war crimes trials in BAOR.'
42 Letter in possession of a former member of the War Crimes Group.
43 WO 32 12197 28.3.47.
44 FO 371 57529/U958.
45 WO 32 12197 12.2.46; WO 32 12202 12.2.46; FO 371 57540 Feb.
    1946.
46 WO 32 12640 29.1.46.
47 WO 32 12197 15.3.46.
48 TB/Cleaver.
49 WO 32 12202 5.4.46.
50 ibid. 11.4.46.
51 FO 371 57458/U5960. Beaumont commented: 'I fear there is little
    to be gained by once more impressing on Commands the high
    priority to be given to this work.'
52 WO 32 12197 Apr.–Sept. 1945.
53 FO 371 57458/U5960.
54 FO 371 55893 24.6.46.
55 FO 371 57528 21.1.46.
56 FO 371 57548/U5960.
57 UNWCC Reports, vol. V.
58 WO 32 12202 20.6.46.
59 TB/Schweiger.
60 FO 371 57671/U5804.
61 FO 371 57458/U5960.
62 FO 371 57671/U5804.

63 *The Times*, 13.6.46.
64 FO 371 57671/U5804.
65 FO 371 50991 3.11.45.
66 TB/Scott-Fox.
67 TB/Garner.
68 WO 32 12197 17.5.46.
69 FO 371 57458 18.6.46.

CHAPTER 10

1 TB/Nightingale, Smith and Lenewski.
2 RG 260 OMGUS AG Decimal File 1945–46 000.5 18.12.45. Extradition from the US zone was approved by JCS 1023/10.
3 RG 260 OMGUS AG Decimal File 1945–46 000.5 (Box 3) 31.10.46.
4 RG 260 OMGUS AG Decimal File 1945–46 000.5 Box 168 25.7.46.
5 As n. 3.
6 See WO 32 11728 14.3.45; WO 32 12197 28.3.45; and WO 32 12202 29.3.45.
7 FO 371 39008/C16300.
8 FO 371 51003/U6167.
9 WO 32 12197 28.3.45 and WO 32 11728 2.5.45.
10 WO 32 11728 2.5.45.
11 WO 32 11171/192A 1.7.45.
12 War Cab. 57(45)2.
13 WO 32 11728/239 8.6.45. Extradition should have been conditional upon the appearance of the wanted man's name on the UNWCC list. The British protested to Washington on seeing that Eisenhower's directive omitted the need for reference to the UNWCC list. In reply, the War Department insisted that the list was 'exceedingly useful', but in practice it was ignored. RG 260 OMGUS AG Decimal File Box 3 29.8.45.
14 WO 32 12197 44A 14.6.45.
15 WO 32 11171 192A 2.7.45.
16 N. Bethell, *The Last Secret*, Andre Deutsch 1974; N. Tolstoy, *Victims of Yalta*, Hodder and Stoughton 1977.
17 WO 32 11171 192A 2.7.45.
18 WO 32 11171 193A 6.7.45.
19 FACS 259 WO 32 11728 35A.
20 FO 371 57527/U992.
21 RG 338 HQ USAREUR JAG, War Crimes Case files, War Crimes

Organization, 1946.
22 RG 260 OMGUS AG Decimal File 1947 2.4.47.
23 As n. 21.
24 FO 945/352 7.2.46.
25 ibid. 22.8.46. The British evidently had more sympathy for the Yugoslavs. Dean wrote on 5.2.47: 'There seems little doubt that taken by and large, the Germans behaved worse in Yugoslavia than almost anywhere else and that the atrocities committed by them and on their behalf were too appalling to imagine. On the other hand, the Yugoslavs spoil a very good case by their insistence on treating all Yugoslavs who are out of sympathy with the present regime as "war criminals and traitors" ' (FO 371 66570/U271).
26 WO 32 12202 64A 22.10.45.
27 WO 32 12197 112A.
28 The Dutch Parliament finally amended its laws to allow the prosecution of war crimes committed outside Holland on 10.7.1947.
29 WO 267/600 Quarterly Historical Report of the War Crimes Investigation Unit 30.9.1946.
30 Andrews, p. 168.
31 FO 371 57647/U5239.
32 ibid.
33 TB/Smith.
34 RG 260 OMGUS AG Decimal File 1947 000.5 15.10.46.
35 ibid.
36 ibid.
37 See later in the chapter.
38 WO 32 12197 103A 24.9.46.
39 WO 32 12197 97A 15.7.46.
40 FO 371 57458/U5960.
41 WO 32 12202 151A 13.8.46.
42 WO 32 12197 101A 21.10.46.
43 WO 32 12202 167A 2.11.46.
44 WO 32 12197 1.1.47.
45 CAB. 94(46)(2).
46 FO 371 64724/C16455.
47 WO 32 12202 167A 2.11.46.
48 FO 945/554.
49 WO 32 12197 17.1.47.
50 WO 32 12200 15A.
51 FO 371 66559 21.1.47.
52 A. Pierrepoint, *Executioner*, p. 147.
53 FO 945/318.
54 WO 32 12210 161A to 164A FO 371 64849 March 1947.

55 UNWCC Reports, vol. 8.
56 Scotland, p. 172; and see Scotland's 1951 pamphlet printed in both English and German in the same cover, 'The Kesselring case', where he argued that Kesselring's conviction was a miscarriage of justice.
57 Halse, unpublished autobiography, 'Forty Years On', p. 45.
58 FO 371 66570/U646. Dean added: 'The protests in the House of Lords against the condemnation of Kesselring who was undoubtedly responsible for some horrible atrocities in Italy against civilians [were] on the ground that he was an excellent soldier' 7.5.47.
59 Germans, both then and now (see for example, *Der Spiegel*, No. 48 1978), were convinced that the British were in reality keeping the Dienstgruppen in reserve for use in a possible war with Russia. The Germans called the 81,358 members of the Dienstgruppen 'the Balck Reichswehr'. At the Council of Foreign Ministers meeting in March 1947, Russia continuously attacked the Dienstgruppen (FO 371 64155 11.3.47 and FO 371 64352/C1637), and while the British admitted that they were a paramilitary force (FO 371 64453/C4217) and policemen (C4507), they insisted that their use was simply to augnent the depleted British forces in guard duties and clearing operations. At that very time, the British kept 87,000 German POWs at work in Egypt because, as Bevin told Attlee: 'the local Egyptian labour is not as efficient as the Germans' (FO 371 64453/C4217). Western Intelligence estimated that the Russians had kept at least two million German POWs as labour, with about 300,000 receiving military training (FO 371 70648D).
60 FO 945/342.
61 FO 371 64724/C16455.
62 FO 371 64713/C8850.
63 PREM 8 707 13.5.47. See PREM 8 707 29.6.47 for Harding's reasons for the commutation of the death sentences on Kesselring and two other German generals. Harding insisted that Kesselring was an excellent soldier, was only obeying orders, was not in full command at the time, and apart from that one instance had behaved very well throughout the war. Kesselring was released from prison in 1952 on the grounds that he was suffering from cancer. After a miraculous 'recovery', he became president of the Stahlhelm, the German veterans' organization.
64 FO 371 64713/C8850.
65 WO 32 12640 87A 17.6.47.
66 FO 371 66570/U384 10.2.47.
67 FO 371 64712/C8534.

68 FO 371 64718/C13259 and FO 945/554 108A 25.10.47; FO 371 64720/C14173 29.10.47; and see FO 371 64724/C16497 for the problems in Holland; and FO 371 64720/C14121 for the special problems in Yugoslavia.

69 WO 267/600 Quarterly Historical Report of the War Crimes Investigation Unit June 1947.

70 RG 260 OMGUS AG Decimal File 1947 000.5 8.7.47.

71 ibid. 9.7.47.

72 ibid. 1.8.47. For one of many Polish protests see 740.00119 Control (Germany) 5–649 6.5.49.

73 RG 260 OMGUS COS 1722, 135½ 000.5.

74 Straight Report, p. 249. Statistics for extradition are: to Poland 1,172, to France 1,397, to UK 592, to Holland 98, to Denmark 21, to Austria 15, to Norway 9, to Italy 2. Italy had posed a serious problem throughout the 1944–45 discussions on extradition because it had been a wartime ally of Germany. Many Germans responsible for atrocities in Italy therefore remained unprosecuted.

75 RG 260 OMGUS AG Sec. Class 1947 250.3 30.8.47.

76 RG 338 HQ USAREUR JAG War Crimes Case Files, Memorandum from Wurm to Clay on 'The Question of War Crimes Trials before American Military Courts', p. 72. Wurm admits that those acquitted were returned to the American zone.

77 Tauber, p. 921.

78 RG 260 OMGUS AG Sec. Class 1947 250.3 7.11.47.

79 Tauber, p. 921.

80 TB/Straight; and see RG 338 HQ USAREUR JAG War Crimes Case file, War Crimes Organization 1947, 21.2.47.

81 RG 338 HQ USAREUR JAG War Crimes case file, War Crimes Organization 1946, 24.6.46. According to a report by Halse (WO 32 12202/133A June 46) Micklewaite had suggested to him that as most other European countries had presented him with an honour in gratitude for the American army's help, 'Micklewaite thought the presentation to him of an O.B.E.' would help Anglo-American relations. Micklewaite was disappointed.

82 RG 338 HQ USAREUR JAG War Crimes Case file, War Crimes Organization, 1946, 18.6.46.

83 FO 371 57596/U4040.

84 US Military Tribunals Case No. 1 (Medical).

85 RG 260 OMGUS COS 1722, 135½, 000.5 11.6.47.

86 ibid.

87 TB/Straight.

88 RG 260 OMGUS AG Sec. Class 1948 250.3 28.3.48 Box 81.

89 RG 260 OMGUS AG Sec. Class Intelligence Report 1945–49

000.5 Box 54.
90 ibid.

CHAPTER 11

1 Clay, p. 348.
2 FO 371 64724/C16337.
3 RG 260 OMGUS COS 1722, 135½ 000.5 19.8.47.
4 R. T. Paget, *Manstein*, p. 50.
5 Hilberg, p. 187.
6 US Military Tribunals Case No. 9 (Einsastzgruppen).
7 FO 371 64474/C12143.
8 ibid.
9 FO 371 64474/C13393.
10 FO 371 64474/C13392.
11 FO 371 64475/C13823.
12 TB/Taylor; T. Taylor, 'Final Report to the Secretary of the Army on the Nuremberg War Crimes Trials Under Control Council Law No. 10', Washington 1949, p. 82 (hereafter Taylor Report); RG 260 OMGUS AG Decimal File 1947 000.5 18.10.47.
13 FO 371 64474 8.10.47.
14 RG 260 OMGUS AG Decimal File 1947 000.5 18.10.47.
15 FO 371 64475/C13823.
16 RG 260 OMGUS AG Decimal File 1947 000.5 29.10.47.
17 FO 371 66564/U291.
18 RG 260 OMGUS COS 1722, 135½ 000.5 7.11.47.
19 FO 371 64475/C14352.
20 FO 371 64475/C14408.
21 FO 371 64475/C15977.
22 ibid.
23 FO 371 64724/C16337; and see Robertson to Pakenham, 15.11.47: 'I am sure we should be well advised to drop the whole question of a trial' (FO 371 64475/C15574).
24 FO 371 64724/C16455 and WO 32 12640 12.1.48.
25 FO 371 70477/C165.
26 FO 371 70815/CG 495, and see Shapcott's comments at FO 371 70815/CG431.
27 FO 371 70815/CG 495.
28 FO 371 70652/C753.
29 ibid.
30 ibid.
31 ibid.

32 FO 371 70798/1548.
33 FO 371 70797/1414.
34 M. Hastings, *Bomber Command*, p. 171.
35 *The Papers of General Lucius D. Clay*, ed. J. E. Smith, vol. II p. 568.
36 FO 371 70817/CG 1642 and WO 32 12640 131A.
37 ibid.
38 FO 371 70817/CG 1642.
39 WO 32 12640 30.4.48 and 8.5.48.
40 FO 371 70819/CG 2221; WO 32 12640 140A; and see FO 371 70822/CG 3534.
41 FO 371 70819/CG 2221.
42 FO 371 70800/CG 2047.
43 FO 371 70801/CG 2349 and Klarsfeld, pp. 141ff.
44 FO 371 70817/CG 1642. But see FO 371 77006, where in January 1949 Robertson was apparently trying to secure the extradition to the Russians of two German generals, Helmuth Dannel and Kurt Erdmann, because of their war crimes. The Russians did not reply to Robertson's two letters.
45 FO 371 70817/CG 1642; 70822/CG 3534; 70822/CG 3605; 70822/CG 3936.
46 CAB. CM (48)47(3) and CP (48)151; CP (48)159; CP (48)165.
47 FO 371 70804/CG 3319. Bevin replied on 24.8.48 in CG 3319.
48 FO 371 70805/CG 3453.
49 FO 371 70805/CG 3469.
50 FO 371 70805/ CG 3479.
51 CM (48)61(2).
52 FO 371 70807.
53 FO 371 70809.
54 FO 371 77026.
55 FO 371 77027.
56 CP (49)73.
57 FO 371 77027.
58 CP (97). The report was discussed at CM 32(49)4.
59 Requests for the extradition of collaborators and traitors from the British zone had to be submited before 1.3.49.
60 House of Commons, 17.5.49.
61 FO 371 77032.
62 *Daily Telegraph*, 18.7.49.
63 FO 371 77030.
64 FO 371 77032.
65 Paget, pp. 89ff.
66 Paget, pp. 20, 127.
67 FO 371 77033.

68 FO 371 77034.
69 United Nations War Crimes Commission, *History of the United Nations War Crimes Commission*, p. 288.
70 FO 371 30916/C4049.
71 War Cab. 86(42)4.
72 FO 371 26540/C11999.
73 740.00116 EW 1939/818 26.2.43.
74 *History of UNWCC*, p. 282; see House of Lords debate 5.5.49, where Simon defended the alteration.
75 740.00116 EW PROSECUTION/6–745.
76 Paget, p. 109.

CHAPTER 12

1 RG 84 59A543 Box 734 820.02a SH.
2 FO 371 66559/U95 7.1.47; FO 371 55893/C11913; Merritt. p. 33; RG 260 OMGUS HQ AG Decimal File 000.5 Box 3; OMGUS 7964, 201²/₁₇ 30.6.48.
3 Unless stated, the factual detail on the Malmédy Massacre is taken from Weingartner's account.
4 Department of the Army, Tab A. Memo for the File, Malmédy Case NA, RG 319.
5 There was definitely violence against a suspect in the Stalag Luft 111 investigation (see Andrews, p. 194, case of Reinhold Bruchardt), and the author was given confirmed reports of serious attacks by another investigator who was reprimanded but not removed.
6 RG 338 USAREUR JAG War Crimes Case Files, War Crimes Organization, 1947, 17.9.47; and see in the 1948 files 21.7.48.
7 RG 338 HQ USAREUR JAG War Crimes Case files, War Crimes Organization, 1948 28.11.47.
8 RG 260 OMGUS HQ COS 1722, 135½, 000.5 5.11.47.
9 RG 338 HQ USAREUR JAG War Crimes Case Files, EXECUTION 1948.
10 War Crimes Board of Review and Recommendations in the case of US v. Valentin Bersin et al. (The Malmédy Case), NRC Box 4–1/11.
11 RG 260 OMGUS HQ COS War Crimes Trials 17.12.47 (Gailey's personal file).
12 Clay Papers, p. 565.
13 *Washington Post*, 30.4.48.
14 Clay Papers, p. 658.
15 TB/Wilkinson.

16 RG 260 OMGUS HQ COS War Crimes Trials 16.3.48.
17 RG 260 OMGUS HQ Box 23 29.1.48.
18 RG 260 OMGUS HQ Box 24 22.4.48.
19 Clay Papers, p. 658.
20 Clay Papers, p. 661.
21 RG 153 War Crimes Division, Administrative Office, Executive Reading File, May 1948 15.3.48.
22 US Military Tribunals Case No. 11 (Ministries case) Trial transcript p. 4976.
23 RG 338 HQ USAREUR JAG War Crimes Case file, 8.6.48.
24 ibid. 20.5.48.
25 ibid. 19.6.48.
26 Clay Papers, p. 671.
27 Administration of Justice Review Board NRC Box 4–1/11; RG 260 OMGUS HQ COS 1722, 135½, 383.3.
28 Memorandum for the Secretary of the Army NA RG 319 14.9.48.
29 RG 260 OMGUS HQ COS War Crimes Trials 12.8.48 (Gailey's personal file).
30 RG 260 OMGUS HQ AG Decimal File 1948 013.3 Box 24 28.9.48.
31 RG 338 USAREUR JAG War Crimes, Execution 1948 11.10.48; for Clay's telegram RG 260 OMGUS HQ AG Decimal File 1948 013.3 Box 25 9.10.48.
32 RG 153 War Crimes Administrative Office Executive Reading File July 1949.
33 Chicago Tribune, 13.10.48.
34 Weingartner, p. 190.
35 'Conduct of Ilse Koch War Crimes Trial', Report No. 1175 Part 3, [80th Congress] Washington 19.6.1948 (hereafter Koch Investigation).
36 20.9.48, quoted in John Mendelsohn, 'From Prosecution to Clemency for War Criminals', p. 7, an unpublished paper kindly lent to the author.
37 1.10.48.
38 Koch Investigation, p. 13.
39 RG 153 War Crimes Division Administrative Office, Executive Reading File, September, 20.9.48; Clay Papers, p. 889.
40 Clay Paper, p. 1007.
41 Philadelphia Inquirer, 27.9.48.
42 RG 260 OMGUS HQ COS Box 75 6.12.48.
43 RG 59 740.00119 Control (Germany)/2–1649.
44 RG 338 HQ USAREUR JAG War Crimes Case file 19.6.48.
45 ibid. 11.12.48.
46 RG 153 War Crimes Division Administrative Office Executive

Reading File September 1949.
47 RG 153 War Crimes Division Administrative Office Executive Reading File, May 1949.
48 RG 260 OMGUS HQ COS, 1722, 135½, 383.3 31.1.49.
49 RG 153 War Crimes Division Administrative Office Executive Reading File, Feb. 49.
50 RG 260 OMGUS HQ COS 1722, 135½, 383.3 8.3.49.
51 ibid. 17.3.49.
52 ibid. March 49.
53 Clay Papers, p. 1041.
54 Tauber, p. 1305 fn. 65.
55 Weingartner, pp. 200ff.
56 RG 338 USAREUR JAG War Crimes Case File, War Crimes Organization 1949 6.10.49.
57 ibid.
58 RG 153 War Crimes Division Adminstrative Office, Executive Reading File December 49 and January 1950 3.1.50.
59 ibid. Feb. 1950.
60 'Malmédy Massacre Investigation, Hearings Before a Subcommittee of the Committee on Armed Services', United States Senate, 1949.
61 RG 260 OMGUS HQ shipment 17, 217–2 15.12.49.

CHAPTER 13

1 RG 260 OMGUS 8012, $217^3/_{17}$ 25.6.48.
2 RG 260 OMGUS 7964, $201^2/_{17}$ 16.7.48.
3 Assistant Secretary of State OCC Area 1946–49 Boxes 15, 16.
4 RG 260 OMGUS 8021, $217^3/_{17}$ 22.7.48; 7964, $201^2/_{17}$ 28.7.48.
5 RG 260 OMGUS HQ AG Decimal File 1948, 383 30.4.48.
6 Josiah E. Du Bois *The Devil's Chemists*, p. 214.
7 FO 371 76691.
8 RG 260 OMGUS 7953 $197^3/_{17}$ 29.8.49.
9 Hilberg, p. 711.
10 F.Kruse, *NS-Prozesse und Restauration*, p. 131.
11 RG 260 OMGUS 7952, $197^2/_{17}$ 21.11.50.
12 RG 260 OMGUS HQ shipment 17, 217–2 15.12.49.
13 RG 260 OMGUS HQ 8011, $217^2/_{17}$ 18.11.46.
14 740.00116 EW 1939/10–2744 27.10.44.
15 FO 371 51017/U2994.
16 WO 32 12202 16A.
17 RG 260 USGCC 1944–45, 383. 6 Oct. 45. See Clay Papers, p. 124,

for Washington's rejection of the idea.

18 FO 371 50995/U9161.
19 The dispute was about Articles 2(1)(b) and 3(1)(d).
20 WO 32 12208 31A.
21 Smith, pp. 91–9.
22 RG 107 1940–47 ASW 000.5 WC 'Criminals'; see RG 338 USAREUR JAG War Crimes Case file, War Crimes Organization 1946, where Clay thought that there would be just 'several hundred' membership cases (18.2.46).
23 RG 260 OMGUS HQ AG Decimal File 1945–46 000.5 Box 3 26.9.46. See also memo to Hildring on 7.10.46, Ass. Sec. of State, 1946–49, Box 156.
24 FO 945/554 66B; WO 32 12208 47C; FO 371 55435 29.3.46.
25 WO 32 12208 p. 9 Part V.
26 WO 32 12208 64B Report of the Heyman Working Party.
27 FO 371 55436/C6491.
28 WO 32 12208 8.4.46.
29 Smith, p. 163.
30 Ass. Sec. of' State 1946–49 Box 156 7.10.46 (draft directive SWNCC 50/1/D); Jackson to Taylor 12.10.46.
31 FO 945/356 2A.
32 FO 55893 7.11.46. For their explanation see FO 371 64712/C7782.
33 FO 945/356 29.11.46.
34 ibid.
35 FO 937/29 11.12.46; FO 371 55893 18.12.46.
36 FO 371 64713/C8850; ORC (47)27 11.6.47.
37 FO 64712/C7782; see Wilberforce at FO 945/356.
38 WO 32 12208 66A.
39 Issued on 18.12.46.
40 FO 945/356 46 and 52A.
41 FO 937/29.
42 ibid.
43 ibid.
44 FO 64712/C8466.
45 FO 371 64720 22.10.47.
46 FO 371 70817 8.4.48.
47 FO 371 70849/C9317.
48 FO 64881/C14141 and C11379; FO 64747/C14541.
49 FO 371 64881/C14450.
50 FO 371 70849/CG400.
51 FO 371 70817 8.4.48; 70849/CG1555.
52 FO 371 77072 26.1.49. It includes the final summary and letters from Robertson and Jowitt praising the success of the Operation.

53 FO 371 70819/CG2624.

CHAPTER 14

1 Account of I.G. Farben's activities taken from Borkin and Du Bois.
2 Borkin, p. 51.
3 J. Martin, *All Honourable Men*, pp. 74ff.
4 FO 371 46894 (SHAEF report); RG 260 OMGUS $17^1/_{11}$, 6262 18.5.45, Report by SHAEF Finance Division.
5 Martin, p. 55.
6 NI 5196 I.G. Farben Trial Papers.
7 Du Bois, p. 345.
8 RG 260 OMGUS 6235 $5^1/_{11}$.
9 See in general and J.S. Poole, *Who Financed Hitler*.
10 Martin, p. 11.
12 RG 260 OMGUS 6264, $17^3/_{11}$.
13 Borkin, p. 177.
14 Martin, p. 163.
15 Joint Declaration of the Reichsgruppe Industrie and F.B.I. on the Results of the Convention held at Düsseldorf (F.B.I. Archives Ref. GER/COMP D.8325).
16 FO 371 46799 16.7.45.
17 FO 371 46975. For his temporary arrest, see same file on 30.11.45.
18 FO 945/26 13.2.47; and see FO 371 57583/U1236, where the Foreign Office considered him to be 'Equally guilty' as Krupp as a war criminal.
19 Martin, p. 46; House of Representatives 26.7.47.
20 FO 371 55696/C524.
21 Martin, p. 185; OSS Profile of 65 leading German businessmen RG 153 War Crimes Division JAG Law Library 1944–49 L-227.
22 FO 371 46801/C9406.
23 FO 371 46973/C7200.
24 TB/Kellam.
25 FO 945/784 2A; but see ORC (46)60, a Memorandum by the Chancellor of the Duchy of Lancaster, 'Denazification is slowing down production' 28.6.46; and see similar protest by Minister of Fuel and Power CP (46)240.
26 FO 371 55437 18.6.46 and FO 371 55436 15.6.46 Appx 'A' to SCD/P(46)40.
27 FO 371 55439 6.11.46.
28 FO 938/73 Jan. 46.
29 ibid. 10.12.46.

30 ibid. 21.12.46. The last message said that the Control Office was 'disturbed by what appears to have been a rather excessive delay',
31 FO 938/73 17.3.47. Chaput de Saintonge minuted: 'We have every reason for feeling that this problem is not being approached with the necessary energy and expedition by our authorities in Germany.' Wilberforce replied: 'I agree entirely.'
32 FO 371 55434 11.3.46.
33 FO 371 55435/C5698 20.3.46. See FO 64353/C4725, the brief for the March 1947 CFM, which justifies the non-denazification of farms as 'not practical' because it would 'dislocate the production and distribution of food'.
34 740.00119 Control (Germany)/4–2049 20.4.49.
35 FO 371 46801 4.12.45 Appx B, 8th Meeting of Standing Committee on Denazification.
36 FO 371 55434 3.1.46.
37 FO 371 46801 8th Meeting Standing Committee on Denazification. An order to denazify the industry by July 1946 was ignored, FO 371 55437/C7621 and C7758.
38 RG 260 OMGUS HQ AG Sec. Class 1945–49, 350.09 13.12.45.
39 RG 260 OMGUS 6243 10³/₁₁ 23.6.47. It was a breach of the moratorium policy.
40 PREM 8/520 20.6.46 'German Economic Problem' quoting ORC (46)54 and see ORC (46)9th 21.6.46.
41 FO 371 64748/C15961.
42 FO 371 64371/C8534; ORC (47)5(9).
43 FO 936/744.
44 FO 936/743.
45 FO 936/748; 'Operation Sparkler' FO 936/741; see also FO 936/746 'The Gentile Case'.
46 FO 936/743.
47 FO 936/743; FO 938/386; CP (46)240 Shinwell memorandum to Attlee; FO 945/303 78A; PREM 8 520 where Normanbrook wrote: 'the scale of British administration in Germany is too lavish.'; Eighth Report, Select Committee on Estimates 1946–47.
48 Zink, p. 138.
49 Martin, p. 155.
50 Martin, pp. 155, 170.
51 Griffith, p. 464, quoting the Hoover Report and many other statements which were pro-German and occasionally, even in Congress, anti-Semitic. But in contrast, an O.S.S. Report, often quoted in Germany (cf. L. Niethammer, *Entnazifizierung in Bayern*, Frankfurt 1972), concluded that the Allied failure to bomb the Ford plant outside Cologne was the product of a capitalist plot. On 30 July 1938

Henry Ford had accepted Hitler's award of the 'Grand Cross of the Golden Eagle' presented by a German diplomat in America on Hitler's behalf (A. Nevins, *Ford Decline and Rebirth*, Scribner's, 1962).

52 Hastings, pp. 107ff.

53 FO 371 71188 5.2.48.

54 TB/Kellam.

55 RG 260 OMGUS 5243 $12^1/_{11}$.

56 TB/Adams.

57 RG 260 OMGUS 6262 $17^1/_{11}$. The breakdown of relations between British and American administrators in Germany became so serious that both sides made a special agreement to improve contacts. British officers apparently refused to implement it, because on 24.5.46 Herbert Morrison, the deputy prime minister, sent a memorandum to his colleagues: 'I am very much disturbed by telegram 3394 from Washington which shows that the agreement which I reached with the President for the common treatment of the British and American Zones in Germany is meeting with some resistance down the line in the American army owing to a real or imaginary grievance by the Americans about the lack of co-operation from the British Zone' FO 945/13 2B; and see FO 945/13 6A, a letter to Robertson about the failure.

58 J. Wheeler-Bennett, and Anthony Nicholls *The Semblance of Peace*, p. 429.

59 Martin, p. 200.

60 Martin, p. 225.

61 FO 371 55702/C7357 and C7870.

62 FO 371 55703/C9504.

63 FO 371 55703/C10323.

64 Martin, p. 198.

65 Martin, p. 199; Draper's reply disagreeing with Clay RG 260 OMGUS 6243 $10^3/_{11}$.

66 FO 371 55703/C13018.

67 FO 371 55703/C15523.

68 US Military Government Law 56; British Military Government Law 78.

69 Martin, p. 277.

70 RG 260 OMGUS 6243 $12^1/_{11}$ 11.1.48.

71 ibid. 14.4.48.

72 ibid. 28.7.49.

73 740.00119 Control (Germany)/3–3149 31.3.49.

74 FO 945/554.

75 WO 32 12208 8.4.46.

76 ibid. 1.5.46.
77 FO 371 55436/C7276.
78 FO 371 55438 17.9.46. Chambers describes in his unpublished memoirs (period 7 p. 48) how he tried to convince the Americans to impose a windfall tax levy on the enormous profits which accrued to the owners of property and merchandise when the deutschmark was introduced in 1948. The Americans rejected his proposal. Chambers is convinced that the Americans bowed to the pressure of wealthy German industrialists. Clay (*Decision in Germany*) admits (p. 210) that the failure to impose the tax allowed the property owners and black marketeers 'to escape unscathed'. In fact, Clay wanted to resign in protest against Washington's (and especially Draper's) refusal to honour Clay's public commitment to impose an equalization tax (Clay Papers, p. 968).

CHAPTER 15

1   Unless otherwise stated, the account of Krupp is based on W. Manchester, *The Arms of Krupp*.
2   Smith, p. 78.
3   PREM 4 100/10 26.6.44 WP(44)345.
4   FO 371 39007/C15544.
5   FO 371 46701 28.11.44.
6   Smith, p. 68.
7   Document 321, Krupp Trial. US Military Trial Case No. 10.
8   B.B.Ferencz, *Less Than Slaves*, p. 90.
9   Manchester, p. 576.
10 UNWCC Report vol. X, p. 95.
11 Manchester, p. 625.
12 Deposition 313 contained in FO 371 57587, Elyyn Jones to Foreign Office 11.10.46.
13 Manchester, p. 883 and Ferencz.
14 Manchester, pp. 626ff.
15 FO 371 57583/U878.
17 ibid.
18 RG 260 OMGUS HQ AG Decimal File 1945–46 000.5 Box 3 30.1.46 and 5.2.46.
19 ibid. 6.2.46.
20 FO 371 57583/U1905.
21 FO 371 57583/U2996; Scott-Fox at 57583/U2439.
22 RG 260 OMGUS HQ AG Decimal File 1945–46 000.5 Box 3 9.4.46.

23 RG 107 1940–47 ASW 000.5 War Crimes 'Criminals' 24.4.46.
24 RG 260 OMGUS COS 2493, 177⅔ 13.5.46.
25 Smith, p. 110.
26 RG 260 OMGUS COS 2493, 177⅔ 13.5.46.
27 ibid.
28 FO 371 57584/U5947.
29 ibid.
30 ibid.
31 RG 260 OMGUS COS 2493, 177⅔ 29.7.46.
32 FO 371 57584/U5947.
33 RG 260 OMGUS COS 2494, 177⅔ 29.7.46.
34 FO 371 57584/U5947.
35 PREM 8 391 10.8.46.
36 RG 260 OMGUS COS 2493, 177⅔ 29.7.46.
37 RG 107 1940–47 ASW 000.5 War Crimes 'Criminals' 6.8.46.
38 PREM 8 391 10.8.46; and see Dean: 'Apparently opposition to a Second Trial (by private enterprise) is very strong in America' FO 371 57586/U6993.
39 PREM 8 391 15.8.46.
40 FO 371 57587/U7918.
41 PREM 8 391 25.7.46. On 11.9. 46 Shawcross wrote to Bevin: 'I am faced with kthe almost complete disappearance of my staff' FO 371 57586/U7183.
42 FO 371 57586/U7295.
43 F. Biddle, *In Brief Authority*, p. 575; Smith, p. 277.
44 Smith, p. 218.
45 FO 371 57587/U7918.
46 ibid.
47 ibid.
48 FO 371 57586/U7888; PREM 8 391 28.10.46.
49 PREM 8 391 29.10.46.
50 PREM 8 391 31.10.46; FO 371 57586/C7904.
51 CAB. 94(46)2 4.11.46.
52 FO 371 57587/U8088.
53 FO 371 57587/U8128.
54 FO 371 70852/CG4647.
55 FO 371 64724/C16343.

CHAPTER 16

1 Borkin, p. 139.
2 Borkin, p. 140.

3 Du Bois, p. 69.
4 FO 371 66564/U634.
5 RG 165 OPD 000.5 (Sec. 11-A) Case 31/1.
6 RG 260 OMGUS HQ AG Decimal File 1945–46 000.5 18.2.46.
7 RG 260 OMGUS 6264, 17³/₁₁ 9.2.46.
8 ibid.
9 RG 260 OMGUS HQ AG Decimal File 1945–46 000.5 3.9.46.
10 ibid. 9.10.46.
11 Taylor Report, p. 84.
12 Taylor Report, p. 74.
13 RG 260 OMGUS HQ AG Decimal File 1945–46 000.5 24.8.46.
14 ibid. 27.7.46. For French complicity see Du Bois, p. 189.
15 RG 84 Polad 810, 31.12.45. For early doubts of Ministerial Collecting Centres, see USGCC 1944–45, 322 29.8.45.
16 Taylor Report, p. 60.
17 RG 260 OMGUS HQ AG Decimal File 1945–46 000.5 23.8.45.
18 RG 238 War Crimes Interrogations.
19 OMGUS Finance Division, Columbia Law School Library.
20 RG 260 OMGUS HQ AG Decimal File 1947 000.5 20.5.47.
21 RG 260 OMGUS HQ Adj.-Gen. 1947 014.311 5.7.47.
22 US Military Tribunal Case No. 5 (the Flick Case).
23 Flick Case, Transcript pp. 1992–4.
24 Taylor Report, p. 187.
25 US Military Tribunal Case No. 11 (Ministries Case), Judgement pp. 485–6; Taylor Report, p. 202.
26 Taylor Report, p. 34.
27 Du Bois, p. 95.
28 RG 153 War Crimes Division, Administrative Office Executive Reading File 24.5.48.
29 TB/Sprecher.
30 ibid.
31 Farben Trial, Transcript p. 144. US Military Tribunal Case No. 6.
32 Borkin, p. 150.
33 Borkin, p. 115.
34 Manchester, p. 735.
35 TB/Abs.
36 TB/Reinstein. Clay had misgivings about Abs because his 'influence as a banker reached its peak during the Nazi regime' (Clay Papers p. 960). In the same message to Washington, Clay says with considerable naïvety that *in Abs's favour* is the testimony of the Deutsche Bank, who say that Abs had been 'fair in their dealings with them'. One can only assume that Clay was ignorant of the facts. To see how by 1948 control had passed to the Germans, see

FO 371 71040, a pessimistic report on the lack of British and even American influence.

CHAPTER 17

1 RG 338 USAREUR JAG War Crimes Case Files, 8.1.51.
2 RG 260 OMGUS 8011, 217²/₁₇ 26.4.50 the Weigert File.
3 RG 153 War Crimes Division Administrative Office Reading File, Jan. 51, 5.1.51.
4 RG 338 USAREUR JAG War Crimes Case File 29.6.50.
5 ibid. Jan. 51.
6 ibid. 10.11.50.
7 ibid. Jan. 51.
8 RG 260 OMGUS 7755, 54³/₁₇, 383.3.
9 RG 238 Peck Report, National Archives Collection of War Crimes Trial Records, HICOG Clemency Board Box 2.
10 Manchester, p. 757.
11 As n. 7.
12 Hilberg, p. 698.
13 TB/McCloy.
14 Manchester, p. 758.
15 Manchester, p. 773.
16 Hilberg, p. 697.
17 As n. 1.
18 RG 338 USAREUR JAG War Crimes, Execution-Death Sentences 9.2.51.
19 Manchester, p. 764, quoted McCloy writing to a friend: 'I am very much puzzled by the English reaction to the release of Krupp. In the first place the English refused to try any industrialists, and rather criticized us for our vindictiveness in doing so. . .Of all places from which I would least have expected criticism in this case England was first.'
20 TB/Hancock.
21 TB/Liddle-Simpson.
22 TB/Possa; TB/Kempner.
23 Engelmann, p. 65.
24 TB/Possa.
25 K. Adenauer, *Memoirs 1945–1953*, p. 445; and see Kruse, p. 115, quoting General Eisenhower in 1951 publicly declaring that German officers had behaved honourably during the war.
26 RG 260 OMGUS 217²/₁₇.
27 RG 338 USAREUR JAG War Crimes Case Files 11.5.54.

28 ibid.
29 ibid.
30 RG 338 USAREUR JAG War Crimes Case Files May 55. Dietrich was later convicted by a West German court for his part in the murders of the SA during the 'Night of the Long Knives' in 1934.
31 Information and documents from Prof. Keith Mant; *Daily Telegraph*, 12.7.58.

CHAPTER 18

1 Engelmann, p. 223.
2 RG 84 Polad 810 20.4.45.
3 ibid. 12.5.45.
4 740.00119 Control (Germany)/12–2049 20.12.49. See also memorandum called 'Investigation into Abs' to determine 'whether Abs was an opportunist who would play with what he thought was the winning side' 21.12.49. There is no filed result.
5 Dahrendorf, pp. 253ff, 'Bureaucracy'. For some seemingly naïve methods adopted by the British to democratize the civil service see *'A Report on some methods used to assist Local Government and the Civil Service in the British Zone in Germany*, HMSO Cmd. 7804.
6 Information supplied by Wolfgang Benz of the Institut für Zeitgeschicht.
7 Interview with author.
8 Tauber, p. 925.
9 ibid. p. 941.
10 ibid. p. 943.
11 Engelmann, pp. 61, 310.
12 A. Rückerl, *The Investigation of Nazi Crimes 1945–1978*.
13 Kruse, p. 125.
14 TB/Simon. The West German government's refusal to accept the Document Centre has several times been the subject of controversy in the Bonn Parliament. See for example, *Der Spiegal*, No. 17/197, p. 41.
15 TB/Kempner.
16 RG 338 USAREUR JAG War Crimes Case File, War Crimes Organization 1949, 19.9.49.
17 Rückerl, *Investigation*, p. 46.
18 ibid. p. 45.
19 TB/Bülow.
20 TB/Massen.
21 Author's interviews with former Ministry of Justice officials and

with E. Bucher, ex-Minister of Justice.

22 Rückerl, *Investigation*, p. 47.
23 *Documents Relating to the Termination of the Occupation Regime in the Federal Republic of Germany*, HMSO Cmd. 9368, 1955; Rückerl, p. 77.
24 Rückerl, *Investigation*, p. 47.
25 Engelmann, p. 108.
26 ibid. pp. 270ff.
27 TB/Rückerl.
28 TB/Schwedersky.
29 TB/Vogel.
30 TB/Pilichowski. Pilichowski has produced a convincing file of memoranda given to him by a sympathetic West German government official, containing letters between the Federal Ministry of Justice in Bonn and the state ministries in Düsseldorf and Wiesbaden. There are other memoranda between those ministries and the state prosecutors. They prove conclusively that the West Germans, for political reasons, deliberately did not ask the Communist governments of Europe for either evidence or assistance.
31 TB/Harel.
32 M. Elkins, *Forged in Fury*.
33 TB/Bucher.
34 Interviews with author.
35 'The Brown Book', published by the DDR government. Engelmann writes that he checked on their research and it proved in the case of the police to be comparatively reliable, pp. 278, 344.
36 Kruse, p. 250.
37 House of Commons 10.7.57, p. 351; 10.3.58, p. 30.
38 Tauber, pp. 958–62.
39 Brown Book, p. 119.
40 The Bonn government does not seen to dispute much of the contents of the Brown Book.
41 Published by the 'Untersuchungsausschuss Freiheitlicher Juristen', a lawyers' organization supported by the Ministry of Inter-German Affairs.
42 Rückerl, *Investigation*, p. 59; R. Vogel, *Ein Weg aus der Vergangenheit*, p. 24.
43 Vogel, p. 25.
44 Rückerl reduces the number to 70,000, *Investigation*, p. 117.
45 Statistics provided by the Federal Ministry of Justice.
46 Vogel, p. 27.
47 Bundesgerichtshof 5 StR 658/58.
48 Rückerl, *Investigation*, pp. 112–3.

49 Author's interview.
50 Author's interview.
51 M. Broszat, 'Basic problems and conditions of Nazi Crime Trials in West Germany'. A paper delivered in Washington, 13.3.75.
52 TB/Rückerl.
53 Rückerl, *Investigation*, p. 117.
54 ibid. p. 102.
55 ibid. p. 109.
56 ibid. p. 106.
57 ibid. p. 108.
58 C. Pilichowski, *The Central Polish Commission for the Investigation of Nazi War Crimes.*
59 FO 371 70794/CG 687; FO 371 70796 4.7.48; FO 371 70797/CG 1472; WO 235/807; RG 260 OMGUS 7964 201²/₁₇ 21.6.48; Taylor Report, pp. 47, 297.

CHAPTER 19

1 S. Cobler, *Law, Order and Politics in West Germany*, pp. 40ff.
2 ibid. p. 44.
3 O. Zierer, *Franz Josef Strauss.*
4 TB/Bock.
5 Stolting on ZDF Television, 27.11.77, 'Die Vergangenheit kehrt zurück'.
6 Rückerl, *Investigation*, p. 100.
7 ZDF, 27.11.77.
8 *Vorwärts*, 2.12.76.

INDEX

Wherever possible, names, titles and ranks are as given in the text, and not updated to include honours or ranks subsequently awarded.

abbreviations:
dnz. = denazification
decart. = decartelization

Aachen: German administration, 141 – 2; mayor, 142 – 3; to British Zone, 145; dnz. failure, 164
Abetz, Otto, 46
Abich, Dr Meyer, 304, 305
Abs, Dr Hermann Josef, 21, 319, 354, 364, 365, 383, 464; banking career, 14 – 20, 328, 364; financial connections with Nazism, 13, 16, 17, 24; Deutsche Bank and other posts, 16, 17, 18, 19, 20, 26; IG Auschwitz, 18; prepares post-defeat plans, 18; rebuilds German banking, 20, 22, 23, 24, 328; Gunston friendship, 20, 23, 24; loses directorships, 25; German recovery, keystone, 364; Marshall aid funds, 364 – 5; vetoed as first foreign minister, 381
war crimes suspicion, 354; arrest, 25 – 6; interrogation, 24; 'Investigation into Abs', 466; trial prospects, 346; Yugoslavia sentence, *in absentia*, 364
'Academy for Economic Leaders', 390
Achenbach, Ernst, 46, 402 – 3
Acht, Major B., 263
Adam, Gen. Sir Ronald, 125, 207, 209, 210
Adams, Foster, 326, 347, 354, 364

Adenauer, Dr Konrad, 385; Landsberg convicted men, 365, 376; govt. appts., former Nazis, 375, 379 – 83; favours rearmament, 375, 376; economic control, 383; protection of Nazis, reasons for, 384 – 5
Adjutant-General, 125, 128, 444; Dept. AG3, coordinates war crimes investigation, 107 – 8, 117, 125; first meeting, 130; closure, 211
Administration of Justice Review Board, 287
Administration of Territories (Europe) Committee, 138, 139
AG3, Department, *see under* Adjutant-General
Albers, Hans, 382
Alexander, Field Marshal, 225, 247
Ambros, Otto, 353, 359, 360, 362, 383
Anerswald, Max, 276
Allen, Dennis, 69, 82, 94, 104, 426, 428; on Jewish extermination reports, 43, 53, 74 – 5; and WCC actions, 52, 60, 65, 80, 99; Majdanek letter dismissed, 63; scorns Gestapo arrest scheme, 68
Allen, Roger, 62, 99, 424; Jewish stateless persons seen as political issue, 69 – 70
Allied Control Council, Berlin, 150 – 1

Allied Criminals Investigation
Department (ACID), 99, 130
Amann, Max, 83
anti-Nazis: 'White' German
refugees, 145, 149 – 50, 441;
discriminated against, 150,
159, 174; fraternization
rejections, 156, 159; minority
element, 158, 164, 169,
180 – 1; distrusted, 164, 192;
1 per cent only, 170; teachers,
184; seen as traitors, 192;
social welfare drawbacks, 384
'Antifa', anti-fascist groups, 175,
443, 445
appeasement policy, 27, 32, 41,
93, 252
*Arbeitskreis für Aussen-
wirtschaftsfragen* (AAF), 18, 19,
26, 380, 383
archives: Document Centre, 304,
386, 409; East European, 386,
388, 392 – 3, 397, 399; IG
Farben, 310 – 11, 312, 353;
govt. documents Collecting
Centre, 353 – 4; Krupps, 339,
353
Armistice Terms and Civil
Administration Committee,
138
Army, Allied: war crimes
directives, 87; 21 Group, 108,
109, 125, 129, 130, 438; US,
60, 121, 123, 144; US
investigating teams, 113, 114,
119, 120, 123; Nazis,
employment of, 164
Army, German, 158; Allied
respect for, 164 – 5, 232 – 4,
255; 'anti-Nazi', 368;
Balts/Ukranians, 223;
captured generals, US
debriefing, 237; Landsberg
internees, release demands,

375, 376, 377; military caste
and Nazism, 242 – 3; leaders,
criminality, 242 – 5;
Wehrmacht-SS links, 242,
244, 246, 263; Western
defence, 368, 369, 375; *see also*
Generals' trial, soldiers *and*
war crimes: military
operations
Aschenauer, Dr Rudolph, 286,
289
Aschke, Aachen coal manager,
142, 144
'Ashcan': centre for V.I.P.
Nazis, 116
atrocity stories: propaganda, 30,
36; Russian, 34
Attlee, Clement, 83, 207; queries
Belsen trial delays, 202, 203,
pursues Shawcross *dictat*, 205,
206; anti-Nazi tycoons, 335;
rejects industrialists' trials,
349; anger at Landsberg
reprieves, 373, 374
Auschwitz camp trial, 403; *see
also* concentration camps,
A – Z
Auschwitz police court, 401 – 2
Australia, 39, 81
Austria, 16, 225, 226
Axmann, Arthur, 83

Baader-Meinhof gang, 406, 408
Babi Yar, massacre, 36
Baden: judiciary, Nazi, 194
Baer, General de, 67, 68, 239
Baldwin, Senator Raymond:
Committee, 288 – 91
Balfour, Michael, 148
Balfour, Maj. Gen. P.M., 189
Baltic States, 57, 63, 224; war
crimes, 223, 240; political
extraditions, 223, 226

Bamberg: *Oberlandesgericht* court, 367
banks and bankers, 13 – 14, 16, 315; dnz., 23, 24, 25, 162, 185; industrial finance, 14, 16 – 18; Jewish, 315; Nazi links, 14 – 18, 20 – 3, 313; postwar plans, 18 – 19, 20, 22; wartime control and wealth retained, 317, 331 – 2; *see also* names of individual banks
    as alleged war criminals, 20, 21, 22, 334, 342, 354 – 5, 410; Anglo-US financiers' protection, 316, 347; loans not war crimes, 357; trials, 356, 364
Barnes, Sir Thomas, 96, 97, 98, 106, 107, 438
Barraclough, Lt. Col. John, 125, 130
Barth, Johann, 415
BASF Chemicals: Abs, deputy chief, 364
Bauer, Fritz, 392, 393
Bausch and Lomb: Zeiss links, 316
Bavaria, 184, 374; judiciary, Nazis return, 294, 295; Schäffer administration, 152 – 3; tribunals, appeals, 170, 171
Bayer Chemicals, 315, 383
Beaticle, Odette, 47 – 8
Beaumont, Sir Richard, 217, 448
Belgium, 227, 254, 401
Bell, Bishop George K.L., 252
Bellenger, Frederick, 229, 230, 246
Belsen trial (1945), 197 – 201; criticisms, British inertia, 199, 200 – 1; *see also* concentration camps, A-Z
Berle, Adolph, 71
Bergmann, Dr Günther, 380
Berlin: blockade, 253, 255, 260, 294, 364
Bernays, Col. Murray, 102, 110, 297; invents new int. crimes, 101; int. tribunal mooted, 110
Bernstein, Col. Bernard, 140, 144, 404; seeks German economy crushed, 21 – 2; demands Abs interrogation, 24; Nazi presence in banking, 152, 317
Bertheimer, Anton, 281
Besekow, Arno, 395
Betts, Gen. E.C., 91, 119, 121, 298
Betts, Brig. Gen. T.J., 86, 115
Bevin, Ernest, 174, 177, 202, 204, 205, 206, 209, 256, 346; effective war crimes programme, 202, 203, 218, 219, 227, 229, 235; trials to continue, 230, 253 – 4, 257 – 8; Generals' trial, 249, 251, 252, 255, 257; Byrnes deal on industrialists, 345, 346, 348
Bickelhaupt, General, 152
Biddle, Francis, 104, 298, 301, 342, 347
Bird, Geoffrey, 185
Birkett, Norman, 298, 342
Birley, Dr Robert, 185
Bishop, Gen. Sir Alec, 147, 178, 234
Blankerhorn, Herbert, 380 – 2
Blatt, Thomas, 56
Blessing, Karl, 15, 18 – 19, 26, 322, 365, 383; interrogations, 354
BMW, company, 17 – 18
Bock, Ludwig, 414

Bogdan, Captain Norbert, 316
Bogen, Judge Günther, 411,
413, 415, 416
Bokum Island: massacre, 369
Boldt, Berthold, 395
Böll, Heinrich, 408
bombing, German cities, 268,
325 – 6, 460 – 1
Bormann, Martin, 379, 380
Bosch, Robert, 313, 314, 353,
355
Böttcher, Hermine, 414, 416
Bovenschen, Sir Frederick, 85,
107, 109, 125, 138, 148, 297;
war crimes, attitude to,
95 – 6, 97, 98, 125, 127, 204,
209; Army commitment
limited, 106; on extraditions,
224, 225, 226
Bradfisch, Dr Otto, 396
Bradshaw, Col. George, 202,
205 – 6, 210, 212, 213, 219,
302
Brand, Joel, 73, 75
Brandt, Dr Karl, 238 – 9
Brandt, Willy, 192
Brauchitsch, Field Marshal
Walther von, 99; trial: Polish
and Russian atrocities, 242,
244 – 5, 247, 251 – 2;
'Commissar Order', 244;
death, 259
Bremen: Nazi mayor and
judiciary, 157, 194
Bresee, Col. Howard, 273 – 4,
275, 281
Bridgeman, Viscount, 205, 206,
207, 261; heads AG3, 128,
132; 500 cases trial, delays,
129, 204, 209, 210, 214
Bridges, Sir Edward, 65, 85, 96
Brimelow, Sir Thomas, 200
British Ally, 200
British Army of the Rhine

(BAOR): war crimes work,
202, 203, 204, 215, 448; 500
cases target, 205, 206, 207 – 9;
failure, 213, 229; success, 230;
and executions, 231 – 2
British Broadcasting Corporation: war crimes, deportations
broadcasts, 35 – 6, 54, 65, 72
British Dominions, 39, 56 – 7,
81
British in Germany, The (book),
185
British Transport Division,
151 – 2, 442
Brod, Pery, 402
Bronson, Richard, 330
Broszat, Martin, 400
'Brown Book' (Communist
propaganda), 397
Buchenwald trial, 282 – 5; see
also concentration camps, A-Z
Bucher, Ewald, 394, 397, 398
Bülow, Dr Arthur, 388
Buna (artificial rubber), 308 – 9,
359, 362
Bundestag, 132, 375; civil service
regulations (1937) re-adopted,
382
Burress, General, 182
Burrows, Bernard, 176
Busch, Dr Fritz: railways
management, 151 – 2
Bütefisch, Heinrich, 383, 404;
trial, 359ff.
Byrnes, James, 327; Bevin deal,
345ff.

Cabinet (UK), 82 – 3; Ruhr
Communist plot, 250;
Shawcross 'riot act' read,
205 – 6' Simon committee,
42; trials, decisions on, 256,
257, 349

Cadogan, Sir Alexander, 34, 37, 39, 59, 68, 73, 75, 81, 99, 428; rules of war, British breaches, 65; war crimes policy committee, 107

Calder, Ritchie, 157, 164 – 5, 441

Canfield, Major L.S.W., 200

Carpenter, Lt. Col. Edwin, 274

Carr, Sir Arthur Comyns, 261

cartels, international, 308, 310; Anglo-US and German, 315 – 16, 318, 321, 351; Four Power law against, 329; *see also* decartelization

Cavendish-Bentinck, Victor, 36, 62, 265, 424

Central Military Pensions Office: SS names, 392

Central Office for the Investigation of War Crimes, Ludwigsburg, 385, 390, 398, 400; 'aiders and abetters', checks on, 398 – 9; East European help, 391, 392 – 3, 397, 399 – 400, 401; background of first director, 390 – 1; research, Nazi crimes, outside Germany only, 391; success rate, 399 – 400

Central Registry of War Criminals and Security Suspects (CROWCASS), Paris, 116; collapse and results, 231; Russia excluded, 118, 220; war crimes register, 117, 118, 134, 188

Chambers, Paul, 22, 23, 331, 332, 462

Chaplin, Dwight, 149 – 50

chemical industry, 321; war footing, 309, 311, 359

Chicago Tribune, 276, 282, 285

Chilton, Maj. Gen. Maurice, 129, 203, 204, 205, 206 – 8, 210

Christian Social Union (CSU), 294, 407

Churches: Catholic: Nazism, coexistence with, 153 – 4, 167 – 8, 172; 'collective guilt', 154 – 5; dnz., opposition to, 172, 180; Vatican Concordat, 154
German, 158, 159; coexistence with Nazism, 142, 153 – 5, 162, 'spotty record', 145 – 6; influence in post-war Germany, 166; war criminals, 271, 285
Protestant, 167 – 8; 'collective guilt' accepted, 155; dnz., opposition to, 180; Nazi Party membership, 167 – 8

Churchill, John, 321

Churchill, Winston, 75, 83, 84, 91, 139, 261, 373, 428; broadcasts, 33, 35, 37, 40; proposes UN Atrocities Commission, 41, 42; plans Moscow Declaration, 59; retribution warnings, 59, 95, 259; shoot top Nazis on sight, 73, 81 – 2, 106, 334; hears Morgenthau proposals, 141; on Kesselring verdict, 234; Generals' trial, 257, defence fund contribution, 261, 373 – 4

Civil Affairs Division, US, 140

civil service, German: dnz., 162, 166 – 7, 409; elitist duopoly, 381 – 2; senior posts, renazified, 380, 382

civil service, Nazi, 158, 159, 167

Clark, Andrew, 105

Clark, William, 196

Clay, Gen. Lucius D., 123, 146,

152, 155, 178, 256, 382, 464;
relations with clergy, 155,
166, 167, 168; dnz.
programme, 164, 168, 169,
172, 179, 181 – 3, 404,
handed to Germans, 170, 182;
Nazism, firm commitment
against, 165 – 6, 229, 299,
387; relations with Russia,
221, 241, 253, 328; urges
power structure shift,
317 – 18, 328 – 9, 330, 404;
industrialists' trials, 352, 364
war crimes work: extradi-
tion issues, 235 – 7; ends
trials, 236; Generals'
trials, 242, 244, 246,
248, 249; Malmédy trial,
270 – 1, 287, 288 – 9;
executions, 273, 277,
280, 282, 288 – 9; cases
reviewed, 276 – 7
Cleaver, Henry, 212 – 13
coal industry, Ruhr, 318; dnz.
failures, 320 – 1; synthetic
fuel, 309
Cohen, Prof. Sir Henry, 260
Collingwood, Mr Justice,
261 – 2
Collins, Henry, 320
Combined Chiefs of Staff, 91;
Directive 1023/10, 96, 97,
108, 113, 119, 121; PHP sub-
committee, 138
'Commissar Order', 244, 401
Committee for Germany Unity:
and West German judges, 396
Communism: Cold War, 241,
253, 327; WCC, Soviet no-go
areas or cases, 63
communists and socialists, 147,
268, 396 – 7; and Churches,
180; and dnz., 170, 174, 178;
Ruhr sabotage plot, 250

concentration camps, 15,17 – 18,
20, 27, 45, 47, 63, 115, 151,
200, 201, 223, 227, 234, 296,
306, 366, 391; British Zone,
203; legal in Germany, 199;
liberation 109, 114; staff, 91,
116, 119, 127, 214, 220 – 2,
228, 231, 239, 295, 306,
336 – 7, 377, 395, 415, 416;
trials, procedural niceties,
213 – 14; village, 131 – 2
concentration camps: named:
Auschwitz, 17, 18, 20, 45,
47, 48, 53, 94, 151, 172, 183,
197 – 8, 234, 286, 295, 402,
Buna plant (Auschwitz),
359 – 60, 404; Belsen, 53,
109, 125 – 6, 129, 198, 240,
339, British nationals, 127,
129, local folk, 153, 157,
epitome of war crimes
mismanagement, 201 – 2;
Buchenwald, 17, 20, 27, 63,
105, 366, 428; guards,
221 – 2, 281, 282 – 3, 287,
306, 368, 375, 395, 404, 412,
428 – 9, liberation publicity,
109, 115, SS investigation,
395; Camp Dora, 112 – 13;
Dachau, 15, 18, 20, 27, 240,
272, 355, townsfolk, 155,
157, trial; 366; Drancy, 45,
47, 49, 116; Majdanek, 20,
413; Monowitz, 360 – 2;
Nordhausen, 221 – 2, 377;
Ravensbrück, 17, 254, 338,
medical atrocities, 377 – 8;
Sobibor, 55 – 6, 116, 223
Constitution, Federal:
extradition barred, German
nationals, 402; prosecutions
inhibited, 388; see also Statute
of Limitations
Consultative Assembly: civil

service reform proposals,
381 – 2
Control Commission (British
Zone), 138, 139, 148, 346;
dnz., 173 – 4, 184 – 5, 318,
321; staff, corruption, lax
morality, 323 – 4; 'White'
Germans excluded, 149 – 50
war crimes (B2), 91, 94,
229; 'German Character'
circular, 147
Control Commission: Legal
Division, 105, 108, 132 – 3,
148, 189, 192 – 3, 299
Control Council: Law 10, 255;
Nazi organizations, conspiracy
charge, 298, 299
Control Office, 131, 138, 321,
322; dnz. achievements, 176,
328; Nazis recruited, 188,
189; war crimes, extradition,
233 – 4
Control Office: Legal Division,
310 – 3, 305
cosmetics: eau-de-cologne
'4711', 323
Counter-Intelligence Corps
(CIC), 121, 124
Courtaulds, company, 323
courts, 58, 127; British Zone,
132; German, 387; allegedly
anti-Nazi, 303; Bizonal High
Court, 294; Federal Supreme
Court: retired judges, immune
from murder charges, 398,
402; German crimes in, 395;
jurisdiction, Allied
Limitations, 386, 388 – 9;
Transition Agreement,
misused, 389; international:
for war crimes, 68, 296;
military, 40, 91, 92, 94, 96,
97, 127, 214; Military
Government, 195 – 6, 208;

Nazi: Rechtstaat, 190, 191,
Special People's Courts, 191,
396; US Zone, 132, 217;
USA, 272, 277, Supreme
Court, Washington, 368; see
also trials
Creditanstalt Wiener
Bankverein, 16
crimes, international: new —
'crimes against humanity",
101; "waging aggressive
war", 101
Crossman, Richard: broadcast,
150
Cruscius, Major, 29
Czechoslovakia, 16, 36, 38, 81,
90, 396; closure, WCC,
Prague, 229; Communist
coup, 253; Lidice, 39; war
crimes investigation and
extraditions, 226, 228, 399,
401

Dachau (US compound): cases
and trials, 202, 238, 271, 275,
278, 280, 291, 412;
'Avenging Angels', 286; see
also Malmédy trial
Dahrendorf, Ralf, 190
Daimler-Benz, company, 383,
410
Dalby, Brig. Gen. Josiah T.,
268, 269
Dalton, Dr Hugh, 34 – 5
Dannecker, Theodor, 46, 47
Darré, Dr Richard, 306
Davis, James, 288
Dean, Patrick, 89, 91, 92, 96,
100, 106, 108, 125, 131,
132 – 3, 205, 450; FO war
crimes action, 93, 94, 118,
219; seeks WO help, 97, 108,
109, 218; on war trials: 200,
203, 213ff., 341, 343 – 4, 345,

General's trial, 233, 246, Nazi
organizations, 297, 298,
wishes industrialists exempted,
335, 344, 346
decartelization, 324, 352; aim of,
313, 317 – 18, 325; Allied
antagonisms, 324, 325,
326 – 9, 330 – 1; British
policy: anti-trust busting,
318 – 20, 325, 326, 328,
330 – 1; Russian reaction,
329; US policy: anti-cartel
section, 316 – 18, 328 – 30;
pro-lobby, 328
Declarations, on war crimes,
54 – 5, 82, 90; Allied, 36 – 9,
42, 424 – 5; Moscow, 59 – 61,
81, 93, 222 – 3: camp guards
excluded, 119 – 20,
extraditions, 220 – 1, 224,
Jews, extermination, 71;
Tripartite (1940), 32
de Crespigny, Air Vice Marshal
H.V.C., 175 – 6
DEGESCH, company, 295
Dehler, Thomas, 291 – 2, 296,
367, 369, 388; prosecution a
German affair, 292, 293
Delbruck, Schickler (bank), 14,
15, 16, 23, 24
DeL'Isle, Viscount, 252, 261
denazification, 21 – 2, 23, 24 – 5,
153, 182; aims, 143, 161,
163 – 4, 168 – 9, 183ff., 268,
404; Anglo – US dissensions,
21 – 5, 139; 'Antifa' organizations, 175, 445; British policy:
139, 143 – 4, 150, 173 – 8,
criticisms of, 173, 177, 179,
181, German help unwanted,
174, 175 – 6, lawyers reinstated, 189, 191 – 3; failure of,
179, 268, 404, 406; "free
election" (1945), Nazi govt.,

170; Germans seconded to
organize, 180, 171, 183;
leftwing part in, 173, 174,
175, 178, 181; Nazis, re-
employment, 143 – 5, 150 – 3,
156 – 7, 165 – 6, 191, 193,
194, 295, 441; Nazis,
removals, 164; postwar
generation, 409; re-Nazification, 151, 157, 293 – 5;
Russian policy, 177 – 8, 228;
US policy: 21 – 2, 24, 25,
146, 164, 165, 168 – 9, 183,
318, army role, 153,
bureaucracy – Law 8,
165 – 6, Nazi categorization,
169, 177, 182, 444, 445,
questionnaires, 163 – 4, 169,
438, statistics, 294
opposition to: German,
156, 159, 166, 168, 169,
171, 173, 179 – 84
passim; Churches, 172,
179 – 80; communist
tool, 170, 179 – 80;
leftist criticisms, 178; by
politicians, 170, 179,
181 – 2; US, 276
denazification groups and
sectors: armed forces, 158,
159, 162, 242 – 4; bankers and
financiers, 14 – 18, 20 – 6,
162, 185; civil service, 158,
162, 409; clergy, 158, 159,
162; coal industry, 320 – 1;
conservatives, 157 – 8; educationalists, 159, 162, 183 – 6,
409; Establishment, 162, 247,
409; farming industry,
322 – 3; industrialists/
industry, 14 – 19, 21, 22 – 4,
159, 162, 321, 323, 409, 459;
legal profession, 162, 190 – 2,
193 – 5, 396, 398, 409;

medical profession, 159, 162;
Nazi categories, 161 – 2:
'Militarists', 144, 445,
'nominal', 144, 158, non-
Party, profiteers, 144, 161 – 3,
172, 331 – 3; oil industry,
322 – 3; Party members, 161;
police purges, 162, 395; professional classes, 158, 159,
162, 409; universities, 183 – 6;
working-class, 158
denazification tribunals and
appeals, 163; Germans on,
'self-cleaning', 168 – 71, 179;
farcial nature, 170 – 3, 181;
local opposition, instances,
171 – 3, 386; Nazi
organizations, 299
Denazification, Standing
Committees, 24 – 5, 176,
184 – 5, 186, 191, 299, 303,
319, 322
de Saintonge, Richard Chaput,
189
Deutsche Bank, 14 – 15, 17, 18,
20, 23, 24, 26, 120, 464;
conduit, Nazi funds, 16 – 19,
313, 314, 319; investigation,
354
Devereux, Frederick, 317
Did Six Million Really Die?, 262
Dienstgruppen, 233, 264, 451
Dietrich, Gen. Sepp, 64, 103,
134, 269, 273, 377; Roehm
conviction, 389, 466
Dillon, Read, bankers, 16, 316
Dinkelbach, Heinrich, 19, 319
Dittrich, Horst, 377
Document Centre, Berlin, 304,
386, 409
Dondero, George A., 351
Donovan, Gen. William, 119
Dorn, Dr Walter: on dnz., 170,
171, 172; investigates

universities, 184, 185
Dorpmüller, Dr Julius, 151
Douglas, Air Marshal William
Sholto, 229, 233, 235; on
Generals' trial, 244, 246, 247,
248
Dow Chemical Company, 351
Draper, Col. Gerald, 126, 129,
133, 210, 215, 234, 256, 261,
266, 374
Draper, William, 316; anti-
decart., 317, 325, 327, 328,
329; Anglo-US Zones,
economic merger, 329
Dratvin, Lt. Gen. M., 239
Dresdener Bank, 313, 314, 406;
directors, charges against,
355, 356
Druit, Rev. Geoffrey, 324
Du Bois, Josiah, 351, 358, 359
Dubost, Charles, 334, 339, 345
Dulles, John Foster, 317
Du Pont, company, 310, 311,
321
Dürrfeld, Walter, 360, 361, 362,
383
Dwinell, John, 273

Ebble, Friedrich, 290
EBIG, consortium, 25
Ecer, Dr, 67
Economic Cooperation, Ministry
for, 383
economy, German, 14, 325, 328,
329, 383; bizonal economic
merger, 329, 330; British
pragmatism toward, 21 – 3,
319 – 20, 325, 326; crisis, 314,
320; recovery and boom
(1948), 151 – 2, 158, 326,
328, 331, 364; US draconian
proposals, 21, 83 – 4, 141,
164, 317ff., 423; see also
decartelization

Eden, Anthony, 93, 148, 426; war crimes, attitudes to, 33, 34, 36 – 7, 39, 43, 59, 74, 87; seeks retribution, 35, 75; Jewish persecutions: anti-Semitism alleged, 36 – 7, 43, 74, 75; on war criminals, 37 – 8, 83; 'Treatment of War Criminals' paper, 40, 41 – 2; proposes EAC, 139

Education Branches, Military, 184, 185, 300 – 1

educationalists and teachers, 143, 159; dnz., 162, 183 – 6, 409

Ehemalige Nationalsozialisten in Pankows Dienstein (book), 397

Eichmann, Adolf, 45 – 8 *passim*, 72, 73, 116, 379, 393 – 5

Einsatzgruppen, 19, 44, 61, 223, 242, 244 – 6, 287, 370ff., 390, 396

Eisele, Hans, 296

Eisenhower, General Dwight D., 60, 61, 109, 164, 376, 449; war crimes directives, 113 – 14, 222; outburst over Nazi reinstatements, 153

Eisenstadt, Robert, 63

Eliot, T.S., 261

Elliot, Roger, 131

Ellis, Lt. Col. Burton, 135, 274

Erhard, Ludwig, 19, 26, 365, 383

Erlangen University, 183 – 4

Erzberger, Matthias, murder, 194, 440

espionage, US, 229

Establishment, 20 – 1, 247; dnz., 409; *Schlusstrich*, 404 – 5; society and morality, unreformed, 405, 408

Ethyl Export Corporation, 309

Europe, Eastern: extraditions, anti-Communist, 224, 226, 228 – 9; war crimes archives, 386, 388

Europe, Western: war crimes, nominal German investigation, 401

European Advisory Committee, 68, 74, 81, 106, 140; British solo belief in, 99 – 100; Eden proposal, 139

euthanasia, 296; institutions, 295

Everett, Col. Willis, 269, 273, 274, 277 – 8, 282

executions, 231 – 2; Malmédy/Landsberg war criminals, 282, 366 – 7; reprievals and reviews, 276 – 7; stay of, 272 – 3, 277, 280; last (257th), 373

extraditions, 228, 233 – 4, 235 – 7, 241, 251, 449, 452; requests and restrictions: anti-Communist 'politicals', 224, 226, 228; collaborators, 226; East European, 224 – 6, 228 – 9; 'fair trial countries' only, 226; occupied countries, 218; POWs, in Britain, 225; Russian, 237, 454; treaty formalization, 224; war criminals, 224, 260; Yugoslavia, 235

Fahy, Charles, 169, 221

Falla, P.S., 105

Fanton, Major Dwight, 133 – 5

farming and food industries: dnz., 322

Faulhaber, Cardinal, 153, 154

Ferenbaugh, General, 376

Ferencz, Benjamin, 370

Fergusson Committee, 330

Filbinger, Hans, 408 – 9

finance: currency reform (1948), 326, 331, 462; reorganization,

423; reparations, 15, 23; reserves (1937), 15

Finance, Ministry of, 380, 382, 383

"Financial and Property Control Technical Manual" (SHAEF), 22

financial institutions: dnz., 23, 185; power and authority, 347 – 8

fingerprint proposal (US Zone), 118 – 19, 164

Finlay, Lord, 107, 109, 130 – 1

Fischer, Karl August, 152 – 3

Fleps, Georg, 135

Flick, Friedrich, 19, 313, 314, 320, 372, 383, 410; trial, 353, 355 – 6, 361, 364

Foreign Affairs, Department of, 380 – 1; diplomats, ex-Nazis, 382

Foreign Ministers meetings: London, 177, 241; Moscow, 233

Foreign Office (UK): arcane belief in diplomacy, 99 – 100

Foreign Office: 'Final Solution', attitudes and policy, 43 – 4, 48 – 9, 53 – 5

(1933 – 42): war crimes policy, 27 – 8, 81, 83, 98, 109; 'detached coolness', 27, 30 – 1, 34, 36, 38, 41, 44, 50, 79, 109, 300, 425; German internal affair only, 27, 75, 104, 132 – 3; Leipzig precedent, caution, 28 – 30, 40; retribution, commitment to, 28, 30 – 42 *passim*, 49, 59 – 60, 74, 75, 92, 95; Quislings sought, 33 – 4; Churchill broadcasts,

anxiety over, 33 – 4, 37; reactions to: prewar crimes, 69 – 73 *passim*, German Jews, 69 – 71, and stateless persons, 69, 70, 71, 73; major criminals listed, 82 – 3; ineffectual policy, 84, 93, 94, 96

(1942 –): Japanese atrocities, effect of, 39, 42; Eden, new proposals, 40, 41, 42; Nazi leadership prosecution, 40, 41, 82, 83; WCC, relations with, 49 – 53, 56 – 7, 62 – 8, 78, 80, 89, 92, 94, 235; and asked to observe Russian no-go areas, 63

(1945 –), 149; commitment, minimal, 128; German crimes against Germans, 132 – 3; and 'political' extraditions, 223, 224, 225, 228

war criminals, 98 – 9, 107, 374; lists of, 33, 34 – 5, 37 – 8, 40, 50, 78, 82 – 3, 98 – 9; ACID proposal, 99; Generals' trial, 251 – 2; industrialists' trials, 335, 339 – 40, 344 – 9; trials generally, 251, 253, 301, 349

Germany, post-war planning, 137 – 8, 188; Control Commission created, 138, 148; dnz. programme, 176, 188

Foster, John, 68, 85 – 6

Four Power Economic Directorate, Berlin, 325

Fragebogen, questionnaires, 163, 168, 304

France, 36, 38, 124, 194, 201; Hackel case, 92; and industrialists' trials, 340, 341, 343, 344; Jews, deportation of, 45 – 9; war crimes and trials, 236, 254, 402

Franco-German Agreement (1954 – 71, 1975 –), 402

Frank, Hans, 55, 382

Franz, Kurt, 391 – 2

fraternization (non-), policy, 156 – 7, 159

Freisler, Roland, 279

Frick, Dr Wilhelm, 380, 384

Fröschmann, Dr Georg, 286

Funk, Walther, 313 – 14

G2, Intelligence Division, 86, 182

Gailey, General, 271, 272, 276, 294, 352

Galen, Bishop von, 154

Ganse, Leonard J., 295 – 6

Ganzenmüller, Theodor, 151

Garner, Frederick, 218 – 19, 228, 346, 349 – 50

Gaus, Dr Friedrich, 278 – 9, 346

Geissler, Kurt, 395

Geisz, Dr Hermann, 152

Generals' trial, 242 – 67; defence fund, 261; not one general executed, 267; opposition, public and military, 247, 249, 250, 252, 255 – 61 *passim; see also* Army, German, Manstein

Geneva Convention, 61, 131, 263, 264; British breaches, 65, 264

Gepp, Cyril, 62, 63, 85

German Affairs, Ministry for, 380

'German Character': circular, 147

German people: 'British justice', regard for, 207, 208, 214, 215, 217, 218, 250, 253; democracy and, 104, 105, 181, 268; failure to understand Allied revulsion, 156; opposition to Allies, 155, 157; and US justice, 268, 270 – 1, 276, 279, 280, 286, 292; war criminals, more credible prosecution, 293; war guilt, collective, 141, 159, 160, 162, 214, 252, 286; war responsibility, 156 – 7, 286; *see also* fraternization *and under* war crimes

Germany: Agricultural Division, 152; Communications Division, 152; refugees, 'White' Germans: 354, discriminated against, 149 – 50, 441; scientific establishment, Allied captures, 111 – 12; United, Potsdam Agreement, 241; war loans, 14, 15, 16, 19, 23

Germany: Military Occupation; Allied Control Council govt., 150 – 1; Armies of Occupation: 20 – 1, 95, Country Unit, 140, German resentment, 158, 159, 253, Nazis, arrest of, 143 – 4, employment (US rules), 143 – 5, resistance movements, 117, 157, 182, 440

Military Government, 159, 352; (British), 147 – 8; Economics Division (Ruhr): oppose decart., 318, 326, dnz. failures, 319, 321, self-interest, shipping, 323; Finance Division, 20, 22 – 3, 24, 25; (Russian), 227; (US) Office of Military Government for Germany, United States (OMGUS), 145 – 6, 165 – 6; German help rejected, 149 – 50, political naivety, 142 – 3, 145; top Nazis back in office, 150 – 3, 194, 295; Economics Division, Cartels Section, 310, decart. opposition, 316 – 18, 324, sexual antics, 324; Finance Division, 24; Legal Division, 193, 194, 195, 196, 295; see also under Courts

Zones: (British): dnz., see that heading; Dienstgruppen, 233, 264, 451; financial aid, 179; Nazis, cooperation with, 147, 186 – 9, 191, 193, 351; war crimes teams, 125 – 6; (Russian): German people, treatment of, 159 – 60; (US): army, 'moral degradation', 276, 324; dnz., and economy, see those headings; financial aid, 179; fingerprint proposal, 118 – 19; Nazis, reinstatement, 150 – 3, 156 – 7, 191, 193, 441; universities, 183 – 4; war crimes investigation, 120 – 4, and totals, 239; see also Control Commission

Germany: Post-War future planning, 163, 178, 179; Anglo-US disagreements, 21ff., 137, 139, 140, 141, 144; East-West tension, 179, 180, 241, 253; economy, see that heading; food and fuel crisis, 178 – 9, 231; government, nature of, 104 – 5, 138, 140, 150 – 1; justice, futile commitment to, 417; Nazism, offices and privileges restored, 20, 150 – 3, 156, 157, 180, 194, 195; Russian reunification offers, 241; Western negativism, 159, 160 British policy, pragmatic, 137 – 8, 140, 145; US, policy forming bodies, 139 – 43, 164; JCS 1067, 316, 317; Washington power struggle, 139 – 41, 164

Germany, East: Nazi eradication, 396; on W. German judiciary, former Nazis, 396 – 7

Germany, Federal Republic, 241, 253, 254, 374; untested by adversity, 405 – 7

Gestapo, 45, 217, 227, 243, 297, 300, 301; arrest for collective responsibility, 68; escape organization, 89; records destruction, 216

Gilchrist, A.G., 249

Glas, Hans, 172

Globke, Dr Hans Maria, 380, 382

Glücks, Richard, 198

Göbell, Kurt, 369

Goebbels, Paul Josef, 60, 83, 158, 265

Goering, Hermann, 83, 116, 268, 308, 309, 315, 319, 355,

358; courtroom victory, 342
Golkel, Captain Karl: trial,
215 – 16
Gollancz, Victor, 252
Gotowicki, Dr Apolinary, 338
Göttingen University, 185
governments-in-exile, 30 – 1, 33,
36, 49, 53, 86; war crimes
reports, 65 – 6, 86, 89
Graham, James, 63 – 4
Grass, Günther, 408
Green, Commander Edward, 229
Grese, Ilse, 200
Grew, Joseph, 105, 381
Grigg, Sir John, 88, 109, 436
Groth, Eward, 286
Gunn, Damon, 238, 369, 376
Gunston, Charles, 14 – 15, 25;
friendship with Abs, 20, 23,
24, 26
Gurney, Maj. Gen. Russell, 128,
132, 209

Hackmann, Hermann, 411 – 12,
416
Hackworth, Green, 66, 67,
69 – 70, 71, 77, 79, 81, 105,
106, 110, 431; approves
Bernays plan, 102
Hagen, Herbert, 46, 47, 48, 254,
402, 403; conviction, 48, 426
Hague Convention (1907),
263 – 4, 424
Halifax, Lord, 31, 32, 102
Halland, Gerald, 187 – 8, 189
Hallstein Doctrine, 388, 391,
397
Halse, Brig. Richard, 127, 438,
451
Hamburg, 174, 256, 259, 387;
dnz., 178; Mayor, 157; re-
Nazification, 192
Hamman, Wilhelm, 239
Hancock, Sir Patrick, 374

Handy, Gen. Thomas: clemency
pleas, 366 – 9
"Hang the Kaiser" (slogan), 28,
38, 128, 426
Hanover, 157; police dnz.,
186 – 7, 189
Harbough, Brig. Gen. James,
121, 270 – 1, 273, 284 – 5
Harel, Isser: Eichmann arrest,
393 – 4
Harford, L.W., 322
Harrison, Geoffrey, 53, 75
Hartman, Alfred, 380
Hartshorne, Dr E., 183 – 4, 185
Harvey, Oliver, 36 – 7, 91, 94,
148, 340; on Lord Simon, 93;
and 'Antifa', 175
Hawkins, Philip, 330
Haynes, Albert, 23
Hays, Maj. Gen, G.P., 239
Heigel, Gustav, 368
Heinemann, Gustav, 375 – 6,
398
Heinrichsohn, Ernst, 45, 46,
116, 403; convicted 48, 426
Heissmeyer, August, 389
Heitgres, Senator, 192
Hellmuth, Edward, 23, 24, 25
Hennessey, Brig. J.B.G.: Golkel
case, 215 – 16
Herbert, Judge Paul: on IG
Farben trial, 362 – 3
Hess, Rudolf, 51, 52, 82, 380
Heydrich, Richard, 36, 39, 44,
45, 46; widow, 383
Heyman, Brig. D.G., 175, 300,
303
Hick, Charles, 171
Hill, Graham, 58
Hilldring, General John, 140,
183
Himmler, Heinrich, 83, 116,
151, 198, 216, 336, 337, 368,
410; bank account, 17, 355;

Circle, 15, 314, 355
Hipp, Otto, 153
history, German contemporary: postwar teaching and re-writing, 183 – 4, 405, 409, 413, 414
Hitler, Adolf, 14, 83, 279, 383; bank accounts, 16, 17, 24, 355; industrialists meeting, 314; July plot, 243, 377, 395; *Mein Kampf* and Christianity, 167; popular acclaim, 157 – 8; on WCC list, 78
Hoare, Ronald, 203, 204, 206, 209, 210
Hodenberg, Freiherr von, 305 – 6
Hodgkin, Brig. A.E., 318
Hodgson, Lt. Col. Joseph V., 77, 78
Hoess, Rudolf, 336, 359, 360
Hoey Committee: war crimes trials, 290 – 1
Hoffman, Hans, 395
Höhn, Reinhard, 389 – 90, 410
Holland, 227, 254, 401, 450
Hollins, R., 322
Hollman, Dr Heinrich, 194
Holzbauer, Dr Andreas, 293 – 5
Home Office (UK), 27, 252, 259
Hoover, Herbert: Report, 325, 460
Hopkins, Harry, 42, 141
Houman, Garret: on OMGUS courts, 195 – 6
Hubert, Peter, 337
Hull, Cordell, 55, 58, 61, 76, 140
Humphrey, Dr Donald, 325
Hungary, 226: Jewish deportations, 54, 72, 73, 74, 75, 76, 337
Hurst, Sir Cecil, 62; WCC, delegate work, 65, 67, 68, 72,

74, 78, 79, 80, 86 – 90, 432; Gestapo arrest suggestion, 68; policy letter to Eden, 72, 73, 74, 80, 102, 435
Hynd, John, 303; 'Progress in Germany', 189

IG Auschwitz, plant, 18, 19, 353, 359 – 63, 383, 404
IG Farben, company, 295, 312, 316, 351; commercial/technical subterfuges, 308 – 10; documents destruction, 310 – 11, 312, 353; Nazism, material support, 308 – 9, 312; slave labour, Monowitz, 359 – 60; subsidiary companies, 310; war crimes trial, 340, 344, 351, 353, 357 – 9, 361 – 3, 372
IG Farben, factories, bomb damage, 326; dnz., 321, 322
Imperial Chemical Industries, 321, 351
industrialists, German, 14, 16, 17 – 18, 315, 351; dnz., 22 – 4, 162, 409; Hitler, meeting, 314; interned, 410; Krupp, most greedy, 339; Nazism, support and financial aid, 17, 19, 20 – 1, 22 – 3, 308, 312ff., 319, 332 – 4, 343, 344, 409 – 10; post-defeat plans, 18 – 19
   war criminals: charges, planning and waging war, 343, 344, 358, spoliation, 356, 358; criminality, 334, 343, 344, 348; defences, 355, 356, 361, 363; property confiscations, 83, 331 – 2, 335
   war trials and cases, 18, 24,

83, 248, 334 – 5,
338 – 40, 342, 345, 347,
352; British
commitment, 341, 344,
346 – 50; British single
conviction, 350;
communist-capitalist
struggle, 343;
extraditions, 346; French
part in, 340, 341, 343,
344; govt. documents,
353 – 4; Russian
demands, 340, 341, 343,
344; US involvement,
judges, 340 – 6, 357 – 8
industrialists, Post-War: power
concentration restored, 19, 26,
313, 318 – 20; wealth intact,
331
industry, German: Allied
bombing, 325 – 6; Anglo-US
aid, 316; Allied policy, see
decartelization; dnz.,
318 – 21, 322, 323, 459;
plunder and reparations,
323 – 4, 331; management,
former Nazis, 383; recovery,
276, 317, 318, 364, 365
Intelligence Services, military and
civilian, 63, 86, 88, 97, 107,
108, 117 – 18, 121, 124, 130,
131, 233, 352; POW
feedbacks, 88, 95 – 6
International Court of Justice,
Hague, 287
internment camps, 116, 131,
134, 165, 182, 200, 410; bedrock Nazis, 300 – 1; guilt,
degrees of, 301 – 2;
interrogations, 131, 134 – 5
(see also Schwäbisch Hall);
numbers involved, 116, 120,
125, 144, 164, 168, 226,
238 – 9, 300; photographs,

231; releases, 235, 307
interpreters: inadequacies of, 216
interrogations, 24, 92, 107, 108,
116, 131; German refugees,
354; mistreatment alleged,
281, 288, 290; trained,
absence of, 130 – 1, 134 – 5;
see also Malmédy
Investigation of Nazi War Crimes
1945 – 1978 (Rückerl), 385
iron and steel industry, Ruhr,
318, 319
Isham, Major V.A.R., 108, 117,
125
Israel: Nazis, search for, 393 – 4
Italy, 235; Nazi crimes, 59,
60 – 1, 232, 249, 393 – 4, 401

Jackson, Judge Robert, 110, 119,
124, 340, 341, 343;
Nuremberg trial, 266, 268,
301, 334, 342; Nazi
organizations, conspiracy
charge, 298 – 9, 300;
industrialists' trials, 342, 345,
352
Jäger, Dr Wilhelm, 337 – 8
Jähne, Friedrich, 361
Japan: war crimes, 39, 219, 229,
425
Jaworski, Leon, 119
Jenkins, Gilmour, 176 – 7
Jewish banks and companies, 16,
315
Jews, European: 'Avenging
Angels'/'Men of 39', 278,
279, 282, 286 – 7, 290
Jews, extermination and
deportation, 43, 44, 53, 54,
223, 295, 304, 370, 382, 383,
402; British public pressure,
49, 70, 73 – 4; Moscow
Declaration, 71; 'rather a wild
story', 43; US policy, 54, 70,
71

Jews: 'Final Solution', 380, 399;
history of, being rewritten,
414
Jews: immigration to Palestine,
54, 55, 70, 72, 73, 76, 101
Jews: Nazi persecutions, 30, 69,
70ff., 379 – 80; 'crimes against
humanity', 71, 72
Joint Chiefs of Staff, 85, 87, 108,
127; Directive 1067, on
employment of Nazis, 143,
316; and postwar Germany,
139, 140; and war crimes, 60,
61, 66, 222
Jones, Elwyn, 248, 261, 262,
346, 348, 349
Jowitt, Lord, 209, 234 – 5, 249,
260; trials, presumption of
guilt, 302 – 3
Judge Advocate-General, 126,
207, 369; Department,
100 – 1, 114, 119, 121,
122, 129, 133, 266, 293;
HQ (Germany), 130,
133, 204, 205, 209, 238;
(London), 127; Review
Board, 273, 287
trials, 213 – 14,
216 – 17, 284; Belsen,
197, 202; decision
making from London
to Germany, 204,
205, 206, 209; lawyers
dispensed with, 205,
206; prosecutors,
army antagonism,
234; war crimes
agency, see War
Crimes Branch
judiciary, British, 208; German:
106, 305; 50% German rule,
303, 367; murder
prosecutions, immunity, 398,
402; Nazi backgrounds, 396,
398; Nazi court decisions
binding, 190, 387; original
order-givers still giving
orders, 403; and war crimes
trials, 106; Nazi: 190, 192,
387; agents of the state,
194 – 5; judicial murders,
190 – 1, 396, 398, 402; none
prosecuted, 191, 194; see also
law and legal profession,
courts and trials
justice: British; 'best traditions
of, 207, 208, 217, 218;
German opinion of, 214, 215,
250; German, post-war: futile
commitment, 76, 79, 104 – 5,
294 – 7, 417; US, 268:
besmirched, 275, 280, 282;
German view of, 270 – 1, 276,
279, 292
Justice, Ministry of, 388, 390,
394, 395, 398; Nazi nominees,
152; Rechtschutzstelle, 388;
criminal proceedings, figures,
398

Kajun-Chan-Veli, 228
Kamark, Major Andrew, 24
Kappler, Col. Hubert, 9, 232
Karl Zeiss, Jena, 315 – 16, 401
Katyn massacre, 60
Keating, Kenneth B., 369
Keegan, Col. Charles, 153
Keenan, Joseph B., 229
Keitel, Field Marshal Wilhelm,
45, 83, 358
Kellam, John, 24, 25 – 6, 320,
326
Kempner, Dr Robert, 278,
386 – 7
Kent, Peter, 62, 89, 98, 107, 127
Keppler, Wilhelm, 314; Kreis,
355

Kerr, Sir Archibald Clark,
51 – 2, 84, 427
Kesselring, Field Marshal Albert:
trial, 232, 234, 247, 451
Kiel, 157; demo, police boycott,
189
Kilgore Committee: Report
(1945), 316
Kirby, Maj. Gen. Stanley W.,
91, 94, 139, 148, 441
Kirkpatrick, Ivonne, 22, 108,
251, 373, 374
Kirschbaum, Joseph, 269, 272,
274, 278
Kleine Arbeitskreis (KA), 18, 19,
383
Kleinwort, bankers, 15, 23
Kneipe, Fritz, 187
Knierem, August von, 361
Knöchlein, Captain Fritz, 250,
254
Knorr, Dr Edouard, 290
Koch, Ilse, 282 – 5, 286, 371
Korean War, 1951, 366, 367,
373
Kössler, Maximilian, 270
Kramer, Josef, 126, 197; trial,
198, 199, 200
Kramer, Karl, 275
Krapf, Franz, 382
Krauch, Carl, 309, 312, 358 – 9,
361, 362
Krech, Stefan: Dachau, stay of
execution petition, 272 – 3
Krupp, Baron Alfried, 344, 383;
Nazism, slavish devotion, 339
trial, 332, 335, 344, 346,
348, 349, 350, 363, 370;
archives destruction,
339, 353; property,
hand-over, 363, 372;
sentence and release, 363,
372, 373, 465; wrong
Krupp charged, 332

Krupp, Gustav, 334; Nazism,
support for, 314 – 15; sues
Vickers, 316
Krupp armament factories, 326;
concentration camp
conditions, 335 – 8, 363

Labour Government (UK), 179;
and dnz. panels, 174
Lächert, Hildergart, 412, 414,
416
LaFollete, Charles, 279
Lambert, Guy, 41, 88 – 9, 92,
96, 98, 201, 202; war crimes,
negative attitude, 97, 99, 108,
109, 125, 203, 204, 209 – 10,
218
Länder governments: prosecution
of Germans, 385ff., 395, 400
Länderrat, 181 – 2
Landsberg prison: war criminals,
286, 290, 291 – 2, 363 – 4,
366; defence ploys, 368, 369;
German support for release,
285 – 6, 291, 292, 365,
369 – 70, 375ff.; political
problems, 367, 375; sentences
and reprievals, 371 – 7; *see also*
executions
Lang, Xavier, 172
Lange, Karl, 153
Langer, William, 288
Laternser, Dr Hans, 260 – 1
Laurich, Emil, 412
Latvia: Reich Finance
Department, 383
Law, Richard, 53, 54, 93, 104,
109
'Law 8': repercussions, 165 – 6,
317
'Law 10', 266, 297, 298, 303,
304
law: presumption of guilt,
301 – 3

INDEX

law, Basic (1949), 375
law, German, 196; customs,
compared to Nuremberg, 279;
doctrines: *lex posterior*, 305 – 6,
Notstand, 304 – 5, 306, *nulla
poena*, 305; on slave labour,
132; war crimes prosecutions,
296 – 7
law, German Administration of
Justice, 193
law, International: bank loans,
357; private property, 335;
textbook, 266 war crimes,
61, 73, 84, 98, 101, 104,
424; Nazi war crimes
not recognised as crimes,
40; leadership beyond
prosecution, 40, 41;
genocide, amendments,
75 – 6; 'new' crimes, 101
law, retrospective: war crimes,
42, 104, 105, 264, 297, 303,
305, 306, 398
Law, rule of, *see Rechtstaat*
"Law for Liberation from
National Socialism and
Militarism', 170
Law Officers, British, 39, 40,
82, 102, 127, 265, 266, 301,
349
Lawrence, Lt. Col. Charles W.,
280
Lawrence, Sir Geoffrey: on
Schacht and Speer's
demeanour, 298, 347
Lawson, John, 202, 203, 204,
205, 206, 212, 218, 229
Lawyers, German Association of
Democratic, 192
Le Druillenec, Harold Osmond,
126
Leeb, Field Marshal Wilhelm
von, 247, 248, 256
Leeper, Sir Reginald, 30

legal profession, German, 132,
143, 190, 212, 305;
conservative character, 190,
381; dnz., 162, 293 – 5, 409,
reinstatement, 189, 191ff.;
links with civil service, 190;
Nazi organizations, pro-
secutions in German courts,
299 – 300, 303 – 6,

prosecutors seen as traitors,
307; Nazism, alignment with,
190, 218, 293ff.; Nazism,
50% rule on, 303, 367;
Nazism, re-editing of, 413,
414; refugee lawyers, 192; re-
nazification, 293 – 5; (US
Zone), 193 – 5, 292; war
criminals, prosecution:
procedural ploys, 297, 304 – 6
Lehmann, Heinrich, 335, 338 – 9
Leipzig, *see* War, 1914 – 18
Lenewski, Joe, 221
Le Paradis, massacre, 230, 250
Lerer, Sam, 56
Lersnera, Baron von, 28
Leverkühn, Dr Paul, 260 – 1
Ley, Dr Robert, 116
Liberal Party (FDP), 367, 402
Liddell Hart, Basil, 243, 257,
267
Lindeiner-Wildau, Col. von, 133
Lischka, Kurt, 45, 46, 47, 48,
403; convicted 48, 426
Loeb, General, 309
London Cage: interrogation
centre, 130, 131, 133, 232
Long, Breckenridge, 67
Lübke, Heinrich, 404
Ludwigsburg, *see under* Central
Office
lunatic asylum, Kaufbeuren:
extermination centre (1945),
160

487

Mcaskie, Nicholas, 189 – 90, 193, 248 – 9, 299, 302, 303, 304, 305

McCarthy, Senton Joseph, 287; Baldwin Committee hearings, 288 – 9

McCloy, John, 100, 101, 102, 139, 144, 293; war criminals, amnesty requests, 291 – 2, 296; executions, clemency pleas, 366, 369 – 73; Krupp, decision, 372 – 3

MacGeagh, Sir Henry, 88, 106, 108, 125 – 7, 132, 205, 206, 207, 214; on JAG efficiency, 129 – 30

Mackensen, Gen. August von, 232

MacLeish, Archibald, 110

MacLeod, Lt. Col. D.: AG3, 107, 130 – 1

McMahon, Col. B.B., 166

Macmillan, Harold, 60

McSherry, Brig. Gen. Frank, 145 – 6

Maelzer, Gen. Kurt, 232

Maier, Reinhold, 181 – 2, 445 – 6

Maisky, Ivan, 53, 54, 56 – 7

Majdanek camp: protracted trial, 411 – 17

Makins, Roger, 31, 34, 35, 38

Malkin Sir William, 33, 34, 35, 39, 53, 63, 65, 70, 96, 98, 106, 425, 427; on WCC actions, 67, 68, 69, 79 – 80; defines WO responsibility, 98

Malkoff, Maj. Gen., 227

Malmédy massacre, SS, 102, 110, 113; investigations, 103 – 4, 133 – 5; a political issue, 136

Malmédy trial, 268 – 9, 366; criticisms, 269, 271, 273, 284; executions, 282, 287; inquiries into, 280 – 1, 287 – 9; interrogation techniques, 267, 270 – 2, 274 – 5, 277, 281, 288, 290; sentences, 270, 272, 277, 281, 372; verdicts, reviews, 269, 270, 272, 273, 277, 281, 287 – 9

Manchester, William, 373

Manchester Guardian, 257, 260

Mannesmann, company, 17, 319, 353

Manstein, Field Marshal Erich von: war crimes trial, 242, 243, 247, 251 – 2, 259 – 62, 401; argument with Hitler, 243, 264, 267; charges, 243, 245 – 6, 262 – 3; defence, 261 – 5, 266; Nuremberg evidence, 256, 258 – 9; public sympathy (fund), 257, 258, 260, 261; verdict, 266 – 7

Mant, Prof. Keith, 377

Marktheidenfeld, village: dnz. panel, 171

Marlowe, Anthony, 218

Marshall, Gen. George, 140; Aid, 331, 364 – 5

Martin, James, 310; trust-busting measures, 317ff., 321, 324, 326, 327, 328, 329; resignation/US campaign, 330

Massen, Hermann, 388

Matthews, Freeman, 57

Maugham, Lord, 49, 252

Maxwell-Fyfe, Sir David, 39, 40, 340

medical profession: dnz., 159, 162; euthanasia, 295 – 6; experiments, 377 – 8

Meldebogen, (questionaries) 169, 438

Mengele, Josef, 394

MI5, agency, 130; MI9, 63, 64, 89, 133

Micklewaite, Col. Claude, 122, 238, 452
Midland Bank: and Deutsche Bank, 23, 25; and EBIG, 25
Milch, Field Marshal Erhard, 346, 383
Military Code, German, 265
Military Governments, see under Germany
Mills, Sir Percy, 318, 326, 329 – 30, 331, 340, 404; anti-decart., 318 – 20, 325; "Robber Mills", 323
Mirbach, Graf von, 382
Mocatta, Colonel, 109, 132
Molotov, V.M., 233, 241, 426 – 7
Montgomery, Field Marshal Bernard, 125, 130, 147, 174, 205, 206, 207, 209, 212; 'high priority' to war crimes, 207, 209, 210, 212
Morgan, Lt. Gen. F.E., 117 – 18
Morgenthau, Henry, 77, 140 – 1, 179, 432 – 3; German industry, perpetual destruction of, 83, 141, 164
Morris, Judge James, 357 – 8, 361, 362
Müchen, Bishop, 369
Müller, Dr Josef, 293, 294
Mundorf, Hans, 413
Mundt, Karl, 291
Munich: judiciary, Nazi, 194
Murphy, Robert, 145 – 6, 164, 323, 381, 402, 441
Murray, George, 185
Mussgeller, Philomena, 295

Nacht und Nebel, decree, 36, 304
National Council for the Prevention of War, 289, 291
National Socialism, 154, 157 – 8, 160, 161, 170, 242; disapproval, latent, 159; national consensus, 157 – 8, 174; opinion polls in favour (1945 – 48), 156
navy: war crimes refusal, 435
Nazi Crimes in Poland, Commission for the Investigation, 392
Nazi leadership, 301; war crimes guilt, 16, 78, 82, 106, 114, 427; a political decision, 40, 41, 42, 52, 81, 83; 'shoot on sight', 81 – 4 passim, 106, 334; trials, 100, 101, 104, 110
Nazi organizations: US criminal conspiracy charge, 297 – 300
Nazism, 412; categories, see denazification; eradication, removed from office, 21, 141, 160, 161, 176; fanatics, re-education, 300 – 1, 307; financial support, 308; Party card index, 312; power, reinstatement to policy making positions, 174, 178, 186 – 9, 194, 195, 294 – 5, 320 – 1, 324, 331, 375, 379ff., 396, 404, 405, 409, 443; profiteers, 144, 161 – 3, 172, 331 – 3; racial theories, 245, 379 – 80, 409 – 10; re-employed, 177ff., 409; Schlusstrich, 404
Nazism, Post-War: rehabilitation by historians, 274, 414; see also history
Neue Ruhr Zeitung, 286
Neuhaüsler, Bishop Johannes, 285, 291
Neumann, Franz, 163, 164
Neumann, Lt. Cmdr. Karl, 29
neutral countries, 89, 90, 433
New York Times, 32, 180, 373

Newton, Basil, 214, 218, 345, 447
Newton, Oliver, 436
Niemöller, Pastor Martin, 155, 279
Nightingale, Alan, 210, 220 – 1, 256, 448
Nixon, Russel, 310, 311 – 12, 317
Norman, Sir Montagu, 14, 15, 347
Nothaft, Maria, 194
Notstand, legal doctrine, 304 – 5, 306
Nuremberg, International Military Tribunal, 10, 119, 120, 124 – 5, 197, 301
   Charter, 132 – 3, 242, 304
   Judgement, 253, 255, 264, 266, 297, 304 – 5;
     criminality, 242; German acceptability, 303 – 4; presumption of guilt, 301
Nuremberg Laws on Race, 379
Nuremberg: subsequent trials, 268, 279, 351 – 2; documentary evidence given to Germans, 386 – 7, 395; German opposition, 279 – 80, 351; purpose of, Nazi criminality, 352; see also IG Farben and Krupp trials

Oberdorf, Mark, 172
Oberg, Karl, 46, 47, 48, 254
Oberhauser, Dr Herte, 377 – 8
Oberländer, Theodor, 383
occupied countries, Western Europe: war crimes teams, 222 – 3; seek political 'collaborators', 223; trials, curious reluctance about, 219 – 20, 227, 236, 254

Office of Strategic Services (OSS), 163, 229, 317, 354; fingerprint idea, 118 – 19
O'Grady, Michael, 241, 250
Ohlendorf, Otto, 19, 262, 286, 292, 340, 370, 371, 380; trial, 245 – 6
oil industry, 322 – 3, 324, 354
O'Neill, Con, 63, 75, 132, 144, 159 – 60, 166; on industrialists' trials, 340, 341
'Operation Bird Dog' (currency reform), 253
'Operation Old Lace' (British Zone), 297 – 306
'Operation Osavakim', Russian, 112
'Operation Sparkler', 324
Oppenhoff, Franz, Aachen mayor, 142 – 3
Otto, Lt. Col. Martin, 133, 135
Overseas Reconstruction Committee (Cabinet), 176, 189, 253

Padover, Saul, 142
Paget, Reginald, 243, 252, 258, 261, 262 – 7
Pakenham, Lord, 247, 252, 307
Palestine: immigration, 54, 55, 70, 72, 73, 76, 101
Palfrey, Lt. Col. William, 117, 118, 231
Parker, Haven, 195, 196
'Parole and Clemency Board ...', 376
Patton, General George, 153, 161
Paulus, Field Marshal Friedrich von, 159
Peck, Judge David: Report (1950), 370 – 1
Pehle, John, 70 – 1, 76 – 7
Peiper, Major Jochen, 103, 134,

135, 366; trial, 269, 273, 275, 278, 284, 367 – 8, 377
Peleus, M.V.: massacre, 76
Pell, Herbert: WCC work, 57, 58, 62, 70 – 1, 72, 74, 86, 121, 137, 428; hostile to FO, 65, 67, 89, 102; Roosevelt, influence with, 70, 72, 77; critical of US apathy, 77, 78, 92, 102, 104; resignation/ martyrdom, 80
Penal Code, German: distortions, 398; extraditions, murder charges, 254; manslaughter, 402; murder, 297; Section 54, 304 – 5
Perl, William, 134, 135, 278; interrogation skills, 136, 269 – 70, 274, 275, 290
Perlizweig, Rabbi, 53
Peters, Dr Carl, 321
Petersen, Dr: Hamburg mayor, 174 – 5
Pfeiffer, Dr Anton, 170, 181, 182
Phillimore, Lt. Col. H.J., 107 – 8
Pierrepoint, Albert, 232
Pietsch, Albert, 17
Pilichowski, Czeslaw, 392 – 3, 399, 402, 467
Pink, Sir Ivor, 137, 177
Pius XII, Pope, 154
Playfair, Edward, 21 – 2, 318, 331 – 2, 423
Pleiger, Paul, 340
Plischke, Lt. Elmer, 164
PM, US publication, 80
Pohl, Oswald, 216, 292, 370, 372
Poland, 30 – 2, 60, 63, 81; and Allied Declarations, 32, 35, 36; intellectuals executed, 399; Warsaw ghetto, 53, 55, 223, 237, 240
war crimes, 30 – 2; archives, 392 – 3, 397, 399; extraditions, 226, 236 – 8, 402; investigation teams, 210; reluctance to prosecute Germans, 237 – 8; trials, 398
Police, 186, 386, 388; dnz. purges, 162, 184, 186 – 9; depoliticize, failure, 189; prosecution of Germans, 385; rebuilding, post-war, 187 – 9; re-nazification, 186 – 9; Schleyer kidnapping, 406 – 7; town chiefs, former Nazi officers, 395
Political Liberation, Ministries for, 169, 170, 181
Political Warfare Department, 150
politics, German, 299; crisis situation, Schleyer episode, 406 – 7; democratic, 405, 408, 410; Left/liberal, 405, 407, 408, 410 – 11; right-wing, 407 – 8, 410 – 11
Pönsegn, Ernst, 313, 319, 340
Ponto, Dr Jurgen, 406
Pooley, Albert, 64
Possa, Dieter, 375
Post Hostilities Planning Sub-Committee, 138
Potsdam Agreement (1945), 150, 151, 179, 316, 317
Pravda, 51, 52
press, Nazi: closures, 143
press, US: on war trials, 276, 282, 283, 285
Preuss, Dr (Erlangen University), 183
Preuss, Lawrence, 66, 67, 70
Prisoner of War Interrogation,

107, 108
prisoners of war: as war
    criminals, law on, 264; Allied:
    reprisals fear, 52, 61, 78, 110;
    repatriation, intelligence
    reports, 88, 95 – 6, 435;
    German, still in custody, 225,
    264, 442, 451
professional classes, 158, 159,
    381; dnz., 162, 409
'Project Paperclip': removal of
    German scientists, 111 – 12,
    437
propaganda, Allied, 155 – 6, 177,
    214 – 15, 234; East German,
    396 – 7; Nazi, 158, 286
Psychological Warfare Division
    (SHAEF), 142, 155
Public Safety Branch, 119, 163,
    164, 170 – 1, 182, 183, 187,
    300; recruit Nazi officers, 186,
    188
Puhl, Emil, 17
Purvis, Col. M., 123 – 4

Quernheim, Gerde, 228
Quislings, 33, 81, 82, 223, 225

Rademacher, Franz, 295, 382
Rademacher, Karl, 46
railways: rebuilding, 151, 326
Rankin, John, 351
Rasche, Karl, 355 – 7, 364
Rathbone, Jack: and German
    lawyers, 189 – 95, 299, 300,
    303 – 5, 307
Raymond, Col. John, 196
Reams, Robert, 54
rearmament, German, 14, 343,
    359, 366, 375 – 6
Rechtschutzstelle, 388
Rechtstaat, rule of law, 394, 408,
    410
Rechtswahrerbund, 190, 191

Reddaway, N., 176
Reemstsma, Phillip, 17, 19
Refugees, Ministry of, 380, 382
Reich Security Office (RSHA),
    399, 400
Reichsbank, Berlin, 14, 15, 17,
    343, 423
Reichstag elections (1932), 157
Reidenburg: appeals tribunal,
    172 – 3
Reinefarth, Gen. Heinz, 237 – 8
Reinstein, Jacques, 364
Renwick, E.D., 305
Resch, Dr Walter, 183 – 4
Reway, Julian, 228
Rhine Coal Syndicate, 320
Ribbentrop, Joachim von, 16,
    83, 116, 382, 427
Riedel, Fritz, 395
Riegner, Gerhart, 43
Rieke, Willie, 273
Rigby, Lt. Col. Paul, 123
Ritchie, William, 329
Roberts, Frank, 32, 35, 36, 41,
    52, 53, 67, 68, 93, 102, 425,
    427, 428, 429, 430, 432; and
    war criminals: lists, 37 – 8;
    WCC liaison, 81, 87;
    clemency programme, 374
Robertson, Gen. Brian, 133,
    179, 241, 329, 330, 332, 404;
    and dnz., 173, 176 – 7; war
    crimes programme, 229, 230,
    231, 298 – 300, 302;
    extraditions, 230, 233 – 5,
    241, 250 – 1, 253, 254, 454;
    trials, 234, 241, 250 – 1, 280;
    Generals' trial, 256 – 7;
    Russian reparations, 328
Robinson, David: on dnz.,
    168 – 70
Rockley, Lord Robert, 23
Rockwell, Alvin, 194, 196
Roehm, Ernst, 389

Roland, Nigel, 438
Ronau, K., 306
Roosevelt, Franklin D., 42, 43, 107, 141; on war crimes, 37, 55, 58, 82; supports summary executions, 82, 83; on Germany's future, 139 – 40, 268
Rose, Colonel, 25
Rosenman, Judge Samuel, 106 – 7, 297
Rosenfeld, Col. Abraham, 268, 269
Rosengarten, Leon, 69, 71
Roth, Capt. Irving, 326 – 7
Rothaug, Judge Oswald, 191
Royal Warrant, 125, 127 – 8, 132, 209, 272; death by hanging, 231
Royall, Kenneth, 276; on executions, 277, 280, 282; Simpson report, 280, 287 – 8
rubber, artificial, see Buna
Rückerl, Adalbert: war crimes investigation, 385, 386ff., 390, 392, 397, 399, 400, 401; heads Ludwigsburg, 391; conviction rate, 400, 401
Ruhr (British Zone), 318, 325 – 6, 348, 350
Rundstedt, Field Marshal Gerd von; trial, 242 – 4, 247, 251 – 2, 259 – 60; feted by WCG, 256
Russia, 139, 177, 425, 451; dnz. policy, 177 – 9, 181; German scientists, seizure, 112, 224; on industrialists' trials, 313 – 14, 340, 341, 343, 344 – 6, 353; reparations, 179, 328
war crimes in, 34, 36, 38 – 9, 50, 52, 61, 118, 236 – 7, 426 – 7; 'Com- misar order', 244; extraditions, suspicion of, 210 – 12, 224 – 8, 236, 239; collaborators only, 228, 454; 'Extraordinary State Commission', 52; Nazis condemned, not German people, 38, 159; one single crime investigated, 401; war crimes investigation, negative response, 220 – 3, 227, 230, 236
Rust, Bernhard, 83
Ryan-Braunsteiner, Hermine, 412, 413

Sachsenhausen, 220 – 1, 395, 412; trial, 236
Sacks, Alexander, 330
Sandberger, Martin, 287
Sass, S.: German expatriate, 149
Sauckel, Fritz, 347
Schacht, Hjalmar, 15, 17, 308, 315; finances rearmament, 14, 23; conduit for secret funds, 16; trial, 342, 343, 347, 348
Schäffer, Dr Fritz, 152 – 3, 383, 390
Schäffer, Liberius, 306
Schafhausen, Dr, 327
Scharfwinkel, Wilhelm, 227 – 8
Schirmer, Hans, 382
Schleyer, Hanns Martin: kidnapping and murder, 406 – 9, 411, 416; Nazi past, 409 – 10
Schlusstrich, 378, 387, 404 – 5, 417
Schmidt, Hans, 287, 368, 372, 373
Schmidt, Heinrich, 416
Schmitz, Hermann, 19, 310,

311, 344, 361 – 2
Schneider, Chritian, 361
Schnell, Dietrich, 290
Schnitzler, Baron von, 311, 344,
    358 1m. dollars Nazi pledge,
    308, 312; trial, 362
Schreibtischtäter, 398
Schröder, Baron Kurt von, 17,
    116, 344; bank, and Nazi
    funds, 314, 316, 355; (Old
    Lace) trial, 340, 350
Schroeder Banking Corporation,
    New York, 16, 316 – 17
Schüle, Erwin, 390 – 1
Schult, Lt. Col. Adolf, 186
Schülter, Kriminalkommisar,
    188
Schumacher, Kurt, 170, 186,
    375
Schuster, Lord, 436
Schwäbisch Hall prison: SS
    detainees, interrogation, 275,
    277, 278, 282, 289, 290
Schweder, Bernhard, 390
Schwedersky, Kurt, 391 – 2
Schweiger, Capt. Harry: and
    JAG, 216 – 17
Scotland, Lt. Col. Alexander,
    232; heads 'London Cage',
    130, 131; and Stalag Luft III,
    133, 227
Scott-Barrett, Brig. David, 129,
    130, 132, 204, 207
Scott-Fox, Sir David, 218,
    339 – 40, 341, 346
Sears, Judge, Charles, 355
Sedillo, Juan, 294
Senteck, Rudolf, 380
Sergeant, Sir Orme, 34, 35, 37,
    38, 60, 225, 226;
    industrialists' trial, 345, 348;
    memo to Attlee, 349; Krupp
    trial, 350
Serov, Col. Gen., I.A., 221

Shaddock, Judge, 376
Shake, Judge Curtis, 312 – 13,
    358, 361, 362
Shapcott, Brig, Henry, 117, 127,
    132, 197, 207, 217, 241: and
    war crimes trials, 128, 213,
    250, 251; on war crimes, 132,
    203, 204, 205; closure of
    AG3, 211
Shawcross, Sir Hartley, 202, 205,
    298; sets 500 cases 'target',
    205, 207, 219; trials, progress
    and conclusion, 208 – 9,
    211 – 12, 219, 229, 230, 346;
    Generals' trial, 255, 258ff;
    industrialists' trials, 334,
    339 – 41, 344, 346; ignorant
    of FO moves, 345, 348 – 9;
    Krupp trial, 334, 350
Sheen, Col. H.G., 86
Shilling, Andreas, 377
Shinwell, Emanuel, 241,
    249 – 51, 255, 260
shipbuilding industry, 323
Siebenlist, Wilhelm, 171
Siemens, company, 17, 177,
    314, 353
Silkin, Samuel, 261, 263
Silverman, Sidney, 43, 53, 54
Simon, Lord, 41, 76, 91 – 2,
    106, 431; 'appeaser', 41, 93;
    ministerial committee, 42, 49,
    56, 85; and WCC, 50, 53, 68,
    69, 73 – 4, 92; Nazi leadership
    and organizations, 82, 83,
    297; on trials and courts, 91,
    102, 106, 128, 258, 266; War
    Crimes Bill, 94 – 5
Simon, Daniel, 386, 409
Simpson, Lt. Gen. Sir Frank, 263
Simpson, Judge Gordon: Com-
    mission, 280, 287 – 8, 370,
    371, 376
Simpson, John Liddle, 302, 374

Siptrott, Sgt., 135
slave labour, 17 – 18, 112 – 13, 116, 216, 298, 304, 335 – 9 (Krupps), 350, 356, 359 – 60, 363, 384, 399; German law on, 132
Smith, Sacha, 220, 228
Snow, Brig. Gen. Conrad B., 370
Social Democrats, 152, 170, 174, 186, 407 – 8
Sokolovsky, Gen. Vassily, 221, 236, 252, 298
soldiers: 'superior orders', defence, 41, 42, 61, 250 – 1, 304, 306, 374; German attitude to, 264 – 7, 387; senior officers, 266; SS, Gestapo, unacceptable for, 216
Somerhough, Group Capt. Tony, 130, 133, 231; commands WCG, 203, 204, 210, 227, 228
Somervell, Sir Donald, 39, 40, 82, 83, 102, 106, 127, 128, 436
Soskice, Frank, 348 – 9
Spain: Nazi escape organization, 89
Special Air Service Regiment (SAS): murder trials, 215, 256
Speer, Albert, 347
Sprecher, Drexel, 341, 354, 358
SS (Schutzstaffel), 161, 216, 223, 301, 302, 307; escape organization, 89; military atrocities, 63 – 4, 102 – 4, 215 – 16, pensions, 383, 384
Stahl, Rudolf, 19
Stalag Luft III: murders, 87 – 8, 89, 111, 133, 227, 230, 255, 430; executions, 250
Stalin, Josef, 51 – 2, 59, 222, 427; Nazi leaders, executions

issue, 84, 95
Standard Oil: IG Farben deal, 309 – 10
Stanislavski, Andrzey, 415 – 16
Stars and Stripes, 134
stateless persons, 69, 73, 74
Statute of Limitations, 389, 393, 394, 397, 398; and manslaughter, 399, 402; to 1979, 399
Steele, Christopher, 150, 174, 175, 180
Stenger, Gen. Erwin, 29
Sterling, Carl L.: on Belsen trial, 200 – 1
Stettinius, Edward, 66, 67, 70, 71, 104, 381
Stimson, Henry, 66, 104, 140, 141, 297, 429; approves JAG war crimes agency, 100
Stinnes, Hugo, 313, 320, 340, 350
Stokes, Richard, 252, 258, 307
Stolting, Hermann, 414
Straight, Col. Clio E., 222, 437, 452; in charge WCB, 114 – 16, 119, 120 – 1; handicaps, 114 – 15, 122; war crimes orders, 119, 121; "turn them loose", 239; war trials: 208, 237 – 9, 284, sentences, 270, 284 – 5, detainees, treatment, 271, 272, Malmédy, 135 – 6, 270, 273
Strang, Sir William, 32, 34, 74, 81, 159; on dnz., 174 – 5, 180 – 1, 320, 322
Strauss, Col. Gen. Adolf: trial, 242, 244, 247, 251 – 2, 256, 259 – 60
Strauss, Franz Josef, 407, 408
Strauss, George, 104
Strauss, Dr Walter, 366 – 7
Strecker, Reinhard, 396

Streicher, Julius, 116
Strong, Maj. Gen. K.W.D., 86
Stuckart, Wilhelm, 380, 389
student revolts, 1968, 186
Sturm-Abteilung, 298, 300
Subsequent Proceedings
    Division, 352 – 3
'superior orders', defence, see
    soldiers
Supreme Headquarters Allied
    Forces Europe (SHAEF), 22,
    25, 430; Nazis, employment
    of, 143 – 4; occupation forces,
    22, 91, 140, 141, 143, 163;
    war crimes, responsibility: 85,
    86, 89, 94, 96, 97, 103 – 4,
    108, 133, courts of inquiry,
    103 – 4, 113, 133, investiga-
    tion groups, 110, 114, 115,
    116, 117, 118, limited to
    Allied personnel only, 113,
    114, and not civilians or
    before D-Day, 86, 95; see also
    war crimes agency, War
    Crimes Commission
        Legal Division, 85, 91, 115

'T Forces', 111 – 13
Taylor, Brig. Gen. Telford, 237,
    242, 246, 247, 276, 352 – 3;
    Generals' trials, 248 – 9;
    industrialists' trials, 341, 344,
    345, 349 – 50, 352, 356, 358
Tengelman, Herbert, 319;
    Wilhelm, 314, 320
Ter Meer, Dr Fritz, 359, 360,
    362, 373
Tesch, Dr Bruno, 295, 350,
    357
textile industry, German, 319
The Times, 29, 32, 218, 261,
    351
Thedieck, Franz, 380
Thiele, Adolf, 337

Thierack, Otto, 249, 346
Thon, Harry, 134, 269
Thorp, Willard, 329
Thummler, Johansen, 401 – 2
Thyssen, Fritz, 313, 314
Tippelskirch, Col. Werner von,
    435
Torrie, Brig. A., 251
trade unions, 314, 321
Transition Agreement (1955):
    Article 3, 389
Treasury Solicitor, 62, 96, 127
Treatment of German Nationals in
    Germany, 27
trials, war crimes, 10, 127 – 8,
    129, 208 – 9, 214, 216 – 17,
    230, 302, 307, 368, 388,
    394 – 5, 447; Anglo-US
    differences, 100; British
    policy, 197; British Zone,
    213 – 18, 233, 234, 251, 253,
    minimum, 500 cases, 205,
    211, 218, 219, 230; to end
    (Sep 1948), 230, 253ff.;
    German controlled, 255,
    386 – 7; guilt, presumption of,
    issue, 301 – 3; 'Hostages' case,
    275 – 6, 278; 'Ministries' case,
    278, 368; moral validity, 253;
    Nazi organizations, 299 – 306;
    Nazi reprisals, fears, 52, 53,
    65; politically counter-
    productive, 241, 250 – 1,
    366 – 71 passim, 373, 376;
    poor results, 216; Russian
    show trial, 236; US Zone,
    236, 247 – 8, 275, 279, 281,
    287; verdicts, 292, 353, 369,
    377, 396; W. German courts,
    396
        German campaign against,
        241, 258, 267, 275, 279,
        281 – 3, 285, 286, 291, 292
Troutbeck, Jack, 76, 106, 137,

150, 226, 298, 441, 443
Truman, Harry S., 325, 327
'trust busters', see decartelization
Turpin, Brig. P.G., 212, 213, 217, 219, 302

U-Boat crimes, 29, 265
Ukraine, 223, 228
Ulm Einsatzgruppen: trial, 390
Ulrich, Franz Heinrich, 17
United Nations: Commission on Atrocities, 41, 42
United Nations War Crimes Commission, see War Crimes Commission
United States of America, 268; anti-semitism and 'new' Americans, 278, 286 – 8, 290; banks, 16; investment in Germany, 278, 316; Jewish lobbyists, 49, 70, 80; pro-German lobby, 277 – 9, 283, 285, 286 – 91
    war crimes policy: agencies, 109 – 10;
        national position on, 76 – 9 passim, 102, 103, 104 – 5, 119, 120; post-war German economy, 83 – 4; public response, 77, 79 – 80
Anti-Trust Division, 308, 310 – 11, 313 Army Department, 113, 114, 276 Foreign Activity Correlation Dept., 77 Justice Department, 224 State Department, 43, 44; 'Eastern Project analysis', generals' debriefing, 237; and 'Final Solution', 48 – 9; and German Jews, 69ff.; visa control section, 110
    war crimes policy, 49, 54, 80, 84, 89, 110;

aligned with Britain, 76 – 7; 'political' crimes, 223, 228; WCC, dealings with, 49, 57, 66 – 9, 77, 79, 89

War Department: war crimes policy, responsibility for, 66, 77, 79, 85, 89, 101 – 2, 128; investigation programme, 109, 115; Nazi organizations conspiracy charge, 298, 299; prosecutions, policy, 102, 104, 113 – 14; see also Judge Advocate-General
United Steel, company, 314
universities, 143, 162; dnz., 183 – 6 (Erlangen), 183 – 4, (Göttingen) 185, (Wurzburg) 184); Nazi studies resumed, 183ff.
Urbich, Franz, 19 – 20

V – 2 rockets, 112 – 13, 404
Vabre, Judge Donnedieu de, 347
van Roden, Judge LeRoy, 280, 282, 287 – 8, 290
Vansittart, Sir Robert: on genocide, 31 – 2
Vatican, 433; Concordat with Hitler, 154, 167
venereal disease, 156
Versailles Treaty, 15, 28, 29, 158, 316
Vialon, Karl, 383
villages: mini-concentration camps, 131 – 2
Vitek, Rudolf, 360 – 1
Vits, Ernst, 319
Vogel, Georg, 382
Vogel, Hans-Jochen, 392
Vögler, Albert, 340

Vyshinsky, Andrei, 341

Wagner, Gustav, 55 – 6, 116
Wagner, Prof. Herbert, 111
Wagner, Pius, 187
Wagner, Robert, 66
Wallenberg, Raoul, 76
Walz, Hans, 355, 356
War, 1914 – 18, 264 – 5, 299, 369; Leipzig trials, 28 – 31; 'superior orders', 264 – 5
War, 1939 – 45; surrender terms, 14, 76, 115, 137
War Crimes, National Office for, 98
war crimes and atrocities, 28 – 31, 42, 127, 128, 129, 223, 224, 265, 266, 424, 427, 428
  Allied policy, first declaration, 251 Allied propaganda, 155 – 6 archives, see that heading British official policy, 27 – 8, 39, 201 – 2, for details, see Foreign Office concentration camps, murder not a crime, 199 concentration camps, staff, see that heading courts, see that heading 'crimes against humanity', 132, 363 Declarations, see that heading early evidence, British collection, 62 – 4 European reports, first, 33 extraditions, see that heading German view of, 267, 272, 274, 277 – 8, 285, 386; communist propaganda, 263; ignorance, innocence etc., 155 – 7; Nazis blamed, 156, 157;

  punishment, moral validity questioned, 75, 252, 253; refusal to accept 'collective guilt', 154, 155, 252 indictment figures, 398, 400 by industrialists, see that heading intelligence reports, early, 88 international law against, 69, and see that heading law, national, no defence against int. law, 101 magnitude, beyond belief, 120, 126, 417 manslaughter, 'aiders and abetters', 398 – 9, 402 military operations, German, 41, 61, 99, 242ff., see also soldiers Nazi leadership, see that heading Nazi organizations, figures representing, 101 pre-1939, 69, 70, 71, 72, 73, 104, 121 public pressure and opinion, 39, 41, 77, 79 – 80, 92, 102, 127ff. retribution, first hints, 33 Russia, see that heading statistics, 239 (US Zone), 385 total war, no such thing, 253 trials, see that heading, and indiv. cases as Generals', IG Farben etc. tribunals, suggestions, 33, 52, 82, 101, 110 US policy, 280 – 1, for details see U.S.A. State and War Departments US protest lobby, 278, 284, 285 W. German investiga-

tions, 385, 387, 388 – 91,
394; inadequacies, com-
placency, 386 – 7, 388,
390, 392, 395, 396
White Paper, record, 27
committed against: Allied
nationals, 75, 128; Allied
servicemen, 63 – 4, 122,
215 – 16, 230, 236, 244,
250, 265, 273, 366, 369
(Malmédy *and* Stalag Luft
III, *see* those headings);
British nationals, 92, 97,
101 – 2, 127; European
Allies, 92, 97, 98, 99;
German/Axis nationals, 27,
67, 69, 70, 71, 76, 77 – 9,
83, 102, 105, 132 – 3, 295;
Jews, *see* that heading, *also*
stateless peoples; UN
nationals, 69, 71; US
nationals, 429
committed by the Allies, 252,
268, 278, 367
war crimes agency (Weir),
100 – 1, 109 – 10
War Crimes Bill (Simon), 94 – 5,
431
War Crimes Branch (US),
Wiesbaden: investigation
agency, sole, 85, 88, 100, 114,
115, 119, 120, 124, 211;
failure to cope, 126 – 9,
131 – 2, 133, 203, 204
War Crimes Bulletins, 122
War Crimes Commission,
United Nations, 41 – 2, 50ff.,
58, 62, 67, 74, 80 – 1, 85, 91,
146, 429 – 30;
Anglo-US cooperation
sought, 62 – 6, 106
beginning of, and title, 49,
69 Belsen camp, barred
from, 109 closure,

suggestions, 81, 94, 235
concentration camps, 109,
438 criticisms of, 92 – 4,
and failures exposed,
press conference, 78 – 9
first meeting, 58, and first
report, 67 – 8 int. tribunal
proposal, 52 investigations,
denials and restrictions,
69 – 74, 76, 79 – 80, 83,
106
Jewish representatives, 72
membership, 56 – 7, 81, 92
'police agency' role sought,
86 – 8, 89, 204 Russia,
excluded from,
50 – 3, 56 – 7, 61, 68,
87, 220, 426, 430, and
no-go areas, 63
SHAEF links, 68, 80,
86 – 9 *passim*, 91 – 5 *passim*
US, attitudes towards,
66 – 7 war crimes lists, 85,
86, 98 – 9, 108,
110, 113, 117, 239, 449;
exclude Axis nationals,
76, 79 – 80, 83; kept out
of Europe, 225, 430; not
one US contribution,
225, 423
war criminals, capture
target, 107; *see also* Foreign
Office *and* under U.S.A.
State *and* War
Departments
War Crimes Executive (British),
218 – 19
War Crimes Group (British),
Bad Oeynhausen, 203, 205,
209, 216, 230 – 1, 254, 269,
293; closure, 242; 500 cases
target failure, 213; one
cohesive agency, 210 – 11,
231; refuse to assist Generals'

trial, 256; results, suspects, 231, 234, 253, 255; Rundstedt dinner, 256

War Crimes Modification Board, Army, 369

'War Crimes Trials, Hints to New Prosecutors', 217

war criminals, 9 – 10, 19, 26, 48, 56, 68, 107, 132 – 3, 215, 228, 235, 428; armistice, and immediate surrender, 49, 426; British clemency programme, 374; British policy, 10% prosecutions aim, 204, 205; collaborators, see extraditions; escape routes, 89 – 90; executions, see that heading; extradition, see that heading; generals, not one executed, 267; German prosecutions of, 79, 104 – 5, 293, 296, 385; interrogations, 92, and see that heading; 'ringleaders or perpetrators', 49; 'superior orders', see soldiers; USA entry, 224

'War Criminals, Punishment of' (Churchill), 81

'War Criminals, Treatment of' (Eden), 40, 41, 42

'War Criminals, Trial of European', 101

War Office, 27, 148, 346; BAOR to investigate war crimes, 203; and Belsen, 109, 201, 202; British troops as witnesses, 65, 88; early evidence collection, 62 – 4, 85, 88, 127; Generals, disinclined to try, 246, 252, 255, 259; rules of war, breaches of, 41; war crimes machinery, unpreparedness, 85, 88 – 9, 204; war crimes responsibility, 96 – 9, 107, 108, 128, 132, 203, 204, 209, 218, 229, 230; see also Adjutant-General Post-War Planning Committees, 138

Ward, John G., 105, 109, 148

Wardrop, James, 80, 94, 98 – 9, 114, 335

Warren, Fletcher, 77, 89, 110

Way, G.R., 88, 95

Wegrezecka, Jadwiga, 415

Wehner, Dr Bernard, 395

Weigert, Hans: and Nazis in 'key positions', 193, 293 – 4

Weimar Republic, 157 – 8, 190, 243, 305, 406

Weir, Brig. Gen., 100 – 1, 106, 109 – 10, 114

Weir, Sir Cecil, 328, 329

Weiss, Klaus, 396

Welles, Sumner, 44

Wennerstrum, Judge Charles, 275 – 6, 278, 357

Werner, Dr Bernard, 296

Westerick, Ludger, 19, 26, 380, 383

Wheeler-Bennett, John, 149

Wiesenthal, Simon, 394

Wilberforce, Richard, 132, 189, 301 – 2, 332

Wilck, Col. Gerhard, 141

Wilkins, Judge, 363

Wilkinson, Lawrence, 276; anti-decart. activities, 328, 330

Williams, Elvyn, 90

Wilson, Col. Keith, 119, 164

Winant, John, 49, 140, 426, 428

Winek, Anton, 239

Winwood, Major T.C.M., 199, 200

Wise, Rabbi Stephen, 43, 44, 54, 71, 72

Wolff, Karl, 151, 249, 359

Wolff, Otto, 313

working class: Party
membership, 158
Wormhoudt, massacre, 230, 250
Wright, Lord, 90, 107, 225, 235
Wurm, Bishop, of
Württemberg, 155, 167, 171,
286; defends civil service,
166 – 7; dnz., opposition to,
155, 166, 168, 179; Law 8
protest, 166; *NYT* interview,
180; on Nuremberg trials,
279 – 80
Würzburg, 293; University, 184
Wysor, Rufus, 317

Yalta Agreement: Russian
repatriations, 224 – 5

youth, German: Marxists, 405,
406, 408
Yugoslavia, 233, 364, 401, 450;
anti-Tito elements, 224, 225,
233; Bergman affair, 235;
extraditions, 225, 226 – 7,
239 – 40

Zach, Sgt. Henry, 104
Zangen, Wilhelm, 17, 19, 313,
318 – 19, 340, 346
Zelle, Johanna, 412
Zink, Harold, 324
Zurlippe, Erbprinz Ernst, 306
Zyklon B gas, 295, 350, 357,
414